T0329758

MERCHANTS, MARKETS, AND EXCHANGE
IN THE PRE-COLUMBIAN WORLD

Dumbarton Oaks Pre-Columbian Symposia and Colloquia

Series Editors
Joanne Pillsbury
Mary E. Pye

Editorial Board
Elizabeth Hill Boone
Tom Cummins
David Webster

MERCHANTS, MARKETS, AND EXCHANGE IN THE PRE-COLUMBIAN WORLD

KENNETH G. HIRTH AND JOANNE PILLSBURY

Editors

DUMBARTON OAKS RESEARCH LIBRARY AND COLLECTION
WASHINGTON, D.C.

Second Printing, 2016

Library of Congress Cataloging-in-Publication Data

Merchants, markets, and exchange in the Pre-Columbian world /

Kenneth G. Hirth and Joanne Pillsbury, editors.

    p. cm. — (Dumbarton Oaks Pre-Columbian symposia and colloquia)

Includes index.

  ISBN 978-0-88402-386-9 (hardcover : alk. paper)

1. Indians of Mexico—Commerce. 2. Indians of Mexico—Economic conditions. 3. Indians of Mexico—
Antiquities. 4. Indians of Central America—Commerce. 5. Indians of Central America—Economic
conditions. 6. Indians of Central America—Antiquities. 7. Indians of South America—Andes Region—
Commerce. 8. Indians of South America—Andes Region—Economic conditions. 9. Indians of South
America—Andes Region—Antiquities. I. Hirth, Ken. II. Pillsbury, Joanne.

F1219.3.C6M49 2013

972´.01—dc23

2012022302

General editors: Joanne Pillsbury and Mary E. Pye

Art director: Kathleen Sparkes

Design and composition: Melissa Tandysh

Managing editor: Sara Taylor

Volume based on papers presented at the Pre-Columbian Studies symposium "Merchants, Trade, and
Exchange in the Pre-Columbian World," held at Dumbarton Oaks Research Library and Collection,
Washington, D.C., on October 8–9, 2010.

Jacket illustration: Disguised merchants on the road to Tzinacantlan. Reproduced from Bernardino de
Sahagún, *Historia de las cosas de Nueva España* (Madrid: Hauser y Menet, 1905–1907).

www.doaks.org/publications

CONTENTS

PREFACE AND ACKNOWLEDGMENTS

The papers in this volume were originally presented at a symposium entitled "Merchants, Trade, and Exchange in the Pre-Columbian World," organized with Ken Hirth at Dumbarton Oaks on October 8th and 9th, 2010. My first acknowledgment must be to Ken, who made the entire process—from planning to publishing—an absolute delight. His great insight into the topic of trade and exchange, as well as his endless intellectual curiosity about and enthusiasm for the subject across the Americas, made the event and the resulting volume especially stimulating. I would also like to thank the authors of this volume for their willingness to share their data and ideas, and for working together to complete this book in a timely fashion.

I am grateful to many individuals who helped organize the symposium and who supported the present volume. In particular, I would like to thank the director of Dumbarton Oaks, Jan Ziolkowski; William L. Fash; and the members of the board of senior fellows, including Barbara Arroyo, Elizabeth Hill Boone, Tom Cummins, Virginia Fields, Charles Stanish, Gary Urton, and David Webster. Emily Gulick Jacobs was pivotal in all stages of the symposium and this publication, and I am eternally in her debt for her contributions, both large and small. Two interns, Ari Caramanica and Michelle Young, were essential to the overall success of the symposium itself, and a third intern, Alexandra Méndez, worked tirelessly to prepare this volume during the summer of 2011. I am grateful to Ben Benus, Kinya Inokuchi, Yuichi Matsumoto, Yoshio Onuki, and Yutaka Yoshii for their help in obtaining images for several chapters.

I offer my sincere thanks to the three anonymous reviewers for their detailed and thoughtful advice on an early draft of this volume. This publication would not have been possible without the assistance of Reiko Ishihara-Brito, whose significant contributions to the final editorial stages were above and beyond the call of duty. I am grateful to Amanda Sparrow for her graceful copyediting and to Melissa Tandysh for her elegant design. Finally, Kathleen Sparkes, director of publications at Dumbarton Oaks, and Sara Taylor, art and archaeology editor, shepherded the book into print with grace, insight, and endless good humor.

Joanne Pillsbury

Merchants, Markets, and Exchange in the Pre-Columbian World

KENNETH G. HIRTH AND JOANNE PILLSBURY

Economics are important because the way that resources were produced and distributed laid the foundation for all state-level societies across the Pre-Columbian world. Although the organization of ancient economies varied greatly from region to region—just as our sources for understanding these systems—all economic models are fundamentally based on common concerns. If there was one point upon which Martin Luther, Karl Marx, and Adam Smith could agree, it was that material goods and their acquisition provided the strongest motivations and temptations in the everyday life of humans. Although American academe has moved away from materialist explanations of culture change in recent years, the economy remains as basic to the emergence of cultural complexity as food and water are to life. The key is to understand how the economy was integrated with social and ideological forces in the Pre-Columbian world.

This volume examines the structure, scale, and complexity of economic systems in three areas: the Mexican Highlands, the Maya region, and the Central Andes. Civilization in those places was characterized by complex political and religious institutions, highly skilled craft production, and the long-distance movement of finished goods. Despite a number of similarities, their economic structures differed significantly from one another. Populations in the Mexican Highlands developed a highly commercial economy and one of the ancient world's most complex market systems. The Maya region, in contrast, appears less commercially developed. There, marketplaces are less apparent, household-level craft production is more difficult to identify, and the palace seems more prominent in the organization of distribution networks. At the far end of the spectrum lie Andean societies, which are often described as having noncommercial economies.[1] Here, forms of centralized redistribution are used to model economic interaction at both the local and interregional levels.

This book explores the role and importance of commercial exchange in these three areas; this

figure 1.1
Location of key sites and areas explored in the volume in Mesoamerica. (Map designed by Reiko Ishihara-Brito based on 90 Meter Global Terrain Map created by Matt Fox of the Google Earth Library [http://www.gelib.com/global-terrain-map.htm]. Ground surface and ocean textures from the Blue Marble Next Generation [NASA]; ground surface elevation data [hole-filled seamless SRTM data v4] from the International Center for Tropical Agriculture—CIAT [http://srtm.csi.cgiar.org]; and bathymetric elevation data [SRTM 30 Plus] from Scripps Institution of Oceanography, University of California, San Diego.)

topic is important for three reasons. First, Pre-Columbian societies occupy a unique position in the study of ancient economies. Unlike the societies of the Old World, with their well-developed maritime and terrestrial transportation networks, Pre-Columbian societies were limited in their ability to move goods. In fact, Mesoamerica had the worst transportation system in the ancient world. It lacked beasts of burden and had few navigable rivers; coastal trade, where it occurred, was limited to small-scale canoe fleets. Although Andean societies could move goods via llama caravans,[2] riverine transportation was impossible in most areas, and maritime transportation remained underdeveloped. Traditional thinking would suggest that these conditions must have limited the formation of complex economic structures, but this was not the case. Rather, the Mexican Highlands created extensive systems of trade and regionally integrated market systems (Blanton, this volume), even though all goods moved overland on the backs of human porters (Hirth, this volume). The same was true across the Andes, where exchange networks and forms of symbiotic interaction developed early between coastal regions, the highlands, and the highland fringe of the Amazon basin (see Burger, this volume; Dillehay, this volume).

The second reason for the current topic is the need to consider models of trade and exchange from a hemispheric perspective. It has been suggested, following the work of Karl Polanyi (1957), that the Andean region was markedly different in economic

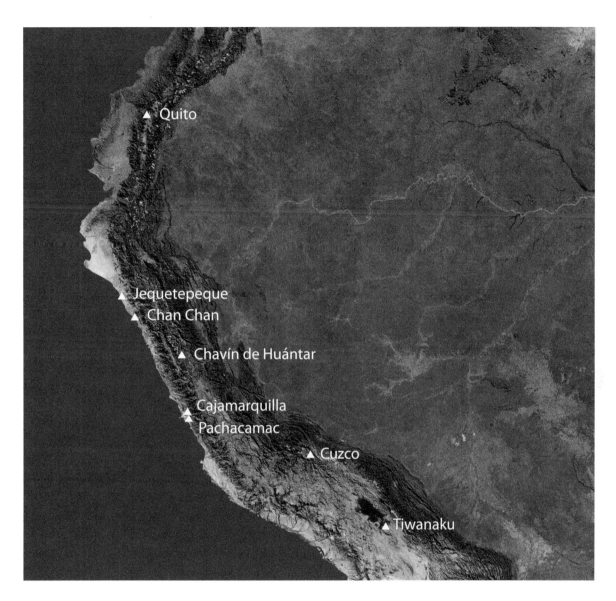

figure 1.2

Location of key sites and areas explored in the volume in the Andes. (Map designed by Reiko Ishihara-Brito based on 90 Meter Global Terrain Map created by Matt Fox of the Google Earth Library [http://www.gelib.com/global-terrain-map.htm]. Ground surface and ocean textures from the Blue Marble Next Generation [NASA]; ground surface elevation data [hole-filled seamless SRTM data v4] from the International Center for Tropical Agriculture—CIAT [http://srtm.csi.cgiar.org]; and bathymetric elevation data [SRTM 30 Plus] from Scripps Institution of Oceanography, University of California, San Diego.)

structure from other areas of the ancient world. The Andes, without question, had its own unique cultural traditions and forms of organization. Traditionally, the region has been characterized as having noncommercial societies. Instead of developing large periodic markets, the Andes achieved economic integration primarily through centrally controlled forms of redistribution (La Lone 1982; Murra 1980 [1955]; Smith 2004). The Andes is the only area where it was believed that complex societies did not establish household-level commercial interaction and some form of market exchange. Recent research, however, suggests that marketplace and household-based exchange were more important in both the Andean and Maya regions than previously thought (Dahlin et al. 2007; D'Altroy and Hastorf 2001; Stanish 2010). The time is right to reexamine the commercial and noncommercial aspects of economic organization throughout the Pre-Columbian world. To this end, the authors in this volume were asked to challenge existing beliefs and models through a critical analysis of available data.

The third and final impetus for the present volume is that Pre-Columbian societies have long been left out of the comparative study of ancient and modern complex economic systems. The reason for this neglect is primarily geographical: Pre-Columbian societies lie outside the historic continuum leading to the Industrial Revolution and the capitalistic world system centered in western Europe (Garraty and Stark 2010; Wallerstein 1976; Wolf 1982). New World economic traditions, while rich in organizational diversity, have rarely been examined comparatively, either with respect to one another or to areas of the Old World (but see Trigger 2003; Wolf 1982). This book aims to redress this lacuna and to prompt a broader comparative conversation about economic systems in the New World.

The title of this volume, *Merchants, Markets, and Exchange in the Pre-Columbian World*, captures a range of economic behaviors. Commercial activity can be found in the actions of the full- and part-time merchants who moved goods to earn their livelihoods. Whether they were Mexican *pochteca*, Ecuadorian *mindalaes*, South Andean caravan traders, or domestic artisans selling the goods they produced, economic gain provided the motive for their actions. At the other end of the spectrum were household-to-household exchange networks organized around barter and gift-giving, designed to even out resource irregularities and to reinforce social relationships. Between these two poles is the marketplace, where all segments of society came together to trade and to convert surpluses into alternative goods. In the marketplace, economic motives blended with social interactions, and all economic institutions—from the household to the palace—converged.

Dual Economy: The Domestic and Institutional Sectors

Comparative study requires that we identify key economic structures common to the regions under discussion. We must first recognize that both simple and complex societies have a dual economic structure composed of domestic and institutional sectors (Hirth 2012; Johnson and Earle 1987; Wilk 1989). The *domestic economy*, as the name implies, is centered on the household and comprises the array of activities that households engage in to provision themselves with the resources needed for demographic and social reproduction. A fundamental feature of the domestic economy is that households are economically conservative. They conduct business for themselves, and a failure to perform effectively threatens the survival of all household members. Two types of behavior characterize household subsistence strategies: 1) they actively strive to maintain access to the resources critical for their survival, and 2) they will not relinquish control over these resources unless they are forced to do so (Hirth 2009a, 2009b). As a result, household production strategies attempt to minimize subsistence risk (O'Shea 1989) while retaining the ability to intensify production when they need to meet subsistence needs (Netting 1990, 1993). As such, they are not as concerned with maximizing individual returns per unit of labor as they are with ensuring a steady and predictable supply of resources for the aggregate household. Not surprisingly, the domestic economy often emphasizes self-sufficiency as a general strategy over market dependency, even though we know archaeologically that households were never completely self-sufficient (Flannery 1976; Wiessner 2002).

All societies have social activities that promote internal cohesion and maintain relationships with neighboring groups (Bray 2003; Dalton 1977). As societies grow in size, they develop institutions that provide services and frame interaction on a regular basis. In complex societies, political and religious institutions often structure social interaction. The *institutional economy*, therefore, refers to the production or mobilization of the resources needed to cover the costs of maintaining these organizations and their social services. The institutional economy includes the political economy and all other social, religious, and economic organizations that operate above the level of the household (Hirth 1996, 2012; Johnson and Earle 1987; Wells and Davis-Salazar 2007). These institutions are easier to identify in antiquity because they were organized as freestanding entities rather than integrated into the operation of elite households, as was the case with palaces (Sheehy 1996). Palace institutions pose special analytical problems since in these situations it is difficult to separate activities intended for domestic maintenance of elite families from the production or accumulation of surpluses needed for society-wide institutional use.[3]

Institutional economies often are organized to support themselves. They produce the resources they need through voluntary contributions and set aside production, situational taxation, and corvée labor drafts (Hirth 1996). Perhaps most importantly, institutions—at least at their inception—usually fund their activities without significantly intruding into what households produce for their own support. Direct taxation of household income only occurred after households lost a significant degree of economic control over their productive resources. This pattern was the basis for the early state economies of Sumeria, Assyria, and Egypt (Postgate 1992; Trigger 2003), and it is how institutional economies were structured among the Aztec, Maya, and Inca. This same trend is evident in our own economic history. In the United States, government agencies are supported by income tax that comes directly out of household income. But income tax was a late development in this country's history and did not appear until 1913, with the passage of the Sixteenth Amendment. Until that time, the government supported itself through a combination of import and export duties, excise taxes, and real-estate taxes that did not directly tax the incomes of individual households.

Domestic and institutional economies coexisted in all premodern complex societies. Moreover, the institutional economy depended on the domestic sector for the majority of the labor used

in institutional production, either in the form of intermittent labor drafts or rotational corvée labor. Institutions favored revenue-producing strategies that minimized costs while maximizing returns and, therefore, periodically drew labor from the domestic sector. Researchers often oversimplify these relationships by focusing on one dimension of the institutional economy, such as the political or religious, and using it to model the structure of the whole economy. Examples of this type of error include labeling the Maya as a palace economy, modeling Andean economies in terms of a centralized Inca political economy, and viewing highland Mexican societies as modern market economies. Palaces, political economies, and marketplaces were components of the broader economy where domestic and institutional structures interface. Understanding this interrelationship is fundamental to understanding how Pre-Columbian economies were organized.

Principles of Pre-Columbian Economy

Certain principles guide the growth and operation of all economic systems. One such principle is that economic systems are essentially accumulative and conservative in structure. Growth in social complexity brings about change in the economic fabric of society. Economic systems are accumulative in that innovations in production and distribution are added, as they appear, to the repertoire of existing economic arrangements. Similarly, economic systems are conservative insofar as they retain simpler forms of production and distribution as societies grow in size, and this is important because it means that even state societies retain the economic structures developed in acephalous and ranked societies. These simpler structures continue to be used in larger states within domestic and small-group settings where they are most appropriate.

Economic change, therefore, tends to be one of degree rather than kind. Preexisting forms of gift exchange, household reciprocity, or cooperative labor exchange are not eliminated when new forms of economic integration (e.g., capitalist market societies) emerge; they simply are modified to fit their new economic circumstances. This growth in complexity is noteworthy because it means that earlier forms of exchange and production never really disappear—they just continue alongside new economic adaptations. It also means that complete economic transformations never occur. Societies do not evolve from reciprocal to redistributive or market societies with the growth of empire and the appearance of marketplaces or full-time professional merchants. Simpler and earlier economic structures are not abandoned but rather are incorporated into new economic structures as they take shape.

Economic systems are also conservative in the way that the movement of resources is embedded in social, political, and religious life. One reason for this embeddedness is that resource movement reinforces the maintenance of social relations. Gift-giving makes friends even if it comes in the form of a bribe. Exchanging gifts and resources is fundamental to alliance formation (Dalton 1977; Mauss 1990 [1924]), and the continual cycle of gifts and countergifts makes the creation of social relationships an ongoing process. The economy is embedded in ancient society not because it is less important than religion or politics, or because it cannot be studied as a separate field of human behavior (sensu Dalton 1977; Polanyi 1957). Economy is embedded in ancient society because it is fundamental to successful adaptation. Rooting the economy in social institutions was one way to ensure that resources were available and en route to those who needed them.

The economy is often defined in functional terms as the production, distribution, and consumption of resources. Because this volume focuses on exchange, it is important to clarify several terms and concepts that pertain to economic distribution. *Merchants*, for example, are distribution specialists who move goods over long distances and provide retail functions between suppliers and consumers. They were prominent in some areas of the Pre-Columbian world because of limitations in transportation technology. Nevertheless, we need to recognize that merchants took many forms, from wealthy retailers and long-distance importers to humble peddlers and producer-vendors who sold the goods they produced directly to the people who consumed them. Merchants may operate independently for their own benefit or be clients of the state or the governing elite. Their position in society depends on the functions they perform and for whom they perform them. Ancient professional merchants generally operated under the radar of history. It was not in their interest to document their routes—especially where their success depended on maintaining control over "trade secrets." Most merchants were not members of the ruling strata, and as a result there is little historical data on their scale and strategies of operation. This is especially true in the Pre-Columbian world, where, aside from the use of simple maps and counting devices, there is no written documentation of indigenous commercial transactions. There is generally little evidence in Pre-Columbian or colonial sources on who merchants were—whether full- or part-time, elite or poor—and on how their activities impacted the ancient economy.

Trade and exchange are forms of dyadic distribution between mutually interacting parties. Depending on the context of the discussion, these terms can have very different meanings to those who employ them. *Trade* is used to refer to balanced and negotiated resource exchanges. It is a form of balanced exchange that may occur within marketplaces and through social partnerships (Heider 1969) and trade networks based on household visitation (Strathern 1971; Wiessner 2002). Archaeologists also use the term *trade* as a pseudonym for long-distance movement of goods. Researchers who speak of trade in this way often mean to imply commercial activity in the absence of the hard evidence needed to confirm it.

Exchange, on the other hand, has a wider range of meanings and usages, as it refers to both the movement of goods and the transfer of ideas, styles, and people. When referring to goods, it can encompass transfers that are balanced or unbalanced, immediate or delayed, and confined to socially established partners or open to all. Exchange is a catchall term that conveys the idea of distribution either in the form of a gift or a premeditated theft.

Its lack of precision makes it applicable in a host of contexts; its ambiguity makes it incumbent on researchers to define it with more precision whenever possible.

Market exchange refers specifically to "exchange transactions where the economic forces of supply and demand are highly visible" (Pryor 1977:437). The key here is that market exchange refers to a negotiated transaction between participating individuals both inside and outside a marketplace. *Barter* is a special type of market exchange whereby goods are directly exchanged for one another without the use of money or some other media of exchange (Garraty 2010:8; Humphrey 1985). This view of barter differs from that of Stanish and Coben (this volume), who use the term in a more specific sense to suggest a type of market system where exchange occurs within the context of traditional or fixed prices without the use of currencies.

Prominent throughout this volume is the topic of the *marketplace*, and the reason for this emphasis is twofold. First, from a comparative perspective, most complex societies in the ancient world had some form of reciprocal, negotiated exchange through which some amount of goods moved. New evidence for pre-Hispanic marketplaces in both the Maya and the Andean regions (Dahlin et al. 2007; Mayer 2002; Stark and Garraty 2010:52–56), where they had long assumed to have been absent (Murra 1985; Potter and King 1995), requires a re-examination of this topic. Second, the marketplace is a specialized institution where the domestic and institutional sectors of the economy could intersect. It is a place of centralized reciprocal exchange where households provisioned themselves independently of elite interference. In Mesoamerica, the marketplace served as the primary place of resource conversion. It was where the state converted tribute goods into other commodities and elite households sold agricultural surpluses for goods from long-distance merchants and household craft specialists (Carrasco 1978). How the marketplace operated in different areas is open to debate, but it is a topic that needs to be addressed in order to further our understanding of the Pre-Columbian commercial world.

Colonial sources do not clearly describe the structure of the domestic economy and the diverse ways in which households provisioned themselves with the resources necessary for survival. The Spanish were unconcerned with how indigenous households operated as long as their members were available for work. The institutional economy is a different story and, as such, is better documented. The Spanish recognized that they could easily expropriate tribute goods, institutional wealth, and elite lands for their own use. Although the institutional sector is more thoroughly recorded, we must take care not to use it as the model for the entire ancient economy.

The economy has always been the foundation upon which complex societies were built. But as central as the economy is, this topic is difficult to address due to the breadth of perspective required to study it. The three areas of civilization discussed in this volume—the Mexican Highlands, the Maya Lowlands, and the Andean region—contrast greatly in how their economic structures are characterized and described. While the economies of the Mexican Highlands were highly commercialized, as one moves south the vibrancy of commercial interaction through merchants and marketplaces appears to decrease.

Economic Issues in the Mexican Highlands

Societies in the Mexican Highlands developed the most commercialized economy in the Pre-Columbian world. Professional merchants known as *pochteca* and *oztomeca* resided in numerous towns across the highlands and played an indispensable role in moving both staple and high-value wealth goods across the terrain. These merchants were not elite; instead, they were wealthy members of the *macehualli* (commoner class), who operated primarily as independent agents to make a profit (Sahagún 1961:42, 59). Common throughout the highlands were marketplaces (Hassig 1982), and most members of society bought and sold goods there as a normal part of household provisioning. An important, but often overlooked, aspect of the marketplace is that it also provided an entrepreneurial environment for participating households. Most craft production was carried out by artisans who worked at home and sold finished goods in the marketplace. As a result, intermittent craft production was a crucial component of many domestic subsistence strategies.

Good research often stimulates additional investigation, but this has not been the case in highland studies. The broad outline of the region's economic structure was established by the 1970s (Berdan 1975, 1989; Berdan and Anawalt 1992; Bittman and Sullivan 1978; Carrasco 1978; Katz 1966), and new research into the economy was slow to follow. Major questions remain, such as: How far did different categories of goods move over space, and who moved them? Likewise, we need to expand our understanding of the breadth of commercial activity and its penetration into the everyday life of ordinary households (e.g., Smith 2010; Smith and Berdan 2003). Similarly, marketplaces are often described as if they were equivalent even though they varied tremendously in type, size, and frequency across the highlands. Most of the available information comes from descriptions of urban marketplaces in the Basin of Mexico, which are not representative of smaller marketplaces found in less densely populated rural areas. Furthermore, considering that the locations of most major marketplaces have not been mapped, more research is needed.

Five chapters in this volume explore some of these unresolved issues. Richard Blanton addresses the nature of the marketplace and the conditions of social cooperation needed to bring it into existence. He argues that the marketplace is a liminal space, where normal social relations must be suspended so that individuals can engage in balanced, negotiated market exchange. The creation of these spaces involves more than just resolving the problems of cheating, safety, and adjudication of disputes that regularly arise in market settings; it involves establishing a place where social identity can be relaxed in order to foster economic interaction. For Blanton, the creation of market spaces requires elite involvement, develops gradually over time, and

may involve the operation of markets piggybacking onto existing organizations like shrines, pilgrimage sites, and temples, where religious authority mandates peaceful behaviors. As part of the discussion, he develops an evolutionary model for market development involving restricted and regionally integrated market systems that is applied to the Maya region, Oaxaca, and Central Mexico during the Postclassic period.

Two papers by Nichols and Hirth explore the topic of highland merchants. Deborah Nichols presents a unique view of a community of professional traders (*pochteca*) in the Basin of Mexico. Her research at the town of Otumba revealed evidence for craft production and the manufacture of a wide range of goods. This finding includes maguey fiber processing; spinning and weaving of maguey and cotton textiles; the production of pottery Red Ware vessels; obsidian blades and bifaces; ground stone tools; lapidary goods (e.g., earspools and labrets); and ceramic manufacture of figurines, spindle whorls, pipes, stamps, earspools, musical instruments, and censers. Her research indicates two important things about these professional merchants. First, the concentration of craft industries at Otumba underscores the close relationship that Bernardino de Sahagún (1959:88) reports between *pochteca* merchants and craftsmen in the barrio of Amantla in Tenochtitlan. Besides trading, the *pochteca* supplied, encouraged, and may have underwritten the manufacture of the goods that they sold. Second, while *pochteca* are often linked to trade in high-value goods, the archaeological evidence suggests that they, as well as other regional merchants, also trafficked in medium- and low-value goods. Evidence for the local distribution of these goods is found throughout the northeastern Basin of Mexico.

Kenneth Hirth broadens the discussion of merchants by looking beyond the *pochteca* to consider whether individuals in other commoner-class, non-*pochteca* households also engaged in trade. He presents and discusses three related issues, beginning with the concept of profit and how many commoner households benefited economically from participation in the marketplace.

Economic differentiation at the household level is underscored by the identification of 112 producer-vendors in the marketplace who sold goods that they produced in their homes or within the marketplace. The variation in these producer-vendors broadens our discussion of who merchants were as well as the range of activities all households engaged in to support themselves. How far did staple goods actually move via trade on the backs of human porters? Hirth addresses this question using ethnohistoric data, and the results indicate that ecological diversity was important in promoting short- and intermediate-scale trade between regional marketplaces. Finally, he constructs a profitability model for itinerant obsidian-blade producers. The model shows that itinerant crafting and intermediate-scale exchange could be a highly profitable venture for households that practiced it as a component of normal domestic subsistence activities.

Teotihuacan was one of Mesoamerica's largest early state centers and a major Pre-Columbian mercantile center. The chapter by David Carballo gives an overview of what the Teotihuacan commercial system looked like. It examines how cotton and lime were processed and where obsidian and ceramic goods were made. Carballo finds evidence for the organization of work at various levels within the city. Obsidian working, weaving of simple cotton garments, and ceramic manufacture were organized at the level of the corporate residence. Elaborate costumes for elites were made in the households of high-ranking barrio leaders, while other goods—like theater braziers and obsidian bifaces and eccentrics—were produced in state and ritual production contexts like those described for the contact-period Aztecs. He discusses those dimensions of the economy that were commercially and politically motivated and examines the most likely transportation routes used to import goods such as obsidian, cotton, lime, and Thin Orange ceramics into Teotihuacan.

Gerardo Gutiérrez provides the final chapter on economic systems in the Mexican Highlands. He examines a tribute registry from the town of Tlapa and explores what it tells us about systems of valuation in the highlands and how they were applied to tribute levies. The Tlapa document is unique because it is a record of what the Tlapa polity paid in tribute to the Aztecs instead of what the Aztec state received in the Valley of Mexico. He shows that tribute levies were not necessarily fixed in specific categories of goods, as previously assumed. Instead, he demonstrates that a system of valuation was in place that provided a degree of flexibility in what was turned in, allowing local tributaries to substitute one good for another of equal value. Although eight different types of tribute goods were demanded by the Aztecs, tribute in Tlapa was only paid in three: gold dust, gold bars, and woven textiles. Gutiérrez shows that the goods turned in had a value 12 percent higher than what was demanded by the Aztec state. This higher value may have been used to support the Aztec *calpixqui,* who perhaps played an active role, along with local elite, in converting tribute paid in gold and textiles into the specific types of products depicted in Aztec tribute records. This arrangement implies that the Aztec tribute system employed a much more flexible method of establishing equivalencies for the goods demanded in tribute that is more in line with equating value using a market mentality.

Economic Issues in the Maya Region

The Maya region boasts a number of striking contrasts with highland economic systems. The traditional view is that the Classic Maya had a non-commercial and largely managed economy bordering on redistribution for some sectors (Henderson 1981:152; Willey and Shimkin 1973). Marketplaces are known to have existed at the time of the arrival of the Spaniards, but their existence is questioned for earlier periods (Potter and King 1995). Where marketplaces did exist, they are assumed to have been small and under direct elite control. Commerce and trade have been seen as limited in scale and monopolized by merchants who—unlike those in Central Mexico—were probably members of high-ranking families, rather than commoners. The Maya economies were incorrectly viewed as small, fragile, and with little internal economic diversification (cf. Fedick 1996). They are perceived as being divided into two parts: a large sector of self-sufficient commoners producing staple goods for tribute and their own use, and a palace economy involved in the procurement and production of prestige goods for use by Maya elites. This noncommercial view of Maya society is derived primarily from political and religious depictions of courtly life found on monuments and polychrome pottery (McAnany 1989:348), rather than from analyses of material remains that define modes of production and distribution.

This traditional view stands in strong contrast to Diego de Landa's description of indigenous life in Yucatan during the early sixteenth century. According to him, the "occupation to which they had the greatest inclination was trade . . . exchanging all they had for cacao and stone beads which were their money . . . and at their markets they traded in everything which there was in that country" (in Tozzer 1941 [ca. 1566]:94–96). Modern scholars have begun to question the traditional, noncommercial model, and a vigorous debate has arisen over whether marketplaces were present among the Classic-period Maya (Dahlin et al. 2007; Freidel 1981; Masson 2002; Masson and Freidel, this volume; West 2002). As a result, researchers are also interested in whether merchants were elite or nonelite and whether they were part of a broader commercial system or simply agents of the palace. Scholars now question, rather than assume, the role of the palace in controlling the economy. This doubt is particularly evident in the discussion of Maya craft production, where numerous authors have argued the case for elite control (Aoyama 1999; Inomata 2001; Kovacevich 2007). Nevertheless, the difficulty in identifying craft workshops (Rice 1987) is a perpetual problem in the Maya area; it suggests that many types of craft goods were probably manufactured by independent specialists who worked in small, domestic contexts in both urban and rural settings.

Four chapters examine economic structure among the Classic lowland Maya. The first is by Alexandre Tokovinine and Dmitri Beliaev, who examine the topic of merchants among the ancient Maya with particular focus on the Classic period. Merchants are not prominent in texts or images anywhere in Mesoamerica, much less in the Maya region, where the focus of courtly expression is on the ruler. Nevertheless, the authors argue that merchants were integral to Maya society based on four types of data: Maya economic vocabularies; representations of merchants in Classic-period courtly scenes; inferences about merchant behavior that can be gleaned from the presence of marketplaces; and depictions of merchant gods during the Classic and Postclassic periods. Tokovinine and Beliaev suggest that merchants in the Classic period were depicted in the visual arts as white-gowned diplomatic emissaries known as *ebeet*. Known to travel, the *ebeet* may have been courtly individuals involved in the long-distance trade of wealth goods. Tokovinine and Beliaev argue that the North Acropolis mural at Calakmul portrays a market scene based on its context, types of goods depicted, and glyphic identification of individuals offering what are likely items for sale. The authors demonstrate that the presence of merchants and the origins of the type of market economy found among the Postclassic Maya at the time of the Conquest stretch back into the Classic and Preclassic periods.

Marilyn Masson and David Freidel build a strong case for the antiquity of marketplaces in the Maya region. They suggest that the Classic-period economy was much like that of Postclassic Yucatan. Evidence for marketplaces is found in plaza arrangements, soil enrichments within plazas, and the murals depicting commercial activity found in the North Acropolis plaza at Calakmul. Masson and Freidel argue that elite redistribution would have been inefficient and that markets provisioned both commoners and elites with a wide variety of local and nonlocal goods, including food. They view the Maya economy as partially commercialized and containing a mixture of trade, tribute, and marketplace exchange, which they believe originated in the Maya Lowlands during the Late Preclassic period. The authors propose that the marketplace was the cornerstone of a multifaceted Maya economy that included, among other things, the use of shell beads, cotton textiles, and cacao as currency.

The palace was a prominent institution in ancient Maya society, and Patricia McAnany addresses its economic role during the Classic period. The palace was the seat of elite power, and its wealth was based on regional tribute systems. Commerce was practiced, but the author argues that relations between merchants and elites were tense because long-distance trade had the ability to destabilize the accumulation of wealth through tribute systems. Tribute was depicted on ceramic vessels and in mural painting. Wealth goods—often cacao, textiles, *Spondylus* shell, jade, and quetzal feathers—are shown on palace steps. Many of these items had to be procured outside of the local domain, implying some reliance on merchants to meet tribute obligations. McAnany suggests that a more commercialized Maya economy emerged during the Late and Terminal Classic, when merchant activity began to be held in higher regard. This change of status is seen in the transformation of merchant God L from a being of disrepute to a morally acceptable one. This change was concurrent with trade becoming a possible royal occupation, which altered the palace by broadening its role as the center of tribute collection, craft production, and trade.

The final chapter in the Maya section by Brigitte Kovacevich explores how elites were involved in the production and control of high-value wealth goods through a case study of jade lapidary production at the site of Cancuen, Guatemala. The manufacture of jade goods here appears to occupy an intermediary position between production in elite households (Widmer 2009) and production in nonelite households (Rochette 2009). Jade production and use was not the exclusive prerogative of the elite. At Cancuen, jade crafting was a segmented operation, with commoners carrying out the early stages of manufacture in their households and elites handling the intricate carving and final finishing. Kovacevich suggests that jade probably moved through multitier exchange spheres: the simple jade beads found in commoner households were procured through market exchange, while elaborately manufactured regalia recovered in elite households moved through gift and emissary trade. Interestingly, foreign ceramics frequently occur in nonelite crafting households, which may reflect their participation in long-distance exchange as merchants if imports are not widely distributed elsewhere throughout the site. Compositional analysis indicates that the jade at Cancuen came from the Alta Verapaz region and not the Motagua Valley, which has long been considered the primary source for jade in the Maya region. Cancuen was in a perfect position to control the flow of jade along river routes into the lowlands. Nevertheless, distributional data show that not all areas in the lowlands received jade, suggesting either the existence of different valuation spheres for jade or some sharp divisions and variations in the routes along which jade goods moved.

Economic Issues in the Central Andes

Turning farther south, from Mesoamerica to the Central Andes, the evidence for marketplaces in the pre-Hispanic period becomes ever more scarce. The traditional and—to a certain degree—still dominant paradigm in modern scholarship is that Central Andean state societies in the pre-Hispanic period were organized as noncommercial economies that lacked both merchants and marketplaces (La Lone 1982; Smith 2004). This model posits that regional economies were organized as redistribution systems along the lines that Karl Polanyi (1957) advocated (for a discussion of the issues surrounding redistribution as a problematical concept, see Earle 1977). John Murra (1972, 1980 [1955], 1985), the major proponent of this model, argued that the economy was organized through reciprocal group colonization into vertically distinct ecological zones in order to gain access to different types of resources. Therefore, resources were moved between community segments by corporately owned llama caravans and redistributed to colonists by regional leaders. Marketplaces were viewed as negative forces for social integration. Implicit in the model is the notion that households were completely dependent on the hierarchy of their ethnic group for resources critical to their survival.

More recent research, however, has revealed the nuances of ancient economies across the Andes. Rather than viewing the Inca economy (or other economies) as a monolithic system, scholars are beginning to understand the complex interactions between different sectors. Prestige goods, for example, may have been managed, centralized, and controlled by the elite (D'Altroy and Earle 1985), but as Stanish and Coben (this volume) show, other goods may have moved via different channels. Nielsen, for example, points out in his chapter that Inca attempts to control the circulation of prestige goods were not entirely successful. Furthermore, scholars have noted that a single economic model cannot be applied uniformly across the Central Andes. For example, the classic "vertical archipelago" model does not include merchants, yet as Frank Salomon (1987) has shown, there is good evidence for merchants in Ecuador. Different regions most likely had highly distinct systems of economic integration. Coastal populations would have undoubtedly availed themselves of maritime transport for the movement of goods, as María Rostworowski (1970) suggested for the Chincha Valley. Farther south, trade caravans were a feature in the Southern Andes, possibly from very early times (Dillehay, this volume; Nielsen, this volume; Nuñez and Dillehay 1995).

There are several problems with the traditional vertical archipelago model of Andean economy. First, most of the discussion has addressed Inca political economy instead of the economy as a whole. This model also overlooks variations in pre-Inca economies and how Andean economic systems developed over time. Although vertical economic integration was important, cross-cultural studies (Pryor 1977) indicate that societies develop multiple forms of distribution as they grow in size. As mentioned above, economic systems are both accumulative and conservative in nature. It is illogical, therefore, to assume that the redistribution of resources associated with the colonization of different ecological zones would completely replace simpler forms of household-to-household exchange. Domestic provisioning relies on the operation of multiple forms of resource acquisition in weakly integrated market systems. It is likely, therefore, that Andean households always provisioned themselves through a variety of mechanisms that included household-to-household reciprocal exchange, barter, limited market exchange, and redistribution based on verticality.

The majority of chapters on the Andes in this volume directly challenge and refute the non-market paradigm using both ethnohistoric and archaeological data (see also Stark and Garraty 2010:52–56). Enrique Mayer, one of Murra's last students, challenged Murra's antimarket approach almost a decade ago when he pointed out evidence for marketplaces and market exchange in Peru at the time of the Conquest (Mayer 2002). Mayer's model was based on five distinct pieces of evidence: 1) the presence of marketplaces in Cuzco and other towns at the time of the Conquest; 2) the regular practice of barter by both local lords (*curacas*) and individual households to procure grain and other resources; 3) the use of periodic marketplaces by households to acquire resources through exchanges with social partners; 4) the practice of delayed reciprocity as a means of masking individual gain; and 5) the use of coca leaf as a type of money to calculate value, facilitate conversions, and actualize economic increase (Mayer 2002:58–65, 105–110, 176). According to Mayer, marketplaces were a regular feature of the Pre-Columbian environment, but they were suppressed by the Inca in order to centralize political control. He argues that marketplaces reappeared soon after the Conquest because Andeans were already used to them: barter was a fundamental and traditional feature of household provisioning within the domestic economy.

Seven papers in this volume examine resource distribution in different areas of Andean South America. Tom Dillehay gives an overview of current models of ancient Andean economy, ranging from transhumance and verticality to political colonization and migration. He argues that mobility and exchange were important provisioning mechanisms as early as the Initial Period. Following the accumulation principle, Dillehay claims that the forms of exchange found among Formative societies were retained and integrated into later states. He challenges the practicality of Murra's verticality model as the primary way of moving resources throughout the Andes. Instead, he feels that other informal forms of exchange certainly existed because of the way resources are distributed through multiple networks in all societies. Some of the possibilities for the Andes include household-to-household reciprocity, mobile traders, cyclical residency, and small-scale barter marketplaces such as the one Dillehay identifies in the Jequetepeque Valley on the North Coast of Peru.

Enrique Mayer examines anew the foundation of "Andean verticality," as the traditional model is often called. He provides an intellectual history of Murra's thinking about Andean economy and reveals Murra's original stance: that both marketplaces and forms of reciprocal exchange were part of the Pre-Columbian economic landscape. Murra developed his verticality model during the late 1960s in tandem with his anticapitalist political views. From the discussion, the image emerges of a scholar committed to defending a polemic rather than constructing a comprehensive model of Andean economies. Murra downplayed the Inca suppression of previously existing market institutions, the role of women in exchange transactions, and the way *curacas* functioned as merchants and entrepreneurs who brokered access to resources in neighboring regions for their local communities. Andean economy was fuller and far more complex than Murra argued, an issue that scholars have only recently begun to appreciate.

Two chapters address the ancient economies of the North-Central Andes and Ecuador. The first, by Richard Burger, examines the structure of economic relations and the existence of merchants and marketplaces in the north-central highlands of Peru. Burger argues that marketplaces were present in the Andes before the Inca suppressed them in order to directly control staple and prestige goods. He suggests that pilgrimage and cult centers were the most likely venues for fairs and early marketplaces because of the demand for goods that pilgrims would have brought to these locales (cf. Abbott 2010). Focusing specifically on the Early Horizon cult center of Chavín de Huántar, Burger

notes that the recovery of many of the imported objects in nonelite contexts indicates the operation of an early marketplace. While pilgrims probably brought gifts to offer to deities, they also would have exchanged imported goods for food and Chavín cult objects. Marketplaces do not require professional merchants in order to operate successfully, and Burger doubts that merchants played a role in the development of early systems of long-distance trade. Nevertheless, the evidence provided makes a strong case for long-distance exchange and market activity in the north-central highlands beginning in the Early Horizon.

The chapter by John Topic expands this discussion by reviewing similarities and differences in exchange practices in northern Peru and Ecuador during pre-Inca times. Evidence for both merchants and marketplaces has been reported for Ecuador (Salomon 1986). Merchants known as *mindalaes* were active in the highlands, and trade via balsa rafts is reported for the coast. *Mindalá* merchants administered the Quito marketplace and were sponsored by elites in addition to trading for themselves. Topic expands our understanding of verticality by discussing the practice of *camayoc,* found in both Ecuador and northern Peru, whereby elites rent land to outside groups for payment in the kinds of goods produced. He shows that colonists in foreign enclaves were required to pay "rent in kind" to the local elite for the products they produced. This scenario changes the view of verticality from simple reciprocal production to one in which the elite could attract and exploit additional labor from outside groups. Of particular importance is the fact that multiple modes of exchange are shown to be operating across the Andean region—from merchants and marketplaces in Ecuador to barter, administered trade, verticality, and redistribution in Peru. Clearly the frontier between these two spheres—modern-day northern Peru and southern Ecuador—was porous; it is likely that many forms of distribution operated to move people, artifacts, and raw material across it.

Two contributors, Paul Goldstein and Axel Nielsen, each discuss the nature of exchange networks in the Southern Andes. Goldstein explores

Tiwanaku economy from AD 500 to 1000 using a more traditional approach. He sees no evidence for merchants, marketplaces, or price-setting traditions and argues for the traditional model of corporate economy in the Southern Andes. He presents evidence for zonal complementarity and identifies two diaspora highland communities from Tiwanaku in the Moquegua Valley in southern coastal Peru. Unlike some of his colleagues, Goldstein does not see the movement of resources between the communities as having been highly centralized. Instead, he argues for the presence of an embedded economy with goods flowing between corporate segments through both reciprocal and redistributive exchange. Goldstein focuses on the *ayllu*, the kin-based corporate landholding unit that was similar in function to the *calpolli* in Mesoamerica. According to the author, *ayllus* located in different areas were trade partners and probably operated independently of one another to obtain the resources they consumed.

Axel Nielsen takes us farther south, into the highlands of Argentina, Bolivia, and Chile, to focus on the role of caravan trade. He uses an "internodal approach" to examine the transport sites found along trade routes—such as campsites and shrines—extending from the coast to the highlands. The method is innovative because it directly examines the goods moving between regions connected by communication corridors. Evidence for trade is found during all the periods between 500 BC and AD 1550. Exchange items include ceramics, lithics, lapidary goods, salt, feathers, ash, and food staples such as fruit, eggs, and game. No evidence is found for either marketplaces or the existence of interzonal complementarity under elite direction. Instead, many goods moved through caravan trade based on reciprocal barter between interested parties. Models of elite control do not work in this area because most trade goods moved through open and decentralized circulation networks. Nielsen also demonstrates that Inca goods traveled along routes outside state control. Stimulated by ecological diversity, the caravan trade was carried out by pastoral groups as a secondary activity embedded in other behaviors related to hunting and gathering. Embedded trade in this sense is distinct from some

form of specialized trade associated with interregional caravans.

Charles Stanish and Lawrence Coben provide an important summary on the role of the Andean marketplace. They expand the discussion of what marketplaces are and argue that marketplaces definitely existed throughout the Andes during Pre-Columbian times. The authors state that Andean markets did not use currencies, set prices, or rely on merchants. Instead, they were barter markets where households produced and exchanged goods to provision themselves with critical resources. The basis for these markets was "rational decision making" by households who participated in them. Household members interacted through durable social relationships that provided the linkages through which goods were exchanged. In the Andean region, the production of goods through labor control was more important than the procurement of goods through trade. Stanish and Coben reorient the discussion back to the domestic economy and the operation of barter to equalize different levels of production among and between households.

Barry Isaac's final overview to the volume asks two fundamental questions: What is a market, and what is the political context in which exchange occurs? He notes that while marketplaces may be located in all three regions, we must exercise caution in defining their structure and function in the respective societies. These were not market societies like our own. There were no separate markets in land, labor, or capital, and, in all but a few cases, most people did not get the bulk of their income from trade in the marketplace. Barter was the foundation of market exchange, which led to more stable prices than when valuation was established using standardized currencies. One major difference between Mesoamerican and Andean markets is that Aztec tribute policies promoted markets, while those of the Inca did not. Isaac argues that redistribution is an outmoded and inaccurate way of describing an economy and one that obscures the specific characteristics of the mobilization and transfer strategies involved. Andean institutional economies were unique because they had to cover the cost of supply and distribution that were handled by the marketplace in Mesoamerica. Most importantly, he calls for an integrated approach to the study of the ancient Pre-Columbian economy, one that recognizes that exchange and production were embedded in various ways in both the domestic and institutional economic sectors.

Toward a New Understanding of Pre-Columbian Economy

The goal of this volume is to stimulate a new understanding of Pre-Columbian economies. Authors were asked to push the limits of what we knew, or thought we knew, about pre-Hispanic economic systems. They demonstrate that it is possible to talk in comparative terms about the economy of the Mexican Highlands, the Maya area, and the Central Andes. As expected, the economy was organized in different ways in each of these three regions. Nevertheless, the contributors expand our understanding and challenge conventional wisdom in a number of important ways. In the space remaining, we explore the inroads they make in creating a better understanding of Pre-Columbian economy.

The Mexican Highlands had a thriving commercial economy centered on the marketplace. What remains unclear is the degree of household participation in the marketplace, especially in rural areas at variable distances from large urban centers (but see Smith 2010; Stark and Ossa 2010). Yet the market was a special place wherever it was located. While Nahua society stressed fairness and humility, the market operated on the principle of competitive profit making (Hirth, this volume). It was also a place of suspended social relations designed to encourage economic interactions. Therefore, it was a liminal place where new rules of conduct had to be learned and enforced (Blanton, this volume; Hutson 2000). Among these rules were new systems of valuation, indispensable both as a *practical means* of encouraging interaction as well as an *abstract scale* for establishing equivalent worth across different products (Gutiérrez, this volume). The marketplace was constructed to permit households to interact and exchange goods

in a secure and efficient manner; in the process, it created the conditions that allowed households to engage in new forms of craft production, resource merchandising, and commercial retailing (Hirth, this volume) that would not have been possible without the concentration of potential consumers that the marketplace attracted.

Merchants were a fixture in the highlands, and the merchants of Tlatelolco have told their story through the words of Sahagún (1959). In their own biased portrayal, they were religious, humble, self-sacrificing, and a great service to society because of the wealth they generated for the state. Of course, they themselves became immensely wealthy in the process. Unfortunately, archaeologists and historians have let Sahagún's words become scholarly gospel, characterizing merchants as specialists who only transported high-value goods over long distances. This portrayal is far from accurate. Merchants trafficked in a range of both staple and inexpensive goods that they sold at both the local and interregional level (Hirth, this volume; Nichols, this volume). Merchants also stimulated a great deal of craft production for the products they wished to sell (Nichols, this volume). The opportunity to profit from trade and intermittent craft production was the same for commoner households as it was for merchant groups (Hirth, this volume) because there were few economies of scale beyond what the marketplace provided as a source of consumer demand. Yet the marketplace had an enormous effect in mobilizing bulk resources over short to intermediate distances of thirty to one hundred fifty kilometers (Hirth, this volume).

Merchants, marketplaces, and specialized forms of craft production probably did not appear simultaneously throughout the Mexican Highlands; instead, each has its own history of development. While not necessary for merchant activity, the marketplace greatly enhanced commercial efficiency and encouraged greater participation by individuals at all levels of society in commercial activities. Increases in commercial intensification appear linked to the development of large communities. Whether it was in large urban centers like Teotihuacan (Carballo, this volume) or medium-sized communities like Otumba (Nichols, this volume), large centers fostered economic diversification. Nevertheless, how rural households were involved in this process needs to be established since the production of many key items occurred in rural areas where natural resources abounded.

Among the Classic Maya, the palace was the center of elite power and governance as well as the heart of its institutional economy (McAnany, this volume). After meeting tribute obligations, commoners were left to their own devices, provisioning themselves through a range of formal and informal distribution networks. The development of the marketplace would have been a boon to Maya domestic economy (Masson and Freidel, this volume). It would have enhanced household resource procurement, helped convert surplus production into other items, and provided a point of sale and distribution for craft goods made in rural households. Jade and shell elite goods may have been produced near their palace consumers (Kovacevich, this volume), but utilitarian items made of ceramic, stone, wood, and fiber probably were not. The dearth of production venues in major centers suggests that utilitarian goods were manufactured across the rural countryside. The Calakmul murals provide visual evidence for marketplaces among the Classic Maya (Tokovinine and Beliaev, this volume), a trait that Thompson (1954:60) assumed was an integral feature of the Maya economy.

Goods certainly moved across the Maya region, but by whom and in what quantity remains unclear. The *Relaciones geográficas* of Yucatan suggest that goods moved with the people who produced them. Salt, for example, was not widely traded within Yucatan, but individuals traveled from towns to the coast to process what they needed (Garza et al. 1983). Despite this circumstance, trade did occur and some of that trade was carried out by merchants operating both as independent operators and as agents for the palace (McAnany, this volume; Tokovinine and Beliaev, this volume). It is just as common cross-culturally for elite to contract with independent merchants for specific goods as it is for government officials and travelers like the *ebeet* to engage in personal trade while on official business.

The evidence implies that trade became an acceptable practice during the Terminal Classic period, and this may be the point when mercantile activities first became acceptable for elite participation. Finally, although the palace was supported through tribute, commoner households almost certainly relied on noncommercial reciprocal exchange networks and periodic marketplaces to meet their domestic needs and desires.

The chapters on the Andean region represent a major paradigm shift in how that area's economy is conceptualized and modeled. They reject environmental complementarity and centralized redistribution as a monolithic economic system in favor of multiple forms of resource distribution (Dillehay, this volume). *Ayllu* segments were certainly linked across different environmental segments (Goldstein, this volume), but internal corporate distributions were probably practiced alongside reciprocal exchanges both in- and outside of marketplaces. Although John Murra maintained a strong antimarket stance, he neither completely disavowed the existence of marketplaces nor rejected other forms of reciprocal exchange (Mayer, this volume). Marketplaces were not confined to Ecuador (Topic, this volume); they occurred widely across the Northern and Central Andes (Burger, this volume; Dillehay, this volume; Stanish and Coben, this volume). Small marketplaces were relatively common before the Inca, who repressed them in favor of direct control over production and distribution networks (Isaac, this volume). Marketplaces can be associated with regional mobility (Dillehay, this volume), cult centers and pilgrimage sites (Burger, this volume), and communities in different ecological zones, where individuals could travel to procure key resources (Mayer 2002; Stanish and Coben, this volume).

The "carrying trade" was a normal part of mobile pastoralism, both in the Andes and in other parts of the ancient world. Herders were informal, part-time merchants (Dillehay, this volume; Nielsen, this volume), moving products both for exchange and to provision members of their corporate group. The role of the professional merchant, however, remains unclear outside of Ecuador (Topic, this volume). The presence of merchant groups in the Chincha

Valley (Rostworowski 1970) remains unconfirmed and controversial despite good evidence for long-distance movement of goods in early periods. If merchants did operate across the Central Andes, they were few in number and probably acted in service to the elite, who sought wealth goods and exotic resources like *Spondylus* (Pillsbury 1996) for use in craft production and other purposes. Formal currencies did not exist, but—as we know from other parts of the ancient world (Dercksen 1996; Veenhof 2003; Weatherford 1997:27)—they were not a prerequisite for either market exchange or systems of formal barter.

Rethinking the Andean economy in this way brings the Andes back in step with all other areas of the ancient world. Environmental complementarity certainly existed, and resources moved between social segments found in different ecological zones. Centralized redistribution, however, is an extremely costly form of distribution that is difficult to maintain except under special circumstances or for a narrow range of goods. Moreover, the acceptance of foreign colonists by a local lord may not be based on altruistic reciprocity and the relocation of local people as colonists to other areas. Instead, foreign colonists paid tax in kind (e.g., *camayoc*) to local lords in some areas of the Andes (Topic, this volume), which was expropriated by local elites for their own use. From a developmental perspective, reformulating Andean distribution systems in this way follows the principles found in other societies around the world (Mauss 1990 [1924]; Pryor 1977). The Andes, therefore, can be considered in a comparative framework with other complex economies where goods were distributed in multiple ways and societies grew in complexity by adding and adapting new forms of production and distribution to existing ones without replacement.

The study of ancient economy is not the "dismal science" that the Victorian historian Thomas Carlyle (1849:531) thought it was. Instead, it is the enlightened science that provides scholars with the means and foundation for understanding how ancient societies were organized and developed over time. The contributions in this volume are a step along the path of developing a broader comparative perspective of ancient economy in the Pre-Columbian world.

NOTES

1 We prefer to use the term *noncommercial* rather than the term *nonmarket,* which is more commonly used in Pre-Columbian studies. *Market society* implies a more capitalistic structure, which is generally inappropriate for the ancient Americas. It could be argued that all Pre-Columbian economies are nonmarket, as they lack a significant market in labor and land (see Isaac, this volume).

2 The limited carrying capacity of llamas is often noted. While a single human porter can carry more than a single llama, two drovers can drive a large group of llamas, thereby exceeding the total cargo of two men by a significant amount.

3 See also Cummins 2002 for a discussion of the ruler as an embodiment of a polity.

REFERENCES CITED

Abbott, David

2010   The Rise and Demise of Marketplace
Exchange among the Prehistoric
Hohokam of Arizona. In *Archaeological
Approaches to Market Exchange in
Ancient Societies,* edited by Christopher P.
Garraty and Barbara L. Stark, pp. 61–83.
University Press of Colorado, Boulder.

Aoyama, Kazuo

1999   *Ancient Maya State, Urbanism, Exchange,
and Craft Specialization: Chipped Stone
Evidence from the Copan Valley and
the La Entrada Region, Honduras /
Estado, urbanismo, intercambio y espe-
cialización artesanal entre los mayas
antiguos: Evidencia de lítica menor del
Valle de Copán y la región de La Entrada,
Honduras.* Memoirs in Latin American
Archaeology 12. University of Pittsburgh,
Pittsburgh.

Berdan, Frances F.

1975   Trade, Tribute, and Market in the Aztec
Empire. PhD dissertation, Department
of Anthropology, University of Texas,
Austin.

1989   Trade and Markets in Precapitalist
States. In *Economic Anthropology,* edited
by Stuart Plattner, pp. 78–107. Stanford
University Press, Stanford.

Berdan, Frances F., and Patricia Rieff Anawalt (editors)

1992   *The Codex Mendoza.* 4 vols. University
of California Press, Berkeley.

Bittman, Bente, and Thelma Sullivan

1978   The Pochteca. In *Mesoamerican
Communication Routes and Cultural
Contacts,* edited by Thomas A. Lee Jr.
and Carlos Navarrete, pp. 211–218. New
World Archaeological Foundation,
Brigham Young University, Provo, Utah.

Bray, Tamara

2003   *The Archaeology and Politics of Food and
Feasting in Early States and Empires.*
Kluwer Academic/Plenum, New York.

Carlyle, Thomas

1849   Occasional Discourse on the Negro
Question. *Fraser's Magazine for Town
and Country* 40:527–538.

Carrasco, Pedro

1978   La economía del México prehispánico.
In *Economía política e ideología en el
México prehispánico,* edited by Pedro
Carrasco and Johanna Broda, pp. 13–74.
Editorial Nueva Imagen, Mexico City.

Cummins, Thomas B. F.

2002   *Toasts with the Inca: Andean Abstraction
and Colonial Images on Quero Vessels.*
University of Michigan Press, Ann Arbor.

Dahlin, Bruce, Christopher Jensen, Richard Terry,
David Wright, and Timothy Beach

2007   In Search of an Ancient Maya Market.
Latin American Antiquity 18:363–384.

Dalton, George

1977   Aboriginal Economies in Stateless
Societies. In *Exchange Systems in
Prehistory,* edited by Timothy K. Earle
and Jonathon E. Ericson, pp. 191–212.
Academic Press, New York.

D'Altroy, Terence, and Timothy K. Earle

1985   Staple Finance, Wealth Finance, and
Storage in the Inca Political Economy.
Current Anthropology 26:187–206.

D'Altroy, Terence, and Christine Hastorf

2001   *Empire and Domestic Economy.* Kluwer
Academic, New York.

Dercksen, Jan

1996   *The Old Assyrian Copper Trade in
Anatolia.* Nederlands Historisch-
Archaeologisch Instituut te Istanbul,
Istanbul.

Earle, Timothy

1977   A Reappraisal of Redistribution: Complex
Hawaiian Chiefdoms. In *Exchange
Systems in Prehistory,* edited by Timothy
K. Earle and Jonathon E. Ericson, pp.
213–229. Academic Press, New York.

Fedick, Scott L.

1996   *The Managed Mosaic: Ancient Maya
Agriculture and Resource Use.* University
of Utah Press, Salt Lake City.

Flannery, Kent V.

1976   The Empirical Determinants of Site
Catchments. In *The Early Mesoamerican
Village,* edited by Kent V. Flannery, pp.
103–117. Academic Press, New York.

Freidel, David A.

1981   The Political Economics of Residential Dispersion among the Lowland Maya. In *Lowland Maya Settlement Patterns*, edited by Wendy Ashmore, pp. 371–384. University of New Mexico Press, Albuquerque.

Garraty, Christopher P.

2010   Investigating Market Exchange in Ancient Societies: A Theoretical Review. In *Archaeological Approaches to Market Exchange in Ancient Societies,* edited by Christopher P. Garraty and Barbara L. Stark, pp. 3–32. University Press of Colorado, Boulder.

Garraty, Christopher P., and Barbara L. Stark (editors)

2010   *Archaeological Approaches to Market Exchange in Ancient Societies.* University Press of Colorado, Boulder.

Garza, Mercedes de la, Ana Luisa Izquierdo, María del Carmen León Cázares, Tolita Figueroa, and Carlos Ontiveros

1983   *Relaciones histórico-geográficas de la gobernación de Yucatán: (Mérida, Valladolid y Tabasco).* 2 vols. Universidad Nacional Autónoma de México, Mexico City.

Hassig, Ross

1982   Periodic Markets in Pre-Columbian Mexico. *American Antiquity* 47:346–355.

Heider, Karl

1969   Visiting Trade Institutions. *American Anthropologist* 71:462–471.

Henderson, John

1981   *The World of the Ancient Maya.* Cornell University Press, Ithaca, N.Y.

Hirth, Kenneth G.

1996   Political Economy and Archaeology: Perspectives on Exchange and Production. *Journal of Archaeological Research* 4:165–229.

2009a   Craft Production, Household Diversification, and Domestic Economy in Prehispanic Mesoamerica. In *Housework: Craft Production and Domestic Economy in Ancient Mesoamerica,* edited by Kenneth G. Hirth, pp. 13–32. Archaeological Papers of the American Anthropological Association 19. Wiley, Hoboken, N.J.

2009b   Craft Production in the Mesoamerican Marketplace. *Ancient Mesoamerica* 20:89–102.

2012   Markets, Merchants, and Systems of Exchange. In *Oxford Handbook of Mesoamerican Archaeology,* edited by Deborah L. Nichols and Christopher A. Pool, pp. 639–652. Oxford University Press, Oxford.

Humphrey, Caroline

1985   Barter and Economic Disintegration. *Man* 20:48–72.

Hutson, Scott

2000   Carnival and Contestation in the Aztec Marketplace. *Dialectical Anthropology* 25:123–149.

Inomata, Takeshi

2001   The Power and Ideology of Artistic Creation: Elite Craft Specialists in Classic Maya Society. *Current Anthropology* 39:451–476.

Johnson, Allen, and Timothy K. Earle

1987   *The Evolution of Human Societies: From Foraging Group to Agrarian State.* Stanford University Press, Stanford.

Katz, Friedrich

1966   *Situación social y económica de los aztecas durante los siglos XV y XVI.* Serie de Cultura Nahuatl, Monografías 8. Universidad Nacional Autónoma de México, Instituto de Investigaciones Históricas, Mexico City.

Kovacevich, Brigitte

2007   Ritual, Crafting, and Agency at the Classic Maya Kingdom of Cancuen. In *Mesoamerican Ritual Economy,* edited by E. Christian Wells and Karla L. Davis-Salazar, pp. 67–114. University of Colorado Press, Boulder.

La Lone, Darrell

1982   The Inca as a Nonmarket Economy: Supply in Command versus Supply and Demand. In *Contexts for Prehistoric Exchange,* edited by Jonathon E. Ericson and Timothy K. Earle, pp. 291–316. Academic Press, New York.

Masson, Marilyn A.

2002   Introduction. In *Ancient Maya Political Economies*, edited by Marilyn A. Masson and David A. Freidel, pp. 1–30. Altamira Press, Walnut Creek, Calif.

Mauss, Marcel

1990 [1924]   *The Gift: The Form and Reason for Exchange in Archaic Societies*. Translated by W. D. Halls. Routledge, London.

Mayer, Enrique

2002   *The Articulated Peasant: Household Economies in the Andes*. Westview Press, Boulder, Colo.

McAnany, Patricia A.

1989   Economic Foundations of Prehistoric Maya Society: Paradigms and Concepts. In *Prehistoric Maya Economies of Belize*, edited by Patricia A. McAnany and Barry L. Isaac, pp. 347–372. Research in Economic Anthropology, Supplement 4. JAI Press, Greenwich, Conn.

Murra, John

1972   El "control vertical" de un máximo de pisos ecológicos en la economía de las sociedades andinas. In *Visitas de la provincia de León de Huánuco en 1562: Iñigo Ortiz de Zuñiga, visitador*, edited by John V. Murra, pp. 429–476. Documentos para la Historia y Etnología de Huánuco y la Selva Central, vol. 2. Facultad de Letras y Educación, Universidad Nacional Hermilio Valdizán, Huánuco, Peru.

1980 [1955]   *The Economic Organization of the Inka State*. JAI Press, Greenwich, Conn.

1985   El Archipelago Revisited. In *Andean Ecology and Civilization: An Interdisciplinary Perspective on Andean Ecological Complementary*, edited by Shozo Masuda, Izumi Shimada, and Craig Morris, pp. 3–13. University of Tokyo Press, Tokyo.

Netting, Robert McC.

1990   Population, Permanent Agriculture, and Polities: Unpacking the Evolutionary Portmanteau. In *The Evolution of Political Systems: Sociopolitics in Small-Scale Sedentary Societies*, edited by Steadman Upham, pp. 21–61. Cambridge University Press, Cambridge.

1993   *Smallholders, Householders: Farm Families and the Ecology of Intensive, Sustainable Agriculture*. Stanford University Press, Stanford.

Nuñez, Atencio Lautaro, and Thomas Dillehay

1995   *Movilidad giratoria, armonía social y desarrollo en los Andes meridonales: Patrones de tráfico e interacción económica*. 2nd ed. Universidad Católica del Norte, Antofagasta, Chile.

O'Shea, John

1989   The Role of Wild Resources in Small-Scale Agricultural Systems: Tales from the Lakes and the Plains. In *Bad Year Economics: Cultural Responses to Risk and Uncertainty*, edited by Paul Halstead and John O'Shea, pp. 57–67. Cambridge University Press, Cambridge.

Pillsbury, Joanne

1996   The Thorny Oyster and the Origins of Empire: Implications of Recently Uncovered *Spondylus* Imagery from Chan Chan, Peru. *Latin American Antiquity* 7:313–340.

Polanyi, Karl

1957   The Economy as an Instituted Process. In *Trade and Market in the Early Empires: Economics in History and Theory*, edited by Karl Polanyi, Conrad M. Arensberg, and Harry W. Person, pp. 243–270. Free Press, New York.

Postgate, J. Nicholas

1992   *Early Mesopotamia: Society and Economy at the Dawn of History*. Routledge, London and New York.

Potter, Daniel, and Eleanor King

1995   A Heterarchical Approach to Lowland Maya Socioeconomies. In *Heterarchy and the Analysis of Complex Societies*, edited by Robert M. Ehrenreich, Carole L. Crumley, and Janet E. Levy, pp. 17–32. American Anthropological Association, Arlington, Va.

Pryor, Frederic

1977   *The Origins of the Economy: A Comparative Study of Distribution in Primitive and Peasant Economies*. Academic Press, New York.

Rice, Prudence

1987 Economic Change in the Lowland Maya Late Classic Period. In *Specialization, Exchange, and Complex Societies*, edited by Elizabeth M. Brumfiel and Timothy K. Earle, pp. 76–85. Cambridge University Press, Cambridge.

Rochette, Erick

2009 The Late Classic Period Organization of Jade Artifact Production in the Middle Motagua Valley, Zacapa, Guatemala. PhD dissertation, Department of Anthropology, Pennsylvania State University, University Park.

Rostworowski de Diez Canseco, María

1970 Mercaderes del valle de Chincha en la época prehispánica: Un documento y unos comentarios. *Revista española de antropología americana* 15:153–177.

Sahagún, Bernardino de

1959 *Florentine Codex: General History of the Things of New Spain*, bk. 9, *The Merchants*. Translated by Arthur J. O. Anderson and Charles E. Dibble. School of American Research, Santa Fe, and University of Utah, Salt Lake City.

1961 *Florentine Codex: General History of the Things of New Spain*, bk. 10, *The People*. Translated by Arthur J. O. Anderson and Charles E. Dibble. School of American Research, Santa Fe, and University of Utah, Salt Lake City.

Salomon, Frank

1986 *Native Lords of Quito in the Age of the Incas: The Political Economy of North-Andean Chiefdoms*. Cambridge University Press, Cambridge.

1987 A North Andean Status Trader Complex under Inca Rule. *Ethnohistory* 34:63–77.

Sheehy, James

1996 Ethnographic Analogy and the Royal Household in Eighth-Century Copan. In *Arqueología mesoamericana: Homenaje a William T. Sanders*, vol. 2, edited by Alba Guadalupe Mastache, Jeffrey Parsons, Robert Santley, and Mari Carmen Serra Puche, pp. 253–276. Instituto Nacional de Antropología e Historia, Mexico City.

Smith, Michael E.

2004 The Archaeology of Ancient State Economies. *Annual Review of Anthropology* 33:73–102.

2010 Regional and Local Market Systems in Aztec-Period Mexico. In *Archaeological Approaches to Market Exchange in Ancient Societies*, edited by Christopher P. Garraty and Barbara L. Stark, pp. 161–182. University Press of Colorado, Boulder.

Smith, Michael E., and Frances F. Berdan

2003 *The Postclassic Mesoamerican World*. University of Utah Press, Salt Lake City.

Stanish, Charles

2010 Labor Taxes, Market Systems, and Urbanization in the Prehispanic Andes: A Comparative Perspective. In *Archaeological Approaches to Market Exchange in Ancient Societies*, edited by Christopher P. Garraty and Barbara L. Stark, pp. 185–205. University Press of Colorado, Boulder.

Stark, Barbara L., and Christopher P. Garraty

2010 Detecting Marketplace Exchange in Archaeology: A Methodological Review. In *Archaeological Approaches to Market Exchange in Ancient Societies*, edited by Christopher P. Garraty and Barbara L. Stark, pp. 33–58. University Press of Colorado, Boulder.

Stark, Barbara L., and Alanna Ossa

2010 Origins and Development of Mesoamerican Marketplaces: Evidence from South-Central Veracruz, Mexico. In *Archaeological Approaches to Market Exchange in Ancient Societies*, edited by Christopher P. Garraty and Barbara L. Stark, pp. 99–126. University Press of Colorado, Boulder.

Strathern, Andrew

1971 *The Rope of Moka: Big-Men and Ceremonial Exchange in Mount Hage, New Guinea*. Cambridge University Press, Cambridge.

Thompson, John Eric Sidney

1954 *The Rise and Fall of Maya Civilization*. University of Oklahoma Press, Norman.

Tozzer, Alfred M.

1941   *Landa's* Relación de las cosas de
[ca. 1566]   Yucatan: *A Translation.* Papers of
            the Peabody Museum of American
            Archaeology and Ethnology 18. The
            Peabody Museum, Cambridge, Mass.

Trigger, Bruce

2003   *Understanding Early Civilizations:*
            A Comparative Study. Cambridge
            University Press, New York.

Veenhof, Klaas

2003   Trade and Politics in Ancient Assur:
            Balancing of Public, Colonial, and
            Entrepreneurial Interests. In *Mercanti*
            e politica nel mondo antico, edited by
            Carlo Zaccagnini, pp. 69–118. L'erma
            di Bretschneider, Rome.

Wallerstein, Immanuel

1976   *The Modern World-System.* Academic
            Press, New York.

Weatherford, Jack

1997   *The History of Money: From Sandstone*
            to Cyberspace. Crown, New York.

Wells, E. Christian, and Karla L. Davis-Salazar

2007   *Mesoamerican Ritual Economy:*
            Archaeological and Ethnological
            Perspectives. University Press of
            Colorado, Boulder.

West, Georgia

2002   Ceramic Exchange in the Late Classic
            and Postclassic Maya Lowlands: A
            Diachronic Approach. In *Ancient Maya*
            Political Economies, edited by Marilyn
            A. Masson and David A. Freidel,
            pp. 140–196. Altamira Press, Walnut
            Creek, Calif.

Widmer, Randolph

2009   Elite Household Multicrafting
            Specialization at 9N8, Patio H, Copan.
            In *Housework: Craft Production*
            and Domestic Economy in Ancient
            Mesoamerica, edited by Kenneth G.
            Hirth, pp. 174–204. Archaeological
            Publications of the American
            Anthropological Society 19. Wiley,
            Hoboken, N.J.

Wiessner, Polly

2002   Hunting, Healing, and Hxaro Exchange:
            A Long-Term Perspective on !Kung
            (Ju/'hoansi) Large-Game Hunting.
            Evolution and Human Behavior
            23:407–436.

Wilk, Richard

1989   *The Household Economy: Reconsidering*
            the Domestic Mode of Production.
            Westview Press, Boulder, Colo.

Willey, Gordon, and Demitri Shimkin

1973   The Maya Collapse: A Summary View.
            In *The Classic Maya Collapse*, edited
            by T. Patrick Culbert, pp. 457–502.
            University of New Mexico Press,
            Albuquerque.

Wolf, Eric

1982   *Europe and the People without History.*
            University of California Press, Berkeley.

2

Cooperation and the Moral Economy of the Marketplace

RICHARD E. BLANTON

ANTHROPOLOGY'S TURN TO PROCESSUALISM more than fifty years ago brought new theory that invigorated research on sociocultural evolution, but processualists erred by neglecting markets. This omission stems from a pervasive antimarket mentality (Cook 1966) that flowed from anthropology's embrace of elements of Marxist-Leninist theory; the claim of German neo-Romanticism that the market, with its anonymity and competitiveness, brings dehumanization (e.g., in the substantivist economic anthropology of Polanyi [1944:71–76]); and the idea that the commercialized West was unique in human experience (Goody 1990:xix). Now anthropologists and historians are acknowledging the ideological and orientalist origins of antimarket thinking (e.g., Blanton and Fargher 2010; Yang 1998; see also Burger, this volume; Mayer, this volume), and some are striving to fill the market-research gap (e.g., Attwood 1997; Berdan 1986; Blanton 1985, 1996; Fargher 2009; Feinman and Garraty 2010; Garraty and Stark 2010). While G. W. Skinner's (1964) pioneering study of Late

Imperial Chinese market systems is acknowledged as an important contribution to the development of contemporary market research in anthropology, the growing corpus of Mesoamericanist literature on markets is also thought of as exemplary (including Beals 1975; Cook and Diskin 1976; Smith 1976). Market research has entered into discussions of pre-Hispanic Mesoamerican civilization in a way that is unusual by comparison with other world regions; a full account is provided later in this chapter, in the introduction by Hirth and Pillsbury, and in the chapters by Nichols, Hirth, Carballo, Masson and Freidel, and McAnany.

It is time to rethink how we understand markets in relation to sociocultural evolution broadly conceived. This reevaluation requires a new theoretical synthesis to counter not only antimarket thinking but also the limitations inherent in traditional economic theory that views market transactions from the perspective of highly rational and individualized economic actors, thus "disembedding" market behavior from social ties and institutions, as the latter are regarded only as frictional drags on economic efficiency (critics of mainstream economic theory include Acheson 1994; Bates 1983; Evensky 2005:245; Granovetter 1992; North 1990; Sugden 1986; Swedberg 2005). To sidestep both anthropology and traditional economics, I propose that we should—as some economists have (e.g., Gintis et al. 2005; North 1990)—consider questions raised by cooperation research. According to this theory, while rational behavior may enhance market efficiency, it also has potentially negative outcomes when market participants aim for short-term gain by cheating (Milgrom et al. 1990:1). This approach is useful because markets inhabited by the highly individualized, competitive, and unregulated *Homo economicus* posited by economic theory likely would suffer from cooperation problems. Rather than *Homo economicus*, the ideal market participant turns out to be a cooperator whose actions, shaped by institutions and organizational structures, engender greater levels of trust necessary for effective market function (Fukuyama 1995; Henrich et al. 2010).[1] In this chapter, I make use of comparative data drawn from history, archaeology, and ethnography to address the question of how market cooperation problems are resolved in premodern conditions; I then evaluate the degree to which a cooperation approach might shed light on the commercial life of the Late Postclassic period of pre-Hispanic Mesoamerica.

Introduction to a Cooperation Theory for Market Study

The scheme I develop makes a distinction between those situations in which market transactions take place between persons who are known to each other directly (or indirectly through reputation) on the one hand, and situations in which the probability is higher that transactions will occur between strangers, on the other hand. Cooperation problems are minimized in the first case by the embeddedness of commercial transactions in diverse kinds of social relationships and ties. The latter situation is inherently problematic in terms of efficient

market functioning and thus presents interesting research questions. Market builders attempting to solve cooperation concerns in these contexts faced numerous impediments that we need to appreciate and understand (e.g., Bridbury 1986:117), most notably, as I argue below, when the intrinsically egalitarian nature of the marketplace challenges prevailing social conventions that reproduce and legitimate inequality.

Typically we know little about the earliest periods of market development, mostly because archaeologists have tended to ignore this aspect of social evolution (the principal New World exceptions include Abbott 2010 for Hohokam; Blanton 1983, Blanton et al. 1982, and Feinman and Nicholas 2010 for Oaxaca; Hirth 1998 for Morelos; Stark and Ossa 2010 for south-central Veracruz; and Dahlin et al. 2007, Dahlin et al. 2009, and Hutson et al. 2010 for the lowland Maya area), but I am able to elucidate the ways that humans have solved market cooperation problems from a comparative study of historical and ethnographic sources from various world areas. From these materials, I identify two key causal factors in market evolution, the first being geographical marginality and the social disembedding of the marketplace from the main political and economic structures of society; these aspects combine to carve out distinct physical and social spaces for marketplaces where cooperation could thrive. I add to these elements the social and cultural construction of paragovernmental organizations that endow marketplaces with forms of social capital suited to the resolution of cooperation problems. By necessity, then, the subject of this paper centers around the social behavior of persons who face cooperation problems in the context of commodity transactions, especially those behaviors found in the marketplace itself. For the premodern societies addressed here, marketplaces are defined as sites where people gather periodically to buy and sell goods and services, usually according to a set schedule of market days (e.g., Skinner 1964).

While this chapter reflects the influence of cooperation research, the approach taken here—because it is empirical and comparative—by necessity deviates from the research by economists on cooperation, which relies heavily on experimental games and mathematical simulations (e.g., Gintis et al. 2005; Greif 2006). Like the economists' *Homo economicus*, whose limited range of expected behaviors can be easily represented through mathematical analysis (Evensky 2005:257–258), game and simulation methods are ideally suited to the study of simple two-person interactions or of small groups in which cooperation is predicated on social knowledge of interacting partners from repeated games (e.g., Bowles and Gintis 2005). North (1990:12) makes the obvious point that "cooperation is more complex when the game is not repeated," which would obtain in many of the kinds of market transactions I will discuss.

Restricted Forms of Market Cooperation

In situations where market cooperation problems have not been fully resolved, market transactions will be limited to the comparatively personalized transactions occurring within what I term "restricted markets." In this category, market transactions are embedded in networks of social relationships in the sense of Granovetter (1992) and thus embody some characteristics of reciprocal gift exchanges (transactions of inalienable goods which aim to reproduce existing social relationships) rather than pure commodity transactions (those involving alienable goods between persons not aiming to build lasting social relationships [e.g., Gregory 1982]). As I describe below, the more embedded framework for market behavior poses numerous limitations and inefficiencies, especially for commoners,[2] so why haven't humans always devised solutions that allow them to transcend restricted markets? To address this dilemma, I point to the many kinds of market cooperation problems that inhibit market development beyond restricted forms. I employ a thought experiment in which I situate restricted market exchange in the kind of sociospatial context generalized from actual well-known cases from ethnographic and archaeological research, and which is exemplified in some of the ethnographic and historical examples I address here.

A typical setting for my thought experiment is a politically fragmented macroregion consisting of a patchwork of loosely connected but largely autonomous chiefdoms or small states—such as Renfrew's (1975) "early state module." Areas surrounding the core regions of the polities consisted of weakly controlled shatter or buffer zones where communities enjoyed some freedom from what James Scott, discussing Southeast Asia, describes as the "oppressions of the state-making projects in the valleys—slavery, conscription, taxes, corvée labor . . ." (Scott 2009:ix). In my thought experiment, shatter-zone marketplaces—for example, border markets situated at points of intersection between regions with differing resource endowments—present difficult market cooperation problems. Here, market transactions will be plagued with uncertainty and opportunism, exacerbated by the fact that participants potentially could include persons from diverse ethnic groups, polities, factions, or clans who may view each other as enemies. Further, marketplace transactions in the main political centers may also be limited if marketplaces are located in strongly fortified political centers that are not readily accessible to strangers (such as marketers from distant regions [e.g., Hill 1966:298]).

Elite Involvement in Border Markets

In the historical and ethnographic materials I investigated, border markets and fairs located in zones of weak sovereignty abound (e.g., Benet 1957:197; Pohl et al. 1997; Sawyer 1986:66), but border market transactions will exemplify my sense of restricted markets if most interpolity commerce rests in the hands of an elite. Here the embeddedness of market transactions reflects social ties stemming from diplomacy, genealogy, intermarriage, and reciprocal gifting (e.g., Feldman 1985:20; Roberts 1970:42) that endow the governing elite with commercially advantageous "network capital" (Fafchamps 2004).[3] A pattern of restricted cooperation will also obtain when merchant groups migrate from regions where more complex forms of market cooperation have developed; such groups use their network capital to organize trade, potentially even displacing the governing elite in trade prowess because of their ability to extend regional trade to a world-system scale (Oka and Fuentes 2010:15–18). Examples include Chinese merchant groups in Southeast Asia (Davis 1973:170–172; Dewey 1962:44–49; T'ien 1953) and Arab and Swahili traders in sub-Saharan Africa (Ensminger 1997; Northrup 1978; Tosh 1970).

Disadvantages abound for commoners in these situations because they lack the comparable sources of network capital that an elite or merchant group can use to dominate interpolity trade and its profits (e.g., Roberts 1970). Market inefficiency is compounded by the disincentives faced by commoners when they attempt to extend their own commercial efforts into the interpolity sphere. In addition to the inherent dangers of travel into foreign territories and shatter zones, problems ensue when disputes arise in market contexts, as they often do given the potential for cheating. In this case, commoners will choose to participate only when they can expect fair adjudication ("adjudicative trust"),[4] but they may be at a disadvantage in comparatively lawless boundary settings and when market judges favor a powerful elite or sectorial interests, such as those based on polity membership or ethnicity (e.g., Benet 1957:202).

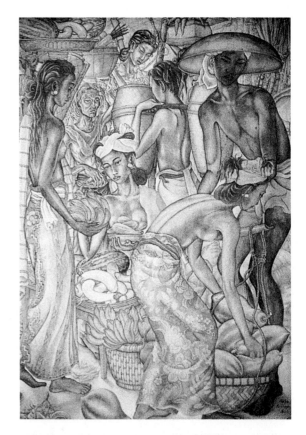

figure 2.1

Local market in Bali. (Reproduced from *Market Scene*, by Sobrat of Padangtegal, in A. A. M. Djelantik, *Balinese Paintings* [1986], plate 5, with permission of Oxford University Press, Hong Kong.)

Local Markets

Unless border market cooperation problems can be resolved, risk and other disincentives to participation leave commoners with few marketing choices beyond their polity boundaries. In this local context, cooperation is assured because commercial exchange takes place in conjunction with other communal activities that bring together members of a local social group (e.g., Smith 1962:309). In this case, market cooperation is enhanced when trade is with persons who are kin or who are known from reputation or from prior interactions. (Polanyi [1944:62–63] describes local markets in similar terms.) Figure 2.1 depicts a local market in Bali, where, in the nineteenth century, commerce featured the restricted pattern. Local intrapolity trade

occurred in "morning markets," where daily staples could be purchased, while intermarket and inter-island trade was in the hands of Balinese rulers and non-Balinese trading groups who were mostly Chinese and Arabs (Geertz 1980).

Transcending Restricted Markets

To the degree that an elite (or a merchant specialist) group is able to maintain its domination of interpolity and world-system scale trade, and if commoners are able to satisfy their consumer needs principally through local markets, the two-tiered commercial system that sharply separates elite and commoner market activities could remain unchanged. Growing demand may stimulate the creation of new institutional arrangements to enhance commoner market participation beyond the local scale, although, from my review of the literature, it is not always clear what forces cause market evolution. The idea that pressure to develop new market arrangements will emanate from a governing elite is questionable since the elite thrive on the interpolity commerce stemming from their superior network capital. I would also note that, in some situations I encountered, the governing elite display little interest in market involvement (e.g., Bridbury 1986:108; Hill 1966:297, 299). In other cases, elite intervention in market management did occur but was not conducive to market development or even functioning (Bridbury 1986:113; Shaw 1981:53) when, for example, local norms of justice are inappropriate in interlocal situations such as border markets (Benet 1957:200). By contrast, commoners often are described as benefiting when they gain direct access to nonlocal goods, sometimes even basic foodstuffs (e.g., Benet 1957:193; Hill 1971; Riddell 1974), which points to the possibility that the incentives to devise new forms of market cooperation were situated at the base of society rather than among the governing elite.[5]

Beyond Restricted Markets

Markets could not survive "unless those who [were] enfranchised . . . [made] some concessions to those who they would rather exclude . . . from opportunities for profitable dealing . . ." (Bridbury 1986:108).

Free people make free markets (Kerridge 1986: 123).[6]

I propose that the market cooperation problem is not fully resolved unless both commoners and elite trust that they will be able to extend marketplace activities beyond the local scale. Because we live in a society with largely free and reasonably well-regulated markets, we take full commercialization for granted, but numerous hurdles had to be overcome by the early market builders who paved the way for our highly developed commercial economies. In this section, I argue that for commoners to participate in nonlocal commercial venues, radical institutional and cultural changes must be made that transform traditional systems of morality and modes of governance. For example, the institutions and ethical codes that make possible adjudicative trust are predicated on an underlying sense that all market participants—across the class divide and between genders and ethnicities—have the requisite moral capacity to distinguish between self-interest and moral obligation to others. If this is present, a diverse group of marketers are free to engage equitably in market transactions and to stand in front of market arbiters as moral equals. When the peasantry are viewed as an exploitable and largely politically and culturally irrelevant subaltern class, these kinds of ideas may not be readily accepted by an elite, making market development a difficult and lengthy process entailing cultural, institutional, and organizational change that is most likely instigated by those who lack control over the customary ideational and material sources of power in society.

I point to medieval European history, where market builders faced "a thousand obstacles, many formidable, others tenuous, [that] impeded their activities at every turn" (Bridbury 1986:117). In this case, such hurdles included dissolving long-established feudal notions of property rights in order for property to be "private to individuals and their families, corporations, and other voluntary associations" (Kerridge 1986:121). This change allowed for mutually profitable trade across social sectors with no fear that profits, or goods bought and sold, could be confiscated according to feudal concepts of fealty or other expressions of elite privilege and domination of commoners. Bridbury (1986:83) sees social equality also in terms of the development of a more pragmatic approach to moral concepts surrounding wealth and its uses. Commoners were not likely to trust the market until a new mentality placed moral restrictions on the uses of wealth because, in the European Middle Ages, "anything could be bought," including justice.

Markets and Liminality

The market brings a state of "absolute depersonalization . . . contrary to all the elementary forms of human relationship . . . [such as those based on] . . . personal fraternization or even blood kinship" (Weber 1978:637).

While the neo-Romanticists thought that the depersonalization of the market was dehumanizing, Max Weber recognized that in the market, people develop new concepts for cooperation based on the "rational legality" of "market ethics" (Weber 1978:636). Further, Weber realized that a market ethic will imply a radical departure from other ethical systems, such as those of the religious and political domains of society, making the market ethic a distinct "value sphere," standing in opposition to the substantive rationality predominating in other spheres, especially the political (e.g., Weber 1946:331–333). While, typically, in the political sphere, social conventions link status to the privileges of power and wealth appropriation, in the market the predominant values emphasize the importance of cooperation among social equals.

But how is it possible to build and maintain a separate, and even contrary, value sphere within the larger framework of society? In part, the answer to this question is found in a spatial logic that requires the physical separation of contrastive value spheres. As Benet (1957:212) describes it for the Berber Highlands, "That both these contexts of Berber life are institutionalized into physically separate places of action, village and market, is important indeed. If they were not, these contraries would come to a head-on collision." Further, the spatial logic of separation is augmented by the identity-transforming power of the liminal process as it is applied to the marketplace. To be in the marketplace is to enter a liminal phase during which the marketer exits, temporarily, from the modes of coercive appropriation of goods and services found in the political community (e.g., Weber 1978:640). For example, as Scott (1990:122) observed, in the medieval European market, "privilege was suspended" so that "the rituals and deference required before lords and clergy

did not apply." Other market-threatening aspects of identity are also abandoned as the liminal phase engenders a collective sentiment of cooperation that substitutes for ethnicity or other possible sources of factionalism and dispute (e.g., Benet 1957:193). It is also of interest to note that in Europe, as elsewhere, the suspension of privilege extended to gender relations. Researchers have often noted that the market is a domain where women's traditional roles are relaxed, allowing them to act to an unusual degree as autonomous economic actors (Boserup 1970:87–95; Hill 1971; Hodder 1961; Wycherley 1978:94). For example, as Benet (1957:205) noted in the Berber Highlands, even in this Islamic society, women engaged independently in market transactions, and "the market is a source of feminine private income." Below, I use the degree of female participation in commercial activities as a barometer of marketplace egalitarianism.

As a liminal zone, the marketplace takes on a sacred character because, in Turner's (1969:128) phraseology, liminality has the power to transgress or dissolve norms and "is accompanied by experiences of unprecedented potency."[7] Sacredness may be highlighted by designating the marketplace's physical boundary as a socially and symbolically meaningful threshold. Among the West African Loango, for example, market entrances were publicly commemorated by constructions that "symbolize this 'truce of God'—mounds fenced in with stakes, memorial posts, and structures of poles intertwined with branches of the large-leaved, spreading fig-tree known as *nzandu*" (Thurnwald 1932:167–168). In classical Athens, the boundary (*perirrhanteria*) of the Agora, a political zone with market functions (it was originally a market area), was signified by stone markers (*horoi*) that read "I am the boundary of the Agora" (Figure 2.2); persons deemed to have questionable moral character were not allowed to cross this boundary (Wycherley 1978:62). In the highland Berber region, markets were enclosed by a "holy perimeter" (*haran*) specifying the limits of a zone of safe passage (Benet 1957:196). As was true for other Arabian sanctuaries, the Ka'ba in the valley of Mecca was surrounded by a sacred limit (*haram*) within which no

figure 2.2
Horos (boundary marker of the Agora), Athens, fifth century BC. (Photograph courtesy of the Agora Excavations, American School of Classical Studies, Athens.)

blood could be shed. As Mecca gained in commercial importance, the market managers, the Koreish (Quraysh, Quraish), "self-consciously sought to extend the sacred precinct as a means for increasing the stability of social relations in their trading territory" (Wolf 1951:337–338).

Marketplace as a Site of Anti-Structure

Liminality is an identity-transforming process present in many societies and often figures into rites of passage, from adolescent to adult roles, or other transitions (Turner 1969; Van Gennep 1909). Similarly, in the market, "liminars" cross a threshold into a market space to, in Turner's (1969:95) words, "elude or slip through systems of classification that normally locate states and positions in cultural space." In this sense, the market becomes a domain of what Turner calls "anti-structure"; there, society is reconfigured "as an unstructured or rudimentarily structured and relatively undifferentiated *comunitas*, community, or even communion of equals," an inversion of the domain of "structure," which he defines as a "differentiated and often hierarchical system of politico-legal-economic position with many types of evaluation, separating men in terms of 'more' or 'less'" (Turner 1969:96).[8]

While no market is totally unstructured, in the historical and ethnographic literature I reviewed markets often were viewed in anti-structural terms in the sense that they are sites where people were freer to engage in alternate political discourses— what Scott (1990:122) refers to as sites of "antihegemonic discourse." Similarly, Benet (1957:193) repeats E. Doutte's claim that in Arab markets, "political information is passed on, the announcements of the authorities are made and the reaction to these are formed . . . political conspiracies started, public outcries raised, broadminded proposals mooted and crimes hatched" (cf. Shaw 1981:56). That the market is in some senses a domain of anti-structure may explain why elitist philosophical discourses often depict the market and its activities as amoral or dangerous (Dilley 1989). For example, Redfield (1986:29–30) notes that in the *Iliad* and the *Odyssey*, commerce is associated with "disreputable" Phoenicians, and he comments on the "tense" relationship of the Greek polis and the market. Aristotle distinguished the "natural" economy of the household (*oikonomia*) from the "unnatural" market economy (*kapelike*) (Parry 1989:84); this duality has been a stimulus to anthropology's antimarket mentality, as expressed by Marx and Polanyi (Booth 1993; Nafissi 2005:3–10). Similar antimarket biases are found in Chinese political thought (e.g., Duyvendak 1928:49–55), in Tokugawa Japan (Hall 1991:3), and in medieval Europe, where church dogma condemned merchants (e.g., Bridbury 1986:84; Le Goff 1980:59–65; Parry 1989:78).

Marketplace and Sociocultural Change

While the early marketplaces may have become, in some senses, sites of anti-structure, this is only part of the story, since a marketplace, to function efficiently, requires "social capital" in the form of institutions (rules of operation) coupled with an organizational structure that enacts rules in social practice. In this respect, although traditional economic theory emphasized how markets are more efficient when there is competition between participants, here I emphasize the importance of competition between marketplaces for bringing about beneficial social change (e.g., Hill 1966:305). The problem of conflict management provides a useful example. In those marketplaces without the requisite social capital to provide adequate public order, one solution is for participants to take matters into their own hands to exercise informal constraints (altruistic punishment) (North 1990:39–40), sometimes violently, as described by Benet (1957:204). But market regulation by altruistic punishment may make markets inherently dangerous places, such as in the "explosive markets" of the Berber Highlands, where episodes of extreme violence are recorded in a "sudden, panicky 'snapping' which breaks the peace of the *suq* [market]: the *nefra'a*" (Benet 1957:203). In my review of the literature, I encountered few instances where altruistic punishment played any meaningful role in solving the

market cooperation problem, perhaps because, as Benet (1957:205) noted for markets in the Berber Highlands, violence "will discredit a *suq* and people will stop coming to it" (cf. Bridbury 1986:111).

A more common and presumably less violent solution than altruistic punishment is "piggybacking" markets on existing organizations capable of maintaining order, especially the sanctifying of markets by linking them to religious sites such as shrines, pilgrimage sites, and churches. As examples, I point to periodic markets that were part of religious festivals (*panegyreis*) in ancient Greece (Spawforth 1996) and the numerous early medieval European markets located near pagan cult centers, Christian churches, and pilgrimage sites (Sawyer 1986:64–69). A fair near the Basilica of Impruneta in the province of Florence, for example, combined commerce with the celebration of a miracle said to have occurred there (Figure 2.3). Scandinavian markets were protected by the "Law of Saint Cuthbert" that guaranteed seven days of safe travel during market days (Sawyer 1986:64; see also Burger, this volume). Another possible benefit from piggybacking on religious sites is that the authority of religious figures allows them to manage markets and adjudicate disputes in a neutral manner (Hill 1966:296). If they are sufficiently free of elite patronage and control—and as long as the increased transaction costs to the religious and host organization are mitigated in some way—religious organizations or specialists can gain from the increased traffic in a well-managed market. In medieval Europe, marketplaces prospered if they were in proximity to a church, and at the same time they benefited church officials who realized revenues from them (e.g., Sawyer 1986:62–64; a similar example is the holy men in the Berber Highlands as described in Shaw 1981:69–70), but this connection created a dilemma because by associating with markets and commerce, clergy were in violation of church canon handed down from the papal offices (Bridbury 1986:86; Le Goff 1980:63–65; cf. Shaw 1981:69). That religious figures could operate effectively and autonomously is illustrated in cases in the Berber Highlands, where some marketplaces housed shrines built to honor religious authorities renowned for their success in market

SERENISSIMO COSMO... MAGNO DVCI ETRVRIÆ...

figure 2.3

Jacques Callot, *The Fair at Impruneta*, 1619. (Reproduced with permission of the Fine Arts Museum of San Francisco, San Francisco.)

management. The shrine symbolized that, even in death, marketplace order could be maintained by a "formidable saint" (Benet 1957:201).

I found altruistic punishment and piggybacking on religious authority in some cases where border market exchanges were economically important but institutional controls were only weakly developed. But cooperation problems are more effectively mitigated when a governing body of market liminars—I call them "market managers"—is present. Market managers develop a paragovernmental mode of governance, separate from political or religious authorities, that is funded by internal market-produced revenues. While economic anthropologists have focused attention on how wealth is generated in premodern societies principally from the reproduction of kinship roles (Gregory 1982) and elite appropriation from a subaltern class (Wolf 1999), market revenues from tolls, space-rental fees, and fines can also generate wealth to fund paragovernmental organizations.

Viewed cross-culturally, a bewildering variety of forms of paragovernmental market management can be found. To illustrate the range of possibilities, I mention only a few examples, including "masters of the market" found in some highland Berber markets (Benet 1957:201) and among the Loango of West Africa (Thurnwald 1932:168); the Maghribi traders' coalitions of medieval North Africa and other merchant guilds described by Greif (2006); "law merchants" who adjudicated disputes and maintained records on the market dealings of merchants in the European early Middle Ages (Milgrom et al. 1990); and specialized market brokers who facilitated trade between strangers in Hausaland (Hill 1971:315). The Diakhanké, located on the margins of the Malian territory (AD 1600–1850), illustrate a type of social arrangement found in several sub-Saharan African polities influenced by Islam (Curtin 1971). The Diakhanké were specialized market managers whose zone of control, though technically within Malian territory, was in a fringe area that they governed somewhat independently as a recognized sanctuary from direct state control. Here, the Diakhanké devoted themselves to religion and market matters, including judicial services and caravan protection. Perhaps the most famous Old World example of paragovernmental market managership is the Koreish, sometimes described as a "tribe of traders," who, beginning around AD 400, managed a major Arabian border market in the environmentally marginal valley of Mecca (Wolf 1951). They engaged in commerce, guarded caravans, and managed markets with such authority that they were able, even in this militarily charged situation, to require market participants to surrender their weapons.

The Evolution of Market Cooperation in Pre-Hispanic Mesoamerica

All of the concepts used or developed in this chapter to characterize variant forms and degrees of market cooperation—restricted markets, border markets, adjudicative trust, market as liminal space, market as anti-structure, and paragovernmental market managers—are applicable, to varying degrees, in the Postclassic period of pre-Hispanic Mesoamerica. Forms of market cooperation differ in this complex civilization, both in space and time, although diachronic change is beyond the scope of this paper; all of the marketplace behavior I discuss below is known from archaeology and from ethnohistoric and early colonial documents that shed light on the Postclassic period. While information on markets is uneven—early Spanish sources focused the most attention on Central Mexico and its notable marketplaces—enough information is available to identify major themes in Postclassic-period market cooperation.

Restricted Markets in the Maya Region

The Epiclassic and Postclassic periods saw a reordering of Mesoamerica's world-system geography (Smith and Berdan 2003) and growing world-system interactions that yielded significant economic changes in the Maya area (Kepecs and Masson 2003; Smith and Berdan 2003; see also McAnany, this volume, for a summary of commercial changes beginning in the Late and Terminal Classic periods). Chichen Itza (Kepecs 2007) and Mayapan (see Masson and Freidel, this volume) emerged as prominent political capitals and world-system trade centers. Endogenous intermarket commerce is evident, for example, at the trade entrepôt at Cozumel, which, interestingly, also featured one of the most important shrines of the period in Yucatan (Rathje and Sabloff 1975:10). Commercial change during the Postclassic period is also evident in the south Gulf coast, where the Nonoalca and Olmeca-Xicallanca intermediated goods exchange and cultural diffusion between the Maya area, Central Mexico, and Oaxaca (McCafferty 2007), and in the activities of commercially active groups such as the Mexicanized Putun (e.g., Kepecs 2007:133–134). There is no question that markets functioned throughout the Maya region; there were local markets (e.g., Feldman 1985:21) as well as border markets located either in neutral sites at the edges of political boundaries, such as Belen in Guatemala (Feldman 1985:15), or in marginal polities controlled by militarily independent but weak states (Feldman 1985:19), including the aforementioned Cozumel. Although there was a network of local and border markets, the evidence supports the conclusion that much aboriginal Maya market cooperation was restricted. In both Yucatan and highland Guatemala (Feldman 1985; Roys 1943:11), markets operated within the context of a patchwork of autonomous and sometimes warring polities (e.g., as described by Bishop Diego de Landa in the mid-sixteenth century [Tozzer 1941 (ca. 1566):96]) that in most respects matches the scenario for a politically fragmented landscape I sketched out previously. I infer a situation of largely restricted modes of commerce from Feldman's (1985:19–21) study of highland Guatemala, in which he distinguished between "petty traders" operating principally within their local districts and the small number of "upper-class" traders who journeyed to distant markets, where their transactions were made on "a more personal basis," occurring in relation to gift exchanges and other kinds of reciprocation among elites (cf. Roys 1943:51). Archaeological data from earlier in the Maya Postclassic period also point to the importance of the governing elite in commerce (Masson et al. 2006:197).

In this largely elite-driven situation, it seems unlikely that commoners could expect fair adjudication, as we see from Landa's comment that "the nobles laughed at the friars because they gave ear to the poor and rich without distinction" (Tozzer 1941 [ca. 1566]:97). Additionally, there is little evidence that paragovernmental market management was present in native Maya commerce. Instead, management was vested in local political authorities whose degree of adjudicative neutrality seems to have been limited, given that they "had cause to fear the merchants from the more powerful states"

(Feldman 1985:19). While Landa noted the presence of women in marketplaces (Tozzer 1941 [ca. 1566]:127), they may have been mostly elites. Landa (in Tozzer 1941 [ca. 1566]:97) describes commoner women as "brief in their conversations, and . . . not accustomed to do any business for themselves, especially if they were poor."

Restricted Markets or Market Cooperation in Oaxaca?

Aboriginal Mixtec maps, early colonial documents, and archaeology provide a partial picture of markets in Postclassic Oaxaca. As in the Maya region, Oaxaca's social landscape was politically fragmented (Byland and Pohl 1994;

figure 2.4
A Mixtec ruler shown with a son who has become a merchant (after Smith and Berdan, eds. 2003:fig. 22.4). (Reproduced with permission of John M. D. Pohl and the University of Utah Press.)

Kowalewski et al. 2009:324), even in the valley of Oaxaca, where only a thin veneer of centralized political control was exercised over a series of what my colleagues and I termed petty kingdoms (Kowalewski et al. 1989:344–348). In the politically fragmented Mixteca Alta region, the social fabric of interpolity exchange reflected principally elite interests that combined marriages, alliances, and diplomacy with the rich trade in prestige goods. It would appear that the principal long-distance merchants were junior members of the great families who governed local polities (Pohl 2003a, 2003b:175) (Figure 2.4),[9] while the degree of commoner participation in border markets or other interpolity exchange is not known with certainty. Especially in the Mixteca Alta region, aboriginal maps depict many activities associated with interpolity boundary zones, including ballcourts, pilgrimage sites, shrines, oracles, sites of shamanic practice, monastic orders, and border markets (Pohl et al. 1997; Smith 1973; cf. Abbott 2010, describing how early Hohokam marketplaces were associated with ballcourt ceremonialism). While local markets possibly were a common feature of the polity (ñuu) centers (Terraciano 2001:248), Pohl and his coauthors suggest that border markets were the main market type (Pohl et al. 1997:215–219). This stance is confirmed from Postclassic settlement pattern data (Kowalewski et al. 2009) analyzed by Pluckhahn (2009), who identified thirty-seven potential Mixteca Alta market plazas, of which the majority were in border locations. Similarly, in the valley of Oaxaca, Appel (1982:147–148) found colonial-period documentary evidence for border markets, while the majority of political centers lacked significant markets.

Archaeological and ethnohistoric data are not clear on the extent of Mixteca Alta market culture and the nature of marketplace social capital, and, as I mentioned, it is not even clear whether commoners regularly attended border markets. Women participated in markets (Terraciano 2001:248), although it is unclear whether this took place beyond the local scale. It does appear to be the case that market cooperation issues may have been resolved to some degree by piggybacking markets onto religious sites, including shrines, divination sites, sacred funerary sites, and sacred caves. Religious specialists (*yahui*, a term that also denotes "market" or "fair") served as both market administrators and "merchant princes" (Pohl et al. 1997:210), and the etymology of the word *yahui* links it to market-related words such as "price" and "gain" (Smith 1973:49). Yet the evidence points to primarily elite participation in intermarket trade (Terraciano 2001:249–251), suggesting something less than full commercialization in the Mixteca Alta region. Tellingly, in the absence of what Terraciano calls "corporate" market regulation, after the Conquest, Spanish administrators took control of local and long-distance trading; it also appears to be the case that pre-Hispanic markets were not taxed, at least judging from the intense opposition to market taxation when it was introduced by the Spanish colonial authorities. By contrast, among the Central Mexican Nahua groups, indigenous systems of market management and taxation were retained in aboriginal hands long after the Spanish conquest (Berdan 1986), even up to the eighteenth century in some provincial towns (Gibson 1964:352–356); I consider this interesting situation next.

Market Cooperation in Central Mexico

The strongly commercialized economy of the Central Mexican Postclassic period is well known from early Spanish accounts and archaeology (Berdan 1985, 1986; Blanton 1996; Charlton 1994; Hassig 1985; Hodge and Smith 1994; Minc 2009; Nichols et al. 2002; Smith and Berdan 2003). While in the Maya area and in Oaxaca, fragmented social landscapes provided social environments suited to border markets, in Central Mexico the region was largely politically integrated by the Aztec Empire. In its imperial core in the Basin of Mexico, a commercial landscape developed that was a hierarchically structured interlocking market system similar to what is predicted from central-place theory (Blanton 1996), and this system extended into adjacent regions such as Morelos (e.g., Smith 2010). Although analysis of archaeological collections points to some degree of regionalism rather than basin-wide exchange in this commercial economy, it was the case that even ordinary goods such as specialist-produced pottery moved long distances through market channels that transcended local political boundaries (Charlton et al. 2008; Garraty 2006; Minc 2009).

This degree of regional integration suggests that commoners had market destination choices beyond the local, and this view is supported by early colonial-period documents that describe how commoners took even multiday trips to distant markets outside their own polity and ethnic group (e.g., Durán 1967 [1570–1581]:1:177). Specialized commoner merchants traveled between different markets, following the schedule of market days (Motolinía 1903 [ca. 1560]:331). Commoners enjoyed a wide range of potential market destinations and goods choices, including what Susan Kepecs (2003:130) has termed "bulk luxury goods"—dyed cotton, cacao, polychrome pottery, green obsidian, and imported fine salt (Blanton et al. 2005). In Nahua society, women played an important role in the marketplaces (Sahagún 1950–1982:10:figs. 119, 120–127). In fact, the market was the major avenue of social advancement for commoner women, who could become wealthy merchants and even serve as market judges (McCafferty and McCafferty 1988:48).

Central Mexican marketplaces boasted elements of market cooperation discussed previously, including the piggybacking of markets on religious sites (signified as "gods of the marketplaces" in Durán [1971 (1574–1579):273]), market liminality, anti-structure and alternate structure, adjudicative trust, and paragovernmental market managers.[10] These features are described most completely in relation to the region's main market at Tlatelolco, a vast walled concourse that served up to an estimated fifty thousand people on major market days (Cortés 1986:103). It is reasonable to see this market as a liminal space in some ways distinct from the central political structure and cultural pattern of neo-Toltec Nahua (Aztec) society. For example, inspired by accounts of the carnival-like atmosphere in European medieval markets (Bakhtin 1984; Scott 1990), Hutson looked for and found

evidence of anti-structure in the Tlatelolco market, concluding that the market "simultaneously represents, contests, and inverts ordinary sites and ideologies of Aztec society" (Hutson 2000:124). The author alludes to the Tlatelolco marketplace's open expression of gender equality as well as tales of women engaging in flirting or other violations of decorum (cf. Joyce 2000:161), possible public drunkenness, and spectacles such as humorous or bawdy performances.[11] Another useful example of the "anti-structural" quality of the market is the fact that a slave who passed into the market boundary and then escaped his owner could become a free person (Durán 1971 [1574–1579]:284–285).

Amazingly, the Tlatelolco market—the most commercially active space in all of pre-Hispanic Mesoamerica at the time—was constituted as a distinct social domain in which the official judicial authority of the powerful Aztec Empire was suspended, leaving market management entirely in the hands of an organization of commoner specialists, the *pochteca* (Sahagún 1950–1982:9:24). The *pochteca* organization, a paragovernmental system functioning within the larger authority structure of the Aztec Empire, consisted of twelve regional subgroups integrated into a hierarchically arranged umbrella organization whose central authorities resided in Tenochtitlan (Van Zantwijk 1985:ch. 7). Although *pochteca* members were commoners, their degree of political influence and autonomous authority is quite striking and unmatched by Maya or Oaxacan organizations. The *pochteca* leader was a member of the Aztec Empire's ruling council, *pochteca* independently governed the important commercial center of Tochtepec in Oaxaca, and *pochteca* had the authority to sentence to death members who violated the code of market ethics (Offner 1983:156). The *pochteca's* judicial neutrality in commercial matters was recognized (Sahagún 1950–1982:8:69; cf. Van Zantwijk 1985:ch. 7), although, outside of the Tlatelolco market, political authorities were likewise concerned that their own, as well as *pochteca,* judicial services were neutral and effective (Sahagún 1950–1982:8:67). Lastly, all persons recruited into the *pochteca* organization were taught to uphold an ethical code that included loyalty to and solidarity with the *pochteca* group; respect and regard for others, including non-Aztec peoples, and their property; and fairness in matters of trade (a more complete account is found in Van Zantwijk 1985:171).

Mythic History and Market Cooperation in Central Mexico

I have pointed to several social and cultural changes—including imperial political integration, market liminality, and paragovernmental market management—that were key to market cooperation and full commercialization in Central Mexico. Underlying these specific changes, however, I suggest that market cooperation was also an outgrowth of Postclassic neo-Toltec Nahua cultural innovation that served to complicate the role of ethnicity as an element of the social solidarity of local groups. At the same time, this ideational system attributed a high level of moral capacity and virtue to commoners, especially when viewed comparatively with Oaxaca and the Maya area.[12] In Oaxaca, local polities were dominated by powerful ruling families who used origin myths and funerary cults to enhance corporate solidarity within their particular territories, linking ancestors to local places or phenomena such as rivers and trees to bolster the claim that "they had always been the stewards of the land" (Pohl 2003a:64). By contrast, in Central Mexico, institutional and cultural changes resulted in a less patchy and fragmented conceptualization of ethnicity and also weakened the divide between noble and commoner. The cultural origins of this Central Mexican pattern is found in the promulgation of a slightly varied but largely uniform mythic history shared among many of the Postclassic Nahua peoples (Fargher et al. 2010; much of the following is summarized from Bernal-García 2007:69; Boone 1991:148; Broda 1991; cf. Gillespie 1989:xxv; Van Zantwijk 1985; Wolf 1999:278).

According to mythic history, many of the different ethnic groups making up the Nahua peoples could trace their origins to "primitive" Chichimecs (desert people) who migrated from a shared origination point (Boone 1991). Not only did they share origins, the different migrating groups eventually colonized distinct regions of Central Mexico to establish polities, but, in the process, they all adopted elements of culture and language from the more "civilized" neo-Toltec Nahua, a clear indication that ethnic identity was viewed as permutable. I suggest that this scheme resulted in a comparatively weak and contingent sense of ethnicity in Central Mexico and thus allowed for extensive interpolity social interaction as well as migration, producing what Barbara Stark (2008:44) refers to as an "ethnic mosaic" (cf. Brumfiel 1994; Van Zantwijk 1985).

In addition to its theory of ethnic origins and change, mythic history also contains an extended discourse on the moral capacity of the common person. The principal feature of this discourse was a Nahua cultural logic that presented authority and moral capacity in relation to a logic of opposition that contrasted two principal deities who together created what the Nahua peoples thought of as the current world. Quetzalcoatl was symbolically associated with the collapsed Toltec civilization and its noble descendants who held most positions of authority (Nicholson 2001), while Tezcatlipoca was often associated with the arid north and the Chichimec peoples (e.g., Van Zantwijk 1985:96–97). In this dual scheme, the neo-Toltec person enjoys a civilized way of life—sedentary, farming, with great material wealth—while the Chichimec person, though closer to a state of nature (and therefore culturally and technologically deprived), may possess a well-developed sense of moral purpose and understanding. Tezcatlipoca's ability to perceive the potential for virtue in all persons illustrates the latter point (Heyden 1991:189; Sahagún 1950–1982:2:5).

These elements of Central Mexican culture change are first evident after about AD 1000 at Tula, where a column on the important Pyramid B on the city's central concourse pairs the earliest known representation of Tezcatlipoca with a representation of Topiltzin Quetzalcoatl (Mastache et al. 2002:303–304). Nearby, a frieze in a colonnaded hall that links Pyramid B to the main concourse is interpreted by Kristan-Graham (1993) as a procession of merchants and evidence of what she calls Tula's emerging "business narrative." This new religion, its associated business narrative, and discourse on moral capacity, combined with a comparatively weak and contingent concept of ethnic identity, I would suggest, served as cultural foundations for the development of the paragovernmental *pochteca* system with its high degree of governmental autonomy, elaborate moral code, and legal norms that provided fair treatment for commoners and nobility alike (e.g., Offner 1983). Hence, persons of different ethnic groups as well as commoners and elite were freer to engage equitably in market transactions and to stand in front of market arbiters with the trust that all categories of persons were thought to possess the potential for moral capacity and could be judged accordingly.

Conclusion

I started this chapter by proposing that a cooperation approach will provide new insights on how markets developed in premodern societies, and I believe the information presented here strengthens that idea and suggests some new avenues to follow for theory building. One advantage of a cooperation perspective is that it focuses attention on how rational but socially and institutionally embedded persons solve cooperation problems in the marketplace. As such, this approach avoids the strong ideological claims of both traditional economic theory—with its individualistic *Homo economicus*—and anthropology's substantivism with its antimarket mentality. Also, the cooperation approach to market behavior that I envision incorporates ideas about the important role of the marginal and liminal in social and economic change. When anthropological archaeologists center their work on the governing elite and their associated public works, texts, and monuments, they privilege what Weber termed the political sphere of society and thus perpetuate what Turner and Turner (1978:1) describe as anthropology's "general disregard of the liminal and marginal."

A cooperation perspective also sheds new light on the nature of social differentiation in premodern societies. Restricted markets serve commoner interests poorly while privileging an elite whose network capital allows them to dominate interpolity exchange. By contrast, "free" unrestricted markets imply broader participation in commercial life and enhanced marketing choices, while increasing the potential of the marketplaces to generate wealth independent of the state or elite privilege.[13] It is this wealth-producing potential of successful well-governed markets that makes them an attractive source of taxable revenue for a governing elite (this is well described for the Central Mexican Postclassic period [e.g., in Blanton 1996:82; Durán 1967 (1570–1581):79, 180; Hicks 1987]) and with it comes the possibility that marketplaces will become decreasingly liminal and more fully incorporated into the political and economic fabric of city and polity. Yet, to do this, the governing elite must bring the egalitarian ethic of the market into society's mainstream culture. This potential of the market as an leveling force is one reason why anthropologists should reconsider their antimarket mentality and, instead, view the marketplace as a force counter to patrician values and other forms of inherited privilege in the long-term social and cultural evolution of societies. In this connection, we should recall that negative characterizations of the market promulgated by Marxist-Leninists and neo-Romanticists, such as Karl Polanyi, are historically specific (see also Mayer, this volume); by contrast, earlier eighteenth- and early nineteenth-century European authors often saw commerce as "a civilizing agent" and society's basis for moral conduct (Hirschman 1982:1464; e.g., Dixon and Wilson 2010). I propose that we should, with care, revisit those ideas but extend them beyond European history.

Market evolution evidently had this kind of equalizing consequence by the end of the Postclassic period in Central Mexico, where the ruler is described as taking "care of the directing of the marketplace and all things sold, for the good of the common folk, the vassals, and all dwellers in the city, the poor, the unfortunate, so that [these] might not be abused, nor suffer harm, nor be deceived, nor disdained" (Sahagún 1950–1982:8:67). An egalitarianizing cultural movement is evident beyond Central Mexico with the Mexicanization of the Postclassic world-system, including the development of new forms of comparatively egalitarian governance at Mayapan, Chichen Itza, and other Maya centers that replaced the old ruler-centered political structures of the Classic period (Cobos 2007). In spite of these changes, however, in both Oaxaca and the Maya area, interpolity and world-system exchange remained largely in the hands of foreign merchant groups or a local elite, while endogenous forms of market management appear to have been weakly developed by comparison with Central Mexico.

Acknowledgments

I am grateful to Stephen Kowalewski, Lane Fargher, Frances Berdan, and Gary Feinman, valued colleagues over many years, whose insightful comments on a draft of this chapter helped me to refine my ideas. My wife, Cindy Bedell, also provided useful comments on an early draft. I thank Joanne Pillsbury and Kenneth Hirth for inviting me to the "Merchants, Trade, and Exchange" conference that also was a source of inspiration as I developed the ideas for this chapter. I also benefited from remarks by two anonymous reviewers and Sara M. Taylor, art and archaeology editor of Dumbarton Oaks. All omissions or errors are the responsibility of the author.

NOTES

1 This is evident from recent ethnographic research applying the Ultimatum and Dictator games in diverse cultural settings that found comparatively high levels of fairness and willingness to punish for unfairness in Western societies; these were not often found in smaller-scale societies where there is little commercialization (Henrich et al. 2004).

2 I link market efficiency to the degree of full commercialization in a society, which goes to, especially, the degree to which commoner families are able to participate in a wide range of commodity transactions and are able to choose between a variety of market destinations. My definition of market efficiency departs from the economist's usual definition of "Pareto Optimality." In the latter, a market change is efficient only if it makes some persons better off without making others worse off. As I point out in this chapter, market change that enhances commoner access to markets and commodities typically will be at the expense of an elite who will find it more difficult to monopolize market transactions.

3 In conditions of low risk, commoners may also engage in trade based on network capital, such as the Buguias trader partners described by Lewis (1989).

4 Adam Smith (2008 [1776]:459) first pointed to the need for a fair judiciary if commerce is to flourish.

5 Bates (1983) evaluates a theory of state formation, first proposed by David Ricardo, in which the market's requirements for peace and order are argued to have been a prime cause of state formation. But as Bates (1983:27) put it: "Ironically, the basic problem with the [Ricardian] argument is that it is insufficiently motivated. As gains from efficiency from the innovation of new institutions are available to everyone, it is in no one's particular interest to provide them." I would change this to read: It is not often in the interest of a governing elite to be innovative in relation to commerce.

6 "Free" market in this sense doesn't refer to the unregulated markets so desired by market fundamentalists in the present day; instead, "free" refers to markets where commoners and an elite participate equally in commercial transactions.

7 Although Victor Turner never addressed liminality as it applies specifically to marketplaces, I think he would not be opposed to my use of his ideas. As I point out in the concluding section, he and his wife were disappointed that anthropologists often ignored the liminal aspects of human experience.

8 Mikhail Bakhtin, following the literature of Rabelais, described behavior in public spaces, including markets, in terms similar to Turner's anti-structure, for example: "Thus, the unofficial folk culture of the Middle Ages and even of the Renaissance has its own territory and its own particular time, the time of fairs and feasts. This territory . . . was a peculiar second world within the official medieval order and was ruled by a special kind of relationship, a free, familiar, marketplace relationship. . . . Officially the palaces, churches, institutions, and private homes were dominated by hierarchy and etiquette, but in the marketplace a special kind of speech was heard, almost a language of its own" (Bakhtin 1984:154).

9 Coixtlahuaca was an important Mixtec polity associated with pan-Mesoamerican traders from Central Mexico (Ball and Brockington 1978:111), but it is unclear to what extent merchants there were involved with the commercial system of the Mixteca Alta.

10 As described by Durán (1971 [1574–1579]:273–286), the materialization of Central Mexican marketplaces shows analogies with some features I earlier alluded to for Africa and Europe. Markets were walled spaces and were symbolized by a specific type of carved stone marker ("fixed round carved stones"). I thank Frances Berdan for reminding me of these stone monuments.

11 Even though the marketplace was to some extent a site of anti-structure, I cannot find much evidence for an antimarket mentality in Nahua culture like that found in other early civilizations, such as ancient Greece. In fact, while in Greek philosophy market morals were considered unlike the moral basis for marriage (Parry 1989:84), in Nahua language the root form of the words relating to market exchange are the same as those for the moral obligations shared by married couples (Joyce 2000:141). This is an interesting difference with the Mixtec word *yahui*, which is etymologically related to concepts of price and gain rather than to a moral concept.

12 In the Central Highlands, there appears to have been much new Postclassic-period cultural production related to matters of religion, ethnicity, commerce, and commoner moral capacity, but at present it is not known to what degree this was a departure from Classic-period culture.

13 This is evident, for example, in the "port polities" or similar trading emporia, such as Malacca in the Malay Peninsula, which offered neutral adjudication and other services to long-distance merchants who were more than willing to pay the required transaction costs; the polity produced no goods for exchange and had only a minimal local agricultural sustaining area, importing even basic food from distant regions, such as Java (Chaudhuri 1985:112–114).

REFERENCES CITED

Abbott, David

2010 The Rise and Demise of Marketplace Exchange among the Prehistoric Hohokam of Arizona. In *Archaeological Approaches to Market Exchange in Ancient Societies,* edited by Christopher P. Garraty and Barbara L. Stark, pp. 61–83. University Press of Colorado, Boulder.

Acheson, James M.

1994 Welcome to the Nobel Country: A Review of Institutional Economics. In *Anthropology and Institutional Economics,* edited by James M.

Acheson, pp. 3-42. Society for Economic Anthropology, Monographs 12. University Press of the Americas, Lanham, Md.

Appel, Jill

1982 Addendum to Chapter Eight: The Postclassic—A Summary of the Ethnohistoric Information Relevant to the Interpretation of Late Postclassic Settlement Pattern Data, the Central and Valley Grande Survey Zones. In *Monte Albán's Hinterland,* pt. 1, *The Prehispanic Settlement Patterns of the Central and Southern Parts of the*

Valley of Oaxaca, Mexico, by Richard
E. Blanton, Stephen A. Kowalewski,
Gary M. Feinman, and Jill Appel,
pp. 139–148. Memoirs of the Museum
of Anthropology, University of
Michigan 15. Museum of Anthropology,
University of Michigan, Ann Arbor.

Attwood, Donald W.

1997   The Invisible Peasant. In *Economic
Analysis Beyond the Local System*,
edited by Richard E. Blanton, Peter
N. Peregrine, Deborah Winslow, and
Thomas D. Hall, pp. 147–169. Society for
Economic Anthropology, Monographs
13. University Press of the Americas,
Lanham, Md.

Bakhtin, Mikhail

1984   *Rabelais and His World*. Translated
by Hélèn Iswolsky. Indiana University
Press, Bloomington.

Ball, Hugh G., and Donald L. Brockington

1978   Trade and Travel in Prehispanic Oaxaca.
In *Mesoamerican Communication
Routes and Cultural Contacts*, edited by
Thomas A. Lee Jr. and Carlos Navarrete,
pp. 107–114. New World Archaeological
Foundation, Brigham Young University,
Provo, Utah.

Bates, Robert H.

1983   *Essays on the Political Economy of Rural
Africa*. Cambridge University Press,
Cambridge.

Beals, Ralph L.

1975   *The Peasant Marketing System of
Oaxaca, Mexico*. University of
California Press, Berkeley.

Benet, Francisco

1957   Explosive Markets: The Berber High-
lands. In *Trade and Markets in the Early
Empires: Economies in History and
Theory*, edited by Karl Polanyi, Conrad
M. Arensberg, and Harry W. Pearson,
pp. 188–217. Free Press, New York.

Berdan, Frances F.

1985   Trade, Tribute, and Market in the Aztec
Empire. PhD dissertation, Department
of Anthropology, University of Texas,
Austin.

1986   Enterprise and Empire in Aztec and
Early Colonial Mexico. *Research in
Economic Anthropology*, Supplement
2:281–302.

Bernal-García, María E.

2007   The Dance of Time, the Procession
of Space at Mexico-Tenochtitlan's
Desert Garden. In *Sacred Gardens and
Landscapes: Ritual and Agency*, edited by
Michel Conan, pp. 69–112. Dumbarton
Oaks Research Library and Collection,
Washington, D.C.

Blanton, Richard E.

1983   Factors Underlying the Origin and
Evolution of Market Systems. In
*Economic Anthropology: Topics and
Theories*, edited by Sutti Ortiz, pp. 51–65.
Society for Economic Anthropology,
Monographs 1. University Press of the
Americas, Lanham, Md.

1985   A Comparison of Market Systems.
In *Markets and Marketing*, edited by
Stuart Plattner, pp. 399–416. Society for
Economic Anthropology, Monographs
4. University Press of the Americas,
Lanham, Md.

1996   The Basin of Mexico Market System and
the Growth of Empire. In *Aztec Imperial
Strategies*, by Frances F. Berdan, Richard
E. Blanton, Elizabeth Hill Boone, Mary
G. Hodge, Michael E. Smith, and Emily
Umberger, pp. 47–84. Dumbarton
Oaks Research Library and Collection,
Washington, D.C.

Blanton, Richard E., and Lane F. Fargher

2010   Evaluating Causal Factors in Market
Development in Premodern States:
A Comparative Study, with Critical
Comments on the History of Ideas. In
*The Evolution of Markets and Market
Systems in the Premodern World*, edited
by Christopher P. Garraty and Barbara
L. Stark, pp. 207–226. University Press
of Colorado, Boulder.

Blanton, Richard E., Lane F. Fargher, and Verenice Y.
Heredia Espinoza

2005   The Mesoamerican World of Goods
and Its Transformations. In *Settlement,
Subsistence, and Social Complexity:
Essays Honoring the Legacy of Jeffrey R.
Parsons*, edited by Richard E. Blanton, pp.
260–294. Cotsen Institute of Archaeology,
University of California, Los Angeles.

Blanton, Richard E., Stephen A. Kowalewski, Gary M. Feinman, and Jill Appel

1982   *Monte Albán's Hinterland,* pt. 1, *The Prehispanic Settlement Patterns of the Central and Southern Parts of the Valley of Oaxaca, Mexico.* Memoirs of the Museum of Anthropology, University of Michigan 15. Museum of Anthropology, University of Michigan, Ann Arbor.

Boone, Elizabeth Hill

1991   Migration Histories as Ritual Performance. In *Aztec Ceremonial Landscapes,* edited by David Carrasco, pp. 121–151. University Press of Colorado, Boulder.

Booth, William James

1993   *Households: On the Moral Architecture of the Economy.* Cornell University Press, Ithaca, N.Y.

Boserup, Ester

1970   *Woman's Role in Economic Development.* St. Martin's Press, New York.

Bowles, Samuel, and Herbert Gintis

2005   Can Self-Interest Explain Cooperation? *Evolutionary and Institutional Economics Review* 2:21–41.

Bridbury, A. R.

1986   Markets and Freedom in the Middle Ages. In *The Market in History,* edited by B. L. Anderson and A. J. H. Latham, pp. 79–120. Croom Helm, London.

Broda, Johanna

1991   The Sacred Landscape of Aztec Calendar Festivals: Myth, Nature, and Society. In *Aztec Ceremonial Landscapes,* edited by David Carrasco, pp. 74–120. University Press of Colorado, Boulder.

Brumfiel, Elizabeth M.

1994   Ethnic Groups and Political Development in Ancient Mexico. In *Factional Competition and Political Development in the New World,* edited by Elizabeth M. Brumfiel and John W. Fox, pp. 89–102. Cambridge University Press, Cambridge.

Byland, Bruce, and John M. D. Pohl

1994   *In the Realm of Eight Deer: The Archaeology of the Mixtec Codices.* University of Oklahoma Press, Norman.

Charlton, Thomas H.

1994   Economic Heterogeneity and State Expansion: The Northeastern Basin of Mexico during the Late Postclassic Period. In *Economies and Polities in the Aztec Realm,* edited by Mary G. Hodge and Michael Smith, pp. 221–256. Institute for Mesoamerican Studies, State University of New York, Albany.

Charlton, Thomas H., Cynthia L. Otis Charlton, Deborah L. Nichols, and Hector Neff

2008   Aztec Otumba, AD 1200–1600: Patterns of the Production, Distribution, and Consumption of Ceramic Products. In *Pottery Economics in Mesoamerica,* edited by Christopher A. Pool and George J. Bey III, pp. 237–266. University of Arizona Press, Tucson.

Chaudhuri, K. N.

1985   *Trade and Civilisation in the Indian Ocean: An Economic History from the Rise of Islam to 1750.* Cambridge University Press, Cambridge.

Cobos, Rafael

2007   Multepal or Centralized Kingship? New Evidence on Governmental Organization at Chichén Itzá. In *Twin Tollans: Chichén Itzá, Tula, and the Epiclassic to Postclassic Mesoamerican World,* edited by Jeff Karl Kowalski and Cynthia Kristan-Graham, pp. 316–343. Dumbarton Oaks Research Library and Collection, Washington, D.C.

Cook, Scott

1966   The Obsolete Antimarket Mentality: A Critique of the Substantivist Approach in Economic Anthropology. *American Anthropologist* 68:323–345.

Cook, Scott, and Martin Diskin

1976   *Markets in Oaxaca.* University of Texas Press, Austin.

Cortés, Hernán

1986   *Hernán Cortés: Letters from Mexico.* Translated by Anthony Pagden. Yale University Press, New Haven.

Curtin, Philip D.

1971   Pre-Colonial Trading Networks and Traders: The Diakhanké. In *The Development of Indigenous Trade and Markets in West Africa,* edited by

Claude Meillassoux and Daryll Forde,
pp. 228–239. Oxford University
Press, Oxford.

Dahlin, Bruce H., Daniel Bair, Timothy Beach,
Matthew Moriarity, and Richard E. Terry

2009   The Dirt on Food: Ancient Feasts
and Markets among the Lowland
Maya. In *Pre-Columbian Foodways:
Interdisciplinary Approaches to Food,
Culture, and Markets in Ancient
Mesoamerica*, pp. 191–232. Springer
Science and Business, New York.

Dahlin, Bruce H., Christopher T. Jensen, Richard E.
Terry, David R. Wright, and Timothy Beach

2007   In Search of an Ancient Maya Market.
Latin American Antiquity 18:363–384.

Davis, William G.

1973   *Social Relations in a Philippine Market:
Self-Interest and Subjectivity*. University
of California Press, Berkeley.

Dewey, Alice G.

1962   *Peasant Marketing in Java*. Free Press of
Glencoe, New York.

Dilley, Roy

1989   Contesting Markets: A General Introduction to Market Ideology, Imagery, and
Discourse. In *Money and the Morality
of Exchange*, edited by Jonathan Parry
and Maurice Bloch, pp. 1–34. Cambridge
University Press, Cambridge.

Dixon, William, and David Wilson

2010   Thomas Chalmers: The Market, Moral
Conduct, and the Social Order. *History
of Political Economy* 42:723–746.

Djelantik, A. A. M.

1986   *Balinese Paintings*. Oxford University
Press, Oxford.

Durán, Diego

1967   *Historia de las indias de Nueva España e
[1570–1581]   islas de la tierra firme*. 2 vols. Edited by
Ángel María Garibay Kintana. Editorial
Porrúa, Mexico City.

1971   *Book of the Gods and Rites and the
[1574–1579]   Ancient Calendar*. Translated by
Fernando Horcasitas and Doris Heyden.
University of Oklahoma Press, Norman.

Duyvendak, J. J. L.

1928   *The Book of Lord Shang: A Classic of
the Chinese School of Law*. University
of Chicago Press, Chicago.

Ensminger, Jean

1997   Transaction Costs and Islam: Explaining
Conversion in Africa. *Journal of Institutional and Theoretical Economics*
153:4–29.

Evensky, Jerry

2005   *Adam Smith's Moral Philosophy: A Historical and Contemporary Perspective
on Markets, Law, Ethics, and Culture*.
Cambridge University Press, New York.

Fafchamps, Marcel

2004   *Market Institutions in Sub-Saharan
Africa: Theory and Evidence*. MIT Press,
Cambridge, Mass.

Fargher, Lane F.

2009   A Comparison of the Spatial Distribution
of Agriculture and Craft Specialization
in Five State-Level Societies. *Journal of
Anthropological Research* 65:353–387.

Fargher, Lane F., Richard E. Blanton, and Verenice Y.
Heredia-Espinoza

2010   Egalitarian Ideology and Political Power
in Prehispanic Central Mexico: The Case
of Tlaxcallan. *Latin American Antiquity*
21:227–251.

Feinman, Gary M., and Christopher P. Garraty

2010   Preindustrial Markets and Marketing:
Archaeological Perspectives. *Annual
Review of Anthropology* 39:167–191.

Feinman, Gary M., and Linda Nicholas

2010   A Multiscalar Perspective on Market
Exchange in the Classic-Period Valley of
Oaxaca. In *Archaeological Approaches
to Market Exchange in Ancient Societies*,
edited by Christopher P. Garraty and
Barbara L. Stark, pp. 85–98. University
Press of Colorado, Boulder.

Feldman, Lawrence H.

1985   *A Tumpline Economy: Production
and Distribution Systems in Sixteenth-
Century Eastern Guatemala*.
Labyrinthos, Culver City, Calif.

Fukuyama, Francis

1995   *Trust: The Social Virtues and the
Creation of Prosperity*. Simon and
Schuster, New York.

Garraty, Christopher P.

2006 The Politics of Commerce: Aztec Pottery Production and Exchange in the Basin of Mexico, AD 1200–1650. PhD dissertation, School of Human Evolution and Social Change, Arizona State University, Tempe.

Garraty, Christopher P., and Barbara L. Stark (editors)

2010 The Evolution of Markets and Market Systems in the Premodern World. University of Colorado Press, Boulder.

Geertz, Clifford

1980 Ports of Trade in Nineteenth-Century Bali. Research in Economic Anthropology 3:109–122.

Gibson, Charles

1964 The Aztecs under Spanish Rule: A History of the Indians of the Valley of Mexico, 1519–1810. Stanford University Press, Stanford.

Gillespie, Susan D.

1989 The Aztec Kings: The Construction of Rulership in Mexica History. University of Arizona Press, Tucson.

Gintis, Herbert, Samuel Bowles, Robert Boyd, and Ernst Fehr

2005 Moral Sentiments and Material Interests: Origins, Evidence, and Consequences. In Moral Sentiments and Material Interests: The Foundations of Cooperation in Economic Life, edited by Herbert Gintis, Samuel Bowles, Robert Boyd, and Ernst Fehr, pp. 3–40. MIT Press, Cambridge, Mass.

Goody, Jack

1990 The Oriental, the Ancient, and the Primitive: Systems of Marriage and the Family in the Pre-Industrial Societies of Eurasia. Cambridge University Press, Cambridge.

Granovetter, Mark

1992 The Nature of Economic Relations. In Understanding Economic Process, edited by Sutti Ortiz and Susan Lees, pp. 21–40. Society for Economic Anthropology, Monographs 10. University Press of the Americas, Lanham, Md.

Gregory, Chris A.

1982 Gifts and Commodities. Cambridge University Press, Cambridge.

Greif, Avner

2006 Institutions and the Path to the Modern Economy: Lessons from the Medieval Trade. Cambridge University Press, Cambridge.

Hall, John W.

1991 Introduction. In The Cambridge History of Japan, vol. 4, Early Modern Japan, edited by John W. Hall, pp. 1–39. Cambridge University Press, Cambridge.

Hassig, Ross

1985 Trade, Tribute, and Transportation: The Sixteenth-Century Political Economy of the Valley of Mexico. University of Oklahoma Press, Norman.

Henrich, Joseph, Robert Boyd, Samuel Bowles, Colin Camerer, Ernst Fehr, and Herbert Gintis (editors)

2004 Foundations of Human Sociality: Economic Experiments and Ethnographic Evidence from Fifteen Small-Scale Societies. Oxford University Press, Oxford.

Henrich, Joseph, Jean Ensminger, Richard McElreath, Abigail Barr, Clark Barrett, Alexander Bolyanatz, Juan Camilo Cardenas, Michael Gurven, Edwins Gwako, Natalie Henrich, Carolyn Lesorogol, Frank Marlowe, David Tracer, and John Ziker

2010 Markets, Religion, Community Size, and the Evolution of Fairness and Punishment. Science 327:1480–1484.

Heyden, Doris

1991 Dryness before the Rain: Toxcatl and Tezcatlipoca. In Aztec Ceremonial Landscapes, edited by David Carrasco, pp. 188–204. University Press of Colorado, Boulder.

Hicks, Frederic

1987 First Steps Toward a Market-Integrated Economy in Aztec Mexico. In Early State Dynamics, edited by Henri J. M. Claessen and Peiter van de Velde, pp. 91–107. E. J. Brill, Leiden.

Hill, Polly

1966 Notes on Traditional Market Authority and Market Periodicity in West Africa. Journal of African History 7:295–311.

1971 Two Types of West African House Trade. In The Development of Indigenous Trade and Markets in West Africa, edited by Claude Meillassoux and Daryll Forde, pp. 303–318. Oxford University Press, Oxford.

Hirschman, Albert O.

1982   Rival Interpretations of Market Society: Civilizing, Destructive, or Feeble? *Journal of Economic Literature* 20:1463–1484.

Hirth, Kenneth G.

1998   The Distributional Approach: A New Way to Identify Marketplace Exchange in the Archaeological Record. *Current Anthropology* 39:451–467.

Hodder, B. W.

1961   Rural Periodic Day Markets in Part of Yorubaland. *Transactions and Papers of the Institute of British Geographers* 29:149–159.

Hodge, Mary G., and Michael Smith

1994   *Economies and Polities in the Aztec Realm.* Institute for Mesoamerican Studies, State University of New York, Albany.

Hutson, Scott R.

2000   Carnival and Contestation in the Aztec Marketplace. *Dialectical Anthropology* 25:123–149.

Hutson, Scott R., Bruce H. Dahlin, and Daniel Mazean

2010   Commerce and Cooperation Among the Classic Maya. In *Cooperation in Social and Economic Life*, edited by Robert C. Marshall, pp. 81–106. Altamira Press, Lanham, Md.

Joyce, Rosemary A.

2000   *Gender and Power in Prehispanic Meso-america.* University of Texas Press, Austin.

Kepecs, Susan

2003   Salt Sources and Production. In *The Postclassic Mesoamerican World*, edited by Michael E. Smith and Frances F. Berdan, pp. 126–130. University of Utah Press, Salt Lake City.

2007   Chichén Itzá, Tula, and the Epiclassic/Early Postclassic Mesoamerican World System. In *Twin Tollans: Chichén Itzá, Tula, and the Epiclassic to Postclassic Mesoamerican World*, edited by Jeff Karl Kowalski and Cynthia Kristan-Graham, pp. 129–150. Dumbarton Oaks Research Library and Collection, Washington, D.C.

Kepecs, Susan, and Marilyn A. Masson

2003   Political Organization in Yucatán and Belize. In *The Postclassic Mesoamerican World*, edited by Michael E. Smith and Frances F. Berdan, pp. 40–44. University of Utah Press, Salt Lake City.

Kerridge, Eric

1986   Early Modern English Markets. In *The Market in History*, edited by B. L. Anderson and A. J. H. Latham, pp. 121–154. Croom Helm, London.

Kowalewski, Stephen A., Andrew Balkansky, Laura R. Stiver, Thomas J. Pluckhahn, John F. Chamblee, Verónica Pérez Rodríguez, Verenice Y. Heredia Espinoza, and Charlotte A. Smith

2009   *Origins of the Ñuu: Archaeology in the Mixteca Alta, Mexico.* University of Colorado Press, Boulder.

Kowalewski, Stephen A., Gary M. Feinman, Laura Finsten, Richard E. Blanton, and Linda Nicholas

1989   *Monte Albán's Hinterland*, pt. 2, *Prehispanic Settlement Patterns in Tlacolula, Etla, and Ocotlán, the Valley of Oaxaca, Mexico.* Memoirs of the Museum of Anthropology, University of Michigan 23. Museum of Anthropology, University of Michigan, Ann Arbor.

Kristan-Graham, Cynthia

1993   The Business Narrative at Tula: An Analysis of the Vestibule Frieze, Trade, and Ritual. *Latin American Antiquity* 4:3–21.

Le Goff, Jacques

1980   *Time, Work, and Culture in the Middle Ages.* Translated by Arthur Goldhammer. University of Chicago Press, Chicago.

Lewis, Martin W.

1989   Commercialization and Community Life: The Geography of Market Exchange in a Small-Scale Philippine Society. *Annals of the Association of American Geographers* 79:390–410.

Masson, Marilyn A., Timothy S. Hare, and Carlos Peraza Lope

2006   Postclassic Maya Society Regenerated at Mayapán. In *After Collapse: The Regeneration of Complex Societies*, edited by Glenn M. Schwartz and

John J. Nichols, pp. 188–207. University of Arizona Press, Tucson.

Mastache, Alba Guadalupe, Robert H. Cobean, and Dan M. Healan

2002   *Ancient Tollan: Tula and the Toltec Heartland.* University Press of Colorado, Boulder.

McCafferty, Geoffrey G.

2007   So What Else is New? A Cholula-Centric Perspective on Lowland-Highland Interaction during the Classic/Postclassic Transition. In *Twin Tollans: Chichén Itzá, Tula, and the Epiclassic to Early Postclassic Mesoamerican World,* edited by Jeff Karl Kowalski and Cynthia Kristan-Graham, pp. 449–479. Dumbarton Oaks Research Library and Collection, Washington, D.C.

McCafferty, Sharisse D., and Geoffrey G. McCafferty

1988   Powerful Women and the Myth of Male Dominance in Aztec Society. *Archaeological Review from Cambridge* 7:46–59.

Milgrom, Paul R., Douglass C. North, and Barry R. Weingast

1990   The Role of Institutions in the Revival of Trade: The Law Merchants, Private Judges, and the Champagne Fairs. *Economics and Politics* 2:1–20.

Minc, Leah D.

2009   Style and Substance: Evidence for Regionalism within the Aztec Market System. *Latin American Antiquity* 20:343–374.

Motolinía, Fray Toribio de Benavente

1903   *Memoriales.* Edited by Luís García
[ca. 1560]   Pimentel. Casa Editorial, Mexico City.

Nafissi, Mohammad

2005   *Ancient Athens and Modern Ideology: Value, Theory, and Evidence in Historical Sciences, Max Weber, Karl Polanyi, and Moses Finley.* Institute of Classical Studies, University of London, London.

Nichols, Deborah L., Elizabeth M. Brumfiel, Hector Neff, Mary G. Hodge, Thomas Charlton, and Michael Glascock

2002   Neutrons, Markets, Cities, and Empires: A 1000-Year Perspective on Ceramic Production and Distribution in the Postclassic Basin of Mexico. *Journal of Anthropological Archaeology* 21:25–82.

Nicholson, Harold B.

2001   *Topiltzin Quetzalcoatl: The Once and Future Lord of the Toltecs.* University Press of Colorado, Boulder.

North, Douglass C.

1990   *Institutions, Institutional Change and Economic Performance.* Cambridge University Press, Cambridge.

Northrup, David

1978   *Trade without Rulers: Pre-Colonial Economic Development in South-Eastern Nigeria.* Clarendon Press, Oxford.

Offner, Jerome A.

1983   *Law and Politics in Aztec Mexico.* Cambridge University Press, Cambridge.

Oka, Rahul, and Augustín Fuentes

2010   From Reciprocity to Trade: How Cooperative Infrastructures Form the Basis of Human Socioeconomic Evolution. In *Cooperation in Economy and Society,* edited by Robert C. Marshall, pp. 3–28. Society for Economic Anthropology Monograph 28. Altamira Press, Lanham, Md.

Parry, Johathan

1989   On the Moral Perils of Exchange. In *Money and the Morality of Exchange,* edited by Johathan Parry and Maurice Bloch, pp. 64–93. Cambridge University Press, Cambridge.

Pluckhahn, Thomas J.

2009   Plazas y mercados en la Mixteca Alta prehispánica. In *Bases de la complejidad social en Oaxaca,* edited by Nelly M. Robles García, pp. 277–293. Instituto Nacional de Antropología e Historia, Dirección General de Publicaciones del Consejo Nacional para la Cultura y las Artes, Mexico City.

Pohl, John M. D.

2003a   Creation Stories, Hero Cults, and Alliance Building: Confederacies of Central and Southern Mexico. In *The Postclassic Mesoamerican World,* edited by Michael E. Smith and Frances F. Berdan, pp. 61–66. University of Utah Press, Salt Lake City.

2003b   Ritual Ideology and Commerce in the Southern Mexican Highlands. In *The Postclassic Mesoamerican World*, edited by Michael E. Smith and Frances F. Berdan, pp. 172–177. University of Utah Press, Salt Lake City.

Pohl, John M. D., John Monaghan, and Laura Stiver

1997   Religion, Economy, and Factionalism in Mixtec Boundary Zones. In *Códices y documentos sobre México: Segundo simposio,* vol. 1, edited by Salvador Rueda Smithers, Constanza Vega Sosa, and Rodrigo Martínez Baracs, pp. 205–232. Instituto Nacional de Antropología e Historia, Dirección General de Publicaciones del Consejo Nacional para la Cultura y las Artes, Mexico City.

Polanyi, Karl

1944   *The Great Transformation: The Political and Economic Origins of Our Time.* Beacon Press, Boston.

Rathje, William L., and Jeremy A. Sabloff

1975   Theoretical Background: General Models and Questions. In *Changing Pre-Columbian Commercial Systems: The 1972–1973 Seasons at Cozumel, Mexico,* edited by Jeremy A. Sabloff and William L. Rathje, pp. 6–20. Peabody Museum of Archaeology and Ethnology, Harvard University, Cambridge, Mass.

Redfield, James M.

1986   The Development of the Market in Archaic Greece. In *The Market in History*, edited by B. L. Anderson and A. J. H. Latham, pp. 29–58. Croom Helm, London.

Renfrew, Colin

1975   Trade as Action at a Distance: Questions of Integration and Communication. In *Ancient Civilization and Trade*, edited by Jeremy A. Sabloff and C. C. Lamberg-Karlovsky, pp. 3–60. University of New Mexico Press, Albuquerque.

Riddell, J. Barry

1974   Periodic Markets in Sierra Leone. *Annals of the Association of American Geographers* 64:54–58.

Roberts, Andrew

1970   Nyamwezi Trade. In *Pre-Colonial African Trade: Essays on Trade in Central and Eastern Africa before 1900*, edited by Richard Gray and David Birmingham, pp. 39–74. Oxford University Press, New York.

Roys, Ralph L.

1943   *The Indian Background of Colonial Yucatan*. Carnegie Institute of Washington Publication 548. Carnegie Institution of Washington, Washington, D.C.

Sahagún, Bernardino de

1950–1982   *Florentine Codex: General History of the Things of New Spain.* Translated by Arthur J. O. Anderson and Charles E. Dibble. School of American Research, Santa Fe, and University of Utah, Salt Lake City.

Sawyer, Peter

1986   Early Fairs and Markets in England and Scandinavia. In *The Market in History*, edited by B. L. Anderson and A. J. H. Latham, pp. 59–78. Croom Helm, London.

Scott, James C.

1990   *Domination and the Arts of Resistance: Hidden Transcripts.* Yale University Press, New Haven.

2009   *The Art of Not Being Governed: An Anarchist History of Upland Southeast Asia.* Yale University Press, New Haven.

Shaw, Brent D.

1981   Rural Markets in North Africa and the Political Economy of the Roman Empire. *Antiquités africaines* 17:37–83.

Skinner, G. William

1964   Marketing and Social Structure in Rural China, Part 1. *Journal of Asian Studies* 24:3–43.

Smith, Adam

2008 [1776]   *An Inquiry into the Nature and Causes of the Wealth of Nations.* Edited by Kathryn Sutherland. Oxford University Press, Oxford.

Smith, Carol A.

1976   Regional Economic Systems: Linking Geographical Models and Socioeconomic Problems. In *Regional Analysis*, vol. 1, *Economic Systems*, edited by Carol A. Smith, pp. 3–68. Academic Press, New York.

Smith, M. G.

1962   Exchange and Marketing among the Hausa. In *Markets in Africa*, edited by Paul Bohannan and George Dalton, pp. 299–334. Northwestern University Press, Evanston, Ill.

Smith, Mary Elizabeth

1973   *Picture Writing from Ancient Southern Mexico: Mixtec Signs and Maps.* University of Oklahoma Press, Norman.

Smith, Michael E.

2010   Regional and Local Market Systems in Aztec-Period Morelos. In *The Evolution of Markets and Market Systems in the Premodern World*, edited by Christopher P. Garraty and Barbara L. Stark, pp. 161–184. University of Colorado Press, Boulder.

Smith, Michael E., and Frances F. Berdan

2003   Postclassic Mesoamerica. In *The Postclassic Mesoamerican World*, edited by Michael E. Smith and Frances F. Berdan, pp. 3–13. University of Utah Press, Salt Lake City.

Smith, Michael E., and Frances F. Berdan (editors)

2003   *The Postclassic Mesoamerican World.* University of Utah Press, Salt Lake City.

Spawforth, Antony J. S.

1996   Markets and Fairs. In *The Oxford Classical Dictionary*, edited by Simon Hornblower and Antony Spawforth, p. 926. Oxford University Press, New York.

Stark, Barbara L.

2008   Archaeology and Ethnicity in Postclassic Mesoamerica. In *Ethnic Identity in Nahua Mesoamerica: The View from Archaeology, Art History, Ethnohistory, and Contemporary Ethnography*, edited by Frances F. Berdan, John K. Chance, Alan R. Sandstrom, Barbara L. Stark, James M. Taggart, and Emily Umberger, pp. 38–63. University of Utah Press, Salt Lake City.

Stark, Barbara L., and Alanna Ossa

2010   Origins and Development of Mesoamerican Marketplaces: Evidence from South-Central Veracruz, Mexico. In *Archaeological Approaches to Market Exchange in Ancient Societies*, edited by Christopher P. Garraty and Barbara L. Stark, pp. 99–126. University Press of Colorado, Boulder.

Sugden, Robert

1986   Labour, Property, and the Morality of Markets. In *The Market in History*, edited by B. L. Anderson and A. J. H. Latham, pp. 9–28. Croom Helm, London.

Swedberg, Richard

2005   Markets in Society. In *The Handbook of Economic Sociology*, edited by Neil J. Smelser and Richard Swedberg, pp. 233–253. Princeton University Press, Princeton.

Terraciano, Kevin

2001   *The Mixtecs of Colonial Oaxaca: Ñudzahui History, Sixteenth Through Eighteenth Centuries.* Stanford University Press, Stanford.

Thurnwald, Richard

1932   *Economics in Primitive Communities.* Oxford University Press, Oxford.

T'ien, Ju-K'ang

1953   *The Chinese of Sarawak: A Study of Social Structure.* London School of Economics and Political Science, Department of Anthropology, London.

Tosh, John

1970   The Northern Interlacustrine Region. In *Pre-Colonial African Trade: Essays on Trade in Central and Eastern Africa before 1900*, edited by Richard Gray and David Birmingham, pp. 103–118. Oxford University Press, New York.

Tozzer, Alfred M.

1941 [ca. 1566]   *Landa's* Relación de las cosas de Yucatan: *A Translation.* Papers of the Peabody Museum of American Archaeology and Ethnology 18. The Peabody Museum, Cambridge, Mass.

Turner, Victor

1969   *The Ritual Process: Structure and Anti-Structure.* Cornell University Press, Ithaca, N.Y.

Turner, Victor, and Edith L. B. Turner

1978   *Image and Pilgrimage in Christian Culture.* Columbia University Press, New York.

Van Gennep, Arnold

    1909   *The Rites of Passage.* Translated by Monika B. Vizedom and Gabrielle L. Caffee. Routledge and Kegan Paul, London.

Van Zantwijk, Rudolph

    1985   *The Aztec Arrangement: The Social History of Pre-Spanish Mexico.* University of Oklahoma Press, Norman.

Weber, Max

    1946   *From Max Weber: Essays in Sociology.* Translated and edited by H. H. Gerth and C. Wright Mills. Oxford University Press, New York.

    1978   *Economy and Society*, vol. 1. Edited by Guenther Roth and Claus Wittich. University of California Press, Berkeley.

Wolf, Eric

    1951   The Social Organization of Mecca and the Origins of Islam. *Southwestern Journal of Anthropology* 7:329–356.

    1999   *Envisioning Power: Ideologies of Dominance and Crisis.* University of California Press, Berkeley.

Wycherley, R. E.

    1978   *The Stones of Athens.* Princeton University Press, Princeton.

Yang, Anand A.

    1998   *Bazaar India: Markets, Society, and the Colonial State in Bihar.* University of California Press, Berkeley.

3

Merchants and Merchandise

The Archaeology of Aztec Commerce at Otumba, Mexico

DEBORAH L. NICHOLS

AN IMPORTANT FORCE IN MODERN ECONO-
mies, commerce began in the ancient world.
The Spanish chroniclers vividly described markets
and merchants as significant elements in the complex economy of the Aztec state, the largest in the
history of pre-Hispanic Mesoamerica (Figure 3.1):
"When we arrived at the great market place, called
Tlatelolco, we were astounded at the number of people and quantity of merchandise that it contained
and at the good order and control that was maintained, for we had never seen such a thing before"
(Díaz del Castillo 1996 [1568]:215). Such markets
were critical to sustaining Aztec cities, towns, and
villages. By the start of the sixteenth century, more
than one million people lived in the Basin of Mexico,
the heartland of the Aztec Empire. Only a century
earlier, the region had been politically fragmented
into a series of city-states (*altepetl*), each ruled by
a hereditary lord or lords (*tlatoani*) (Charlton and
Nichols 1997:199–202; Hodge 1994, 1997).

By AD 1400, the Acolhua of Texcoco in the
eastern basin and the Tepenaca of Azcapotzalco

in the western basin each had formed fragile tributary empires (Figure 3.2). In 1428, the Mexica of
Tenochtitlan broke away from the Tepenaca and
initiated a military alliance with Texcoco and the
small city-state of Tlacopan to defeat the Tepenaca.
After consolidating control over city-states within
the Basin of Mexico, the Aztecs began to conquer
areas outside of it, starting in Morelos immediately to the south; over the next eighty years, they
would extend their conquests to the Pacific and
Gulf coasts and the Southern Highlands of Mexico
(Davies 1973; Hassig 1988). Although the Mexica
dominated this Triple Alliance with Texcoco and
Tlacopan, the Acolhua of Texcoco maintained a
strong hold over the eastern basin.

These developments took place amid a climate of increasing commerce and an economy that
involved intensive agriculture, specialization, and
a complex division of labor, taxation, markets, and
merchants. Much research on the Aztec economy
and the role of markets has been couched in terms
of larger debates about the sociopolitical versus

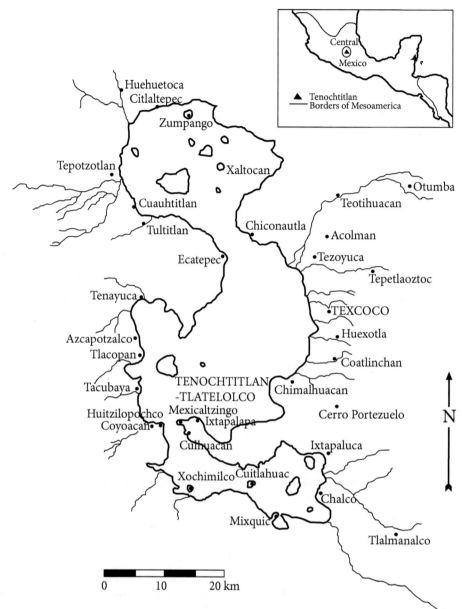

figure 3.1
Basin of Mexico, showing major Aztec sites. (Drawing courtesy of Deborah L. Nichols.)

the commercial dimensions of premodern state economies (Brumfiel 1987; Oka and Kusimba 2008; Smith 2004). In the 1980s, Thomas Charlton and I directed a project of intensive archaeological survey and excavations at Otumba, an Aztec city-state capital in the northeastern basin, to address some of these issues. Our work showed that a variety of craft industries were concentrated in an urban center that, according to documentary sources, was one of twelve cities or towns in the basin with a resident group of professional long-distance merchants, or *pochteca*. Otumba is the only provincial Aztec center in the Basin of Mexico where *pochteca* resided that archaeologists have investigated intensively. This paper will review debates about commerce in the Aztec economy, discuss the documentary evidence of merchants, and draw on archaeological data from Otumba as a case study. I will argue that, although the *pochteca* were important to Aztec commerce and Otumba's urban economy, because of the richness of documentary accounts about them and their focus on wealth goods, their roles have overshadowed those of regional merchants and producer-vendors in Aztec commerce.

Markets and Merchants

Smith (2004:79) characterizes the Aztec economy as one of "intermediate commercialization." Such economies have "interlocking central-place market systems for goods and services, and they have commercial institutions such as money and professional entrepreneurs." Typically, however, little land is privately held, and labor is not commoditized (Hicks 1987; Isaac, this volume). A standard feature of Aztec towns and cities, marketplaces were where producers and merchants sold goods, and a regional hierarchy of markets existed (Berdan 1985; Blanton 1996; Evans 1980; Hassig 1985; Smith 1979, 1980). The large imperial cities of Tenochtitlan-Tlatelolco and Texcoco held daily markets, while smaller cities and towns had

a market once every five days (an Aztec week). Some markets specialized to attract buyers and sellers, such as the famous dog market at Acolman (Durán 1967 [1570–1581]:278). Markets were organized by type of goods, and most exchanges took place through bartering, but cacao beans, cotton cloth, copper axes, and gold-filled quills served as standards of exchange (Sahagún 1950–1982:10:64). The presence of markets in the Aztec economy is not disputed; however, scholars differ on the weight they assign to economic and sociopolitical factors in market development (Nichols et al. 2009). Some researchers see evidence of the development of a fully integrated regional or complex interlocking market system in the Basin of Mexico by the Late Postclassic period (Blanton et al. 1993; Smith 2003). For example, at Cerro Portezuelo in the southern Texcoco region, substantial amounts of the Aztec III Black-on-Orange serving wares were made in the Tenochtitlan area, with many others from workshops in the Texcoco area. Tenochtitlan-area potters also supplied large ceramic griddles (*comals*) to Cerro Portezuelo (Garraty 2006, n.d.).

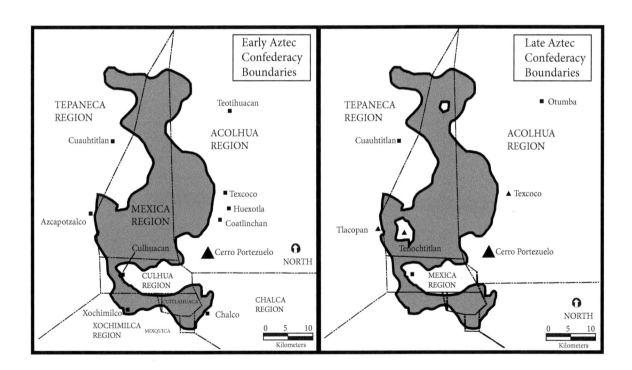

figure 3.2
Aztec confederations of the Basin of Mexico (after Hodge 1996:figs. 2.2–2.3; Garraty 2006:31).

Other scholars see strong indications of political control of markets and merchants (Carrasco 1980, 1983). Hodge, Minc, and colleagues (Hodge and Minc 1990; Hodge et al. 1992, 1993; Minc 2006, 2009; Minc et al. 1994) argue that political—confederation—boundaries constrained exchanges of Aztec pottery, limiting merchants' access to markets. Looking at Red Ware pottery, Minc (2006) divides the basin into two hierarchical dendritic networks that conformed to the boundaries of the Acolhua and Mexica territories (Figure 3.2). Other authors emphasize increasing market integration and expanding exchange between imperial capitals and hinterlands, but note persistent regionalism on the basin's northeast periphery (Charlton et al. 2000a; Nichols et al. 2002).

All economies were and are embedded (Feinman and Garraty 2010:173; Isaac, this volume). Although we may debate the degrees to which Aztec regional markets were integrated and the extent to which politics influenced them, we gain from these studies a fuller appreciation of the complexity of the market system and the volume of domestic goods, which were mostly manufactured in household workshops and traded in Aztec markets. Understanding ancient state economies, such as that of the Aztecs, requires multiple scales of analysis.

Sellers and Merchants

Three types of sellers frequented Aztec marketplaces: *tlanamacac*, the producer-vendors; *tlanecuilo*, the itinerant regional merchants also referred to as retailers, dealers, or peddlers; and the famous *pochteca*, or guild merchants (Berdan 1975:204, 1988:645). Intricate webs linked producer-vendors to regional and guild merchants (Berdan 1988:645–647). Producers directly sold crops, fish, game, and goods created in their households and craft workshops (Hirth, this volume). Most manufacturing took place in households—as it did at Otumba—although some producers also made goods in the marketplace. In the sixteenth century, Bernardino de Sahagún (1950–1982:10:85) noted that "the obsidian seller, is one who, [with] a staff, with a cross

piece, forces off blades." Some manufacturing, such as maguey-fiber processing, involved suprahousehold organization or cooperation (Nichols et al. 2000; Parsons and Parsons 1990).

Producer-vendors could be either men or women, and they are usually characterized as having been "small-scale" and having sold goods in small lots (e.g., Berdan 1986; Hirth, this volume; Van Zantwijk 1985:131). But at Otumba, household workshops employed methods of mass production—such as molds—and took advantage of family labor to make large quantities of goods. Workshop operations might have been small in terms of the absolute number of personnel, but output could be quite substantial (Parry 2001). The participation of both women and men as sellers in the market further reinforced gender parallelism in Aztec society and provided commoners some economic autonomy.

In addition to producer-vendors, regional merchants (*tlanecuilo*) also traded many of these goods (Table 3.1). They were independent middlemen: "a retailer, a retailer of diverse objects: one who procures things in wholesale lots, who peddles them" (Sahagún 1950–1982:10:91). *Tlanecuilo* exchanged goods of "modest to medium value" (Berdan 1986:288). Such items included foods—cacao, maize, and amaranth seeds—and household items—sandals, palm fibers, baskets, gourd bowls, and salt (Berdan 1975:374–380). *Pochteca*, along with producers and regional merchants, also traded cacao and textiles. Some *tlanecuilo* specialized in particular commodities—usually ones that were geographically restricted (Berdan 1988). For example, the salt seller (Figure 3.3) "sets out on the road, travels with it, goes from market to market, sells salt. He sells salt, balls, salt bars, salt ollas" (Sahagún 1950–1982:10:85). Van Zantwijk (1985:131–132) groups together producer-vendors and regional merchants because both were composed of commoners who belonged to *calpolli* (a landholding corporate group that could also be a ward or barrio of a town or city) and who also engaged in farming, fishing, hunting, or craft manufacturing but were not organized into corporate groups as sellers or traders. They mostly sold goods produced by households or in household-based workshops and "as a rule . . . operated within

table 3.1
Coyoacan market tax records pre-1571, names of towns underscored (Berdan 1975:374–380)

SELLERS	DEALERS	MAKERS
clay-dye sellers	wood dealers	stew-pot makers and sellers
medicine sellers	chia dealers	large-basket makers
tamale sellers	salt dealers	mat makers
smoking-tube sellers	merchants <u>Oztomecan</u>	smoking-tube makers
chia sellers	merchants <u>Tetitlacalque</u>	cane makers
pottery sellers	merchants Mixcouac	pine-torch splitters
mortar and pestle sellers	merchants A(n)tocon	spindle makers
clay-dye sellers	merchants Tequemecan	tumpline makers
lime sellers	merchants Atoyac	sandal makers
bark with dark clay and *uixachin*-leaves sellers	merchants Nexpilcon	metalworkers
rabbit-hair sellers	merchants Aticpac	candlemakers
feather sellers		garment makers
lake-scum sellers		maguey-garment makers
broom sellers		maguey-fiber shirt maker
candle sellers		warping-frame makers
cigar sellers		cloth-border makers
spilt-oak sellers		small-bell makers
cacao sellers		obsidian-blade makers
tumpline sellers		carpenters
hide sellers		salt breakers
		collar maker

small areas, leaving their villages for only a few days at time" (Van Zantwijk 1985:132).

Although household-based producer-vendors and regional merchants did not travel far, they supplied most of the goods sold in Aztec marketplaces. As purveyors of the wealth goods essential to validating status and class and negotiating Aztec social relations, the *pochteca*—or guild of professional long-distance merchants of the Aztecs—have especially attracted attention (e.g., Acosta Saignes 1945; Berdan 1975:141–191; Hassig 1985). Spanish chroniclers wrote of them in some detail; Sahagún (1950–1982:9:1) devoted the ninth book of his Florentine Codex to "telleth of the merchant and artisans."

The *pochteca* themselves enjoyed a higher status than that of the makers and vendors of most household goods, and they also provided diplomatic and military aid to rulers.

The *pochteca* (or *oztemeca* [Berdan 1975:156–157]) were professional merchants who traveled on foot and by canoe with porters in large caravans within and beyond the borders of the expanding Aztec Empire (Acosta Saignes 1945; Berdan 1986, 1988). They traded in large amounts of low-bulk, high-value wealth goods. From the Basin of Mexico, they exported gold jewelry; gold spinning bowls; earplugs of gold, rock crystal, copper, and obsidian; obsidian razors with leather handles;

figure 3.3
Salt selling in the Basin of Mexico, 1938. (Photograph courtesy of Jeffrey R. Parsons.)

obsidian blades; shells; needles; cochineal; alum; rabbit fur; fancy garments; and medicinal herbs, such as birthwort and *cosmos sulphureus* (Sahagún 1950–1982:9:17–18). They exchanged manufactured goods in regional markets and neutral ports of trade for exotic raw materials, which they imported to the Basin of Mexico (Berdan 1975:144; Chapman 1957). During the early years of the Triple Alliance, Aztec nobles depended on *pochteca* to supply raw materials to the artisans who manufactured their sumptuary goods, which were vital to validating an elevated status in political negotiations and state rituals (Isaac 1986:333). *Pochteca* imported gold, feathers, cacao, fine gourd bowls, sumptuous textiles and thread, jade, turquoise, shells, mosaic shields, animal skins, and slaves (Berdan 1975:169, 1988:640; Durán 1967 [1570–1581]:7:85; Sahagún 1950–1982:8:18). As the empire expanded, tribute

also supplied such raw materials; however, most of the trade in wealth goods passed through the *pochteca*'s hands, and their monopoly of foreign trade remained essential in supplying raw materials from the Maya Lowlands (Berdan 1975:276–279). The *pochteca* were private entrepreneurs; on rare occasions, rulers sometimes supplied merchants, at least those based in Tenochtitlan (Berdan 1975:331; Isaac 1986:331, this volume).

The *pochteca* were politically and militarily valuable to rulers, providing them with information about enemies and unconquered territories, acting as spies, and serving as ambassadors. They could even declare war. At home, they also served as judges in marketplaces (Berdan 2005:38–39; Sahagún 1950–1982:bk. 9).

Chroniclers reported that in the imperial cities of Tenochtitlan-Tlatelolco and Texcoco, merchants

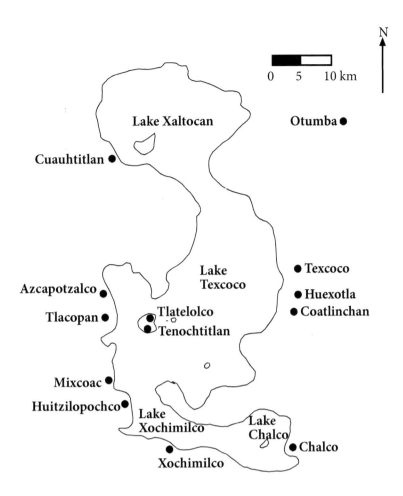

figure 3.4
Cities in the Basin of Mexico where *pochteca* were reported to reside. (Drawing courtesy of Deborah L. Nichols.)

resided in their own barrios and belonged to their own *calpolli*. By the early sixteenth century, *pochteca* were present in a dozen basin cities or towns (Figure 3.4). Berdan (1975:148) thinks the guild merchants in each of these cities were similarly organized and belonged to an overarching merchant organization. The city guilds were not equal in rank, however, and only five—Tenochtitlan, Tlatelolco, Azcapotzalco, Cuauhtitlan, and Uitzilopcho—were permitted to trade outside of the empire (Berdan 1975:164). Interestingly, none of the *pochteca* towns or cities in the Acolhua region of the eastern Basin of Mexico under Texcoco was designated as allowed to trade outside of the empire, although Berdan (1986:284) speculates that they may have acted as foreign emissaries for Texcoco's rulers. Though much attention is paid to the *pochteca's* foreign trade (Acosta Saignes

1945; Chapman 1957), these merchants also operated extensively within the empire (Berdan 1975:116–117, 166–169, 1977:93–94, 1986; Isaac 1986:334).

Pochteca occupied an intermediary social status between nobles and commoners. As guild members, they were required to pay tribute only in goods, although the guild also presented lavish gifts to rulers in conjunction with certain ceremonies (Berdan 1975:165). *Pochteca* also were allowed to sacrifice slaves. They were the only group permitted to establish their own internal laws and courts outside the imperial system (Berdan 1977). In addition, the guild regulated its membership and developed an internal system of ranking (Berdan 1975).

Pochteca could amass considerable wealth. They were accorded certain privileges, but unlike Aztec nobles who routinely displayed their wealth, *pochteca* were prohibited from doing so in public. They were expected to appear humble except on particular public occasions. At home, however, *pochteca* lavishly competed for prestige and rank. The *pochteca* were a close-knit group (Bittman and Sullivan 1978); ranking within the guild distinguished between principal merchants, vanguard merchants, disguised merchants, spying merchants, slave dealers, and slave bathers (Table 3.2). The principal merchants stood at the apex of the hierarchy, and moving up in rank required successful trading in order to sponsor opulent feasts, make lavish gifts, and offer sacrifices (Berdan 1975:178; Sahagún 1950–1982:9:48). During an annual ceremony honoring Panquetzaliztli, Sahagún (1950–1982:9:48) reports that some *pochteca* gave highly ranked nobles and other merchants twelve hundred precious cloaks; four hundred decorated loincloths; skirts; tunics; bins of maize; beans; chia; between eighty and one hundred turkeys; between twenty and forty dogs; twenty sacks of cacao beans; two thousand to four thousand chocolate stirrers; chilies, tomatoes, squash, and other ingredients for sauces; baskets; and firewood. Perhaps to conceal trading expeditions from each other as well as to hide their wealth from public view, *pochteca* began and ended their journeys under the cloak of darkness: "And when things had been arranged in order in their house; when all were about to go on the road, when darkness had fallen, when it was already night, then all the boats were filled" (Sahagún 1950–1982:9:15).

The ban on public displays of wealth shows that political elites saw the *pochteca* and their wealth as a potential threat (Bittman and Sullivan 1978:214). Sahagún's words reveal this attitude clearly: "And when they became proud and haughty and were corrupted by the favors and honors of [their] riches, the king was saddened and began to hate them. He sought false or trumped up reasons to oppress and kill them although they were guiltless, out of hatred for their pride and arrogance" (Sahagún 1950–1982:3:37). Merchants acquired their wealth, whereas most nobles derived their position from their elevated class and the income attached to offices they held (Soustelle 1972 [1961]:82). Although

trading was a means of upward economic mobility, by prohibiting merchants from publicly displaying their wealth, political elites curtailed the *pochteca*'s influence (Katz 1972:214).

Oka and Kusimba (2008:359) identified typical attributes of traders in premodern economies, and *pochteca* exhibited all of them: 1) marginalization by political elites, distrusted but "regarded as necessary evils in most parts of the world"; 2) widespread trading diasporas; 3) residence in delimited areas in or near cities but separate from political centers; 4) frequent differentiation as professionals and ethnically distinct; and 5) trade networks that extended across geographic, cultural, and natural borders. Traders invested in maintaining networks, which tended to be long-lived, and passed them down to ensure the flow of goods and services.

Pochteca trade within the empire provided a vital articulation between the market and tribute systems (Isaac 1986). Hassig (1985:118) also points out that young *pochteca* started out trading in household goods, thus blurring some of the distinction between guild-based merchants and retailers and producer-vendors.

Complex webs of exchange linked household consumers, producer-vendors, regional merchants or retailers, and the colorful guild-based merchants. Documentary sources give fewer details about the household-based producer-vendors and retailers (*tlanecuilo*); most likely some of them were artisans themselves or members of artisan households who took their own products and those of other crafters to market (Carrasco 1980:258). Archaeology provides a complementary perspective, and Otumba offers an especially important case study as a regional market and craft-production center where *pochteca* were present.

Otumba

The Otumba *altepetl*, or city-state, developed in the eastern end of the Teotihuacan Valley in the northeastern Basin of Mexico. The archaeological remains of the capital of the Late Postclassic–period (AD 1350–1521) city-state Otumba encompasses

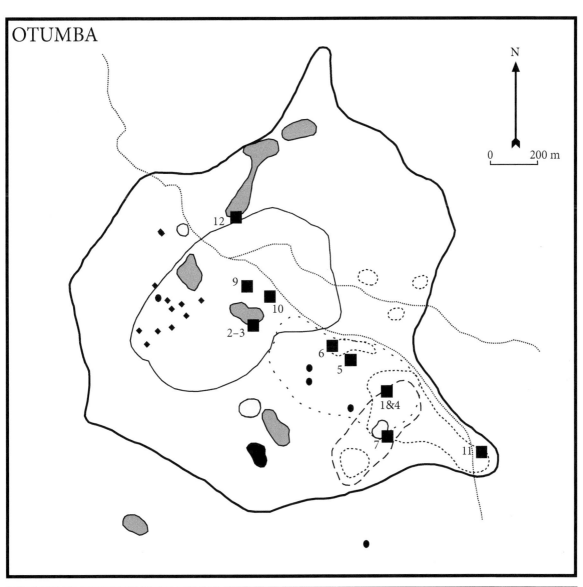

OTUMBA

N

0   200 m

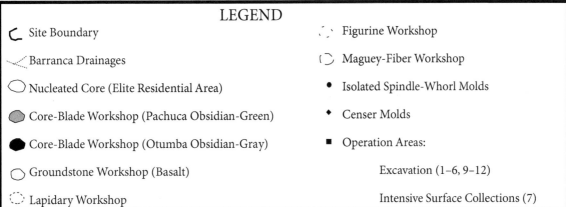

LEGEND

⊏ Site Boundary

⤍ Barranca Drainages

◯ Nucleated Core (Elite Residential Area)

⬤ Core-Blade Workshop (Pachuca Obsidian-Green)

⬤ Core-Blade Workshop (Otumba Obsidian-Gray)

◯ Groundstone Workshop (Basalt)

◌ Lapidary Workshop

◌ Figurine Workshop

◖ Maguey-Fiber Workshop

• Isolated Spindle-Whorl Molds

◆ Censer Molds

■ Operation Areas:

Excavation (1–6, 9–12)

Intensive Surface Collections (7)

figure 3.5
The Otumba town site. (Drawing courtesy of Deborah L. Nichols.)

figure 3.6
Dump of obsidian cores from Otumba. (Photograph by Deborah L. Nichols.)

220 hectares on the edge of a gently sloping piedmont above the alluvial plain, twelve kilometers east of the Early Classic city of Teotihuacan. Two major divisions comprise the town (Figure 3.5). A nucleated core of forty hectares includes several large mounds and the remains of elite residences (with plaster floors), a mound that likely formed the base of a temple-pyramid, and an open area or plaza that may have served as a marketplace. A dispersed residential zone makes up the rest of the archaeological site. Here, erosion and plowing leveled most houses and other buildings to concentrations of rubble and artifacts (Figures 3.5–3.6). To the north, east, south, and southwest lie Otumba's dependent villages (Charlton et al. 1993; Charlton et al. 1991, 2000a, 2000b; Evans 2001). The city-state also encompassed the Otumba obsidian source area (Charlton and Spence 1983).

Documentary sources offer few details about Otumba and its hinterland settlements. Mention of Otumba begins with the reign of Techotlalatzin of

Texcoco (AD 1357–1409), who allowed Otomi refugees fleeing Xaltocan in the northwestern Basin of Mexico to settle at Otumba after their defeat by the Tepaneca of Azcapotzalco (Gibson 1964:10; Ixtlilxochitl 1965 [1891–1892]:1:167–168, 2:82–83). As the Acolhua confederation in the eastern basin and the Tepaneca in the western basin competed for control of the area, Otumba was the site of two battles in the early fifteenth century. Following the defeat of Azcapotzalco by the Triple Alliance in 1428, Nezahuacoyotl consolidated control of the Acolhua confederation, and Otumba became the largest Late Postclassic city-state in both area and population in the Teotihuacan Valley and an important administrative center under Texcoco, the Late Postclassic Acolhua capital.

When archaeologists surveyed the Otumba site in the late 1960s (Sanders and Evans 2001), they recognized substantial evidence of craft manufacturing that Thomas Charlton confirmed in subsequent surveys. In contrast, documentary sources make no mention of these industries, although they indicate that a weekly market noted for the sale of turkeys was held in the town (Blanton and Hodge 1996:244–245; Charlton et al. 2000b). The survey data suggested that the development of craft industries in the town paralleled Otumba's growth as a city-state center.

In 1987 and 1988, the Otumba Project that the late Thomas Charlton and I directed undertook archaeological investigations of the Aztec town and several of its hinterland villages with the goal of examining the role of craft production and exchange in the development of Aztec city-states (Charlton et al. 1991, 2000a, 2000b; Nichols 1994). A subsequent project expanded the scope of our analyses and used instrumental neutron activation analysis (INAA) of obsidian and ceramics from Otumba and other Aztec sites in the eastern and northern Basin of Mexico (Charlton et al. 2000a; Charlton et al. 2008; Neff et al. 2000; Nichols and Charlton 1996; Nichols et al. 2000).

A dispersed, light occupation of Otumba took place during the Early Postclassic period (AD 950–1150), when a city-state centered at Teotihuacan and with ties to Tula dominated the Teotihuacan Valley. The region fragmented after AD 1150, and the beginnings of Aztec city-states in the Teotihuacan Valley can be traced to the Middle Postclassic period (AD 1150–1350) with a dispersed settlement at Otumba. Pottery production began at this time in the town. Otumba and its hinterland settlements grew substantially in the Late Postclassic period, and an estimated 3,600 to 5,500 people lived in the town (Sanders and Evans 2001:997). People continued to reside at Otumba following the defeat of Tenochtitlan, although they abandoned most of the Aztec urban center, and the Spanish shifted the focus of settlement north of the *barrancas* (Charlton et al. 2000a:256–257; Nichols and Charlton 1996).

Otumba Craft Industries

We documented at least six craft industries in the urban center: obsidian core-blade manufacturing; lapidary production; groundstone-tool manufacturing; maguey-fiber processing; spinning (and

presumably weaving) of both maguey and cotton thread; and manufacturing of ceramic figurines, spindle whorls, musical instruments, pipes, stamps, earspools, a local type of Red Ware bowl, and censers (Biskowski 2000; Charlton 1993, 1994; Charlton et al. 1993; Charlton et al. 1991, 2000a, 2000b; Charlton et al. 2008; McClung de Tapia and Aguillar Hernández 2001; Nichols 1994; Nichols et al. 2000; Parry 2001, 2002). Farmers also lived in town and, like rural villagers elsewhere in the Otumba city-state, they intensively cultivated maize and specialized by focusing on nopals and maguey and its products.

The craft-specialist barrios at Otumba are the first such identified places at an Aztec provincial center by archaeologists (Figure 3.5). Their development was linked to the expansion of craft specialization and the importance of *calpolli* organization in the Late Postclassic period. Otumba also provides an example of an Aztec neighborhood organization based on occupation and shows how neighborhoods can be identified through artifact-distribution studies, survey, and excavation (Smith 2010:147).

Obsidian

At Otumba, we found at least seven substantial concentrations of debris from manufacturing prismatic obsidian blades and large polyhedral cores (Parry 2001:104, 2002). The concentrations occur in both the nucleated core and in the dispersed residential zone along the town's southern edge (Figure 3.6). In each case, manufacturing debris was mixed with household artifacts and building materials, indicating that these were domestic workshops. All but one of the core-blade concentrations consist of green obsidian imported from the Pachuca source area; one used the local gray Otumba obsidian. Parry (2001:105) calculated that each concentration represents refuse from forging millions of blades. Production was geared for consumers in the town and surrounding villages, and for export beyond the Teotihuacan Valley, as the Otumba workshops were not the only ones that supplied blades to the Teotihuacan Valley; workshops also were present at nearby Teotihuacan (Spence 1985).

We excavated one obsidian concentration in the nucleated core and found a refuse dump from a workshop that made rectangular blades for everyday use (Parry 2002:43). Just to the south of the dump lay a midden containing intact cores and other obsidian debris mixed with Aztec III (Late Postclassic) and Aztec IV (early colonial) pottery, other domestic refuse, and pieces of painted plaster from a destroyed building. Associated with the midden were a small altar, patio, and postholes; a residence was likely present nearby, but our permit did not allow further excavation. The placement of core-blade workshops in both the town center and in the dispersed residential zones indicates that both elites and commoners were involved with Pachuca core-blade production.

Closely linked to core-blade workshops were Otumba's obsidian lapidaries (Charlton 1993, 1994, 2007; Charlton et al. 1993). Residential workshops fashioned exhausted cores of green Pachuca obsidian into earspools and specialized lapidary tools, which were also sometimes made of imported chert (Figure 3.7). Workshops also manufactured lip plugs of gray obsidian and sometimes of rock crystal. Artisans occasionally made their own blades from cores and turned prismatic blades into disks, eccentrics, and tiny lip plugs; they also produced chert beads. In addition to green obsidian from Pachuca and the local gray obsidian, artisans also used, in lesser amounts, gray obsidian from Paredon, Tulancingo, and Tepolzingo (Glascock et al. n.d.).

Lapidaries made jewelry in household workshops and lived in one-room dwellings that formed a barrio or ward in the southeastern part of the dispersed residential zone at Otumba that likely represents a *calpolli* (Charlton 1994). Lapidaries in Tenochtitlan likewise resided in their own wards, and occupied an intermediate social status (Berdan 2005:31; Charlton 1994:202; Hicks 1987:96). Otumba's lapidary workshops had higher concentrations of decorated pottery than did other households in the dispersed residential zone, indicating that Otumba lapidaries also occupied an intermediary status within the town (Hare 1994).

figure 3.7
Obsidian perforators and earspool blanks from Otumba. (Photograph by William J. Parry.)

Lapidary working required considerable skill and perhaps offers an example of continuous or year-round production (Charlton 1994; Hirth 2009: 22–23). We found little of the finished jewelry at Otumba or other sites in the city-state. Although such wealth objects would have been highly curated, most pieces were intended for export. *Pochteca* in Tenochtitlan-Tlatelolco maintained close relations with lapidaries (Sahagún 1950–1982:8:18). These merchants exported, among other things, obsidian blades and jewelry from the Basin of Mexico and imported exotic stones, such as rock crystal, to be used by Otumba's lapidaries.

Some rural villagers in the Otumba city-state specialized in making bifaces; urban lapidaries perhaps also made bifaces in small quantities. Evans (1988) excavated one biface-workshop midden that adjoined a residential mound in the hinterland village of Cihuatecpan (Abrahms 1988). Bifaces produced there supplied local consumers in the Otumba city-state and were exported as well (Parry 2001).

The only places where archaeologists have discovered concentrations of finished bifaces of Otumba obsidian are in the Templo Mayor in Tenochtitlan and the palace at Chiconautla—an important lakeshore trading center at the mouth of the Teotihuacan Valley (Nichols et al. 2009; Parry 2001).

At Otumba we also found two obsidian concentrations with unusual densities of blades. The blades had been used and consumed, but we do not know what good(s) they fashioned. Like other blades, they were associated with domestic debris, indicating household-based workshops.

Basalt

Small concentrations of debris from manufacturing basalt tools, intermixed with domestic artifacts, are found in the dispersed residential zone all in areas badly disturbed by plowing. Each concentration probably represents the remains of a house and its associated outdoor work areas. The workshops made common household implements—*manos*,

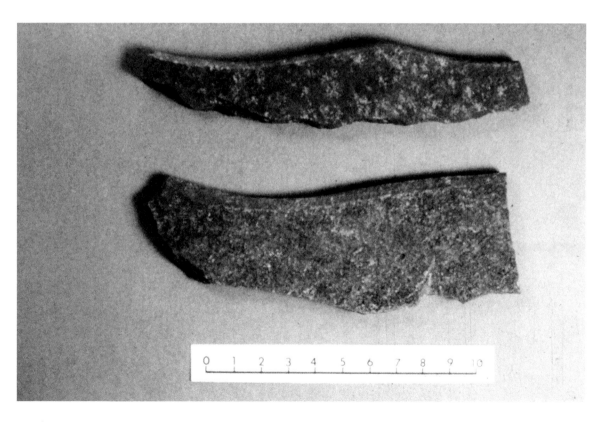

figure 3.8
Basalt polisher from Otumba. (Photograph by Martin Biskowski.)

metates, mortars, and scrapers used on maguey plants—but they also created specialized grinding tools for lapidaries (Figure 3.8). One of these concentrations occurs in the maguey-fiber barrio, providing another example of household multicrafting. The workshops supplied households in the town and surrounding settlements (Biskowski 2000).

Ceramic Barrio

A barrio of ceramic producers lies to the east of the lapidary workshops that were first identified as figurine workshops because of their large concentration of figurines and open-backed figurine molds (Figure 3.9) (Charlton 1994; Charlton et al. 1993:163–165). Our investigations determined that the workshops produced a variety of other ceramic goods.

figure 3.9
Figurine mold from Otumba. (Photograph courtesy of the Otumba Project.)

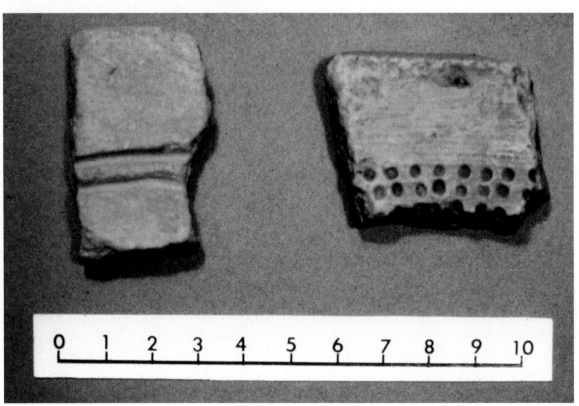

figure 3.10
Censer molds from Otumba. (Photograph courtesy of the Otumba Project.)

They include pipes, flutes, whistles, bells, rattle balls (musical instruments, like figurines, that were used in rituals), and serpent-handled censers, as well as mold-made cotton and maguey spindle whorls, stamps, and a local Red Ware pottery type known as Otumba Polished Tan bowls (Charlton 1994; Charlton et al. 1993:163–165; Charlton et al. 2008). The concentrations exhibited very high surface densities of manufacturing debris—sixty-seven to ninety-eight figurine and mold fragments per twenty-five square meters. These workshops supplied the town and hinterland settlements and likely exported beyond the city-state (Charlton 1994; Charlton et al. 1993:163–165; Charlton et al. 2008). Cynthia Otis Charlton excavated two houses in the barrio. Although the sites have been disturbed by plowing, the remains are fairly typical of Aztec commoner houses in the northeast Basin of Mexico, and each house was associated with various kinds of manufacturing debris, molds, overfired ceramics, and lumps of clay. Figurine workshops have been present in the northeast basin since at least the Early Classic period at Teotihuacan (Sullivan 2006), but this is the first barrio of figurine makers recorded by archaeologists.

Separate from the figurine makers were potters who produced mold-made, long-handled censers (Texcoco Molded and Texcoco Filleted) for household rituals (Figure 3.10). These potters apparently lived and worked in a small barrio in the southwest part of the nucleated core, but unlike the figurine makers, they were associated with elite households (Figure 3.5). It is also possible that the manufacturing debris came from potters making censers as a form of labor tax.

Fibers

Nearly every household in both the town and hinterland villages (and throughout Central Mexico) spun and wove imported cotton as well as locally grown maguey (Evans 1990; Parsons and Parsons 1990). We discovered a barrio of households adjoining Otumba's figurine barrio to the south that engaged in producing, spinning, presumably weaving, and maybe dyeing maguey fibers along with making spindle-whorl molds and spindle

a

b

figure 3.11
a) Cotton and maguey spindle whorls from Otumba; and b) spindle-whorl molds from Otumba. (Photographs courtesy of the Otumba Project.)

whorls—we recovered thirteen hundred spindle-whorl fragments along with molds in surface collections from the largest concentration (Nichols et al. 2000). (Intact maguey whorls are rare on the surface anywhere at Otumba as people have scavenged them from the site for centuries.) These findings constitute the first reported maguey-fiber workshops and barrio of such specialists in Central Mexico. Plowing and erosion had destroyed the architecture of this part of the town, but the manufacturing debris was intermixed with domestic artifacts, which indicated household-based workshops

(Figure 3.11). Some maguey-fiber households also engaged in lapidary work, others made figurines, and there also was one concentration of basalt manufacturing debris from forging maguey scrapers. In addition to spinning thread for clothing (and probably weaving and dyeing), the households produced cordage for sandals, carrying bags, and rope.

The maguey-fiber barrio, along with the adjoining ceramic ward, offers a good example of Aztec multicrafting households (Hirth 2009). This group at Otumba intensified a widespread household craft—that of maguey-fiber processing, spinning, and weaving—and combined it with the production of weaving implements, spindle whorls, molds, and, in some cases, the manufacture of lesser amounts of other goods, including figurines, lapidary work, and basalt tools. Since every household in the Teotihuacan Valley spun thread and wove cloth, it is likely that the maguey-fiber goods produced at Otumba were intended for market.

Farming

Otumba's farmers also intensified agricultural production in the Late Postclassic period, both in the urban center and in hinterland villages. Charlton and colleagues (2000b) had previously identified the remains of floodwater irrigation canals along the edge of the Aztec town (Figure 3.12). Maguey terrace cultivation of the piedmont was an important complement to maize agriculture (Blanton 1996; Evans 1990; Parsons and Parsons 1990). Otumba's farmers also cultivated nopals and beans, as well as wild and domesticated amaranth and chenopods (Genotte 2001:144; McClung de Tapia and Aguillar Hernández 2001:116).

In addition to the regional specialization in maguey, Otumba very likely also manufactured cochineal, a dye made from the dried bodies of insects that live on the leaves of the nopal cactus. In the colonial period, Otumba was part of one of the major cochineal-producing areas, and we know

figure 3.12
Otumba irrigation features exposed by road cut. (Photograph by Deborah L. Nichols.)

from tribute lists that cochineal nopals were produced in the Teotihuacan Valley in Aztec times (Evans 2001:95; Gibson 1964:354). Nopal was cultivated in Aztec times, and the *Mapa de Otumba,* dating to between 1550 and 1575, describes a house that stored nopal fruits (Genotte 2001). Perhaps the maguey-fiber workshops at Otumba also prepared cochineal and dyed cloth.

Mining

The Otumba obsidian source area lies five kilometers from the town (Figure 3.13). This source had been mined since at least the Formative period, and it was heavily worked in Aztec times. Charlton

and Spence (1983:45) think workshops were located at the source area but were separate from the mining sites. An Aztec village that processed obsidian was nearby. Charlton and Spence suggested that Otumba likely exerted some central control over the obsidian source, an idea supported by subsequent source studies (Glascock et al. 2001; Parry 2001).

During the Late Postclassic period, the Otumba town and city-state experienced a large population growth that was fueled both internally and by Otomí immigrants. Households at Otumba responded to and took advantage of the related increase in commerce and tribute by intensifying farming activities. There were landscape modifications in the

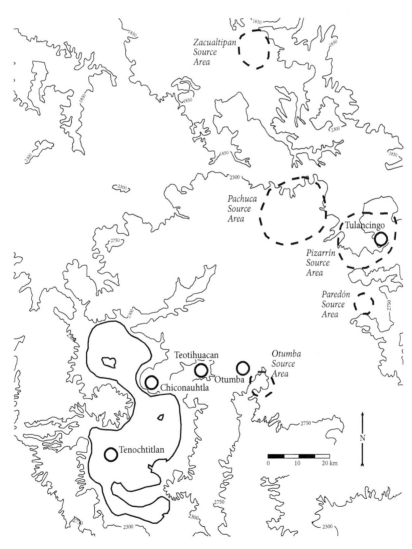

figure 3.13
Obsidian sources used at Otumba (after Charlton and Spence 1983; Parry 2002).

form of irrigation canals and terraces, expanded mining of mineral resources (obsidian and basalt), and increased crafting through greater specialization and diversification as well as a larger overall scale of production.

Source Studies

To expand the scope of our studies beyond Otumba's workshops and households, and to link goods at Otumba with market networks, we conducted source studies using instrumental neutron activation analysis (INAA) of ceramics and obsidian from Otumba (Tables 3.3–3.6) and sites elsewhere in the northern and eastern Basin of Mexico (Charlton et al. 2000a; Charlton et al. 2008; Neff and Glascock 2000; Neff et al. 2000; Nichols et al. 2000). Our studies complement the work of Hodge, Minc, and colleagues (Brumfiel and Hodge 1996; Hodge 1992; Hodge and Minc 1990; Hodge and Neff 2005; Hodge et al. 1992, 1993; Neff et al. 1994; Neff and Hodge 2008) on Aztec ceramics and markets in the eastern and southern basin. Subsequent research has further expanded the INAA database of Aztec ceramics (García Chávez 2004; Garraty 2006, n.d.; Ma 2003; Minc 2006, 2009; Nichols et al. 2002; Nichols et al. 2009; Nichols et al. n.d.).

Middle Postclassic

During the Middle Postclassic period, some low-level manufacturing of chert bifaces and Red Ware, and perhaps Orange Ware, pottery took place at Otumba in household workshops that supplied people in the town and city-state (Table 3.4). Otumba also imported decorated and plain cooking and serving vessels from elsewhere in the Teotihuacan Valley and from the Texcoco, Chalco, Cuauhtitlan, and Tenochtitlan areas—most likely Culhuacan, as it was a major producer of Aztec II Black-on-Orange pottery (Figure 3.14). Substantial amounts of pottery moved between overlapping market networks (Figure 3.15). Garraty (2006:176) found that the market networks for Plain Orange wares were integrated horizontally, while the networks for Aztec II decorated pottery show more hierarchy (Nichols et al. 2002; Nichols et al. 2009). In some parts of the basin, subregional market networks for Aztec Red Ware coincided with city-state confederation boundaries (Minc 2009), while in others traders moved pottery and obsidian across volatile political borders (Nichols et al. 2009). For example, at Chiconautla under Acolhua domain, Early Aztec pottery came from the Cuauhtitlan and Tenochtitlan production zones as well as the Teotihuacan Valley (Nichols et al. 2002; Nichols et al. 2009). Xaltocan also saw high levels of imports of Early Aztec decorated

table 3.2
Aztec merchants (from Hassig 1985:117)

NAME	DESCRIPTION
Tiamicqueh	traders, dealers
Tlanamacanimeh	peddlers
Tlacohocohualnamacqueh	peddlers
Pochetcah	merchants
Pochtecatleahotohequeh	principal merchants
Oztomecas	vanguard merchants
Nahualoztomecah	disguised merchants
Teyahualoanimeh	spying merchants
Tecohanimeh	slave dealers
Tealtianimeh	slave bathers

table 3.3

Sources of obsidian in the Otumba city-state listed in percent (Glascock et al. 2001)

SAMPLE	PACHUCA	OTUMBA	PAREDON	TULANCINGO	MALPAIS	OTHER
25 random samples, Otumba core-blade workshop surface collection	3.2	96.8	0.0	0.0	0.0	0.0
22 non-green, Otumba excavated elite residence	89.6	10.4	0.0	0.0	0.0	0.0
25 non-green, surface coll. TA-37	60.6	39.4	0.0	0.0	0.0	0.0
25 random samples, biface workshop surface coll. TA-37m Sq. 29	0.6	99.4	0.0	0.0	0.0	0.0
25, surface coll., 3 house mounds, TA-57	75.0	25.0	0.0	0.0	0.0	0.0
20 samples, surface coll. TA-71. Sq. 3	33.3	66.7	0.0	0.0	0.0	0.0
50 random samples, Otumba lapidary workshop Op. 11	75.0	16.0	1.5	3.5	0.0	4.0

table 3.4

Otumba: Frequency of Aztec II ceramics by composition group

	CHALCO	TEOHUACAN VALLEY	TEOHUACAN VALLEY MACRO	TEOHUACAN 2	TEXCOCO	SOUTHERN BASIN 1	TRADE ROUTE 1	UNASSIGNED	N
AZTEC II BLACK-ON-ORANGE	9.1 (2)	4.5 (1)	18.2 (4)	9.1 (2)	31.8 (7)			27.3 (6)	22
AZTEC II–III BLACK-ON-ORANGE		33.3 (1)	33.3 (1)		33.3 (1)				3
BLACK-ON-RED	50.0 (1)		50.0 (1)						2
BLACK-ON-WHITE/RED		20.0 (1)	60.0 (3)					20.0 (1)	5
MISCELLANEOUS RED WARE		33.3 (5)		6.6 (1)		26.7 (4)	6.6 (1)	26.7 (4)	15
FIGURINE								100 (1)	1
PRODUCTION DEBRIS			100.0 (1)						1

table 3.5

Otumba: Frequency of Aztec III ceramics by composition group

	PORTEZUELO	CUAUHTITLAN	TENOCHTITLAN	TEOHUACAN VALLEY	TEOHUACAN VALLEY MACRO	TEOHUACAN 2	SOUTHERN BASIN 1	TRADE ROUTE 1	PUEBLA-MORELOS	UNASSIGNED	N
AZTEC III BLACK-ON-ORANGE		5.3 (1)	15.8 (3)	52.6 (10)	21.1 (4)	5.3 (1)					19
AZTEC III–IV BLACK-ON-ORANGE				100.0 (1)							1
BLACK-ON-RED			16.7 (2)	25.0 (3)	41.7 (5)					8.3 (1)	12
BLACK-ON-WHITE/ RED			12.5 (1)	25.0 (2)	25.0 (2)			8.3 (1)		25.0 (2)	8
MISCELLANEOUS RED WARE				1	1						
OTUMBA POLISHED TAN				69.2 (18)	26.9 (7)					3.8 (1)	26
CENSER	4.3 (1)			8.7 (2)	65.2 (15)	4.3 (1)				17.4 (4)	23
CENSER MOLD				25.0 (1)	25.0 (1)						
SPINDLE WHORL				44.4 (8)	50.0 (9)					5.6 (1)	18
SPINDLE-WHORL MOLD					100.0 (2)						2
FIGURINE			1.1 (1)	63.8 (60)	21.3 (20)				1.1 (1)	12.8 (12)	94
AZTEC III PRODUCTION DEBRIS					50.0 (1)					50.0 (1)	2
AZTEC PRODUCTION DEBRIS										100.0 (7)	7

table 3.6

Otumba: Frequency of Aztec IV and colonial ceramics by composition group

	TENOCHTITLAN	TEOHUACAN VALLEY	TEOHUACAN VALLEY MACRO	TEOHUACAN 4	TEXCOCO	UNASSIGNED	N
BLACK-ON-ORANGE	11.1 (1)	11.1 (1)	33.3 (3)	11.1 (1)	22.2 (2)	11.1 (1)	9
COLONIAL GLAZED		50.0 (1)				50.0 (1)	2
FIGURINE		100.0 (1)					1

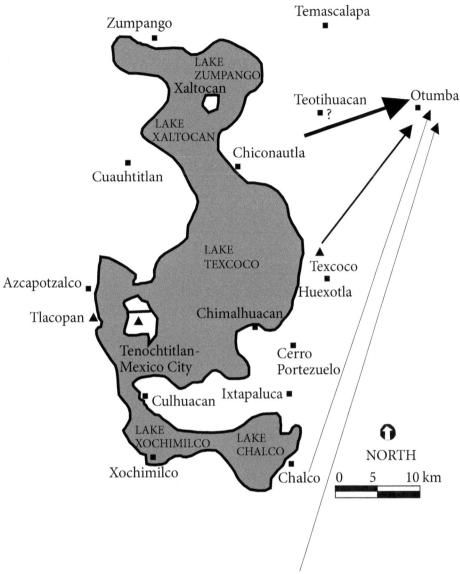

figure 3.14
Middle Postclassic ceramic composition groups at Otumba. (Drawing courtesy of Deborah L. Nichols.)

pottery (Nichols et al. 2002). Otumba, located farther inland, likewise imported some Early Aztec decorated pottery, mostly from the Texcoco area, but also from Chalco.

Late Postclassic

Following regional trends, the population of Otumba and its hinterlands grew in the Late Postclassic period, commerce intensified, and Otumba households expanded craft manufacturing and intensified farming practices. (Increased tribute demands also

encouraged the growth of markets and more craft specialization.) Most of the goods made at Otumba were exchanged in markets, although textiles were also a major Aztec tribute item. Core-blade production with a heavy reliance on imported Pachuca rose, although some blades were made of the local gray obsidian. Rural households specialized in making bifaces of obsidian quarried from the Otumba source area. While obsidian from the Pachuca source area within the domain of the Acolhua confederation was widely available, political boundaries

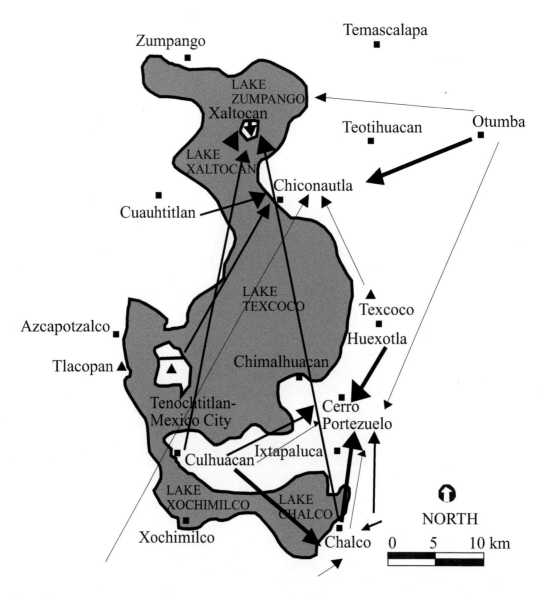

figure 3.15

Middle Postclassic ceramic compositions groups at Cerro Portezuelo, Chalco, Chiconautla, and Xaltocan (INAA data from Garraty n.d.; Nichols et al. 2002, 2009). (Drawing courtesy of Deborah L. Nichols.)

impeded the trade of gray obsidian (Parry 2002). *Pochteca* exported to many parts of Mesoamerica obsidian blades along with earspools, and green obsidian earspools have been found as far away as Oaxaca and the Pacific coast (Parry 2001:109; Smith 1990).

Ceramic workshops at Otumba grew by specializing in household ritual objects (figurines, figurine molds, censers, and musical instruments),

textile implements (spindle whorls and molds), and a local variety of Red Ware pottery. The lapidary industry recycled products from blade workshops and imported stones to create jewelry, while other households in the town focused on maguey-fiber processing, thread making, and probably weaving and dyeing, along with producing spinning tools. Women throughout the city-state also spun and wove in their households.

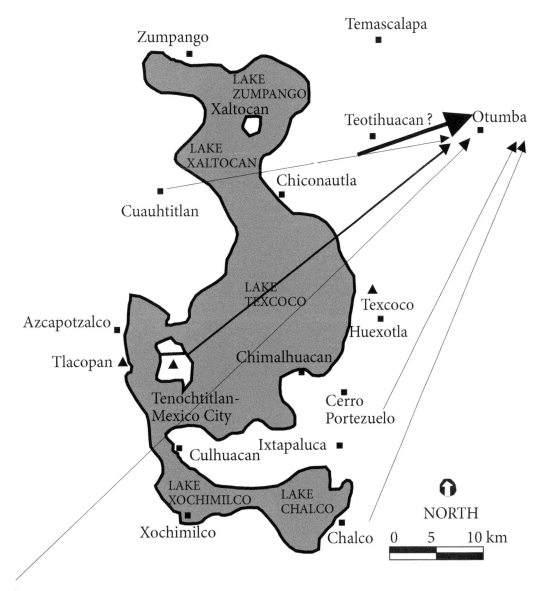

figure 3.16
Late Postclassic ceramic composition groups at Otumba. (Drawing courtesy of Deborah L. Nichols.)

The Otumba potters supplied the town and hinterland villages and also exported to other markets mainly in the Teotihuacan Valley. Most figurines, for example, found in the Teotihuacan Valley were made in the valley, perhaps at Otumba, as it has the valley's only known Aztec workshops (Figure 3.16). Some figurines manufactured in the Teotihuacan Valley, however, reached as far as the site of Cerro Portezuelo on the southern edge of the Texcoco region (Nichols et al. 2002). The Teotihuacan Valley supplied most of the decorated pottery at Charlton's (1978) Trade Route sites in the northeast periphery of the Basin of Mexico. Spindle whorls had a restricted distribution and circulated mostly within their home production zones; 82 percent of the spindle whorls analyzed from the Teotihuacan Valley were locally manufactured (Charlton et al. 2008; Neff et al. 2000; Nichols et al. 2000).

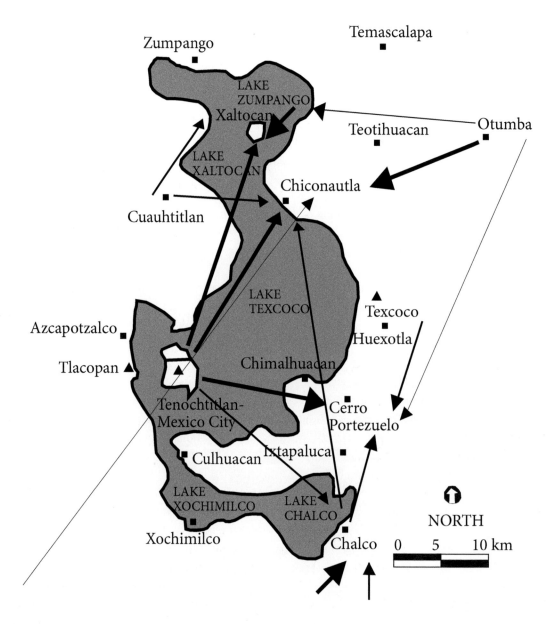

figure 3.17
Late Postclassic ceramic composition groups at Cerro Portezuelo, Chalco, Chiconautla, and Xaltocan (INAA data from Garraty n.d.; Nichols et al. 2002; Nichols et al. 2009). (Drawing courtesy of Deborah L. Nichols.)

The market area for Otumba Polished Tan bowls was even smaller—mostly the Otumba city-state and a few places elsewhere in the Teotihuacan Valley. Brumfiel (2004:252) thinks that Aztecs primarily used Red Ware bowls for drinking, particularly pulque. Otumba obtained most of its serving and cooking wares from elsewhere. In addition to the wares made in the Teotihuacan Valley (and Aztec Teotihuacan is a likely place for such workshops), *tlanecuilo* brought Red Ware bowls, chocolate drinking goblets, and Aztec III Black-on-Orange serving plates, bowls, dishes, and grater bowls (*molcajetes*) from the Tenochtitlan area to Otumba. Plain Orange cooking, storage, and serving wares came mostly from the Teotihuacan Valley, but Otumba also imported some from the Texcoco region.

In the Late Postclassic period, the Tenochtitlan ceramic production zone underwent a huge expansion in pottery manufacturing (Figure 3.17). Much of the trade from the Tenochtitlan area to the eastern Basin of Mexico was funneled through lakeshore centers such as Chimalhuacan; at nearby Cerro Portezuelo, most of the Late Postclassic pottery analyzed by INAA came from the Tenochtitlan composition group (Garraty n.d.). The amount of Aztec III Black-on-Orange from the Tenochtitlan area is similarly high at Chiconautla (Nichols et al. 2009). Not only did the Tenochtitlan workshops manufacture decorated wares for export to other parts of the basin, Central Mexico, and beyond, but they also became a major supplier of some plain wares, including *comals* to villages such as Cerro Portezuelo (Garraty 2006, n.d.). From lakeshore ports merchants brought pottery to inland markets, such as Otumba. On average, 15–30 percent of Aztec III Black-on-Orange pottery from the Tenochtitlan composition group is found in rural villages, as well as in urban centers such as Otumba in the eastern and northern Basin of Mexico.

Charlton's Trade Route sites in the far northeast periphery of the basin are an exception, as the analyzed sample from these places contained almost no Aztec pottery from the Tenochtitlan composition group. The northeast periphery seems to have been beyond the market range of those regional merchants, although they imported Aztec III Black-on-Orange from the Texcoco area as well as the Teotihuacan Valley.

During the Late Postclassic period, the great expansion in pottery manufacturing in the Tenochtitlan area was linked to the growth in lakeshore trade. Additionally, the further development of *chinampas* (raised field agricultural plots) in the southern Basin of Mexico and flow of tribute from the imperial domain perhaps increased the security of the urban food supply enough to allow households in the Tenochtitlan area to shift from intermittent to continuous production. Calnek (1976) concluded that, beyond gardens, craft specialists and others living in Tenochtitlan did not produce food. In contrast, at most other towns, cities, and villages in the basin, Aztec households that specialized in manufacturing domestic goods usually also engaged in farming and/or other subsistence strategies.

Salt that came in unique containers of Texcoco Fabric Marked pottery constitutes another documented import to Otumba. Salt-making communities dotted the shores of Lake Texcoco, and regional merchants brought the salts to markets (Parsons and Parsons 1990).

The market areas for Aztec goods manufactured at Otumba ranged from local to international. Craft specialization at Otumba was done by independent household workshops and grew out of the domestic household economy. The Otumba data largely support Oka and Kusimba's (2008:361) argument that the centralization of some manufacturing in early urban centers was due to location rather than overt political control. Centralization benefited specialists because it provided access to other specialists and their products, to consumers, and to merchants; it also benefited elites, who gained from market tax revenues and had access to both household and wealth goods.

Traders

All the various types of traders in Aztec society—producer-vendors, regional merchants, and the guild-based *pochteca*—contributed to Otumba's economy. Otumba's craft specialists and farmers would have sold their goods and produce at the town's weekly market. Blanton (1996) points out, however, that the development of a weekly market at Otumba is anomalous because of its proximity to the Aztec town of Teotihuacan, a long-standing regional market and craft-production center. Here, politics enters the picture. Otumba had close ties to the Acolhua leadership, and Blanton sees this relationship as part of the Acolhua leader's strategy to undermine Teotihuacan by encouraging Otumba's economic and political development. Having *pochteca,* who probably oversaw the marketplace, based at Otumba rather than at Teotihuacan enhanced Otumba's position as a commercial center. In addition to its location on a major trade route to the Gulf coast, Otumba offered another advantage for *pochteca* as the only *altepetl* in the Basin of

Mexico with its own obsidian source. Glascock et al. (n.d.) see evidence of significant political control of gray obsidian sources. For example, although figurines and censers made in the Teotihuacan Valley and probably at Otumba were traded to Tepeapulco, no obsidian from the Otumba mines made its way to Tepeapulco's workshops; they therefore had to rely on obsidian from twice as far away as the Otumba source.

Beyond noting the *pochteca* presence at Otumba, historical records give neither details about these merchants nor information on how or where those outside of Tenochtitlan obtained their export goods. We now know that Otumba's workshops manufactured many of the *pochteca's* most important export goods: obsidian knives and blades, earspools, lip plugs of obsidian and rock crystal, other ornaments, cochineal, and textiles. *Pochteca* gave Otumba's craft specialists access to much larger markets, encouraged further specialization, and perhaps also presented some opportunities for upward mobility.

In Tenochtitlan, *pochteca* and lapidaries formed close relations, as they probably did at Otumba (Charlton 1993, 1994); both groups also occupied positions of intermediate status. *Pochteca* supplied lapidaries directly or indirectly with rare stones, such as rock crystal, and a wider array of gray or obsidian sources than what could be found in other households and workshops. From excavations of a palace at Chiconaulta, we see some of the other materials *pochteca* might have imported to the Teotihuacan Valley, including Gulf-coast shell, copper bells, and turquoise (Nichols et al. 2009:463).

In Tenochtitlan, *pochteca* resided in their own barrio, and Berdan (1975:148) thinks they were similarly organized in other cities. A *pochteca* barrio most likely would have been located in the dispersed residential sector at Otumba, separated from the nobility. There are two areas within this zone—one in the southeast part of the site near the lapidaries and another in the northwest part of the site near a workshop with large numbers of obsidian blades—that have relatively high concentrations of fancy and imported polychrome pottery that might represent a *pochteca* barrio (Figure 3.18).

Unfortunately, we did not have the opportunity to excavate in either of those areas.

Pochteca would have purchased goods at Otumba's weekly market where artisans and farmers sold their wares. *Tlanecuilo* also would have been present to buy and sell pottery and other goods. In addition to trading in the marketplace, merchants also would have purchased items directly from workshops.

Pochteca and long-distance trade in wealth goods formed an important component of Otumba's economy and contributed to its urban growth. The production and distribution of domestic goods also strengthened Otumba's economy and spurred Aztec commerce. The movement of substantial amounts of domestic goods through Aztec markets was by no means unique to Otumba. For example, blades made of Pachuca obsidian were available to all Aztec households in the Basin of Mexico, even in city-states without blade workshops (Millhauser 2005:267). Regional merchants exported pottery from Tenochtitlan, Texcoco, Chalco, and Cuauhtitlan to the Teotihuacan Valley. Nevertheless, political boundaries and an emphasis on local production sometimes inhibited the movement of merchants; for instance, regional pottery merchants from the Acolhua territories, including the Teotihuacan Valley, seem to have been restricted from markets in the western basin (Nichols et al. 2002).

Archaeological investigations of Aztec provincial sites, such as Otumba, along with source studies are providing new details about commerce in the Aztec economy and how commoner households contributed to it. Along with the growth in lake transportation, the increased integration of the Late Postclassic market system and expanded volume of trade went hand in hand. At the same time, the manufacture of at least some types of goods (e.g., Black-on-Orange pottery) became more centralized as market integration improved. Even though the wide distribution of clay sources in the basin and the cost of moving heavy, fragile pottery favored decentralized manufacturing, producer-vendors and regional merchants traded substantial amounts of Aztec pottery. Contrary to previous expectations, Garraty (2006) has

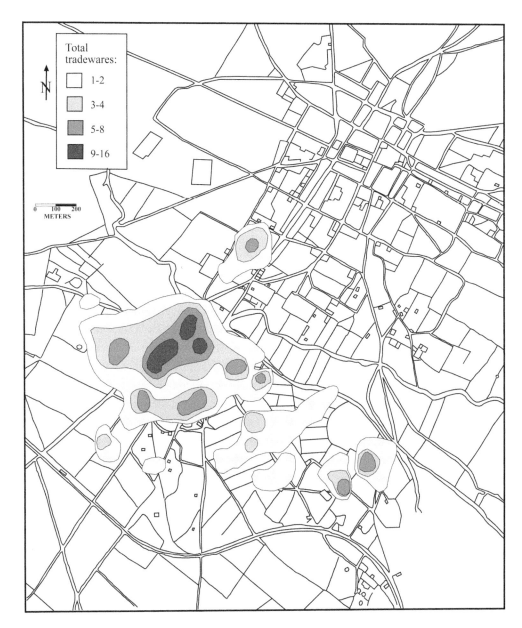

figure 3.18
Trade wares (Xochimlco, Huastec, Gulf coast, and Chalco Cholula) smoothed density plot from surface collections at Otumba. (Drawing by Deborah L. Nichols, after Hirst et al. 1990:42.)

documented considerable trade across subregions of the basin in Plain Orange pottery, such as *comals*, not just decorated serving wares (Garraty n.d.; Nichols et al. 2002). Despite the limited transportation, the volume of Aztec ceramic exchange was substantial (Smith 1990:162; cf. Drennan 1984; Sanders and Santley 1983).

Producer-vendors and retailers were assumed to have only supplied a relatively small number of consumers because of high transportation costs, but the lakes in the basin facilitated the bulk movement of goods (e.g., Sanders and Santley 1983). Nonetheless, the total volume of goods traded by commoner retailers and producer-vendors was high and significant to the Aztec economy. Garraty (2006:209) estimates that about four to five and a half million pots, plain and decorated, were exchanged through the market system each year in the Basin of Mexico, and this number represents only one commodity. These findings highlight the roles of commoner households as craft producers and farmers, vendors, and merchants in the commercial economy of the Aztecs. Merchants also exported Aztec ceramics from the Basin of Mexico in the Late Postclassic period to other parts of the empire (e.g., Gulf coast, Pacific coast, and Southern Highlands) and some even made its way into Tlaxcala, a major Aztec enemy to the east (Skoglund et al. 2006; Smith 1990:163–164).

Unfortunately, in contrast to the *pochteca*, we know little about the social identities of itinerant regional merchants. They were commoners. Some regional merchants were retailers or middlemen who exchanged various commodities, while others belonged to craft-specialist households, barrios, and villages, and they traded goods (and produce) made by their household or barrio, like the salt sellers who brought salt to Otumba in specialized pots (Texcoco Fabric Marked) and traveled a circuit of markets.

Conclusions

Sanders and Santley (1983:274) concluded that *pochteca* with their guild organization were "probably the largest and most important economic institution in Aztec society, other than the state." The development of *pochteca* at Otumba paralleled the town's growth as a market and craft production center. They provided new and larger markets for craft specialists at Otumba. Clearly the presence of *pochteca* fostered the growth in obsidian core-blade and lapidary industries at Otumba and linked these household-based industries to an international market. Politics had a hand in this development, but proximity to an obisidian source especially valued by the Aztecs for jewelry and bifaces, to skilled artisans, and to a major trade route was also important.

Although the *pochteca*'s role in Otumba's economy diminished with the Spanish conquest, and new traders replaced them, Nahua producer-vendors and regional merchants continued to sell goods (Gibson 1964:358). At Otumba, the lapidary industry collapsed under Spanish norms of body

ornamentation, and figurine makers shifted to the production of Hispanic figures rather than Aztec deities (Charlton 2007; Charlton and Charlton 1994). Otumba obsidian continued to be mined, but Aztec distribution networks for Pachuca obsidian began to break down. Workshops still manufactured many types of Aztec pottery, but potters also incorporated new technologies and adjusted to new consumers. Production of Aztec IV Black-on-Orange pottery declined in the Tenochtitlan area but expanded around Texcoco and Otumba's weekly market, and continued, albeit in a new location, when the Spanish relocated the town's center.

The importance of *pochteca* in the Aztec economy and what the development of professional merchants signals about commerce should not overshadow the role of regional merchants, producer-vendors, and household workshops that supplied most goods in Aztec markets. Until recent decades, we have underestimated this trade because of a tendency to associate households and the domestic sphere with low productivity (Brumfiel and Nichols 2009; Hirth 2009). As we have seen, archaeological data from Otumba and other Aztec sites indicate otherwise. At Otumba, specialization in manufacturing domestic goods provided a means for households to diversify their economic base in the face of growing populations, an enlarging consumer base, and rising tribute demands. From recent archaeological work we can gain a fuller appreciation of the contribution of commoner households to Aztec commerce and of commerce outside the imperial cities.

Acknowledgments

The archaeological field research in the Otumba city-state was carried out with permission of the Instituto Nacional de Antropología e Historia, and with support from the National Science Foundation (BNS-87195665 and SBR-9714583, BNS-8718140, and SBR-9707462) and the National Endowment for the Humanities (R-21705-88). Additional funding came from the Dartmouth Class of 1962, the Rockefeller Center of the Social Sciences Reiss Senior Faculty

Grant, the Clair Garber Goodman Fund, the University of Iowa Faculty Development Fund, and the Missouri University Research Reactor. I dedicate this article to Thomas H. Charlton, who invited me to collaborate with him in developing our research. The project also owed its success to Cynthia Otis Charlton's many contributions as well as those of Martin Biskowski and William Parry. Dan Healan directed excavations of the obsidian workshop. Hector Neff and Michael Glascock collaborated on the INAA studies of obsidian and ceramics. Kristin Sullivan assisted with the preparation of figures. I also thank Ken Hirth and Joanne Pillsbury for the opportunity to participate in this symposium and Emily Jacobs for all her assistance. When Tom and I undertook the materials analysis project, my son, Aaron, then age five, described the modern Otumba site as "just a place all covered in cactus." My heartfelt thanks go to John Watanabe and to Gary M. Schwartz for his patience with patients.

REFERENCES CITED

Abrahms, Elliot M.

1988   Investigation of an Obsidian Midden at Cihuatecpan, Mexico. In *Excavations at Cihuatecpan: An Aztec Village in the Teotihuacan Valley*, edited by Susan Toby Evans, pp. 235–238. Vanderbilt University Publications in Anthropology 36. Vanderbilt University, Nashville, Tenn.

Acosta Saignes, Miguel

1945   *Los pochteca: Ubicación de los mercaderes en la estructura social tenochca.* Acta anthropologica 1, no. 1. Sociedad de Alumnos de la Escuela Nacional de Antropología e Historia, Mexico City.

Berdan, Frances F.

1975   Trade, Tribute, and Market in the Aztec Empire. PhD dissertation, Department of Anthropology, University of Texas, Austin.

1977   Distributive Mechanisms in the Aztec Economy. In *Peasant Livelihood: Studies in Economic Anthropology and Cultural Ecology*, edited by Rhoda Halperin and James Dow, pp. 91–101. St. Martin's Press, New York.

1985   Markets in the Economy of Aztec Mexico. In *Markets and Marketing*, edited by Stuart Plattner, pp. 339–367. Monographs in Economic Anthropology 4. University Press of America, Lanham, Md.

1986   Enterprise and Empire in Aztec and Early Colonial Mexico. In *Economic Aspects of Prehispanic Highland Mexico*, edited by Barry L. Isaac, pp. 281–302. Research in Economic Anthropology, Supplement 2. JAI Press, Greenwich, Conn.

1988   Principles of Regional and Long-Distance Trade in the Aztec Empire. In *Smoke and Mist: Mesoamerican Studies in Memory of Thelma D. Sullivan*, edited by J. Kathryn Josserand and Karen Dakin, pp. 639–656. BAR International Series 402(2). BAR, Oxford.

2005   *The Aztecs of Central Mexico: An Imperial Society.* Thomson Wadsworth, Belmont, Calif.

Biskowski, Martin

2000   Maize Preparation and the Aztec Subsistence Economy. *Ancient Mesoamerica* 11:293–306.

Bittman, Bente, and Thelma D. Sullivan

1978   The Pochteca. In *Mesoamerican Communication Routes and Cultural Contacts*, edited by Thomas A. Lee Jr. and Carlos Navarrete, pp. 211–218. New World Archaeological Foundation, Brigham Young University, Provo, Utah.

Blanton, Richard E.

1996   The Basin of Mexico Market System and the Growth of Empire. In *Aztec Imperial Strategies*, edited by Frances F. Berdan,

Richard E. Blanton, Elizabeth Hill Boone, Mary G. Hodge, Michael E. Smith, and Emily Umberger, pp. 47–84. Dumbarton Oaks Research Library and Collection, Washington, D.C.

Blanton, Richard E., and Mary G. Hodge

1996   Appendix 2: Data on Market Activities and Production Specializations of Tlatoani Centers. In *Aztec Imperial Strategies*, edited by Frances F. Berdan, Richard E. Blanton, Elizabeth Hill Boone, Mary G. Hodge, Michael E. Smith, and Emily Umberger, pp. 243–246. Dumbarton Oaks Research Library and Collection, Washington, D.C.

Blanton, Richard E., Stephen A. Kowalewski, Gary M. Feinman, and Laura M. Finsten

1993   *Ancient Mesoamerica: A Comparison of Change in Three Regions*. 2nd ed. Cambridge University Press, Cambridge.

Brumfiel, Elizabeth M.

1987   Elite and Utilitarian Crafts in the Aztec State. In *Specialization, Exchange, and Complex Societies*, edited by Elizabeth M. Brumfiel and Timothy K. Earle, pp. 102–118. Cambridge University Press, Cambridge.

2004   Meaning by Design: Ceramics, Feasting, and Figured Worlds in Postclassic Mexico. In *Mesoamerican Archaeology: Theory and Practice*, edited by Julia A. Hendon and Rosemary A. Joyce, pp. 238–263. Blackwell, Oxford.

Brumfiel, Elizabeth M., and Mary D. Hodge

1996   Interaction in the Basin of Mexico: The Case of Postclassic Xaltocan. In *Arqueología mesoamericana: Homenaje a William T. Sanders*, edited by Alba Guadalupe Mastache, Jeffery R. Parsons, Robert S. Santley, Mari Carmen Sera Puce, pp. 417–437. Instituto Nacional de Antropología e Historia, Mexico City.

Brumfiel, Elizabeth M., and Deborah L. Nichols

2009   Bitumen, Blades, and Beads: Prehispanic Craft Production and the Domestic Economy. In *Housework: Craft Production and Domestic Economy in Ancient Mesoamerica*, edited by Kenneth G. Hirth, pp. 239–251. Archaeological Papers of the American Anthropological Association 19. Wiley, Hoboken, N.J.

Calnek, Edward E.

1976   The Internal Structure of Tenochtitlan. In *The Valley of Mexico: Studies in Prehispanic Ecology and Society*, edited by Eric R. Wolf, pp. 287–302. University of New Mexico Press, Albuquerque.

Carrasco, Pedro

1980   Markets and Merchants in the Aztec Economy. *Journal of the Steward Anthropological Society* 11:249–269.

1983   Some Theoretical Considerations about the Role of the Market in Ancient Mexico. In *Economic Anthropology: Topics and Theories*, edited by Sutti Ortiz, pp. 67–81. Monographs in Economic Anthropology 1. Society for Economic Anthropology, Smithsonian Institution, and University Press of America, Lanham, Md.

Chapman, Anne M.

1957   Port of Trade Enclaves in Aztec and Maya Civilizations. In *Trade and Market in the Early Empires: Economies in History and Theory*, edited by Karl Polanyi, Conrad M. Arensberg, and Harry W. Pearson, pp. 114–153. Collier-MacMillan, London, and Free Press, New York.

Charlton, Cynthia Otis

1993   Obsidian as Jewelry: Lapidary Production in Aztec Otumba, Mexico. *Ancient Mesoamerica* 4:231–243.

1994   Plebeians and Patricians: Contrasting Patterns of Production and Distribution in the Aztec Figurine and Lapidary Industries. In *Economies and Polities in the Aztec Realm*, edited by Mary G. Hodge and Michael E. Smith, pp. 195–220. Studies on Culture and Society 6. Institute for Mesoamerican Studies, State University of New York, Albany, and University of Texas Press, Austin.

2007   Artesanos y barro: Figurillas y alfarería en Otompan, estado de México. *Arqueología* 14(83):71–76.

Charlton, Cynthia Otis, Thomas H. Charlton, and Deborah L. Nichols

1993   Aztec Household-Based Craft Production: Archaeological Evidence from the City-State of Otumba, Mexico. In *Prehispanic Domestic Units in Western*

*Mesoamerica: Studies in Household,
Compound, and Residence*, edited by
Robert S. Santley and Kenneth. G. Hirth,
pp. 147–172. CRC Press, Boca Raton, Fla.

Charlton, Thomas H.

1978　Teotihuacan, Tepeapulco, and Obsidian
Exploitation. *Science* 200:1227–1236.

Charlton, Thomas H., and Cynthia Otis Charlton

1994　Aztec Craft Production at Otumba, AD
1470–1570: Reflections of a Changing
World. In *Chipping Away on Earth:
Studies in Prehispanic and Colonial
Mexico in Honor of Arthur J. O.
Anderson and Charles E. Dibble*, edited
by Eloise Quiñones Keber, pp. 241–251.
Labyrinthos, Lancaster, Calif.

Charlton, Thomas H., Cynthia Otis Charlton,
Deborah L. Nichols, and Hector Neff

2008　Aztec Otumba, AD 1200–1600: Patterns
of the Production, Distribution, and
Consumption of Ceramic Products.
In *Pottery Economics in Mesoamerica*,
edited by Christopher A. Pool and
George J. Bey III, pp. 237–266. University
of Arizona Press, Tucson.

Charlton, Thomas H., and Deborah L. Nichols

1997　Diachronic Studies of City-States:
Permuations on a Theme—Central
Mexico from 1700 BC to AD 1600. In
*The Archaeology of City-States: Cross-
Cultural Approaches*, edited by Deborah
L. Nichols and Thomas H. Charlton,
pp. 169–208. Smithsonian Institution
Press, Washington, D.C.

Charlton, Thomas H., Deborah L. Nichols, and
Cynthia Otis Charlton

1991　Craft Specialization within the Aztec
City-State of Otumba, Mexico: The
Archaeological Evidence. *World Archae-
ology* 23:98–114.

2000a　Otumba and Its Neighbors: Ex oriente
lux. *Ancient Mesoamerica* 11:247–265.

2000b　The Otumba Project: A Review and
Status Report. In *The Teotihuacan Valley
Project Final Report: The Aztec Period
Occupation of the Valley*, pt. 2, edited
by William T. Sanders, pp. 875–887.
Occasional Papers in Anthropology
26. Department of Anthropology,
Pennsylvania State University,
University Park.

Charlton, Thomas H., and Michael W. Spence

1983　Obsidian Exploitation and Civilization
in the Basin of Mexico. In *Mining
and Mining Techniques in Ancient
Mesoamerica*, edited by Phil C.
Weigand and Gretchen Gwynne,
pp. 7–86. Anthropology 4, nos. 1–2.
Department of Anthropology, State
University of New York, Stony Brook.

Davies, Nigel

1973　*The Aztecs: A History.* University of
Oklahoma Press, Norman.

Díaz del Castillo, Bernal

1996 [1568]　*The Discovery and Conquest of Mexico,
1517–1521.* Edited by Genaro García;
translated by Alfred P. Maudslay. Da
Capo Press, New York.

Drennan, Robert D.

1984　Long-Distance Transport Coasts in
Pre-Hispanic Mesoamerica. *American
Anthropologist* 86:105–112.

Durán, Fray Diego

1967
[1570–1581]　*Historia de las indias de Nueva-España
y islas de la tierra firme.* 2 vols. Edited by
Ángel María Garibay Kintana. Editorial
Porrúa, Mexico City.

Evans, Susan Toby

1980　Spatial Analysis of Basin of Mexico
Settlement: Problems with the Use
of Central Place Models. *American
Antiquity* 45:866–875.

1988　*Excavations at Cihuatecpan: An Aztec
Village in the Teotihuacan Valley.*
Vanderbilt University Publications in
Anthropology 36. Vanderbilt University,
Nashville, Tenn.

1990　The Productivity of Maguey Terrace
Agriculture in Central Mexico dur-
ing the Aztec Period. *Latin American
Antiquity* 1:117–132.

2001　Aztec-Period Political Organization
in the Teotihuacan Valley: Otumba
as a City-State. *Ancient Mesoamerica*
12:89–100.

Feinman, Gary M., and Christopher P. Garraty

2010　Preindustrial Markets and Marketing:
An Archaeological Perspective. *Annual
Review of Anthropology* 39:167–191.

García Chávez, Raul E.

2004   De Tula a Azcapotzalco: Caaracter-
ización arqueológica de los altepetl
de la Cuenca de México del posclásico
temprano y medio, a travéz del estudio cerámico regional. PhD dissertation, Facultad de Filosofía y Letras,
Universidad Nacional Autónoma de
México, Mexico City.

Garraty, Christopher P.

2006   The Politics of Commerce: Aztec Pottery
Production and Exchange in the Basin of
Mexico, AD 1200–1650. PhD dissertation,
School of Human Evolution and Social
Change, Arizona State University, Tempe.

n.d.   Market Development and Expansion
under Aztec and Spanish Rule in Cerro
Portezuelo. *Ancient Mesoamerica*, in
press.

Genotte, Jean François

2001   The Mapa de Otumba: New Hypotheses.
Ancient Mesoamerica 12:127–147.

Gibson, Charles

1964   *Aztecs under Spanish Rule: A History
of the Indians of the Valley of Mexico.*
Stanford University Press, Stanford.

Glascock, Michael D., William J. Parry, Thomas H.
Charlton, Cynthia Otis Charlton, and Hector Neff

2001   Obsidian Artifacts. In *Processes of State
Formation in the Northeastern Basin
of Mexico: Materials Analysis*, edited
by Deborah L. Nichols and Thomas
H. Charlton, pp. 38–42. Final Report
to the National Science Foundation,
Arlington, Va.

n.d.   Evidence for Control of the Obsidian
Economy at Otumba and Tepeapulco.
Manuscript on file, Research Reactor
Center, University of Missouri, Columbia.

Hare, Timothy

1994   Lapidary Craft Specialists at Otumba
(TA80): A Case Study in the Organization
of Craft Production in Late Aztec Mexico.
MA thesis, Department of Anthropology,
University of Iowa, Iowa City.

Hassig, Ross

1985   *Trade, Tribute, and Transportation: The
Sixteenth-Century Political Economy
of the Valley of Mexico.* University of
Oklahoma Press, Norman.

1988   *Aztec Warfare: Imperial Expansion
and Political Control.* University of
Oklahoma Press, Norman.

Hicks, Frederic

1987   First Steps Toward a Market-Integrated
Economy in Aztec Mexico. In *Early State
Dynamics*, edited by Henri J. M. Claessen
and Pieter van de Velde, pp. 91–107. E. J.
Brill, Leiden and New York.

Hirst, K. Kris, Marcela Mendoza, and Thomas H.
Charlton

1990   Analysis of Pottery from the 1% Surface
Collection. In *Early State Formation
Processes: The Aztec City-State of
Otumba Mexico*, vol. 1, edited by Thomas
Charlton and Deborah L. Nichols,
pp. 31–44. Final Report to the National
Science Foundation, Arlington, Va.

Hirth, Kenneth G.

2009   Craft Production, Household
Diversification, and Domestic
Economy in Prehispanic Mesoamerica.
In *Housework: Craft Production
and Domestic Economy in Ancient
Mesoamerica*, edited by Kenneth G.
Hirth, pp. 13–32. Archaeological Papers
of the American Anthropological
Association 19. Wiley, Hoboken, N.J.

Hodge, Mary G.

1992   The Geographical Structure of Aztec
Imperial-Period Market Systems.
*National Geographic Research and
Exploration* 8:428–445.

1994   Polities Composing the Aztec Empire's
Core. In *Economies and Polities in
the Aztec Realm*, edited by Mary G.
Hodge and Michael E. Smith, pp. 43–72.
Institute for Mesoamerican Studies,
State University of New York, Albany,
and University of Texas Press, Austin.

1996   Political Organization of the Central
Provinces. In *Aztec Imperial Strategies*,
edited by Frances F. Berdan, Richard
E. Blanton, Elizabeth Hill Boone,
Mary G. Hodge, Michael E. Smith, and
Emily Umberger, pp. 17–45. Dumbarton
Oaks Research Library and Collection,
Washington, D.C.

1997 When Is a City-State? Archaeological Measures of Aztec City-States and Aztec City-State Systems. In *The Archaeology of City-States: Cross-Cultural Approaches*, edited by Deborah L. Nichols and Thomas H. Charlton, pp. 209–228. Smithsonian Institution Press, Washington, D.C.

Hodge, Mary G., and Leah D. Minc

1990 The Spatial Patterning of Aztec Ceramics: Implications for Prehispanic Exchange Systems in the Valley of Mexico. *Journal of Field Archaeology* 17:415–437.

Hodge, Mary G., and Hector Neff

2005 Xaltocan in the Economy of the Basin of Mexico: A View from Ceramic Tradewares. In *La producción local y el poder en el Xaltocan posclásico / Production and Power at Postclassic Xaltocan*, edited by Elizabeth M. Brumfiel, pp. 320–348. Instituto Nacional de Antropología e Historia, Mexico City, and University of Pittsburgh, Pittsburgh.

Hodge, Mary G., Hector Neff, M. James Blackman, and Leah D. Minc

1992 A Compositional Perspective on Ceramic Production in the Aztec Empire. In *Chemical Characterization of Ceramic Pastes in Archaeology*, edited by Hector Neff, pp. 203–231. Monographs in World Archaeology 7. Prehistory Press, Madison, Wis.

1993 Black-on-Orange Ceramic Production in the Aztec Empire's Heartland. *Latin American Antiquity* 4:130–157.

Isaac, Barry L.

1986 Notes on Obsidian, the Pochteca, and the Position of Tlatelolco in the Aztec Empire. In *Economic Aspects of Prehispanic Highland Mexico,* edited by Barry L. Isaac, pp. 319–346. Research in Economic Anthropology Supplement 2. JAI Press, Greenwich, Conn.

Ixtlilxochitl, Fernando de Alva

1965 *Obras históricas.* 2 vols. Editora
[1891–1892] Nacional, Mexico City.

Katz, Friedrich

1972 *The Ancient American Civilizations.* Translated by K. M. Lois Simpson. Phoenix Press, London.

Ma, Marina K. S.

2003 Examining Prehispanic Ceramic Exchange in the Basin of Mexico: A Chemical Source Analysis from Azcapotzalco. Senior Honors thesis in Anthropology, Dartmouth College, Hanover, N.H.

McClung de Tapia, Emily, and Boris Aramis Aguillar Hernández

2001 Vegetation and Plant Use in Postclassic Otumba. *Ancient Mesoamerica* 12:113–125.

Millhauser, John

2005 Classic and Postclassic Chipped Stone at Xaltocan. In *La producción local y el poder en el Xaltocan posclásico / Production and Power at Postclassic Xaltocan*, edited by Elizabeth M. Brumfiel, pp. 267–318. Instituto Nacional de Antropología e Historia, Mexico City, and University of Pittsburgh, Pittsburgh.

Minc, Leah D.

2006 Monitoring Regional Market Systems in Prehistory: Models, Methods, and Metrics. *Journal of Anthropological Archaeology* 25:82–116.

2009 Style and Substance: Evidence for Regionalism within the Aztec Market System. *Latin American Antiquity* 2:343–374.

Minc, Leah D., Mary G. Hodge, and M. James Blackman

1994 Stylistic and Spatial Variability in Early Aztec Ceramics: Insights into Pre-Imperial Exchange Systems. In *Economies and Polities in the Aztec Realm*, edited by Mary G. Hodge and Michael E. Smith, pp. 134–173. Institute for Mesoamerican Studies, State University of New York, Albany, and University of Texas Press, Austin.

Neff, Hector, Ronald L. Bishop, Edward B. Sisson, Michael D. Glascock, and P. R. Sisson

1994 Neutron Activation Analysis of Late Postclassic Polychrome Pottery from Central Mexico. In *Mixteca-Puebla:*

Discoveries and Research in Mesoamerican Art and Archaeology, edited by H. B. Nicholson and Eloise Quiñones Keber, pp. 117–142. Labyrinthos, Culver City, Calif.

Neff, Hector, and Michael D. Glascock

2000   Provenance Analysis of Aztec-Period Ceramics from the Basin of Mexico. Manuscript on file, Research Reactor Center, University of Missouri, Columbia.

Neff, Hector, Michael D. Glascock, Thomas H. Charlton, Cynthia Otis Charlton, and Deborah L. Nichols

2000   Provenience Investigation of Ceramics and Obsidian from Otumba. *Ancient Mesoamerica* 11:207–322.

Neff, Hector, and Mary G. Hodge

2008   Serving Vessel Production at Chalco: Evidence from Neutron Activation Analysis. In *Place of Jade: Society and Economy in Ancient Chalco*, edited by Mary G. Hodge, pp. 185–224. Instituto Nacional de Antropología e Historia, Mexico City, and University of Pittsburgh, Pittsburgh.

Nichols, Deborah L.

1994   The Organization of Provincial Craft Production and the Aztec City-State Otumba. In *Economies and Polities in the Aztec Realm*, edited by Mary G. Hodge and Michael E. Smith, pp. 175–194. Studies on Culture and Society 6. Institute for Mesoamerican Studies, State University of New York, Albany, and University of Texas Press, Austin.

Nichols, Deborah L., Elizabeth M. Brumfiel, Hector Neff, Mary G. Hodge, Thomas H. Charlton, and Michael D. Glascock

2002   Neutrons, Markets, Cities, and Empires: A 1000-Year Perspective on Ceramic Production and Distribution in the Postclassic Basin of Mexico. *Journal of Anthropological Archaeology* 21:25–82.

Nichols, Deborah L., and Thomas H. Charlton

1996   The Postclassic Occupation at Otumba: A Chronological Assessment. *Ancient Mesoamerica* 7:231–244.

Nichols, Deborah L., Christina Elson, Leslie G. Cecil, Nina Neivens de Estrada, Michael D. Glascock, and Paula Mikkelsen

2009   Chiconautla Mexico: A Crossroads of Aztec Trade and Politics. *Latin American Antiquity* 20:443–472.

Nichols, Deborah L., Mary Jane McLaughlin, and Maura Benton

2000   Production Intensification and Regional Specialization: Maguey Fibers and Textiles in the Aztec City-State of Otumba. *Ancient Mesoamerica* 11:267–292.

Nichols, Deborah L., Hector Neff, and George L. Cowgill

n.d.   Cerro Portezuelo: An Overview. *Ancient Mesoamerica*, in press.

Oka, Rahul, and Chapurukha M. Kusimba

2008   The Archaeology of Trading Systems, Part 1: Towards a New Trade Synthesis. *Journal of Archaeological Research* 16:340–395.

Parry, William J.

2001   Production and Exchange of Obsidian Tools in Late Aztec City-States. *Ancient Mesoamerica* 12:101–111.

2002   Aztec Blade Production Strategies in the Eastern Basin of Mexico. In *Pathways to Prismatic Blades: A Study in Mesoamerican Obsidian Core-Blade Technology*, edited by Kenneth G. Hirth and Bradford Andrews, pp. 39–48. Cotsen Institute of Archaeology, University of California, Los Angeles.

Parsons, Jeffrey R., and Mary H. Parsons

1990   *Otomí Maguey Utilization: An Ethnoarchaeological Perspective*. Museum of Anthropology Papers 82. University of Michigan, Ann Arbor.

Sahagún, Bernardino de

1950–1982   *Florentine Codex: General History of the Things of New Spain*. Translated by Arthur J. O. Anderson and Charles E. Dibble. School of American Research, Santa Fe, and University of Utah, Salt Lake City.

Sanders, William T., and Susan Toby Evans

2001   The Teotihuacan Valley and the Temas-
        calapa Region during the Aztec Period. In
        The Aztec Period Occupation of the Valley,
        pt. 3, *Syntheses and General Bibliography*,
        edited by William T. Sanders and Susan
        Toby Evans, pp. 932–1078. Department
        of Anthropology, Pennsylvania State
        University, University Park.

Sanders, William T., and Robert S. Santley

1983   A Tale of Three Cities: Energetics and
        Urbanization in Pre-Hispanic Central
        Mexico. In *Prehistoric Settlement
        Patterns: Essays in Honor of Gordon
        R. Willey*, edited by Evon Z. Vogt and
        Richard M. Leventhal, pp. 243–291.
        Peabody Museum of Archaeology
        and Ethnology, Harvard University,
        Cambridge, Mass.

Skoglund, Thanet, Barbara L. Stark, Hector Neff,
   and Michael D. Glascock

2006   Compositional and Stylistic Analysis
        of Aztec-Era Ceramics: Provincial
        Strategies at the Edge of Empire,
        South-Central Veracruz, Mexico.
        Latin American Antiquity 17:541–560.

Smith, Michael E.

1979   The Aztec Marketing System and
        Settlement Pattern in the Valley of
        Mexico: A Central Place Analysis.
        American Antiquity 44:110–125.

1980   The Role of the Marketing System in
        Aztec Society and Economy: Reply to
        Evans. *American Antiquity* 44:110–124.

1990   The Role of Long-Distance Trade
        Under the Aztec Empire: A View from
        the Provinces. *Ancient Mesoamerica*
        1:153–169.

2003   *The Aztecs*. 2nd ed. Blackwell, Malden,
        Mass.

2004   The Archaeology of Ancient State
        Economies. *Annual Review of Anthro-
        pology* 33:73–102.

2010   The Archaeological Study of Neighbor-
        hoods and Districts in Ancient Cities.
        Journal of Anthropological Archaeology
        29:137–154.

Soustelle, Jacques

1970 [1961] *Daily Life of the Aztecs on the Eve
        of the Spanish Conquest*. Translated
        by Patrick O'Brien. Penguin Books,
        Harmondsworth.

Spence, Michael W.

1985   Specialized Production in Rural Aztec
        Society: Obsidian Workshops of the
        Teotihuacan Valley. In *Contributions
        to the Archaeology and Ethnohistory of
        Greater Mesoamerica*, edited by William
        J. Folan, pp. 76–125. Southern Illinois
        University Press, Carbondale.

Sullivan, Kristin S.

2006   Making and Manipulating Ritual in the
        City of the Gods: Figurine Production
        and Use at Teotihuacán, México. Elec-
        tronic document, http://www.famsi.
        org/reports/03021/index.html, accessed
        February 4, 2011.

Zantwijk, Rudolf van

1985   *The Aztec Arrangement: The Social
        History of Pre-Spanish Mexico*. Univer-
        sity of Oklahoma Press, Norman.

4

The Merchant's World

Commercial Diversity and the Economics
of Interregional Exchange in Highland Mesoamerica

KENNETH G. HIRTH

MESOAMERICA PROVIDES AN INTRIGU-
ing case in the study of ancient economic
structure because it contradicts how preindustrial economies are assumed to operate. Although
Mesoamerica lacked well-developed transportation networks, it still supported a thriving system
of interregional exchange and resource movement.
Furthermore, while craft production appeared
at the same time that settled village life began, it
remained essentially a domestic activity with limited full-time specialization.

Three dimensions of the Mesoamerican
economy make it unique in comparison to other
complex societies in the ancient world. First,
Mesoamerica had the ancient world's worst transportation system. It lacked beasts of burden, which
meant that most goods moved on the backs of
human porters (Figure 4.1). There were few navigable rivers and little maritime commerce except
around the Yucatan Peninsula. Second, one would
think that poor transportation systems would
have depressed interregional interaction, but

exactly the opposite occurred. By the time of the
Spanish conquest, most areas of Mesoamerica
were linked by a vibrant system of marketplaces
that operated largely through the initiative of individual households with minimal elite involvement.
Third, within the marketplace a rich entrepreneurial economy emerged that, despite transportation
limitations, was highly differentiated from and
more complex than what is known from many
other parts of the ancient world. High transportation costs did not create specialized production
and distribution sectors as might be expected.
Instead, the economy was based on a rich array of
small-scale producer-vendors, artisans, and retail
vendors operating at the household level. Rather
than maintain a simple economy, Mesoamerica
developed a complex market system and a significant degree of interregional exchange. The area
demonstrates the level of economic development
that was possible across the ancient world even
with simple and inefficient forms of transportation, like human portage.

85

figure 4.1
Merchants on the road, carrying goods with tumplines. (Reproduced from Sahagún 1959:pl. 13.)

This paper has three objectives. First, it asks who operated as a merchant in the Pre-Columbian world. I am concerned here with both the indigenous definition of merchants as well as how contemporary scholars see them. My discussion draws upon Bernardino de Sahagún's description of market vendors found in the Tlatelolco marketplace in the mid-sixteenth century. This account provides a general framework for identifying the types of "merchants"—those individuals who sold goods in marketplaces across the central and southern Mexican Highlands. Second, I am interested in how far staple goods like grain, fruit, salt, and ceramics moved between regions. Answering this question is important for modeling the scale and extent of interregional exchange systems. In particular, I am interested in the question of how far goods moved through household-based distribution systems where items moved on the backs of

human porters. Finally, I construct a "profitability" model for itinerant obsidian-blade production. This model illustrates the incentives for and returns from household-based economic retailing of staple goods within and between regions of Mesoamerica. Obsidian-blade production is discussed here not only because there is very good information on this topic, but also because this staple good was made by craft specialists who often produced them on a part-time basis as part of their domestic subsistence regime. As such, it serves as a proxy for the type of part-time commercial activities in which households could engage. Although I model profitability in terms of itinerant, mobile retailing, the same forces would have been at work for stationary retailing and other forms of interhousehold exchange.

This chapter focuses on the commercial activities of commoner households and the profitability of trading goods over relatively short distances under conditions of high transportation costs before the Spanish conquest. From a comparative perspective, transportation in Central Mexico was much more restrictive than it was in either the Maya or the Andean regions, where riverine conveyance and llama caravans made trade and the movement of goods more efficient. Households in these three areas used somewhat different economic strategies to mobilize resources and to meet their economic needs. Nevertheless, the same economic logic pervaded domestic settings throughout the Pre-Columbian world, and households met their resource needs through independent, entrepreneurial activities geared toward enhancing

their economic well-being and ensuring their survival (Hirth 2009a). In this regard, Central Mexico exemplifies what enterprising households could achieve within the sphere of the domestic economy and serves as a point of comparison for examining domestic economic strategies in other pre-Hispanic societies.

Who Were Pre-Columbian Merchants?

Most discussions of Mesoamerican merchants have focused on groups like the Aztec *pochteca* and *oztomeca,* who specialized in long-distance trade of high-value goods (Acosta Saignes 1945;

figure 4.2
Pochteca merchants with high-value goods. (Reproduced from Sahagún 1959:pl. 14.)

Berdan 1975; Bittman and Sullivan 1978; Cardos de Méndez 1959; Carrasco 1978; Katz 1966; León-Portilla 1962). Deborah Nichols provides a good review of *pochteca* merchants in chapter three of this volume and I will not repeat that discussion here. Long-distance *pochteca* merchants were crucial to the Pre-Columbian commercial world (Figure 4.2). They were not, however, the only—or even the dominant or most numerous—group of individuals buying, selling, and moving commodities across the landscape. Individual commoner households who were not members of the *pochteca* community conducted a great deal of commerce. The best way to understand the structure of this ancient commercial world is to look inside a Pre-Columbian marketplace. There, we can profile commercial activity in terms of the range of commercial sellers found in the marketplace and the diversity of items that they sold.

Who qualified as a merchant in Mesoamerica? Merriam-Webster defines a merchant as "an individual who buys and sells goods for profit." This definition is simple and to the point, and emphasizes the merchant's function as a purveyor of wares that can be sold at a profit. While this is a modern view of who a merchant is, it fits the sixteenth-century description of the indigenous merchant provided by Bernardino de Sahagún's native informants:

> In puchtecatl ca tlanamacani, tlanamacac, thanecuilo, tlaixtlapanqui, tlaixtlapanani, tlatennonotzani, tlamixitiani, tlapilhoatiani. In qualli puchtecatl, tlaotlatoctiani, tlanênemitiani, çan tlaipantiliani, tlanamictiani, tlaimacazqui teimacazqui.
>
> In puchtecatl ca tlanamacani, tiamiquini.... tlaixtlapanani, tlamixiuitiani, tlapiloatiani, molpiliani, melaoacatlatoani, tlatolmelaoac, melaoac in iiollo, teuimacaci....tlanamaca, tlatennonotza, tlatentotoca, tenanamiqui.

> The merchant is a seller, a merchandiser, a retailer; [he is] one who profits, who gains; who has reached an agreement on prices; who secures increase, who multiplies [his possessions]. The good merchant

[is] a follower of the routes, a traveler [with merchandise; he is] one who sets correct prices, who gives equal value (Sahagún 1961:42–43).

> The merchant [is] a vendor, a seller, a practiser of commerce ... a maker of profits, a securer of increase, a multiplier [of his possessions]—one who holds fast [to the profits. He is] a straightforward dealer, honest, reliable. He negotiates contracts, he makes agreements, he helps others (Sahagún 1961:59).

Three aspects of Sahagún's description are important. First, it defines a merchant as an individual whose primary motivation for exchange is profit. The Nahuatl word for profit is *tlaixtlapana*. Its literal meaning is "to split or divide things (i.e., goods or money) in a face-to-face setting" like those found in negotiated exchanges within Mesoamerican marketplaces (see appendix for a Nahuatl economic vocabulary). It establishes that the profit motive was a central feature of economic exchange. It also clarifies that negotiation was the method of "setting correct prices," obtaining "equal value," and arranging contracts and agreements.

A second feature of Sahagún's description is that his informants identify a range of types of vendors in market settings. These include the producer-vendor (*tlachiuhqui*), the general merchandiser (*tlanamacac*), and the retailer (*tlanecuilo*). Sahagún's discussion underscores two important aspects of Pre-Columbian commercial activity: 1) vendors operated at different commercial scales within the Tlatelolco marketplace; and 2) individuals who sold what they produced differed from retailers who resold goods bought from others, including imports obtained from outside the region. These distinctions shed light on the structure of commercial exchange and the identities of those involved in it.

A third and final aspect of Sahagún's description is his identification of a merchant as one who travels. Because his descriptions tend to be holistic and inclusive, I believe this is more than just a reference to long-distance *pochteca* merchants. Sahagún's informants stated that travel constituted a general feature of commercial behavior. As will be discussed below, many producer-vendors journeyed between regions with goods to sell. Yet travel was not a necessary part of merchant behavior since many retailers (*tlanecuiloque*) were regular, if not permanent, fixtures in the Tlatelolco market; others circulated among regional markets without ever leaving the Basin of Mexico (Anderson et al. 1976:138–149). Therefore, measuring economic complexity is difficult. One way to do it is to examine the diversity of economic activities found in a society and determine whether specialized practitioners carried them out. This Durkheimian approach assumes that specialization is a product of the organic solidarity or economic interdependence of different segments within society (Durkheim 1933). It is in this regard that Sahagún's description of the marketplace provides a vibrant picture of commercial activity in highland society.

Several features of Sahagún's discussion of the Tlatelolco marketplace are particularly noteworthy. It was intended as an encyclopedic summary, so many of the descriptions are categorical and generic in nature, obscuring differences in the scale, complexity, and range of vendor activities. Sahagún's Tlatelolco informants, who very likely were members of its *pochteca* community, provided these categories. This fact means that the terminology used reflects the commercial categories that the merchants themselves recognized as distinct classes of market vendors. Finally, we need to remember that the Tlatelolco marketplace was arguably the largest urban market in the Aztec Empire and possessed greater internal economic differentiation than was found in other marketplaces in highland Mesoamerica. Nevertheless, Sahagún's description of the Tlatelolco marketplace offers a cross section of the commercial diversity and the level of economic complexity found in Central Mexico at the time of the Conquest.

Inside the Tlatelolco Marketplace

Sahagún discusses six general types of vendors operating inside the marketplace in addition to long-distance *pochteca* merchants. These include producer-vendors, artisans, retailers, peddlers, exchange agents, and commercial agents (Figure 4.3). These were non-*pochteca* merchandisers and they were the backbone of the highland commercial

figure 4.3
A Tarascan marketplace. (Illustration modified from Craine and Reindorp 1970:pl. 29.)

economy. They were all small-scale merchants because, like the *pochteca*, they trafficked in goods to make a profit as part of their day-to-day livelihood. Moreover, they produced the greatest number and assortment of goods sold and represented the majority of commercial vendors who sold their wares in the marketplace. How far they traveled to buy and sell products is unclear, although the *Relaciones geográficas* indicate that producer-vendors regularly participated in intermediate-scale exchange networks throughout the sixteenth century (see below).

As the name implies, producer-vendors were small-scale operators who sold what they grew (farmers), processed (food vendors), collected (hunters and fishers), or manufactured (artisans). I have identified 112 different categories, or types, of producer-vendors in Central Mexican marketplaces. These vendors include men and women who produced goods for sale both in their homes and within the marketplace. Table 4.1 groups these market participants into five broad categories based on the kind of item sold. These categories include: sixteen types of food producers who sold unprocessed grains, fruit, and vegetables; fifteen types of food vendors who sold cooked food and beverages; sixteen types of foragers who hunted, fished, collected, and processed natural resources into products such as resin, dye, glue, and lime; fifty-four types of artisans; and eleven types of service providers who transported goods and performed personal services ranging from barbering to prostitution. Mostly,

these individuals sold goods used by the indigenous population, but the rapidity with which specialty items were created for Spanish consumers certainly testifies to the vendors' commercial acumen.

Artisans constitute nearly one-half of all the producer-vendors found in the marketplace. Nahuatl makes it easy to identify these artisans because they are distinguished by words using the agentive suffix –*chiuhqui*, which translates loosely as "maker of." An artisan selling the ceramic griddles (*comal*) or salt (*iztatl*) that he or she has made would be identified as a *comalchiuhqui* or *iztachiuhqui*. The tempo of production for the marketplace varied from artisan to artisan, depending on how commercial activities fit into the overall domestic economy and an individual's involvement in subsistence farming (Hirth 2009a). Artisans' commercial production could be intermittent or cyclical in nature (Hirth 2009a). Still, even such part-time involvement constituted the source for the majority of goods sold in regional markets throughout Central Mexico (Anderson et al. 1976; Rojas 1986; Sahagún 1961).

A second block of merchants in the marketplace are retail vendors who were identified by the term *tlanecuilo*. They bought goods for resale either directly from producers or from other merchant intermediaries. Retailers dealt in both high- and low-value items produced locally or imported from distant regions. They could also be wholesalers and importers (*tlaquixtiani*, see appendix) who bought goods in lots for resale to other merchants who hawked such wares in the marketplace.

table 4.1

Types of producer-vendors found in Central Mexican marketplaces

TYPES OF PRODUCER-VENDORS	NUMBER	PERCENT
FOOD PRODUCERS	16	14.3
FOOD VENDORS	15	13.4
FORAGERS AND COLLECTORS	16	14.3
CRAFTSMEN	54	48.0
SERVICE PROVIDERS	11	10.0
TOTAL PRODUCER-VENDORS	112	100.0

TYPES OF RETAIL MERCHANTS	NUMBER	PERCENT
FOOD RETAILERS	11	29.7
STAPLE GOODS RETAILERS	4	13.5
TEXTILE SUPPLIERS	11	29.7
WEALTH GOOD RETAILERS	7	18.9
SPECIALTY VENDORS	4	8.2
TOTAL RETAIL MERCHANTS	37	100.0

I have identified thirty-seven types of retailers in Central Mexican marketplaces during the sixteenth century that are grouped into five broad categories based on the type of goods sold (Table 4.2). These include: eleven types of food retailers; four categories of retailers who sold staple goods (salt, medicines, wood products, and gourds); eleven textile suppliers selling finished garments, footwear, dyes, weaving supplies, and spun thread; seven dealers of high-value commodities such as slaves, feather work, and goods made of jade, gold, and shell; and four specialty vendors of sundries like paper, tobacco, rubber, and musical instruments. While most categories reflect precontact commercial activity, others—like the wool-cloth dealer (*tomitilmatli*) and wheat trader (*trigonamacac*)—were postcontact innovations.

As might be expected, the boundary between producer-vendors and retailers is vague, both due to the nature of the descriptions and the types of activities undertaken. Basket and reed-mat makers, for example, are described as both fabricators and resellers of these goods. More importantly, however, reselling items received in barter was probably a regular practice within Mesoamerican marketplaces because barter almost certainly occurred alongside the use of multiple currencies like cacao, textiles, and metals.

Three other kinds of economic practitioners existed in Central Mexico. Itinerant peddlers (*tlacôcoalnamac*) operated as mobile retailers who bought items to sell in regional marketplaces as well as house-to-house in rural areas of low population. Exchange merchants (*tlapatlac*), or money changers, were wealthy individuals, probably from *pochteca* families, who converted goods into cacao or textiles to facilitate exchange within the marketplace. Solicitors and purchasing agents (*tlaciuitiani, tlaciuiti*) supplied retailers with goods and probably represent a type of wholesaler. The existence of a law forbidding purchases outside of the marketplace (Alba 1949:48) suggests that these agents regularly bought wares from rural providers at wholesale prices for resale in the marketplace.

Members of the *pochteca* were certainly involved in all levels of the marketplace, from governance and regulation to wholesale and retail activity (Acosta Saignes 1945; Berdan 1989; Carrasco 1978). Despite their importance, *pochteca* merchants formed a specialized group and a clear minority among the nearly one hundred and fifty different vendors in the marketplace. Simple producer-vendors were the most common merchandisers in the marketplace, outnumbering retailers three to one. While the *pochteca* focused on buying and transporting goods for resale, many other small-scale operators also worked for profit and supported their families from what they grew, processed, made, and sold. We need to recognize the role of this broader array of producer-vendors and itinerant sellers if we are to accurately characterize the full array of participants in the Pre-Columbian commercial world.

The Transportation Problem: How Far Did Goods Actually Move?

The highlands of Mesoamerica are distinctive in that the vast majority of goods moved between regions via human porters (*tlameme*). Under these conditions, resource movement is based on the amount a porter can carry and the associated energetic costs. Because human porters are energetically inefficient, it is assumed that bulk goods did not move very far except through tribute obligations, where transportation costs were absorbed by conquered groups (Drennan 1984b; Sluyter 1993). Instead, it often is argued that most interregional trade consisted of lightweight, high-value goods that could readily handle the high transportation costs imposed by using human porters (Blanton and Feinman 1984; Drennan 1984a; Katz 1966:66).

One of the primary obstacles in modeling *tlameme* transportation systems has been the use of unrealistically conservative estimates of the weight a porter normally carried. Most scholars have favored the two-arroba (twenty-three kilograms) cargo amount that Bernal Díaz del Castillo (1974 [1568]:99) observed for rapid relays. While this figure constituted the normal load associated with public service (*tequitl*) during the colonial period (Hassig 1985), it does not reflect the loads that native porters could or did carry when they moved goods for themselves. Mendieta (1945 [ca. 1571–1596]:1:122) in another sixteenth-century report claims that natives normally carried three to four arrobas

(thirty-four and a half to forty-six kilograms). Likewise, nineteenth- and twentieth-century ethnographic information indicates that tumpline *huacaleros* across Mesoamerica regularly carried loads of forty to seventy kilograms with maximum loads reaching eighty-five to ninety kilograms (Table 4.3). Porters also managed loads of up to three arrobas (thirty-four and a half kilograms) in the Andean region, and D'Altroy (1992:85–88) uses thirty kilograms as an average porter load in this area. These data suggest that native porters regularly bore loads significantly heavier than twenty-three kilograms when it was economically beneficial for them to do so.[1] Of course, porters also incurred the additional cost of feeding themselves when they were on the road. But the same was often also the case when they used pack mules to haul freight.[2]

But the question addressed here is empirical: How far did staple goods actually move via human porters, irrespective of the amount of weight they carried? The staples I examine to answer this question are maize, fruit, chili, salt, unprocessed cotton, and ceramic vessels. Four of these (maize, fruit, chili, and salt) are dietary staples, while cotton was used in the manufacture of textiles. As a group, these items represent a range of low- to moderate-value goods with low to high transportation costs. Knowing the actual distance goods traveled helps establish the empirical limits for modeling merchant behavior based on human porters. Most of this data was compiled from the *Relaciones geográficas* (Acuña 1985a [1579–1581],

table 4.3
Cargo loads in Mesoamerica

REGION	CENTURY	LOAD	LOAD (KG)	SOURCE
CENTRAL MEXICO	sixteenth	normal	34.5–46	Mendieta 1945 [ca. 1571–1596]:1:122
GUATEMALA	early seventeenth	normal	50–60	Gage 1929 [1648]:234
MICHOACAN	late nineteenth	normal	63	Lumholtz 1902
MICHOACAN	late nineteenth	maximum	86	Lumholtz 1902
GUATEMALA	mid-twentieth	normal	68	Bunzel 1959:30
GUATEMALA	mid-twentieth	normal	45	Hammond 1978
GUATEMALA	mid-twentieth	maximum	91	Tax and Hinshaw 1969:83

1985b [1579–1581]), which records a time when households and indigenous merchants still moved many goods using *tlameme* porters. Information on the movement of ceramics was compiled from archaeological sources.

Maize was grown everywhere in Mesoamerica and normally would not have moved very far except in periods of shortfall or to meet institutional demand. Drennan (1984a, 1984b, 1985) has suggested that maize and other staple grains probably did not travel farther than two hundred and seventy-five kilometers because such movement would have been energetically inefficient. The ethnohistoric data support this conclusion for both maize and chia. Sahagún reports that retail vendors in the Basin of Mexico sold imported maize and chia from Guerrero, Morelos, Puebla, Tlaxcala, and Michoacán (Sahagún 1961:66), which suggests that these grains moved regularly enough over distances of seventy-five to two hundred kilometers to be standard items for market retailers to sell (Sahagún 1961:66–67). The *Relaciones geográficas* confirm this assumption: households in fourteen highland towns traveled fifty to one hundred sixty kilometers to buy or sell maize when necessary. Likewise, Durán (1994 [1570–1581]:240) reports that Totonac merchants transported maize two hundred kilometers to the Basin of Mexico in order to buy slaves during the famine of 1454.

Crop failure and insufficient yields were common in Central Mexico and undoubtedly stimulated exchange in maize and other staples over distances of fifty to sixty kilometers. The important point is not the exact distance over which staple grains moved (sensu Drennan 1984a, 1984b), but rather that a demand for maize existed at the household level and that it could regularly move over distances just under one hundred kilometers to even out normal variation in harvest cycles. This demand created a series of intersecting and overlapping regional exchange networks through which a range of other products also moved.

Fruit was another important dietary component that we would not expect to have moved very far given its weight and perishability. Nonetheless, intermediate-scale trade networks existed for its

sale. Sahagún (1961:79) classified the fruit seller (*suchiqualpan tlacatl*) as a producer-vendor, "a fruit owner [who] . . . carrie[d] fruit upon his back— transports it . . . he picks, harvests, produces fruit." The *Relaciones geográficas* indicate that households produced fresh and dried fruit and carried it twenty to eighty kilometers to sell in regional market centers on a regular basis.[3] Trade in fruit across different ecological zones was common throughout the colonial era: Gormsen (1978) documented an eighty-five-year-old merchant who covered a one hundred thirty-kilometer circuit (two hundred sixty kilometers round-trip) on foot with his mule in six days. He bought tropical fruit in Zacapoaxtla and sold it in Tepeaca.[4] While the merchant used a mule, this same level of intermediate-scale trade would have been possible in Pre-Columbian times, since Lumholtz (1902:2:367–370) notes that indigenous merchants using tumplines often carried loads equal to that of mules (up to ninety kilograms) and could cover more territory in a day. Provisioning on the road for these types of short trips would not have been a problem since traveling merchants could carry lightweight *pinole* (Sahagún 1959:14)—like ethnographically documented merchants did (Lumholtz 1902:1:41)—or stay with trade partners and family members located along their commercial circuits.

Salt, another dietary staple, was traded in a variety of forms including grains, bars, balls, and jars (Sahagún 1961:84). Salt was processed through solar evaporation along the coast (Andrews 1983; Ewald 1985; Good 1995; Kepecs 1998), but in the highlands a variety of techniques, including boiling brine, was used (Castellón Huerta 2011; De León 2009; Parsons 2001). The *Relaciones geográficas* provide good information on indigenous salt production. Question thirty asks where indigenous populations got their salt. Responses usually name specific salt-producing towns, suggesting that merchants or itinerant producer-vendors sold salt from the area where it was produced (Horn 1998:71).

Figures 4.4 and 4.5 plot the locations of salt producer and consumer sites mentioned in the *Relaciones geográficas*. References to one hundred and twenty-two salt sources and one hundred and ninety-six consumer sites make it possible to reconstruct the

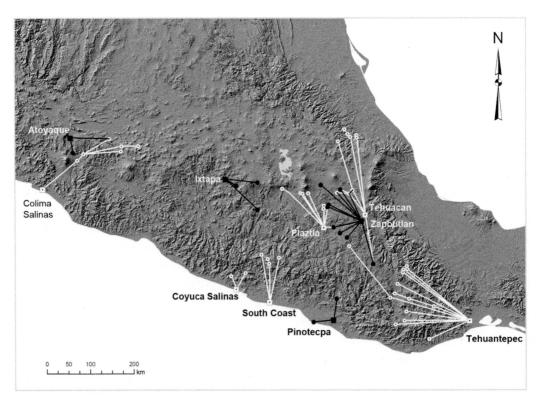

figure 4.4
Highland Mexican and south coast salt sources and their consumers. (Drawing by Kenneth G. Hirth.)

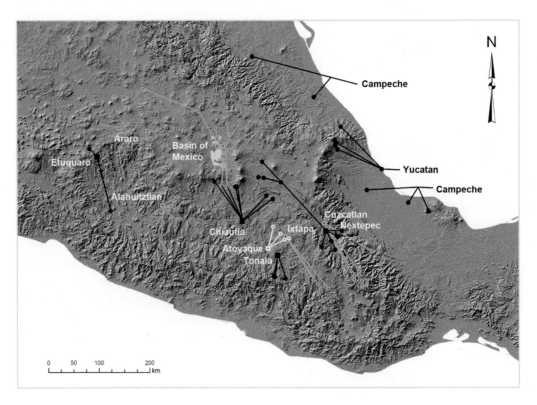

figure 4.5
Highland Mexican and Yucatecan salt sources and their consumers. (Drawing by Kenneth G. Hirth.)

distribution spheres of the major salt-producing towns (Figures 4.4–4.5). Salt from highland sources was produced at the household level and regularly traded over distances of fifty to one hundred fifty kilometers. Merchants from the large producing areas of Tehuacan and Tehuantepec traveled even farther, going anywhere from one hundred seventy-five to three hundred twenty-five kilometers to sell their salt. Merchants from these towns traversed service areas that varied greatly in size: small producers might cover just eight hundred to one thousand square kilometers, while merchants from the largest producing towns covered areas as large as six to ten thousand square kilometers (Figures 4.4–4.5). Some of these service areas overlap, indicating competition between producers or the need for multiple suppliers to meet regional demand. Sahagún confirms these distances, reporting all kinds of salt, including sea salt, being sold in the Tlatelolco market (Sahagún 1961:84). Ethnographic research documents household production and sale of salt well into the early twentieth century, with mestizo merchants moving it by both mule and tumpline over more than one hundred fifty kilometers between coastal and inland areas of Guerrero (Good 1995:9).

Chili peppers and cotton, lightweight consumables, moved with ease over longer distances between regions. Chili peppers were a culinary staple of the Mesoamerican diet. Although they were grown in all areas of Mesoamerica, the range of flavors that different varieties produce made them a favorite item of interregional exchange. Sahagún reports that chili was imported and sold in the Tlatelolco market from Morelos, Puebla, Michoacan, and the Huaxteca, a trade circuit of seventy-five to two hundred kilometers.

Raw cotton was an important trade item because it was used to create high-value textiles. Cotton is native to the *tierra caliente* and was traded interregionally by specialized producer-importers (*ichcanamacac*) and merchant retailers (*ichcanecuilo*) from both the Pacific and Gulf coasts. Figure 4.6

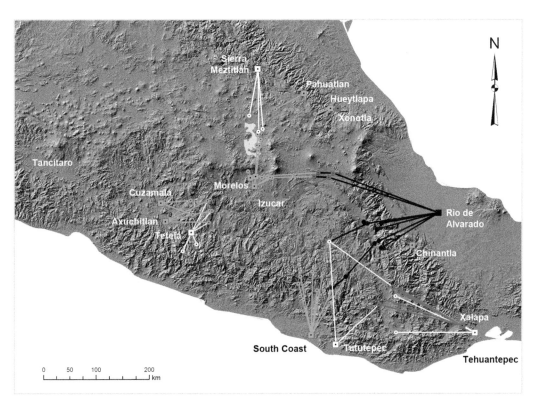

figure 4.6
Cotton sources and service areas in the Mexican Highlands. (Drawing by Kenneth G. Hirth.)

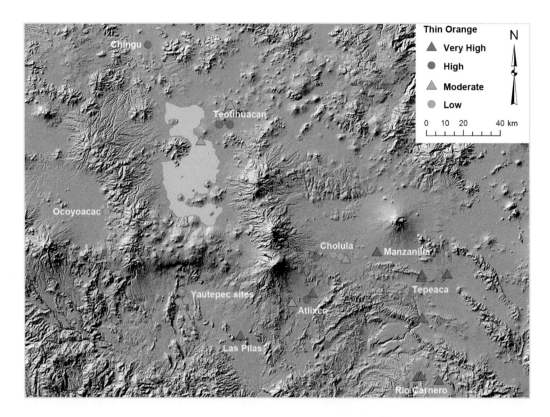

figure 4.7
Thin Orange distribution in Central Mexico. (Drawing by Kenneth G. Hirth.)

summarizes the service ranges for cotton-producing areas mentioned in the *Relaciones geográficas*. A total of one hundred and eight production areas and eighty-one consumer points were plotted, revealing that merchants regularly traded cotton over distances of fifty to one hundred fifty kilometers. The Río Alvarado and the Isthmus of Tehuantepec were especially important production regions, with cotton from these areas being traded distances of two hundred to three hundred kilometers or farther. Cotton also moved through the tribute network, with four provinces in the Codex Mendoza supplying Tenochtitlan with raw cotton from areas located two hundred to three hundred kilometers away from the city (Berdan 1992:map 7).[5]

Pottery is the mainstay of archaeological analysis. A key question is: How far did ceramic vessels move in volume through commercial exchange? Pottery was manufactured everywhere in Mesoamerica and, in theory, should not have moved very far. Nonetheless, certain ceramic types were widely

traded either because of superior manufacturing technology, aesthetic appeal, the ideological significance of their makers, or because they were containers that held other trade goods (e.g., salt, honey, and lime).

Thin Orange, one of Mesoamerica's most important commercial trade wares, circulated widely during the Middle Classic period (AD 300–600), the height of Teotihuacan's power and influence. We can readily identify it as a trade ware by its distinctive paste, its unique color, and its manufacture in standardized forms suitable for compact interregional exchange (Rattray 1990; Rattray and Harbottle 1992; Sotomayor and Castillo Tejero 1963). Thin Orange was produced in the Río Carnero region of southern Puebla, and Figure 4.7 shows the distribution of Thin Orange in select sites across Central Mexico. I have identified five categories based on the frequency of occurrence of Thin Orange within ceramic assemblages. These categories are very high (≥20 percent); high (10–19.9 percent);

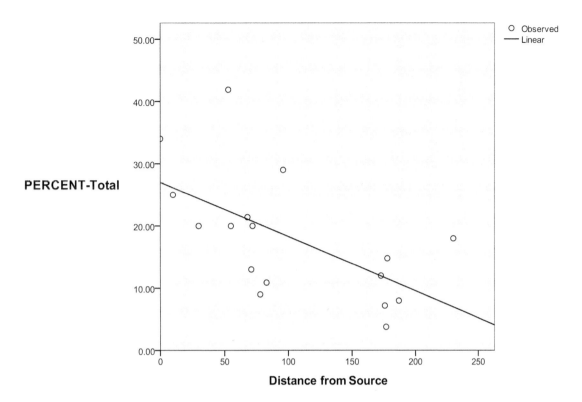

figure 4.8
Falloff graph of Thin Orange over space, derived from Figure 4.7. (Drawing by Kenneth G. Hirth.)

moderate (5–9.9 percent); low (1–4.9 percent); and trace/none (< 1 percent). Although quantifiable data are limited, they reveal that Thin Orange is concentrated in Central Mexico, where it can comprise anywhere from 5–20 percent or more of domestic assemblages at large and small sites. The data show that export-style Thin Orange in the form of ring-base hemispherical bowls moved in large quantities more than two hundred and twenty-five kilometers from its production center.

Interestingly, the distributional data show a clear and steady decline in Thin Orange frequency from its production source toward the northwest into the Valley of Mexico (Figure 4.8). This result is not what we would expect if Thin Orange entered Teotihuacan primarily as a tribute item. Tribute demand should produce a highly localized ceramic concentration at Teotihuacan with relatively few ceramic concentrations between the point of production and the point of delivery of tribute goods. Instead, we find a distance decay function compatible with a commercial

distribution (Renfrew 1975, 1977). These data suggest that ceramics moved commercially over distances of more than two hundred kilometers. This conclusion should not be surprising since Lumholtz (1902:2:890) reported that Tarascan merchants carrying loads with tumplines profitably traded ceramics from Michoacán to Acapulco over a distance of more than three hundred fifty kilometers.

This information reflects important scalar differences in the movement of goods within and between regions throughout Central Mexico. Although the size of exchange circuits varied from commodity to commodity, it is clear that much intermediate-scale exchange moved goods over distances of fifty to one hundred fifty kilometers. Commodities like ceramics, cotton, maize, chia, salt, and chili moved with regularity over two hundred kilometers or more to meet local needs. But it was not long-distance exchange per se that was significant. I believe that short-distance trade and movement of goods only twenty to thirty kilometers was

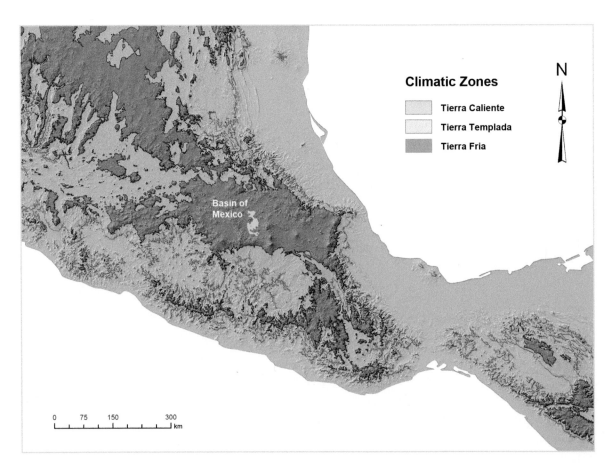

figure 4.9
Climatic zones in Mesoamerica: Tierra Caliente 0–1,000 masl; Tierra Templada 1,000–2,000 masl; and Tierra Fria, above 2,000 masl. (Drawing by Kenneth G. Hirth.)

more important for interregional exchange because it created multiple intersecting commodity spheres that linked environments of vastly different resource potential. Most households in Mesoamerica participated in short-distance exchange over distances as small as twenty to thirty kilometers. Short-distance trade carried out by multiple individual households created strong symbiotic interaction between communities located in different ecological zones and with varying levels of crop risk and resource maturation cycles.

Figure 4.9 illustrates the three major climatic-vegetation zones of the *tierra caliente, tierra templada,* and *tierra fria* found in Central Mexico between Lake Cuitzeo and the Isthmus of Tehuantepec. All areas of this region are within ninety kilometers of a different vegetative zone. This number

is well within the one hundred fifty-kilometer range of intermediate-scale trade found within the highlands. More significantly, however, the vast majority of pre-Hispanic communities in this region were located within one day's journey of another major climatic-vegetation zone or the coast. If settlements were distributed randomly across this area, then fully 86.6 percent of all towns and villages would have been located within thirty kilometers or less of another major climatic-vegetation zone at least one square kilometer in size (Figure 4.10).

The closeness of these zones created an astounding degree of ecological diversity and symbiotic interaction. These environmental conditions suggest that ecological diversity stimulated many peasant households and small-scale merchants to engage in trade, offering products from

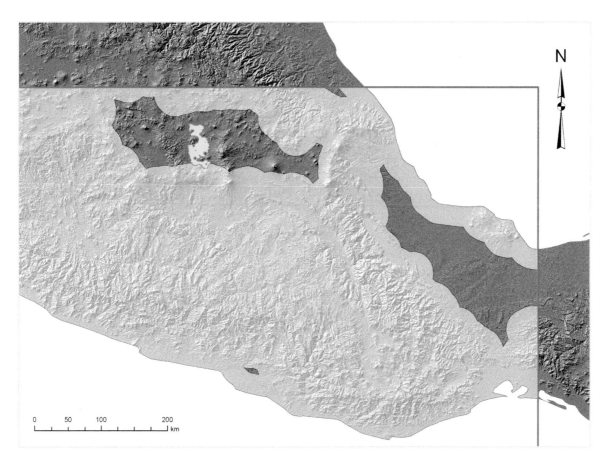

figure 4.10
Areas of the Mexican Highlands within thirty kilometers of another ecological interface. (Drawing by
Kenneth G. Hirth.)

different environmental zones for sale in regional marketplaces as part of their normal domestic routine. These exchanges created networks and relays through which households bought and sold a range of craft goods, specialty crops, and non-local raw materials. It was this type of interaction that William Sanders (1956) distinguished in his discussion of the Central Mexican Symbiotic region (see also Sanders and Price 1968). While Sanders identified these interregional interactions, he never considered the scale or the role they played in the organization of subsistence and commercial production at the level of individual households. Examination of itinerant obsidian-blade production illustrates why households would have found small-scale interregional exchange profitable for a host of varied commodities.

Profitability Model of Itinerant Obsidian-Blade Production

Obsidian was a valuable Pre-Columbian commodity because it could be formed into razor-sharp cutting tools used at all levels of society. Metal tools were rare in Mesoamerica, and what emerged instead was a sophisticated technology geared to the production of standardized obsidian prismatic blades. Obsidian blades were the cutting tool of choice at the time of the Conquest and were consumed in large quantities by households and the state, and used in a range of different craft activities. They were sold by artisans who worked in the marketplace and by peddlers who sold goods as they moved across the landscape.

The importance of obsidian has made the

control of obsidian-blade production an important topic in models of Pre-Columbian political economy (Clark 1987, 1989; Santley 1983, 1984). Unfortunately, the jump to large theory (Santley 1983) preceded careful modeling of the scale and organization of actual production-distribution networks (Hirth 2008). Over the past decade, scholars have learned that most obsidian-blade manufacture consisted of small-scale domestic production by independent male artisans who, as producer-vendors, marketed their finished goods in local marketplaces (Hirth 2006, 2009b). The presence of itinerant obsidian craftsmen in the highlands has been conclusively identified at Xochicalco, Morelos (Hirth 2006, 2008) and El Durazno, Michoacán (Darras 2009), eight hundred years before the Spanish conquest. It is, therefore, likely that itinerant craftsmen who worked in the marketplace created the majority of obsidian blades at the time of the Conquest.

How profitable was itinerant crafting for the craftsmen who practiced it? I examine this issue from a profitability perspective because Sahagún (1961:42–43) clearly states that merchants took to the road to "secure an increase." This would have been just as true for small-scale producer-vendors as it was for *pochteca*.

Profitability modeling goes beyond quantifying activities in energetic terms and examines the actual economic return from the energy expended. Here, I evaluate profitability as a simple gross profit model of return on effort. It does not attempt to calculate the cost of all relevant inputs; instead, it focuses on the value of the finished obsidian blades and, thus, reduces gross profit to a simple calculation of the quantity of goods produced times the price of goods sold. This formula is expressed as:

$$GP = (P \times Q), \text{ where}$$

GP = gross profit of obsidian blades
P = price of obsidian blades
Q = quantity of blades produced

In this simplified model, we need only two types of information to calculate gross profit: the quantity of blades produced and the price of obsidian blades sold to consumers. Fortunately, Gerónimo de Mendieta (1945 [ca. 1571–1596]) gives the price of obsidian blades in his *Historia eclesiastica indiana,* where he links it to the cost of a shave and a haircut. In his own words:

> Cortarán y rasparán la barba y cabello con ellas, y de la primera vez y primero tajo, poco menos que con una navaja acerada; mas al segunda corte pierden los filos, y luego es menester otra y otra para acabar de raparse el cabello o barba, aunque a la verdad son baratas, que por un real darán veinte de ellas (Mendieta 1945 [ca. 1571–1596]:58).

> With these they cut and scrape the beard and hair, and upon the first time and first cut, a bit less then with a steel blade; yet, at the second cut they lose all sharpness, and then another and another is necessary to finish shaving the hair and beard, although in truth they are cheap, since for one real they give twenty of them.

In this account, Mendieta indicates that obsidian blades were cheap, and twenty of them sold for one Spanish real. This price probably dates to sometime around 1565 to 1575, since Mendieta began writing the *Historia* in 1571. This cost is an applicable proxy for the precontact value of blades because, although they were still employed, demand was falling throughout the colonial period as a result of the increased use of Spanish steel and overall population declines. If anything, demand and price may have been higher during Pre-Columbian periods. Since one real was valued at one hundred cacao beans during the early sixteenth century, individual blades are often considered to have been worth five cacao beans each (Smith 1996:124). Mendieta's commentary identified obsidian blades as an inexpensive commodity, although this price certainly reflects his Spanish bias as much as it does the use of multiple blades in trimming and shaving a man's beard. If we use the cost of obsidian blades supplied by Mendieta, the remaining variable needed for the model is the quantity of goods produced.

Production Output for Obsidian Blades

To model the quantity of obsidian blades produced requires an estimate of the number of blades a craftsman could make. Since the quantity of goods produced is dependent upon time and resources, I estimated output in terms of the number of obsidian blades that could be produced from a single load of obsidian carried by an itinerant craftsman. I used both archaeological data and experimental data derived from lithic technology studies to make this estimate.

Archaeological analyses have demonstrated that the obsidian used to make prismatic blades moved across the landscape as preformed polyhedral cores rather than as raw material (Clark 1989; Hay 1978; Healan 1997; Hirth 2008; Pastrana and Domínguez 2009; Sanders and Santley 1983). There are several reasons for this. First, obsidian is heavy, weighing 2.22 kilograms per liter.[6] Transporting obsidian as preformed cores maximized the number of blades that could be made from the load carried by an itinerant craftsman. Second, Mendieta relates that obsidian blades dull quickly with use. Producing blades on demand for the consumers constituted the most efficient way to provide sharp cutting tools with a minimum of waste.

At the time of the Conquest, obsidian from the Pachuca source was widely used for blades throughout Central Mexico. Most of these blades were manufactured from preformed pressure cores that were eight to eleven centimeters long (Parry 2002) and eight to ten centimeters in diameter. Based on experimental research (Hirth and Andrews 2006), the number of blades that could be obtained from cores of this size was calculated using the formula:

B = CSCA/CSA, where
B = number of pressure blades removed
  from a core
CSCA = cross-sectional core area available for
  blade removal
CSA = cross-sectional area of prismatic blades

This can be transformed into the formula:

$$B = \frac{\pi(Di/2)^2 - \pi(Do/2)^2}{(A+B)C/2}$$

where CSCA is represented by

Di = the average diameter of cores at the
  beginning of production
Do = the average diameter of cores when
  production stops
π = the pi numerical constant of 3.1416

and where CSA is calculated from

A = distance between dorsal arris on
  a prismatic blade
B = width of the blade
C = thickness of the blade

This formula allows analysts to conceptualize pressure cores as bundles of unremoved pressure blades (Figure 4.11). In simple terms, the mass of the core at the end of the production cycle (Do) is subtracted from the mass of the core at the beginning. This relationship is illustrated in Figure 4.12.

Once the CSCA mass is calculated, the estimate of the number of blades produced can be divided by the average cross-sectional area or mass (CSA) of the blades produced. Figure 4.13 illustrates where these measurements are taken on a normal prismatic blade to calculate CSA. (For a detailed discussion of the procedure used to calculate blade production with these formula, see Hirth and Andrews 2006.)

The parameters used to make these estimates employ data for Aztec-period obsidian-blade production (Parry 2002). An obsidian pressure core that was ninety millimeters (nine centimeters) in diameter, and that was used to produce obsidian blades until it had a forty-millimeter diameter, would have a cross-sectional core area (CSCA) of 5,105.1 square millimeters. A sample of Aztec-period blades with a CSA of twenty-six square millimeters from consumer contexts at the site of Calixtlahuaca, Mexico, was used to compute blade

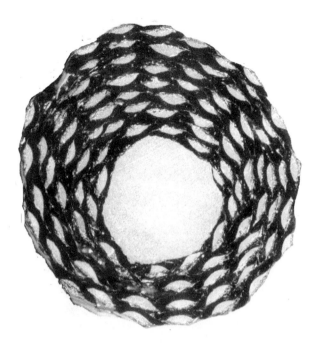

figure 4.11
Refit obsidian core. (Photograph by Kenneth G. Hirth.)

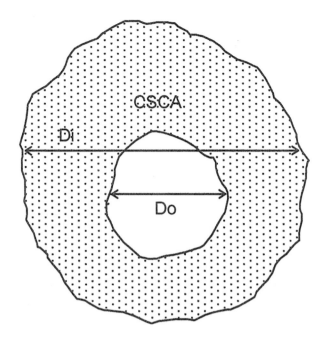

figure 4.12
Dimensions needed to calculate the cross-sectional core area of an obsidian core. (Drawing by Kenneth G. Hirth.)

output.[7] Dividing the CSCA (5,105.1 square millimeters) by the CSA (twenty-six square millimeters) produces an estimate of 196 blades per core. Not all of the CSCA would normally be usable, however, since some core mass would be lost to production errors, in-transit damage, and the normal core maintenance and error-recovery operations. If 10–15 percent of the CSCA were lost to these problems, then production would be reduced to 166 to 176 blades per core. To simplify calculations, I used the figure 170 to estimate the number of blades produced from each core.

If 170 blades were produced per core, then how many blades could an itinerant craftsman sell from one load of obsidian cores? A slightly conical obsidian core ten centimeters long and nine centimeters in diameter at the platform would weigh about 1.4 kilograms.[8] If the itinerant craftsman carried a load of thirty kilograms, he would have twenty to twenty-one cores in his pack. At 170 blades per core, a load of twenty-one obsidian cores would produce an average of 3,570 pressure blades. At a sales price of twenty blades for one real, the blades sold would net 178.5 Spanish reales.

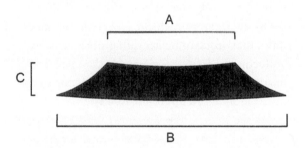

figure 4.13
Dimensions needed to calculate the cross-sectional area of a prismatic blade. (Drawing by Kenneth G. Hirth.)

The real question is: How productive was itinerant crafting for the individuals who practiced it? In terms of the price of labor, 178.5 reales were the equivalent to sixty-eight to seventy weeks of minimum-wage labor, which in the year 1578 was four reales per week (six *granos* of gold per day) (Borah and Cook 1958:44). Because the goal of craftsmen was to support their families, we converted the value of these 178.5 reales into maize equivalents using the price of maize during the sixteenth century. This calculation provided a measure of standard return and the relative purchasing power of itinerant crafting in relation to the standard return from maize agriculture.

Although economic data are limited, the retail price of maize between 1565 and 1580 averaged around six reales per fanega.[9] In practical terms, this means that the obsidian blades the itinerant craftsman sold could buy 29.75 fanegas of maize. At forty-six kilograms per fanega (Borah and Cook 1958:19; Gibson 1964:357; Hassig 1985:294n64; Rojas 1995:262) this represents a total of 1,368.5 kilograms of maize. According to Flannery (1976:106), the average Mesoamerican household of five persons required one metric ton (one thousand kilograms) of maize for normal annual subsistence needs. This means that the blades produced from a small load of just thirty kilograms of obsidian (twenty-one cores) was worth 35 percent more in maize than a family of five needed for an entire year! Even if itinerant crafting was carried out for only one month, the potential return to the household would have been enormous, even after deducting all the costs of procuring obsidian and feeding the craftsman during his time on the road. (This does not mean, of course, that craftsmen could become immensely wealthy; they did not, for reasons too extensive to discuss here.) Nevertheless, even small-scale obsidian craftsmen at the Epiclassic site of Xochicalco, Morelos, appear to have been well-off compared to other households (sensu Hirth 2009c; Hirth and Webb 2006).

One issue immediately becomes apparent from the profitability of obsidian-blade production: How would an itinerant craftsman capitalize on the returns from his efforts? He certainly could not transport 1.3 metric tons of maize back to his home without the help of a large group of porters. The answer, of course, is that he doesn't move his profit in the form of maize. Instead, he uses the power of the marketplace and converts the maize, or the other products he receives for his blades, into cacao or cotton mantles that are lightweight, high-value goods that fit well into his pack and are, thus, much easier to transport. These types of items would be accumulated gradually over time. Upon the end of his trip, the itinerant craftsman has two options: either he

can convert all of his proceeds into low-bulk, high-value goods like cotton textiles, or he can purchase another type of cargo, such as raw cotton, or salt, that can be sold upon his return home. In any event, the key to this system is that goods can be converted into higher- or lower-value items in the marketplace to facilitate transactions as well as their movement over space. Even if the ultimate goal of the itinerant craftsman is maize for his family, he converts his products into high-value, lightweight goods during the course of his travels—and then reconverts them into maize in a local marketplace at home.

Clearly, the economic returns from itinerant obsidian crafting were potentially high. While the profitability model was accurately modeled, the conclusions would be the same even if the actual profit was two or three times smaller than that calculated here because it still would have been a highly profitable activity for households. The same was probably also true for other forms of domestic crafting. Nevertheless, crafting typically constituted a secondary activity for households because of the risks involved in economic specialization, the high cost of moving finished products over space, and the inability of a household to engage in economies of scale in domestic production. Since craft production could be practiced during the nonagricultural cycle (Hirth 2009a), seasonally available labor could be used to provide household income. Whatever the level of production, intermittent or periodic crafting offered valuable supplemental income for households that typically engaged in subsistence agriculture.

Conclusion

The foregoing discussion has illustrated four important aspects about the Pre-Columbian merchant's world. First, it was a commercial one, and participation in the marketplace was profit oriented. In the words of Sahagún's informants, the merchant was "one who profits, who gains; who has reached an agreement on prices; who secures [an] increase" (Sahagún 1961:42–43). Profit was a recognized and motivating force for interaction in the marketplace.

It was not the only reason sellers went to the marketplace, but it was an important one.

Second, individuals who sold items for profit included a wide array of producer-vendors, local retailers, commercial agents, peddlers, and *pochteca*. Sahagún listed 112 small-scale producer-vendors and thirty-seven retailer-dealers in the Tlatelolco marketplace. The greater body of retailers selling high-value goods probably included merchants who obtained these items in their commercial travels. Nevertheless, the majority of the vendors in the marketplace sold food staples and craft goods to the greater consuming public. These vendors did not belong to the wealthy *pochteca* groups but instead were peasant producers and artisans working out of their households to support their families.

Third, it is clear that virtually all products, from grain to fruit and salt to ceramics, moved through interregional trade. The distances that goods moved differed from commodity to commodity. Nevertheless, overlapping trade circuits in the range of fifty to one hundred fifty kilometers were common for staple goods. These circuits converged on key market centers, creating trade relays through which different commodities moved. Ecological diversity provided the engine behind these trade circuits. Trade circuits like these were common in many areas of the ancient world including Africa, Anatolia, and southern Mesopotamia, bridging different ecological zones and moving goods across hostile state boundaries (Adams 1974:246; Berdan 1989:104, fig. 4.1; Curtin 1984:17). In Mesoamerica, they created spheres of symbiotic interaction by which tropical products moved to the highlands and highland products moved to the lowlands. Furthermore, the intersection of short- and intermediate-distance trade circuits established the long-distance trade routes traveled by merchants across Mesoamerica.

Fourth and finally, I have offered a profitability model for itinerant obsidian-blade production based on the price of obsidian blades recorded by Gerónimo de Mendieta in the mid-sixteenth century. Although obsidian was considered inexpensive, the blades produced from a single load of obsidian cores provided a very high return from the labor invested. Itinerant obsidian crafting was indeed a profitable enterprise. Obsidian-blade production illustrates why intermittent craft production was such an important part of the domestic economy: it was a very profitable addition to normal subsistence agriculture. While sales opportunities certainly varied from item to item, the marginal economic return from collecting, producing, preparing, and selling goods in the marketplace greatly contributed to the annual subsistence budget of enterprising households.

The marketplace has often been cited as the main institution involved in provisioning households with subsistence goods. It certainly did that, but the marketplace also provided an arena where households engaged in trade for their individual economic benefit. The ethnohistoric record sheds light on the interregional movement of resources like maize, fruit, and salt, products that often escape archaeological detection. While this information varies greatly in quality from region to region, it provides valuable insight into the economic activities in which individual households engaged.

Commerce was important in Mesoamerica, and goods moved widely on the backs of human porters. All levels of society—from the simplest households to the wealthy *pochteca*—were involved in trade. We need to recognize the breadth of this commerce if we are to fully understand the structure of interregional exchange in ancient Mesoamerica.

NOTES

1 These loads are compatible with loads of fifty-eight to eighty-eight kilograms documented for highland porters in Tibet and eastern Nepal. Malville et al. (2001) found that commercial incentives prompted porters paid by weight to carry heavier loads than porters who hauled goods for household

consumption. Commercial Tibetan tea porters carried some of the heaviest loads on record. In the 1900s, these tea porters regularly carried loads of seventy-six to one hundred twenty kilograms more than 226 kilometers from Yacho to Tatsienlu, with the heaviest burdens reaching 164 kilograms (Malville et al. 2001:53). In the Andes, D'Altroy (1992:85) reports that porters often haul loads equivalent to their body weight over long distances and up steep slopes, although moderate loads in the range of twenty-one to thirty-four kilograms are most common (D'Altroy 1992:85).

2 Archaeologists often forget that pack animals such as mules often had to carry their own fodder when they were hauling freight because of the lack of suitable grazing lands or the time or opportunity to take advantage of them in the areas traversed. Grain was commonly used for this purpose and was a significant factor in the cost of transporting goods (Committee on Military Affairs 1864; Essin 1997:52, 69, 71–72). In fact, to supply the Army of the Cumberland during the American Civil War, quartermaster records show that it took twice the number of wagons to supply the mules and horses in Grant's army than it did to supply his entire complement of 114,000 soldiers (Essin 1997:71). Even when grazing was available en route, it could be limited when mules had to be picketed in the evenings (Daly 1917:161).

3 The towns mentioned in the *Relaciones geográficas* as fruit sellers include Anecuilco, Ceuctla Coatzinco, Cuicatlan, Guayneo, Necotlan, Nochiztlan, Ocopetayuca, Quautlatlauc, Sirandaro, Tancítaro, Tepuztlan, Texalucan, and Zoyatitlanapa (Acuña 1985a [1579–1581], 1985b [1579–1581]).

4 The trader packed garlic and onions in Acatzingo and traveled on foot with his mule on Sunday to make the market at Oriental on Monday (fifty-six kilometers). On Tuesday he arrived at Zaragosa (forty-six kilometers), reaching the market at Zacapoaxtla on Wednesday where he bought fruit (fourteen kilometers). He then headed home to make the Tepeaca market to sell his fruit on Friday. On Saturday he rested at home in Acatzingo, fourteen kilometers from Tepeaca, before setting out again on Sunday for the fruit market at Zacapoaxtla (Gormsen 1978:251). While Tepeaca is in the highlands, Zacapoaxtla was the terminus of an interregional network that connected the highlands of

eastern Puebla to the lower Gulf-coast plain via the Apulco-Tecolutla River.

5 Provinces that paid their tribute in raw cotton included Cihuatlan from the Pacific coast and Tzicoac, Atlan, and Quauhtochco on the Gulf coast. Their annual tribute consisted of 4,400 loads or 101,217.61 kilograms in transport weight (Berdan 1987:252). The distances from Tenochtitlan for these provinces were: Cihuatlan (300 km), Tzicoac (230 km), Atlan (200 km), and Quauhtochco (240 km).

6 The weight for obsidian was calculated from a cut square block of Pachuca obsidian that was 12.0 × 6.1 × 4.3 centimeters in size (314.76 cc). This block weighed exactly seven hundred grams. The weight per liter (1000 cc) was then calculated as 2.22 kg/liter.

7 The mean diameter of exhausted cores used in this calculation was 4.0 centimeters. This number is realistic since exhausted Aztec-period cores at the site of Otumba (TA-80) range from 3.1 to 6.4 centimeters in diameter (Parry 2002:42). Bradford Andrews graciously provided the metric information for Aztec-period pressure blades from Calixtlahuaca. These blades averaged 12.0 millimeters wide and 3.0 millimeters thick. The sample consisted of 161 final series pressure blades and two initial series pressure blades of mixed gray and green obsidian. Average blade dimensions in millimeters used in the calculation of CSA were: A=4.98, B=12.01, C=3.00. The CSA for all 163 blades was 25.996 millimeters. The CSA for only the green obsidian blade was 27.14 millimeters.

8 The volume of a cylinder nine centimeters in diameter and ten centimeters in height is 636.2 cubic centimeters (cc). A slightly conical core with these dimensions would be slightly smaller, and 620 cubic centimeters was used as the estimate for its volume. At 2.22 grams/cc, a slightly conical core with these dimensions would weigh 1376.4 grams or 1.38 kilograms. For calculation purposes, I used 1.4 kilograms as the weight of these cores.

9 The wholesale price of maize ranged from 4.5 to 5.5 reales per fanega between 1565 and 1580. I conservatively estimated the average retail price at six reales per fanega, which is 20 percent higher than the midpoint of this range. This is realistic considering the wholesale price of maize was 4.8 reales per fanega shortly after Mendieta started writing the *Historia eclesiastica indiana* in 1571 (Borah and Cook 1958).

APPENDIX: A NAHUATL ECONOMIC VOCABULARY

MARK CHRISTENSEN AND KENNETH G. HIRTH

Nahuatl has a rich and diversified commercial vocabulary used in buying and selling both inside and outside of the marketplace. The following economic vocabulary is not exhaustive; it is intended simply to show the diversity of Nahuatl words found in early colonial documents that were likely in use across the Mexican Highlands at Spanish contact. The vocabulary is derived primarily using Molina's sixteenth-century dictionary (Molina 1977 [1571]), Lockhart (1992), and books nine and ten of Sahagún's Florentine Codex (1959, 1961). Although many close equivalents existed, we should not assume that there existed a Nahuatl word for every European economic concept. Thus, the definitions given represent those prescribed to them in a colonial context and not necessarily precontact understandings of the terms. The subject in general deserves much more scholarly attention.

Nahuatl creates composite words to create meaningful sentences and ideas. In the list that follows, *tla–* is an indefinite nonpersonal object prefix. The nominalizing construction *–liztli* suffixed to a verb creates a noun that means the action of the verb, much like a gerund. Nahuatl also creates agentives (nouns derived from verbs) through the present agentive suffix *–ni* and preterit agentive suffixes *–c* and *–qui*. The causative suffix of verbs is *–tia* or *–ltia*. The applicative ending adds an object to a verb with the ending *–lia* (e.g., for him). Location where action takes place is expressed by the locatives *–yan*, *–can*, or *–co*. We want to thank James Lockhart for his invaluable help with the Nahuatl. Any error or misunderstandings are our own.

NAHUATL VERBS	MORPHOLOGY AND LITERAL DEFINITION	COLONIAL ECONOMIC CONTEXT
cemana	*cem*, entirely, as a whole; *ana*, to take. "to take whole amounts"	to wholesale
chihua	*chihua*. "to do, make, perform, engender"	to manufacture, to make
cohua	*cohua*. "to buy something" (*co–* has implications of "turning" or "returning" in many Nahuatl words, indicating that the term possibly had an archaic reciprocal meaning "to trade")	to buy
huiquilia	*huica*, to take, accompany, be responsible for; *–lia*. "to take, carry something for someone"	to owe (money)
namaca	*na–*, archaic form of the indefinite reflexive *ne–* and was originally a reciprocal; *maca*, to give. "to sell something," although archaically it possibly meant "to give in return for something"	to sell
necuiloa	*necuiloa*. "to bow, bend, twist something, to engage in commerce"	to deal
pialia	*pia*, to keep, have custody of; *–lia*. "to keep something for someone"	to owe (money)
–tech necuiloa	*–tech*; *necuiloa*. "to make an investment with someone"	to loan with interest, to invest
–tech tlaixtlapana	*–tech*; *tla–*; *ix–* (not identified); *tlapana*, to split or divide something	to loan with interest, to invest, to profit
tiamiqui	origin of the *tianquiztli*, market.	to engage in commerce
tlanehuia	originally seems to have meant to borrow and return the same thing	to rent from someone for money (land), to borrow

NAHUATL VERBS	MORPHOLOGY AND LITERAL DEFINITION	COLONIAL ECONOMIC CONTEXT
tlaneuhtia	*tlanehuia*; *–tia*. "to cause something to be borrowed"	to lease something to someone for money, to lend
tlapatilia	given as reflexive (*nino–*); *tla–*; *patla*, to exchange something; *–lia*. "I exchange things for myself"	to exchange, to operate in the market
tlaquehualtia	*tlaquehua*, to hire someone; *–ltia*. "to hire someone"	to hire someone
tlaxtlahua	*tla–*; *ixtlahua*, to pay for something. "to pay for something"	to pay for something

NAHUATL NOUNS	MORPHOLOGY AND LITERAL DEFINITION	COLONIAL ECONOMIC CONTEXT
patiuhtli	*patla–* usually appears possessed (*i-pati-uh*), meaning "its price" and refers to what something could be exchanged for	price, worth
tiamicoyan	*tiamiqui*; passive *–o*; locative *–yan*. "place where trade or business takes place"	market, places where trading occurs
tiamictli	from *tiamiqui*	merchandise
tiamiquiztli	*tiamiqui*; *–liztli*. "the act of selling and buying or doing business"	the act of selling and buying
tianquizcayotl	*tianquiztli*; *–ca–*; nominal suffix *–yo*. "the essence of the market, something characteristic of the market"	market merchandise
tianquiztli	from *tiamiqui*	market
tlacemanani	*tla–*; *cem*; *ana*. "one who takes whole amounts"	wholesaler
tlachiuhqui	*tla–*; *chihua*; *–qui*. "maker of things"	producer, vendor, craftsman
tlacocoaliztli	*tla–*; *co–*, distributive of *cohua* implying many repetitions; *–cohua*; *–liztli*. "the act of buying things"	the act of buying
tlacocohualoni	*tla–*; *co–*, distributive of *cohua* implying many repetitions; *cohua*; nonactive agentive *–loni*. "instrument for buying things"	currency
tlacohualli	from *cohua*. "something bought"	a purchase
tlacohuani	*tla–*; *cohua*; *–ni*. "he who buys things"	buyer
tlaixtlapanqui	*tla–*; *ix–* (not identified); *tlapana*; *–qui*.	investor, profiteer
tlamama, tlameme	from *mama* and *meme*, to carry something	porter
tlanamacac	*tla–*; *namaca*; *–c*. "seller of things"	seller, vendor, merchandiser
tlanamacaliztli	*tla–*; *namaca*; *–liztli*. "the act of selling things"	sale, act of selling something
tlanecuilo	*tla–*; *necuiloa*. "he who bends, twists things, engages in commerce"	dealer, also swindler, sharp dealer
tlaquehualli	from *tlaquehua*	a person hired to do something
tlaquixtiani	*tla–*; *quixtia*; *–ni*. "one who removes things"	importer, distributor
tlaxtlahuilli	from *ixtlahuia*	payment to someone (salary)

Acosta Saignes, Miguel

1945   *Los pochteca: Ubicación de los merca-*
        deres en la estructura social tenochca.
        Acta anthropologica 1, no. 1. Sociedad
        de Alumnos de la Escuela Nacional de
        Antropología e Historia, Mexico City.

Acuña, René

1985a   *Relaciones geográficas del siglo*
[1579–1581] *XVI: Mexico tomo primero.* Serie
        Antropológica 63. Universidad
        Nacional Autónoma de México,
        Instituto de Investigaciones
        Antropológicas, Mexico City.

1985b   *Relaciones geográficas del siglo*
[1579–1581] *XVI: Tlaxcala tomo segundo.* Serie
        Antropológica 59. Universidad
        Nacional Autónoma de México,
        Instituto de Investigaciones
        Antropológicas, Mexico City.

Adams, Robert McC.

1974   Anthropological Perspectives on
        Ancient Trade. *Current Anthropology*
        15:239–258.

Alba, Carlos

1949   *Estudio comparativo entre el derecho*
        azteca y el derecho positivo mexicano.
        Ediciones Especiales del Instituto
        Indigenista Interamericano 3.
        Mexico City.

Anderson, Arthur, Frances F. Berdan, and James
Lockhart

1976   *Beyond the Codices: The Nahua View*
        of Colonial Mexico. University of
        California Press, Berkeley.

Andrews, Anthony

1983   *Maya Salt Production and Trade.*
        University of Arizona Press, Tucson.

Berdan, Frances F.

1975   Trade, Tribute, and Market in the Aztec
        Empire. PhD dissertation, Department
        of Anthropology, University of Texas,
        Austin.

1987   Cotton in Aztec Mexico: Production,
        Distribution, and Use. *Mexican Studies /*
        Estudios mexicanos 3:235–262.

1989   Trade and Markets in Precapitalist
        States. In *Economic Anthropology*, edited

by Stuart Plattner, pp. 78–107. Stanford
University Press, Stanford.

1992   The Imperial Tribute Roll of the Codex
        Mendoza. In *The Codex Mendoza*, vol. 1,
        edited by Frances F. Berdan and Patricia
        Rieff Anawalt, pp. 55–79. University of
        California Press, Berkeley.

Bittman, Bente, and Thelma Sullivan

1978   The Pochteca. In *Mesoamerican*
        Communication Routes and Culture
        Contacts, edited by Thomas Lee and
        Carlos Navarrete, pp. 211–218. Papers
        of the New World Archaeological
        Foundation 40. Brigham Young
        University, Provo, Utah.

Blanton, Richard E., and Gary M. Feinman

1984   The Mesoamerican World System.
        American Antiquity 86:673–682.

Borah, Woodrow, and Sherburne Cook

1958   *Price Trends of Some Basic Commodities*
        in Central Mexico, 1531–1570. University
        of California Press, Berkeley and
        Los Angeles.

Bunzel, Ruth

1959   *Chichicastenango.* University of
        Washington Press, Seattle.

Cardos de Méndez, Amalia

1959   El comercio de los mayas antiguos. *Acta*
        anthropologica, segunda epoca, 2(7).

Carrasco, Pedro

1978   La economía del México prehispánico.
        In *Economía política e ideología en el*
        México prehispánico, edited by Pedro
        Carrasco and Johanna Broda, pp. 13–74.
        Editorial Nueva Imagen, Mexico City.

Castellón Huerta, Blas

2011   Procesos tecnológicos y especialización
        en la producción de panes de sal en el
        sur de Puebla. In *Producción artesanal y*
        especializada en Mesoamérica: Áreas de
        actividad y procesos productivos, edited
        by Linda Manzanilla and Kenneth G.
        Hirth, pp. 283–311. Universidad Nacional
        Autonóma de Mexico, Mexico City.

Clark, John

1987   Politics, Prismatic Blades, and
        Mesoamerican Civilization. In *The*

Organization of Core Technology, edited by Jay Johnson and Carol Morrow, pp. 259–285. Westview Press, Boulder, Colo.

1989   Obsidian: The Primary Mesoamerican Sources. In *La obsidiana en Mesoamérica*, edited by Margarita Gaxiola and John Clark, pp. 299–319. Colección científica 176. Instituto Nacional de Antropología e Historia, Mexico City.

Committee on Military Affairs

1861   *Concentrated Feed for Horses and Mules*. The Senate of the United States, Washington, D.C.

Craine, Eugene, and Reginald Reindorp

1970   *The Chronicles of Michacán*. University of Oklahoma Press, Norman.

Curtin, Philip

1984   *Cross-Cultural Trade in World History*. Cambridge University Press, Cambridge.

D'Altroy, Terence

1992   *Provincial Power in the Inka Empire*. Smithsonian Institution Press, Washington, D.C.

Daly, Henry

1917   *Manual of Pack Transportation*. Quartermaster Corps, U.S. Army, Government Printing Office, Washington, D.C.

Darras, Veronique

2009   Peasant Artisans: Household Prismatic Blade Production in the Zacapu Region, Michoacan (Milpillas Phase 1200–1450 AD). In *Housework: Craft Production and Domestic Economy in Ancient Mesoamerica*, edited by Kenneth G. Hirth, pp. 92–114. Archaeological Papers of the American Anthropological Association 19. Wiley, Hoboken, N.J.

De León, Jason

2009   Rethinking the Organization of Aztec Salt Production: A Domestic Perspective. In *Housework: Craft Production and Domestic Economy in Ancient Mesoamerica*, edited by Kenneth G. Hirth, pp. 45–57. Archaeological Papers of the American Anthropological Association 19. Wiley, Hoboken, N.J.

Díaz del Castillo, Bernal

1974 [1568]   *Historia verdadera de la conquista de Nueva España*. Editorial Porrúa, Mexico City.

Drennan, Robert

1984a   Long-Distance Movement of Goods in the Mesoamerican Formative and Classic. *American Antiquity* 49:27–43.

1984b   Long-Distance Transport Costs in Pre-Hispanic Mesoamerica. *American Anthropologist* 86:105–112.

1985   Porters, Pots, and Profit: The Economics of Long-Distance Exchange in Mesoamerica. *American Anthropologist* 87:891–893.

Durán, Diego

1994 [1570–1581]   *The History of the Indies of New Spain*. University of Oklahoma Press, Norman.

Durkheim, Emile

1933   *The Division of Labor in Society*. Free Press, New York.

Essin, Emmett

1997   *Shavetails and Bell Sharps: The History of the Army Mule*. University of Nebraska Press, Lincoln.

Ewald, Ursula

1985   *The Mexican Salt Industry, 1560–1980: A Study in Change*. Gustave Fischer Verlag, Stuttgart.

Flannery, Kent

1976   The Empirical Determinants of Site Catchments. In *The Early Mesoamerican Village*, edited by Kent Flannery, pp. 103–117. Academic Press, New York.

Gage, Thomas

1929 [1648]   *A New Survey of the West Indies, 1648: The English-American*. Robert McBride and Company, New York.

Gibson, Charles

1964   *The Aztecs under Spanish Rule: A History of the Indians of the Valley of Mexico*. Stanford University Press, Stanford.

Good, Catherine

1995   Salt Production and Commerce in Guerrero, Mexico: An Ethnographic Contribution to Historical Reconstruction. *Ancient Mesoamerica* 6:1–13.

Gormsen, Erdmann

1978   Weekly Markets in the Puebla Region of Mexico. In *Market-Place Trade: Periodic Markets, Hawkers, and Traders in Africa, Asia, and Latin America,* edited by Robert Smith, pp. 240–253. Centre for Transportation Studies, University of British Columbia, Vancouver.

Hammond, Norman

1978   Cacao and Cobaneros: An Overland Trade Route between the Maya Highlands and Lowlands. In *Mesoamerican Communication Routes and Culture Contacts*, edited by Thomas Lee and Carlos Navarrete, pp. 19–25. Papers of the New World Archaeological Foundation 40. Brigham Young University, Provo, Utah.

Hassig, Ross

1985   *Trade, Tribute, and Transportation: The Sixteenth-Century Political Economy of the Valley of Mexico.* University of Oklahoma Press, Norman.

Hay, Conran Alexander

1978   Kaminaljuyu Obsidian: Lithic Analysis and the Economic Organization of a Prehistoric Maya Chiefdom. PhD dissertation, Department of Anthropology, Pennsylvania State University, University Park.

Healan, Dan

1997   Pre-Hispanic Quarrying in the Ucareo-Zinapecuaro Obsidian Source Area. *Ancient Mesoamerica* 8:77–100.

Hirth, Kenneth G.

2006   *Obsidian Craft Production in Ancient Central Mexico: Archaeological Research at Xochicalco.* University of Utah Press, Salt Lake City.

2008   The Economy of Supply: Modeling Obsidian Procurement and Craft Provisioning at a Central Mexican Urban Center. *Latin American Antiquity* 19:435–457.

2009a   Craft Production, Household Diversification, and Domestic Economy in Prehispanic Mesoamerica. In *Housework: Craft Production and Domestic Economy in Ancient Mesoamerica*, edited by Kenneth G. Hirth, pp. 13–32.

Archaeological Papers of the American Anthropological Association 19. Wiley, Hoboken, N.J.

2009b   Craft Production in the Mesoamerican Marketplace. *Ancient Mesoamerica* 20:89–102.

2009c   Household, Workshop, Guild, and Barrio: The Organization of Obsidian Craft Production in a Prehispanic Urban Center. In *Domestic Life in Prehispanic Capitals: A Study of Specialization, Hierarchy, and Ethnicity*, edited by Linda Manzanilla and Claude Chapdelaine, pp. 43–65. Museum of Anthropology, University of Michigan, Ann Arbor.

Hirth, Kenneth G., and Bradford Andrews

2006   Estimating Production Output in Domestic Craft Workshops. In *Obsidian Craft Production in Ancient Central Mexico: Archaeological Research at Xochicalco*, edited by Kenneth G. Hirth, pp. 202–217. University of Utah Press, Salt Lake City.

Hirth, Kenneth G., and Ronald Webb

2006   Households and Plazas: The Contexts of Obsidian Craft Production at Xochicalco. In *Obsidian Craft Production in Ancient Central Mexico: Archaeological Research at Xochicalco,* edited by Kenneth G. Hirth, pp. 18–62. University of Utah Press, Salt Lake City.

Horn, Rebecca

1998   Testaments and Trade: Interethnic Ties among Petty Traders in Central Mexico (Coyoacán 1550–1620). In *Dead Giveaways: Indigenous Testaments of Colonial Mexico and the Andes*, edited by Susan Kellogg and Matthew Restall, pp. 59–83. University of Utah Press, Salt Lake City.

Katz, Friedrich

1966   *Situación social y económica de los aztecas durante los siglos XV y XVI.* Universidad Nacional Autónoma de México, Instituto de Investigaciones Históricas, Mexico City.

Kepecs, Susan

1998   *The Political Economy of Chikinchel, Yucatan, Mexico: A Diachroinic Analysis from the Prehispanic Era through the Age of Spanish Administration.* PhD dissertation, Department of Anthropology, University of Wisconsin, Madison.

León-Portilla, Miguel

1962   La institución cultural del comercio prehispánico. *Estudios de cultura náhuatl* 3:23–54.

Lockhart, James

1992   *The Nahuas after the Conquest: A Social and Cultural History of the Indians of Central Mexico, Sixteenth through Eighteenth Centuries*. Stanford University Press, Stanford.

Lumholtz, Carl

1902   *Unknown Mexico: A Record of Five Years' Exploration among the Tribes of the Western Sierra Madre, in the Tierra Caliente of Tepic and Jalisco, and among the Tarascos of Michoacan*. 2 vols. C. Scribner's Sons, New York.

Malville, Nancy, William Byrnes, H. Allen Lim, and Ramesh Basnyat

2001   Commercial Porters of Eastern Nepal: Health Status, Physical Work Capacity, and Energy Expenditure. *American Journal of Human Biology* 13:44–56.

Mendieta, Gerónimo de

1945   *Historia eclesiástica indiana, com-*
[ca. 1571–1596]   *puesta por el padre fray Gerónimo de Mendieta . . . con algunas advertencias del p. fray Joan de Domayquíar el padre fray Gerónimo de Mendieta . . . sacadas de cartas y otros borradores del autor*. 4 vols. Salvador Chávez Hayhoe, Mexico City.

Molina, Alonso de

1977 [1571]   *Vocabulario en lengua castellana y mexicana y mexicana y castellana*. 2nd ed. Editorial Porrúa, Mexico City.

Parry, William

2002   Aztec Blade Production Strategies in the Eastern Basin of Mexico. In *Pathways to Prismatic Blades: A Study in Mesoamerican Obsidian Core-Blade Technology*, edited by Kenneth G. Hirth and Bradford Andrews, pp. 37–45. Cotsen Institute of Archaeology, University of California, Los Angeles.

Parsons, Jeffrey

2001   *The Last Saltmakers of Nexquipayac, Mexico: An Archaeological Ethnography*.

Anthropological Papers 92. Museum of Anthropology, University of Michigan, Ann Arbor.

Pastrana, Alejandro, and Silvia Domínguez

2009   Cambios en la estrategia de la explotación de la obsidiana de Pachuca: Tenochtitlan, Tula, y la Triple Alianza. *Ancient Mesoamerica* 20:129–148.

Rattray, Evelyn

1990   New Findings on the Origins of Thin Orange Ceramics. *Ancient Mesoamerica* 1:181–195.

Rattray, Evelyn, and Garman Harbottle

1992   Neutron Activation Analysis and Numerical Taxonomy of Thin Orange Ceramics from the Manufacturing Sites of Rio Carnero, Puebla, Mexico. In *Chemical Characterization of Ceramic Pastes in Archaeology*, edited by Hector Neff, pp. 221–231. Monographs in World Archaeology 7. Prehistory Press, Madison, Wis.

Renfrew, Colin

1975   Trade as Action at a Distance. In *Ancient Civilization and Trade*, edited by Jeremy Sabloff and C. C. Lamberg-Karlovsky, pp. 3–59. University of New Mexico Press, Albuquerque.

1977   Alternative Models for Exchange and Spatial Distribution. In *Exchange Systems in Prehistory*, edited by Timothy K. Earle and Jonathon E. Ericson, pp. 71–90. Academic Press, New York.

Rojas, José Luis de

1986   *México Tenochtitlan, economía y sociedad en el siglo XVI*. Fondo de Cultura Económica, Mexico City, and Colegio de Michoacán, Zamora, Michoacán.

1995   *México Tenochtitlan, economía y sociedad en el siglo XVI*. 2nd ed. Fondo de Cultura Económica, Mexico City, and Colegio de Michoacán, Zamora.

Sahagún, Bernardino de

1959   *Florentine Codex: General History of the Things of New Spain*, bk. 9, *The Merchants*. Translated by Arthur J. O. Anderson and Charles E. Dibble. School of American Research, Santa Fe, and University of Utah, Salt Lake City.

1961   *Florentine Codex: General History of the Things of New Spain,* bk. 10, *The People.* Translated by Arthur J. O. Anderson and Charles E. Dibble. School of American Research, Santa Fe, and University of Utah, Salt Lake City.

Sanders, William

1956   The Central Mexican Symbiotic Region: A Study in Prehistoric Settlement Patterns. In *Prehistoric Settlement Patterns in the New World*, edited by Gordon Willey, pp. 115–127. Viking Fund Publications in Anthropology 23. Wenner-Gren Foundation for Anthropological Research, New York.

Sanders, William, and Barbara Price

1968   *Mesoamerica: The Evolution of a Civilization.* Random House, New York.

Sanders, William, and Robert Santley

1983   A Tale of Three Cities: Energetics and Urbanization in Pre-Hispanic Central Mexico. In *Prehistoric Settlement Patterns: Essays in Honor of Gordon R. Willey*, edited by Evon Z. Vogt and Richard M. Leventhal, pp. 243–291. University of New Mexico Press, Albuquerque, and Peabody Museum of Archaeology and Ethnology, Harvard University, Cambridge, Mass.

Santley, Robert

1983   Obsidian Trade and Teotihuacan Influence in Mesoamerica. In *Highland-Lowland Interaction in Mesoamerica: Interdisciplinary Approaches*, edited by Arthur Miller, pp. 69–124. Dumbarton Oaks Research Library and Collection, Washington, D.C.

1984   Obsidian Exchange, Economic Stratification, and the Evolution of Complex Society in the Basin of Mexico. In *Trade and Exchange in Early Mesoamerica*, edited by Kenneth G. Hirth, pp. 43–86. University of New Mexico Press, Albuquerque.

Sluyter, Andrew

1993   Long-Distance Staple Transport in Western Mesoamerica: Insights through Quantitative Modeling. *Ancient Mesoamerica* 4:193–199.

Smith, Michael

1996   *The Aztecs.* Blackwell, Oxford, and Cambridge, Mass.

Sotomayor, Alfredo, and Noemí Castillo Tejero

1963   *Estudio petrográfico de la cerámica "anarajado delgado."* Instituto Nacional de Antropología e Historia, Mexico City.

Tax, Sol, and Robert Hinshaw

1969   Maya of the Midwestern Highlands. In *Ethnology*, edited by Evon Vogt. Vol. 7 of *Handbook of Middle American Indians*, edited by Robert Wauchope. University of Texas Press, Austin.

5

The Social Organization of Craft Production
and Interregional Exchange at Teotihuacan

DAVID M. CARBALLO

O NE NEED ONLY GAZE UPON THE RUINS OF Teotihuacan to appreciate their magnitude and decidedly planned layout (Figure 5.1). These features of the ancient city bespeak a highly centralized government with an influence beyond the ceremonial core to the very residences its inhabitants occupied. But just how overarching was this influence? Although Teotihuacan served as a hub for the most robust economic system in Classic-period Mesoamerica, its organization remains a topic of spirited debate. While some propose that the Teotihuacano economy was tightly managed, with political and religious agents responsible for mobilizing most production and distribution, others suggest that it was strongly commercialized, with more significant roles for independent household crafting and market exchange (cf. Kurtz 1987; Manzanilla 1992; Millon 1992; Sanders and Santley 1983).

In this study, I model landscape usage between the city and areas of acquisition and distribution, and examine production contexts both at Teotihuacan and within adjacent regions in order to assess potential interregional exchange routes and what dimensions of the Teotihuacano economy were more likely to have been commercially, rather than politically, motivated. Production and exchange should be considered as embedded within multiple, crosscutting social institutions such as household, market, temple, and state, which may be heuristically separated as domestic and institutional facets of a complex web of economic relations (see Hirth and Pillsbury, this volume). Economic opportunities attracted migrants to the city from throughout Mesoamerica, making it the most ethnically diverse and polyglot population of the Americas in its day (Figure 5.2), with more than one hundred thousand inhabitants speaking five or more languages (Cowgill 1997, 2008; Manzanilla 1999; Millon 1992). The macroregional scope of the economy is distilled here by considering four major commodities that circulated widely: obsidian, lime, cotton, and export ceramics. I evaluate potential exchange routes and mercantile activities involving these commodities after first outlining the economic base of the city.

figure 5.1
Teotihuacan viewed from Cerro Gordo in the early 1960s. (Photograph courtesy of William G. Mather III.)

figure 5.2
Teotihuacan
chronology.
(Chronology
by David M.
Carballo.)

Period			Date	Ceramic Phase	Cultural Attributes
	Epi		700	Coyotlatelco	Still sizable populations live around former center
	Late	CLASSIC	600	Metepec	Political decentralization and demographic collapse
			500	Late Xolalpan	
			400	Early Xolalpan	Height of influence abroad
	Early		300	Late Tlamimilolpa	
			200	Early Tlamimilolpa	Construction of: Apartment compounds Feathered Serpent Pyramid Moon Pyramid Sun Pyramid
				Miccaotli	
			100		
				Tzacualli	
	Terminal	FORMATIVE	AD BC		Urbanization
				Patlachique	
			100		
				Tezoyuca	
	Late		200		Possibly several competing centers in Teotihuacan Valley
				Late Cuanalan	
			300		

Economic Foundations

The immediate resource base that Teotihuacanos exploited was the semiarid highlands of Central Mexico (see McClung de Tapia 2009) (Figure 5.3). At 2,250 meters above sea level (masl), the small rivers of the Teotihuacan Valley drained into the lake system at the center of the Basin of Mexico. Although the valley receives less precipitation than do regions to the south, three of its characteristics were conducive to economic development. First, springs flowed at approximately five hundred to fifteen hundred liters of water per second, permitting permanent irrigation of more than three thousand hectares of farmland (Sanders et al. 1979:256–260, 386–389). This fertile land within an otherwise agriculturally

risky landscape encouraged the nucleation of early farming villages, while the digging and maintenance of canals may have stimulated larger-scale group coordination (Webster 1996). Second, the valley forms a natural opening in the basin, connecting with the adjacent Puebla-Tlaxcala region to provide the easiest route to the resources of the Gulf of Mexico as well as to all other points east and south. I refer to this route as the Tlaxcala Corridor, and build from a previous study (Carballo and Pluckhahn 2007) with new analyses here to assess its utility for exchange. Third, the eastern valley contains its own obsidian sources and has unimpeded passage to additional sources to the north (Charlton 1978). As metals were not used in Classic-period Central Mexico, these obsidian quarries

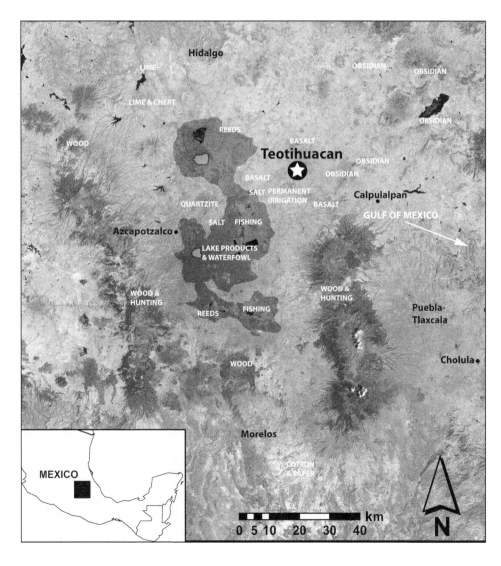

figure 5.3
Resources and regions surrounding Teotihuacan (after Sanders et al. 1979:maps 24–25). (LANDSAT ETM+ image source: Global Land Cover Facility [http://www.landcover.org].)

provided Teotihuacanos with a highly desired trade commodity. Together with the lake resources and other highland products of the Basin of Mexico, this combination of springs, transportation corridors, and obsidian formed the city's economic foundation.

Like other traditional societies, the primary unit of production at Teotihuacan was the household; however, most Teotihuacanos lived in exceptionally large houses known as apartment compounds (Figure 5.4), within which dozens of individuals cohabitated (Cowgill 2007; Manzanilla 1996; Millon 1976). Craft production was primarily undertaken within apartment compounds or in the common spaces of neighborhoods (termed "barrios" in most of the literature on Teotihuacan), and the construction and maintenance of apartments themselves also involved specialists for

stuccoing walls and painting them with vibrant pigments. Under this residential system, domestic production became economies of scale in which labor tasks were divided for efficiency (Manzanilla 2009; Millon 1981). Such a system requires that its participants trust those with whom they cooperate (Blanton, this volume; Ostrom and Walker 2003). Household and barrio rituals cemented the bonds of this trust at Teotihuacan (Manzanilla 2002). The city's leaders also inculcated an ideology of work involving a corporate identity that did not celebrate particular ethnic groups or individuals (Kurtz and Nunley 1993). These integrative mechanisms provided some degree of cohesion for a cosmopolitan population that included immigrants from different regions of Mesoamerica, including west Mexico, the Gulf coast, Oaxaca, and the Maya region (Gómez Chávez 2002; Gómez Chávez

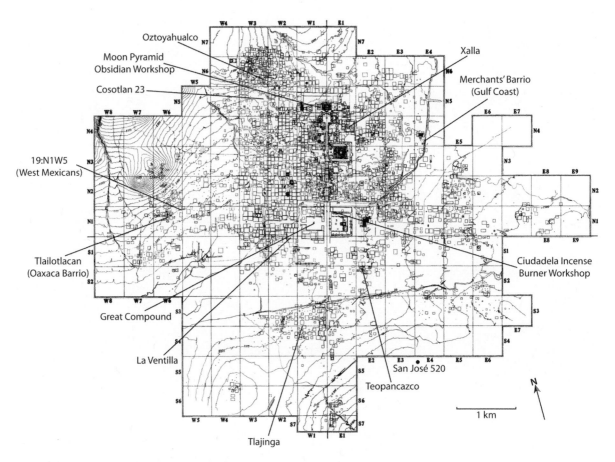

figure 5.4
Map of Teotihuacan with locations mentioned in text (after Millon 1973).

and Gazzola 2009; Price et al. 2000; Rattray 1990a; Spence et al. 2005; Taube 2003; White et al. 2004).

The art of Teotihuacan privileges religious and martial themes, flora and fauna, and geometric patterns, shedding little light on economic issues. Jorge Angulo (1995:113–133) made a noteworthy attempt to glean insights, but certain reconstructions make considerable leaps from existing material evidence. Nonlocal resources, such as tropical feathers and shell, are emphasized in art, and some acquisition activities are depicted—such as individuals picking fruit trees, including lowland cacao, and divers collecting marine shells (Figure 5.5). Obsidian is represented

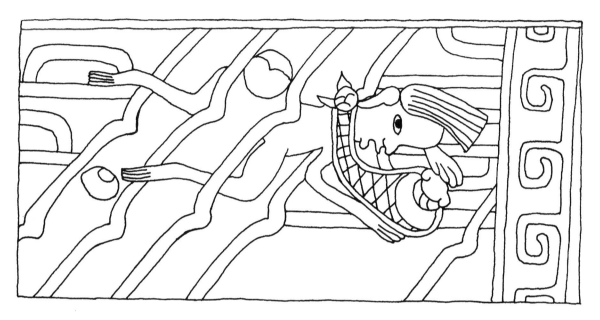

figure 5.5
Shell diver from Tetitla mural (redrawn from Fuente 1995b:fig. 19.24).

figure 5.6
Storm God with woven container carried on back from Zacuala mural (redrawn from Fuente 1995c:fig. 21.4).

figure 5.7
Exchange, either redistribution or trade, depicted on Temple of Agriculture mural (redrawn from Fuente 1995a:fig. 10.3 and lám. 5).

as weaponry, but the production and use of utilitarian tools or other types of craft production are not portrayed. Burdens carried on the back to transport goods, like those Aztec merchants used, are depicted (Figure 5.6), but the individuals carrying them are not iconographically designated as merchants (Von Winning 1987:153–154). While individuals are shown exchanging goods, it is unclear if the exchange is market based or redistributive. Most notably, a mural from the Temple of Agriculture includes a central scene in which individuals face each other as if involved in exchange (Figure 5.7) while others make offerings to figures that have been interpreted as deities or mortuary bundles. Linda Manzanilla (1992:328) suggests the image depicts redistribution, but the central figures could also be interpreted as engaged in trade (cf. Angulo 1995:99; Millon 1967).

The scale of market exchange at Teotihuacan remains a contested issue, and only limited excavations have been undertaken in the Great Compound—the most likely location for a central marketplace if one existed (Millon 1992). This chapter will not resolve the market-redistribution debate for Teotihuacan, which can only be addressed through multiscalar studies combining extensive investigations at the Great Compound, additional work on production and consumption

within apartment compounds, and similar research at contemporary communities within Central Mexico (see Feinman and Garraty 2010; Hirth 1998; Rodríguez García 1991). Scholars must also consider a broader spectrum of types of market exchange (e.g., Blanton, this volume; Isaac, this volume; Stanish and Coben, this volume), rather than framing the issue as an either/or question hinging on the operation of a large central marketplace akin to Tlatelolco during the Postclassic period. Progress in this direction is being made, and new information is available on how production and exchange were organized.

Transportation and Interregional Exchange

In reviewing the history of the railroad, historian John Coatsworth (1981:12) noted: "Mexico is a country where geography conspires against economy. Since the pre-rail transport system depended on overland movement using animal power or on foot, transportation costs were high." Many scholars have similarly emphasized transportation possibilities in investigating Pre-Columbian economies, as these relied exclusively on human porters except for a few select instances of lacustrine or riverine transport (Drennan 1984; Hassig 1985; Hirth and

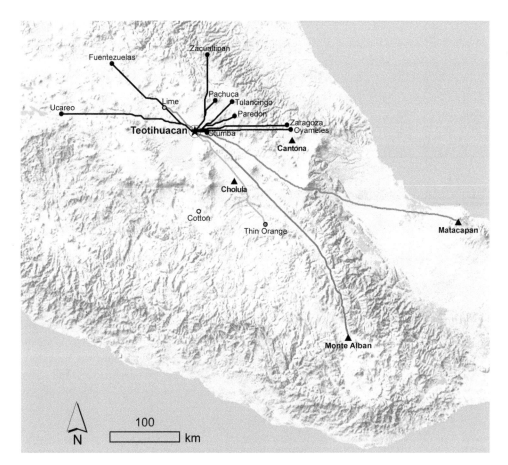

figure 5.8
Least-cost paths calculated using SRTM (90 m) satellite data with Tobler (1993) hiker function. Data available from U.S. Geological Survey, EROS Data Center, Sioux Falls, S. Dak. (http://seamless.usgs.gov/). (Map by David M. Carballo.)

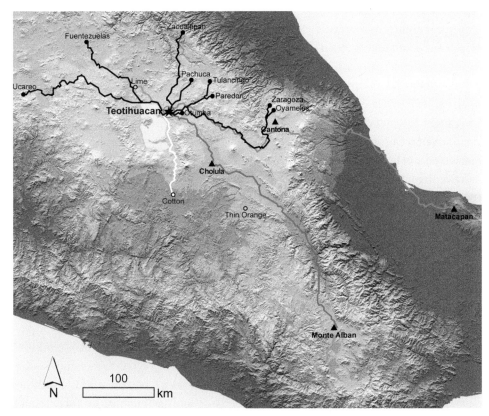

figure 5.9
Least-cost paths calculated using ASTER (30 m) satellite data with Tobler (1993) hiker function. ASTER GDEM is a product of METI and NASA (https://wist.echo.nasa.gov/). (Map by David M. Carballo.)

table 5.1

Distance and estimated travel time between Teotihuacan and selected resources and sites

	OBSIDIAN						
	Otumba	Pachuca	Tulancingo	Paredon	Oyameles	Zaragoza	
EUCLIDIAN DISTANCE (KM)	18	53	68	61	140	134	
TRAVEL TIME (HR, 4KM/HR)	4.5	13.3	17.0	15.3	35.0	33.5	
PATH COST SRTM (HR)	3.9	11.6	14.4	13.3	31.6	30.8	
PATH COST ASTER (HR)	5.4	17.4	16.9	12.8	38.3	38.3	

Notes: Travel time is estimated simply at a rate of four kilometers per hour over linear routes (Euclidian distance), whereas the relative costs of slope travel are registered in the different estimates using digital terrain models incorporating the Tobler (1993) hiker function for least-cost path. All travel times are calculated from Teotihuacan. The higher resolution ASTER data (thirty meters) results in routes that are more slope adverse than those produced using SRTM data (ninety meters). In most cases, this difference accounts for the longer time estimates with ASTER data, most of which are likely more accurate than are those based on SRTM data. The Basin of Mexico lake system was modeled as a barrier since this study focuses on foot travel outside of the basin. When not modeled as a barrier, only the Ucareo paths and Morelos cotton path based on ASTER data passed through the lakes.

Pillsbury, this volume; Sanders and Santley 1983). Analyses incorporating geographic information systems (GIS) further this line of inquiry by modeling possible routes across Mexico's mountainous landscape. The new analyses presented in this study build from an earlier one (Carballo and Pluckhahn 2007) to highlight some of the routes that Teotihuacanos may have taken for acquiring and exchanging raw materials and finished goods.

Two separate terrain models were derived from Shuttle Radar Topographic Mission (SRTM) elevation data with ninety-meter resolution (Figure 5.8) and Advanced Spaceborne Thermal Emission and Reflection Radiometer (ASTER) elevation data with thirty-meter resolution (Figure 5.9). The combination of two sources permits corroborative assessment of suggested least-cost paths over an anisotropic friction surface calculated using the hiker function developed by Tobler (1993) for modeling the time of travel through mountainous terrain. Destination points were chosen by virtue of being resource zones of established importance or

contemporary communities with documented ties to Teotihuacan. The Basin of Mexico lake system was modeled as a barrier because the destination points in the study all lay outside of the basin (but see Gorenflo and Gale 1990). Results of the analyses are summarized in Table 5.1.

It should be emphasized that cost-path analysis provides a measure of estimated optimal routes in energetic terms that must then be matched with archaeological indices of cultural interaction to be of analytical value. Accordingly, the analyses are tethered to recently documented studies of craft production and exchange within apartment compounds, barrio centers, and temples. Manzanilla (2009) provides a useful tripartite division of production within the city: 1) utilitarian goods often produced in the urban fringe; 2) elite dress and regalia often produced in barrio centers; and 3) implements of governance and rulership often produced at temple and palace precincts. Rossend Rovira Morgado (n.d.) gives an equally useful classification of exchange within Teotihuacan: 1) household

OBSIDIAN			CHINGU LIME	MORELOS COTTON	THIN ORANGE	MONTE ALBÁN	GULF-COTTON MATACAPAN
Zacualtipan	Ucareo	Fuentezuelas					
110	193	144	55	113	167	368	403
27.5	48.3	36.0	13.8	28.3	41.8	92.0	100.8
24.8	41.1	31.8	11.3	22.9	36.0	80.2	86.8
32.2	50.2	36.9	10.8	27.0	38.5	88.7	78.2

barter, 2) institutionalized redistribution, 3) market exchange within barrio plazas or formal marketplaces, and 4) long-distance trade. To round out the city's economy we should add two forms of exchange that would have been organized by governing authorities: 5) tribute in goods and 6) temple labor obligations (for comparative frameworks, see Feinman and Garraty 2010; Hirth and Pillsbury, this volume).

Four Commodities

Obsidian, lime, cotton, and export pottery provide useful perspectives on economic activities at Teotihuacan because of their relatively well-defined places of origin and widespread consumption. These commodities also had the potential for labor-added value, as they could be made into quotidian items and sumptuary or ritual goods with restricted circulation based on the amount of labor involved in their transformation. Elaborate transformations included fashioning ceremonial artifacts from obsidian; maintaining the walls of elite residences with fresh coats of lime stucco painted with Teotihuacan's famous murals; fancy cotton vestments worn by social elites; and finely made ceramic vessels for food service and mortuary deposits. Additionally, these commodities had variable degrees of elasticity—meaning the relationship between their value and demand (Wilk and Cliggett 2007:64–66). In the absence of metals, demand for obsidian was relatively inelastic, as it was essential to many daily tasks. The relative elasticity of lime depended on its usage. Stuccoing buildings with lime plaster was an entrenched cultural norm at Teotihuacan but was not a necessity for survival; yet treating maize with lime water (nixtamalization) was an important dietary practice in Mesoamerica. Cotton was used for clothing and other textiles, but its production occurred at a distance from Teotihuacan. Its value was more elastic, as woven cotton could have been substituted with cloth made from local maguey (*Agave* spp.) fiber. Export pottery likely had high elasticity: Teotihuacanos or societies with which they traded could simply manufacture pots from local clays. Consideration of relative labor-added value, degrees of elasticity, and possibilities of substitution is important as we turn to the production and exchange of these four commodities.

Obsidian

Based on the volume of literature on obsidian, a nonspecialist may be led to believe that either Teotihuacanos were obsessed with the material or that scholars are; neither is the case. Obsidian has been one of the primary materials used in explorations of Teotihuacan's economy because its place of origin can be easily traced (Cobean 2002)

table 5.2

Summary of three obsidian-sourcing studies for Teotihuacan

STUDY	SOURCE/NUMBER				
	OTUMBA	PACHUCA	TULANCINGO	PAREDON	
GAZZOLA (2009) INAA & PIXE (N=85)	53 (62%)	12 (14%)		17 (20%)	
GLASCOCK AND NEFF (1993) INAA (N=109)	79 (72%)	21 (19%)		5 (5%)	
CARBALLO ET AL. (2007) LA-ICP-MS (N=55)	26 (47%)	12 (22%)	14 (25%)	1 (2%)	

Note: Percentages are rounded.

and because it held importance in the absence of developed metallurgy. Its ubiquity and indelibility ensures that production, distribution, and consumption may be evaluated from a number of social contexts. For these reasons, obsidian has been emphasized at Teotihuacan and used as a proxy for inferring other less conspicuous economic activities.

Perspectives on the organization of obsidian industries range from those that hold Teotihuacanos monopolized all or most nearby sources, including state management of a large portion of production and distribution, to those that view these activities as having been mostly market driven and independent of political ties (cf. Andrews 2002; Charlton 1978; Clark 1986; Drennan et al. 1990; Santley 1983; Spence 1981, 1996). The initially proposed figure of four hundred obsidian workshops within Teotihuacan during its apogee is almost certainly too high (Spence 1996:30). Yet the position taken by John Clark (1986) for the scale of production in the city, extrapolating from only a superficial cover of debitage, has been shown to be just as unlikely by several excavations that have unearthed exceedingly dense subsurface deposits (Andrade Olvera and Arellano Álvarez 2011; Carballo 2011; Paredes Cetino 2000; Paz Bautista 1996; Trinidad Meléndez 1996). An accurate reconstruction lies somewhere in between, and the comprehensive excavation of an apartment compound inhabited by obsidian workers is needed to advance current understanding.

Literature on Teotihuacano obsidian exploitation has focused primarily on just two quarries within Central Mexico: the Pachuca source, with its valued green obsidian, and the nearby Otumba source of gray obsidian, located within a day's round-trip journey. Quarrying and production activities have only been well documented at the Pachuca mines, where Pastrana and Domínguez (2009) report on small Classic-period apartment compounds and campsites, which they attribute to Teotihuacano involvement in making preforms and tools for export back to the city and elsewhere. Chemical variability between different flows in the quarry has been defined (Ponamarenko 2004; Spence et al. 1984), but compositional analyses of artifacts found at Teotihuacan remain scarce. Obsidian sourcing studies for Teotihuacan artifacts of which I am aware include the analysis of samples from the Feathered Serpent Pyramid, dating to the midpoint of the city's occupation, by Michael Glascock and Hector Neff (1993); our analysis of samples from workshop dumps and construction fill next to the Moon Pyramid, which are later in the occupation (Carballo et al. 2007); and the analysis of samples from early construction episodes underneath the Ciudadela by Julie Gazzola (2009). It should be noted that though the three studies nicely span the city's primary occupation, they are all biased in originating in or next to major monuments. The results of these studies (summarized in Table 5.2) suggest that, while Otumba and Pachuca

		SOURCE/NUMBER		
OYAMELES	ZARAGOZA	ZACUALTIPAN	UCAREO	FUENTEZUELAS
	1 (1%)	1 (1%)		
	2 (2%)		1 (1%)	1 (1%)
2 (4%)				

obsidian were most important, material from the Tulancingo and Paredon sources made it to the city in significant amounts. These four sources are followed in much lower quantities by others along the Mexican Neovolcanic Belt.

Potential routes to the primary obsidian sources may be inferred by the cost-path analyses and compared with contemporary roads, for which a distinction between divided highways and undivided highways is relevant, as the construction of the former often involved dynamiting through slopes while the latter more often follow natural topography. The route suggested by the ASTER terrain model to Pachuca quickly forks from the route to Tulancingo and Paredon, with the modern divided highway running between these two possibilities, whereas the route to Tulancingo nearly mirrors the undivided highway between Teotihuacan and that city. The routes suggested by the SRTM terrain model to the four most utilized sources are similar but straighter. The high exploitation of these sources and their accessibility within four to seventeen hours, suggested by the Tobler hiker function, lend additional support and resolution to Charlton's (1978) pioneering work on trade routes. Charlton noted the importance of sites near Calpulalpan, in northwestern Tlaxcala, for the transshipment of obsidian and other goods that Teotihuacanos would have traded in easterly and southerly directions. More recent work near Calpulalpan affirms that communities there were part of Teotihuacan's

immediate core zone (Martínez Vargas and Jarquín Pacheco 1998). It is, therefore, likely that Calpulalpan's modern identity as a gateway community has roots extending back two millennia.

The geochemical studies indicate that other obsidian sources are uncommon at Teotihuacan, but the least-cost analyses are illustrative of potential exchange at lower scales in obsidian or other goods. The routes to the eastern sources run through the Tlaxcala Corridor in the ASTER-based model, largely following Mexico's first railroad, linking Mexico City and Veracruz, as well as the undivided highway passing through Apizaco. Following the SRTM-based model, these eastern routes originate in the Tlaxcala Corridor as well, but then they traverse part of Sierra de Ixtacamaxtitlan. Such a course is inconsistent with settlement and artifact inventories in northern Tlaxcala (Carballo and Pluckhahn 2007; García Cook and Merino Carrión 1996), which instead support the route from the ASTER analysis.

Once procured, the obsidian from these sources was reduced into varied artifact types at Teotihuacan. Our excavations next to the Moon Pyramid demonstrate that artisans engaged in large-scale but episodic production of dart points, large knives, and eccentrics depicting martial symbols (Carballo 2007, 2011) (Figure 5.10). The high quantities of by-products attest to the intensity of these activities. In the most completely excavated deposit, more than 170 kilograms of debris was recovered from an estimated third to sixth of the

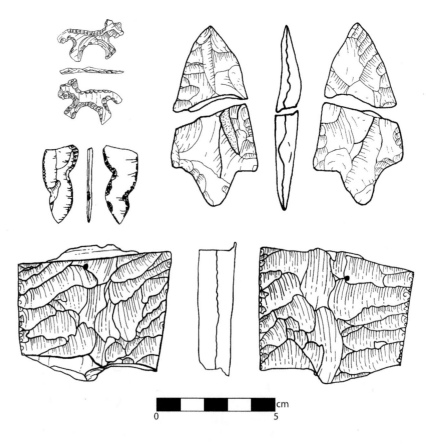

figure 5.10
Obsidian debris
from Moon
Pyramid workshop
deposits, including
canid and serpent
eccentric, refitting
dart-point preform,
and fragment
of large knife.
(Drawing by
David M. Carballo.)

0   5 cm

original dump. We encountered millions of waste flakes, along with pieces of dart points and eccentrics broken during manufacture. The episodic nature of the activity is apparent from the depositional contexts of the three deposits, which were discarded within depressions in compacted, sterile substrate (*tepetate*) during remodeling episodes at the pyramid. Artisans were well supplied with raw obsidian and could be characterized as having been wasteful in its reduction. This is particularly apparent in the large biface production activities: blocks and large pieces broken during production could have been recycled into other tools but were not. Such wastefulness within specialized and symbolically charged production activities is more consistent—in this one particular case—with centralized provisioning of raw material and/or ritual production rather than with commercially oriented, household production (see Schortman and Urban 2004).

Domestic production of obsidian tools was likely much more common than was temple production, but further study is needed. Excavations at the La Ventilla Barrio recovered abundant green obsidian, likely associated with the manufacture of prismatic blades (Cabrera Castro and Gómez Chávez 2008; Trinidad Meléndez 1996). Further, a technological reanalysis conducted by Brad Andrews (2002) for the San Martín complex and new excavations by Davíd Andrade support domestically organized production intended for exchange (Andrade Olvera and Arellano Álvarez 2011). Consumption patterns also suggest that production was more likely to have been independently, rather than politically, organized. For instance, in a study of 284 burials containing grave offerings, Martha Sempowski (1994:130, 154–155, 252) tallies approximately 20 percent having blades, 6 percent having points, and less than 1 percent having eccentrics. These data imply that blades and other utilitarian items circulated relatively freely in the Teotihuacano economy, while the movement of eccentrics was more restricted. Yet eccentric production was not confined to temple contexts, such as the Moon Pyramid, as Andrews (2002) has demonstrated.

figure 5.11
Lime-plastered mural fragment from Temple of the Feathered Shells. (Photograph by David M. Carballo.)

Lime

A second major industry at Teotihuacan centered on lime, which would have been consumed in staggering quantities for basic food processing and for making plaster or stucco to cover walls (Figure 5.11) and certain ceramics (Barba Pingarrón and Córdova Frunz 1999, 2010; Murakami 2010). Limestone deposits are scarce within the Basin of Mexico but can be found in the Zumpango region of the northern basin and in adjacent areas of Hidalgo, Puebla, and Morelos. The chemical analyses of Luis Barba and associates have been at the forefront of understanding this industry. They suggest that elevated levels of carbonates within the floor of a room at Azcapotzalco may indicate the draining of water associated with the nixtamalization (Barba et al. 1999). Higher carbonate levels were also detected in certain rooms of the Oztoyahualco compound at

Teotihuacan, but in this case production activities appear to be associated with plaster making, since excavations also recovered large quantities of stone smoothers used for applying plaster to walls, floors, and other surfaces (Lizárraga and Ortiz Butrón 1993; Ortiz Butrón and Barba 1993). These authors propose that plastering would have been one of the trades in which inhabitants of the compound specialized. A similar group of artisans likely occupied the Oaxaca Barrio (Rattray 1995:71), but here Zapotecs appear to have migrated from their homeland to work on construction projects at Teotihuacan.

The vast quantities of lime used in stuccoing Teotihuacan would have necessitated coordinated acquisition networks and large amounts of fuel to convert limestone into powdered quicklime. Barba Pingarrón and Córdova Frunz (2010:147) estimate that some six hundred thousand tons of lime would have been necessary to plaster the temples, plazas, and apartment compounds of the city. They extrapolate that such an amount necessitated one hundred forty porters daily in order to move lime between a quarry and the city during its height. Burning this much limestone would have required tens of thousands of tons of fuel per year (Barba Pingarrón and Córdova Frunz 2010:114–117). Nevertheless, Carmen Adriano-Morán and Emily McClung de Tapia (2008) suggest that Teotihuacanos successfully managed forest resources throughout the Classic period. Although these authors register significant landscape modification, including the retreat of nearby forests at the expense of agricultural fields, their study does not support deforestation as a primary factor in Teotihuacan's collapse, even with such intensive lime processing (see also McClung de Tapia 2009).

Barba and colleagues (2009) combined compositional analyses with petrographic characterization in determining that the lime used to plaster the main courtyard at Teopancazco originated from the Chingú region of southern Hidalgo, as opposed to other possible sources in the states of Puebla and Morelos. The authors reason that the transformation of limestone to quicklime would have occurred near the source, a proximity that would have been energetically sensible and consistent with Adriano-Morán and McClung de Tapia's (2008) documentation of sustained wood resources near Teotihuacan. The source region is near the eventual Toltec capital of Tula; therefore, it appears that Classic-period contacts with Teotihuacan stimulated population growth and increased social complexity during the Postclassic period, as was suggested by Clara Díaz Oyarzábal (1981). The least-cost path to the Chingú region lime source proceeds in a fairly straight line northwest from Teotihuacan. An estimated travel time of eleven hours implies that the trip could be made in a single day.

It is interesting to note that the least-cost routes match the distribution of documented sixteenth-century communities involved in lime exchange much more accurately than do contemporary roads, which are oriented toward Mexico City for historical reasons (see Barba Pingarrón and Cordóva Frunz 1999:fig. 1). They also pass directly through the Zumpango region, which Tatsuya Murakami (2010:191–192) notes may have been a second important source of lime for Teotihuacan at half the distance, but source material from this region was not included in the study by Barba and colleagues (2009). In either case, the least-cost path distribution raises the possibility that the demand Teotihuacan exerted for lime created a sort of "lime corridor" of production communities that persisted along this route into the Postclassic period.

Cotton

Cotton represents another nonlocal resource. It was grown in the more humid, adjacent state of Morelos or in more distant lowland regions. Drawing comparisons to the Mexica strategy of early expansion, Hirth (1978) suggested that significant reorganization of settlement between the Terminal Formative and Early Classic periods in eastern Morelos was stimulated by the intensification of cotton production related to Teotihuacan. While it is likely that cotton arrived to Teotihuacan from greater distances, particularly due to its low weight and ease of packing (see Hirth, this volume), eastern Morelos would have been the most accessible source. It was also the nearest source for more temperate fruits, including avocados. The least-cost paths derived from both terrain models follow a similar route south of the city, exiting the basin through the Amecameca pass and mimicking the undivided highway to Cuautla. As with other cases, the SRTM-derived path is straighter because subtle changes in slope are obscured by the coarser resolution of the data.

Although Morelos is closer to Teotihuacan, manufacture of cotton textiles is better documented at two barrios that exhibit greater ties to the Gulf coast. Manzanilla (2007, 2009) recovered abundant remains associated with the tailoring of elaborate costumes at Teopancazco. Cotton *mantas* appear to have been imported along with Gulf of Mexico fauna, and the small eyes on needles suggest that raw cotton thread was also imported and used for sewing decorative elements onto costumes (Manzanilla 2009:32). The sex and strontium ratios of six individuals buried in the barrio center lead Manzanilla

figure 5.12
Priest wearing an elaborate cotton garment in a mural from Tepantitla (reconstruction, Museo Nacional de Antropología, Mexico City). (Photograph by David M. Carballo.)

to conclude that the tailors were men who migrated from the Gulf coast, possibly originating from the Nautla region in northern Veracruz (Manzanilla 2011). In a related case that is interesting for contrast, Spence and colleagues (2005:163) suggest that textile working at the Merchants' Barrio was performed by women and that their role in this socially valued labor contributed to their relatively high status. Men in the Merchants' Barrio appear to have been the long-distance traders, moving between their Gulf-coast homeland and Teotihuacan, while local-born Teotihuacanas maintained a matrilocal household, a pattern seen in urban merchant enclaves elsewhere in the world (Spence et al. 2005:179). The potentially divergent exchange and production practices in these two barrios provide insights into possible gender and ethnic variability in mercantile activities. The cotton-weaving women of the Merchants' Barrio may have enjoyed an elevated

status relative to that of women involved in crafting with local resources, such as maguey fiber or clay, but the textiles that the women of the Merchants' Barrio produced appear to have been utilitarian and geared toward general consumption. More ornate costumes were made at Teopancazco (Figure 5.12).

At the macroregional scale, intensified Gulf-coast cotton industries, possibly associated with demand from Teotihuacan, have been documented in the Mixtequilla (Stark et al. 1998) and Tuxtla (Hall 1997) regions. Trade routes to these areas may be inferred through the least-cost analyses between Teotihuacan and Matacapan, building from our previous study plotting three equidistant destinations along the gulf (Carballo and Pluckhahn 2007). Matacapan is also appropriate as a destination because it is centrally located along the Gulf coast and has been proposed as a Teotihuacan colony with a small resident population of ethnic Teotihuacanos involved in coastal–highland exchange (Santley 2007). People from other areas of the Gulf coast certainly exchanged with Teotihuacanos (Ruiz Gallut and Pascual Soto 2004), and energetically optimal routes for them would likely pass through the Sierra Madre Oriental closer to Xalapa (north) or to Orizaba (south), based on their final destination.

The ASTER-derived route to Matacapan passes through the Tlaxcala Corridor and crosses the Sierra Madre south of the Cofre de Perote volcano before hugging the coast. The SRTM route passes through the Tlaxcala Corridor, Oriental Valley, and Maltrata Valley, following the Mexico City–Veracruz rail line. Recent archaeology in the Oriental Valley and Maltrata region suggests that the Maltrata route was of greater importance to Teotihuacan. Survey and excavations by Yamile Lira López (2010) have demonstrated settlement disruption in the region during the Formative-Classic transition, followed by the appearance of Teotihuacano materials. Further, the corpus of radiocarbon assays presented by Ángel García Cook (2004, 2009) for Cantona shows that the city was a large contemporary of Teotihuacan. If Cantonecos challenged Teotihuacano passage through the northern Oriental Valley, the Maltrata route likely would have been a less contested option for merchants. Yet if Manzanilla's (2011) postulated ties between inhabitants of Teopancazco and the Nautla region are correct, then this northerly route or another around Cantona may have also been used. In any case, the journey between Teotihuacan and the central Gulf coast would have taken approximately ten days and would have represented a portion of farther-flung exchange relations and hegemonic alliances with certain Maya kingdoms (see Freidel et al. 2007).

Ceramic Trade Wares

Unlike obsidian, lime, and cotton, most pottery was not conducive to long-distance trade since it was bulky and fragile and since most people could find suitable potting clay close to home. Nonetheless, Teotihuacan is notable for two ceramic types that circulated widely throughout its sphere of interaction and reached more distant parts of Mesoamerica:

Thin Orange ware and theater-style incense burners. Thin Orange, produced in southern Puebla, is one of the best studied and most widely distributed ceramic types from Mesoamerica (Kolb 1977, 1986; Rattray 1990b, 2001). Its defining attributes—thin vessel walls of orange paste—appear to have been desirable for Central Mexicans in the Late Formative period, but the ware became standardized due to the volume of demand from Teotihuacan and its economic networks (Plunket and Uruñuela 2012; Uruñuela and Plunket 2010).

Thin Orange is more commonly found in burials than in fill contexts, suggesting that vessels were reserved for ritual consumption events, passed along as heirlooms, and taken out of circulation by mortuary rites and limited accidental breakage (Kolb 1986; Uruñuela and Plunket 2010). An example is provided by a tomb from Los Teteles de Ocotítla that contained thirteen Thin Orange vessels mixed with 291 vessels of other, mostly local, types (Vega Sosa 1981). Given the positioning of the site along the Tlaxcala Corridor, the presence of these vessels suggests that locals engaged in trade relations with wider networks involving southern Puebla and Teotihuacan. Thin Orange wares are found as far away as Honduras (Sharer 2003), demonstrating that their social value as an index of contacts with Central Mexico—and likely Teotihuacan in particular—outweighed the challenges inherent in moving vessels long distances. Charles Kolb (1986:190–191) has noted that the standardized dimensions and open form of one of the most commonly traded Thin Orange vessels—annular-based hemispherical bowls—permitted them to be stacked for efficient packaging (Figure 5.13). Based on a survey of Thin Orange deposits throughout Central Mexico, Hirth (this volume) contends that the decreasing frequency from the Río Carnero manufacturing region toward Teotihuacan is more suggestive of commercially based exchange than of tribute, which should result in discrete concentrations at some distance from where the pottery was produced.

Both least-cost path analyses for Thin Orange support a route between the production zone and Teotihuacan that passes east into the Tlaxcala

Corridor before descending south through the Puebla-Tlaxcala Valley. The ASTER route runs directly through the sites of Cholula and Cacaxtla-Xochitecatl, while the SRTM route passes slightly east of the former and through the latter. Both routes' general paths nicely match Kolb's (1986:178–179) favored possibility. They also initially parallel those between Teotihuacan and Monte Albán, which then branch through the Tehuacan Valley following the modern undivided highway. Other than Thin Orange, ceramics from the Gulf coast and Oaxaca are two of the more common foreign wares in the city. The sourcing study of George Cowgill and Hector Neff (2004) documents imported ceramics from the southern Gulf coast and suggests possible origins of one group in the vicinity of Matacapan; the other is more to the east near Tabasco. Kolb (1986:193–194) noted that the Calpulalpan region would have served as a gateway for Thin Orange exchange, to which we may add ceramics from the Gulf coast and Oaxaca.

The composite ceramic incense burners called "theater-style"—for their resemblance to a stage (likely a temple) with a human face or figure (Figure 5.14)—emphasize iconographic themes related to Teotihuacan's state and religious hierarchy (Sugiyama 2002). These burners are found not only

in most apartment compounds at Teotihuacan but also in distant communities, such as the potential colony of Montana along the Pacific coast of Guatemala (Berlo 1984; Bove and Medrano Busto 2003). Associated production debris has been encountered within certain apartments at Teotihuacan (Sullivan 2007), but it was also abundant at a workshop attached to the northern facade of the Ciudadela. Here, Carlos Múnera Bermúdez (1985) recovered a complete production sequence including molds, broken decorative plaques, polishers, wasters, sheet-mica, and pigment grinders used in the process of adorning burners. Accordingly, the manufacture of theater-style incense burners appears to have been organized both at the domestic and state/temple levels. Although these items were predominantly destined for use in domestic rituals, their iconography, exportation abroad, and temple workshop suggest that the politico-religious hierarchy of the Teotihuacan state oversaw a significant portion of their production.

Ceramic manufacture within the city that likely operated independently from its institutional economies has been investigated recently at several apartment compounds. Kristin Sullivan's (2006) analysis of San Martín Orange pottery from the Tlajinga Barrio suggests that this utility ware from

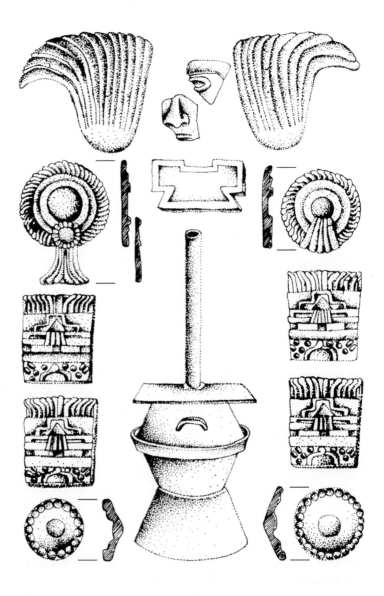

figure 5.14
Components of a theater-style incense burner, showing mold-made adornments (redrawn from Ségourné [1966:fig. 24]).

the Xolalpan-Metepec phase was produced by individual households working cooperatively as part of larger neighborhood collectives, as does her analysis of figurine and censer production at Cosotlan 23 (Sullivan 2005, 2007). Site 520, located just southeast of the mapped portions of the city, has been explored by Oralia Cabrera Cortés (2006), who documents domestic potting by a low-ranking household occupying residences made of more modest materials than those of the apartment compounds. Yet burial offerings suggest that the inhabitants of Site 520 were integrated into Teotihuacan's urban economy, likely by exchanging the ceramics they manufactured. Lastly, the production strategies

of potters who fashioned elegant cylinder tripods have been studied by Cynthia Conides (1997). She proposes that the increased frequency of stuccoing and painting relative to more labor-intensive excising during the late occupation of Teotihuacan may be attributed to potters attempting to increase output and reach more consumers.

Discussion

Viewed through four commodities, the heterogeneity in Teotihuacan's economy and the organization of different production and exchange activities are apparent. Given our incomplete record, it is not surprising that little consensus exists on the degree to which economic institutions were organized by political-religious authorities as opposed to a more commercial system; yet recent investigations have moved the debate beyond polarizing positions. In fact, the anthropological focus of Teotihuacan studies has led to sophisticated explorations of a scale of economic activity that economists often ignore: those social arrangements that mediate between the household and state or market, such as corporate kin groups and guildlike trade organizations. In an article titled "Neither Markets nor States," the economist Elinor Ostrom and colleagues (1997) emphasize precisely these types of institutions and call attention to the importance of face-to-face interactions, mutual monitoring, and sanctioning in organizing collective economic relations of an intermediate scale. Scholars of Teotihuacan largely agree on this fundamental scale of economic organization within the city but debate the relative importance of other institutions (cf. Manzanilla 1992, 2009; Millon 1992).

In considering production near the Moon Pyramid and Ciudadela, I argue that ethnohistoric analogy to the Mexica best matches the production contexts and remains. It is clear in both cases that these craft activities were not undertaken at temples exclusively; obsidian points and eccentrics as well as theater-style incense burners were also produced within households. Nevertheless, the symbolic themes, specialized distribution networks, and large-scale manufacture at temples connect these activities to the state religious system, and historical documents from the Aztec period may reveal the mechanism by which such production was organized. Mexica labor duties involving work as part of a collectivity were termed *tequitl*, and are detailed by Pedro Carrasco (1978) and Teresa Rojas Rabiela (1977, 1986). A similar institution may have organized production among the social units that occupied the apartment compounds and barrios of Teotihuacan. Mexica political or religious labor obligations were usually designated *coatequitl* ("public works"), which were a form of rotating, obligatory labor tribute in duties such as digging irrigation canals or making crafts next to temples (Molina 2008 [1571]:23). One form of Mexica *coatequitl* was directed at the manufacture of arms for state armories called *tlacochcalco* ("house of darts") (Díaz del Castillo 1956 [1568]:211–212). Claudia García-Des Lauriers (2008) has identified iconographic elements suggestive of the presence of armories at Teotihuacan and, based on the scale of dart-point production at the Moon Pyramid, one of the structures within the Moon Precinct would certainly seem to be the best candidate for such a building. In the case of public labor duties and state armories, therefore, the analogy between Teotihuacan and the Mexica seems appropriate, and such production was likely rendered as part of the labor tribute required of households within the city itself (see Millon 1992:377).

The organization of other mercantile activities at Teotihuacan depends largely on the robustness of market exchange within the city and its sphere, and the characteristics of the goods and resources that were exchanged. Useful frameworks have been developed by Randolph Widmer (1996) and Linda Manzanilla (2009). Widmer begins by noting that a nonelite compound at Maquixco Bajo, located outside of the city but within the Teotihuacan Valley, possessed one of the densest concentrations of imported *Spondylus* shell excavated in highland Mesoamerica (see also Kolb 1987). He contrasts this pattern with pottery production using local clays at the Tlajinga Barrio at Teotihuacan. Unlike mined resources, shell is less easily monopolized since it is widely dispersed along coasts. Shell was used for adornment at Teotihuacan and, therefore, had relatively high elasticity as a commodity. Widmer (1996) proposes that a material like shell would have moved through several exchange nodes before arriving to Teotihuacan, where traders would have distributed some portion as a tax to ruling elites and others as a market commodity. Manzanilla's (2009) synthetic reconstruction elaborates further, suggesting a division between the production of utilitarian goods in the urban fringe, the production of elite vestments and adornments often in barrio centers, and the production of items relating to governance and rulership within temple and palace precincts.

Extrapolating from the potential exchange routes and production contexts reviewed in this study, the organization of mercantile activities relating to many utilitarian obsidian tools, lime used for treating maize, simpler cotton garments, and most pottery appears to have been organized at an intermediate, corporate-kin scale, rather than by the noble heads of barrios or by temple or state institutions. These goods would have likely circulated as commercial commodities within periodic, barrio-centered markets as Manzanilla (2009) proposes and may also have been exchanged in a centralized market within the Great Compound (Millon 1992). Plastering temples, palaces, and other civic-ceremonial structures certainly would have been a form of production related to governance and rulership, consistent with Manzanilla's model, and lime was a relatively circumscribed resource that would be easy to monopolize, consistent with Widmer's model. Why Teotihuacano rulers would manage the plastering of houses is less clear, however, unless we consider the highly planned apartments of Teotihuacan to have been a massive public housing project. Most convincing in this regard is René Millon's (1981:209) observation that, like Pachuca obsidian and theater-style incense burners, apartment compounds do not survive the collapse of the state. Central Mexicans continued to live in relatively large quadrangular residences after Teotihuacan, but not at the scale and level of orthogonal precision seen during the Classic period. Centralized oversight of the construction and maintenance of apartment compounds may have been an effective way for Teotihuacano rulers to have organized labor tribute and taxed goods (Kurtz and Nunley 1993; Millon 1976, 1981), and lime plaster was one part of these more involved relationships. But lime-plaster production was likely another activity organized by independent households along the lime corridor as well as by state/temple tribute demands, as it was for the Mexica (Rojas Rabiela 1986:142).

Both Michael Spence (1986:95) and Ian Robertson (2001:225–227) have noted that the construction of apartment compounds in a massive urban-planning project during the middle of the city's history would have required state oversight for leveling most existing residences to raise new ones, but the building program also may have allowed households to relocate to parts of the city that better suited their needs. This possibility could help explain a pattern to emerge from the least-cost path analysis presented here: that certain compounds appear to be conveniently positioned with respect to trade routes associated with the economies of those compounds. Examples include the western location of Oztoyahualco and the Zapotec Barrio, near the route to lime; the eastern location of the Merchants' Barrio and Teopancazco, near the route to the Gulf coast; and the greater number of potential obsidian workshops in northern sectors of the city, closer to the four primary sources (Spence 1981, 1986). Alternatively or additionally, households may have adopted economic strategies based partially on their proximity to the terminus of certain exchange routes.

At the macroregional scale, the cost-path analyses demonstrates the profound impact that the Teotihuacano economy had on neighboring areas, as hypothesized optimal routes coincide with major settlement shifts and changes in material culture more often than not. The analyses underscore the importance of the Puebla-Tlaxcala region for Teotihuacan contacts to the east and south: the Tlaxcala Corridor to the east/southeast and the Puebla-Tlaxcala Valley to the south. Obsidian routes to the northeast cover the four quarries of greatest importance, and the Calpulalpan region appears an enduring node for transshipment. Northwest of the city, a possible linear network of sites may represent a route of lime processing that was a Classic-period legacy of the Teotihuacan economy still operational a millennium later when the Spanish arrived.

The political and mercantile activities of Teotihuacanos in other regions of Mesoamerica would have stimulated and maintained the ethnic migrations that replenished the city. These migrations indicate that economic opportunities were available at Teotihuacan for merchants who do not appear to have been closely affiliated with the state.

For instance, Spence and colleagues (2005:176) note the striking difference between the Gulf-coast traders of the Merchants' Barrio and the *pochteca* of Tenochtitlan: while the latter were politically and ethnically affiliated with the city of their residence, the former lived primarily as foreigners in an adopted city while maintaining close ties to their homelands. This mercantile cosmopolitanism is remarkable for its time and place among societies that faced many challenges to staying interconnected—and is surely one of Teotihuacan's most notable historical legacies.

Acknowledgments

Sincere thanks go to Ken Hirth, Joanne Pillsbury, Amanda Sparrow, Sara Taylor, and the staff of Dumbarton Oaks for organizing the symposium and present volume, and for their helpful suggestions on earlier drafts of this chapter. I am also grateful to George Cowgill, Gary Feinman, and an anonymous reviewer for their useful comments; to Nico Tripcevich for his assistance in applying the Tobler function in ArcGIS; and to William Mather for sharing his photo.

REFERENCES CITED

Adriano-Morán, Carmen Cristina, and Emily McClung de Tapia

2008   Trees and Shrubs: The Use of Wood in Prehispanic Teotihuacan. *Journal of Archaeological Science* 35:2927–2936.

Andrade Olvera, Davíd, and Victor G. Arellano Álvarez

2011   Artesanos en el sector noreste de la antigua ciudad de Teotihuacan. Paper presented at the Fifth Mesa Redonda de Teotihuacan, San Juán Teotihuacan.

Andrews, Bradford W.

2002   Stone Tool Production at Teotihuacan: What More Can We Learn from Surface Collections? In *Pathways to Prismatic Blades: A Study in Mesoamerican Core-Blade Technology*, edited by Kenneth G. Hirth and Bradford W. Andrews, pp. 47–60. Cotsen Institute of Archaeology, University of California, Los Angeles.

Angulo, Jorge

1995   Teotihuacán: Aspectos de la cultura a través de su expresión pictórica. In *La pintura mural prehispánica en México*, vol. 1, *Teotihuacan*, bk. 2, *Estudios*, edited by Beatriz de la Fuente, pp. 65–186. Universidad Nacional Autónoma de México, Mexico City.

Barba Pingarrón, Luis A., J. Blancas, L. R. Manzanilla, A. Ortíz, D. Barca, G. M. Crisci, D. Miriello, and A. Pecci

2009   Provenance of the Limestone Used in Teotihuacan (Mexico): A Methodological Approach. *Archaeometry* 51:525–545.

Barba Pingarrón, Luis A., and José Luís Córdova Frunz

1999   Estudios energéticos de la producción de cal en tiempos teotihuacanos y sus implicaciones. *Latin American Antiquity* 10:168–179.

2010   *Materiales y energía en la arquitectura de Teotihuacan.* Universidad Nacional Autónoma de México, Mexico City.

Barba Pingarrón, Luis A., R. García, E. Mejía, and M. Martínez

1999   Determinación de áreas de actividad en una unidad habitacional del Clásico en Azcapotzalco, D.F. *Anales de antropología* 33:69–89.

Berlo, Janet Catherine

1984   *Teotihuacan Art Abroad: A Study of the Metropolitan Style and Provincial Transformation in Incensario Workshops.* BAR, Oxford.

Bove, Frederick J., and Sonia Medrano Busto

2003   Teotihuacan, Militarism, and Pacific Guatemala. In *The Maya and Teotihuacan: Reinterpreting Early Classic Interaction,* edited by Geoffrey E. Braswell, pp. 45–79. University of Texas Press, Austin.

Cabrera Castro, Rubén, and Sergio Gómez Chávez

2008   La Ventilla: A Model for a Barrio in the Urban Structure of Teotihuacan. In *Urbanism in Mesoamerica,* vol. 2, edited by Alba Guadalupe Mastache, Robert H. Cobean, Ángel García Cook, and Kenneth G. Hirth, pp. 37–84. Instituto Nacional de Antropología e Historia, Mexico City, and Pennsylvania State University, University Park.

Cabrera Cortés, M. Oralia

2006   Craft Production and Socioeconomic Marginality: Living on the Periphery of Teotihuacán, México. Electronic document, http://www.famsi.org/reports/03090/03090CabreraCortes01.pdf, accessed December 17, 2010.

Carballo, David M.

2007   Implements of State Power: Weaponry and Martially Themed Obsidian Production near the Moon Pyramid, Teotihuacan. *Ancient Mesoamerica* 18:173–190.

2011   *Obsidian and the Teotihuacan State: Weaponry and Ritual Production at the Moon Pyramid / La obsidiana y el estado teotihuacano: La producción militar y ritual en la Pirámide de la Luna.* University of Pittsburgh Memoirs in Latin American Archaeology 21. Center for Comparative Archaeology, Department of Anthropology, University of Pittsburgh, Pittsburgh, and Instituto de Investigaciones Antropológicas, Universidad Nacional Autónoma de México, Mexico City.

Carballo, David M., Jennifer Carballo, and Hector Neff

2007   Formative and Classic Period Obsidian Procurement in Central Mexico: A Compositional Study Using Laser Ablation-Inductively Coupled Plasma-Mass Spectrometry. *Latin American Antiquity* 18:27–43.

Carballo, David M., and Thomas Pluckhahn

2007   Transportation Corridors and Political Evolution in Highland Mesoamerica: Settlement Analyses Incorporating GIS for Northern Tlaxcala, Mexico. *Journal of Anthropological Archaeology* 26:607–629.

Carrasco, Pedro

1978   La economía del México prehispánico. In *Economía política e ideología en el México prehispánico,* edited by Pedro Carrasco and Johanna Broda, pp. 13–74. Editorial Nueva Imagen, Mexico City.

Charlton, Thomas H.

1978   Teotihuacan, Tepeapulco, and Obsidian Exploitation. *Science* 200:1227–1236.

Clark, John E.

1986   From Mountains to Molehills: A Critical Review of Teotihuacan's Obsidian Industry. In *Research in Economic Anthropology,* supplement 2, *Economic Aspects of Prehispanic Highland Mexico,* edited by Barry L. Isaac, pp. 23–74. JAI Press, Greenwich, Conn.

Coatsworth, John H.

1981   *Growth against Development: The Economic Impact of Railroads in Porfirian Mexico.* Northern Illinois University, DeKalb.

Cobean, Robert H.

2002   *A World of Obsidian: The Mining and Trade of a Volcanic Glass in Ancient Mexico.* University of Pittsburgh, Pittsburgh, and Instituto Nacional de Antropología e Historia, Mexico City.

Conides, Cynthia A.

1997   Social Relations among Potters in Teotihuacan, Mexico. *Museum Anthropology* 21:39–54.

Cowgill, George L.

1997   State and Society at Teotihuacan. *Annual Review of Anthropology* 26:126–161.

2007   The Urban Organization of Teotihuacan, Mexico. In *Settlement and Society: Essays Dedicated to Robert McCormick Adams,* edited by Elizabeth L. Stone, pp. 261–295. Cotsen Institute of Archaeology, University of California, Los Angeles, and Oriental Institute, University of Chicago, Chicago.

2008   An Update on Teotihuacan. *Antiquity*
        82:962–975.

Cowgill, George L., and Hector Neff

2004   Algunos resultados del análisis por acti-
        vación neutrónica de la ceramic foránea
        de Teotihuacan. In *La costa del golfo
        en tiempos teotihuacanos: Propuestas
        y perspectivas*, edited by María Elena
        Ruiz Gallut and Arturo Pascual
        Soto, pp. 63–75. Instituto Nacional de
        Antropología e Historia, Mexico City.

Díaz del Castillo, Bernal

1956 [1568]   *The Discovery and Conquest of Mexico,
               1517–1521*. Translated by Alfred P.
               Maudslay. Farrar, Straus, and Cudahy,
               New York.

Díaz Oyarzábal, Clara Luz

1981   Chingú y la expansión teotihuacana. In
        Interacción cultural en México central,
        edited by Evelyn Childs Rattray, Jaime
        Litvak King, and Clara Díaz Oyarzábal,
        pp. 107–112. Universidad Nacional
        Autónoma de México, Mexico City.

Drennan, Robert D.

1984   Long-Distance Movement of Goods
        in the Mesoamerican Formative and
        Classic. *American Antiquity* 49:27–43.

Drennan, Robert D., Philip T. Fitzgibbons, and Heinz
Dehn

1990   Imports and Exports in Classic
        Mesoamerican Political Economy: The
        Tehuacan Valley and the Teotihuacan
        Obsidian Industry. In *Research in
        Economic Anthropology*, edited by
        Barry L. Isaac, pp. 177–199. JAI Press,
        Greenwich, Conn.

Feinman, Gary M., and Christopher P. Garraty

2010   Preindustrial Markets and Marketing:
        Archaeological Perspectives. *Annual
        Review of Anthropology* 39:167–191.

Freidel, David A., Hector L. Escobedo, and Stanley P.
Guenter

2007   A Crossroads of Conquerors: Waka'
        and Gordon Willey's "Rehearsal for
        the Collapse" Hypothesis. In *Gordon
        R. Willey and American Archaeology:
        Contemporary Perspectives*, edited by
        Jeremy A. Sabloff and William L. Fash,
        pp. 187–208. University of Oklahoma
        Press, Norman.

Fuente, Beatriz de la

1995a   Zona 2. Templo de la Agricultura. In *La
        pintura mural prehispánica en México*,
        vol. 1, *Teotihuacan*, bk. 1, *Catálogo*,
        edited by Beatriz de la Fuente, pp. 103–
        107. Universidad Nacional Autónoma de
        México, Mexico City.

1995b   Tetitla. In *La pintura mural prehispánica
        en México*, vol. 1, *Teotihuacan*, bk. 1,
        Catálogo, edited by Beatriz de la Fuente,
        pp. 259–311. Universidad Nacional
        Autónoma de México, Mexico City.

1995c   Zacuala. In *La pintura mural prehis-
        pánica en México*, vol. 1, *Teotihuacan*,
        bk. 1, *Catálogo*, edited by Beatriz de la
        Fuente, pp. 321–341. Universidad Nacional
        Autónoma de México, Mexico City.

García Cook, Ángel

2004   Cantona: Ubicación temporal y generali-
        dades. *Arqueología* 33:91–108.

2009   El Formativo en la mitad norte de
        la Cuenca de Oriental. *Arqueología*
        40:115–152.

García Cook, Ángel, and Beatriz Leonor Merino
Carrión

1996   Situación cultural en Tlaxcala durante el
        apogeo de Teotihuacan. In *Homenaje a
        William T. Sanders*, vol. 1, edited by Alba
        Guadalupe Mastache, Jeffery Parsons,
        Robert Santley and Mari Carmen Serra
        Puche, pp. 281–316. Instituto Nacional de
        Antropología e Historia, Mexico City.

García-Des Lauriers, Claudia

2008   The "House of Darts": The Classic
        Period Origins of the Tlacochcalco.
        Mesoamerican Voices 3:3–21.

Gazzola, Julie

2009   Fuentes de abastecimiento de obsidi-
        ana en fases tempranas en Teotihuacán,
        México. *Arqueología* 41:47–63.

Glascock, Michael, and Hector Neff

1993   Sources of Obsidian Offerings at the
        Temple of Quetzalcoatl, Teotihuacan.
        Manuscript on file, Research Reactor
        Center, University of Missouri,
        Columbia.

Gómez Chávez, Sergio

2002   Presencia del occidente de México
        en Teotihuacan: Aproximaciones a la
        política exterior del estado teotihuacano.

In *Ideología y política a través de materiales, imágenes y símbolos: Memoria de la Primera Mesa Redonda de Teotihuacan,* edited by María Elena Ruiz Gallut, pp. 563–626. Instituto Nacional de Antropología e Historia, Mexico City.

Gómez Chávez, Sergio, and Julie Gazzola

2009 Los barrios foráneos de Teotihuacan. In *Teotihuacan: Ciudad de los dioses,* pp. 71–77. Instituto Nacional de Antropología e Historia, Mexico City.

Gorenflo, Larry J., and Nathan Gale

1990 Mapping Regional Settlement in Information Space. *Journal of Anthropological Archaeology* 9:240–274.

Hall, Barbara Ann

1997 Spindle Whorls and Cotton Production at Middle Classic Matacapan and in the Gulf Lowlands. In *Olmec to Aztec: Settlement Pattern Research in the Ancient Gulf Lowlands,* edited by Barbara L. Stark and Philip J. Arnold III, pp. 115–135. University of Arizona Press, Tucson.

Hassig, Ross

1985 *Trade, Tribute, and Transportation: The Sixteenth-Century Political Economy of the Valley of Mexico.* University of Oklahoma Press, Norman.

Hirth, Kenneth G.

1978 Teotihuacan Regional Population Administration in Eastern Morelos. *World Archaeology* 9:320–333.

1998 The Distributional Approach: A New Way to Identify Marketplace Exchange in the Archaeological Record. *Current Anthropology* 39:451–476.

Kolb, Charles C.

1977 Technological Investigations of Mesoamerican "Thin Orange" Ceramics. *Current Anthropology* 18:534–536.

1986 Commercial Aspects of Classic Teotihuacan Period "Thin Orange" Wares. In *Research in Economic Anthropology,* supplement 2, *Economic Aspects of Prehispanic Highland Mexico,* edited by Barry L. Isaac, pp. 155–205. JAI Press, Greenwich, Conn.

1987 *Marine Shell Trade and Classic Teotihuacan, Mexico.* BAR, Oxford.

Kurtz, Donald V.

1987 The Economics of Urbanization and State Formation at Teotihuacan. *Current Anthropology* 28:329–353.

Kurtz, Donald V., and Mary Christopher Nunley

1993 Ideology and Work at Teotihuacan: A Hermeneutic Interpretation. *Man* 28:761–778.

Lira López, Yamile

2010 El valle de Maltrata, Veracruz: Ruta de comunicación y comercio durante más de 2000 años. In *Caminos y mercados de México,* edited by Janet Long Towell and Amalia Attolini Lecón, pp. 129–149. Instituto Nacional de Antropología e Historia, Mexico City.

Lizárraga, Yara, and Agustín Ortiz Butrón

1993 Hacia una reinterpretación de los "pulidores de estuco." In *Anatomía de un conjunto residencial teotihuacano en Oztoyahualco,* vol. 1, *Las excavaciones,* edited by Linda Manzanilla, pp. 468–493. Instituto de Investigaciones Antropológicas, Universidad Nacional Autónoma de México, Mexico City.

Manzanilla, Linda

1992 The Economic Organization of the Teotihuacan Priesthood: Hypotheses and Considerations. In *Art, Ideology, and the City of Teotihuacan,* edited by Janet Catherine Berlo, pp. 321–333. Dumbarton Oaks Research Library and Collection, Washington, D.C.

1996 Corporate Groups and Domestic Activities at Teotihuacan. *Latin American Antiquity* 7:228–246.

1999 The Emergence of Complex Urban Societies in Central Mexico: The Case of Teotihuacan. In *Archaeology in Latin America,* edited by Gustavo G. Politis and Benjamin Alberti, pp. 93–129. Routledge, New York.

2002 Living with the Ancestors and Offering to the Gods: Domestic Ritual at Teotihuacan. In *Domestic Ritual in Ancient Mesoamerica,* edited by Patricia Plunket, pp. 43–52. Cotsen Insitute of Archaeology, University of California, Los Angeles.

2007   Las "casas" nobles de los barrios de Teotihuacan: Estructuras exclusionistas en un entorno corporativo. *Memoria 2007 de El Colegio Nacional, México*:453–470.

2009   Corporate Life in Apartment and Barrio Compounds at Teotihuacan, Central Mexico: Craft Specialization, Hierarchy, and Ethnicity. In *Domestic Life in Prehispanic Capitals: A Study of Specialization, Hierarchy, and Ethnicity*, edited by Linda R. Manzanilla and Claude Chapdelaine, pp. 21–42. Museum of Anthropology, University of Michigan, Ann Arbor.

2011   Sistemas de control de mano de obra y del intercambio de bienes suntuarios en el corredor teotihuacano hasta la costa del golfo en el Clásico. *Anales de antropología* 45:9–32.

Martínez Vargas, Enrique, and Ana María Jarquín Pacheco

1998   *Materiales arqueológicos del noroeste de Tlaxcala*. Instituto Nacional de Antropología e Historia, Mexico City.

McClung de Tapia, Emily

2009   Los ecosistemas del Valle de Teotihuacan a lo largo de su historia. In *Teotihuacan: Ciudad de los dioses*, pp. 37–45. Instituto Nacional de Antropología e Historia, Mexico City.

Millon, René

1967   Cronología y periodificación: Datos estratigráficos sobre períodos cerámicos y sus relaciones con la pintura mural. In *Teotihuacan: XI Mesa Redonda*, vol. 1, pp. 1–18. Sociedad Mexicana de Antropología, Mexico City.

1973   *Urbanization at Teotihucán, Mexico*, vol. 1, *The Teotihuacan Map*, pt. 1, *Text*. University of Texas Press, Austin.

1976   Social Relations in Ancient Teotihuacan. In *The Valley of Mexico: Studies in Pre-Hispanic Ecology and Society*, edited by Eric R. Wolf, pp. 205–248. University of New Mexico Press, Albuquerque.

1981   Teotihuacan: City, State, and Civilization. In *Supplement to the Handbook of Middle American Indians*, vol. 1, *Archaeology*, edited by Jeremy Sabloff, pp. 198–243. University of Texas Press, Austin.

1992   Teotihuacan Studies: From 1950 to 1990 and Beyond. In *Art, Ideology, and the City of Teotihuacan*, edited by Janet Catherine Berlo, pp. 339–429. Dumbarton Oaks Research Library and Collection, Washington, D.C.

Molina, Alonso de

2008 [1571]   *Vocabulario en lengua castellana y mexicana y mexicana y castellana*. Editorial Porrúa, Mexico City.

Múnera Bermúdez, Luis Carlos

1985   Un taller de cerámica ritual en la Ciudadela, Teotihuacan. Licentiate thesis, Escuela Nacional de Antropología e Historia, Mexico City.

Murakami, Tatsuya

2010   Power Relations and Urban Landscape Formation: A Study of Construction Labor and Resources at Teotihuacan. PhD dissertation, School of Human Evolution and Social Change, Arizona State University, Tempe.

Ortiz Butrón, Agustín, and Luis A. Barba Pingarrón

1993   La química en el estudio de áreas de actividad. In *Anatomía de un conjunto residencial teotihuacano en Oztoyahualco,* vol. 2, *Los estudios específicos*, edited by Linda Manzanilla, pp. 617–660. Universidad Nacional Autónoma de México, Mexico City.

Ostrom, Elinor, Roy Gardner, and James M. Walker

1997   Neither Markets nor States: Linking Transformation Processes in Collective Action Arenas. In *Perspectives on Public Choice: A Handbook*, edited by Dennis C. Mueller, pp. 35–72. Cambridge University Press, Cambridge.

Ostrom, Elinor, and James M. Walker (editors)

2003   *Trust and Reciprocity: Interdisciplinary Lessons from Experimental Research*. Russell Sage Foundation, New York.

Paredes Cetino, Rodrigo Néstor

2000   Vestigios culturales en "El Corzo" de la zona arqueológica de Teotihuacan. *Antropológicas* 17:79–86.

Pastrana, Alejandro, and Silvia Domínguez

2009   Cambios en la estrategia de la explotación de obsidiana de Pachuca: Teotihuacan, Tula y la Triple Alianza. *Ancient Mesoamerica* 20:129–148.

Paz Bautista, Clara

1996   El grupo 5, un conjunto de tres templos miccaotli-tlamimilolpa temprano en Teotihuacan. *Revista mexicana de estudios antropológicos* 42:109–120.

Plunket, Patricia, and Gabriela Uruñuela

2012   Where East Meets West: The Formative in Mexico's Central Highlands. *Journal of Archaeological Research* 20:1–51.

Ponamarenko, Alyson Lighthart

2004   The Pachuca Obsidian Source, Hidalgo, Mexico: A Geoarchaeological Perspective. *Geoarchaeology* 19:71–91.

Price, T. Douglas, Linda Manzanilla, and William D. Middleton

2000   Immigration and the Ancient City of Teotihuacan in Mexico: A Study Using Strontium Isotope Ratios in Human Bone and Teeth. *Journal of Archaeological Science* 27:903–913.

Rattray, Evelyn Childs

1990a   The Identification of Ethnic Affiliation at the Merchants' "Barrio," Teotihuacan. In *Etnoarqueología*, vol. 1, *Coloquio Pedro Bosch Gimpera*, edited by Yoko Suguira and Mari Carmen Serra Puche, pp. 113–138. Universidad Nacional Autónoma de México, Mexico City.

1990b   New Findings on the Origins of Thin Orange Ceramics. *Ancient Mesoamerica* 1:181–195.

1995   *The Oaxaca Barrio at Teotihuacan*. Instituto de Estudios Avanzados, Universidad de las Américas, Puebla.

2001   *Teotihuacan: Ceramics, Chronology, and Cultural Trends*. University of Pittsburgh, Pittsburgh, and Instituto Nacional de Antropología e Historia, Mexico City.

Robertson, Ian G.

2001   Mapping the Social Landscape of an Early Urban Center: Social-Spatial Variation in Teotihuacan. PhD dissertation, Department of Anthropology, Arizona State University, Tempe.

Rodríguez García, Ignacio

1991   Un modelo para la investigación arqueológica: A propósito del Gran Conjunto. In *Teotihuacan 1980–1982: Nuevas interpretaciones*, edited by Rubén Cabrera Castro, Ignacio Rodríguez García, and Noel Morelos García, pp. 377–385. Instituto Nacional de Antropología e Historia, Mexico City.

Rojas Rabiela, Teresa

1977   La organización del trabajo para las obras públicas: El coatequitl y las cuadrillas de trabajadores. In *El trabajo y los trabajadores en la historia de México*, edited by Elsa Cecilia Frost, Michael C. Meyer, Josefina Zoraida Vázquez, and Lilia Díaz, pp. 41–66. El Colegio de Mexico City, Mexico City, and University of Arizona Press, Tucson.

1986   El sistema de organización en cuadrillas. In *Origen y formación del estado en Mesoamérica*, edited by Andrés Medina, Alfredo López Austín, and Mari Carmen Serra Puche, pp. 135–150. Universidad Nacional Autónoma de México, Mexico City.

Rovira Morgado, Rossend

n.d.   Niveles de circulación económica en los barrios de Teotihuacan: Propuestas teóricas y métodos de análisis. *Tezontle*, in press.

Ruiz Gallut, María Elena, and Arturo Pascual Soto (editors)

2004   *La costa del golfo en tiempos teotihuacanos: Propuestas y perspectivas*. Instituto Nacional de Antropología e Historia, Mexico City.

Sanders, William T., Jeffrey Parsons, and Robert S. Santley

1979   *The Basin of Mexico: Ecological Processes in the Evolution of a Civilization*. Academic Press, New York.

Sanders, William T., and Robert S. Santley

1983   A Tale of Three Cities: Energetics and Urbanization in Pre-Hispanic Central Mexico. In *Prehistoric Settlement Patterns: Essays in Honor of Gordon R. Willey*, edited by Evon Vogt and Richard Leventhal, pp. 243–291. University of New Mexico Press, Albuquerque, and Peabody Museum of Archaeology and Ethnology, Harvard University, Cambridge, Mass.

Santley, Robert S.

1983   Obsidian Trade and Teotihuacan
        Influence in Mesoamerica. In *Inter-
        disciplinary Approaches to the Study of
        Highland-Lowland Interaction*, edited by
        Arthur Miller, pp. 69–124. Dumbarton
        Oaks Research Library and Collection,
        Washington, D.C.

2007   *The Prehistory of the Tuxtlas*. University
        of New Mexico Press, Albuquerque.

Schortman, Edward M., and Patricia A. Urban

2004   Modeling the Roles of Craft Production
        in Ancient Political Economies. *Journal
        of Archaeological Research* 12:185–226.

Séjourné, Laurette

1966   *Arqueología de Teotihuacan: La
        cerámica*. Fondo de Cultura Económica,
        Mexico City.

Sempowski, Martha L.

1994   Mortuary Practices at Teotihuacan.
        In *Mortuary Practices and Skeletal
        Remains at Teotihuacan*, by Martha L.
        Sempowski and Michael W. Spence,
        pp. 1–275. University of Utah Press,
        Salt Lake City.

Sharer, Robert J.

2003   Founding Events and Teotihuacan
        Connections at Copán, Honduras. In
        *The Maya and Teotihuacan: Reinterpret-
        ing Early Classic Interaction*, edited
        by Geoffrey E. Braswell, pp. 143–166.
        University of Texas Press, Austin.

Spence, Michael W.

1981   Obsidian Production and the State
        in Teotihuacan. *American Antiquity*
        46:769–788.

1986   Locational Analysis of Craft
        Specialization Areas in Teotihuacan.
        In *Research in Economic Anthropology*,
        supplement 2, *Economic Aspects of
        Prehispanic Highland Mexico*, edited
        by Barry L. Isaac, pp. 75–100. JAI Press,
        Greenwich, Conn.

1996   Commodity or Gift: Teotihuacan
        Obsidian in the Maya Region. *Latin
        American Antiquity* 7:21–39.

Spence, Michael W., Jerome Kimberlin, and Garman
Harbottle

1984   State-Controlled Procurement and the
        Obsidian Workshops of Teotihuacán,
        Mexico. In *Prehistoric Quarries and
        Lithic Production,* edited by Jonathan E.
        Ericson and Barbara A. Purdy, pp. 97–105.
        Cambridge University Press, Cambridge.

Spence, Michael W., Christine D. White, Evelyn
Childs Rattray, and Fred J. Longstaffe

2005   Past Lives in Different Places:
        The Origins and Relationships of
        Teotihuacan's Foreign Residents. In
        *Settlement, Subsistence, and Social
        Complexity: Essays Honoring the Legacy
        of Jeffrey R. Parsons*, edited by Richard
        E. Blanton, pp. 155–197. Cotsen Institute
        of Archaeology, University of California,
        Los Angeles.

Stark, Barbara L., Lynette Heller, and Michael A.
Ohnersorgen

1998   People with Cloth: Mesoamerican
        Economic Change from the Perspective
        of Cotton in South-Central Veracruz.
        Latin American Antiquity 9:7–36.

Sugiyama, Saburo

2002   Censer Symbolism and the State Polity
        in Teotihuacán. Electronic document,
        http://www.famsi.org/reports/97050/
        index.html, accessed December 17, 2010.

Sullivan, Kristin Susan

2005   Making and Manipulating Ritual in the
        City of the Gods: Figurine Production
        and Use at Teotihuacán, México. Elec-
        tronic document, http://www.famsi.
        org/reports/03021/index.html, accessed
        December 17, 2010.

2006   Specialized Production of San Martín
        Orange Ware at Teotihuacan, Mexico.
        Latin American Antiquity 17:23–53.

2007   Commercialization in Early State
        Economies: Craft Specialization and
        Market Exchange in Classic Period
        Teotihuacan. PhD dissertation, School
        of Human Evolution and Social Change,
        Arizona State University, Tempe.

Taube, Karl A.

2003   Tetitla and the Maya Presence at Teotihuacan. In *The Maya and Teotihuacan: Reinterpreting Early Classic Interaction*, edited by Geoffrey E. Braswell, pp. 273–314. University of Texas Press, Austin.

Tobler, Waldo

1993   *Three Representations of Geographical Analysis and Modeling.* National Center for Geographic Information and Analysis, Technical Report 93-1.

Trinidad Meléndez, Miguel Ángel

1996   Análisis lítico de una unidad habitacional en La Ventilla: Resultados preliminares. *Revista mexicana de estudios antropológicos* 42:49–61.

Uruñuela, Gabriela, and Patricia Plunket

2010   The Standardization of the Thin Orange Ceramic Tradition: The Formative to Classic Transition. Paper presented at the 75th Annual Meeting for the Society for American Archaeology, Saint Louis.

Vega Sosa, Constanza

1981   Comparaciones entre los Teteles de Ocotítla, Tlaxcala y Teotihuacan a través de materiales cerámicos. In *Interacción cultural en México central*, edited by Evelyn Childs Rattray, Jaime Litvak King, and Clara Díaz Oyarzábal, pp. 43–53. Universidad Nacional Autónoma de México, Mexico City.

Von Winning, Hasso

1987   *La iconografía de Teotihuacan: Los dioses y los signos,* vol. 1. Universidad Nacional Autónoma de México, Mexico City.

Webster, David

1996   Economic Differentiation, Stratification, and the Evolution of Complex Societies: A Teotihuacan Case Example. In *Homenaje a William T. Sanders,* vol. 1, edited by Alba Guadalupe Mastache, Jeffery Parsons, Robert S. Santley and Mari Carmen Serra Puche, pp. 111–134. Instituto Nacional de Antropología e Historia, Mexico City.

White, Christine D., Rebecca Storey, Fred J. Longstaffe, and Michael W. Spence

2004   Immigration, Assimilation, and Status in the Ancient City of Teotihuacan: Stable Isotopic Evidence from Tlajinga 33. *Latin American Antiquity* 15:176–198.

Widmer, Randolph J.

1996   Procurement, Exchange, and Production of Foreign Commodities at Teotihuacan: State Monopoly or Local Control? In *Homenaje a William T. Sanders*, vol. 1, edited by Alba Guadalupe Mastache, Jeffery Parsons, Robert S. Santley and Mari Carmen Serra Puche, pp. 271–279. Instituto Nacional de Antropología e Historia, Mexico City.

Wilk, Richard R., and Lisa C. Cliggett

2007   *Economies and Cultures: Foundations of Economic Anthropology.* 2nd ed. Westview Press, Boulder, Colo.

6

Negotiating Aztec Tributary Demands in the *Tribute Record of Tlapa*

GERARDO GUTIÉRREZ

L ATE POSTCLASSIC–PERIOD CENTRAL MEXICO
cannot be understood without a detailed analysis of the arrangements made by the Aztecs in
the conceptual triad of empire, tribute, and trade
(Hassig 1988). The Aztec Empire was created by
the military subjugation of many polities subsequently forced into economic relationships based
on the required periodic delivery of goods and
services (tribute). The realization of this master-
subject dynamic involved economic processes of
production, distribution (including transportation and storage), and consumption that affected
the economy of both the conqueror and the conquered. With each conquest, the ancient market
tradition of Central Mexico scaled up, as tribute
obligations often forced more exchange (Berdan
1994:306; Hassig 1985:109).[1] Aztec imperial economy
follows the Pre-Columbian principles of being conservative (absorbing preexisting political tributary
entities) and accumulative (increasing in scale), as
outlined in the introductory chapter of this volume
by Hirth and Pillsbury.

In addition, Aztec political expansion resulted
in the takeover of trade routes, which reduced the
risk of transporting goods across the empire and
facilitated the movement of items destined for small
and large marketplaces. Imperial tribute collectors
(*calpixque*), small peddlers (*tlapatlani*), and long-
distance traders (*pochteca*) all mobilized goods
using the same routes and village circuits, resting
and obtaining supplies in some places and buying
and selling items in others. It was inevitable that the
Aztec imperial *calpixque* would overlap with the
Aztec *pochteca,* and both *calpixque* and *pochteca*
with a myriad of local tribute collectors, regional
merchants, and local buyers and sellers.

Economically, tribute functioned as a sub-
sidy for the final recipients, who, by consuming
and redistributing it, stimulated many other sectors of the market and the political and ideological realms as well. Using the province of Tlapa as
a case study, this paper analyzes how tribute complemented and reinforced the Aztec economic system. The Aztec Empire marshaled vast quantities of

both staple and wealth finance. This financing was required by marketplaces for convertibility and to maintain a steady stream of goods into the political and economic system. The constant influx of goods stabilized rates of exchange and facilitated the acceptance of standard exchange units based on *quachtli*, or *mantas de tributo* (tributary cloth), cacao, and gold. Notably, the most complete lists of exchange values for all Mesoamerican goods come from tributary documents and not from market records. Here, I will analyze how tribute in kind was "negotiated" in the broadest sense by: 1) two parties conferring so as to arrive at an agreement on quantity and periodicity; and 2) converting the tribute into other goods. I will highlight those moments in which the Aztecs and their subjects likely negotiated the assessment, allocation, and collection of tribute.

Tributary obligations of the Aztec provinces have generally been assumed to be fixed in quantity as well as in the kind of goods delivered to the empire (Barlow 1949; Berdan 1992, 1994, 1996; Hassig 1985; Kobayashi 1993). Nonetheless, I will argue here that the tribute paid to the Aztecs was not static or fixed in quantity, quality, or type. Indeed, I underscore that one of the most obvious negotiations in the tributary system was the possibility of substituting or swapping tributary items for others of similar value. Evidence to support this proposal is derived from three sources: 1) the valuation system recorded in the *Información de 1554* (Rojas 1997; Scholes and Adams 1957), in which native informants provided exchange values for almost all tributary items given to the Aztec Empire in the abstract exchange unit of *mantas*; 2) the list of goods assessed as tribute to the Tlapa province according to Aztec tributary records; and 3) the list of goods given to the Aztecs according to the tributary tally created by the Tlapa province; here, I refer to the *Tribute Record of Tlapa*, the only known example of a province's record of tribute paid to the Aztec Empire (Gutiérrez et al. 2009a, 2009b).

I begin by presenting the basic operation of the Aztec tributary system, followed by a brief explanation of the structure, content, and way of reading the *Tribute Record of Tlapa*. Finally, I will convert into a *manta* standard all of the tribute demanded by the Aztecs from the Tlapa province as depicted in the *Matrícula de Tributos*, the Codex Mendoza, and the *Información de 1554,* and then compare these tallies with those reported in the *Tribute Record of Tlapa*. This exercise allows comparison of tributary demands by converting the goods into an abstract unit of exchange, in this case into *mantas*, thereby addressing variability in quantities and types of goods depicted in the four sources. The results of this comparison reveal the flexibility of the Aztec tributary system in converting or negotiating tributary goods using the same exchange values as those of the marketplaces. Contrasting these sources provides empirical evidence that: 1) the imperial tribute was always fluctuating and being adjusted; 2) the tributary items paid were not necessarily those depicted in the sources of Central Mexico as long as overall equivalence was maintained; 3) the tributary demands fostered specializations in the production of some goods; and 4) the Aztec tribute collector may have been engaged in complex processes of exchanging and swapping tributary goods as part of an intricate network between local lords, long-distance traders, and regional merchants. Finally, for the first time, an estimate of the logistical costs of maintaining an Aztec *calpixque* can be made, which I propose was on the order of 12 percent of the total tribute paid by the Tlapa province.

Some Aspects of the Aztec Tributary System

I refer to the Aztec Empire as the complex political-spatial entity created by the confederation of Tenochtitlan, Texcoco, and Tacuba, also known as the Triple Alliance (Barlow 1949; Berdan and Anawalt 1992; Carrasco 1999; Davies 1968, 1987; Matos Moctezuma 1988; Zantwijk 1985). Thus, the "Aztec people" is an abstraction referencing all nobles and commoners recognized as members of these three original *huey tlatocayotl* (large native dynastic states) that comprised the core of the empire. The Mexica-Tenochca people, the dominant political partner of the Aztec Empire, did not invent the tributary system of Central Mexico, since it had already been in place long before their arrival in the Basin of Mexico. As immigrants, the Mexica-Tenochca experienced the system first as tribute payers to the rulers of Colhuacan, and, later, to those of Azcapotzalco. Before the Aztecs coalesced into an empire, the typical tributary organization of the Postclassic period was structured at the local level, where each segment (*calpulli* or *tlaxilacalli*) of a political unit had at least one *tequitlato,* a local officer in charge of organizing all things related to tribute (Velasco 1958 [1562]:30). This *tequitlato* was responsible for allocating and collecting the tribute owed by each tributary unit, defined by a composite of houses and coresidents. Tributary units were variable in size and demographic structure (Cline 1993:103; Prem 1974), a fact that has complicated simple explanations of their operation. The tribute, or *tequitl,* was paid in goods (*tlacalaquilli*) or in labor (*coatequitl*) based on lists of tributaries, as detailed in the Morelos census of tributes, for example (Cline 1993). After the Aztecs experienced a successful program of political expansion, they created a network of political operators and tribute collectors to oversee the compliance of local lords to their demands (Kobayashi 1993:53). Imperial governors and *calpixque* operated with autonomy, living in the provinces with their family and a few retainers (Durán 1994 [1570–1581]:181).

Aztec provincial *calpixque* reported constantly to the *petlacalcatl,* or high steward in charge of the *petlacalco* (the main storage facility) of Tenochtitlan. Bernal Díaz del Castillo (1986 [1568]:168) vividly recalls how the *petlacalcatl* had a large house full of tribute books and was in charge of all accounting for the entire Aztec tributary system, recording everything in the vast archive of painted assessments and receipts. Tragically, this tributary library was "lost" during the conquest of Mexico, as Hernán Cortés puts it (1988 [1519–1526]:61), and thus, most of our knowledge about the structure of the Aztec tributary system is based on only three primary sources: 1) the *Matrícula de Tributos* (Reyes 1997); 2) the Codex Mendoza (Berdan and Anawalt 1992); and 3) the *Información sobre los tributos que*

los indios pagaban a Moctezuma, año 1554 (also known and referred to here as the *Información de 1554*) (Rojas 1997; Scholes and Adams 1957). All academic narratives of how the Aztec Empire operated have been constructed primarily from these three surviving tallies.

Problems in the Reconstruction of the Aztec Tributary System

It should be remembered that the *Matrícula de Tributos,* the Codex Mendoza, and the *Información de 1554* reflect the final state of tributary relationships on the eve of the Spanish conquest.[2] In other words, these documents offer no insight on how the tribute system was created and developed over time. Were the quantities depicted in these documents always the same after each place was conquered, or were there changes? What was the logic of taxation for each province, and under what circumstances did tribute vary? Since there are only three surviving sources, evaluating the veracity of their contents is difficult. The most serious problems for analyzing the tribute system of the Aztec Empire can be summarized in three points:

1) It is impossible to test the historical accuracy of the content and quantities listed as tribute in the three sources.
2) The ethnocentric narrative of the three sources silences the accounts of the presumably conquered peoples. Did the Aztec Empire conquer all of the places mentioned in these sources? Did these places, in fact, pay the tribute in the quantities and on the dates specified according to the Aztec sources?
3) The static nature of these tribute records does not allow for a diachronic study of the creation of and key moments in the evolution of the tribute system of the Aztec Empire.

Berdan (1992:63) has already noted that these problems cannot be answered solely from the three mentioned sources, and so listing the obvious weaknesses of these primary documents does not contribute much. It would be better to ask how we might mitigate these problems.

Archaeological investigations have greatly assisted in corroborating or detecting Aztec domination as well as understanding diachronic changes experienced by the economies of the conquered places (Brumfiel 1980; Nichols 1994). Unfortunately, in-depth studies have been restricted to just a few locales in the empire, particularly Morelos and the Valley of Mexico (Brumfiel 1987; Hodge and Minc 1991; Smith 1987, 1994), while for other distant provinces we continue to rely on Aztec documents. A possible solution to this problem would be the use of alternative sources, independent of the Aztecs, with the following requirements:

1) Records that detail the exact quantities and types of products paid and the frequency with which they were delivered.
2) Sources that have been created locally by the conquered province. This would eliminate doubts as to the veracity of Aztec domination and amend the Aztec ethnocentric vision.
3) Sources with information on annual tribute payments through time, beginning with the moment when the province was conquered.

Unfortunately, this type of record is not easily found. The only known surviving tally describing the payments made by a local province to the Aztecs is the *Tribute Record of Tlapa* (Gutiérrez et al. 2009b). Analysis of this record provides the singular opportunity to at least contrast the data from the Tlapa province with that of the Codex Mendoza, the *Matrícula de Tributos*, and the *Información de 1554*. The *Tribute Record of Tlapa* can aid in understanding the tribute system of the Aztec Empire from the perspective of a conquered province.

The *Tribute Record of Tlapa*

The *Tribute Record of Tlapa* is an indigenous tally depicting thirty-six years of tributary payments from the Tlapa province of eastern Guerrero to the Aztec Empire from 1486 to 1522. An extraordinary feature of this document is that it breaks down the annual fiscal obligations of the province into quarterly payments; therefore, a detailed study of changes in tributary demands required from this province is possible. The *Tribute Record of Tlapa* did not come to us as a single document. It is composed of two surviving fragments: the *Codex Azoyú 2-Reverse* and the *Codex Humboldt Fragment 1* (Gutiérrez et al. 2009a:57–61). The *Tribute Record* is organized into a kind of spreadsheet, and each tributary item can be located through a system of coordinates, depending on the position each element occupies with respect to the intersection of a particular column and row (Figure 6.1). The reading order is unidimensional (Boone 2000:61); in other words, it follows a preestablished order for each timeline and event. The *Tribute Record* is read from left to right and from bottom to top. The document is structured into a grid with five columns and one hundred forty-five rows. Each folio contains five rows with tributary entries (Gutiérrez et al. 2009a:65). The division of the columns begins with Row 2, using the nomenclature of letters from left to right, E, D, C, B, and A, as was done by Seler (1904) in his study of the *Codex Humboldt Fragment 1*. The rows are numbered from one (in Folio 1) to one hundred forty-five (in Folio 29). Hence, the grid contains seven hundred twenty cells (the intersection of five columns multiplied by one hundred forty-four rows), plus one row that is not segmented by the columns and forms a large cell across the width of the folio (a color reproduction of the *Tribute Record* can be consulted in Gutiérrez et al. 2009b).

The narrative of the *Tribute Record* is organized as a chronological guide for an annual cycle composed of four quarters: a group of four rows comprises a year of three hundred sixty days. Given that there are one hundred forty-four chronological rows, we are dealing with thirty-six years of tribute payments made by the Tlapa province to the Triple Alliance. The first tribute payment (Row 2) occurred during the festival of Tlacaxipehualiztli during the final quarter of the year 7 Deer (around February 22, 1487). Column A presents the passing of annual cycles, using the Type II year-bearer signs (Wind, Deer, Grass, Movement). Column B is used to refine

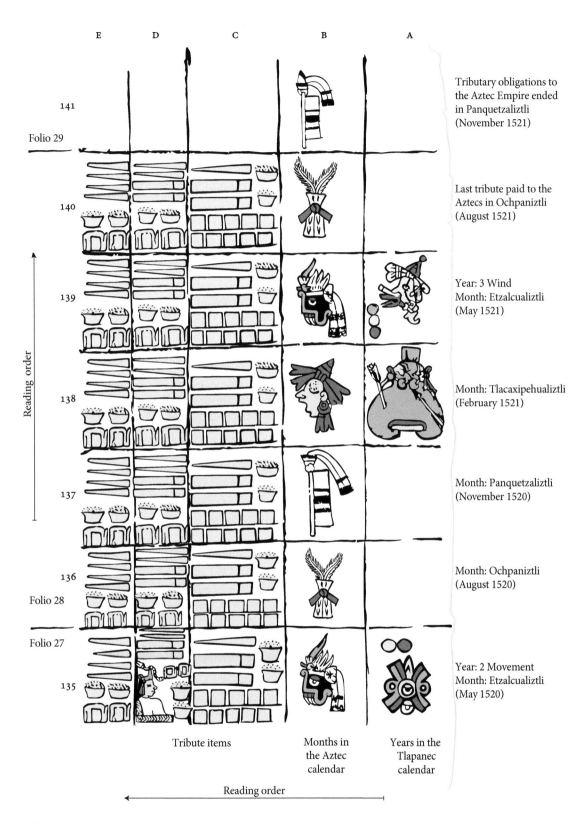

Column labels (top): E D C B A

141
Folio 29

Tributary obligations to
the Aztec Empire ended
in Panquetzaliztli
(November 1521)

140

Last tribute paid to the
Aztecs in Ochpaniztli
(August 1521)

139

Year: 3 Wind
Month: Etzalcualiztli
(May 1521)

138

Month: Tlacaxipehualiztli
(February 1521)

137

Month: Panquetzaliztli
(November 1520)

136
Folio 28

Month: Ochpaniztli
(August 1520)

Folio 27

135

Year: 2 Movement
Month: Etzalcualiztli
(May 1520)

Reading order

Tribute items

Months in
the Aztec
calendar

Years in the
Tlapanec
calendar

Reading order

figure 6.1

Tribute given to the Aztecs in the Tlapanec year 2 Movement (1520–1521), detail from Folios 27 and 28 of the
Tribute Record of Tlapa. (Illustrations by Gerardo Gutiérrez, after Gutiérrez et al. 2009b.)

Tlapa Cozcatepec Hueycatenango

Place names

Local rulers Local *calpixqui*

Aztec *calpixque* Aztec imperial governor

Tlacaxipehualiztli Etzalcualiztli Ochpaniztli Panquetzaliztli

Aztec months

Grass Earthquake Wind Deer

Tlapanec years: year bearers Type II.

figure 6.2
Some key pictorial elements in the *Tribute Record of Tlapa*. (Illustrations by Gerardo Gutiérrez.)

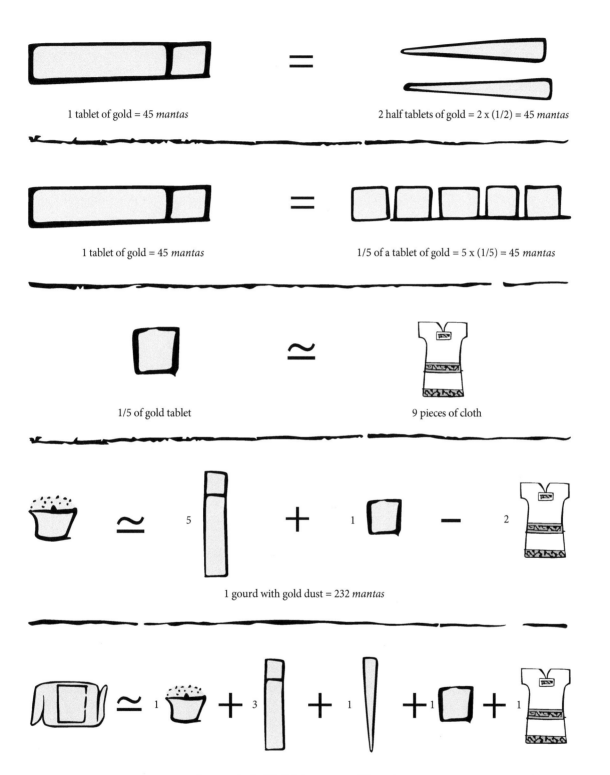

1 tablet of gold = 45 *mantas*

2 half tablets of gold = 2 x (1/2) = 45 *mantas*

1 tablet of gold = 45 *mantas*

1/5 of a tablet of gold = 5 x (1/5) = 45 *mantas*

1/5 of gold tablet

9 pieces of cloth

1 gourd with gold dust = 232 *mantas*

1 *cempoalquimilli* of plain *mantas* = 400 *mantas*

figure 6.3

Interpretations of the quantities of tributary goods and their equivalents in the *Tribute Record of Tlapa*.
(Illustrations by Gerardo Gutiérrez.)

the chronological scale by dividing each year into four quarters (Figure 6.2). Each row is accompanied by one of the following glyphs: Tlacaxipehualiztli, Etzalcualiztli, Ochpaniztli, Panquetzaliztli. These glyphs mark the four major festivals of the indigenous calendar and, at the same time, define four months of the annual calendar of eighteen months. Columns C, D, and E depict items given in tribute, which gradually increases in quantity over the years. The only items shown in these columns are gold and bundles of cloth. Gold is depicted in one of two ways—as tablets of different sizes[3] or as gourds filled with gold dust (Figure 6.3).[4]

Practice and Historicity of the Aztec Tributary System from the Perspective of the Subject Tlapa Province

In multiple passages, Durán (1994 [1570–1581]) reports how local lords and commoners who initially opposed the Aztecs quickly became supplicants once they perceived their chances of surviving an armed conflict were low. Surrender to the Aztecs involved a complex series of ceremonies in which the conquered accepted the domination of the Aztec king and the supremacy of the Aztec tribal god (Huitzilopochtli) and agreed to give tribute to the Aztecs. The defeated people typically volunteered an instant quota of tribute goods to appease the immediate fury of Aztec armies. Unfortunately, none of Durán's plates capture this seemingly

common ceremony of capitulation; however, the very first row of the *Tribute Record of Tlapa* does depict such a ceremony of local rulers submitting to the Aztec Empire (Figure 6.4). The scene presents four individuals, each in different attire. Two of them are shown wearing turquoise diadems (*xihuitzolli*), and are seated on *petate* thrones (*petlaicpalli*), which identify them as dynastic rulers of Tlapa-Tlachinollan. The other two individuals are depicted with hairstyles characteristic of officials in charge of tribute allocation and collection, or *calpixque*. The Aztec *calpixque*, on the far right, is shown in rich dress with a red stole around his neck; the stole drapes behind him and seemingly holds a large flag. The other tribute collector, a Tlapanec (third from left), is dressed more simply: he wears a white tunic with a turquoise border along the hem of his garment.

Another important image here is the mountain decorated with a rhomboidal net of black lines. In the center of the mountain, a red circle has been painted, and below it there is a throne draped with a jaguar skin. The red circle within the mountain is the toponym for Tlapa (Gutiérrez and Medina 2008:88), and the entire glyph makes reference to the seat of authority of Tlapa-Tlachinollan, an ancient and powerful Tlapanec-Mixtec realm (Gutiérrez 2002). This scene indicates that in the year 7 Deer (at the end of 1486), the Aztec *calpixqui*[5] fixed the value of tribute for the *altepetl* of Tlapa, together with its subject pueblos (Gutiérrez et al. 2009a:67). The Tlapanec *calpixqui*, named Rain,

Folio 1, Row 1

Tlapanec rulers   Tlapanec *calpixqui*   *Altepetl* of Tlapa   Aztec *calpixqui*

figure 6.4
Ceremony of subordination of the lords of Tlapa to the Aztec Empire (after Gutiérrez et al. 2009b). Note the rich attire of the Aztec *calpixqui*. (Illustrations by Gerardo Gutiérrez.)

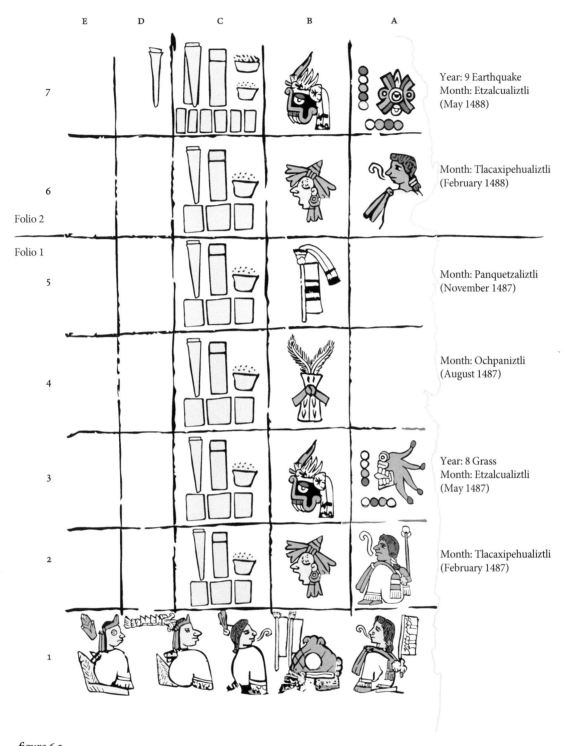

	E	D	C	B	A
7					Year: 9 Earthquake Month: Etzalcualiztli (May 1488)
6					Month: Tlacaxipehualiztli (February 1488)

Folio 2

Folio 1

	E	D	C	B	A
5					Month: Panquetzaliztli (November 1487)
4					Month: Ochpaniztli (August 1487)
3					Year: 8 Grass Month: Etzalcualiztli (May 1487)
2					Month: Tlacaxipehualiztli (February 1487)
1					

figure 6.5

First year of tributary obligations, from Folio 1 of the *Tribute Record of Tlapa*. (Illustrations by Gerardo Gutiérrez, after Gutiérrez et al. 2009b.)

submitted to these terms, which were solemnly witnessed by the ruler of Tlapa-Tlachinollan, Lord Turquoise Serpent (Xiuhcoatl), and his dynastic successor, Lord Jilote (Xilomantzin) (Vega Sosa 1991:84–85). The occurrence of a ceremony of submission documented in the local tributary document reaffirms the credibility of the Aztec sources, at least with reference to the fact that Tlapa historically accepted Aztec domination. After this scene of submission, subsequent images inform us that an Aztec *calpixqui*, as richly attired as the previous one, arrived in Tlapa to receive the first tribute payment during the festival of Tlacaxipehualiztli (around February 22, 1487) (see Figure 6.5, Column A, Row 2, Folio 1; Gutiérrez et al. 2009b).[6]

The first tributary assessment does not appear to have been extreme; during the Tlapanec year 8 Grass (1487–1488), only four gourds of gold dust and 8.4 tablets of gold were paid—the equivalent of 1,306 pieces of cloth (the amount of tribute presented when adding the quantities depicted in Rows 3, 4, 5, and 6 in Figure 6.5). This might suggest it was a relatively easy war with a quick surrender. Notably, Durán does not elaborate on

the conquest of Tlapa, although he does mention the Tlapanec prisoners who were sacrificed during Ahuitzotl's dedication of the Great Temple of Tenochtitlan (Durán 1994 [1570–1581]:235).[7] In the third week of February of 1508 (Column A, Row 86, Folio 18; Gutiérrez et al. 2009b), a *tlacatecatl,* or provincial governor, from Tenochtitlan was assigned to Tlapa, an action that signals the growing importance of this province (Figure 6.6). It appears that this provincial governor lived in Tlapa until his death in February of 1519, when he is depicted in his mortuary bundle (Column A, Row 130, Folio 26; Gutiérrez et al. 2009b). This suggests that Aztec provincial governors could remain in their positions for life, since this particular individual seems to have lived in Tlapa for eleven years. The historical prologue at the opening of the tributary tally highlights the ideological importance of the submission ceremony. In Mesoamerican worldview, acceptance of dominion was the most relevant part of the conquest, and the subsequent tribute to be paid was a necessary consequence of accepting a subordinate position (Durán 1994 [1570–1581]:212).

figure 6.6
Appointment of the Aztec imperial governor in February of 1508, Column A, Row 86, Folio 18 of the *Tribute Record of Tlapa*. (Illustrations by Gerardo Gutiérrez, after Gutiérrez et al. 2009b.)

Exchangeability of Tributary Obligations: The Tlapa Province According to the Four Sources

According to the Codex Mendoza and the *Matrícula de Tributos*, the Tlapa province at the moment of the Spanish conquest consisted of fourteen towns: Tlapa, Xocotla, Ichcateopan, Amaxac, Ahuacatla, Acocozpan, Yoallan, Ocoapan, Huitzamola, Acuitlapan, Malinaltepec, Totomixtlahuacan, Tetenanco, and Chiepetlan. With respect to the amount of tribute the province was expected to pay, there are some discrepancies in the glosses between the *Matrícula de Tributos*, the Codex Mendoza, and the *Información de 1554* (Table 6.1). The *Matrícula de Tributos*, considered the oldest document of the three, states that the Tlapa province gave the following annual tribute to the Triple Alliance (Figure 6.7): 1) eight hundred gourds; 2) two warrior costumes with shields; 3) ten bars[8] of gold; 4) twenty *tecomates* (gourd containers) of gold dust; 5) four hundred women's garments (*huipiles*); 6) four hundred items of cloth decorated with stripes; and 7) eight hundred items of plain cloth (*tilmas*). The glosses of the *Matrícula de Tributos* clarify that the warrior costumes were given once a year, while the textiles were given every eighty days. It does not specify the interval of time between the deliveries of gold bars or *tecomates* with gold dust.

The Codex Mendoza presents exactly the same tribute items; however, the glosses specify that the textiles were delivered every six months. The two warrior costumes with shields, the ten tablets of gold, and the gourds of gold dust were delivered only once a year (Berdan and Anawalt 1992). When referring to the textiles, the glosses of the Codex Mendoza depict larger quantities—interpretations of these glosses have the Tlapa province delivering sixteen hundred "loads" of cloth every six months, each load consisting of twenty individual items of cloth. If this reading is correct, the total tribute in textiles for the province would have been sixty-four thousand items annually, which seems excessive; I argue that the glosses of the Codex Mendoza were incorrect in their depiction of textile quantities paid in tribute (Berdan 1980, 1992). As previously mentioned, the glosses of the *Matrícula de Tributos* note that the textile tribute comprised only four bundles of four hundred individual items, with four such bundles delivered every eighty days—in total, sixty-four hundred individual cloth items per year—only a tenth of what the Codex Mendoza describes.

The *Información of 1554* reported that the Tlapa province gave Tenochtitlan almost exactly what was painted in the Codex Mendoza and *Matrícula de Tributos* with, however, the addition of other items not mentioned in the other two

table 6.1

The amounts recorded in the four tributary sources, by type of tribute item

ITEM/SOURCE	MATRÍCULA DE TRIBUTOS	CODEX MENDOZA	INFORMACIÓN DE 1554	TRIBUTE RECORD OF TLAPA
GOLD TABLETS	10	10	10	38
GOURDS OF GOLD DUST	20	20	20	24
ITEMS OF CLOTH	6,400	64,000	3,200	6,400
WARRIOR COSTUMES	2	2	2	0
SHIELDS	2	2	2	0
TECOMATES	800	1,600	400	0
CAKES OF RUBBER	0	0	2,000	0
HUMAN FIGURES OF RUBBER	0	0	400	0

figure 6.7

Tribute paid by the Tlapa province, from Plate 10r of the *Matrícula de Tributos*. (Illustrations by Gerardo Gutiérrez.)

table 6.2

The amounts Tlapa reported having paid to the Aztecs for the Tlapanec year 2 Movement (1520–1521) (see also Figure 6.1, Rows 135–138 of the *Tribute Record of Tlapa* [Gutiérrez et al. 2009b])

FOLIO	ROW	TLAPANEC YEAR	FESTIVAL	GOURDS OF GOLD DUST	GOLD TABLETS	PLAIN CLOTH[1]	DECORATED CLOTH
27	135	2 Movement	Etzalcualiztli	6	9.5	4	0
28	136	2 Movement	Ochpaniztli	6	9.5	4	0
28	137	2 Movement	Panquetzaliztli	6	9.5	4	0
28	138	2 Movement	Tlacaxipehualiztli	6	9.5	4	0
			Totals	24	38.0	16	0

1 In this year they gave only plain cloth, which we assume consisted of bundles containing four hundred individual items.

sources. According to the native witnesses, Tlapa delivered the following each year: 1) two richly decorated warrior costumes; 2) two richly decorated shields; 3) ten pieces of gold with the thickness of adobe bricks; 4) twenty *tecomates* of gold dust; 5) four hundred *tecomates*; 6) two thousand cakes of rubber; and 7) four hundred human forms made of rubber to offer to the idols. This same document also states that Tlapa delivered eight hundred items of cloth every eighty days. This would equal only thirty-two hundred items of cloth each year, half that stated in the *Matrícula de Tributos* and one-twentieth of that noted in the glosses of the Codex Mendoza. In addition to the items listed above, Tlapa delivered daily "a great number of chickens" (turkeys), as many as requested. This last item perhaps went directly toward the maintenance of the provincial governor.

I now turn to an analysis of the materials and quantities that Tlapa gave to the Triple Alliance, according to its local record, so as to understand the historicity of these changes. Of course, the local record is likely to express the interests of the local polity; thus, the *Tribute Record of Tlapa* may contain biases as to what materials and quantities were given. Table 6.2 shows what Tlapa reported having paid to the Aztecs for the Tlapanec year 2 Movement (1520–1521) (Figure 6.1, Rows 135–138).

The twenty-four gourds of gold dust correspond to the twenty reported in the Aztec tribute records (Table 6.1). Such is not the case for the gold tablets, where it seems the Aztecs demanded only ten, while the Tlapanecs report having given thirty-eight. I have argued elsewhere that the tablets depicted in the *Tribute Record of Tlapa* are of equal size to those depicted in the Codex Mendoza (62.5 centimeters in length by 7 centimeters in width, with a thickness averaging 1.5 millimeters, containing 1.266 kilograms of gold per tablet [Gutiérrez et al. 2009a:73–81]), and, therefore, the Tlapanecs are claiming that in 1520, they paid thirty-eight gold tablets to the Triple Alliance, which would equal 48.1 kilograms of gold.

The number of textiles reported in the *Tribute Record of Tlapa* coincides with the Aztec documents—sixteen bundles per year—but textiles are not accompanied by any numerical symbol to indicate how many *mantas* are contained in each bundle. Assuming each bundle held four hundred individual items, according to the *Matrícula de Tributos*, there would have been an annual tribute of sixty-four hundred items of cloth.[9] With respect to the qualitative attributes of the textiles, there exists an important difference between the sources of Central Mexico and the *Tribute Record of Tlapa*. According to the Aztecs, Tlapa was paying decorated cloth as well as plain cloth—not so, according to the *Tribute Record*. Decorated cloth was paid in tribute only between the years 1511 and 1514. After these dates, and until the last payment,

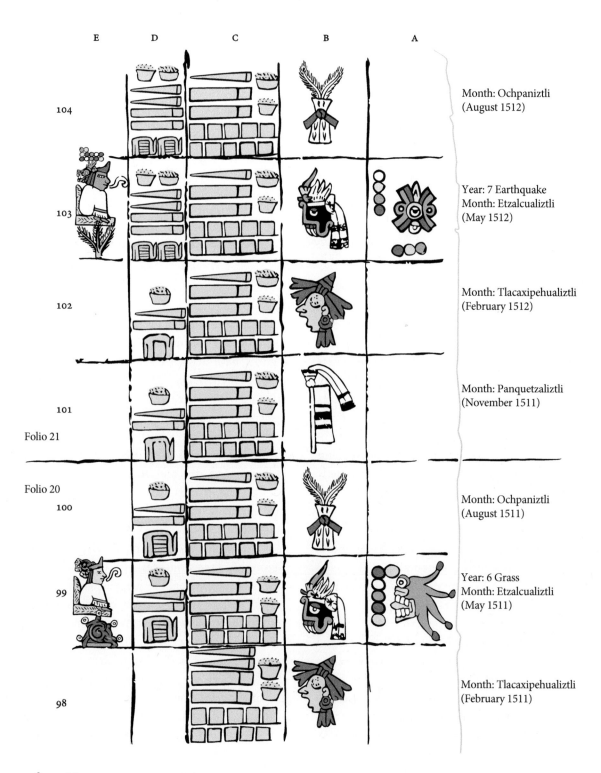

E D C B A

104   Month: Ochpaniztli
(August 1512)

103   Year: 7 Earthquake
Month: Etzalcualiztli
(May 1512)

102   Month: Tlacaxipehualiztli
(February 1512)

101   Month: Panquetzaliztli
(November 1511)

Folio 21

Folio 20

100   Month: Ochpaniztli
(August 1511)

99   Year: 6 Grass
Month: Etzalcualiztli
(May 1511)

98   Month: Tlacaxipehualiztli
(February 1511)

figure 6.8
Annexations of the realms of Lord Jaguar (Column E, Row 99, Folio 20) and Lord 12 Deer (Column E, Row 103, Folio 21) in the *Tribute Record of Tlapa*. (Illustrations by Gerardo Gutiérrez, after Gutiérrez et al. 2009b.) Note the increase in tribute for the whole province, but also note the reduction of one-half a gold tablet from Column C between Rows 98 to 99, while Column D presents new tribute.

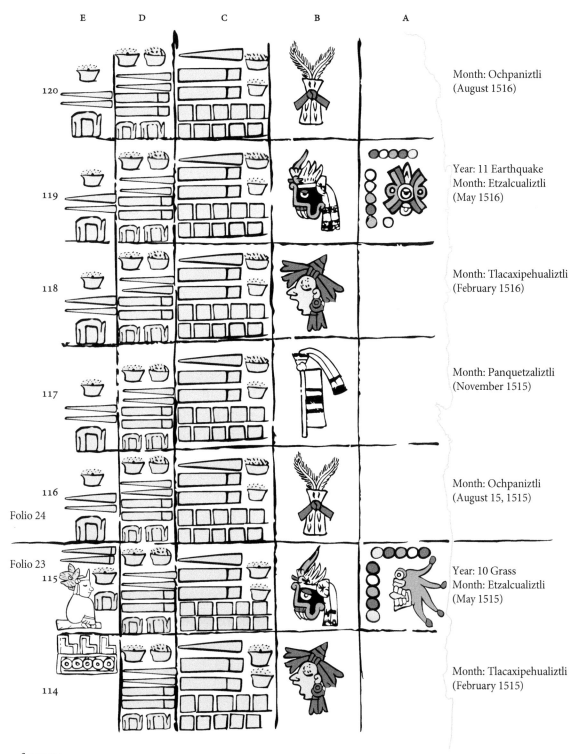

Columns (left to right): E, D, C, B, A

Row 120 — Month: Ochpaniztli (August 1516)

Row 119 — Year: 11 Earthquake / Month: Etzalcualiztli (May 1516)

Row 118 — Month: Tlacaxipehualiztli (February 1516)

Row 117 — Month: Panquetzaliztli (November 1515)

Row 116 — Month: Ochpaniztli (August 15, 1515)

Folio 24

Folio 23

Row 115 — Year: 10 Grass / Month: Etzalcualiztli (May 1515)

Row 114 — Month: Tlacaxipehualiztli (February 1515)

figure 6.9

Annexation of the realm of Lord Rabbit of Hueycatenango, Column E, Row 115, Folio 24 of the *Tribute Record of Tlapa*. (Illustrations by Gerardo Gutiérrez, after Gutiérrez et al. 2009b.) Note the increase in tribute for the whole province, but also note that Column C depicts the same tribute from Rows 114 to 115. Column D shows an increase in tribute, and Column E is used for the first time to present tribute.

Tlapa only paid in plain cloth (Figure 6.8). This fact leads me to believe that after 1514, payment in decorated cloth was modified, and only plain cloth was paid through some type of negotiation. In effect, note that in 1515 the *Tribute Record* depicts increases in all categories of tribute, but the decorated cloth tribute has disappeared (Figure 6.9). This remarkable detail sheds light on the flexibility of the Aztecs' tribute collection: perhaps deals were cut on the spot based on perceived or actual resistance, albeit masked as respectful requests, from their subjects.

The Value of Tribute in Cloth

With the objective of visualizing the differences between the sources, I now reduce the various kinds of articles into a single, comparable medium of exchange. I will use the conversion factor of *mantas* as reported in the *Información de 1554* for the Tlapa province, according to Table 6.3 (see also Figure 6.3), and I will refer to the converted quantity as "*manta*-equivalents."

After performing this exercise (Table 6.4), one can see that the Codex Mendoza is the only source with a significantly different total value of tribute paid annually by the Tlapa province. I highlight once again the extraordinary quantities documented in the Codex Mendoza based on a literal interpretation of its glosses and the discrepancy between it and the other Aztec sources, and the *Tribute Record of Tlapa*. Instead, if one ignores the Codex Mendoza's glosses with regard to textiles (Berdan 1992), and one assigns a value of four hundred items to each of the bundle of cloth glyphs depicted in Folio 39r, the total 69,000 *mantas* would be reduced to 12,100 *mantas* and would then coincide with the totals from the other sources.

It is also interesting that in 1520 the province says it delivered at least sixteen hundred more *mantas* than what was documented in the *Matrícula de Tributos* and the *Información de 1554*. This seems strange: if the Tlapanecs are playing with the numbers for some political reason, why would a province consciously inflate their tribute payments, knowing that the Spaniards could then use this exaggerated tribute record as a basis for demanding higher colonial taxes? Perhaps the Tlapa record documents the total payments made by the province to the Aztec *calpixqui*, including the *calpixqui*'s personal demands and other local administrative costs. I believe the *Matrícula de Tributos* is only depicting what was actually delivered to the imperial coffers in the *petlacalco* of Tenochtitlan and not the total payment made by the province, for which a series of costs must be subtracted, the most notable being the maintenance for the *calpixqui* and his household.[10] If this were the case, then one could infer that the operating costs for the Aztec

table 6.3

Conversion formulas for tributary items given by Tlapa province, according to the *Información de 1554*

1 gold tablet = 45 *mantas*
10 gold tablets = 450 items of cloth
1 item of cloth = 1 peso of common gold (during the early years after the Conquest)
1 warrior costume = 112.5 *mantas* (highly variable, example taken from Tlalcozauhtitlan, Guerrero)
1 shield = 112.5 *mantas* (example taken from Tlalcozauhtitlan, Guerrero)
1 gourd of gold dust = 232 *mantas*
10 *tecomates* for drinking cacao = 1 *manta*
1 cake of rubber = 0.05 *mantas*
1 human figure of rubber = 8 *mantas*

table 6.4

Tribute given by Tlapa for the year 1520, standardized into items of cloth (*mantas*)

ITEM/SOURCE	MATRÍCULA DE TRIBUTOS	CODEX MENDOZA	INFORMACIÓN DE 1554	TRIBUTE RECORD OF TLAPA
GOLD TABLETS	450	450	450	1,710
GOURDS OF GOLD DUST	4,640	4,640	4,640	5,568
ITEMS OF CLOTH	6,400	64,000	3,200	6,400
WARRIOR COSTUMES	225	225	225	0
SHIELDS	225	225	225	0
TECOMATES	80	160	40	0
CAKES OF RUBBER	0	0	100	0
HUMAN FIGURES OF RUBBER	0	0	3,200	0
TOTAL IN *MANTAS*	12,020	69,700	12,080	13,678

calpixque in Tlapa would be on the order of 12 percent of the total tribute delivered by the province. I would further note that this figure is close to the 10 percent that the *tepantlato* (litigant attorney) was given from tribute for performing a good job in the native court system (Sahagún 1961:37). If other sources confirm the existence of this kind of remuneration for provincial *calpixque*, then we should begin taking this into account when analyzing other native tallies. Otherwise, our studies will overlook the hidden costs of administering tributary networks that were becoming more logistically complex over time.

Perhaps most revealing is that the *Tribute Record of Tlapa* does not document items that imperial sources maintain they received from this province, specifically finely decorated warrior costumes and shields, *tecomates* for consuming cacao, cakes of rubber, rubber in the shape of human figures, and daily "chickens"; however, it does document the delivery of more tablets of gold and gourds filled with gold dust than the Central Mexican sources. I do not believe this is a scribal mistake; on the contrary, I suggest this discrepancy represents acceptable negotiated flexibility in the operations of imperial tribute. Despite the "missing" products, the amount given in tribute (translated into the value of *mantas*) fulfills and exceeds the expected

tribute payment to the Triple Alliance. The extra tablets and gold dust may have compensated for the sumptuary objects, which, in theory, the province was supposed to provide.

I would further propose that these sumptuary products (perhaps actually demanded by the *petlacalco* of Tenochtitlan) were acquired in other provinces through exchange or, more likely, through the great regional markets of Central Mexico. These exchanges may have been done by the local Tlapanec *tequitlato*, but perhaps the Aztec *calpixque* was also involved in these conversions of tribute items, since they would be in a key position to contact *calpixque* in other provinces to assist in swapping tributary goods. This is an area of research that requires further study, since the Spanish *granjería*, or "working of the tribute," may not have been a European introduction as has been interpreted (Miranda 1952:35) but rather had a pre-Hispanic prototype. The concept of "working of the tribute" meant the taking of some tribute in kind (*tlacalaquilli*) from a coastal pueblo (for instance, raw cotton), and transporting it (using the tribute in labor of a second pueblo located in the piedmont) to a third pueblo in the highlands to be woven into *mantas* (again using tribute in labor [*coatequitl*] owed by the third pueblo). Once the *mantas* were woven, they were taken to the market to acquire other products. With each exchange, there was always an attempt to multiply the value of the item (Patch 1994:95) (see the existence of a pre-Hispanic concept for profit in Hirth, this volume). One document from the early colonial period indicates that this practice took place among the natives in specific situations. In a particular case documented in the *Codex of Tepeucila*, the *caciques* and *tequitlato* of the pueblo had to borrow forty-five pesos of gold from the *pochteca* of Mexico and Texcoco to pay their tribute. The interest asked from the *pochteca* of Central Mexico was at least 100 percent, so the Indians of Tepeucila promised to pay double the borrowed gold (Herrera Meza and Ruíz Medrano 1997:33). Tepeucila borrowed constantly from the *pochteca* of Mexico and Texcoco from 1535 to 1540, to a point where they fell behind in their repayments. It is reported that one hundred *pochteca* from Central Mexico were sent to Tepeucila to collect the debt, chasing the *cacique* and *principales* out of town (Herrera Meza and Ruíz Medrano 1997:36).

One wonders if such arrangements like this existed in the late Aztec period between Aztec *calpixque* and *pochteca* with local rulers and *tequitlatoque*. It suggests, for example, that there were standardized practices whereby some type of *mantas* from one area of the empire, considered desirable elsewhere, were produced in higher quantities than what was actually owed in tribute, but the extras were taken to other provinces by Aztec *pochteca* or other merchants to be exchanged with local *tequitlatoque* for other items in order to pay the specific tribute owed to the Aztec *calpixque*. With this exchange mechanism, even *mantas* and goods awarded to valiant warriors could have found their way to distant provinces, recycled into the tributary system as a kind of incipient mercantile venture. A celebrated case of economic enterprise was reported when Ahuitzotl gave sixteen hundred *mantas* to the *pochteca* of Tenochtitlan and Tlatelolco to be traded along the southern frontier of the empire for precious stones and other rare products not found in Central Mexico (Sahagún 1959:7–8).

Transformations in the Tribute History of the Province of Tlapa

According to data reported by the *Información de 1554*, on the eve of the Spanish conquest, Tlapa paid a tribute equivalent to 12,080 *mantas* (some 1.9 percent of the total Aztec revenue reported in that source). This is an enormous increase from the original assessment of 1,306 *manta*-equivalents reported for 1487 by the *Tribute Record of Tlapa*. Since tribute is the material manifestation of a dominate-subordinate relationship, changes in assessments indicate moments of tension and negotiation. Thus, it is revealing to analyze specific historical transformations in the ever-changing master-subject bond by assessing variations in tributary demands.

I have calculated the cumulative total of thirty-six years of tribute paid by Tlapa to the Aztec Empire to have included 390 gourds with gold dust and 759.8 tablets of gold. They would have also delivered some 117 bundles of cloth, equaling 46,800 individual cloth items (assuming each bundle contained four hundred items). All of these goods, translated into the standardized unit of *mantas*, equal 171,471 *manta*-equivalents, and so this would have been the total tribute paid by Tlapa from 1487 to 1522 (Table 6.5).

I estimate that over these thirty-six years of Aztec domination, the tribute requirement for the Tlapa province increased by 947 percent, beginning in 1487 with the original tribute valued at 1,306 *manta*-equivalents (four gourds of gold dust and 8.4 tablets of beaten gold), which ended in 1520 with a tribute of 13,678 *manta*-equivalents (twenty-four gourds of gold dust, thirty-nine tablets of beaten gold, and sixteen bundles of cloth) (Figures 6.10–6.11).

The most significant increases in tribute occurred at seven key moments. First, with the original assessment of four gourds of gold dust and 8.4 tablets of beaten gold (standardized to 1,306 *manta*-equivalents) in 1487, when the tributary relationship imposed by conquest began. Second, in 1488, the tributary demand increased to seven gourds of gold dust and 11.7 tablets of beaten gold

table 6.5

Standardization in *mantas* for each item given in tribute by Tlapa per year

YEAR	VALUE OF GOURDS IN *MANTAS*	VALUE OF GOLD TABLETS IN *MANTAS*	VALUE OF ITEMS OF CLOTH IN *MANTAS*	ANNUAL VALUE OF TRIBUTE IN *MANTAS*
1487	928	378	0	1,306
1488	1,624	526.5	0	2,150.5
1489	1,856	636.75	0	2,492.75
1490	1,856	657	0	2,513
1491	1,856	677.25	0	2,533.25
1492	1,856	738	0	2,594
1493	1,856	738	0	2,594
1494	1,856	738	0	2,594
1495	1,856	738	0	2,594
1496	1,856	738	0	2,594
1497	1,856	738	0	2,594
1498	1,856	738	0	2,594
1499	1,856	798.75	0	2,654.75
1500	1,856	819	0	2,675
1501	1,856	819	0	2,675
1502	1,856	819	0	2,675
1503	1,856	819	0	2,675
1504	1,856	879.75	0	2,735.75
1505	1,856	900	0	2,756
1506	1,856	900	0	2,756
1507	1,856	900	0	2,756
1508	1,856	900	0	2,756
1509	1,856	900	0	2,756
1510	1,856	900	0	2,756
1511	2,552	1,035	1,200	4,787
1512	3,480	1,282.5	2,800	7,562.5
1513	3,712	1,350	3,200	8,262
1514	3,712	1,350	3,200	8,262
1515	4,408	1,485	4,400	10,293
1516	4,640	1,530	4,800	10,970
1517	4,640	1,530	4,800	10,970
1518	4,640	1,530	4,800	10,970
1519	5,568	1,710	6,400	13,678
1520	5,568	1,710	6,400	13,678
1521	4,176	1,282.5	4,800	10,258.5
TOTALS	90,480	34,191	46,800	171,471

figure 6.10
Yearly increments of each type of tribute item. (Illustration by Gerardo Guriérrez.)

figure 6.11
Historical trend of the tributary obligations of the Tlapa province by year. (Illustration by Gerardo Guriérrez.)

(standardized to 2,150 *manta*-equivalents), which was a 64 percent increase and might represent the actual assessment assigned directly from the *petla-calcatl*, or high steward in charge of the *petlacalco* of Tenochtitlan. As mentioned previously, in some reported cases, once a province surrendered to the Aztec armies, temporary tribute was assigned on the spot until the actual tribute was assessed by Tenochtitlan after more ceremonies of submission were performed. Third, from 1489 to 1492, tribute was increased almost every year but only in small amounts equivalent to half a tablet of gold (some twenty to twenty-five *manta*-equivalents). Overall, the tribute was increased 20 percent from some 2,150 to 2,593 *manta*-equivalents. This cycle of small increments is followed by seven years of stability (no increases).

A fourth cycle of small yearly increments begins in 1499 and ends in 1505. The increases for all tribute of this period can be calculated as 6 percent, from 2,594 to 2,756 *manta*-equivalents. The year 1502 marks the succession of Moctezuma II to *huey tlatoani*, but this seems not to have greatly affected the tributary demands of Tlapa. The situation worsened for Tlapa in 1511, when there were large increases in the demand for gourds with gold dust and gold tablets. Besides this, the province was requested for the first time to provide tribute in cloth, beginning with three bundles per year. The increase is dramatic—a 73 percent increase (from 2,756 to 4,787 *manta*-equivalents). A similar increase occurred during the years 1512 and 1513, with a composite raise of 72.6 percent (from 4,787 to 8,262 *manta*-equivalents). These higher demands are likely associated with the enlargement of the tributary base through the annexation of defeated lords to the Tlapa province. Specifically, the realms of Lord Jaguar in 1511 (Column E, Row 99, Folio 20) and Lord 12 Deer in 1512 (Column E, Row 103, Folio 21) are listed as new tributaries (see Figure 6.8). This information indicates that tributary "provinces" were not static and could grow (and perhaps also decrease) in a modular fashion, leading to reassessments in the tribute load. Who received the credit for the annexation of newly defeated local polities? Perhaps the imperial

governor, local lords, or local armies directed by a small detachment of Aztec warriors in the same way later Spanish forces operated.

During the year 1515, Lord Rabbit of Hueycatenango was also annexed to the province (Figure 6.9), and thus a new tributary assessment was added to the previous tribute. This time the tribute was augmented from 8,262 to 10,293 *manta*-equivalents, an increase of 24.5 percent, indicating that the Aztec Empire, including its provinces, was still growing. If the Aztecs calculated their tributary demands based on the number of household-families under the command of a local lord, given a formula of one tribute payer equaling one *manta* yearly, then we might assume that at the time of the forced incorporation of Hueycatenango into the Tlapa province, Lord Rabbit, ruler of Hueycatenango, brought with him some two thousand commoners; this speculation is likely simplistic but still sheds light on demographics and tribute.

Finally, the last phase of tributary demands occurs from 1516 until the siege of Tenochtitlan. Without any apparent explanation (such as the annexation of new lords), tribute was increased first to an estimated equivalent of 10,970 *manta*-equivalents and then jumped to 13,678 *manta*-equivalents in 1519, a combined increase of 32.8 percent. In relative numbers this increase might not seem as dramatic as that of the period of 1511 to 1513; however, in absolute terms this was an addition of some 3,385 *manta*-equivalents, which were only ninety *mantas* short of the absolute increase of 1511 to 1513 (3,475 *manta*-equivalents). The big difference here is that one cannot attribute this rise to local causes, which may suggest the Aztecs were in need of more resources, perhaps due to the formation of a larger imperial bureaucracy, more ambitious construction programs in Tenochtitlan, or the never-ending elaboration of ritual life in the imperial capital (Durán 1994 [1570–1581]:394–401).

From these key moments, I interpret the early years of Aztec domination as a learning period for understanding the Tlapa province's economic capacity, which then saw slight annual adjustments. These adjustments were initially brought about through increased demands in gold tablets, since

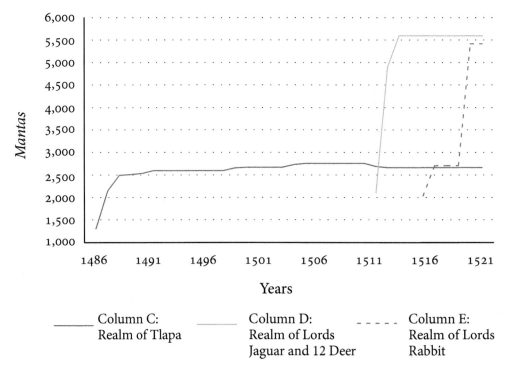

figure 6.12
Breakdown of tribute paid by component realms of the Tlapa province. (Illustration by Gerardo Gutiérrez.)

these were a more flexible unit of exchange of lesser value (forty-five items of cloth equals one tablet of beaten gold). After the amount of gourds with gold dust doubled in the second year, tribute remained fairly stable for some time, since each adjustment for one gourd would equal an increase in 232 items of cloth. From 1490 to 1510, there is relative stability in Aztec tribute demands with slight changes in the number of gold tablets. In 1511, there is a significant increase in tribute demand for all items, in addition to demanding textiles for the first time. From 1513 onward, large increases continue until the maximum level of tribute was reached in 1519.

High sumptuary costs at the courts of the Triple Alliance during the rule of Moctezuma II may explain the external push for large tributary increases after 1517. Nevertheless, local factors associated with the incorporation of new lords into the Tlapa province probably also account for the enormous rise in tribute beginning in 1511. I believe the tribute presented in Columns C, D, and E can be interpreted as contributions given by different political entities or tributary modules headed by

different lords. If this were the case, I believe the tributary province can be broken down into three or four large districts that encompassed all the pueblos of the Tlapa province as depicted in the *Matrícula de Tributos* (Figure 6.12). Indeed, Column C must represent the realm of Tlapa-Tlachinollan itself, given that this was the first column used at the beginning of the Aztec conquest all the way to the last tribute delivered to the Aztecs. Column D shows the combined tribute of two lords: Jaguar from Atepec/Cuitlapan (conquered in 1511) and 12 Deer from Ocoapan (conquered in 1512) (Figure 6.8). Column E would represent the tribute coming from the *altepetl* of the lord of Hueycatenango, which was conquered in 1515 (Figure 6.9). All of these newly annexed lords are depicted together in Folio 31 of the *Codex Azoyú 1* (Vega Sosa 1991). If this interpretation is correct, during Aztec domination, the realm of Tlapa-Tlachinollan absorbed all tributary demands, from 1487 to 1510, beginning with the equivalent of 1,306 *manta*-equivalents and ending with an assessment of 2,756 *manta*-equivalents per year. Notably, after the annexation of Lord Jaguar's *altepetl*, the tribute of Tlapa was reduced symbolically by half a tablet of gold (22.5 *manta*-equivalents) and was kept at that assessment for the remainder of Aztec rule. The conquered rulers, Lord Jaguar and 12 Deer, had to pay heavy tribute that began with 2,098 *manta*-equivalents in 1511 and jumped to 5,596 *manta*-equivalents in 1513, remaining stable at that level until the fall of the Aztecs. In 1515, Lord Rabbit provided all the new tributary increases, starting with 2,031 *manta*-equivalents and ending with an obligation of 5,416 *manta*-equivalents in 1519. Tlapa, the older tributary realm, experienced a small reduction of tribute, while the new tributary groups were charged with heavy increases.

The year 1520 was the last in which the Aztecs enjoyed annual tribute (four payments) from the Tlapa province. After this came the debacle of the Spanish conquest. The Tlapanecs continued making payments to the Aztec *calpixque* until August of 1521, when the island of Tenochtitlan finally succumbed to the Spanish siege. The Tlapanecs did not make any payment in November of 1521, nor in February of 1522, despite the apparent presence of some Aztec *calpixque* in the province. The Aztec Empire was no more, and none of the subject provinces seemed to have assisted their Aztec overlords. The fact that the Aztecs faced their last fight alone amid the ruins of Tenochtitlan and Tlatelolco is the most irrefutable display of resistance from their unhappy subjects, particularly if Tlapa's tributary trends were comparable in other regions of Mesoamerica.

Tribute Negotiation in the Aztec Realm: Some Conclusions

The Nahuatl word *tequiyotl*, "all things or actions related to tribute," also means "all things or actions related to negotiation"; thus, *tequitl* (tribute) and *tequiti* or *tequitiliztli* (to negotiate and negotiation) come from the same root. This linguistic insight signals that the most important financial contribution of commoners to native polities has its origin in negotiated agreements as to what and how

much labor or goods were needed to accomplish goals related to the survival and reproduction of these polities. The Aztec tributary system co-opted local tributary practices of existing polities in central and southern Mexico, and, as much as possible, the Aztecs did not seemingly intervene with local practices of tribute organization and collection. Nonetheless, they certainly affected the provinces by subtracting vast quantities of wealth from local consumption. The *Tribute Record of Tlapa* demonstrates how each tributary province was likely formed by specific historic events with unforeseen and unexpected consequences. The step-by-step analysis of how Aztec domination was materialized in Tlapa through tributary practices provides a fresh view of the empire. The provincial tribute tally offers insight on issues that are often unclear in the sources from Central Mexico; fundamentally, it provides a way of calculating the rates of tribute increases in specific years. It also sheds light on the permanent positions of some Aztec officials in the Tlapa province while suggesting clues as to mechanisms for economic exchange of tribute items. The fact that it may have been possible to exchange some tribute items for others (e.g., pay in gold instead of warrior costumes) would undoubtedly have been an enormous benefit for the market system of Mesoamerica, facilitating some standard mediums of exchange and accepted rates of convertibility. No doubt, an unexpected consequence of a tributary system as large and complex as that administered by the Aztecs was an increase in market transactions that stimulated economic regional specialization. This change would have had many consequences, since some provinces may have been willing to pay more of one particular product abundant in their region in exchange for products that were not. Thus, the Tlapa province became specialized in mining, gold extraction, and some basic metallurgic processes (González de Cossío 1952:511–512; Sahagún 1961:187). Tlapa cultivated some cotton, but it is likely that many of their tribute *mantas* and richly decorated warrior suits and shields were acquired in the market. Extra gold made up the difference for the lack of cotton and feathers. At this point, the agency of imperial and local *calpixque*, in association with Aztec traders, could have played a critical role in bartering interprovincial products.

As to the rate of change in tribute payments for the Tlapa province, there was a 947 percent increase over the thirty-six years of Aztec subjugation, perhaps partly a result of the constant demands required for the operation of the imperial system and the growing size of the nobility of Tenochtitlan, Texcoco, and Tacuba. Additionally, some of this increase undoubtedly came with the annexation of additional provinces. Indeed, some local agency may also have been operating in which subject lords might have pursued the forced annexation of recalcitrant neighbors to their province, and thus to the empire, knowing it would benefit them as well. How much the Aztec Empire was a creation of local politics and regional factionalism remains an open line of research.

By means of this study I also suggest the imperial governor of Tlapa kept 12 percent of the total tribute paid by Tlapa. Essentially, the Tlapanecs would have paid the total reported in the *Tribute Record of Tlapa* directly to the Aztec *calpixque* in Tlapa, who then subtracted this 12 percent

for his household and sent the rest on to Central Mexico. This amount might have been his profit, since daily living was provided by the local lords through tribute in labor and special food tribute as reported in the *Información de 1554*. If this hypothesis is correct, then it offers some understanding on the logistical costs of running the empire. By permitting the conversion of tributary goods, the Aztec *calpixque* provided opportunities for trade, exchange, and profit on a scale never before seen. As long as the coffers of Tenochtitlan received the tribute assessed for each province, the Aztec *calpixque* enjoyed great autonomy and—besides being political officials—they also became powerful economic agents.

Acknowledgments

I would like to thank Ken Hirth and Joanne Pillsbury for inviting me to participate in this volume. In addition, I thank Ken Hirth, Mary Pye, and the two anonymous reviewers for their comments on this work.

NOTES

1 In Nahuatl, there are three sets of concepts for market and exchange: 1) *tlapatlaloyan* ("barter" and "marketplace"); 2) *tlanamaquiliztli* ("to sell"), and thus *tlanamacoyan* ("marketplace"); and 3) *tiamiquistli* ("to sell and buy") and thus *tianquistli* ("marketplace") (see Molina 1977 [1571]).

2 Barlow (1949:4) first proposed that these tributary tallies, especially the *Matrícula de Tributos*, recorded tribute payments between 1511 and 1520. Berdan (1992:65) has since narrowed that range to the years 1516 to 1518.

3 For a discussion on the depiction of gold in different size and possible values, see Gutiérrez et al. 2009a:73–81.

4 For a detailed explanation of my interpretations of the tributary quantities represented in the *Tribute Record of Tlapa*, see Gutiérrez et al. 2009a:73–81.

5 *Calpixqui* is the singular for *calpixque*.

6 Tlapa's first tribute payment was given in late February of 1487. The month glyphs in the *Tribute Record of Tlapa* correspond to the tributary festivals imposed by Tenochtitlan and operated according to the Aztec calendar. With respect to these tributary festivals, consult the statements by witnesses in the *Información de 1554* (Rojas 1997:112–113).

7 In a previous work (Gutiérrez 2002), I argue that there existed a pact of "friendship" beginning in 1461 between the lords of Tlapa and Tenochtitlan. This pact was broken during an internal succession dispute in Tlapa around 1480; the local conflict was used by the Aztecs to justify their conquest of the province in 1486.

8 Interpretation of the lexical variation between tablets, bars, and bricks in the different sources is

addressed in detail in Gutiérrez et al. 2009a:109–116. Here, I will use tablets as the primary quantity.

9 Using the depictions in the *Codex of Otlazpan*, Rojas (1997:41) has argued that the glyph for a bundle of *mantas* actually represents a load of twenty *mantas*, and, therefore, the glosses of the Codex Mendoza are correct in their assessment of four hundred loads of twenty pieces of *manta*. Nonetheless, the *Tribute Record of Tlapa* contradicts the *Codex of Otlazpan*. Before making any claim about scribal errors (often everyone's first assumption), let us instead assume for the moment that there might have been bundles of twenty, or four hundred, *mantas* represented with the same glyph. There is no rule imposing a fixed unit of twenty *mantas* to all bundles at all times. All we know is that the glyph in question might indicate what Molina (1977 [1571]) identified as one *atadura* (the binding of things together, *tlaneunilpilli, tlatzouazilpilli*), one *nudo* (the tying of things tightly with a knot, *ilpilli, tlatlalpilli*), or one *emboltorio* (bundle, *quimilli*), while the specific number of items in the bundle varied, depending on particular contexts. Thus, there could have been bundles of twenty, forty, sixty, all the way up to four hundred *mantas* or more. Even in spoken Nahuatl, apart from the specific *cenquimilli* (one load of *mantas* or twenty *mantas*), Molina recorded the other *quimilli* of *mantas* with a confusing and perhaps context-specific double meaning: 1) *onquimilli* (forty "*mantas*" or forty "large bundles of cloth"); 2) *yequimilli* (sixty "loads" of *mantas* or sixty "*mantas*"); 3) *macuilquimilli* (one hundred "loads" of *mantas* or one hundred "*mantas*"); 4) *matlacquimilli* (two hundred "loads" of *mantas* or two hundred "*mantas*"); and 5) *cempoalquimilli* ("four hundred *mantas*" or "four hundred loads of *mantas*"). This variation reminds us that pictographies were only mnemonic devices that assisted native interpreters to orally recite complex details not depicted in the paintings. That is why there was an explosion in the use of glosses in colonial records.

10 See Rojas (1997) and Berdan (1992) for discussions on the question as to whether the surviving tallies are assessments or receipts.

REFERENCES CITED

Barlow, Robert H.
    1949   *The Extent of the Empire of the Culhua Mexica.* AMS Press, New York.

Berdan, Frances F.
    1980   Aztec Merchants and Markets: Local-Level Economic Activity in a Non-Industrial Empire. *Mexicon* 2(3):37–41.
    1992   The Imperial Tribute Roll of the Codex Mendoza. In *The Codex Mendoza*, vol. 1, edited by Frances F. Berdan and Patricia Reiff Anawalt, pp. 55–79. University of California Press, Berkeley.
    1994   Economic Alternatives under Imperial Rule: The Eastern Aztec Empire. In *Economies and Polities in the Aztec Real*, edited by Mary G. Hodge and Michael E. Smith, pp. 291–312. Institute for Mesoamerican Studies, State University of New York, Albany.
    1996   The Tributary Provinces. In *Aztec Imperial Strategies*, by Frances F. Berdan, Richard E. Blanton, Elizabeth Hill Boone, Mary G. Hodge, Michael E. Smith, and Emily Umberger, pp. 115–135. Dumbarton Oaks Research Library and Collection, Washington, D.C.

Berdan, Frances F., and Patricia Rieff Anawalt (editors)
    1992   *The Codex Mendoza.* 4 vols. University of California Press, Berkeley.

Boone, Elizabeth Hill
    2000   *Stories in Red and Black: Pictorial Histories of the Aztecs and Mixtecs.* University of Texas Press, Austin.

Brumfiel, Elizabeth M.
    1980   Specialization, Market Exchange, and the Aztec State: A View from Huexotla. *Current Anthropology* 21:459–478.

1987   Elite and Utilitarian Crafts in the Aztec State. In *Specialization, Exchange, and Complex Societies*, edited by Elizabeth M. Brumfiel and Timothy K. Earle, pp. 102–118. Cambridge University Press, Cambridge.

Carrasco, Pedro

1999   *The Tenochca Empire of Ancient Mexico: The Triple Alliance of Tenochtitlan, Tezcoco, and Tlacoapan.* University of Oklahoma Press, Norman.

Cline, S. L.

1993   *The Book of Tributes: Early Sixteenth-Century Nahuatl Censuses from Morelos.* Nahuatl Study Series 4. UCLA Latin American Center, University of California Press, Los Angeles.

Cortés, Hernán

1988   *Cartas de relación.* Editorial Porrúa,
[1519–1526]   Mexico City.

Davies, Claude Nigel

1968   *Los señoríos independientes del imperio azteca.* Instituto Nacional de Antropología e Historia, Mexico City.

1987   *The Aztec Empire.* Oklahoma University Press, Norman.

Díaz del Castillo, Bernal

1986 [1568]   *Historia de la conquista de la Nueva España.* Editorial Porrúa, Mexico City.

Durán, Diego

1994   *The History of the Indies of New Spain.*
[1570–1581]   Translated, annotated, and with an introduction by Doris Heyden. University of Oklahoma Press, Norman.

González de Cossío, Francisco

1952   *El libro de las tasaciones de los pueblos de la Nueva España, siglo XVII.* Archivo General de la Nación, Mexico City.

Gutiérrez, Gerardo

2002   *The Expanding Polity: Patterns of the Territorial Expansion of the Post-Classic Señorío of Tlapa-Tlachinollan in the Mixteca-Nahuatl-Tlapaneca Region of Guerrero.* PhD dissertation, Department of Anthropology, Pennsylvania State University, University Park.

Gutiérrez, Gerardo, Viola Koenig, and Baltazar Brito

2009a   *Códice Humboldt Fragmento 1 (Ms. amer. 1) y Códice Azoyú 2 reverso. Nómina de tributos de Tlapa y su provincia al imperio mexicano.* Bilingual edition. Centro de Investigaciones e Estudios Superiores en Antropología Social, Mexico City, and Stiftung Preussischer Kulturbesitz, Berlin.

2009b   *Códice Humboldt Fragmento 1 (Ms. amer. 1) y Códice Azoyú 2 reverso. Nómina de tributos de Tlapa y su provincia al imperio mexicano. Facsimile.* Bilingual edition. Centro de Investigaciones e Estudios Superiores en Antropología Social, Mexico City, and Stiftung Preussischer Kulturbesitz, Berlin.

Gutiérrez, Gerardo, and Constantino Medina

2008   *Toponimia náhuatl en los códices de Azoyú 1 y 2. Un estudio crítico.* Centro de Investigaciones e Estudios Superiores en Antropología Social, Mexico City.

Hassig, Ross

1985   *Trade, Tribute, and Transportation: The Sixteenth-Century Political Economy of the Valley of Mexico.* University of Oklahoma Press, Norman.

1988   *Aztec Warfare: Imperial Expansion and Political Control.* University of Oklahoma Press, Norman.

Herrera Meza, María del Carmen, and Ethelia Ruíz Medrano

1997   *El códice de Tepeucila: El entintado mundo de la fijeza imaginaria.* Instituto Nacional de Antropología e Historia, Mexico City.

Hodge, Mary G., and Leah D. Minc

1991   The Spatial Patterning of Aztec Ceramics: Implications for Pre-Hispanic Exchange in the Valley of Mexico. *Journal of Field Archaeology* 17(4):415–437.

Kobayashi, Munehiro

1993   *Tres estudios sobre el sistema tributario de los mexicas.* Centro de Investigaciones e Estudios Superiores en Antropología Social, Mexico City.

Matos Moctezuma, Eduardo

1988   *The Great Temple of the Aztecs: Treasures of Tenochtitlan.* Thames and Hudson, London.

Miranda, José

1952   *El tributo indígena en Nueva España durante el siglo XVI.* Colegio de México, Mexico City.

Molina, Alonso de

1977 [1571]   *Vocabulario en lengua castellana y mexicana y mexicana y castellana.* Editorial Porrúa, Mexico City.

Nichols, Deborah L.

1994   The Organization of Provincial Craft Production and the Aztec City-State of Otumba. In *Economies and Polities in the Aztec Real*, edited by Mary G. Hodge and Michael E. Smith, pp. 175–193. Institute for Mesoamerican Studies, State University of New York, Albany.

Patch, Robert W.

1994   Imperial Politics and Local Economy in Colonial Central America, 1670–1770. *Past and Present* (May):77–107.

Prem, Hanns J.

1974   *Matrícula de Huexotzinco.* Akademische Druck- und Verlagsanstalt, Graz.

Reyes, García Luís

1997   *Matrícula de tributos o códice Moctezuma.* Akademische Druck- und Verlagsanstalt, Graz, and Fondo de Cultura Económica, Mexico City.

Rojas, José Luís de

1997   *Información de 1554 sobre los tributos que los indios pagaban a Moctezuma.* Secretaria de Educación Pública and Centro de Investigaciones e Estudios Superiores en Antropología Social, Mexico City.

Sahagún, Bernardino de

1959   *Florentine Codex: General History of the Things of New Spain,* bk. 9, *The Merchants.* Translated by Arthur J. O. Anderson and Charles E. Dibble. School of American Research, Santa Fe, and University of Utah, Salt Lake City.

1961   *Florentine Codex: General History of the Things of New Spain,* bk. 10, *The People.* Translated by Arthur J. O. Anderson and Charles E. Dibble. School of American Research, Santa Fe, and University of Utah, Salt Lake City.

Scholes, France V., and Eleanor B. Adams (editors)

1957   *Información sobre los tributos que los indios pagaban a Moctezuma. Año de 1554.* José Porrúa e Hijos, Mexico City.

Seler, Eduard

1904   Mexican Picture Writings of Alexander von Humboldt. In *Mexican and Central American Antiquities, Calendar Systems, and History*, edited by Charles P. Bowditch, pp. 123–229. Bureau of American Ethnology Bulletin 28. Smithsonian Institution Press, Washington, D.C.

Smith, Michael E.

1987   The Expansion of the Aztec Empire: A Case Study in the Correlation of Diachronic Archaeological and Ethnohistorical Data. *American Antiquity* 52:37–54.

1994   Economies and Polities in Aztec-Period Morelos: Ethnohistoric Overview. In *Economies and Polities in the Aztec Realm*, edited by Mary G. Hodge and Michael E. Smith, pp. 313–348. Institute for Mesoamerican Studies, State University of New York, Albany.

Vega Sosa, Constanza

1991   *Códice Azoyú 1: El reino de Tlachinollan.* Fondo de Cultura Económica, Mexico City.

Velasco, Luís de

1958 [1562]   Parecer del virrey don Luis de Velasco sobre lo del tributar los indios de Mexico. Mexico, ultimo de febrero, 1562. [Archivo General de Indias, Patronato, legajo 182, ramo 2]. In *Sobre el modo de tributar los indios de Nueva España a su majestad, 1561–1564*, edited by Frances V. Scholes and Eleanor B. Adams, pp. 29–32. José Porrúa e Hijos, Mexico City.

Zantwijk, Rudolph van

1985   *The Aztec Arrangement: The Social History of Pre-Spanish Mexico.* University of Oklahoma Press, Norman.

7

People of the Road

Traders and Travelers in Ancient Maya Words and Images

ALEXANDRE TOKOVININE AND DMITRI BELIAEV

The occupation to which they had the greatest inclination was trade...and at their markets they traded in everything which there was in that country.

DIEGO DE LANDA
Relación de las cosas de Yucatan
(Tozzer 1941 [ca. 1566]:94–96)

ACCORDING TO DIEGO DE LANDA'S (TOZZER 1941 [ca. 1566]) influential sixteenth-century account on the customs of the Maya shortly after the Conquest, no other occupation appealed to the hearts and minds of the indigenous population of Yucatan more than trade. Canoes and caravans with salt, cloth, and slaves would leave the peninsula and return with cacao and precious stones. Everything could be bought and sold in the markets with cacao beans and certain shells as currency, paid on the spot or on credit. The *Relaciones histórico-geográficas* of the Yucatan province (Garza 1983) paint a similar picture of widespread trading activity, though acknowledging that most things were produced and consumed locally.

This paper explores representations of trade and traders in ancient Maya texts and images. It begins by looking at the available ethnohistorical sources, which reflect the importance of trade and merchants in the social and economic fabric of the Late Postclassic–early colonial Maya world. The discussion then shifts to much less documented merchants of the Classic period and their divine patrons.

Ethnohistorical Sources on Trade and Traders

The relative complexity of the Maya market economy shortly before and after the Spanish conquest is evidenced in early colonial dictionaries from northern Yucatan and highland Chiapas. These sources identify different kinds of transactions, including wholesale operations. A clear distinction is made between local, itinerant, and professional long-distance traders. Traveling and business are often semantically related. Several glosses attest to the presence of marketplaces.

In northern Yucatan, *Calepino de Motul* (Ciudad Real 1995 [ca. 1590]:11, 19, 28, 42, 43, 45, 60, 91, 251, 269, 325, 427, 472, 536, 585, 588, 663) and *Diccionario de San Francisco* (Pérez 1976 [1866–1877]:178, 179) record a variety of terms for different business activities. They include buying and selling on credit (*atcabtah, boolman*) and on behalf of a third person (*lukzahmantah, luksah conol*). Dictionaries mention transactions involving small amounts (*ppeppel conol, ppeppel con*), groups of twenty, or items in bulk (*hukmantah, mux contah, mux mantah, otzmantah*). The sources also distinguish between various kinds of merchants and trade: long-distance merchants (*chuy contah*), sometimes classified by their place of origin as a "trader who goes or comes from Campeche" (*ah campech yoc*), professional and itinerant traders who may or may not have to travel (*ah zut* "rescatador que compra y vende por los pueblos," *ah kakayah* "rescatador, que vende y compra por los pueblos," *ah ppolom* "mercader, que compra y vende," *ah ppolom yok* "mercader así que anda de una parte a otra") as well as intermediaries (*ah tatacchii man, ah tatacchii conol, chumuccabal*). Traveling and business are not just associated; "traveling" means "business" with the same gloss for *camino* and *negocio* (*ocil*). A special term refers to "tianguis, fair, market, square for selling and buying" (*kiuic*) and "trading in a market or fair" (*kiuicyah*).

A colonial Tzeltal dictionary from highland Chiapas (Ara 1986 [1571]:250, 269, 270, 283, 296, 305, 312, 332, 362, 364–365, 367, 379, 386, 388, 406) also references various commercial activities. "To retail" is *chughun ta batel* as well as *mebachonon* and *tuculchon*. A number of terms and expressions highlight specific market transactions: "to lower a price" (*yamagh ztohol* and *uetz*), "to buy in small amounts" (*tuculmanoghon*), "very high in price" (*toyol*), "to buy or sell trade goods" (*polmaghon*), "to gain in trading" (*elaghpolmal*), and "to pass a debt or rulership or duty" (*yoquin*). The same dictionary lists different terms for merchants and travelers (*beyon, ghbeel, ueyom*), those who "sell in exchange" (*ghchonpolmalil*), and "negotiants" (*ghpolmalon*). As in Yukatek, "road" also means "business." The glosses for "market" (*chiuich*) and "marketplace" (*chihuichighibal*) are attested along with derived terms like "to organize a market" (*chihuichighibal*) and "occupation of buying and selling" (*chiuich-ighel*). Of great interest are counting words: *picuy* "to count by *xiquipiles* or units of eight thousand," *picbul* "counted this way," *piz* "weight, *libra*," *olil piz, paot piz* "half of a *libra*," and *teel* "a half of *hanega*."

Colonial Tzotzil also reflects the importance of indigenous trade and merchants shortly after the Conquest. Valuable information on this issue is provided in the *Diccionario grande del siglo XVI*. According to this document (Calnek 1988:22–23), colonial Tzotzil speakers distinguished between long-distance "walking traders" (*xanbil*) and local merchants "who don't walk but stay in their shops," literally "exchangers" and "sellers" (*quexoghel, chonoghel*).

These rich linguistic data suggest a somewhat similar picture of extended trading activities compared to the better-documented area of the Guatemala Highlands. In his study of the region's early colonial economy, Lawrence Feldman (1985:15–21) notes the presence of professional long-distance merchants alongside itinerant, petty traders. He also highlights the significant role of regular markets associated with distinct exchange regions as well as fairs that acted as ports of trade for long-distance operations. According to Feldman, early colonial Maya professional merchants were less organized and less independent when compared to their Aztec counterparts, whereas elites were more directly involved in the patronage of markets and traders and even participated in the long-distance exchange themselves. Feldman (1985:21–23, 84–94) argues that most high-value objects, such as precious feathers, stones, and cacao beans, circulated in a highly restricted and controlled manner. On the other hand, he reports market-based distribution for common food, pottery, cotton, salt, and various nonelite items (Feldman 1985:56–72, 76–80). Even when resources such as maize were initially obtained as tribute, they were redistributed through sale in the market (Feldman 1985:30).

To the north and west of the Guatemala Highlands, commerce sometimes appeared to be the primary occupation of entire communities. Friar Tomás de la Torre—who accompanied Bartolomé de las Casas during his visit to the Chiapas province in 1545–1546—described the principal Tzotzil town of Sinacantlan (known today as Zinacantan) as inhabited mostly by merchants: "Being itself so infertile, this town abounds in all things because others come here to buy what they need and to sell what they bring. They are very haughty and they boast of not planting or doing crafts, because they say they are merchants" (Ximénez 1929:360). According to Tomás de la Torre, Zinacantecos were "by their nature more noble than the rest of their nation" and "all or the most part of them" were merchants. The high social status of traders was also something peculiar to the Zinacantan community: "they from this town in all this land are like principal people in every other town and only by being from Sinacantlan they make themselves proud by saying that they are merchants."

In the Chontal-speaking area of Acalan, one of the four divisions of the city of Itzamk'anak seemed to have been named after Tachabte, "a place of honey/bee wax trees" (cf. *chabi' te'* "any wax producing tree" in Ch'orti' [Wisdom 1950:695]). Honey and wax were the most important local tradable products. Consequently, it is significant that the divine patron of the said city division was the god of merchants: Ik' Chawa (Scholes and Roys 1968:395; Smailus 1975:82–85). Colonial sources also indicate that even members of the most powerful and noble families of Yucatan engaged in long-distance trade. Landa mentions that some Kokom lords organized trading expeditions to Honduras (Tozzer 1941 [ca. 1566]:39). Trading and traders appeared to be prominent enough for a *k'atun* to be remembered as the one when "merchants were dispersed" in the *Book of Chilam Balam of Chumayel* (Roys 1967 [1782]:141).

Despite this apparent importance of trade and traders, there is a remarkable lack of detail about actual trading routes and operations, as well as about merchants themselves. The latter, owing probably to the inherent secrecy of commercial operations, left us with no written testimonies of their

own—nor were their specific activities reported in early colonial documents. It seems that merchants provided Spanish expeditions with some firsthand knowledge about territory and ways to get to certain places by land or water, and even served as guides (Avendaño y Loyola 1987 [1696]:5; Marjil de Jesús et al. 1984:10; Scholes and Adams 1991:19–20). Some traders clearly operated across political boundaries, and the accounts of Cano (1984 [1696]:10) and Avendaño y Loyola (1987 [1696]:47) on the encounters with the Itza testify to that. Details of actual trade operations, however, were harder to extract from these merchants. Moreover, such details would probably not have been of much interest to the Spaniards, whose notion of "business" with the indigenous population often amounted to little more than the expropriation of goods and labor (Scholes and Adams 1991:33).

Trade and Merchants in Classic Maya Texts and Imagery

This situation of limited data does not improve as we move back in time: Classic Maya visual and written narratives are even more reluctant to mention merchants and commerce. Out of thousands of known Classic Maya historical individuals (Colas 2004), nobody takes the titles and epithets of merchants attested in the colonial sources. One dubious candidate is the owner of the unprovenienced drinking cup (K633) painted in the style of the Naranjo workshop (see Reents-Budet 1994:62–63, fig. 2.31). His name includes a title spelled as /a-k'i-wi/ni-ki/ (Figure 7.1). If the reading of the third letter in it is /wi/, then the whole word may be read as *aj-k'iwik*, or "man of/from *k'iwik*," potentially involving the term *k'iwik* for "plaza" and "market" known from colonial Yukatek dictionaries (e.g., Ciudad Real 1995 [ca. 1590]:427, 500, 703). However, given that the potential /wi/ looks rather like other /ni/ signs in the same inscription, it is more likely that the title should be read as *aj-k'inik* and, therefore, does have any connection to trade or markets.

Available linguistic evidence (Table 7.1) points to some form of exchange as far back as the time

figure 7.1

Detail of the dedicatory text on a Late Classic vessel. (Drawing by Alexandre Tokovinine, after a photograph in the Dumbarton Oaks Pre-Columbian Photography and Fieldwork Archive, LC.CB2.408.2).

of the Proto-Mayan language (around the second millennium BC). Kaufman (2002:792) reconstructs a Proto-Mayan gloss *k'aay* as "to sell." In Ch'olan and Tzeltalan languages, however, the only comparable gloss is *k'ay*, meaning "song" (Kaufman 1972:106; Kaufman and Norman 1984:123). The use of *k'aay* as "to sell" is attested only in Eastern Mayan and Yukatekan languages. The most plausible explanation is that it is the same gloss that either lost or obtained additional meanings. In Yukatek (Barrera Vásquez et al. 1995:391; Ciudad Real 1995 [ca. 1590]:27), the primary meaning of *k'aay* is still "to sing," but the same word is also used to describe all kinds of activities when shouting (*voceando*) is involved: begging, auctioning, and selling in the streets. This is a perfect term for the most basic and, presumably, the earliest kinds of informal trading activities with itinerant merchants and no dedicated markets.

Greater Tzeltalan and Yukatekan languages share glosses for buying (*man*), selling (*kon*), trading for profit (*p'ol*), and market (*k'iwik*). The emergence of these new terms must postdate the breakdown of the Proto-Mayan and predate the separation of Yukatekan and Western Mayan languages in the first millennium BC (Campbell 1984; Kaufman 1972:13–14, 1976:107). On the other hand, the Q'anjobalan gloss for selling and its derivations appear to have been loaned from Ch'olan languages (Kaufman 2002:795–796). Therefore, linguistic data suggest that key market-related activities in the Maya Lowlands emerged in the Preclassic period. Borrowing of Ch'olan terms into other Mayan languages implicates the extent of the trading operations by Classic Maya Ch'olan-speaking merchants.

As comparative linguistic data indicate, market exchange played a significant role in Classic Maya society, with all the essential terms for trade-related activities already in place by the first millennium AD. Therefore, the scarcity of visual and written evidence may be due to the status of Classic-period merchants and representational conventions in the surviving media of painted vessels and stone monuments. Most of the imagery on these objects deals with the life of royal courts (Houston and Inomata 2009). Classic Maya merchants may have not held a place prominent enough to be portrayed in the presence of rulers. In fact, courtly officials of all ranks often remained unmentioned and unrepresented, particularly at the courts of powerful royal dynasties like those of Tikal and Calakmul. One would look in vain for a court scene with Yihk'in Chan K'awiil, the greatest Late Classic lord of Tikal. The only vase with a text that mentions him as its owner (K8008; Culbert 1993:fig. 83c, 84) shows, appropriately, the celestial court of God D. On the other hand, there seems to be no problem with depicting a roughly contemporaneous court of K'awiil Chan K'inich from the offshoot of the Tikal dynasty that established itself at Dos Pilas and Aguateca (K1599, K2697). Yet even these scenes represent a limited selection of people and objects. There is a preference to display exquisite possessions like inscribed vessels, jewelry, and mirrors.

This lack of explicit references to merchants in Classic Maya imagery and texts has contributed to the widely held view that market exchange played a minor role in the palace economies, which centered on the tightly controlled circulation of

table 7.1

Trade-related terms in greater lowland Maya languages

LANGUAGE/SOURCE	WORDS							
	BUY	SELL	BARTER	TRADE/ PROFIT	PAY	LOAN	PRICE	MARKET
PM (Kaufman 2002)		*k'aay	*k'ex		*toj	*majaan		
GLL (Kaufman 2002)	*man		*k'ex	*p'ol	*toj			k'iwik
PCh (Kaufman and Norman 1984)	*män	*chon	*k'ex	*p'ol	*toj	*majnä		
YUK (Bricker et al. 1998)	man	kon	k'eš		b'ó'ol	mahàan	tohol	k'íiwiik
YUK (Cuidad Real 1995 [ca. 1590])	man	con	kex	ppolmal	bool	páay mahan	tohol	kiuic
ITZ(A?) (Hofling and Tesucún 1997)	män	kaayah kon	k'exik	naal	b'o'ol	pay majan	tulul tool	
TZO (Laughlin and Haviland 1988)	man	chon	k'ex	p'olmal	toj	pay ch'amol	tojol	ch'ivit
TZE (Ara 1986 [1571])	man	chon		polmal	toghol	maghan	toghol	chiuich
CHT (Robertson et al. 2010)	man	chon	quex	eçomagh polom / polon	toho			
CHR (Wisdom 1950)	man	chon		b'or	tohoma'ar	mahan	toy	
CHR (Tuyuc Sucuc 2001)					toy		choher tujr	
CHN (Keller and Luciano 1997)	man	chon	q'uex		toje'	majan	toj / tojquiba	
						q'uex	choj / cho'an	
CHL (Aulie and Aulie 1978)	mΛn	chon	q'uex	p'olmΛj	tojolan	majan	tojol	

Abbreviations: PM—Proto-Mayan; GLL—Greater Lowland Languages; PCh—Proto-Ch'olan; YUK—Yukatek; ITZ— Itzaj; TZO—Tzotzil; TZE—Tzeltal; CHT—Ch'olti'; CHR—Ch'orti'; CHN—Chontal; CHL—Ch'ol

high-valued items (see Blanton, this volume; Hirth and Pillsbury, this volume). There is a tendency to interpret as tribute scenes all contexts in which such items as jade jewelry, mantles, cacao beans, painted vessels, and feathers are displayed in Classic-period elite households (see McAnany, this volume).

According to David Stuart (1998:409–417, 2006:128–137), *ikaatz* or *ikitz* (spelled /i-ka-tzi/ or /i-ki-tzi/) is a key term for objects in elite transactions. It is used to label jade artifacts (Stuart 2006:figs. 4–5), so its primary meaning seems to be fine jade jewelry, not the raw material. This semantic distinction fits well with the archaeological data on the production and distribution of jade (see Kovacevich, this volume). Bundles labeled as *ikaatz* appear in a variety of narratives and depictions of courtly settings. Stuart's initial interpretation of *ikaatz* was that it referred to gifts and tribute (1998:409–416). The tribute part was largely based on an otherwise unique inscription on Naranjo Stela 12 (see also McAnany, this volume) that described the presentation of the *ikaatz* of the defeated Yaxha lord ordered by the victorious Naranjo ruler (*na[h]waj yikaatz yaxa' ajaw ukabjiiy k'uhul ajsa'aal*).

But Stuart's (2006) later interpretation of *ikaatz* transactions emphasizes gift exchange. Once again, it is based on a text from Naranjo. An inscription on the steps of a palanquin depicted on Naranjo Stela 32 reports how a certain K'uk' Bahlam "gave" (*yak'aw*) two unknown units (*k'aw*) and later five "scores" (*k'al*) of *ikaatz* (Stuart 2006:133, fig. 6). Stuart (2006:129–130) notes that *ikaatz* bundles appear in a host of contexts: they are held by royal consorts during public dances depicted on Yaxchilan monuments (Stuart 2006:fig. 2), carried by Hero Twins in the watery underworld (Stuart 2006:fig. 3a), and displayed behind the thrones of God L (Stuart 2006:fig. 3b) and God D (Boot 2008:15, figs. 1a, 8). *Ikaatz* may be precious objects that leave with the exiled king and return under the supervision of the new ruler, as in the text on Piedras Negras Throne 1 (Stuart 2006:133–135, fig. 7). Other textual references—such as "celestial *ikaatz*, terrestrial *ikaatz*" (*chanal ikaatz kabal ikaatz*) on the middle panel in the Temple of the Inscriptions at Palenque—are, as Stuart points out (2006:136–137,

fig. 8), even cosmological in nature. The bundle in the celestial court of God D is labeled as *chanal ikaatz* (Boot 2008:15, fig. 1a), so it is tempting to suggest that its terrestrial counterpart is the *ikaatz* bundle in the mountain/cave palace of God L.

The variety of contexts and meanings attached to the *ikaatz* bundles in Classic Maya texts and images suggests that we have to be very cautious in approaching the topic of Classic Maya palace economic transactions. The same care should be taken in dealing with other kinds of objects that may be interpreted as part of the institutionalized political economy. According to Stuart (2006:137–141, figs. 9, 11–12), bundles with units of eight thousand (*pik*) depicted in Classic Maya art contain cacao beans, and the quantities sometimes correspond to ethnohistorically known standard loads of cacao beans. Nevertheless, there is no Classic Maya textual reference to cacao offered as tribute. Depictions of cacao bundles in courtly settings are somewhat ambiguous. In the case of the scenes with emissaries on Bonampak murals (see McAnany, this volume) and one Late Classic vessel (K5453, see below), the bundles are placed directly below the seated ruler and not in front, within the ruler's sight (*ichnal*) (Houston et al. 2006:173–175; Stone and Zender 2011:14–15), as might be expected of tribute. It seems as if the bundles were there for the visitors and for those who view the image. Consequently, these cacao bundles might have been gifts of tribute, but they also might have constituted a display of wealth in its most universal and countable form.

We should also be careful in interpreting the significance of documented elite transactions. The largest amount of fine ceramic vessels, apparently given away as gifts by Naranjo rulers, corresponds to the reign of K'ahk' Tiliw Chan Chahk (AD 693–ca. 728) (Tokovinine 2006). The greatest volume and spatial distribution of exclusive pottery gifts of Motul de San José rulers date back to the reign of Tayel Chan K'inich (ca. AD 712–734) (Tokovinine and Zender 2012). In both cases, these were periods of prosperity and increased geopolitical prominence for Naranjo and Motul de San José. Consequently, giving precious gifts to clients, allies, and neighbors seems to be part of an assertive geopolitical stance and not a sign of subordinate status or weakness. The nature of the gifts—drinking vessels—is probably important because it may be assumed that such gifts were exchanged during feasts, when new alliances were made and old ones reinforced. Scenes of feasting, such as on Piedras Negras Panel 3 (Houston et al. 2006:128–129, fig. 3.26), show drinking vessels changing hands and beverages likely shared between participants. Such events were potentially even more politically significant and religiously charged than the gift itself.

That said, some images on Classic Maya pottery do show transactions described as "tribute" and "payment." One such scene on a vessel from the court of Ik'a' lords of Motul de San José (K4996) deals with presentation of tribute by ward or district governors known as *lakam* (Houston and Stuart 2001; Lacadena 2008; Stuart 2006:127–128, fig. 1). The tribute is called *patan* (Figure 7.2a), the most common term for tribute in the form of goods or labor (Stuart 2006:127–128). The tribute is "piled up" (*tz'ahpaj*), and at least one bundle is visible between the *lakam* officials and the high throne of the ruler. Unfortunately, the rest of this section of the vessel is eroded. "Piling up" is clearly not the same action as the still untranslated "presenting" verb (spelled /na-wa-ja/) reserved for the *ikaatz* objects, captives, and brides—the implication being that different settings and acts are involved.

Another scene on the vessel from the same polity (K1728) shows a seated lord who appears to be receiving four individuals (Houston et al. 2006:243, fig. 7.23). The caption (Figure 7.2b) remains partially undeciphered, but it more or less states that the image deals with the presentation of "tribute mantles" (*yubte'*) as a "payment" (*tojool*) from an individual holding the office of *sajal*, most likely a provincial ruler. It seems that the white-mantled man seated before the king and named Chij Lam in the accompanying caption was responsible for delivering this "payment" to the ruler on behalf of the *sajal*. Even though in colonial Yukatek the term *yubte'* refers to "tribute mantles" ("*mantas de tributo*" [Barrera Vásquez et al. 1995:981]), no cotton mantles are depicted here. Visitors brought

two large bundles topped with *Spondylus* shells; these objects are watched over by a man holding what looks like a staff and litters (Figure 7.2c). The glyphic caption identifies him as "he of mantles, young man" (*aj-[y]ubte' ch'ok*).

Tojool—"payment," "cost (of work)," and "price"—is a term attested in many Mayan languages (see Table 7.1), including colonial Yukatek (Ciudad Real 1995 [ca. 1590]:723) and colonial Tzeltal (Ara 1986 [1571]1385 386). Another example of *tojool* in Classic Maya inscriptions appears on a panel fragment that likely came from Jonuta (Figure 7.2d). One of the protagonists—he carries the title of "head youth" (*baah ch'ok*)—is possibly adorned or presented (the verb remains undeciphered) "with *ikitz*." The final sentence of the text begins with the undeciphered verb that likely connects it to the preceding clause because of its –*ij/ji* suffix. The subject is "his payment" (*u-tojool*). Therefore, the inscription likely deals with a presentation of precious objects as a "payment."

The use of two terms, *patan* and *tojool*, potentially implies different types of transactions. It is probably significant that *patan* may also designate labor (but not in the context where it is mentioned on the vase discussed above), whereas *tojool* may involve *yubte'* tribute mantles as well as precious *ikitz/ikaatz* jade or other extremely high-value items. Consequently, *tojool* might have been a more generic term encompassing tribute proper and more exclusive gifts of *ikaatz*. Unfortunately, there is simply not enough evidence to advance the interpretation of these passages any further.

The other subset of scenes in various media involves messengers or emissaries known as *ebeet* (for the decipherment and original interpretation of this term, see Houston et al. 2006:241–249). In one depiction (Figure 7.3; K5453/MS0071), K'ahk' Hiix Muut, a messenger of the "holy Kaanu'l lord" Yuhkno'm Yich'aak K'ahk' (Martin and Grube 2008), kneels before an otherwise unknown Dos Pilas or Tikal lord Ch'ok Wayis. The glyphic commentary locates the event in Topoxte and dates it to AD 691. The event predates Yuhkno'm Yich'aak K'ahk's defeat in AD 695, so the visiting messenger represents the most powerful Classic Maya ruler of

a

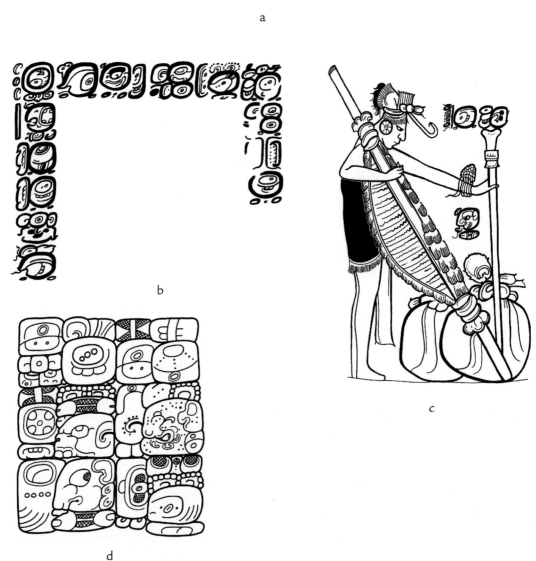

b

c

d

figure 7.2

Classic Maya tribute and payment references: a) detail of the caption on a Late Classic vase (κ4996) (/tz'a-pa-ja
u-pa-ta-na 3-LAKAM-ma yi-chi-NAL ta-ye-le CHAN-na-K'INICH K'UH-IK'-AJAW/, *tz'a[h]paj upatan hux lakam
yichnal tayel chan k'inich k'uh[ul] ik'[a'] ajaw*); b) detail of the caption on a Late Classic vase (κ1728) (/na-tzi na-ja
yu-bu TE' k'e be-la-ja mu-ti u-to-jo-li ti-ki-?-ja mu-ti sa ja-la/, *naatznaj yubte' k'eblaj muut utojool . . . muut sajal*);
c) detail of the scene on a Late Classic vase (κ1728); and d) detail of the Jonuta panel fragment (/i-yu-wa-la ?-ja ta-i-
ki-tzi ta-K'AN-na-to-ko-JOL ?-TI'-?BAHLAM ba-ch'o-ko ?-ji-u-to-jo-li/, *iyuwal . . . ta ikitz ta k'an jol . . . ti' bahlam
ba[ah] ch'ok . . . utojool*) (after Proskouriakoff 1950:fig. 69b). (Drawings by Alexandre Tokovinine.)

figure 7.3
Detail of a Late Classic vessel (к5453) (*k'ahk' hix muut yebeet yuhkno'm yich'aak k'ahk' k'uh[ul] kaanu'l ajaw baah kab*). (Drawing by Alexandre Tokovinine.)

the time. What is of particular interest to us is that the messenger seems to be passing something to the seated lord and also carries a bundle marked by a bar in a rectangle—possibly a reference to quantity (five or fifteen). Ch'ok Wayis's seat displays a bundle of plain square mantles, a bunch of feathers, and possibly a bag of cacao beans marked with the quantity of *huux pik*, or 3 × 8,000; according to early colonial sources, cacao and mantles were the two most common forms of currency. A much larger scene in the upper register of Room 1 of Structure 1 at Bonampak depicts as many as fourteen emissaries, in characteristic capes with shells, facing an enthroned ruler and possibly a designated heir (Houston et al. 2006:248, fig. 7.25a). The only objects next to the throne are several large sacks of cacao beans marked with quantities like 5 × 8,000 (Stuart 2006:fig. 11). The third known scene with messengers appears on a painted

stucco vase from Tikal (Culbert 1993:fig. 68A). It shows caped dignitaries watching a plate with gifts presented to the seated ruler. The captions to most figures are too eroded to identify the ruler and the location, but the *waxak winik* ("28") title of one of the emissaries suggests that the vase is from Petexbatun or the area farther east (Tokovinine 2008).

Ebeet are rarely cited in monumental inscriptions. Fragments of a Terminal Classic–period stucco text from the royal palace of Caracol refer to the *ebeet* of Papamalil (Grube 1994:fig. 9.18; Houston et al. 2006:244, fig. 7.24). The context of the reference is lost, although Papamalil seems to be an important individual associated with the site of Ucanal. He is depicted and mentioned on Caracol Altars 12 and 13 and plays a prominent role in the narrative on Naranjo Stela 32 (Grube 1994:95). Grube has further suggested that Caracol

figure 7.4

Reference to canoes:
a) Piedras Negras Panel 2
(/CHAN-NAL-la CHAK-
chi-wo ?jo AJ-pa-ya-li-?
ju-ku-bi xu/tz'i-ka-la-
NAAH-AJAW/); and
b) Bonampak Miscellaneous
Sculptured Stone 5 (/tu-ta-ja
?NAB-hu-k'a u-KAB-
ji-ya AJ-SAK-la-ka-la
AJ-?JUKUUB/). (Drawings
by Alexandre Tokovinine.)

a

b

Altar 12 and Naranjo Stela 32 might have celebrated the same event that took place at Ucanal, according to the inscription on Stela 32.

The combination of precious objects and bags of cacao beans in the scenes with visiting *ebeet* dignitaries is intriguing. Of all members of the courtly elite known from Classic Maya imagery and inscriptions, *ebeet* are the only ones whose task was essentially to travel, sometimes long distances (e.g., at least 120 kilometers between Calakmul and Topoxte), and pass messages and gifts from one ruler to another. Their dress is consistently a white cape and a necklace of *Spondylus* shells. This uniform suggests that there was some kind of international dress code for emissaries, possibly evoking mantles and shells offered as gifts and tribute (Houston et al. 2006:247). The garments also make one's identification easier in case messengers had to move across otherwise hostile areas. *Ebeet* officials do not carry additional titles; the role of emissaries seems to be their only connection to the court. We do not find the king's own emissaries among the officials present at any internal court event depicted on painted vessels.

It is unclear whether being one's *ebeet* was a singular task or a long-term occupation, but it clearly involved some knowledge of how to get from one place to another. Of all Classic Maya court dignitaries, *ebeet* are the likeliest to have been involved not only in diplomacy but also in long-distance exchange of valuable objects, just like their later Central Mexican counterparts. The display of cacao beans in scenes with *ebeet* seems to support this assertion.

People associated with canoes constitute another likely group who might have been involved in trade. While canoes abound in Classic Maya imagery, the contexts of such scenes tend to be mostly religious or mythological, such as the depictions of the death of the maize god or rain deities fishing (e.g., Moholy-Nagy and Coe 2008:figs. 189–192). Titles like "he of canoe" (*aj-jukuub*) are attested in the Usumacinta River basin, but it is not clear if these are references to trading activities or to military offices. One of the subordinate warriors kneeling before a Piedras Negras ruler on Panel 2 from that site carries the title of *aj-payal-jukuub* (/AJ-pa-ya-li-? ju-ku-bi/) and is identified as a member of the Bonampak-area royal family (/xu/tz'i-ka-la-NAAH-AJAW/; Figure 7.4a). Another *aj-jukuub* person is mentioned on the Miscellaneous Sculptured Stone 5 from Bonampak (Figure 7.4b) as a protagonist of an attack against a small polity somewhere between Bonampak and Yaxchilan (see

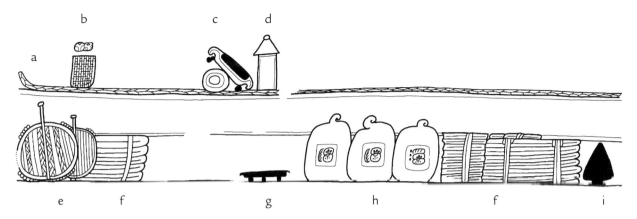

figure 7.5

Objects depicted in the scene on a Late Classic vase (K2914): a) mat; b) *chaach* basket; c) mirror; d) lidded vessel; e) fans; f) mantles; g) plate; h) bean bags; and i) unidentified object. (Drawing by Alexandre Tokovinine.)

figure 7.6

Traveling scene on a Chama-style vase (K594). (Drawing by Alexandre Tokovinine.)

Beliaev and Safronov n.d.). The third example of this title is cited in the text on the unprovenienced "Berman panel" (Mayer 1989:pl. 76).

Classic Maya portrayals of subroyal households are rare. An unprovenienced vase (K2914) that belonged to a district governor or *lakam* (Lacadena 2008) from the Río Azul area, however, offers a rare glimpse of a middle-class household with an unusual emphasis on the quantity of tradable commodities (Figure 7.5). The dwelling (*otoot*, as specified in the caption) of this dignitary features a few exquisite items, such as a mirror and a fine drinking vase, but also several bundles of tribute mantles, fans, and even three large sacks of beans

(labeled as "our beans, our beans, three [bags of] our beans"). Unfortunately, such scenes accompanied by hieroglyphic captions are extremely rare, but they point to different values and economic practices among the elites just below the level of Classic Maya royalty.

Traveling itself is almost never depicted on Classic Maya pottery, although two Chama-style vessels (K594 and K5534) show what looks like a procession of travelers (Figure 7.6). The nature of this procession is unclear (Houston et al. 2006:260–261; Kerr 2001). Is it a rendering of actual travelers or a metaphor of the underworld journey? Both scenes feature a lord carried in a litter, a porter with a tumpline backpack, and trumpeters and other retainers, all wearing travelers' hats.

Our knowledge of Classic Maya travelers and traders can be expanded by looking at other media and genres. One of the earliest of such windows into the world of trade and travel are murals at the archaeological site of La Sufricaya, which were painted around AD 379 in the context of the brief period of Teotihuacan intervention in the political life of the Southern Maya Lowlands (Estrada Belli et al. 2009; Hurst 2009; Stuart 2000; Tokovinine 2008). Mural 1 in Room 1 of Structure 1 at the

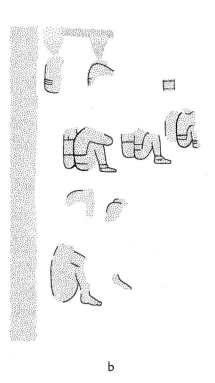

b

a

figure 7.7
Traveling scenes on La Sufricaya murals 6N (a) and 8 (b). (Drawings by Alexandre Tokovinine, after Hurst 2009:figs. 48 and 104 and photographs by Alexandre Tokovinine).

site shows what looks like Maya nobles standing and offering various objects in front of rows of Teotihuacan warriors. Mural 6N presents a maplike landscape with a road connecting two places shown as temples above and below, a group of travelers conducting a ritual in the middle of the road, and a larger figure ascending to the upper temple (Figure 7.7a). The vertical arrangement of these features possibly evokes the west-to-east movement. The road connects this scene with another larger processional representation, at left, that shows more Maya-looking characters and Teotihuacan warriors. The adjacent scene, at right, reveals rows of large bundles and unadorned, seated individuals, possibly with backpacks (Figure 7.7b). The three scenes, therefore, seem to link political events, travel, and trade and/or tribute. The all-glyphic Mural 7, painted in the nearby building, states that the whole complex was dedicated on the one-year anniversary of the arrival of Sihyaj K'ahk' to Tikal, the pivotal event in the Teotihuacan intrusion (Estrada Belli et al. 2009). A similar set of murals with depictions of traveling possibly decorated Hunal, the residence of Copan's founder, who also had a connection to Teotihuacan. But these murals were almost completely obliterated in antiquity (Bell 2007:figs. 5.13–5.14; Hurst 2009:218).

Perhaps the most important set of images related to Classic Maya trade and traders comes from the recently discovered murals adorning the facade of Structure Sub 1-4 in the North Acropolis at Calakmul in Campeche, Mexico (Boucher and Quiñones 2007; Carrasco Vargas and Colón González 2005; Carrasco Vargas et al. 2009). Calakmul Structure 1, a three-terraced platform, is the tallest structure inside the North Acropolis—a large walled compound characterized by a number of low and long platforms that could have easily been part of a large permanent market with stalls and galleries. One wall around the complex was also painted, and the surviving captions (Carrasco Vargas and Colón González 2005:45) seem to label it as *chiik nahb kot*, "the Chiik Nahb wall" (Yurii Polyukhovych, personal communication 2006), linking the complex with one of the two place names associated with Calakmul and its surrounding area (Martin 1997, 2005a; Tokovinine 2007). The layout of the North Acropolis is remarkably similar to some depictions of markets in early colonial sources and also resembles other suspected market areas, such as East Plaza at Tikal (see Masson and Freidel, this volume).

While their significance is open to interpretation, the murals of Structure Sub 1-4 are the closest we come to a depiction of market scenes in Classic

figure 7.8
Detail of the mural on Structure 1 of the Calakmul North Acropolis. (Drawing by Alexandre Tokovinine.)

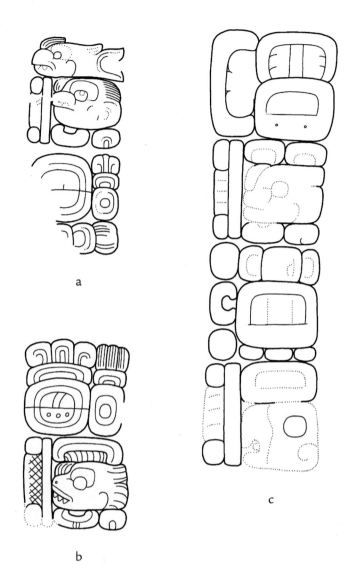

figure 7.9
The *aj-kakaw* title in Classic Maya inscriptions: a) Itzimte altar fragment; b) Itzimte Stela 7; and c) Tonina Monument 89. (Drawings by Alexandre Tokovinine.)

a

b

c

Maya art (Boucher and Quiñones 2007:48). The images mostly show pairs of individuals. One figure presents (or sells) a particular item; the other examines or tastes it (Figure 7.8). Presenters/sellers sit in front of their products, which are placed in various ceramic or basket containers. Most sellers are women wearing wide-brimmed hats as if to protect their faces from sunlight. Every seller is marked by a caption that identifies her or him with the respective product as "person of such-and-such." The list of goods, sold or presented, includes *atole* (*ul*), tamales (*waaj*), tobacco (*may*), maize grains (*ixiim*), salt (*atz'aam*), and serving vessels (*jaay*). These captions are clearly not personal names and suggest a classification of people based on their associated

products. The choice of generic terms over specific (e.g., *jaay*, "thin-walled vessels," but not functional *yuk'ib*, "drinking utensil") also indicates a broader classification. In addition, there are individuals with stretched pieces of cloth, cords, and some kind of pins. The murals feature images of porters or traders with tumplines.

Scenes on the Calakmul murals differ from depictions of courtly life on vessels and monuments in a number of ways. The setting seems to be some kind of open space with no architectural elements, and the protagonists are dressed for long exposure to the sun. The range of products is significant, as some of them are almost never mentioned or portrayed in courtly settings. The baskets stacked with clay vessels and other large containers—present in the murals—are absent in the Classic Maya depictions of palace environments. As Simon Martin (n.d.) points out, if North Acropolis was a market, then Structure 1 could be something like a market shrine, and that would explain the unusual theme of its murals.

While the Calakmul murals really stand out in terms of the nature of the depicted activities and the protagonists, individuals with similar titles suggesting a connection to production or distribution of goods are attested at two other Classic Maya sites. It is potentially significant that both examples involve cacao (*kakaw*), one of the most precious commodities, yet in the names of people of nonroyal rank. Carver's signatures on the altar fragment and Stela 7 from Itzimte (Figure 7.9a–b) identify him as "he of cacao" and "wise man" (/AJ-ka-ka-wa i-tz'a-ti/) (Mejía and García Campillo 2004:822–824). Another example of the same title comes from an inscribed sculpture of a hairless dog (Monument 89) found on the floor of the residential Late Classic Structure F4-6, possibly in association with the nearby Burial III-1, at Tonina (Bequelin and Baudez 1979:105, 134–136, figs. 106–107; Graham 1996:118; see also Stuart 1987:8–10). According to the text on the back of the dog (Figure 7.9c), its owner was *aj-kakaw* (/AJ-ka-ka-wa/). His name continues with a "two *k'atun*" (/2-WINIK. HAAB/) collocation that is usually part of titles like "two *k'atun* lord." Unfortunately, the middle sign in the following block is eroded, so only

a   b   c

d

figure 7.10

Depictions of merchants and travelers at Chichen Itza: a–b) details of the Area 31 of the murals in the Temple of the Warriors; c) detail of the Area 15–16 of the murals in the Temple of the Warriors; and d) detail of the stuccoed and painted vessel (after Villar 1999:60). (Drawings by Alexandre Tokovinine.)

the first and the last glyphs may be read: /AJ-?-a/. The *aj*– prefix and the *-a* ending suggest a toponym, but the two *k'atun* title seems to contradict such identification. The archaeologists described Structure F4-6 as a dwelling of those "who were not very poor," although it did not match fancier structures linked to Tonina royalty (Bequelin and Baudez 1979:105, 134–136).

Murals in the Temple of the Warriors Areas 15-16 and 31 at Chichen Itza (Figure 7.10) (Morris et al. 1931:1:386–395, 418–426, 2:pls. 139, 140b, 159, 160b; see also Finamore and Houston 2010:198–199) are the last known representations of merchants in ancient Maya monumental art. Dated to the Late Terminal Classic–Early Postclassic period, these scenes, not unlike La Sufricaya murals, incorporate figures with walking sticks and tumplines. They are shown in larger landscapes, this time those of coastal communities. The scene in Area 15–16 appears to depict a coastal village of people with striped body paint—a potential clue to their specific ethnic identity. They are under attack by "Toltec" warriors. The latter approach the village, fight, and take captives. Locals are portrayed in the foreground: they scream and flee their dwellings, with bundles on their backs. In the background, daily activities continue uninterrupted: a probable merchant walks along the seashore (Figure 7.10c).

The narrative in the Area 31 Mural is more peaceful. Warriors sail in canoes past a "Maya" coastal community with a "Toltec" temple, and there is no apparent confrontation. Two groups of merchants with speech scrolls are visible in the background—a single figure with a tumpline (Figure 7.10a) and a pair of figures of which only one is the bearer (Figure 7.10b). Although both murals feature canoes, they are empty of merchants and goods. If we assume that these two landscapes follow common Mesoamerican map conventions, the warriors in the foreground come from the west, whereas the merchants walk north and south—an implication that trading and warfare do not happen between the same communities. In addition to murals, at least one stuccoed and painted vessel found at Chichen Itza (Villar 1999:60) shows two travelers with tumpline backpacks: a male and a

female who also carries a baby (Figure 7.10d). As in the case of the earlier La Sufricaya Room 1 murals, traders are depicted as a background to military engagement and travel, this time by land and by sea.

Divine Patrons of Merchants

Although, as we have made clear, Classic Maya merchants are not particularly visible in courtly settings, a number of visual and written narratives reveal the supernatural and mythical side of trade. One of the most prominent protagonists of these narratives is God L. This deity is distinguished by his aged look and a wide-brimmed feather hat adorned with an owl-like bird (Figure 7.11) (Taube 1992:79–81). He is commonly portrayed with large square eyes and jaguar ears, attributes he shares with the Jaguar God of the Underworld (JGU). Smoking a cigar seems to be another of God L's traits. His body is often painted black (Figure 7.12). As pointed out by Taube (1992:81, fig. 40), God L may be shown with a walking staff and a merchant's tumpline, sometimes with a bird on top (Figure 7.12).

Most representations of God L are on Chochola-style vessels and on monuments from the area of Campeche and southern Yucatan (Coe 1973; Mayer 1987:pls. 133, 157, 159, 160, 1989:pl. 39; Robicsek 1978:fig. 41; Tate 1985; Taube 1992). The abundance of God L imagery in this region possibly suggests his greater importance in the local pantheon and, consequently, increased prominence of trade and traders in the social and political fabric. By contrast, God L is not depicted on monuments in most of the Peten, and his representations on pottery are restricted to vases from the workshops in the vicinity of Naranjo (e.g., K7750; see below) and to codex-style vessels possibly from the area of Nakbe (Reents-Budet 1994), although the latter are also found at Calakmul in Campeche (García Barrios and Carrasco Vargas 2006).

Sometimes God L appears to be trying to catch the bird on a stick, possibly with glue (Figure 7.12b), a way of catching birds without killing them or damaging their precious feathers (Feldman 1985:90;

a

b

figure 7.11
Early and Late Classic
representations of God L:
a) detail of the Early Classic
ceramic box (after a photograph
in the Dumbarton Oaks Pre-
Columbian Photography and
Fieldwork Archive, PC.M.EC.
CB4.56.10); and b) detail of the
sanctuary of the Temple of the
Sun at Palenque (after Miller
and Martin 2004:fig.20).
(Drawings by Alexandre
Tokovinine.)

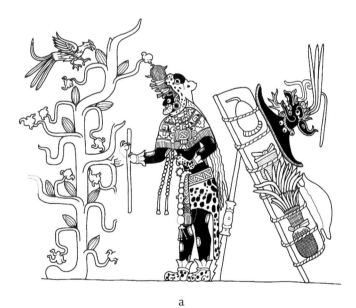

a   b

figure 7.12
God L as a merchant catching birds for their feathers: a) detail of the Cacaxtla murals (after Martin 2006a:fig. 8.12);
and b) detail of the Late Classic plate (after Robicsek 1978:fig. 159). (Drawings by Alexandre Tokovinine.)

Houston et al. 2009:49). He also may be accompanied by human merchants (Taube 1992:fig. 40b). Moreover, some depictions of God L are complete with an idealized representation of the road, which is attached to his belt. Such portrayals include an Early Classic image of the deity on the unprovenienced ceramic box (Figure 7.11a) and the famous Late Classic representation in the sanctuary of the Temple of the Sun at Palenque (Figure 7.11b). God L walks with two kinds of staffs—with and without a pointed end (Figures 7.11a and 7.14).

The Epiclassic murals at Cacaxtla in Puebla, which were painted in a distinctively Maya style (Robertson 1985), also present a revealing image of God L. He has jaguar ears, a jaguar-skinned chin, and jaguar paws, and he presides over maize and cacao plants with a large merchant's backpack propped behind him (Figure 7.12a). As we have mentioned, he seems to be hunting birds. He holds a stick, possibly covered with glue, while a quetzal descends on the cacao tree before him. The contents of God L's backpack underlines his lowland origin: a turtle carapace, a strange gourdlike object, a bundle of cotton mantles, a bunch of long blue-green (evidently quetzal) feathers, and a tied bundle

(possibly with cacao beans). It is worth noting that this bundle is identical to the one of the Calakmul *ebeet* messengers on the vase K5453 (Figure 7.3). The backpack is propped against God L's staff, which is pointed on one edge like the merchant's staff from the Chichen Itza stuccoed and painted vessel discussed earlier (Figure 7.10d). Apparently, the staff could serve as a walking stick, a weapon, and a support for the backpack (Santana Sandoval et al. 1990:333).

God L's name (Figure 7.13) and his relation to other deities are not well understood. One of his names seems to begin with the logogram /ITZAM/, identifying him as a manifestation of the old creator deity along with the celestial God D—Itzam "Principal Bird Deity"—and terrestrial/aquatic God N—Itzam K'an Ahk, Itzam "Snail" (Martin 2006b; Stuart 2007 [1994]). The second part of God L's name is the /AAT/ logogram, so his full name may be Itzam Aat (Figure 7.13a). That said, God L's name in the codices (e.g., Dresden Codex, pages 14b, 14c, 23c) is written with a single distinct logogram (Figure 7.13b) and what look like additional appellatives that possibly indicate overlap or fusion with other gods.

a

b

c

d

e

figure 7.13

Names of God L and his owl hat:
a) detail of the caption on a Late Classic vase (K1398); b) detail of page 14 of the Dresden Codex; c) detail of the caption on a Late Classic vase (K5359); d) detail of page 7 of the Dresden Codex; and e) detail of the caption on a Late Classic vase (K1398). (Drawings by Alexandre Tokovinine.)

God L's specific headdress depicts an owl widely (but erroneously) known as a "Moan Bird." Some representations of God L feature a /13-CHAN-NAL/ collocation on top of the owl head, referring to *huuxlajuun chan(nal) kuy* ("13 Sky Place Owl") who appears in the codices as a separate entity (Dresden Codex, pages 7c, 10a; Figure 7.13d). A caption on the unprovenienced vase in the Kerr database (K5359) identifies God L as /13-? yu-CHAN-na/ (Figure 7.13c) (Miller and Martin 2004:58–63). God L's statement on another unprovenienced vessel mentioned previously (K1398; Beliaev and Davletshin 2007:24, fig. 2) refers to the headdress as "my owl" (*ni-kuy*) (Figure 7.13e), confirming the identification of the headdress as Huxlajuun Chanal Kuy. Consequently, there is probably no connection between God L's name, his headdress, and Tamoachan, contrary to some earlier suggestions (Taube 1992:85).

God L and the sun god refer to each other as "my *mam*" (grandfather/grandson) (Beliaev and Davletshin 2007:25, figs. 4–5). The sixth-century Stela 43 at Naranjo (photographs on file in the Corpus of Maya Hieroglyphic Inscriptions archive, Peabody Museum of Archaeology and Ethnology, Harvard University) shows its ruler, "Aj Wosaj" Chan K'inich, and his predecessor (and father) Pik Chan Ahk as diurnal and nocturnal solar deities, with God L hovering above as one of their ancestors. When God L is not traveling, he is represented as a lord seated in a palace that seems to be inside a mountain complete with water bands, crossed bones, disembodied eyes, and other underworld indicia (Miller and Martin 2004:58–63; Velásquez García 2009). Two such scenes, also on vases from the vicinity of Naranjo (K2796 and K7750), feature God L seated on a throne and gesturing toward six deities before him. A caption to the image describes the "ordering" (*tz'akaj*) of six groups of deities on the creation day of 4 Ajaw 8 Kumk'u. God L's prosperity is indicated by the *ikaatz* bundle—a convention that usually refers to prized jade jewelry, the ultimate expression of wealth (Stuart 2006). In another palatial scene ("Princeton vase," or K511), four young wives attend to God L; two of them make chocolate.

At least three Classic Maya narratives deal with what may be described as the humiliation of God L, and it remains unclear whether these are interconnected stories or regional variants. In all of them, God L loses his possessions or even his life. In some versions, he recovers his wealth, but only after submitting himself to the authority of other deities. The most widespread myth evokes the theme of the resurrection of the maize god. According to Martin, who has discussed this narrative in a number of publications (Martin 2006a, 2010; Miller and Martin 2004:58–63), the story involves the maize god's death and descent into the underworld, where he apparently becomes a cacao/maize tree, the source of God L's wealth. The lightning god K'awiil descends into the underworld and retrieves cacao and maize seeds.

The earliest evidence of this narrative can be traced to the aforementioned Early Classic ceramic box that shows God L (Figure 7.11a) and K'awiil with the seeds. Late Classic allusions to the narrative, particularly in Campeche, also abound. The story is clearly important during the Terminal Classic–Early Postclassic period, as revealed in the decorations of the Temple of the Owls at Chichen Itza (Martin 2006a:174–175, figs. 8.14–8.15). As pointed out by Martin (2006a), the legend likely evokes the agricultural cycle, and although God L and K'awiil appear as adversaries, their roles are complementary to the point that the imagery overlaps. For example, a column from Bakna, Campeche, shows God L carrying K'awiil in a backpack (Figure 7.14). A set of columns possibly looted from the same structure features God L and K'awiil next to a merchant's bundle (Mayer 1987:pls. 157, 159–160). Some scenes on Chochola-style vessels present God L with K'awiil's head in his hand or on his back (Robicsek 1978:pls. 154, 205–206, 215–217, figs. 137, 188–189).

Another myth also discussed by Martin (2006a) features the Hero Twins and the maize god as the main actors in God L's downfall. The Hero Twins' involvement is hinted at in the scene on the Princeton vase and made very clear on an unprovenienced Late Classic vessel (K5359), where they strip God L of his clothes and jewels and disembowel his underworld companion (see also Miller

figure 7.14
Detail of the column from Bakna, Campeche.
(Drawing by Alexandre Tokovinine, after Taube
1992:fig. 41a and Villar 2003:53).

and Martin 2004:58–63; Velásquez García 2009).
The maize god version is presented on another
unprovenienced vase (к1560; Miller and Martin
2004:fig. 22) that seems to show maize god's tri-
umph over three aged deities, including God L,
who are forced to part with their jewelry and clothing. Unfortunately, the captions to the scenes still
evade secure translation.

In the third version or third part of the story,
God L falls to some kind of mischief orchestrated
by the rabbit and the Moon Goddess, and loses his

clothes, jewelry, hat, and "tribute" (*patan*). Two
scenes on an unprovenienced vase from the Naranjo
area (к1398; Beliaev and Davletshin 2007:fig. 1;
Miller and Martin 2004:fig. 23; Stuart 1993) apparently show a rather rude dialogue between the
rabbit and a naked God L, followed by God L's
unsuccessful attempt to seek help at the court of
his grandson, the sun deity (Beliaev and Davletshin
2007:22–29). In this instance, the story seemingly
ends at the court of the Moon Goddess's husband,
God D, whom God L, with the help of other underworld deities, successfully petitions for the return
of his possessions (Figure 7.15) (Tokovinine 2006).
Feasting is evoked, and some scenes show tribute
mantles or bundles, possibly those stolen from
God L (Taube 1992:fig.43c–d).

There are probably more versions of the narrative about God L's destruction. For instance,
Martin (2010) argues that scenes in the Dresden
Codex (page 46c) may be interpreted as God L falling victim to the flood, his possessions recovered by
Chahk in a canoe (see Figure 7.20b). What is important for the present discussion, however, is the relationship between God L, as a wealthy merchant
god, and deities who essentially represent royal
authority and the very idea of kingship—K'awiil,
Hero Twins, maize god, sun god, and God D. These
myths seemingly reveal, according to Martin
(2010), a rather ambivalent attitude toward merchants and a clear emphasis on who has authority.
In the end, God L has to plead for help at the courts
of the sun god and God D. God L's subordination
or even servility to the solar deity is also suggested
by the imagery of the central panel in the sanctuary
of the Temple of the Sun at Palenque, where he and
another jaguar-eared underworld deity support
the insignia of the sun god—the flint-pointed spear
and the shield (Schele and Freidel 1990:259).

The rabbit narrative is particularly interesting given that a large portion of these objects
come from the area of Naranjo. One of the 4 Ajaw
8 Kumk'u vases mentioned above (к7750) identifies the location of God L's court as K'inchil—one
of the places previously conquered by the rulers
of Naranjo according to the inscription on Stela
22 at the site (Graham 1975:56; Martin and Grube

figure 7.15
Detail of the Late Classic vessel (K5166). (Drawing by Alexandre Tokovinine.)

2008). One may only wonder whether God L was the K'inchil's patron deity. The emphasis on God L's downfall in the rhetoric of Naranjo inscriptions would have been directly linked to the region's military conquests, not unlike the narrative imagery, which celebrated Naranjo's victories in campaigns against the Yaxha lords (Grube 2000b:363–365; Martin and Grube 2008).

God L was not the only protagonist of Classic Maya myths involving merchants. One of these narratives is revealed on a Late Classic vase of unknown provenience (K7727; Tunesi 2008:fig. 3). The protagonists are a toad-like creature with a merchant's tumpline (Figure 7.16), a Hero Twin (Juun Ajaw), and God D. In one section of this vase, Juun Ajaw appears to confront the creature with a tumpline

topped by a hat and with a gourd and a jar attached (Figure 7.16b). A hat attached to the tumpline is a common iconographic motif related to trade. It can be found at Cacaxtla in the scene discussed previously and in the murals of North Acropolis at Calakmul (Carrasco Vargas et al. 2009:fig. 4). An accompanying commentary informs that "his *ikaatz* is eight thousand," probably referring to the contents of the unusual merchant's backpack. The second image on the same vase shows God D appraising a macaw and a quetzal, which are presented by a dwarf. This particular episode is known from at least two more vessels (Tunesi 2008:figs. 1, 7). The captions to all three scenes are very similar and seem to record God D's speech as he rejoices in the arrival of "good (things)." Tunesi (2008:23, fig. 8)

a

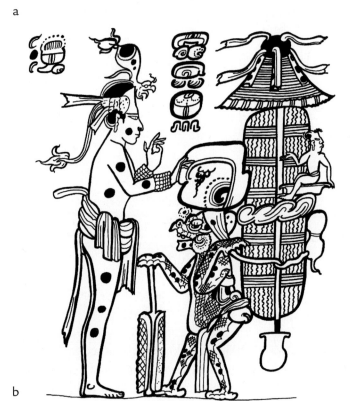

b

figure 7.16
Toad merchant narrative on
a) Late Classic panel in the Museo
de la Escultura Maya in Campeche
(after Tunesi 2008:fig. 8); and b) Late
Classic vase (after photographs in the
Dumbarton Oaks Pre-Columbian
Photography and Fieldwork Archive,
LC.CB2.364.03-04). (Drawings by
Alexandre Tokovinine.)

also identified a scene on the unprovenienced Late Classic panel in the Museo de la Escultura Maya in Campeche that may represent an earlier episode of the same narrative. In this scene (Figure 7.16a), the toad-like merchant is tying a backpack with the help of God L, who places a bird on its top. The contents of this backpack appear to differ from those shown on K7727. The bird might well have been the same bird that would be subsequently appraised by God D. It is tempting to speculate that the attack

on the toad merchant depicted on the vase K7727 corresponds to his return journey from God D's to God L's court. Yet another part of the same myth may be shown on the unprovenienced Late Classic incised vessel photographed by Justin Kerr (K732). It shows the same merchant toad (who appears to be in distress) behind the Hero Twins, who taste pulque before the seated God D.

Finally, a somewhat more sinister aspect of travel is revealed in the depictions of demons or

figure 7.17
Detail of a Late Classic
vessel (K791). (Drawing by
Alexandre Tokovinine.)

wahy (Grube and Nahm 1994; Houston and Stuart 1989) on the unprovenienced Ik'a' vase in the Princeton University Art Museum (Figure 7.17). The demon of the lords of Hux Witznal—Caracol or an unidentified Peten site with the same name—is called "dead man on the road" (*tahn bihil chamiiy*). He is depicted accordingly: a skeleton with blades in his joints (an indication of joint pain). The presumed ability of this particular royal dynasty to make one's trip over land very unpleasant and potentially lethal perhaps suggests its real-world control over land transportation.

As we have noted already, God L was an important deity in Campeche and Yucatan, and continued to be so in the later part of the Terminal Classic and Early Postclassic period. He appears in the Dresden Codex (pages 14b, 14c, 23c), where his omens are usually "good" (*utzil*). The exception occurs on page 49, where God L's form of Venus spears K'awiil. Nevertheless, the Postclassic period sees the introduction of a new deity associated with trade—God M, who is distinguished by his black body paint and grotesque long nose. God M appears on a gilt copper disc found in the Great

Cenote at Chichen Itza, in the Santa Rita murals, and on Mayapan incense burners. Most information about this deity, however, comes from the codices, particularly the later Madrid Codex, where he is depicted in a variety of contexts (Taube 1992:88–92). Most commonly, he is shown with a spear or a pointed staff and a tumpline backpack (Figure 7.18a–b). He also often appears on the road, where he drills fire (Figure 7.18c) and is attacked by various enemies, including God Q (Figure 7.18d; Madrid Codex, pages 51a, 52a, 53ab–55ab, 83a–84a, 91a). These contexts led Paul Schellhas (1904) and, later, Karl Taube (1992:89–92) to conclude that God M should correspond to the Postclassic divine patron of merchants and cacao groves, Ek' Chuwah, whose unusual facial features possibly stem from a partial conflation with a foreign merchant deity, such as the Aztec merchant god Yacatecuhtli who likewise has a long pointed nose.

God M's name, however, consists of just one logogram that looks identical to the appellative of the Classic Maya Jaguar God of the Underworld (Figure 7.19) (Grube 2000a:98–99; Thompson 1960:283). The latter is spelled with two logograms

figure 7.18

God M in the codices: a) Dresden Codex, page 46; b) Madrid Codex, page 52; c) Madrid Codex, page 51; and d) Madrid Codex, page 54. (Drawings by Alexandre Tokovinine.)

(Figure 7.19a–b), the second of which is the same as in the name of God M (Figure 7.19c). Moreover, the earliest images of God M, such as the Chichen Itza disc, show attributes of God L or JGU: an aged look, long canines, spots around the mouth, and jaguar ears (Taube 1992:fig. 44b–e, 45a). Later God M images also display signs of advanced age, such as a nearly toothless mouth. God M's association with weapons is another potential link to JGU. God M's representation in the Dresden Codex (Figure 7.18a) appears to be somewhat out of the canon because he is shown just as an aged character, walking on a road, with a tumpline and without any grotesque facial features. JGU's name is not deciphered, although it may be complemented by the /ji/ syllable. Consequently, God M's name in the codices could be *chuwaaj, but then it would also be JGU's name (Lopes 2002). Since JGU is not attested in the Postclassic imagery, God M may as well be his full substitute (see Martin 2005b, 2006b). One scene with God M includes a full phonetic spelling /si/ti-o K'UH/ (Figure 7.19d), but it may be an

figure 7.19
Names of Jaguar God of the Underworld and God M: a) Naranjo Stela 30:A7; b) Naranjo Stela 21:B13; c) Madrid Codex, page 52; and d) Madrid Codex, page 109. (Drawings by Alexandre Tokovinine.)

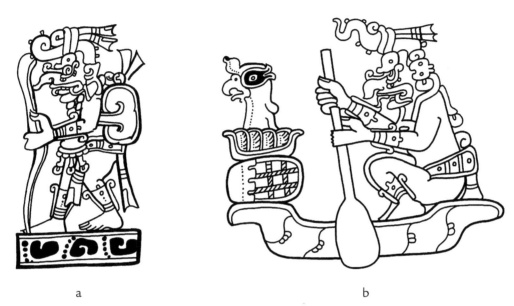

a   b

figure 7.20
Chahk as a merchant in the Dresden Codex: a) page 69; and b) page 46. (Drawings by Alexandre Tokovinine.)

additional title and not a substitution for the JGU name logogram. In any case, there is no one-to-one correspondence between God M's name and the Postclassic merchant deity known from the early colonial sources. The situation is complicated by the fact that the etymology of the word *chuwaj* is unclear. Ralph Roys reports it in the name of a kind of black scorpion (in Barrera Vásquez et al. 1995:151), and the Motul dictionary cites it as part of the name of a kind of wild bee (Ciudad Real 1995 [ca. 1590]:21). Either example makes sense because God M may appear with a scorpion tail (M82a–83a), and he is one of the deities mentioned in the beekeeping section of the Madrid Codex. But these contexts of the *chuwaj* gloss seem to be secondary to the deity's name and do not explain its significance. There is

no such gloss for scorpion or bee in any other Maya language. Given that JGU's name is attested since the Early Classic period, the gloss in his name should be more widespread. According to colonial authors, the Chontal version of the deity's name seems to be Ik' Chawa (see above) and the Chol-speaking Lacandon's version is Chua (Marjil de Jesús et al. 1984 [1695]:12).

Taube suggested another parallel between God M and God L, noting that, according to Landa, the cacao ceremony in honor of Ek Chuah was organized in the month Muan (Taube 1992:92). But as shown above, "Moan Bird" associations for God L should be discarded. Except for the overlapping of functions as trade patrons and merchants, there is no evidence that some attributes of God M were derived from those of God L of the Classic period.

God M is not the only Postclassic deity linked to travel. The Dresden Codex shows Chahk as a traveler walking down the road with a tumpline backpack (Figure 7.20a). Chahk is also shown in a canoe loaded with God L's possessions (Figure 7.20b). The latter scene, as we have discussed, may be interpreted as a kind of postapocalyptic recovery of God L's things, but it may also be seen as a link between Chahk and trade. It is also the only image that establishes some association between traveling in canoe and trading. Despite the prominence of maritime trade in the Postclassic period, there is no clear sign of it when it comes to trade-related deities in the codices. They all seem to be walking. It is potentially significant that Landa's account of pretravel rituals also seems to deal exclusively with land travel (Tozzer 1941 [ca. 1566]:107).

Concluding Remarks

As we have made clear, the main obstacle in exploring the lives of merchants in ancient Maya society is the social and political context of the surviving written and visual narratives, which do not appear to be particularly concerned with trade and traders. On the other hand, linguistic data suggest the emergence of key trade-related activities during the Preclassic period and the subsequent prominence of Ch'olan-speaking merchants in the Late Classic period. Rare glimpses into the world of trade and traveling provided by murals at Calakmul, La Sufricaya, and Chichen Itza indicate that trade and traders were part of the social, political, and economic fabric of the Classic Maya world. Classic Maya merchants, nevertheless, were clearly not as prominent politically and socially as their Postclassic counterparts. There is no evidence that Classic Maya rulers and their families were directly involved in trade. Among various courtly officials, *ebeet* messengers are the likeliest candidates for individuals who could have taken the role of long-distance traders. *Aj-kakaw* titles of some carvers and other subroyal individuals also suggest possible engagement in trade.

The world of Classic Maya deities and lesser supernatural creatures offers another perspective on traders and travelers that hints at greater importance of these activities in certain regions and communities, such as parts of Campeche and areas near Palenque and Naranjo. God L's interactions with the divine patrons of royalty—including the sun god, the maize god, the Moon Goddess, and the Hero Twins—reflect some ambivalence in the Classic Maya attitude toward trade and traders. God L is apparently rich and powerful, and yet he and his associates are constantly humiliated and stripped of their possessions by various divine patrons of Classic Maya rulers, forced to present gifts or tribute and to seek patronage at their courts.

Visual and written narratives also imply a gradual shift in emphasis from the Classic pantheon to the deities known from early colonial sources, although there is no one-to-one match between the early colonial Ek' Chuwaaj and his potential representation, known as God M, in the codices. It is tempting to link this change in the pantheon to the increased role of merchants in Postclassic social and political life.

Acknowledgments

We would like to express our gratitude to Kenneth Hirth and Joanne Pillsbury for organizing this remarkable symposium and for inviting us to participate in it. Our deep appreciation goes to Emily Gulick Jacobs and all the Dumbarton Oaks staff who made this event possible. Discussions and conversations with the symposium organizers, participants, and audience have contributed to the substantial improvement of the original manuscript. We also would like to extend our gratitude to Simon Martin, Albert Davletshin, John Justeson, and the anonymous reviewer for many valuable comments, suggestions, and critique. Dmitri Beliaev's research was supported by the Fellowship Council of the President of the Russian Federation for the state support of young scholars and leading research schools (Project MK-1459.2009.6 "Dictionary of Hieroglyphic Mayan").

REFERENCES CITED

Ara, Domingo de

1986 [1571]   *Vocabulario de lengua tzeldal segun el
orden de Copanabastla.* Universidad
Nacional Autónoma de México, Mexico
City.

Aulie, H. Wilbur, and Evelyn W. de Aulie

1978   *Diccionario Ch'ol: Ch'ol-español,
español-ch'ol.* Instituto Lingüístico de
Verano, In coordination with Secretaría
de Educación Pública, Dirección
General de Servicios Educativos en
el Medio Indígena, Mexico City.

Avendaño y Loyola, Andrés de

1987 [1696]   *Relation of Two Trips to Petén: Made for
the Conversion of the Heathen Ytzaex
and Cehaches.* Translated by Charles
P. Bowditch and Guillermo Rivera,
with additional comments by Adela C.
Breton; edited and with notes by Frank
E. Comparato. Labyrinthos, Culver City,
Calif.

Barrera Vásquez, Alfredo, Juan Ramón Bastarrachea
Manzano, and William Brito Sansores

1995   *Diccionario mayacordemex: Maya-
español, español-maya.* Editorial Porrúa,
Mexico City.

Beliaev, Dmitri, and Albert Davletshin

2007   Los sujetos novelísticos y las palabras
obscenas: Los mitos, los cuentos y las
anécdotas en los textos mayas sobre la
cerámica del periodo clásico. In *Sacred
Books, Sacred Languages: Two Thousand
Years of Ritual and Religious Maya
Literature*, edited by Rogelio Valencia
Rivera and Geneviève Le Fort, pp. 21–44.
Acta Mesoamericana 18. Verlag Anton
Saurwein, Markt Schwaben.

Beliaev, Dmitri, and Alexander Safronov

n.d.   *Saktz'i', 'Ak'e', and Xukalnaah:*
Reinterpreting the Political Geography
of the Upper Usumasinta Region. In
Maya Political Relations and Strategies,
edited by Jaroslaw Zralka and
W. Koskul. Jagiellonian University,
Krakow, in press.

Bell, Ellen E.

2007   *Early Classic Ritual Deposits within
the Copan Acropolis: The Material
Foundations of Political Power at a
Classic Period Maya Center.* PhD
dissertation, Department of
Anthropology, University of
Pennsylvania, Philadelphia.

Bequelin, Pierre, and Claude F. Baudez

1979   *Tonina, une cité maya du Chiapas
(Mexique)*, vol. 1. Mission Archeologique
et Ethnologique Française au Mexique,
Mexico City.

Boot, Erik

2008   At the Court of Itzam Nah Yax Kokaj
Mut: Preliminary Iconographic and
Epigraphic Analysis of a Late Classic
Vessel. Electronic document, http://
www.mayavase.com/God-D-Court-
Vessel.pdf, accessed August 25, 2011.

Boucher, Sylviane, and Lucía Quiñones

2007   Entre mercados, ferias y festines: Los
murales de la Sub 1-4 de *Chiik Nahb*,
Calakmul. *Mayab* 19:27–50.

Bricker, Victoria R., Eleuterio Po'ot Yah, and Ofelia
Dzul de Po'ot

1998   *A Dictionary of the Maya Language: As
Spoken in Hocabá, Yucatán.* University
of Utah Press, Salt Lake City.

Calnek, Edward E.

1988   *Highland Chiapas before the Spanish
Conquest.* New World Archaeological
Foundation, Brigham Young University,
Provo, Utah.

Campbell, Lyle

1984   Implications of Mayan Historical
Linguistics for Glyphic Research. In
*Phoneticism in Mayan Hieroglyphic
Writing*, edited by John Justeson and
Lyle Campbell, pp. 1–16. Institute for
Mesoamerican Studies, State University
of New York, Albany.

Cano, Agustín

1984 [1696]   *Manche and Peten: The Hazards of Itza
Deceit and Barbarity.* Translated by
Charles P. Bowditch and Guillermo
Rivera, with additional comments by
Adela C. Breton; edited and with notes
by Frank E. Comparato. Labyrinthos,
Culver City, Calif.

Carrasco Vargas, Ramón, and Marinés Colón González

2005   El reino de Kaan y la antigua ciudad maya de Calakmul. *Arqueología mexicana* 13(75):40–47.

Carrasco Vargas, Ramón, Verónica A. Vásquez López, and Simon Martin

2009   Daily Life of the Ancient Maya Recorded on Murals at Calakmul, Mexico. *Proceedings of the National Academy of Sciences of the United States of America* 106(46):19245–19249.

Ciudad Real, Antonio de

1995   *Calepino de Motul: Diccionario*
[ca. 1590] *maya-español.* Universidad Nacional Autónoma de México, Dirección General de Asuntos del Personal Académico, Instituto de Investigaciones Antropológicas, Mexico City.

Coe, Michael D.

1973   *The Maya Scribe and His World.* Grolier Club, New York.

Colas, Pierre Robert

2004   Sinn und Bedeutung klassischer Maya-Personennamen: Typologische Analyse von Anthroponymphrasen in den Hieroglypheninschriften der klassischen Maya-Kultur als Beitrag zur allgemeinen Onomastik. PhD dissertation, Universität zu Bonn, Bonn.

Culbert, T. Patrick

1993   *The Ceramics of Tikal.* University of Pennsylvania Museum of Archaeology and Anthropology, Philadelphia.

Estrada Belli, Francisco, Alexandre Tokovinine, Jennifer M. Foley, Heather Hurst, Gene A. Ware, David Stuart, and Nikolai Grube

2009   A Maya Palace at Holmul, Peten, Guatemala, and the Teotihuacan "Entrada": Evidence from Murals 7 and 9. *Latin American Antiquity* 20(1):228–529.

Feldman, Lawrence H.

1985   *A Tumpline Economy: Production and Distribution Systems in Sixteenth-Century Eastern Guatemala.* Labyrinthos, Culver City, Calif.

Finamore, Daniel, and Stephen D. Houston (editors)

2010   *Fiery Pool: The Maya and the Mythic Sea.* Peabody Essex Museum, Salem, Mass., and Yale University Press, New Haven.

García Barrios, Ana, and Ramón Carrasco Vargas

2006   Algunos fragmentos cerámicos de estilo códice procedentes de Calakmul. *Los investigadores de la cultura maya* 14(1):126–136.

Garza, Mercedes de la

1983   *Relaciones histórico-geográficas de la gobernación de Yucatán (Mérida, Valladolid y Tabasco).* Universidad Nacional Autónoma de México, Instituto de Investigaciones Filológicas, Centro de Estudios Mayas, Mexico City.

Graham, Ian

1975   *Corpus of Maya Hieroglyphic Inscriptions,* vol. 2, pt. 1, *Naranjo.* Peabody Museum of Archaeology and Ethnology, Harvard University, Cambridge, Mass.

1996   *Corpus of Maya Hieroglyphic Inscriptions,* vol. 6, pt. 2, *Tonina.* Peabody Museum of Archaeology and Ethnology, Harvard University, Cambridge, Mass.

Grube, Nikolai

1994   Epigraphic Research at Caracol, Belize. In *Studies in the Archaeology of Caracol,* edited by Diane Z. Chase and Arlen F. Chase, pp. 83–122. Pre-Columbian Art Research Institute, San Francisco.

2000a   Fire Rituals in the Context of Classic Maya Initial Series. In *Sacred and the Profane: Architecture and Identity in the Maya Lowlands,* edited by Pierre Robert Colas, pp. 93–109. Verlag von Flemming, Berlin.

2000b   Monumentos esculpidos e inscripciones jeroglíficas en el triángulo Yaxhá-Nakum-Naranjo. In *El sitio maya de Topoxté: Investigaciones en una isla del lago Yaxhá, Petén, Guatemala,* edited by Wolfgang W. Wurster, pp. 249–267. Verlag Philipp von Zabern, Mainz am Rhein.

Grube, Nikolai, and Werner Nahm

1994   A Census of Xibalba: A Complete Inventory of Way Characters on Maya Ceramics. In *The Maya Vase Book,* vol. 4, edited by Barbara Kerr and Justin Kerr, pp. 686–715. Kerr Associates, New York.

Hofling, Charles Andrew, and Félix Fernando Tesucún

1997   *Itzaj Maya-Spanish-English Dictionary = Diccionario maya itzaj-español-inglés.* University of Utah Press, Salt Lake City.

Houston, Stephen D., Claudia Brittenham, Cassandra Mesick, Alexandre Tokovinine, and Christina Warinner

2009   *Veiled Brightness: A History of Ancient Maya Color.* University of Texas Press, Austin.

Houston, Stephen D., and Takeshi Inomata

2009   *The Classic Maya.* Cambridge University Press, New York.

Houston, Stephen D., and David Stuart

1989   *The Way Glyph: Evidence for "Co-essences" among the Classic Maya.* Research Reports on Ancient Maya Writing 30. Center for Maya Research, Washington, D.C.

2001   Peopling the Classic Maya Court. In *Royal Courts of the Ancient Maya*, vol. 1, *Theory, Comparison, and Synthesis*, edited by Takeshi Inomata and Stephen D. Houston, pp. 54–83. Westview Press, Boulder, Colo.

Houston, Stephen D., David Stuart, and Karl A. Taube

2006   *The Memory of Bones: Body, Being, and Experience among the Classic Maya.* University of Texas Press, Austin.

Hurst, Heather

2009   Murals and the Ancient Maya Artist: A Study of Art Production in the Guatemalan Lowlands. PhD dissertation, Department of Anthropology, Yale University, New Haven.

Kaufman, Terrence

1972   *El proto-tzeltal-tzotzil; Fonología comparada y diccionario reconstruido. Versión española e índice español.* Universidad Nacional Autónoma de México Coordinacíon de Humanidades, Mexico City.

1976   Archaeological and Linguistic Correlations in Mayaland and Associated Areas of Mesoamerica. *World Archaeology* 8:101–118.

2002   A Preliminary Mayan Etymological Dictionary. Electronic document, http:// www.famsi.org/reports/01051/index. html, accessed February 22, 2011.

Kaufman, Terrence, and William M. Norman

1984   An Outline of Proto-Cholan Phonology, Morphology, and Vocabulary. In *Phoneticism in Mayan Hieroglyphic Writing*, edited by John Justeson and Lyle Campbell, pp. 77–166. Institute for Mesoamerican Studies, State University of New York, Albany.

Keller, Kathryn C., and G. Placido Luciano

1997   *Diccionario chontal de Tabasco.* Instituto Lingüístico de Verano, Tucson, Ariz.

Kerr, Justin

2001   The Last Journey: Reflections on the Ratinlinxul Vase and Others of the Same Theme. Electronic document, http:// www.mayavase.com/jour/journey.html, accessed July 2, 2010.

Lacadena, Alfonso

2008   El título lakam: Evidencia epigráfica sobre la organización tributaria y militar interna de los reinos mayas del clásico. *Mayab* 20:23–44.

Laughlin, Robert M., and John B. Haviland

1988   *The Great Tzotzil Dictionary of Santo Domingo Zinacantán: With Grammatical Analysis and Historical Commentary*, vol. 1. Smithsonian Institution Press, Washington, D.C.

Lopes, Luís

2002   Some Notes on the Jaguar God of the Underworld. Unpublished manuscript in the possession of the author.

Marjil de Jesús, Antonio, Lázaro de Mazariegos, and Blas Guillén

1984 [1695]   *A Spanish Manuscript Letter on the Lacandones in the Archives of the Indies at Seville.* Translated and with notes by Alfred M. Tozzer; with additional notes by Frank E. Comparato. Labyrinthos, Culver City, Calif.

Martin, Simon

1997   Painted King List: A Commentary on Codex-Style Dynastic Vases. In *Maya Vase Book: A Corpus of Rollout Photographs of Maya Vases*, vol. 5, edited by Barbara Kerr and Justin Kerr, pp. 847–867. Kerr Associates, New York.

2005a   Of Snakes and Bats: Shifting Identities at Calakmul. *PARI Journal* 6(2):5–15.

2005b   The Mesoamerican Flood: Myth and Metaphor. Paper presented at the 10th European Maya Conference, "The Maya and Their Neighbors," University of Leiden, Netherlands.

2006a   Cacao in Ancient Maya Religion: First Fruit from the Maize Tree and Other Tales from the Underworld. In *Chocolate in Mesoamerica: A Cultural History of Cacao*, edited by Cameron L. McNeil, pp. 154–183. University Press of Florida, Gainesville.

2006b   The Old Man of the Maya Universe: Towards an Understanding of God N. Paper presented at 30th Maya Meetings at Texas, University of Texas, Austin.

2010   The Dark Lord of Maya Trade. In *Fiery Pool: The Maya and the Mythic Sea*, edited by Daniel Finamore and Stephen D. Houston, pp. 160–162. Peabody Essex Museum, Salem, Mass., and Yale University Press, New Haven.

n.d.   Hieroglyphs and the Painted Pyramid: The Epigraphy of Chiik Nahb Structure Sub 1-4, Calakmul. In *Maya Archaeology 2*, edited by Charles Golden, Stephen D. Houston, and Joel Skidmore. Precolumbia Mesoweb Press, San Francisco, in press.

Martin, Simon, and Nikolai Grube

2008   *Chronicle of the Maya Kings and Queens: Deciphering the Dynasties of the Ancient Maya*. 2nd ed. Thames and Hudson, London.

Mayer, Karl Herbert

1987   *Maya Monuments: Sculptures of Unknown Provenance*, supplement 1. Verlag von Flemming, Berlin.

1989   *Maya Monuments: Sculptures of Unknown Provenance*, supplement 2. Verlag von Flemming, Berlin.

Mejía, Héctor E., and José Miguel García Campillo

2004   Dos nuevos monumentos de Itzimte, Petén. In *XVII Simposio de Investigaciones Arqueológicas en Guatemala, 2003*, edited by Juan Pedro Laporte, Bárbara Arroyo, Héctor Escobedo, and Héctor E. Mejía,

pp. 810–828. Museo Nacional de Arqueología y Etnología, Guatemala City.

Miller, Mary Ellen, and Simon Martin

2004   *Courtly Art of the Ancient Maya*. Fine Arts Museums of San Francisco, San Francisco, and Thames and Hudson, New York.

Moholy-Nagy, Hattula, and William R. Coe

2008   *The Artifacts of Tikal: Ornamental and Ceremonial Artifacts and Unworked Material*. Tikal Report 27, pt. A. University of Pennsylvania Museum of Archaeology and Anthropology, Philadelphia.

Morris, Earl Halstead, Jean Charlot, and Ann Axtell Morris

1931   *The Temple of the Warriors at Chichen Itzá, Yucatan*. 2 vols. Carnegie Institution of Washington, Washington, D.C.

Pérez, Juan Pío

1976   *Diccionario de San Francisco.*
[1866–1877]   Akademische Druck- und Verlagsanst, Graz.

Proskouriakoff, Tatiana

1950   *A Study of Classic Maya Sculpture.* Carnegie Institute of Washington Publication 593. Carnegie Institute of Washington, Washington, D.C.

Reents-Budet, Dorie

1994   *Painting the Maya Universe: Royal Ceramics of the Classic Period*. Duke University Press, Durham, N.C.

Robertson, Donald

1985   Cacaxtla Murals. In *Fourth Palenque Round Table, 1980*, edited by Elizabeth P. Benson, pp. 291–302. Pre-Columbian Art Research Institute, San Francisco.

Robertson, John S., Danny Law, and Robbie A. Haertel

2010   *Colonial Ch'olti': The Seventeenth-Century Morán Manuscript*. University of Oklahoma Press, Norman.

Robicsek, Francis

1978   *The Smoking Gods: Tobacco in Maya Art, History, and Religion*. University of Oklahoma Press, Norman.

Roys, Ralph

1967 [1782]   *The Book of Chilam Balam of Chumayel*. University of Oklahoma Press, Norman.

Santana Sandoval, Andrés, Sergio de la L. Vergara
Verdejo, and Rosalba Delgadillo Torres

  1990   Cacaxtla, su arquitectura y pintura
          mural: Nuevos elementos para análisis. In
          La epoca clásica: Nuevos hallazgos, nue-
          vas ideas, coordinated by Amalia Cardos
          de Mendez, pp. 329–350. Museo Nacional
          de Antropología, Instituto Nacional de
          Antropología e Historia, Mexico City.

Schele, Linda, and David A. Freidel

  1990   *A Forest of Kings: The Untold Story of*
          the Ancient Maya. William Morrow,
          New York.

Schellhas, Paul

  1904   *Representation of Deities of the Maya*
          Manuscripts. Papers of the Peabody
          Museum of American Archaeology and
          Ethnology 4, no. 1. Peabody Museum of
          American Archaeology and Ethnology,
          Harvard University, Cambridge, Mass.

Scholes, France V., and Eleanor B. Adams

  1991   *Documents Relating to the Mirones*
          Expedition to the Interior of Yucatan,
          1621–1624. Translated by Robert D.
          Wood, with additional notes by Frank
          E. Comparato. Labyrinthos, Culver City,
          Calif.

Scholes, France V., and Ralph Loveland Roys

  1968   *The Maya Chontal Indians of Acalan-*
          Tixchel: A Contribution to the History
          and Ethnography of the Yucatan
          Peninsula. University of Oklahoma
          Press, Norman.

Smailus, Ortwin

  1975   *El maya-chontal de Acalán: Análisis*
          lingüístico de un documento de los
          años 1610–1612. Universidad Nacional
          Autónoma de México, Coordinación
          de Humanidades, Mexico City.

Stone, Andrea, and Marc Zender

  2011   *Reading Maya Art: A Hieroglyphic Guide*
          to Ancient Maya Painting and Sculpture.
          Thames and Hudson, New York.

Stuart, David

  1987   *Ten Phonetic Syllables.* Research Reports
          on Ancient Maya Writing 14. Center for
          Maya Research, Washington, D.C.

  1993   Breaking the Code: Rabbit Story. In
          Lost Kingdoms of the Maya, edited by
          Gene S. Stuart and George E. Stuart,
          pp. 170–171. National Geographic
          Society, Washington, D.C.

  1998   "The Fire Enters His House":
          Architecture and Ritual in Classic
          Maya Texts. In *Function and Meaning*
          in Classic Maya Architecture, edited
          by Stephen D. Houston, pp. 373–425.
          Dumbarton Oaks Research Library and
          Collection, Washington, D.C.

  2000   The Arrival of Strangers: Teotihuacan
          and Tollan in Classic Maya History.
          In *Mesoamerica's Classic Heritage:*
          Teotihuacán to the Aztecs, edited by
          Davíd Carrasco, Lindsay Jones, and
          Scott Sessions, pp. 465–513. University
          Press of Colorado, Boulder.

  2006   Jade and Chocolate: Bundles of Wealth
          in Classic Maya Economics and Ritual.
          In *Sacred Bundles: Ritual Acts of*
          Wrapping and Binding in Mesoamerica,
          edited by Julia Guernsey and F.
          Kent Reilly, pp. 127–144. Boundary
          End Archaeology Research Center,
          Barnardsville, N.C.

2007 [1994] Old Notes on the Possible ITZAM Sign.
          Maya Decipherment. Electronic docu-
          ment, http://decipherment.wordpress.
          com/2007/09/29/old-notes-on-the-
          possible-itzam-sign, accessed
          September 2, 2011.

Tate, Carolyn E.

  1985   Carved Ceramics Called Chochola. In
          Fifth Palenque Round Table, 1983, edited
          by Virginia M. Fields, pp. 123–133. Pre-
          Columbian Art Research Institute,
          San Francisco.

Taube, Karl A.

  1992   *The Major Gods of Ancient Yucatan.*
          Dumbarton Oaks Research Library
          and Collection, Washington, D.C.

Thompson, J. Eric S.

  1960   *Maya Hieroglyphic Writing: An Intro-*
          duction. University of Oklahoma Press,
          Norman.

Tokovinine, Alexandre

2006   Reporte preliminar del análisis epigrá-
        fico e iconográfico de algunas vasijas
        del Proyecto Atlas Arqueológico de
        Guatemala, Dolores, Petén. In *Reporte
        20, Atlas Arqueológico de Guatemala:
        Exploraciones arqueológicas en el
        sureste y centro-oeste de Petén*, edited
        by Juan Pedro Laporte and Héctor E.
        Mejía, pp. 364–383. Dirección General
        del Patrimonio Cultural y Natural,
        Ministerio de Cultura y Deportes,
        Guatemala City.

2007   Of Snake Kings and Cannibals: A Fresh
        Look at the Naranjo Hieroglyphic
        Stairway. *The PARI Journal* 7(4):15–22.

2008   The Power of Place: Political Landscape
        and Identity in Classic Maya Inscrip-
        tions, Imagery, and Architecture.
        PhD dissertation, Department of
        Anthropology, Harvard University,
        Cambridge, Mass.

Tokovinine, Alexandre, and Marc Zender

2012   Lords of Windy Water: The Royal Court
        of Motul de San José in Classic Maya
        Inscriptions. In *Politics, History, and
        Economy at the Classic Maya Center of
        Motul de San José, Guatemala*, edited
        by Antonia Foias and Kitty Emery,
        pp. 30–66. University Press of Florida,
        Gainesville.

Tozzer, Alfred M.

1941 [ca. 1566]   *Landa's* Relación de las cosas de
        Yucatan: *A Translation*. Papers of
        the Peabody Museum of American
        Archaeology and Ethnology 18. The
        Peabody Museum, Cambridge, Mass.

Tunesi, Raphael

2008   Some Thoughts About a Vase and an Old
        God. *The PARI Journal* 9(2):18–23.

Tuyuc Sucue, Cecilio

2001   Ojronerob' Ch'orti' = Vocabulario
        ch'orti': Ch'orti'-español, español-
        ch'orti'. Academia de Lenguas Mayas
        de Guatemala (Comunidad Lingüística
        Ch'orti'), Guatemala City.

Velásquez García, Erik

2009   Reflections on the Codex Style and the
        Princeton Vessel. *The PARI Journal*
        10(1):1–16.

Villar, Mónica del (editor)

1999   *Imágenes de los mayas en San Ildefonso.*
        Arqueología mexicana, edición especial
        no. 3. Editorial Raíces and Instituto
        Nacional de Antropología e Historia,
        Mexico City.

2003   *Sala maya, Museo Nacional de
        Antropología.* Arqueología mexicana,
        edición especial no. 15. Editorial Raíces
        and Instituto Nacional de Antropología
        e Historia, Mexico City.

Wisdom, Charles

1950   *Materials on the Chorti Language.*
        University of Chicago Library, Chicago.

Ximénez, Francisco

1929   *Historia de la provincia de San Vicente
        de Chiapa y Guatemala de la orden de
        nuestro glorioso padre Santo Domingo,*
        vol. 1. Tipografía Nacional, Guatemala
        City.

8

Wide Open Spaces

A Long View of the Importance of Maya Market Exchange

MARILYN A. MASSON AND DAVID A. FREIDEL

Maya archaeologists argue about everything of importance, but they do so within the context of some basic consensual understandings. One of them is that for all of the clear evidence of cultural and social disjunction over the three millennia or more of Maya presence in the lowlands, there is also clear evidence of continuity. Pioneer scholars who pursued this thread, such as Robert Wauchope (1938) in his study of Maya housing, have been followed by generations of archaeologists looking at long-term continuities in subsistence agriculture, craft production, settlements, and institutionalized cultural constructions in politics and religion. Periods marked by profound disjunction, like the Spanish conquest and the ninth-century era of social discord commonly termed the "collapse," are of particular interest in discerning continuity and disjunction. Both of us have been inspired by William Rathje's theoretical work on Maya economics. He, in collaboration with Jeremy Sabloff, outlined some broad patterns of evolutionary change

to describe the transition from the Classic period to the Postclassic period in the lowlands (Sabloff and Rathje 1975). In essence, these patterns hinged on two events: 1) the rise of a new Postclassic merchant class in the wake of the breakdown of Classic elite governments; and 2) the geographic shift of power from the interior to the peripheries for their superior potential for waterborne bulk transport. That shift in power was accompanied by a pragmatic migration of people to those peripheries. The Classic economy was modeled as fundamentally redistributive in regard to long-distance commodities, and it was administered by ritually charged governments. The Postclassic economy, however, was market based and managed by merchants, both noble and commoner.

This model of Classic and Postclassic economies is influential and enduring. It is represented in Patricia McAnany's contribution to the present volume and in her recent article, coauthored with Tomás Gallareta, on Maya resilience in the face of the ninth-century crisis (McAnany and Gallareta

2009). In the following pages, we offer an alternative model of Classic Maya economy, one in which marketplaces and the activities of marketing figure prominently despite the difficulty of identifying these archaeologically—a difficulty which is no more insurmountable than other things archaeologists look for in the record of the Classic Maya past today, such as evidence of court activities (see Tokovinine and Beliaev, this volume). One of the features of Rathje's (1972) original cultural ecological model for the rise of complex society in the lowlands of Mesoamerica that we bring back to the table in the discussion of the Classic–Postclassic transition is the necessary connection between what Terence D'Altroy and Timothy Earle (1985) termed Staple and Wealth finance in their seminal consideration of preindustrial political economies in archaeological contexts. In Rathje's view, Classic Maya governments first administered the long-distance trade and redistribution of vital resources—salt and stone among them—and then capitalized on increasing power and prestige to market ritually charged wealth items. Long questioned in the Maya field (see Marcus 1983), this perspective nevertheless has the merit of maintaining the vital link between Staple and Wealth finance that has significantly slackened in the current models of Classic redistributive economy. Now, the notion that the Maya divine kings and queens competed for status and prestige among themselves by manipulating wealth items satisfies many of our colleagues as an explanation for the manufacture and distribution of such labor-intensive precious commodities in the record. At the same time, Staple finance has been generally relegated to the affairs of ordinary people operating outside of royal courts (see Tourtellot and Sabloff 1972 for a prescient theoretical consideration of this view). Whatever means such people may have employed, be they markets or more casual barter, they bear little explanatory relationship to the rise and fall of governments. Rather, it was endemic warfare among elites attacking communities, drought, and other such direct assaults on ordinary people that account for their ultimate disenchantment with

divine kingship, and perforce the fall of governments of divine kings followed by the rise of merchant princes. We do not doubt the hubris of Maya divine kings in putting their own interests ahead of those of their people; unfortunately, they were indeed human, just like politicians in all times and places. In what follows, we challenge the disconnect between Staple and Wealth finance in Classic Maya political economies.

The materialist core of our argument here is that we now have enough well-contextualized artifactual information to compare the distribution of key commodities in a large Classic-period city, Tikal, and a large Postclassic-period city, Mayapan, with regard to the political and economic institutions that might account for these patterns. Our major finding is that the patterns are strikingly similar, and, in our view, the parsimonious explanation for this finding is that the institutions generating the archaeological patterns were also alike. As has been the case for generations of Maya scholars, we propose that such similarity is the result of continuity in institutional design. That institutional design is a political economy in which Staples have equivalences in Wealth items of a kind generally termed currency, and in which Classic governments maintained marketplaces and peace of the trade routes moving commodities over the lowland landscape. In short, we see no major political-economic disjunction between the Classic and Postclassic periods. What happened in the ninth century, in our view, was generated by centuries of military and diplomatic competition between major regional factions in lowland Maya elite society, factions whose ultimate ambitions for hegemony ended in disarray and chaos rather than in a regional Pax, as in some other ancient civilizations. This is, of course, a paradigmatic constellation of working hypotheses subject to ongoing test. We can only address some aspects of this paradigm in the following pages, but we encourage consultation with the chapter by Tokovinine and Beliaev for germane insight on Classic economy and also with our other articles in the process of preparation and publication.

Comparing Maya and Aztec Market Economies

The existence of marketplaces is increasingly recognized at Classic-period Maya sites, and models of administered (elite-controlled) central markets or informal, local commoner markets have been proposed for the Maya area. But few studies have considered how significant market institutions may have been to daily life as well as to the courtly realm alongside the accumulated practices of tribute, redistribution, or reciprocal exchange (Hirth and Pillsbury, this volume). Although we infer below that models of Postclassic-period Maya market institutions are strong, based on testimonies in colonial-era documentary accounts, the degree of commercial development for this period can seem to pale in comparison to better-documented developments in Aztec-period Central Mexico (e.g., Blanton, this volume; Hirth and Pillsbury, this volume). We do not contest that Tenochtitlan-centered Aztec market systems represented the most complex commercial scale documented for the New World, but the Maya area was probably more commercialized than conventional models acknowledge. For the Maya Lowlands, several contingencies fog the lens of the deeper Maya past, including the passage of the zenith of Postclassic-period centralization at the time of the Mayapan confederacy, which collapsed around AD 1448, more than a half-century before the first Spanish shipwreck victims floated ashore on the Caribbean coast. The northern Maya area at contact was recovering from a civil war that fractured regional polities in the context of a brutal sequence of plagues, droughts, famines, and other disasters that brought Yucatan (and Mayapan with it) to its knees in the late fourteenth and fifteenth centuries (Masson and Peraza Lope n.d.). Spanish conquest in the Maya area was delayed thirty years from the Valdivia shipwreck in 1511 to the founding of Mérida, time enough for new European epidemics to sweep the region, decimate the population, and impact all manner of societal institutions. Despite these setbacks, references to complex market institutions abound in Spanish-era documents that reflect, at minimum, their characteristics a century earlier, when Mayapan united much of the northern peninsula. As is widely acknowledged, ethnohistorical records are best evaluated against archaeological data, as we attempt to do in this chapter.

A Plug for the Importance of Regional-Scale Commerce

A methodological hurdle to understanding the importance of Maya markets seems to be one of scale. Regional exchange in a populous landscape was likely of great significance, as boundaries and networks of allied polities that extended across expansive terrain probably formed the most unimpeded networks for market trade. To provide one example of many, for much of the Classic period, Tikal's political and economic influence was strong in a corridor extending from the city to northwestern Belize, some one hundred kilometers away; this is not the only zone that reveals strong ties to Tikal. Links with sites in northwestern Belize shifted through time to other equally distant areas (Sullivan 2002). Blanton's arguments earlier in this book about the prohibitive social and geographic factors that suppressed commoners' options for traveling to marketplaces are insightful, certainly for boundary markets or other distant venues. But if hometown polities or nearby political capitals hosted regularly scheduled, large, and diverse regional markets, then opportunities to obtain goods might have been easier for local peasants who lacked transportation or social ties. Intermediate distances and scales of merchant movement of goods merit consideration along with patterns involving long-distance interregional luxury trafficking or casual trade among local petty vendors. Indeed, the distributions of pottery styles conform well to networks of allied polities within each temporal interval of the Classic era, and these politico-geographic spheres were broad, encompassing hundreds of settlements of various sizes ranging from political capitals to rural hamlets (Masson 2001). Exchanges among regional merchants probably provisioned hometown consumers with nonlocal, subluxury desirables—such as marine shell objects or nonlocal ground stone (and countless perishables)—without the need for considerable travel or face-to-face producer-consumer interaction. It is also probable that networks of hinterland towns situated near polity boundaries engaged in formal or informal exchanges of goods across these territories, and that such networks augmented the flow of nonlocal goods into the realm of a given kingdom, such as that of Tikal.

Some prior works dismiss the importance of ancient Maya markets due to a lack of interregional dependencies on goods in "common use" (Blanton et al. 1993:221–222), or on the grounds that significant imports are not observed from outside of the Maya area (Braswell 2010). We emphasize here that the Maya area is extensive, and the presence of large proportions of nonlocal materials in ordinary domestic contexts that originate from well beyond the boundaries of political capitals and their subject towns constitutes the type of evidence that is needed to identify significant market institutions. The terrain from the Basin of Mexico and extending to Teotihuacan and Otumba is roughly equivalent to the geographic extent of Tikal's adjoined subject towns and closest allies (Figure 8.1) during the city's peak, not counting more distant, nonadjacent allied kingdoms. Tikal and its associated secondary centers imported abundant quantities of nonlocal goods, such as ground stone from at least ninety kilometers away, marine shell from coasts at least one hundred fifty kilometers distant, and obsidian from sources at least three hundred kilometers to the south (Freidel 1978). Tikal, one of several large cities of the Classic period, boasted a population of sixty thousand (McAnany, this volume) and was nearly two-thirds the size of Teotihuacan (Carballo, this volume) and lay within a few days' walk of Caracol, which had more than one hundred thousand inhabitants, and Calakmul, with its population of around fifty thousand inhabitants. The terrain between these central cities was punctuated with towns, some with thousands of occupants. Populous settlements scattered across diverse resource zones fostered trade dependencies even within concentrated geographic areas (Stark 1997:280).

Contrasting Views

The political economy of the Maya area has traditionally been contrasted with that of Central Mexico. In this dichotomy, Classic Maya polities were exclusionary, heavily reliant on prestige-goods exchanges among elites (Blanton et al. 1996; Blanton et al. 2005; Sanders and Webster 1988:526, 534), and the Maya area had nonluxury production economies that were outside of political control (Potter and King 1995:25–26, 28–29; Scarborough and Valdez 2009). Maya-area production activities were said to be undifferentiated due to redundant regional resources, and the urban status of political centers was also questioned (Sanders 1973:350–351; Sanders and Webster 1988:526, 534). The latter characterization is relevant to this discussion as urban life is cross-culturally correlated with at least part-time occupational specialization. Central Mexican polities on the other hand were corporate, were less concerned with prestige-goods exchanges, exhibited highly nucleated and urban settlement, had centrally controlled production, and had diverse resources (e.g., Blanton et al. 1996; Sanders 1973:351; Sanders and Webster 1988).

Some of these general characterizations of the Maya region have been refuted. In particular, the diversity of agricultural and raw material resources across the Maya Lowlands has been well established (Dunning et al. n.d.; Potter and King 1995; Rice 1993; Scarborough and Valdez 2003, 2009), and accordingly, household archaeology has recognized craft and agrarian production diversity within and outside of Maya centers. In fact, it is this kind of diversification that lends itself cross-culturally to the development and prosperity of regional market systems (Hirth 1998:452; Minc 2006:83; Smith 1976:333; Stark and Garraty 2010:43–45).

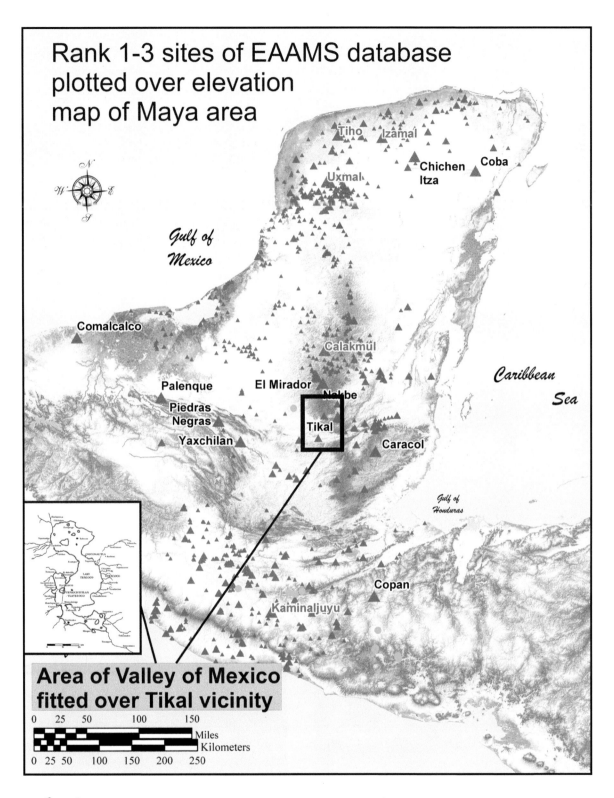

Rank 1-3 sites of EAAMS database
plotted over elevation
map of Maya area

Gulf of
Mexico

Tiho Izamal
Chichen Coba
Itza
Uxmal

Comalcalco

Calakmul

Caribbean
Sea

Palenque   El Mirador   Nakbe

Piedras
Negras   Tikal

Yaxchilan   Caracol

Gulf of
Honduras

Area of Valley of Mexico
fitted over Tikal vicinity

Copan

Kaminaljuyu

0   25   50   100   150
                                    Miles
                                    Kilometers
0 25 50   100   150   200   250

figure 8.1
Comparison of the Basin of Mexico with the area surrounding Tikal. (Map courtesy of Walter R. T. Witschey and
Clifford T. Brown, The Electronic Atlas of Ancient Maya Sites.)

Production versus Distribution Control

A central impediment to understanding political involvement in an integrated Maya economy is the assumption that the production of essential goods must be controlled by elites if their power rests in any significant way on agrarian or basic craft sectors. Elite oversight of luxury-craft production is a given for the Maya area and is excluded from this chapter's discussion (refer to Kovacevich, this volume; McAnany, this volume). Reaches of the institutional economy (Hirth and Pillsbury, this volume) are hinted at by some urban productive activities, such as investment in large-scale infrastructural projects, some of which improved agricultural activity even though most cultivation was probably independent of elite oversight (Dunning et al. n.d.).

Complexity is also seen in the types and contexts of ordinary craft production to an extent that one cannot generalize about the urban versus rural contexts of surplus crafting. A variety of entrepreneurial opportunities—including patronage, vending, and marketplace trading—probably drew craftspersons to large cities. Urban production, much of which was not under elite supervision,

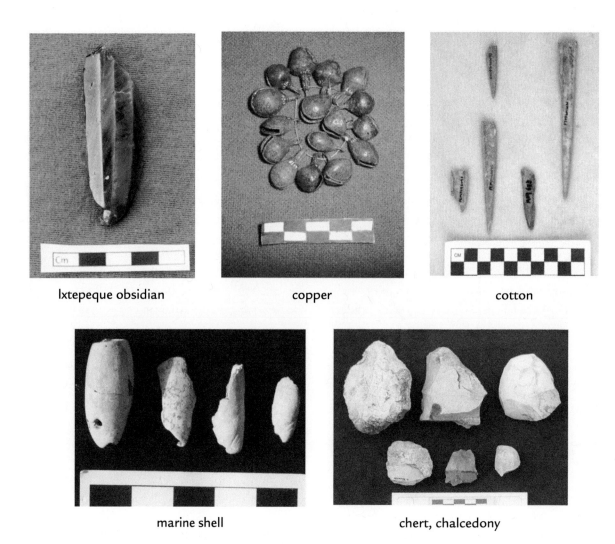

Ixtepeque obsidian   copper   cotton

marine shell   chert, chalcedony

figure 8.2
Imported raw materials found at Mayapan, such as obsidian, copper, marine shell, cotton thread and plain mantles (that were embellished using bone tools), chert, and chalcedony. (Photographs courtesy of the PEMY Mayapan project.)

focused regularly on final stages of manufacture of shell, stone, and cloth items (Fedick 1991; Masson et al. 2006). Raw materials, such as whole shells or preformed cores, were exchanged into these cities, where they were converted to more valuable items (Figure 8.2). Without these supplies, the specific craft industries that depended on them would have ceased. Most residents of Mayapan, like the earlier cases discussed by McAnany (this volume), did not spin cotton but instead focused on more intricate textile-making activities, such as weaving and embroidery (Masson et al. 2006). These finishers are reported from many types of Maya settlements, including political capitals, secondary towns, and rural villages (e.g., Chase and Chase 2004:144; Kidder 1950:12; McKillop 1989; Scarborough and Valdez 2003; Speal 2009). Specialized communities also tended to focus on late-stage production or to segregate phases of manufacture (e.g., Shafer and Hester 1983), a process also described by Kovacevich (this volume).

Freidel (1981) argued many years ago that the control of distribution made more sense for the dispersed landscape of resources, settlement, and production activities of the Maya area. Cross-culturally, control of exchange can be more important than the control of basic goods production for emergent political leaders in ancient agrarian states (Smith 1976:309–310). Elite redistribution has sometimes been proposed as a significant mechanism for Maya centers (Aoyama 2001:355; Sanders and Webster 1988:534; Sidrys 1976; Yaeger and Robin 2004:155–156, 162), but we agree with those who dismiss this institution as not feasible for Maya polities, based on the prohibitively large scale of the undertaking (e.g., Dahlin et al. 2010; Smith 1976:334; Stark and Garraty 2010:44). The ideal type of a redistributive economy is inaccurate even for the chiefdom-like societies for which it was initially defined (Earle 1977; Smith 1976:334; Stark and Garraty 2010:44). Where this model has been promoted at Maya sites, authors are forced to acknowledge that market systems or differential purchasing power could also explain distributional patterns (Aoyama 2001:354; Sidrys 1976:454). Feinman and Garraty (2010:174) remark that "despite an absence

of historical evidence that redistribution was ever a critical mechanism for large-scale provisioning of everyday domestic goods ... except possibly during times of crisis," Mesoamerican archaeologists have tried to find evidence for this mechanism rather than market exchange. This point is crucial. Contact-period Maya accounts do not mention widespread redistribution of food or craft goods except in the context of religious ceremonies, such as rites of passage for children (Tozzer 1941 [ca. 1566]:106); famine relief would also have been important (Freidel and Shaw 2000). These accounts are explicit, however, about markets.

Market Organization and Administration

Central questions must be asked about the importance of market systems to elite economic foundations: How might nobles have controlled market institutions, and how might they have benefited from them? Ethnohistorical analogies may provide relevant answers, and key parallels can be found in descriptions of Central Mexican and Maya systems, even if they varied in scale or magnitude (Table 8.1). In both societies, markets were nested geographically and differed in size, diversity, frequency, and significance (Blanton 1996; Feldman 1978). For both regions, markets were sometimes—but not always—"piggybacked" with religious events (Berdan et al. 2003:101; Blanton, this volume; Freidel 1981:381; Piña Chan 1978:42). In both areas, officials resolved disputes at markets and prohibited trade outside of the marketplace (Blanton 1996:82–83; Feldman 1978:12; Piña Chan 1978:40; Tozzer 1941 [ca. 1566]1:96). Markets were critical for supplying Aztec rulers with the luxuries needed to cement political bonds (Berdan et al. 2003:106; Blanton 1996:83). To this end, tribute was sometimes requested in goods not made locally in the Aztec and Maya areas (Berdan et al. 2003:107; Piña Chan 1978:41), which promoted market trade between subject polities.

Transactions were taxed at Aztec markets to varying degrees (Blanton 1996:82), but we have no evidence of this practice in the Maya area. The masking of tax payments as tribute in Spanish accounts

table 8.1

Attributes of contact-period markets in the Maya area and Central Mexico (citations provided in text)

Variation in scale and timing of markets
Variation in diversity of goods at markets
Restriction of trading to marketplace locales
Judges preside over disputes, weights, and measures
Control exerted over exchange rather than most types of production
Widely used standardized currencies
Market activities poorly represented in pictorial/glyphic records
Tiered ranks of merchants operated at different scales
Commoners acquired abundant, diverse nonlocal valuables
Commoners produced surplus for market exchange (and tribute)

can obscure this distinction (Isaac, this volume; Smith 2010). Aztec elites meddled in regional market organization with the goal of holding the largest, most diverse events in their hometowns and relegating smaller, specialized market operations to potential political competitors (Blanton 1996:82). In the Maya case, there is no record of meddling, but we suspect that Maya elites would have also vied for the opportunity to host the most significant markets at their political capitals in order to derive similar benefits. Hosting major markets improved exchange options for elites, as such events attracted the most accomplished merchants and artisans (Blanton 1996:83). These marketplaces conferred prestige on their hosts and reinforced polity identity. Prosperous markets also allowed supporting populations to exchange and get provisions. Small-scale shortages due to localized crop failures could be mitigated through mutual commoner trade (Freidel and Shaw 2000), lending economic stability to the kingdom with little direct involvement of elites. Evidence for trade blocks or embargoes in the Classic-period Maya political landscape may attest to meddling, as we discuss later in this chapter for the Calakmul and Tikal enmity.

Hosting and organizing markets did not involve oversight of all transactions, which would

have occurred among familiar trading partners as well as strangers, as was the case for the contact period (Berdan et al. 2003:106–107; Hirth 1998:452). A passage selected by Frans Blom (1932:545) from the *Historia de la provincia de San Vicente de Chiapa y Guatemala* sheds light on a contact-period market system:

The rulers took great pains that there should be held great and celebrated and very rich fairs and markets, because at these come together many things; those who are in need of something will find it there and can be exchanged with those other necessary things: they held their fairs and exhibited what they had for sale close to the temples. The selling and buying is to exchange which is the most natural form of trade; they gave maize for black beans and black beans for cacao, exchanged salt for spices which were *ají* or chile . . . also they exchanged meat and game for other things to eat; they swapped cotton cloth for gold and for some hatchets of copper, and gold for emeralds, turquoises and feathers. A judge presided over the market, to see that nobody was exploited. He appraised the prices and he knew of everything, which was presented at the market (Ximénez 1929–1931:1:94).

Challenges to Recognizing Maya Market Institutions

The existence and the significance of market exchange are most often simply omitted from consideration, rather than being directly challenged, in ancient Maya studies. But considerable support for Classic-era market systems can be tracked in the literature (Chase and Chase 2001; Culbert 2003; Dahlin et al. 2010; Fry 2003; Kidder 1950:12; Moholy-Nagy 2003a:108; Rathje 1972:373, 389; Sharer and Traxler 2006:84–85, 634, 714; Sheets 2000). Some suggest that lowland markets were important during the Preclassic period (Clark 2007:37; King n.d.:47; Moholy-Nagy 2003a:87–88, 107; Shaw 1999:95). Recent work advances the idea that solar central-place market models best fit the Classic period (Braswell 2010; West 2002), but the strict parameters of this model may need to be refined in order to accommodate the complexities and variation found in the archaeological record (Masson and Freidel 2012).

Hierarchical versus Heterarchical Perspectives

Still, the question of Maya market institutions evokes little consensus. A large proportion of Maya archaeology focuses on epicentral public and residential architecture, and palace and temple contexts lend themselves to the study of luxury manufacture and exchanges, as well as to an emphasis on the importance of tribute and gifting as primary modes of exchange (e.g., Aoyama 2001; Ball 1993; Foias 2002; see critique by Dahlin et al. 2010:192–193). Michael Smith (2004:89) cautions against confusing prestige-goods models with luxury exchanges among elites, as the latter occurred in all ancient complex societies. Well-documented market societies, like the Aztec, also had sumptuary or market laws that restricted the circulation of the highest-value luxury items, such as turquoise or gold (Berdan 1988:642). Elite culture and symbolically imbued regalia were important for determining the value of objects that were manufactured along continua of inalienable-to-alienable categories of worth (Freidel et al. n.d.; Freidel et al. 2002). As Landa noted for the contact-period Maya, "certain red shells" were used "for money, and as jewels to adorn their persons" (Tozzer 1941 [ca. 1566]:94–96).

Work at smaller sites outside of Maya centers has tended to emphasize commoner autonomy in production and exchange in the exploration of heterarchical principles of organization (Potter and King 1995; Scarborough and Valdez 2003, 2009:211). These different frames of study—palace/temple archaeology and household archaeology—independently foster the view that each sector was profoundly disconnected from the other. A "dual economy" model promotes the view of near social-class independence except through tribute or corvée obligations (Scarborough and Valdez 2009). Market exchange was attributed to low-level interchanges among peripheral or rural "resource specialized" communities and was accorded little political significance (Scarborough and Valdez 2009:212).

As hieroglyphic texts fail to mention markets, the relevance of commercial activities to Classic-period elites tends to be dismissed (Potter and King 1995:25), yet market glyphs and images are also absent in precontact Central Mexican and Maya codices during periods when marketing was widespread. Without ethnohistorical documents, the case for Aztec market institutions might also be contentious. The *momoztli* symbol (round, altar-like stone) that marked marketplaces (*tianquitzli*) occurs only three times in the contact-period Codex Mendoza, and the symbol is used as a place-marker without direct or extensive reference to marketing institutions (Berdan and Anawalt 1992:2:156, 4:120). The perceived threat that merchants posed to patrician elites in many ancient states goes far toward explaining why royal art and writing, including that of the Classic Maya period, hampers our knowledge of the commercial realm (Blanton, this volume; McAnany, this volume; Tokovinine and Beliaev, this volume).

Marketplaces

Ramón Carrasco and colleagues (2009) discovered new murals at Calakmul next to a probable market plaza (Figure 8.3). The images refer hieroglyphically to personages associated with basic goods, and this represents the most direct evidence in Maya art and writing for market activities yet revealed (Martin 2007; Tokovinine and Beliaev, this volume). But the word "market" does not appear once in this 2009 *Proceedings of the National Academy of Science* article. A recent paper by Bruce Dahlin, Richard Terry, and colleagues (2007), which identified soil chemistry signatures that matched expectations of a marketplace at the Classic-period site

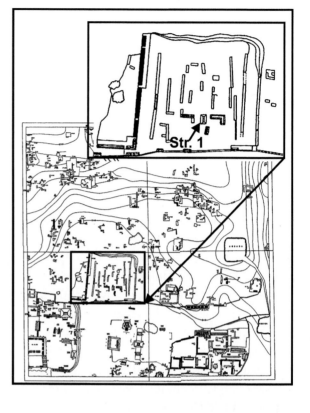

figure 8.3
North plaza at Calakmul (after Folan et al. 2001a: appendix C).

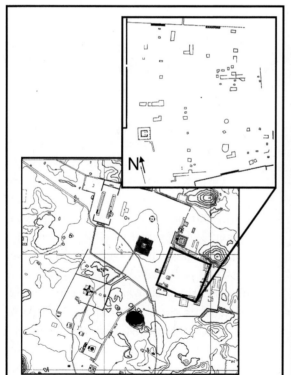

figure 8.4
Chichen Itza's Court of One-Thousand Columns (after Ruppert 1943:230, 1952:fig. 45).

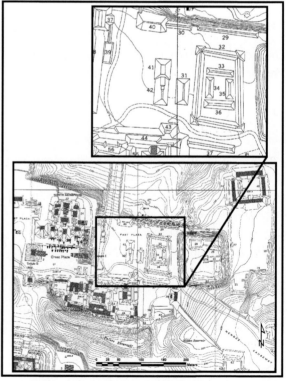

figure 8.5
Tikal's East Market Plaza (Jones 1996:86–87, 91, after Carr and Hazard 1961:map 11).

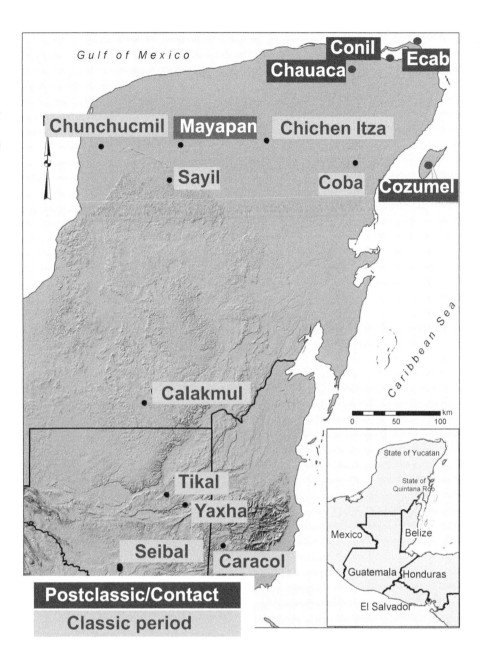

figure 8.6
Maya sites with
plazas linked to
market functions.
(Map courtesy of
Timothy S. Hare.)

of Chunchucmil, was so revolutionary that it was announced in the *New York Times* in 2008.

The most common approach to the study of ancient market systems in the Maya area has been to identify marketplaces at central cities. Evidence in the support of plazas dedicated to exchange includes prominent nonresidential, open or enclosed spaces with stall-like alignments or arcades as illustrated for Calakmul (Folan et al. 2001b:234), Chichen Itza (Ruppert 1943:230), and Tikal (Jones 1996:86–87, 91) in Figures 8.3 to 8.5.

A total of nine Classic-era and four Postclassic-and/or colonial-period Maya sites are shown in Figure 8.6, where plazas linked to market functions have been potentially identified (fully discussed in Dahlin et al. 2010; Masson and Freidel 2012:table 1). Chunchucmil dates primarily to the early part of the Classic era, while Chichen Itza primarily dates to the Terminal Classic period (ninth and tenth centuries AD); the other sites were at their height during much of the Classic period. Mayapan's potential market plaza, located

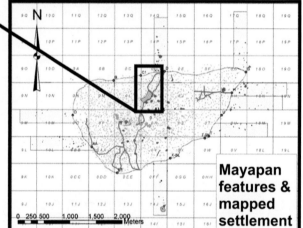

figure 8.7
The Square K rectangular plaza at Mayapan. (Map courtesy of Timothy S. Hare.)

midway between Major Gate D and the monumental center (Figure 8.7), is a large rectangular area devoid of domestic structures and houselot boundary walls that cover most of the residential zone; it has low stall-like alignment features, and patterns of soil chemistry suggest market operations (Bair et al. 2009).

Soil chemistry has proven to be effective at verifying the functions of such plazas as market spaces (Dahlin et al. 2007; Dahlin et al. 2010), but additional studies of economic production and exchange patterns are needed to gauge the importance of these facilities (Garraty 2010:10; Hirth 1998; Stark and Garraty 2010). Below, we offer an example of how analyzing the distribution of artifacts at Maya sites may begin to supply the necessary data. The study of counting artifacts and palettes utilized by numerate literati in noble contexts represents an additional line of investigation that opens up inquiries into the tabulation of commercial exchanges, as does the long-term use of standard currency units from the Preclassic-through contact-period times (Freidel et al. n.d.; Freidel and Reilly 2010; Stuart 2006).

Craft Production at Tikal and Mayapan

Occupational heterogeneity characterizes many dwellings tested at central and peripheral Tikal. Domestic workshops made chert, obsidian blades, shell, pottery, and wooden objects (Becker 1973; Chase et al. 1990:501; Culbert 2003:65–66; Fedick 1991; Fry 2003:151, 157, 167; Haviland 1985:177–178, 184; Moholy-Nagy 2003a:106). Complexity has been tracked in pottery production and distribution. Slipped serving vessels created at specific locales were broadly recovered, and Fry (2003:150) infers that they were acquired in the city's central marketplace, while coarse jars have more limited spatial distributions and are inferred to have been obtained directly from neighborhood producers or from small neighborhood markets. Hence, consumers had options to acquire certain goods from more local vendors as well as to purchase finer vessels in a citywide marketplace. Further evidence in support of the latter is offered by Culbert (2003:65), who notes that polychromes were widely consumed and are present in significant numbers in small houses. Fry (2003:150) concludes that "the most parsimonious explanation for the observed distribution is a complex marketing system."

At Mayapan, a survey of thirty-six cleared milpas from across the settlement zone has led to the identification of twenty-eight workshops associated with residential groups. Like Tikal (Fry 2003:156–167; Moholy-Nagy 2003a:106), craft activities were more intense in downtown Mayapan, near the monumental center where thirteen of twenty-eight workshops were concentrated in the Milpa 1 sample area, but significant workshops are also found in outlying residential zones of the city (Figure 8.8). Comparisons

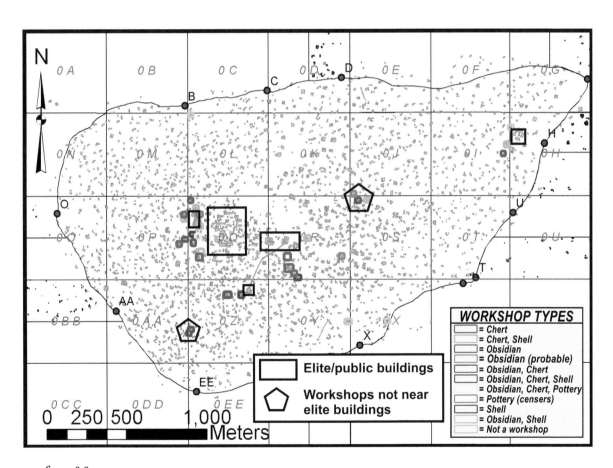

figure 8.8
Distribution of surplus household craft production workshops at Mayapan. (Map by Bradley W. Russell.)

of quantities of debris reveal that the scale of surplus production did not vary significantly between downtown and outlying locales (Masson and Peraza Lope n.d.) Many of the workshops engaged in multicrafting and made more than one type of product (Figure 8.8). All were located at independent commoner households, with one exception—an effigy incense-burner workshop within the houselot walls of an elite palace compound Q-41. As described above, these workshops made craft goods from raw materials that had to be exchanged into the city from elsewhere in the Yucatan Peninsula or beyond (Figure 8.2).

Consumption of Valuables at Tikal and Mayapan

Nonlocal valuables at Tikal and Mayapan exhibit relatively equitable distributions (Tables 8.2–8.3). Hattula Moholy-Nagy (2003b, 2008a, 2008b) has recently published the Tikal data that is employed for these comparisons. Although volumetric comparisons are ideal, as are other methods—such as ratios of materials to pottery—the Tikal data was not reported in a way that allows these full comparisons. While such data are available from Mayapan (Masson and Peraza Lope n.d.), tabulations offered here are presented in comparable format to those of Tikal. We cannot resolve the issue of whether materials from Tikal structures may derive from primary or secondary deposits, although significant quantities of fill probably come from similar nearby edifices. Thus, our comparisons using Tikal data represent a preliminary effort to quantify distributions by context. We are encouraged by affirmation of our results in more recent investigations at Classic-era Maya sites that also report comparable distributions of valuables at elite and commoner dwellings (discussed below).

Most of the Tikal obsidian is of Classic-period date (85.6 percent; Moholy-Nagy 2008a:appendix 6, table 3.24), and a ratio of 9.9 obsidian pieces per chert tool can be calculated for this site (Moholy-Nagy 1997:table 2). Small structure groups at Tikal yielded 40.7 percent of all obsidian blades

recovered at Tikal (Figure 8.9), and a nearly equivalent quantity are from civic-ceremonial and range structures (long, narrow, multiroom buildings that often housed elite families) combined (45.8 percent) (Moholy-Nagy 2008a:appendix 6, table 3.22). This distribution is notable considering that the Tikal project sampled more large public buildings than small structures. The proportion of green obsidian (Table 8.2) of all obsidian is not significantly greater in elite or public buildings (1.3 to 5 percent) compared to small structures (1.9 to 12.5 percent), according to Moholy-Nagy's data (2008a:appendix 5). Similar comparisons (Table 8.2) of thin obsidian bifaces, nonlocal *metates*, *manos*, axes, chisels, and finished shell objects do not indicate concentrations primarily in upperstatus contexts (Moholy-Nagy 2008a:appendices 5–6, tables 3.4, 4.32, 4.34). Rathje (1971) reported an imported rate of 85 percent for nonlocal *manos* and *metates*, a figure that agrees with our own calculations (Figure 8.10). He points out that forty-five of forty-eight peripheral house mounds at Tikal had imported *metates*. The nearest source for these materials is the Maya mountains, at least ninety kilometers away. Quartzite makes up 38–61 percent of the *manos* and *metates*, and these were probably obtained from the Guatemala Highlands (Figure 8.10). Quartzite materials occur in similar proportions at civic-ceremonial and range structures (57 percent, 46 percent) compared to small central or peripheral structures (63 percent, 60 percent) (Moholy-Nagy 2008a:appendix 5). Higher-value marine shells, like *Spondylus*, were more concentrated in elite/public contexts, and olive tinklers were more common in small structures, but building types had overlapping quantities of shell objects and small epicentral structures had great diversity in shell assemblages (e.g., Masson and Freidel 2012:figs. 1, 6).

At Mayapan, imported pottery from the Gulf coast (Matillas Fine Orange) was found as regularly in ordinary houselots as in elite dwellings or public buildings (Table 8.3, Figure 8.11). The same patterns are observed for other nonimported fancy serving wares, such as Chapab Modeled and Sulche Black (Hare and Masson 2010). Comparisons

table 8.2

Equitable distributions of valuables at Tikal. Data is from Moholy-Nagy (2003b:appendix G, tables 3.4, 4.32, 4.34, 2008a: appendices 5–6, F). Values indicate the percentage per structure type of the composite sample of each artifact category.

TIKAL	SMALL STRUCTURES	CIVIC-RANGE STRUCTURES
Green obsidian (percent of all obsidian per structure type)	12%, 3%, 2% (epicenter, central, peripheral)	1%, 5%
Obsidian (percent of all Tikal obsidian recovered)	41%	37%, 9%
Thin obsidian bifaces (percent of all recovered)	33%	30%, 24%
Nonlocal *manos*, *metates* (percent per structure type)	74–85%	78–79%
Nonlocal ground stone axes/chisel (percent per structure type)	41%	13–14%
Finished shell objects (percent of all shell per structure type)	28%, 42% (peripheral, central)	20–42%

table 8.3

Equitable distributions of valuables at Mayapan

MAYAPAN	COMMONER	ELITES	CRAFTING COMMONERS*
Greenstone (surface collection)	1 object (8 cases)	2 objects (1 case)	1–5 objects (7 cases)
Greenstone (fully excavated structures)	Houses 0–1 objects	Houses and public buildings, 1–6	Houses, 1–5 objects
Finished shell (fully excavated structures)	0.03–0.05/m²	0.02–0.03/m²	n/a**
Copper objects (fully excavated structures)	2 objects (1 case)	1–2 objects (3 cases)	1 objects (4 cases)
Obsidian (test pits)	5–22/m² (mean = 5)	12–17/m² (mean = 15)	9–24/m² (mean = 19)

* Cases shown for shell and obsidian frequencies are consumer contexts that were not engaged in surplus shell or obsidian production.

** Not shown due to high frequencies linked to shell production.

for additional categories of nonlocal valuables—including greenstone (serpentine) celts, finished marine shell objects, copper bells, and obsidian—parallel these results (Table 8.3).

There are six pieces of obsidian for every chert or chalcedony tool (including utilized and retouched chert flakes) at Mayapan. Excluding houselots where surplus quantities of obsidian blades were produced (Figure 8.12), some commoners possessed obsidian in equal amounts to elite houses,

with ranges of nine to twenty-three obsidian pieces per square meter of excavation. Most commoners possessed less obsidian, and test-pit frequencies fall within interval ranges of 1–3.5 or 4–8 pieces per square meter (Figure 8.12). Commoner houselots producing obsidian blades had an average of 42.3 pieces of obsidian per square meter, far more than elite houses, which averaged 14.7. Crafting houselots making surplus goods other than obsidian had 11.1 pieces per square meter, and noncrafting

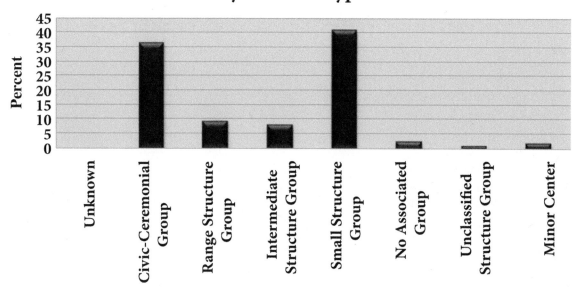

figure 8.9
Distribution of all obsidian blades recovered from Tikal. (Graph by Marilyn A. Masson, derived from Moholy-Nagy 2003b:appendix G, table 3.22).

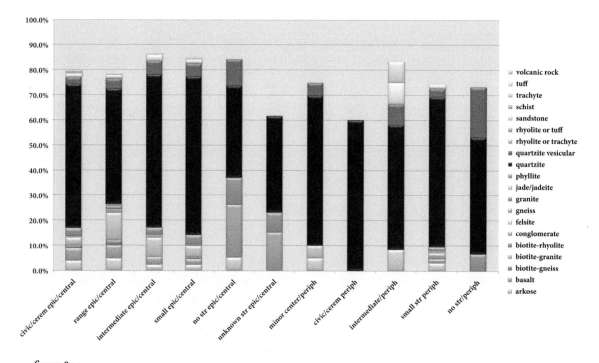

figure 8.10
Distribution of nonlocal ground stone at Tikal. Nonlocal quartzite, the dominant class, is shown in black and dark gray. (Graph by Marilyn A. Masson, derived from Moholy-Nagy 2008a:appendix 5–6, tables 3.4, 4.32, 4.34).

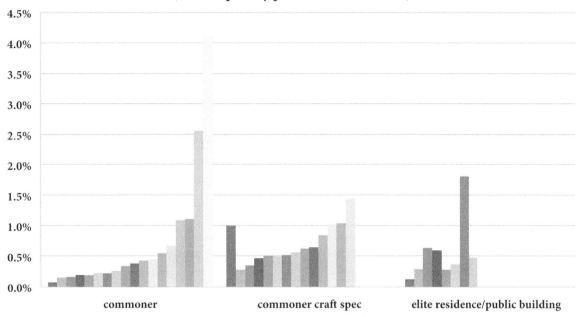

Imported Matillas Fine Orange Pottery at Mayapan
(% of all pottery per excavation context)

figure 8.11
Distribution of imported Gulf-coast Matillas Fine Orange pottery (of all pottery per context) at Mayapan. (Graph and data supplied by Marilyn A. Masson.)

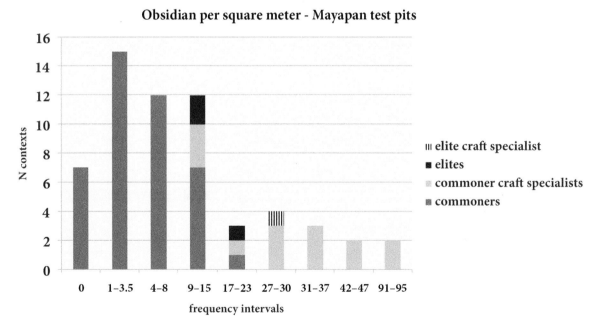

Obsidian per square meter - Mayapan test pits

figure 8.12
Frequency intervals of obsidian per square meter of excavation at Mayapan. (Graph and data supplied by Marilyn A. Masson.)

houselots averaged 4.8 pieces per square meter (Figure 8.12). In test pits that sampled sixty contexts, only seven lacked obsidian. These data refute Braswell's (2010:137) claims that obsidian is concentrated at Mayapan's monumental center; he did not quantify obsidian from any contexts outside of the epicenter to support this inference.

It is important to acknowledge that variation exists among commoner houselots in the quantity of nonlocal valuables recovered (Figures 8.10–8.12). Some discrepancies should be expected in market systems due to the greater purchasing power of wealthier families (Hirth 1998:471), including commoners engaged in surplus craft making at Mayapan. The overall expectation that valuables were obtained by commoners in some abundance remains a key criterion for identifying market distribution (Hirth 1998; Smith 1999:529). The patterns observed here for Tikal's small structures have been reported at a range of Mesoamerican sites—for example, Cuexcomate and Capilco (Smith 1999:tables 1–2), Chunchucmil (Hutson et al. n.d.), settlements in the Chikinchel region (Kepecs 2003:263), Ceren (Sheets 2000:223), and Copan (Aoyama 2001:354; Webster et al. 1997:56, 58). Wide distribution of nonlocal *manos, metates,* and obsidian are also reported from small agrarian sites of Chan Noohol and San Lorenzo in western Belize (Yaeger and Robin 2004:151, 154, 160). The Postclassic hamlet of Laguna de On has more relative obsidian (ratios to chert and to ceramic sherds) than Mayapan (Masson et al. 2006). Additional studies of small settlements are needed.

Discussion

Occupational specialization is an important correlate of urban life, and it is an indicator of household interdependence on local, polity, and interpolity trade (Childe 1950:11). Craft production at the political capitals of Tikal and Mayapan evokes comparisons with Landa's contact-period (Tozzer 1941 [ca. 1566]:94–96) list of specialists that includes potters, carpenters, idol makers, farmers, fishers, and merchants. Coastal salt production

and fishing industries were especially large-scale (Kepecs 2003:264; Tozzer 1941 [ca. 1566]:190), and not only during the Postclassic period (Andrews and Mock 2002). Although most Mesoamerican craft production would have been part-time, this scale was sufficient to support regional market systems (Feinman and Nicholas 2000:136–138, 2004:170, 187). Crafting is documented within Maya cities as well as at secondary centers, villages, and hamlets, as is expected for a complex and integrated market economy. Neither the consumer city model nor the autonomous commoner model is supported by this pattern. The distribution of nonlocal goods at Tikal and Mayapan indicates that ordinary citizens were linked by market networks over considerable regional distances across the Maya area. Commoners obtained significant quantities of marine shell, obsidian, and ground stone from destinations well beyond the borders of the polities with which they were affiliated.

Markets, as Mayer (this volume) reminds us, were diverse and variable entities. Tikal's distribution patterns summarized here differ from those at its primary rival Calakmul, which has little obsidian (Braswell 2010). Competitive and warring alliance networks of these major centers seem to have impeded and shaped the regional flow of goods, as has been suggested for networks within the Basin of Mexico (e.g., Minc 2006:84). Calakmul's dearth of obsidian blades implies that the well-documented conflicts of Calakmul and Tikal had resounding economic consequences. Political competition for access to key trade resources (Demarest et al. 2008; Kovacevich, this volume; Speal 2009:111) and the most diverse and prosperous market events, as described for the Aztec realm (Blanton 1996), would have been important in the deeper Maya past.

Although perishable foodstuffs are more difficult to track (Dahlin et al. 2010), we infer that maize and other staples were also traded across major swaths of the lowlands during the Classic period. A limit of one hundred fifty to two hundred seventy-five kilometers was calculated for cost-effective exchange of agricultural staples (Drennan 1984; Sanders and Santley 1983:246–249), and these distances from Tikal and Mayapan crossed many

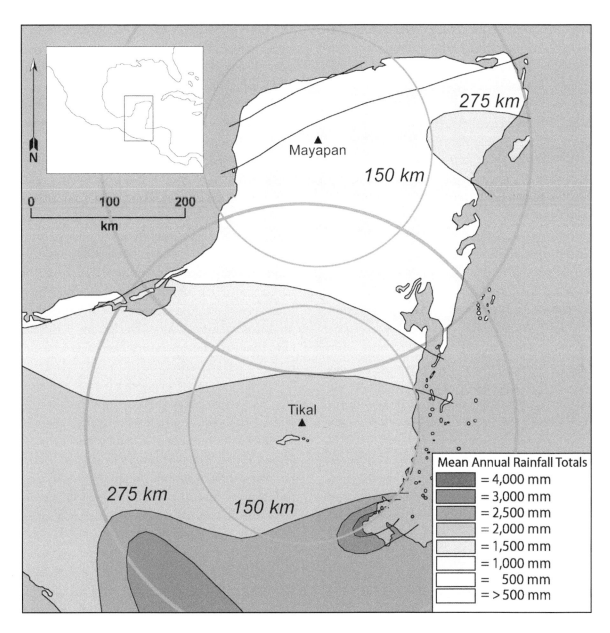

figure 8.13
Rainfall map and transport distances from Tikal and Mayapan. (Map by Bradley W. Russell, after Folan 1983:fig. 3; Sharer and Traxler 2006:fig. 1.6.)

diverse environmental and rainfall zones (Figure 8.13). Riverine routes shortened these distances further in the Southern Lowlands. Quintana Roo has fifty centimeters more rainfall annually than does Mayapan. Similarly, Tikal was also within trading reach of well-watered zones of Belize and Uaymil, Quintana Roo, where settlements are associated with significant surplus agricultural production that could have been traded into

urban centers (Dunning et al. n.d.). Rainfall varies widely in restricted parts of the Maya area, which would have promoted food interdependency (Rice 1993; Scarborough and Valdez 2003:7), such as that recorded between Zoque, Chontalpa, and lower Grijalva towns during the contact period (Scholes and Roys 1968:31, 318). In these cases, food trade was ongoing even without local shortfalls. Regular climatic events, particularly small-scale droughts or hurricanes, in the Maya area can manifest very different effects among neighboring areas.

Maize was difficult to store over a lengthy period in the tropical lowlands, and the ability to move and purchase surpluses across considerable distances would have been critical for mitigating shortages. Freidel and Shaw (2000) have argued that Maya royalty may have stored wealth in durable currency units that could have been used to purchase maize when local disasters struck. Clearly, Maya rulers associated themselves with the icon of agricultural prosperity, the maize god, an identification that implies an obligatory relationship with their subjects (Freidel and Reilly 2010). In support of Freidel and Shaw's argument, Gaspar Antonio Chi reported in the sixteenth century that prices for goods in Yucatan were always the same, "except for maize, which sometimes (rose in price when the crop failed)" (Tozzer 1941 [ca. 1566]:231). Landa also observes that maize was stored in granaries to sell "at the proper time" (Tozzer 1941 [ca. 1566]:96). Famine relief represents an exception to a system where supporting populations usually grew their own food or obtained it in markets (Isaac, this volume; Stark and Garraty 2010:43). While dire prolonged droughts or other extensive disasters tapped the limits of even the most complex agrarian states or empires, famine relief may have been effective for fluctuations of a smaller scale. Even symbolic gestures were good for morale.

Currencies may have had great time depth in the Maya area. Red and white shell beads and other suspended ornaments served as currency units at Spanish contact, along with greenstone beads, cacao beans, cotton mantles, and copper bells; all but copper were significant in the Maya area from the Late Preclassic period onward (Freidel et al. 2002; Stuart 2006). This argument is presented in full detail elsewhere (Freidel et al. n.d.). Cacao, shell, and stone bead currencies were used in sales of salt, cloth, slaves, and "everything which there was in that country" (Tozzer 1941 [ca. 1566]:94–96); food, condiments, and valuables were exchanged for one another (Ximénez 1929–1931:1:94). These descriptions do not suggest strong restrictions on luxury-goods acquisition.

How might markets have been organized and administered? Aspects of Carol Smith's (1976) solar central-place market model fit Classic-era Maya exchange (Braswell 2010; Chase and Chase 2001; West 2002), including such forms of elite oversight as sponsorship, security, dispute negotiation, rules, and restriction of trade to formal marketplaces. Yet Isaac (this volume) suggests that fully elite-administered systems may be an ideal model that is no longer accurate or useful. The ubiquity of nonlocal goods at commoner dwellings is a pattern that diverges most visibly from the elite-centric, monopolistic solar central-place model that carries the expectation of suppressed opportunities for rural wealth. In the Maya area, monopolies may have been weak, and the presence of secondary markets within or along political boundaries may have afforded commoners further options for trade (Masson and Freidel 2012).

It is important to consider a variety of exchanged goods in reconstructing market systems (Smith 1999:528). Studies that primarily analyze the distribution of common pottery types (e.g., Minc 2006; West 2002) consider the least transportable artifact category and result in the identification of more spatially bounded exchange networks. In contrast, Braswell (2010) relies primarily on obsidian—particularly types exchanged from outside of the Maya area—which inhibits the recognition of key long-distance exchanges within the Maya realm between the lowlands and highlands, the interior, and the coasts. The inferences of these specific studies highlight the problem of analytical scale that we raised at the beginning of this chapter. We reiterate here that the geographic extent, population, and resource diversity across the political boundaries of Maya kingdom alliance networks were considerable and suitable for fostering market dependencies among households and settlements.

One fact emerges from Carol Smith's (1976) landmark treatise: the production and exchange activities of small, peripheral households hold the essential data for identifying the importance and type of market exchange because major central markets are held in both simple and more commercialized systems. To what degree did rural producers have the option to trade at more than one central market or at a set of markets? More research is needed, but determining commoner access to marine shell, nonlocal ground stone, and obsidian (at some sites) measures such participation. We already know that important variation existed: Chunchucmil was a market town with much more obsidian than any other northern site yet studied (Hutson et al. n.d.); Tikal accessed an inordinate amount of obsidian compared to Calakmul (Braswell 2010), which implies the existence of trade blocks; ceramic production and exchange spheres defined sets of allied polities and trade partners across the Maya area (Masson 2001); and an array of diverse, multiple productive strategies connected smaller sites into regional exchange networks. Contact-period markets ranged from small, local affairs to large and formal events at major cities and towns. Determining the links between economic activities of commoners and elites through marketplace exchange represents an ongoing challenge for continued investigations. It is reasonable to expect different levels of market integration across pockets of the Maya area according to factors of political or geographic contingencies as for many societies (Blanton 1996; Garraty 2010:18; McAnany 2010:266; Minc 2006; Rice 2009:81; Smith and Berdan 2003), and elite involvement in regulation, while common, also varies cross-culturally (Smith 1980:878). Characterizing ancient economies in terms of their degree of commercialization may be more productive; Classic Maya economies were

probably partially commercialized (Smith 1976; Smith and Berdan 2003:7).

When the Spanish arrived in Yucatan, well-developed market systems existed, and we argue that these institutions were not invented for the Maya by Chichen Itza. While an approach informed by heterarchy principles breaks free of Western tendencies to impose models of hierarchical domination on ancient societies (King n.d.; McAnany 2010:4), a recognition of the degree of commercialization of Maya states also liberates economic studies from antimarket biases projected onto premodern societies (Dahlin et al. 2010; Freidel and Reilly 2010). We encourage further inquiry into the complexity and integration of ancient Maya economies and market systems.

Acknowledgments

We thank the editors of this volume for the opportunity to participate in this important project. We are grateful to Clifford Brown and Walter Witschey for generating Figure 8.1 for us from their electronic database of Maya sites and to Bradley Russell for help with preparing other figures. Thanks are also due to Eleanor King for many insightful comments on our initial manuscript. Economic research at Mayapan has been funded with NSF support since 2001. It has been performed with the permission of Mexico's Consejo de Arqueología, Instituto Nacional de Antropología e Historia, in collaboration with Carlos Peraza Lope and Timothy S. Hare.

REFERENCES CITED

Andrews, Anthony P., and Shirley B. Mock

2002   New Perspectives on the Prehispanic Maya Salt Trade. In *Ancient Maya Political Economies*, edited by Marilyn A. Masson and David A. Freidel, pp. 307–334. Altamira Press, Walnut Creek, Calif.

Aoyama, Kazuo

2001   Classic Maya State, Urbanism, and Exchange: Chipped Stone Evidence of the Copán Valley and Its Hinterland. *American Anthropologist* 103:346–360.

Bair, Daniel A., Eric Coronel, and Richard E. Terry

2009 Estudios geoquímicos de suelo en Mayapán, Temporada 2008. In *Proyecto los fundamentos del poder económico de Mayapán, Temporada 2008*, edited by Marilyn A. Masson, Carlos Peraza Lope, and Timothy S. Hare, pp. 377–383. Report submitted to Consejo de Arqueología, Instituto Nacional de Antropología e Historia, Mexico City, and Department of Anthropology, State University of New York, Albany.

Ball, Joseph W.

1993 Pottery, Potters, Palaces, and Polities: Some Socioeconomic and Political Implications of Late Classic Maya Ceramic Industries. In *Lowland Maya Civilization in the Eighth Century AD*, edited by Jeremy A. Sabloff and John Henderson, pp. 243–272. Dumbarton Oaks Research Library and Collection, Washington, D.C.

Becker, Marshall Joseph

1973 Archaeological Evidence for Occupational Specialization among the Classic Period Maya at Tikal, Guatemala. *American Antiquity* 38:396–406.

Berdan, Frances F.

1988 Principles of Regional and Long-Distance Trade in the Aztec Empire. In *Smoke and Mist: Mesoamerican Studies in Memory of Thelma D. Sullivan*, edited by J. Kathryn Josserand and Karen Dakin, pp. 639–656. BAR, Oxford.

Berdan, Frances F., and Patricia Rieff Anawalt (editors)

1992 *The Codex Mendoza*. 4 vols. University of California Press, Berkeley.

Berdan, Frances F., Marilyn A. Masson, Janine Gasco, and Michael E. Smith

2003 An International Economy. In *The Postclassic Mesoamerican World*, edited by Michael E. Smith and Frances F. Berdan, pp. 96–108. University of Utah Press, Salt Lake City.

Blanton, Richard E.

1996 The Basin of Mexico Market System and the Growth of Empire. In *Aztec Imperial Strategies*, by Frances F. Berdan, Richard E. Blanton, Elizabeth Hill Boone, Mary G. Hodge, Michael E.

Smith, and Emily Umberger, pp. 47–84. Dumbarton Oaks Research Library and Collection, Washington, D.C.

Blanton, Richard E., Lane F. Fargher, and Verenice Y. Heredia Espinoza

2005 The Mesoamerican World of Goods and Its Transformations. In *Settlement, Subsistence, and Complexity: Essays Honoring the Legacy of Jeffrey R. Parsons*, edited by Richard E. Blanton, pp. 260–294. Cotsen Institute of Archaeology, University of California, Los Angeles.

Blanton, Richard E., Gary M. Feinman, Stephen A. Kowalewski, and Peter N. Peregrine

1996 A Dual-Processual Theory for the Evolution of Mesoamerican Civilization. *Current Anthropology* 37(1):1–14.

Blanton, Richard E., Stephen A. Kowalewski, Gary M. Feinman, and Laura M. Finsten

1993 *Ancient Mesoamerica: A Comparison of Change in Three Regions*. 2nd ed. Cambridge University Press, Cambridge.

Blom, Frans

1932 Commerce, Trade, and Monetary Units of the Maya. In *Middle American Papers*, pp. 533–556. Middle American Research Series 4. Department of Middle American Research, Tulane University, New Orleans.

Braswell, Geoffrey E.

2010 The Rise and Fall of Market Exchange: A Dynamic Approach to Ancient Maya Economy. In *Archaeological Approaches to Market Exchange in Ancient Societies*, edited by Christopher P. Garraty and Barbara L. Stark, pp. 127–139. University Press of Colorado, Boulder.

Brown, Clifford T., and Walter R. T. Witschey

2008 Electronic Atlas of Ancient Maya Sites. Electronic document, http://mayaGIS.smv.org, accessed September 2, 2011.

Carr, Robert F., and James E. Hazard

1961 *Map of the Ruins of Tikal, El Peten, Guatemala*. Tikal Report 11. University of Pennsylvania Museum of Archaeology and Anthropology, Philadelphia.

Carrasco Vargas, Ramón, Verónica A. Vásquez López, and Simon Martin

2009   Daily Life of the Ancient Maya Recorded on Murals at Calakmul, Mexico. *Proceedings of the National Academy of Science* 106:19245–19249.

Chase, Arlen F., and Diane Z. Chase

2001   Ancient Maya Causeways and Site Organization at Caracol, Belize. *Ancient Mesoamerica* 12:1–9.

Chase, Diane Z., and Arlen F. Chase

2004   Archaeological Perspectives on Classic Maya Social Organization from Caracol, Belize. *Ancient Mesoamerica* 15:139–147.

Chase, Diane Z., Arlen F. Chase, and William A. Haviland

1990   The Classic Maya City: Reconsidering the "Mesoamerican Urban Tradition." *American Anthropologist* 92:499–506.

Childe, V. Gordon

1950   The Urban Revolution. *Town Planning Review* 21:3–17.

Clark, John E.

2007   Mesoamerica's First State. In *The Political Economy of Ancient Mesoamerica: Transformations during the Formative and Classic Periods*, edited by Vernon L. Scarborough and John E. Clark, pp. 11–46. University of New Mexico Press, Albuquerque.

Culbert, T. Patrick

2003   The Ceramics of Tikal. In *Tikal: Dynasties, Foreigners, and Affairs of State*, edited by Jeremy A. Sabloff, pp. 47–82. School of American Research, Santa Fe.

Dahlin, Bruce H., Daniel Bair, Tim Beach, Matthew Moriarty, and Richard Terry

2010   The Dirt on Food: Ancient Feasts and Markets among the Lowland Maya. In *Pre-Columbian Foodways: Interdisciplinary Approaches to Food, Culture, and Markets in Mesoamerica*, edited by John Edward Staller and Michael Carrasco, pp. 191–232. Springer, New York.

Dahlin, Bruce H., Christopher T. Jensen, Richard E. Terry, David R. Wright, and Timothy Beach

2007   In Search of an Ancient Maya Market. *Latin American Antiquity* 18:363–384.

D'Altroy, Terence N., and Timothy K. Earle

1985   Staple Finance, Wealth Finance, and Storage in the Inka Economy. *Current Anthropology* 26:187–197.

Demarest, Arthur, Melanie Forne, Ronald Bishop, Marc Wolf, and Erin Sears

2008   High Elites, Economy, Production, and Exchange along the Late Classic Maya Western Trade Route. Paper presented at the Annual Meeting of the Society for American Archaeology, Vancouver.

Drennan, Robert D.

1984   Long Distance Movement of Goods in the Mesoamerican Formative and Classic. *American Antiquity* 49:27–43.

Dunning, Nicholas, Timothy Beach, and Sheryl Luzadder-Beach

n.d.   Environmental Variability, Instability, and Ancient Maya Settlement. In *El Urbanismo en Mesoamerica / Urbanism in Mesoamerica,* vol. 3, edited by Robert Cobean, Eric Taladoire, Ángel García Cook, and Kenneth G. Hirth. Instituto Nacional de Antropología e Historia, Mexico City, and Pennsylvania State University, University Park.

Earle, Timothy K.

1977   A Reappraisal of Redistribution: Complex Hawaiian Chiefdoms. In *Exchange Systems in Prehistory*, edited by Timothy K. Earle and Jonathon E. Ericson, pp. 213–229. Academic Press, New York.

Fedick, Scott L.

1991   Chert Production and Consumption among Classic Period Maya Households. In *Maya Stone Tools*, edited by Thomas R. Hester and Harry J. Shafer, pp. 103–118. Prehistory Press, Madison, Wis.

Feinman, Gary M., and Christopher P. Garraty

2010   Preindustrial Markets and Marketing: Archaeological Perspectives. *Annual Review of Anthropology* 39:167–191.

Feinman, Gary M., and Linda M. Nicholas

2000   High-Intensity Household-Scale Production in Ancient Mesoamerica: A Perspective from Ejutla, Oaxaca. In *Cultural Evolution: Contemporary Viewpoints*, edited by Gary M. Feinman and Linda Manzanilla, pp. 119–144. Kluwer Academic/Plenum Publishers, New York.

2004 Unraveling the Prehispanic Highland
Mesoamerican Economy: Production,
Exchange, and Consumption in the
Classic Period Valley of Oaxaca. In
*Archaeological Perspectives on Political
Economies,* edited by Gary M. Feinman
and Linda M. Nicholas, pp. 167–188.
University of Utah Press, Salt Lake City.

Feldman, Lawrence H.

1978 Moving Merchandise in Protohistoric
Central Quauhtemallan. In *Meso-
american Communication Routes and
Cultural Contacts*, edited by Thomas A.
Lee Jr. and Carlos Navarrete, pp. 7–17.
New World Archaeological Foundation,
Brigham Young University, Provo, Utah.

Foias, Antonia E.

2002 At the Crossroads: The Economic Basis
of Political Power in the Petexbatun
Region, Southwest Peten, Guatemala.
In *Ancient Maya Political Economies*,
edited by Marilyn A. Masson and David
A. Freidel, pp. 223–248. Altamira Press,
Walnut Creek, Calif.

Folan, William J.

1983 Urban Organization and Social
Structure of Coba. In *Coba: A Classic
Maya Metropolis*, by William J. Folan,
Ellen R. Kintz, and Laraine A. Fletcher,
pp. 49–63. Academic Press, New York.

Folan, William J., Laraine A. Fletcher, Jacinto May
Hau, and Lynda Florey Folan

2001a *Las ruinas de Calakmul, Campeche,
México: Un lugar central y su paisaje
cultural.* Universidad Autónoma de
Campeche, Centro de Investigaciones
Históricas y Sociales, Campeche.

Folan, William J., Joel D. Gunn, and María del
Rosario Domínguez Carrasco

2001b Triadic Temples, Central Plazas, and
Dynastic Palaces: A Diachronic Analysis
of the Royal Court Complex, Calakmul,
Campeche, Mexico. In *Royal Courts
of the Maya,* vol. 2, edited by Takeshi
Inomata and Stephen D. Houston, pp.
223–265. Westview Press, Boulder, Colo.

Freidel, David A.

1978 Maritime Adaptation and the Rise
of Maya Civilization: The View from
Cerros, Belize. In *Prehistoric Coastal
Adaptations: The Economy and Ecology*

of Maritime Middle America, edited by
Barbara L. Stark and Barbara Voorhies,
pp. 239–265. Academic Press, New York.

1981 The Political Economics of Residential
Dispersion among the Lowland Maya.
In *Lowland Maya Settlement Patterns*,
edited by Wendy Ashmore, pp. 371–
382. University of New Mexico Press,
Albuquerque.

Freidel, David A., Marilyn A. Masson, Michelle Rich,
and F. Kent Reilly III

n.d. Imagining a Complex Maya Political
Economy: Currencies, Images, and
Texts. *Cambridge Archaeological
Journal*, in press.

Freidel, David A., Kathryn Reese-Taylor, and David
Mora-Marin

2002 The Origins of Maya Civilization:
The Old Shell Game, Commodity,
Treasure, and Kingship. In *Ancient
Maya Political Economies,* edited by
Marilyn A. Masson and David A.
Freidel, pp. 41–86. Altamira Press,
Walnut Creek, Calif.

Freidel, David A., and F. Kent Reilly III

2010 The Flesh of the God: Cosmology,
Food, and the Origins of Political
Power in Ancient Southeastern Meso-
america. In *Pre-Columbian Foodways:
Interdisciplinary Approaches to Food,
Culture, and Markets in Mesoamerica*,
edited by John Edward Staller and
Michael Carrasco, pp. 635–680.
Springer, New York.

Freidel, David A., and Justine Shaw

2000 The Lowland Maya Civilization:
Historical Consciousness and
Environment. In *The Way the Wind
Blows: Climate, History, and Human
Action*, edited by Roderick J. McIntosh,
Joseph A. Tainter, and Susan Keech
McIntosh, pp. 271–300. Columbia
University Press, New York.

Fry, Robert E.

2003 The Peripheries of Tikal. In *Tikal:
Dynasties, Foreigners, and Affairs of
State*, edited by Jeremy A. Sabloff, pp.
143–170. School of American Research,
Santa Fe.

Garraty, Christopher P.

2010   Investigating Market Exchange in Ancient Societies: A Theoretical Review. In *Archaeological Approaches to Market Exchange in Ancient Societies*, edited by Christopher P. Garraty and Barbara L. Stark, pp. 3–32. University Press of Colorado, Boulder.

Hare, Timothy S., and Marilyn A. Masson

2010   Pottery Assemblage Variation at Mayapán Residences. Paper presented at the Annual Meeting of the Society for American Archaeology, Saint Louis.

Haviland, William A.

1985   *Excavations in Small Residential Groups of Tikal, Groups 4F-1 and 4F-2.* Tikal Report 19. University of Pennsylvania Museum of Archaeology and Anthropology, Philadelphia.

Hirth, Kenneth G.

1998   The Distributional Approach: A New Way to Identify Marketplace Exchange in the Archaeological Record. *Current Anthropology* 39:451–476.

Hutson, Scott R., Bruce H. Dahlin, and Daniel Mazeau

n.d.   Commerce and Cooperation among the Classic Maya: The Chunchucmil Case. In *Cooperation in Social and Economic Life*, edited by Robert Marshall. Altamira Press, Lanham, Md., in press.

Jones, Christopher

1996   *Excavations in the East Plaza of Tikal.* Tikal Report 16, vol. 1. University Museum Monograph 92. University of Pennsylvania Museum of Archaeology and Anthropology, Philadephia.

Kepecs, Susan M.

2003   Chikinchel. In *The Postclassic Meso-american World*, edited by Michael E. Smith and Frances F. Berdan, pp. 259–268. University of Utah Press, Salt Lake City.

Kidder, Alfred V.

1950   Introduction. In *Uaxactun, Guatemala: Excavations of 1931–1937*, by A. Ledyard Smith, pp. 1–12. Carnegie Institution of Washington Publication 588. Carnegie Institution of Washington, Washington, D.C.

King, Eleanor M.

n.d.   Rethinking the Role of Early Economics in the Rise of Maya States: A View from the Lowlands. In *The Origins of Maya States*, edited by Robert Sharer, Loa Traxler, and Jeremy Sabloff. University of Pennsylvania Museum of Archaeology and Anthropology, Philadelphia, in press.

Marcus, Joyce

1983   Lowland Maya Archaeology at the Crossroads. *American Antiquity* 48(3):454–488.

Martin, Simon

2007   Un informe provisional sobre los murales de la Estructura I de la acrópolis de Chiik Nahb. Manuscript on file, Archivo del Proyecto Arqueológico Calakmul, Instituto Nacional de Antropología e Historia, Sureste, Mérida, Yucatan.

Masson, Marilyn A.

2001   Changing Patterns of Ceramic Stylistic Diversity in the Pre-Hispanic Maya Lowlands. *Acta archaeologica* 72:159–188.

Masson, Marilyn A., and David A. Freidel

2012   An Argument for Classic-Era Maya Market Exchange. *Journal of Anthropological Archaeology*, in press, http://dx.doi.org/10.1016/j.jaa2012.03.007.

Masson, Marilyn A., Timothy S. Hare, and Carlos Peraza Lope

2006   Postclassic Maya Society Regenerated at Mayapán. In *After Collapse: The Regeneration of Complex Societies*, edited by Glenn M. Schwartz and John J. Nichols, pp. 188–207. University of Arizona Press, Tucson.

Masson, Marilyn A., and Carlos Peraza Lope

n.d.   *Kukulkan's Realm: Urban Life at Ancient Mayapan.* University Press of Colorado, Boulder, in press.

McAnany, Patricia A.

2010   *Ancestral Maya Economies in Archae-ological Perspective.* Cambridge University Press, Cambridge.

McAnany, Patricia A., and Tomás Gallareta Negrón

2009   Bellicose Rulers and Climatological Peril? Retrofitting Twenty-First Century Woes on Eighth Century Maya Society. In *Questioning Collapse: Human*

Resilience, Ecological Variability, and the Aftermath of Empire, edited by Patricia A. McAnany and Norman Yoffee, pp. 142–175. Cambridge University Press, Cambridge.

McKillop, Heather I.

1989   Coastal Maya Trade: Obsidian Densities at Wild Cane Cay, Belize. In *Prehistoric Maya Economies of Belize, Research in Economic Anthropology*, supplement 4, edited by Patricia McAnany and Barry Isaac, pp. 17–56. JAI Press, Greenwich, Conn.

Minc, Leah D.

2006   Monitoring Regional Market Systems in Prehistory: Models, Methods, and Metrics. *Journal of Anthropological Archaeology* 25:82–116.

Moholy-Nagy, Hattula

1997   Middens, Construction Fill, and Offerings: Evidence for the Organization of Classic Period Craft Production at Tikal, Guatemala. *Journal of Field Archaeology* 24:293–313.

2003a   Beyond the Catalog: The Chronology and Contexts of Tikal Artifacts. In *Tikal: Dynasties, Foreigners, and Affairs of State*, edited by Jeremy A. Sabloff, pp. 83–110. School of American Research, Santa Fe.

2003b   *The Artifacts of Tikal: Utilitarian Artifacts and Unworked Material.* Tikal Report 27, pt. B. University of Pennsylvania Museum of Archaeology and Anthropology, Philadelphia.

2008a   Appendices 5 and 6. In *The Artifacts of Tikal: Ornamental and Ceremonial Artifacts and Unworked Material.* Tikal Report 27, pt. A. University of Pennsylvania Museum of Archaeology and Anthropology, Philadelphia.

2008b   *The Artifacts of Tikal: Ornamental and Ceremonial Artifacts and Unworked Material.* Tikal Report 27, pt. A. University of Pennsylvania Museum of Archaeology and Anthropology, Philadelphia.

Piña Chan, Román

1978   Commerce in the Yucatec Peninsula: The Conquest and Colonial Period. In *Mesoamerican Communication Routes and Culture Contacts*, edited by Thomas A. Lee Jr. and Carlos Navarrete, pp. 37–48. Papers of the New World Archaeological Foundation 40. Brigham Young University, Provo, Utah.

Potter, Daniel R., and Eleanor M. King

1995   A Heterarchical Approach to Lowland Maya Socioeconomies. In *Heterarchy and the Analysis of Complex Societies*, edited by Robert M. Ehrenreich, Carole L. Crumley, and Janet E. Levy, pp. 17–32. American Anthropological Association, Arlington, Va.

Rathje, William L.

1971   Lowland Classic Maya Socio-Political Organization: Degree and Form Through Space and Time. PhD dissertation, Department of Anthropology, Harvard University, Cambridge, Mass.

1972   Praise the Gods and Pass the Metates: A Hypothesis of the Development of Lowland Rainforest Civilizations in Mesoamerica. In *Contemporary Archaeology: A Guide to Theory and Contributions*, edited by Mark P. Leone, pp. 365–392. Southern Illinois University Press, Carbondale.

Rice, Don S.

1993   Eighth-Century Physical Geography, Environment, and Natural Resources in the Maya Lowlands. In *Lowland Maya Civilization in the Eighth Century AD*, edited by Jeremy A. Sabloff and John S. Henderson, pp. 11–64. Dumbarton Oaks Research Library and Collection, Washington, D.C.

Rice, Prudence M.

2009   On Classic Maya Political Economies. *Journal of Anthropological Archaeology* 28:70–84.

Ruppert, Karl

1943   *The Mercado, Chichen Itza, Yucatan.* Carnegie Institution of Washington Publication 546. Carnegie Institution of Washington, Washington, D.C.

1952   *Chichen Itza Architectural Notes and Plans.* Carnegie Institution of Washington Publication 595. Carnegie Institution of Washington, Washington, D.C.

Sabloff, Jeremy A., and William L. Rathje

1975   The Rise of a Maya Merchant Class. *Scientific American* 233:72–82.

Sanders, William T.

1973   The Cultural Ecology of the Lowland Maya: A Reevaluation. In *The Classic Maya Collapse*, edited by T. Patrick Culbert, pp. 325–366. School of American Research, University of New Mexico Press, Albuquerque.

Sanders, William T., and Robert S. Santley

1983   A Tale of Three Cities: Energetics and Urbanization in Pre-Hispanic Central Mexico. In *Prehistoric Settlement Patterns: Essays in Honor of Gordon R. Willey*, edited by Evon Z. Vogt and Richard Leventhal, pp. 243–291. University of New Mexico Press, Albuquerque.

Sanders, William T., and David Webster

1988   The Mesoamerican Urban Tradition. *American Anthropologist* 90:521–546.

Scarborough, Vernon L., and Fred Valdez Jr.

2003   The Engineered Environment and Political Economy of the Three Rivers Region. In *Heterarchy, Political Economy, and the Ancient Maya: The Three Rivers Region of the East-Central Yucatán Peninsula*, edited by Vernon L. Scarborough, Fred Valdez Jr., and Nicholas Dunning, pp. 3–13. University of Arizona Press, Tempe.

2009   An Alternative Order: The Dualistic Economies of the Ancient Maya. *Latin American Antiquity* 20:207–227.

Scholes, Frances V., and Ralph L. Roys

1968   *The Maya Chontal Indians of Acalan-Tixchel: A Contribution to the History and Ethnography of the Yucatan Peninsula*. 2nd ed. University of Oklahoma Press, Norman.

Shafer, Harry J., and Thomas R. Hester

1983   Ancient Maya Chert Workshops in Northern Belize, Central America. *American Antiquity* 48(3):519–543.

Sharer, Robert J., and Loa Traxler

2006   *The Ancient Maya*. 6th ed. Stanford University Press, Stanford.

Shaw, Leslie

1999   Social and Ecological Aspects of Preclassic Maya Meat Consumption at Colha, Belize. In *Reconstructing Ancient Maya Diet*, edited by Christine D. White, pp. 83–100. University of Utah Press, Salt Lake City.

Sheets, Payson

2000   Provisioning the Ceren Household: The Vertical Economy, Village Economy, and Household Economy in the Southeast Maya Periphery. *Ancient Mesoamerica* 11:217–230.

Sidrys, Raymond

1976   Classic Maya Obsidian Trade. *American Antiquity* 41:449–464.

Smith, Carol A.

1976   Exchange Systems and the Spatial Distribution of Elites: The Organization of Stratification in Agrarian Societies. In *Regional Analysis*, vol. 2, edited by Carol A. Smith, pp. 309–374. Academic Press, New York.

Smith, Michael E.

1980   The Role of the Marketing System in Aztec Society and Economy: Reply to Evans. *American Antiquity* 45:876–883.

1999   On Hirth's "Distributional Approach." *Current Anthropology* 40:528–530.

2004   The Archaeology of Ancient State Economies. *Annual Review of Anthropology* 33:73–102.

2010   Aztec Taxation at the City-State and Imperial Levels. Paper presented at the conference "Fiscal Regimes and the Political Economy of Early States," Stanford University, Stanford.

Smith, Michael E., and Frances F. Berdan

2003   Postclassic Mesoamerica. In *The Postclassic Mesoamerican World*, edited by Michael E. Smith and Frances F. Berdan, pp. 3–13. University of Utah Press, Salt Lake City.

Speal, C. Scott

2009   The Economic Geography of Chert Lithic Production in the Southern Maya Lowlands: A Comparative Examination of Early-Stage Reduction Debris. *Latin American Antiquity* 20:91–119.

Stark, Barbara L.

1997 Gulf Lowland Styles and Political Geography in Ancient Veracruz. In *Olmec to Aztec: Settlement Patterns in the Ancient Gulf Lowlands*, edited by Barbara L. Stark and Philip J. Arnold III, pp. 278–309. University of Arizona Press, Tucson.

Stark, Barbara L., and Christopher P. Garraty

2010 Detecting Marketplace Exchange in Archaeology: A Methodological Review. In *Archaeological Approaches to Market Exchange in Ancient Societies*, edited by Christopher P. Garraty and Barbara L. Stark, pp. 33–58. University Press of Colorado, Boulder.

Stuart, David

2006 Jade and Chocolate: Bundles of Wealth in Classic Maya Economics and Ritual. In *Sacred Acts of Wrapping and Binding in Mesoamerica*, edited by Julia Guernsey and F. Kent Reilly III, pp. 127–144. Boundary End Archaeology Research Center, Barnardsville, N.C.

Sullivan, Lauren A.

2002 Dynamics of Regional Organization in Northwest Belize. In *Ancient Maya Political Economies*, edited by Marilyn A. Masson and David A. Freidel, pp. 197–222. Altamira Press, Walnut Creek, Calif.

Tourtellot, Gair, and Jeremy A. Sabloff

1972 Exchange Systems among the Ancient Maya. *American Antiquity* 37(1):125–135.

Tozzer, Alfred M.

1941 [ca. 1566] *Landa's* Relación de las cosas de Yucatan: *A Translation.* Papers of the Peabody Museum of American Archaeology and Ethnology 18. The Peabody Museum, Cambridge, Mass.

Wauchope, Robert

1938 *Modern Maya Houses: A Study of Their Archaeological Significance.* Carnegie Institution of Washington Publication 502. Carnegie Institution of Washington, Washington, D.C.

Webster, David, Nancy Gonlin, and Payson Sheets

1997 Copan and Cerén: Two Perspectives on Ancient Mesoamerican Households. *Ancient Mesoamerica* 8:43–61.

West, Georgia

2002 Ceramic Exchange in the Late Classic and Postclassic Maya Lowlands: A Diachronic Approach. In *Ancient Maya Political Economies*, edited by Marilyn A. Masson and David A. Freidel, pp. 141–196. Altamira Press, Walnut Creek, Calif.

Ximénez, Francisco

1929–1931 *Historia de la provincia de San Vicente de Chiapa y Guatemala de la orden de predicadores.* 3 vols. Biblioteca "Goathemala" de la Sociedad de Geografía e Historia, Guatemala City.

Yaeger, Jason, and Cynthia Robin

2004 Heterogenous Hinterlands: The Social and Political Organization of Commoner Settlements near Xunantunich, Belize. In *Ancient Maya Commoners,* edited by Jon C. Lohse and Fred Valdez Jr., pp. 148–173. University of Texas Press, Austin.

9

Artisans, *Ikatz*, and Statecraft

Provisioning Classic Maya Royal Courts

PATRICIA A. MCANANY

I N A *TIME* MAGAZINE COLUMN ENTITLED "THE Curious Capitalist," Zachary Karabell (2010:67) notes that "the world is simply more complex than our ability to measure it in *real time*" (emphasis mine). Although referring to twenty-first-century economies of nanosecond trading, derivative algorithms, and global outsourcing, Karabell's observation might give us pause as we go about the business of characterizing merchants, markets, and trade in *unreal time*, based on fragmentary evidence from Pre-Columbian places. Mesoamerican and Andean worlds before Spanish incursion increasingly are recognized as places of great complexity, economic dynamism, and historical contingency. These times and places have been simplified primarily by our analytical models and measures. Several contributors to this volume confront and challenge received wisdom on topics such as the lack of marketplace exchange in the Maya region and the Andes (see Masson and Freidel, this volume; see also Burger, this volume; Dillehay, this volume) or the assumption that imperial Inca suppression of marketplace

exchange can be retrofitted onto deeper time (see Mayer, this volume; see also Stanish and Coben, this volume). Typological distinctions—such as the contrast between commercial and noncommercial economies—can powerfully frame research but also falsely polarize past economic arrangements. Such polarities also negate the principle of economic change as cumulative (rather than substitutive; see Hirth and Pillsbury, this volume) and ignore the thermodynamic properties of social complexity (Braswell 2010:127).

In this chapter, I adopt the perspective of the "The Curious Noncapitalist" and suggest that Classic Maya economies were more varied and heterodoxic than our current analytical frameworks indicate. Within the Maya region, the nuanced character of production and exchange relations and their near hieroglyphic opacity pose a challenge to interpretation, but a monolithic model of "the ancient Maya" that homogenizes lived realities of the past further impedes understanding. Fortunately, three decades of extremely active fieldwork coupled with rigorous study of royal texts and iconography combine to dislodge simplistic models (although not apocalyptic scenarios). Here, my goal is to explore complexity with particular attention to the sources of conflict and vulnerability that arose in the process of provisioning Classic Maya royal courts.

As a nexus of statecraft throughout the Classic Maya region, the court was neither purely residential nor purely administrative (Inomata and Houston 2001a). This hybrid institution incorporated both the domestic and institutional sectors of the economy (see Hirth and Pillsbury, this volume, for discussion of terms) to create something that projected and emphasized difference while at the same time grappled with challenges—such as provisioning and survival—that also characterized the domestic economy of commoners (McAnany and Plank 2001). Since a large and visible part of Classic Maya statecraft pivoted on the royal court, exploring how this entity was financed and provisioned is central to the theme of this book. I aim to contextualize this topic within the conflictive fields of power that once existed and to suggest that the remarkable, hybrid institution of the Classic Maya court proved vulnerable to more heterodoxic and open economic arrangements that emerged during the Terminal Classic period. To provide evidentiary support for this final point, I draw from research at Terminal Classic places in the Sibun Valley of central Belize.

Archaeological evidence from royal courts of Classic Maya capitals such as Aguateca, Copan, and Cancuen (Hendon 2006; Inomata 2001; Widmer 2009; see also Kovacevich, this volume) suggests that production and crafting were critically important court activities. Weaving cotton and working jade are two of the most conspicuous activities of the court, as is detailed later in this essay. The significance of these production activities went beyond provisioning because the items crafted not only materialized difference and compounded social capital (Bourdieu 1977:89, 171–173; Inomata 2001:324) but also provided a type of currency within an intercourt political economy. Crafting was part of the calculus of state finance (more on this shortly).

Modern nation-states are funded through a complex network that includes taxation of livelihood, of most commodity and real estate exchanges, and of corporate gains. As Hirth and Pillsbury (this volume) discuss, taxing livelihood (income tax) is an invention of the modern state. The instruments of finance available to rulers of most archaic states consisted primarily of labor drafts and in-kind taxation, the "harvest" of resources under direct control, the accrual of resources through negotiated diplomacy (often following martial aggression), and trade. But financing a kingdom through trading activities posed considerable challenges, and rulers of archaic states and empires had fabulously complicated relations with long-distance traders who operated outside of their control (Fleisher 2010:145; Yoffee 2005). I suggest that there was pronounced tension between traders and court participants over the conveyance of goods. Drawing upon morality tales embedded within Classic Maya royal iconography, I explore both the problems and opportunities posed by long-distance traders. Tokovinine and Beliaev (this volume) provide additional hieroglyphic and iconographic detail relevant to the role of long-distance traders.

Hirth and Pillsbury (this volume) note that as large communities developed, commercial intensification generally occurred. At many times and places, commercialization took the form of marketplaces; the ethnohistorical record of Postclassic-period highland Mexico offers several well-known examples (see Hirth, this volume). With population estimates of some Maya cities—such as Tikal—hovering at or above sixty thousand, marketplaces likely existed in the Classic Maya world unless they were actively depressed by the state, which apparently happened in the Andean region when provinces fell under Inca control (see Mayer, this volume). The remarkable murals from a royal context at Classic-period Calakmul—although variously interpreted—suggest engagement on the part of royalty in dyadic exchanges of everything from salt to thin-walled pottery (Boucher and Quiñones 2007; Carrasco Vargas and Colón González 2005; Martin 2007). Dahlin and colleagues (2007) argued for the presence of marketplaces at Classic Maya sites, and this position is given additional support by Masson and Freidel in this volume.

Characterized by Hutson (2000:123) as arenas of carnival and contestation, marketplaces momentarily concentrate but ultimately distribute goods. The centrifugal result of marketplace activities is somewhat antithetical to the goals of royal courts that emphasize centralization of goods for the purpose of compounding wealth. In reference to the main concern of this chapter—provisioning courts—a key question is whether or not markets, as places of resource conversion (Carrasco 1978), played a role in provisioning courts as they apparently did among the Postclassic Mexica. In this regard, Gutiérrez (this volume) gives an intriguing perspective on the entanglement between Aztec tribute and marketplace exchange. In brief, he argues that the flow of tribute enabled the marketplace by stabilizing rates of exchange and ensuring acceptance of standardized exchange units based primarily on tributary cloth, cacao, and gold. As noted below, cloth and cacao were also key items of tribute during Classic Maya times.

Although this chapter focuses on the provision of royal courts through artisan production and by negotiated transfer of tributary items between courts (expressed hieroglyphically as *ikatz*), marketplace exchange likely existed for the conversion of generic tribute items to those specifically needed at royal courts. Empirical data on the distribution of artifacts throughout Maya sites support the thesis of marketplace exchange (see Masson and Freidel, this volume). In short, the matrix of this noncapitalistic economy appears to have been more complex (and more similar to highland Mexico) than earlier models suggest.

In the final section of this chapter, I turn to forces that destabilized the competitive tribute system that financed royal courts. During Terminal Classic times—when this institution struggled, and ultimately failed, to survive, heterodoxic practices can be detected along the Caribbean seaboard, which was a key supplier of resources essential to Classic Maya courts. Material indicators of martial sodalities and of new ritual and trading practices (materialized in circular shrines) point toward new economic arrangements that challenged the authority of Southern Lowland royal courts.

An Economy of Difference

In order to shed light on relations of production and conveyance within a world of highly structured social difference, I consider the term "palace economy." Employed by Colin Renfrew (1972) to characterize a kind of state finance in which the institutional sector is embedded within a suprahousehold, palace economies are purported to have existed in the Aegean during the Bronze Age. During this time, monumental architecture was primarily residential and accompanied by clear-cut storage facilities and a writing system that "spelled out" in-kind vertical appropriations (Renfrew 1972:296). Many features of the Aegean Bronze Age contrast strikingly with the Maya Lowlands—particularly the seemingly detailed administrative structure and the overtly economic content of the Linear B writing system (Chadwick 1976:15–33). Nonetheless, in both cases a royal court or palatial precinct functioned as a suprahousehold and seat of power within a milieu of competitive peer polities. Less well understood in the Maya region are the myriad ways in which the sustaining populations arrayed around royal courts were entangled with palace provisioning and maintenance in addition to their likely participation in a marketplace economy. Based on hieroglyphic decipherment of the title *lakam*, which appears at several Late Classic royal courts of the eastern Peten, Lacadena (2008) suggests that this honor belonged to high-ranking but nonroyal persons who were responsible for intrapolity taxation payments and military recruitment. Although this translation may be contested, it provides an intriguing hint of formalized relationships between royal courts and the people whose labor and production gave it vital support.

The terms "royal court" and "palace" are subject to ongoing debate over definition and strategic deployment within Maya archaeology (Christie 2003; Evans and Pillsbury 2004; Inomata and Houston 2001b, 2001c). The corpus of iconographic, hieroglyphic, and architectural information now at hand indicates that royal courts and palaces materialized power and privilege during the Classic and Postclassic periods and possibly earlier, although the webs of power relations that centered on "a big house" changed greatly across time and through space. In concrete terms, the distinction between an elevated, multiroomed palace roofed with a corbeled vault and a commoner residence built of perishable materials at or near ground level is starkly apparent, but there is a considerable amount of ambiguity in midrange structures. In reference to the Minoan/Mycenaean world, Chadwick (1976:70) invokes the presence of written texts as the litmus test for identifying a palace complex. To a certain extent, Mayanists follow Chadwick's lead. Inomata and Houston (2001a:7) define a royal court in terms of the physical proximity of a ruler. Since one of the major signaling devices of a ruler was the commissioning of texts, an architectural complex without texts is suspect as a royal court. For palace structures in the Maya region, however, there is considerably more latitude. Large buildings at Preclassic sites that predate the common presence of glyphic texts have been labeled palaces (e.g., San Bartolo [Saturno et al. 2005:4] and Chiapa de Corzo [Clark and Hansen 2001:27]) and, during the Classic period, there existed many palace complexes inhabited by subroyalty, elites, and even wealthy commoners that do not meet the litmus test for a royal court—that is, they do not contain carved or painted hieroglyphic texts. Here, emphasis is placed on well-established royal courts of Late Classic times with full acknowledgement that similar processes and practices prevailed in less monumental residential contexts and that the palace sector represents but one part of a multinodal economy.

Stone structures adorned with sacred texts and cosmologically rich iconography provided the built environment within which the social difference of palace inhabitants was shaped, performed, and reproduced; daily practice within it served to instantiate palace authority, particularly within the politically competitive milieu of Late Classic times. The exclusionary nature of sacred texts and

their calligraphic crafting by a small group of literati encoded symbolic capital (Bourdieu 1977:89, 171–173) that further materialized hierarchy and naturalized difference. Elsewhere (McAnany 2008, 2010:159), I have suggested that the concept of social speciation provides a way of comprehending the profound social distinctions that existed within Classic Maya society. Such distinctions created and maintained an ethos of nobility and of rulership that was foundational to Maya statecraft.

Hierarchy existed not only in the architectonics and scripting of the Classic Maya built environment but also in a person's dress, food, scent, appearance, and activities. An aesthetic of authority was wielded as a "weapon of exclusion" (Douglas and Isherwood 1996:95). The presence of a preferential "palace diet"—possibly from corn-fed animals—has been proposed based on isotopic and paleopathological analysis of human bone at Caracol, Lamanai, Pacbitun, and other sites as well (Chase and Chase 2001; Coyston et al. 1999; Cucina and Tiesler 2003; Tykot 2002). Increasingly, archaeologists are interpreting as indicators of exclusionary feasting the sizable midden deposits that contain large numbers of conjoinable pottery sherds and animal bones, and that are located adjacent to palace and ballcourt structures (Houston et al. 1992; Reents-Budet 2000). The central role of cacao seeds (Figure 9.1) in ceremonial feasting is well attested (e.g., Panel 3 from Piedras Negras [Houston and Stuart 2001:69–73]; see also Stuart 2006b and other contributions in McNeil 2006). As we shall see in this chapter, provisioning courts with sufficient amounts of cacao was a major challenge of palace economies and a key activity of merchants and tribute bearers.

Prevalent among the distinctive activities of prominent members of the royal court was the impersonation of deities and ancestors, something that required a ready supply of costuming materials, such as quetzal feathers and marine shell. These items—acquired from afar through both trade and tribute—augmented the visual and acoustical experience of "deity concurrence," which is known from more than fifty separate hieroglyphic texts (Houston 2006:148).

Sun-drying cacao seeds on a prepared surface in front of the Chun residence in San Antonio, Toledo District, Belize. Ms. Chun is rotating the drying seeds. (Photograph by Patricia A. McAnany.)

As more exacting excavation techniques are used to investigate palaces and royal courts, it has become obvious that these spaces were veritable hives of crafting activity (e.g., Aoyama 2007:24; Inomata 2001; Widmer 2009). The centrality and pervasiveness of palace artisans—particularly in the realm of gendered textile production—is particularly notable (Hendon 2006). In contrast, the incidence of spindle whorls in commoner domestic contexts is strikingly low (Halperin 2008, 2011; McAnany 2010:115–124). Thus, gendered performance of textile crafting appears to have been another way in which social difference was expressed through a medium of production.

Hieroglyphic evidence only serves to strengthen the association between weaving and royal identity. Miller and Martin (2004:94) note that the "connection between weaving and high status is reiterated on the fine bones from more than one royal court

inscribed with *upuutz' b'aak*, 'the weaving bone of'" followed by the name of a royal female (as deciphered by Houston and Stuart 2001:64). Elsewhere (McAnany 2010:201–206), I examine the implications of these findings for our understanding of crafting and artisan work. An important take-away message from the excavation of countless spindle whorls and brocade picks from elite residences and royal tombs—as well as the fifty-four unique brocade patterns recorded by Looper and Tolles (2000:39–104) from Classic Maya sculpture and paintings—is the intended inalienability of many of these crafted masterpieces. Annette Weiner's (1992) consideration of value and inalienability, and her assertion that inalienable possessions are the oldest form of human currency, strike a resonant chord here. Quite likely, the brocaded *huipiles* worn by Lady K'ab'aal Xook of Yaxchilan (see Tate 1992) were bequeathed to her daughter(s) and only would have been bartered or released as part of a tribute obligation if the royal family fell into difficult circumstances. Lesser textiles as well as other items fabricated at court were given away to cement alliances, settle disputes, or meet tribute obligations. There is a sufficient sample of provenienced, nonperishable artifacts—such as the Buenavista del Cayo vase (Houston et al. 1992)—to suggest the presence of such diplomatic transfers. Would items crafted at court, particularly textiles, have been bartered in a local marketplace or traded to merchants passing through?

Traders certainly brought raw materials to the palace, but did they take away finished goods? There is a high probability that many items crafted in palatial precincts remained under the control of royals and über-elites. In this sphere of conveyance, the preeminent object histories and social context of conveyance were somewhat antithetical to the ethic of trading. Items created in palaces instantiated social difference and power relations, and so were imbued with a quality that traders could not provide. Classic-period royal courts certainly participated in commercial trading, particularly in obsidian (Braswell 2010:135–136), but glyphic and iconographic evidence discussed below indicates that an unknowable percentage of the production at royal courts was destined for self-provisioning or conveyance through mechanisms of the political economy (i.e., tribute offerings and diplomatic transfers). Once transferred, items originally produced within a court for a royal treasury might make their way into a wider variety of contexts, including a marketplace.

In short, the palace sector of Classic Maya economies was built upon principles of hierarchy, social difference, wealth accumulation, and the active maintenance of authority materialized through crafting, feasting, rituals of deity concurrence, and other embodied practices. These fields of action created a totality that did not interact particularly smoothly with the commercial interests of traders. I suggest that the economic tension between traders and rulers was expressed in moral terms of mythic proportions and is detectable in depictions of God L, the Classic-period merchant

deity who was a denizen of the underworld. As we shall see, one of the salient characteristics of royal iconography is the depiction of deities as human-like and humans as godlike.

Deities and Underworld Traders

The aesthetics of beauty in Classic Maya society can be glimpsed in the maize deity, the sun deity, and the nobility who represented themselves with features of these deities. The young maize god, in particular, embodied the foundational processes of fruition, death, and renewal. Taube (1985:172–173; see also Houston et al. 2006:45–49) likens the maize god to a sprouting maize plant with a long, sloping forehead and a headdress that mimics corn silks. The sprouting ears of corn on the maize stalks painted on the murals of Epiclassic Cacaxtla (Piña Chán 1998) are the face of the maize deity himself. Although maize might be the "staff of life," there is nothing mundane or pedestrian about the maize deity, who embodies the epic struggle of humanity for survival and regeneration. Miller and Martin (2004:25) observe that "[t]he Maya usually represented high nobility with the body and face of the Maize God, eternally young and beautiful . . . with exaggerated nose, crossed eyes, and tapering forehead." The tapering forehead was achieved through cranial shaping that is found far more frequently in skeletal remains of nobility.

In addition to the royal appropriation of fertility and regeneration, there is the diurnal cycle represented by the powerful sun god K'inich Ajaw. As the ultimate natural power in the cosmos, the sun has been linked to authority in the earthly realm from the sun kings of ancient Egypt to the southeastern Mississippian kingdoms of the United States and Louis the XIVth of France. Of the 105 named rulers listed by Simon Martin and Nikolai Grube (2008) in *Chronicle of the Maya Kings and Queens*, roughly a third (thirty) bore regal names that included *k'inich*, sun-faced or radiant, in their title. Colas (2003) discussed the manner in which the divinity of the king was reinforced through hieroglyphic appellation of the title *k'inich*, particularly in self-referential texts. Those who did not take *k'inich* in their title string might closely identify with the sun deity and adorn themselves with images of K'inich Ajaw, as do Itzamnaaj B'ahlam and Lady K'ab'aal Xook of Yaxchilan, who wear pendants of K'inich Ajaw on Lintel 24 (Miller and Martin 2004:100). The sun god often is shown with T-shaped incisors, a dental feature that became increasingly popular among the upper sector of society during the Late Classic period and that often was accompanied by inlays of jade (symbolizing "first" and "fertile") on canine teeth. The sun provided more than a power trope for Maya rulers; some were described as possessing a radiance or vital force (*ip*) akin to the sun (Houston 2000:167; Houston and Stuart 2001:55). For Maya royalty, metaphors of agricultural abundance suggested by the youthful and fecund maize deity and of the radiance of the sun—so vital to plant maturation—allude to the value of a bounteous harvest and the high regard in which agricultural wealth was held (see also Freidel and Reilly 2011).

In contrast, the deity of trading—God L—was not an exulted or a handsome member of the Classic Maya deity set: he was depicted as elderly, wrinkled, lascivious, and a denizen of the underworld (see Tokovinine and Beliaev, this volume). A shrewd trader who smoked a big cigar (useful for deterring insects when traveling through forested and estuarine places), he wore rakish yet very luxurious clothing, sported a large-brimmed hat (also an indicator of a forest traveler or hunter), and often was accompanied by a bird. Piecing together an ancient narrative from a series of pictorial vessels, Miller and Martin (2004:58–61, 76; see also Martin 2006) relate a Classic-period tale in which the Hero Twins brought down the arrogant and wealthy God L, stripped him (literally) of his finery, and forced him to pay tribute to the sun god (presumably, a thinly guised reference to a "radiant" ruler). Tokovinine and Beliaev (this volume) recount additional versions of this morality tale, which can be interpreted to suggest that riches—in the absence of sacred power—were dangerous, unbalanced, and needed to be controlled. The story also conveys the sense that Classic-period royals were wary of the wealth that came

from trading activities that they did not control but upon which they were greatly dependent in order to express the social difference that formed the heart of their authority. In short, the human counterpart of God L was probably as popular at Classic Maya royal courts as a Wall Street derivatives trader at a retirement party for a university professor.

Although morality tales based on exploits of deities are not equivalent to the lived experiences of royals and nonroyals alike, such stories arguably reveal fault lines within societies. The Classic-period narratives about God L indicate tension between the wealthy traders who transported raw, crafted, and harvested goods to a wide-ranging clientele and the ruling families who accumulated agricultural wealth and crafted accoutrements of authority, identity, and luxury. Although it is likely that a careful tally was kept of all things coming into and going out of a palace precinct, there was much that circulated beyond the radar of royal oversight in marketplaces and along trade routes that laced together large capitals and small settlements throughout the lowlands. Given this situation, royal courts pursued other strategies that insured a stream of revenue. Tribute provided one means of state finance by which courts could be provisioned with people and items that not only were valuable but also convertible.

Provisioning Courts through Martial Competition and Tribute Extraction

In his 2003 magnum opus *Understanding Early Civilizations*, Bruce Trigger (2003:385) considers that "almost nothing is known about how the Maya upper classes extracted surplus wealth from commoners. The vastness of state projects and the opulent life of Maya rulers suggest, however, that the Maya upper class, and kings in particular, did it very effectively." A decade after this publication, we arguably have not yet developed a clear notion of how royal courts were provisioned, although the Calakmul murals provide some visual clues, as does Lacadena's (2008) interpretation of the subordinate title *lakam*. Notably, a modest corpus of hieroglyphic texts and royal pictorial scenes indicates an important role for the lucrative practice of tribute extraction wedded to martial competition and a carefully calculated dominance hierarchy among Late Classic Maya royal courts. This method of finance—which included the ransom of high-status captives—appears to have been particularly popular throughout the time span of pictorial polychrome vessels, circa AD 600 to 800. As Reents-Budet (2001), Foias (2004), and others have noted, tribute presentation is a frequent topic on pictorial polychrome vessels.

Despite early assertions that hieroglyphic texts lack reference to economic transactions, more recent decipherment reveals the machinations of a political economy organized around the royal court and linked to warfare (Houston 2000:173–174). Stuart (1998:410–416) notes that the co-occurrence of the so-called step glyph with axe events (suggestive of warfare). References to *patan* (tribute or labor service) and to *ikatz* (i-ka-tz'i; cargo or burden borne in Tzeltal Mayan) also co-occur with step glyphs and axe events, most notably on Naranjo Stela 12 (Figure 9.2). Although the step glyph has not been deciphered securely, it probably reads *t'ab'ay* (t'ab'-yi; Stuart 2006a:131) and refers to the act of ascending and offering gifts and tribute. Likewise, Stela 32 from Naranjo (Figure 9.3) not only depicts a stairway leading to a throne but also refers to the delivery (*y-ak'aw*, ya-k'a-wa) of tribute (*ikatz*) (Houston and Escobedo 1996:468; Le Fort and Wald 1995:112). Stairways accentuate themes of hierarchy and subordination; they frequently function as the frame around the protagonists on polychrome vessels. An excellent example is found on a vessel from the burial of Jasaw Chan K'awiil I of Tikal. Two figures climb hieroglyphic steps to offer precious green quetzal feathers and a platter heaped with valuables to a seated ruler, possibly Jasaw Chan K'awiil I himself (Figure 9.4). Such hierarchical compositions with associated texts are particularly significant when the *ikatz* is identified as that of another *k'uhul ajaw*, as on Stela 12 from Naranjo, in which the phrase *y-ikatz* (yi-ka-tz'i, "his cargo") is followed by the title of the conquered

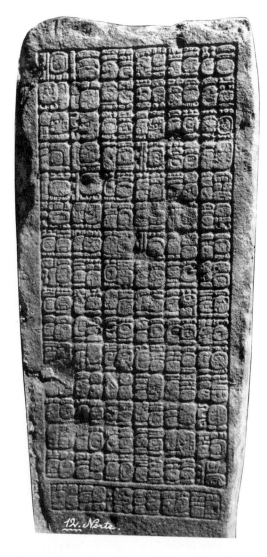

figure 9.2
Naranjo Stela 12 with tribute-related glyphs: axe events (martial conflict), *patan* (tribute), and *ikatz* ("cargo" bundles). (Photograph from Ian Graham and Eric von Euw, *Corpus of Maya Hieroglyphic Inscriptions*, vol. 2, pt. 1, *Naranjo*; courtesy of the President and Fellows of Harvard University.)

lord of Yaxha (Figure 9.2; Stuart 1998:414). Of further interest is the fact that the "foot-ascending-steps" verb, or semantic variants of it, also occurs on glyph bands painted on ceramics and other objects (Stuart 1998:412). This association suggests that many of these objects were crafted and inscribed either as part of a tribute transfer or were created as a testament to such a transfer.

Architecturally, stairways present the perfect spatial geometry in which hierarchy, and thus social order, could be showcased and performed. As Stuart (1998:414) notes, "warfare and captives are dominant themes of inscriptions on steps [of royal courts]." Houston (1998:360–361) suggests that staircases themselves—often overbuilt in proportion to surrounding architecture—are profoundly dramaturgical and were the locales for activities such as "the heaping of tribute . . . or the display of captive[s]."

Additional clues to the workings of the Classic Maya political economy come from identification of the standing and kneeling persons in the pictorial polychrome from the burial of Jasaw Chan

figure 9.3

Naranjo Stela 32 showing stairway at base of stela lightly inscribed with text that refers to the delivery (ya-k'a-wa) of tribute (i-ka-tz'i). (Photograph from Ian Graham, *Corpus of Maya Hieroglyphic Inscriptions*, vol. 2, pt. 2, *Naranjo Chunhuitz Xunantunich*; courtesy of the President and Fellows of Harvard University.)

figure 9.4

Court presentation scene painted on a pictorial polychrome vessel from the tomb of Jasaw Chan K'awiil I (Burial 116) of Tikal (reprinted from Culbert 1993:fig. 68A). (Courtesy of the University of Pennsylvania Museum of Archaeology and Anthropology, image no. 64-5-108.)

K'awiil I. They are dressed in oversized white mantles (unusual attire in a court scene) trimmed with brocaded sky bands and feather edging, and they wear necklaces of jadeite and large *Spondylus* shells, as well as headdresses of quetzal feathers. Elsewhere (on a looted vessel, unfortunately), figures dressed this way are identified as *ybeet* (variant orthographies of this term abound), which is deciphered by Houston and colleagues (2006:243) as "his [bird] messenger." The messenger and the cacao he offers are described as coming to the royal court of Tikal from a lord of Calakmul (Houston et al. 2006:243, fig. 7.22). These two Maya capitals were mortal enemies, and a major achievement of Jasaw Chan K'awiil I of Tikal is generally considered to have been his decisive military victory over Calakmul in AD 695.

References to *ebeet* abound at royal courts with a strong tradition of martial activity, such as those of Naranjo and Caracol. At the latter, the phrase *ybeet papamil*, "the messenger of papamil," has been recorded, although the identity of "papamil" is unknown (Houston et al. 2006:244). These examples pale in comparison to the scale, pomp, and grandeur of *ebeet* who appear in the Bonampak murals. The walls of Room 1, formerly thought to depict an heir-designation scene (Miller 2001:210), actually showcase *ebeet* figures clad, once again, in large white mantles with finely adorned edging, *Spondylus* shells, jadeite ornaments, and quetzal feathers. Bags of cacao, labeled as containing 5-pik (5 × 8,000), or forty thousand cacao seeds, are conspicuously displayed in front of a throne scene painted on the end wall of Room 1 (Houston 1997; Stuart 2006b:190). At Bonampak and elsewhere, *ebeet* are not called by personal names or royal titles, but rather by their role as messengers and their "possessed" affiliation with a noble lord; one Bonampak glyph band reads *ybeet chak-ha ajaw*, or "messenger of the Red or Great Water Lord" (Houston et al. 2006:248). Tokovinine and Beliaev (this volume) suggest that *ebeet* may have been traders—human counterparts of God L—while Houston and others (2006:247) believe that these nonroyal figures likely represented a liege who could not or would not be present. Significantly,

ebeet are shown dressed in raiment that includes valuable tribute items, such as cotton mantles, jadeite, *Spondylus* shells, and quetzal feathers. Are *ebeet* walking tribute bundles, as per Houston and colleagues (2006:247), or wealthy traders modeling their merchandise? The fact that the term *ebeet* is firmly translated as "messenger" and that *ebeet* are not shown with the accoutrements of a long-distance trader (wide-brimmed hat, backrack, or cigar) suggests that *ebeet* played a diplomatic role in relaying messages and goods between royal courts and likely were key players in the negotiations that took place in the throne rooms of royal courts.

The repeated co-occurrence of glyphic logograms for martial conflict (such as the so-called axe glyph) with the step glyph and to references to *patan* or *ikatz*, as noted by Stuart (1998:410–416) and illustrated by Naranjo Stela 12 (Figure 9.2), indicates that tribute may not have been offered on a voluntary basis. Here I suggest a causal linkage between captive taking and tribute offering. David Freidel (1986) and, more recently, Elizabeth Graham (2006) note that the point of martial competition between Classic Maya warriors was to take captives rather than inflict death. Miller and Martin (2004:170) observe that, in several instances, captives of noble rank appear to have survived a period of captivity and returned to their throne in a much-diminished state. Yich'aak Bahlam ("Jaguar Claw") of Ceibal was captured by Dos Pilas in AD 735, yet there is a reference to his rule at Ceibal with a Long Count date of AD 747 (Martin and Grube 2008:61, 63). Likewise, Palenque ruler K'an Joy Chitam II was captured by Tonina in AD 711, but he apparently was restored to the throne of Palenque and ruled until AD 720 (Miller and Martin 2004:183). Also from Palenque, a miniature wall panel—colloquially known as the Bundle Panel (Martin and Grube 2000:173)—features an unusual carved scene dated to AD 731. It shows the successor to K'an Joy Chitam II, Ahkul Mo' Nahb III, managing a huge textile-covered bundle thought to contain tribute (González Cruz and Fernández Martínez 1994; Stuart 1998:413). This image suggests the possibility that even a decade after the death of the once-captive ruler, Palenque still serviced a tribute obligation to Tonina. Likewise, a jadeite cube that is inscribed as the burden, or *y-ikatz,* of a ruler nick-named Sunraiser Jaguar of Pomona was excavated from a tomb at Palenque and includes a Calendar Round date that postdates the death of Sunraiser Jaguar (Miller and Martin 2004:234).

The notion that a royal combatant is more valuable alive is reinforced by the fact that *"chuh-kaj,* 'he is seized/roped,' is the most common of all verbs referring to warfare" (Miller and Martin 2004:166). A captured member of a royal family or a high-ranking soldier and/or scribe rep-resented the wealth of a kingdom and could be used to extract that wealth in the form of goods, labor, land, advantageous marital alliances, and more (Miller and Martin 2004:166). Premodern European history is full of such accounts. As the wages of war took their toll on one kingdom after another, rulers such as Richard the Lionheart, Jean of France, and Francis I of France were held for a "king's ransom" (Gillingham 1978; Knecht 1994; Tuchman 1978). According to Tuchman (1978:84), the taking of high-ranking captives for ransom in fourteenth-century England and France "became a commercial enterprise." With this observation from a faraway time and place, we glimpse how a political economy might become commercialized.

Items Frequently Shown in Court Presentation Scenes

Ebeet advertised the fine quality of the woven tex-tiles, lapidary works of art, and precious marine shell with which they were adorned for court. In Late Classic painted scenes of court presenta-tion—including the Bonampak mural—five items of tribute consistently recur: cacao, cotton man-tles, *Spondylus* shell, jadeite, and quetzal feathers. Among these five, there exist dramatic contrasts in terms of availability, transformational intensivity, and accessibility of knowledge necessary for creat-ing these highly valued items. The varying charac-teristics of these paradigmatic items highlight the complexities of provisioning royal courts.

Cacao, the seed of a tropical forest tree species (*Theobroma cacao* L.), can be grown wherever there is no danger of frost and there is adequate mois-ture—even in moist *rejolladas* in the relatively dry northern Yucatan Peninsula (Gómez-Pompa et al. 1990; Kepecs and Boucher 1996; Perez Romero 1988). Concentrated production of high-quality cacao was restricted to the alluvial soils of river valleys in the lower Usumacinta delta, along the southern Caribbean coast, and the piedmont flanks of the Pacific coast. Stuart (2006b:191–199) enter-tains the notion that regionally specific varieties of cacao—as well as different additives to the drink—may be at the base of the somewhat enigmatic epithets that co-occur with the frequent ka-(ka)-wa (*kakaw*) glyph, particularly on the text bands rimming pictorial polychrome vessels. Cacao can be understood to have been a naturally circum-scribed resource. For the early colonial period, Caso Barrera and Aliphat F. (2006:303) describe the Itza—who inhabited central Peten, where cacao did not grow well—as resorting to "trade, raiding, and control of the cacao-producing areas" in order to ensure a continuous supply for the royal court at Tah Itza. Unlike the compressed scheduling har-vest of a maize field, a grove of cacao trees can be harvested over several months, which means that royal courts could be supplied continuously with moderate amounts of cacao for most of the year. The *kakaw* sacks shown in the Bonampak murals were labeled with the *kakaw* glyph surmounted by a number that Stuart (2006a:139) deciphers as 5-pik (forty thousand seeds). Stuart (2006a:138–141) notes the frequent use of a 3-pik (twenty-four thousand seeds) label, which coincides with a count of cacao seeds that was considered a "carga" in Postclassic-period highland Mexico.

Cotton cloth, in contrast, was fabricated in royal courts. But like cacao, cotton could be grown in many parts of the lowlands, although this spe-cies (*Gossypium hirsutum*) prefers a hot, somewhat dry climate and tolerates salty soils. Cotton grows as a wild perennial bush along the eastern littoral of the Yucatan Peninsula; this fact has prompted some plant biologists to suggest that the Yucatan was the site of its initial domestication in Mesoamerica

(Piperno and Pearsall 1998:151). The transformation of cotton bolls into cloth involves the tedious separation of fibers from constituent plant parts and the washing of the bolls. Clean cotton fibers likely were delivered to palace precincts, where skilled female labor spun and wove the fibers into cloth. Of all the items of tribute, cloth may be the most labor intensive, closely matched by jadeite, which is discussed below. Among Postclassic Mexica, weaving and wearing cotton were recognized status markers, but there has been little discussion of such embodied practices during Classic Maya times.

Evans (2010:13) notes that spindle whorls do not occur at Teotihuacan before the end of the Classic period. Ardren and colleagues (2010) document a significant increase in spindle whorls in Terminal Classic deposits at the site of Xuenkal in Yucatan; the pertinent deposits are associated with Sotuta (Chichen Itza–related) ceramics. Thus, evidence from Teotihuacan, Xuenkal, and other sites indicate that spinning thread was not a universal activity of Mesoamerican females, particularly before the Postclassic period. The lived experience of women was historically and status contingent. In the royal courts of the lowland Maya, however, the gendered production of cloth and the female artisans who participated in it drove the tribute economy of the Late Classic period and those of more recent times (Ardren et al. 2010:287; McAnany 2010:296–297).

A semiprecious gemstone, jadeite appears to have moved—as a tribute item—in finished form. The only jadeite sources currently known for Mesoamerica occur in the metamorphic rock of the southeast, in and around the Motagua Valley of Guatemala (Foshag 1984 [1957]:fig. 13; Hammond et al. 1977; Taube 2005). Most royal courts would have engaged in trade to secure the raw material from which to fabricate jadeite beads, pendants, earspools, and so forth—common items of tribute. Excavations at Cancuen have yielded a large sample of worked jadeite preforms that were removed from boulders via string-saw technology (Kovacevich 2007, this volume). Jadeite inscribed with some variant of *ikatz* or the "tribute" glyph is known from Piedras Negras (Burial 5) as well as Palenque (specifically, a tomb within Temple 12 [Miller and

Martin 2004:234] and the sarcophagus of K'inich Janahb' Pakal I [Houston and Escobedo 1996:467, figs. 2–3]). Complex networks of trade, tribute, and other types of transfer stretched across the Maya region, leaving a residual mosaic pattern of places with ready access to jadeite—such as Cancuen—and other places to which access appears to have been blocked. Carving this precious greenstone with time-intensive calligraphic inscription renders the *ikatz*-engraved stones particularly important for signaling the presence (and the burdens) of a royal court. Stuart (2006a) considers jadeite, along with cacao, to have been a significant wealth item in Classic Maya courts and suggests that most hieroglyphic mentions of bundled *ikatz* are references to precious carved jade that was transferred from one royal court to another via gifting or tribute extraction.

Blended trade and tribute probably accounts for the circulation of *Spondylus* shells, a deepwater species available off both the Caribbean and Pacific coasts (*Spondylus americanus* Hermann and *Spondylus princeps* Broderip, respectively; Andrews 1969:25–26; Vokes and Vokes 1983:62). *Spondylus* harvesting likely was a specialized activity (see Pillsbury 1996:317–319 for review of *Spondylus* habitat). The shell arrived at royal courts essentially unmodified and often was worn as such, as part of a necklace or a belt ensemble. Unworked *Spondylus* shells are also found in elite burials and caches, where they are thought to represent fertility and renewal. The paired "clam shells" of *Spondylus princeps* were used to hold small, precious objects (i.e., "jewel boxes" [Andrews 1969:25]; see also Chase and Chase 1998:315). Although difficult to acquire, *Spondylus* shells are very durable and enjoy a long shelf life. Presumably the use demands of a royal mortuary interment or a building dedication initiated a cycle of procurement; *Spondylus* shells often are depicted in court presentation scenes.

Today, quetzal birds—with their long, elegant green tail feathers—are an endangered species that live in Alta Verapaz, a cloud forest region of limestone karst where the lowlands meet the igneous mountains of the Guatemala Highlands. Thompson (1964:32) asserted that trapping rights once existed at places where the birds came to drink. Based on ethnohistorical documents, Feldman (1985:90) states that "killing quetzal birds was a more heinous crime than murdering quetzal feather collectors." Apparently, birds were trapped at waterholes during the dry season using an ingenious trap that allowed the bird to escape but not with its tail feathers (Feldman 1985:90). Only lowland sites situated close to Alta Verapaz would have been reasonably close to this extremely valuable resource; other places would have procured quetzal feathers via trade or tribute demands. A frequently depicted element of noble costuming—as a backrack or headdress element—quetzal feathers could not have enjoyed a long shelf life in the humid tropics and must have been replaced more regularly than *Spondylus* shell or jadeite. In the painted court presentation scene from the tomb of Jasaw Chan K'awiil I (Figure 9.4), a figure holding a bundle of quetzal feathers ascends the steps to the throne.

These paradigmatic five items—cacao, cotton mantles, jadeite, *Spondylus* shells, and quetzal feathers—are often characterized as luxury or sumptuary goods (as opposed to items of staple finance) but an underappreciated fact is that three of the five—cacao, cotton mantles, and *Spondylus* (or red) shell—are mentioned in ethnohistorical accounts of Mexica markets as items of extreme convertibility for which equivalencies were widely agreed upon. While I cannot definitively assert that these items were valued in the same way during Classic Maya times, the parallel is intriguing and suggests the likelihood that Classic Maya tribute goods circulated into other spheres of conveyance, much as Mexica elites traded tribute mantles for maize in the Tlatelolco marketplace. David Freidel (see Masson and Freidel 2002) has advocated for acknowledgment of deeply rooted media of convertibility within the Maya region; Classic Maya court presentation scenes provide support for this proposition.

Positing that tribute was an important mechanism by which Classic Maya royal courts were provisioned means that persons identified iconographically as "scribes" might have held more broadly construed positions—that is, some of the royal figures wearing a bulbous headdress pierced with pen quills (as in Figure 9.4) probably were tribute collectors and accountants. Ethnohistorically, K'iche' royalty who occupied the "tribute collector" role held the title of *ajpop k'amja*, "Keeper of the Reception House Mat" (Tedlock 1985:315). Braswell (2001:312), following Bartolomé de las Casas (1909 [1552–1561]:615–616), identifies the Keeper of the Reception House Mat as "king-elect," an indication that the role of tribute collector was one of extremely high status and not that of a lowly palace functionary or bureaucrat. The last K'iche' to hold this noble title, don Juan Cortés, traveled to Spain in 1557 in an unsuccessful bid to persuade the Crown to restore the right of K'iche' lords to collect tribute (Carrasco 1967; Tedlock 1985:315). Jackson and Stuart (2001:225) suggest that the hieroglyphically attested title of *aj k'uhun* may refer to one who guards, keeps, or oversees tribute collection and presentation for a named ruler.

When successful, provisioning through tribute would have lessened the need for long-distance traders since items that were not locally available to a royal court (such as cacao or *Spondylus* shell) could be acquired through negotiated tribute. If one kingdom could dominate another through martial victories or shrewd diplomacy, then items essential to the performance of nobility could be secured with only limited interaction with long-distance traders. Clear-cut military victories, however, seldom followed martial hostilities. In reference to the Hundred Years War between France and England, Tuchman (1978:83, 199) notes that "medieval armies had no means of achieving a decisive result" but rather aimed at "seizure of dynastic rule at the top by inflicting enough damage to bring about downfall of the opponent." Maya hieroglyphic texts—known for vague and inconclusive references to martial conflict—may be reflecting actual ambiguities.

The indecisiveness of war and the labor to prepare tribute items—if one was militarily or diplomatically vanquished—must have greatly taxed royal courts, rendering them vulnerable to short amplitude perturbations as well as external challenges to authority. Iconographic evidence suggests that women of the court seldom entered the battle-field, but their labor in weaving cotton into highly valued cloth played a critical role in the political economy and was entangled with a masculinist ethos of warfare. Ironically, subjugated polities that bore the brunt of amassing items of tribute gained considerable expertise in large-scale production and transportation of the very items that came to play a prominent role in the Postclassic Mesoamerican "world system" (Smith and Berdan 2000). With this thought in mind, I turn to evidence from Terminal Classic places that shed light on shifts in the movement of goods and construal of authority that challenged business-as-usual in Classic Maya royal courts.

Terminal Classic Heterodoxy and the Dissolution of Royal Courts

How and why did Classic Maya nobility ultimately fail to maintain their radiant authority and ability to attract and hold thousands of followers? How apocalyptic was the ninth-century dissolution of royal courts, and what is the significance of increasingly documented "termination" rituals that purposely deanimated and decommissioned monumental structures at the core of so many Classic Maya political capitals (Stanton and Magnoni 2008)? Although this profound transformation of Classic Maya society often is represented as societal failure or, worst yet, extinction (Diamond 2005), it does represent in hindsight a spectacular implosion of a political order (McAnany and Gallareta Negrón 2009). Poorly understood events of the ninth century overwhelmed the ability of royal courts to maintain social order, to squelch challenges to authority, and to provide thousands of followers with a reason to stay and continue to support—through labor and goods—both the royal court and the smaller palace precincts (Lucero 2007).

This process can be examined by pivoting away from Classic Maya royal courts and focusing on Terminal Classic places such as Cacaxtla, Chichen Itza, and recently documented sites within the Sibun Valley. Research in the Sibun Valley has yielded intriguing clues to the destabilization of Classic Maya courts. Situated along the resource-rich Caribbean seaboard, the Sibun Valley is one of many coastal locations that thrived during the Terminal Classic period (for discussion of others, see Masson and Mock 2004). At all locations under consideration, merchants are implicated in a power shift of sea change proportions that took place between the Late and Terminal Classic periods (discussed in more detail below). The Terminal Classic construction of a network of circular shrine structures from Chichen Itza to the Sibun Valley materialized this power shift and the introduction of ritual practices that diverged from Classic Maya orthodoxy (McAnany 2012).

In this regard, a Terminal Classic representation of God L—the deity of trading—is enlightening. At the highland site of Cacaxtla in Tlaxcala, Mexico, a series of polychrome murals depict scenes of martial conflict and sacrifice along with a representation of God L (Figure 9.5). In this image, God L, complete with a *cacaste* backrack brimming with valuable trade goods, leans slightly to inspect a cacao tree (although none could survive in this dry highland climate). He appears to have lost his rakish clothing and foppish hat. Looking almost regal, he wears a jaguar costume that includes a headdress, loincloth, mittens, and booties. He affects a hand gesture commonly associated with royalty. Has God L been rehabilitated?

Other sources suggest that royalty embraced rather than scorned identity as a merchant during Terminal and Postclassic times. We learn from colonial-period accounts that one of the royal Kokom princes was spared certain death when Postclassic Mayapan was sacked and burned because he was absent on a trading mission in Honduras (Tozzer 1941 [ca. 1566]:37–39). A second example from early colonial times is provided by Restall (1997:185), who translates a Yukatek legal document of 1580 in which Diego Pox makes a claim on his father's estate with the following statement: "I have also sustained my father, for four times I went to trade in Bacalar, that I might bring cacao, half of which I gave to my father, as the principal men of my *cah* [town and community] well known [*sic*]."

figure 9.5
Terminal Classic version of the merchant deity God L from the murals of Cacaxtla. (Drawing by Simon Martin.)

These accounts imply that trading activities were subsumed within a Postclassic elite identity.

Evidence of trading as an elite occupation begins to appear during the latter part of the Classic period. Conceivably, an increasingly commercialized tribute economy facilitated a change in the perception of traders. Such a shift appears to have been linked to a greater openness to heterodoxic and pan-Mesoamerican trading and ritual practices. Based on evidence of a far-flung obsidian-trading network, Braswell (2010:137) characterizes the economy of Chichen Itza during this time as part of a "fully commercialized, interregional, and open market economy." Architecture, iconography, and hieroglyphic texts of Chichen Itza, in particular, project two ideologies and modes of

governance: one that was congruent with Classic Maya orthodoxy, and one that was more heterodoxic and is thought to have signaled the presence of a Mesoamerican Tollan—a supraregional pilgrimage center for initiates seeking investiture into military sodalities or a kind of political legitimization that was recognized throughout Mesoamerica (Kowalski and Kristan-Graham 2007; Ringle 2004; Ringle and Bey 2009).

At Chichen Itza, a circular shrine called the Caracol occupies a pivotal space between the two "faces" of this extraordinary place and appears to mediate between the two. This nonresidential architectural form often is associated with the feathered serpent of the Mexican Highlands (Carrasco 2000; Florescano 1999; Masson and Peraza Lope 2007:80;

Nicholson 2000; Ringle et al. 1998; Taube 2000); yet, starting in the ninth century, circular shrines were built along the Caribbean seaboard at locales that were strategic to canoe navigation and the acquisition of such resources as cacao (Harrison-Buck and McAnany 2006; McAnany 2007, 2012). There is increasing evidence that these Caribbean locales—on the edge of the heartland of Late Classic royal courts—were actively involved in the promotion of an ideology that de-emphasized royal genealogy and actively encouraged large-scale and long-distance trade (McAnany 2012). Such a development could not help but weaken nobles' ability to provision royal courts and to retain followers. Drastic demographic shifts ensued, coupled with the transformation of political, religious, and economic practice.

Research in one cacao-producing area of the Caribbean seaboard—the Sibun Valley—has so far uncovered circular shrines built at three sites: Samuel Oshon, Augustine Obispo, and Pechtun Ha (Figure 9.6). All three sites appear to have been founded during the Terminal Classic period; they contain no underlying Early Classic or Preclassic constructions. The circular shrines are integrated into the plaza plans rather than added as a later,

figure 9.6
Partially excavated circular shrine structure at the Augustine Obispo site, Sibun Valley. (Photograph by Patricia A. McAnany.)

Bench

Doorway

Arc of Earlier Str.

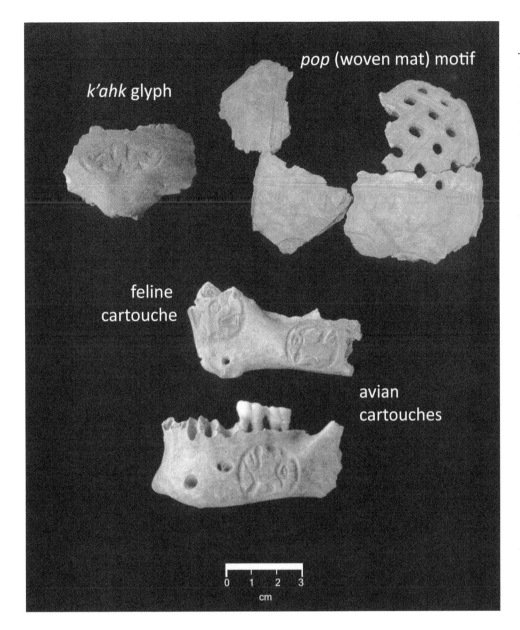

k'ahk glyph

pop (woven mat) motif

feline cartouche

avian cartouches

figure 9.7
Fragments of a human skull mask and carved mandible placed with the burial of an older male at Pakal Na, Sibun Valley. (Photograph by Patricia A. McAnany.)

intrusive building, as documented at Nohmul (Chase and Chase 1982). Upriver from the shrines, a place called Pakal Na contained the burial of an older, robust male interred with an evocative suite of materials that suggest he was a soldier with a sodality-like affiliation. On a ledge within the burial pit were the remains of a carved human skull mask and mandible. Bird and canine cartouches were carved on the sides of the mandible, the glyph for *k'ahk* ("smoke" or "fire") appears on the forehead, and a *pop* (woven mat) motif covers the top of the cranium (Figure 9.7) (Harrison-Buck et al.

2007; McAnany 2007). A radiocarbon assay on charcoal from a smoking/burning ritual conducted during interment yielded a two-sigma calibrated date range of AD 687–959. The temporal overlap among this burial interment with warrior sodality paraphernalia, the circular shrines constructed in this cacao-producing valley, and the termination deposits at royal courts of Classic-period capitals are not likely to be coincidental. The forces ushering in these winds of change defy facile understanding but appear to have been political and economic rather than environmental.

Discussion and Conclusions

Findings in the Sibun Valley suggest that during Terminal Classic times, the rules of martial engagement, the axes of power, and the role of merchants shifted dramatically. The vulnerability of royal courts to this change in the construal of authority is demonstrated by their gradual abandonment. For the preceding two hundred years, the prevailing orthodoxy of lowland Maya statecraft had centered on the royal court and ancillary palace precincts. The manner in which the courts—exemplary of social difference—were provisioned appears to have included a blend of exchanges that included production at court through valuation of artisanship, tribute presentation that was linked to martial competition, and trade. Classic Maya royal iconography contains evidence of a conflictive relationship between nobility and merchants. The five items frequently shown on tribute presentation scenes—cacao, cotton mantles, jadeite, *Spondylus* shells, and quetzal feathers—overlap with items recognized for their exchangeability (for food and other items at marketplaces) among the Postclassic Mexica. This fact suggests that typological distinctions between staple and wealth finance (D'Altroy and Earle 1985) or corporate versus exclusionary states (Blanton et al. 1996) obscure important complexities and hinder, rather than facilitate, knowledge production. Likewise, categorizing Maya economies as noncommercial (Smith 2004) rules out the possibility of marketplace exchange before it can be explored, ignores the commercial intensity of tribute negotiation, and misses the historical dynamism of Maya exchange networks, particularly after AD 800.

Although in common usage, the term "the ancient Maya" is too monolithic to do justice to the diverse and historically contingent character of merchant and artisan identities. Likewise, the entanglements of exchange relationships within which trading, gifting, and offering compulsory tribute coexisted seem poorly served by such a singular term. On the other hand, the term does accurately project the orthodoxy (almost a fundamentalism) of the royal court, which was the most vulnerable and most conspicuous part of Classic Maya society.

Acknowledgments

I wish to extend my gratitude to Kenneth Hirth and Joanne Pillsbury for organizing a stimulating, comparative symposium and for extending to me an invitation to participate. Emily Jacobs and the staff of Dumbarton Oaks worked tirelessly to ensure a smooth-running conference and to encourage promptly submitted papers. My chapter is much improved thanks to comments and responses from session organizers, fellow speakers, informed members of the audience, anonymous peer-reviewers, and the Dumbarton Oaks copyeditors. I acknowledge the reviewer who, in a brilliant fashion, saw a link between an increasingly commercialized tribute system and the expansive Postclassic trading networks that followed. I especially wish to thank Barry Isaac for his constructive comments on my chapter. Over the years, Barry has nurtured my interest in economic anthropology, suffered through my prose (at times long-winded), and encouraged me to push the limits (but only if I could muster empirical support). Field research in the Sibun Valley was funded by the National Science Foundation (BCS-0096603) and graciously permitted by the National Institute of Culture and History, Institute of Archaeology, in Belmopan, Belize.

REFERENCES CITED

Andrews, E. Wyllys

    1969   *The Archaeological Use and Distribution of Mollusca in the Maya Lowlands.* Middle American Research Institute, Tulane University, New Orleans.

Aoyama, Kazuo

    2007   Elite Artists and Craft Producers in Classic Maya Society: Lithic Evidence from Aguateca, Guatemala. *Latin American Antiquity* 18(1):3–26.

Ardren, Traci, T. Kam Manahan, Julie Kay Wesp, and Alejandra Alonso

    2010   Cloth Production and Economic Intensification in the Area Surrounding Chichen Itza. *Latin American Antiquity* 21:274–289.

Blanton, Richard E., Gary M. Feinman, Stephen A. Kowalewski, and Peter N. Peregrine

    1996   A Dual-Processual Theory for the Evolution of Mesoamerican Civilization. *Current Anthropology* 37(1):1–86.

Boucher, Sylviane, and Lucía Quiñones

    2007   Entre mercados, ferias y festines: Los murales de la Sub 1-4 de Chiik Nahb, Calakmul. *Mayab* 19:27–50.

Bourdieu, Pierre

    1977   *Outline of a Theory of Practice.* Cambridge University Press, Cambridge.

Braswell, Geoffrey E.

    2001   Post-Classic Maya Courts of the Guatemalan Highlands: Archaeological and Ethnohistorical Approaches. In *Royal Courts of the Ancient Maya*, vol. 2, *Data and Case Studies*, edited by Takeshi Inomata and Stephen D. Houston, pp. 308–334. Westview Press, Boulder, Colo.

    2010   The Rise and Fall of Market Exchange: A Dynamic Approach to Ancient Maya Economy. In *Archaeological Approaches to Market Exchange in Ancient Societies*, edited by Christopher P. Garraty and Barbara L. Stark, pp. 127–140. University Press of Colorado, Boulder.

Carrasco, Davíd

    2000   *Quetzalcoatl and the Irony of Empire: Myths and Prophecies in the Aztec Tradition.* University Press of Colorado, Boulder.

Carrasco, Pedro

    1967   Don Juan Cortés, Cacique de Santa Cruz Quiché. *Estudios de cultura maya* 6:251–266.

    1978   La economía del México prehispánico. In *Economía política e ideología en el México prehispánico*, edited by Pedro Carrasco and Johanna Broda, pp. 13–76. Editorial Nueva Imagen, Mexico City.

Carrasco Vargas, Ramón, and Marinés Colón González

    2005   El reino de Kaan y la antigua ciudad maya de Calakmul. *Arqueología mexicana* 13(75):40–47.

Casas, Bartolomé de las

    1909   Apologética historia de las Indias de
    [1552–1561]   Fr. Bartolomé de las Casas. In *Historiadores de Indias*, vol. 1, edited by Manuel Serrano y Sanz. Nueva Biblioteca de Autores Españoles 13 and 15. Bailly, Bailliére é Hijos, Madrid.

Caso Barrera, Laura, and Mario Aliphat F.

    2006   The Itza Maya Control over Cacao: Politics, Commerce, and War in the Sixteenth and Seventeenth Centuries. In *Chocolate in Mesoamerica: A Cultural History of Cacao*, edited by Cameron L. McNeil, pp. 289–306. University Press of Florida, Gainesville.

Chadwick, John

    1976   *The Mycenaean World.* Cambridge University Press, Cambridge.

Chase, Arlen F., and Diane Z. Chase

    2001   The Royal Court of Caracol, Belize: Its Palaces and People. In *Royal Courts of the Ancient Maya*, vol. 2, *Data and Case Studies*, edited by Takeshi Inomata and Stephen D. Houston, pp. 102–137. Westview Press, Boulder, Colo.

Chase, Diane Z., and Arlen F. Chase

    1982   Yucatec Influence in Terminal Classic Northern Belize. *American Antiquity* 47:596–614.

    1998   The Architectural Context of Caches, Burials, and Other Ritual Activities for the Classic Period Maya (as Reflected at Caracol, Belize). In *Function and Meaning in Classic Maya Architecture*,

edited by Stephen D. Houston,
pp. 299–332. Dumbarton Oaks
Research Library and Collection,
Washington, D.C.

Christie, Jessica Joyce (editor)

2003   *Maya Palaces and Elite Residences: An
Interdisciplinary Approach.* University
of Texas Press, Austin.

Clark, John E., and Richard D. Hansen

2001   The Architecture of Early Kingship:
Comparative Perspectives on the Origins
of the Maya Royal Court. In *Royal Courts
of the Ancient Maya*, vol. 2, *Data and
Case Studies*, edited by Takeshi Inomata
and Stephen D. Houston, pp. 1–45.
Westview Press, Boulder, Colo.

Colas, Pierre R.

2003   K'inich and King: Naming Self and
Person among Classic Maya Rulers.
Ancient Mesoamerica 14(2):269–283.

Coyston, Shannon, Christine D. White, and Henry P.
Schwarcz

1999   Dietary Carbonate Analysis of Bone
and Enamel for Two Sites in Belize.
In *Reconstructing Ancient Maya Diet*,
edited by Christine D. White, pp. 221–
243. University of Utah Press, Salt
Lake City.

Cucina, Andrea, and Vera Tiesler

2003   Dental Caries and Antemortem Tooth
Loss in the Northern Peten Area,
Mexico: A Biocultural Perspective on
Social Status Differences among the
Classic Maya. *American Journal of
Physical Anthropology* 122:1–10.

Culbert, T. Patrick

1993   *The Ceramics of Tikal: Vessels from the
Burials, Caches, and Problematical
Deposits.* Tikal Report 25, pt. A. Uni-
versity Museum Monographs 81. The
University Museum, University
of Pennsylvania, Philadelphia.

Dahlin, Bruce H., Christopher T. Jensen, R. E. Terry,
David R. Wright, and Timothy Beach

2007   In Search of an Ancient Maya Market.
Latin American Antiquity 18(4):363–384.

D'Altroy, Terence N., and Timothy K. Earle

1985   Staple Finance, Wealth Finance, and
Storage in the Inka Political Economy.
Current Anthropology 26(2):187–206.

Diamond, Jared

2005   *Collapse: How Societies Choose to Fail or
Succeed.* Viking, New York.

Douglas, Mary, and Baron Isherwood

1996   *The World of Goods: Towards an
Anthropology of Consumption.*
Routledge, London and New York.

Evans, Susan Toby

2010   Teotihuacan: Art from the City Where
Time Began. In *Ancient Mexican Art at
Dumbarton Oaks: Central Highlands,
Southwestern Highlands, Gulf Lowlands*,
edited by Susan Toby Evans, pp. 11–14.
Dumbarton Oaks Research Library and
Collection, Washington, D.C.

Evans, Susan Toby, and Joanne Pillsbury (editors)

2004   *Palaces of the Ancient New World.*
Dumbarton Oaks Research Library
and Collection, Washington, D.C.

Feldman, Lawrence H.

1985   *A Tumpline Economy: Production and
Distribution Systems in Sixteenth-
Century Eastern Guatemala.*
Labyrinthos, Culver City, Calif.

Fleisher, Jeffrey B.

2010   Housing the Market: Swahili Merchants
and Regional Marketing on the East
African Coast, Seventh to Sixteenth
Centuries AD. In *Archaeological
Approaches to Market Exchange in
Ancient Societies*, edited by Christopher P.
Garraty and Barbara L. Stark, pp. 141–159.
University Press of Colorado, Boulder.

Florescano, Enrique

1999   *The Myth of Quetzalcoatl.* Translated by
L. Hochroth. Johns Hopkins University
Press, Baltimore.

Foias, Antonia E.

2004   The Past and Future of Maya Ceramic
Studies. In *Continuities and Changes
in Maya Archaeology: Perspectives at
the Millennium*, edited by Charles W.
Golden and Greg Borgstede, pp. 143–175.
Routledge, New York.

Foshag, William F.

1984 [1957]   *Mineralogical Studies on Guatemalan
Jade.* Smithsonian Institution Press,
Washington, D.C.

Freidel, David A.

1986 Maya Warfare: An Example of Peer Polity Interaction. In *Peer Polity Interaction and Socio-Political Change*, edited by Colin Renfrew and John F. Cherry, pp. 93–108. Cambridge University Press, Cambridge.

Freidel, David A., and F. Kent Reilly III

2011 The Flesh of God: Cosmology, Food, and the Origins of Political Power in Ancient Southeastern Mesoamerica. In *Pre-Columbian Foodways: Interdisciplinary Approaches to Food, Culture, and Markets in Ancient Mesoamerica*, edited by John Edward Staller and Michael Carrasco, pp. 635–680. Springer, New York.

Gillingham, John

1978 *Richard the Lionheart.* Times Books, New York.

Gómez-Pompa, Arturo, José Salvador Flores, and Mario Aliphat Fernández

1990 The Sacred Cacao Groves of the Maya. *Latin American Antiquity* 1:247–257.

González Cruz, Arnoldo, and Gerardo Fernández Martínez

1994 Inscripciones calendáricas encontradas en Palenque, Chiapas. *Arqueología mexicana* 2(8):60–62.

Graham, Elizabeth

2006 An Ethnicity to Know. In *Maya Ethnicity: The Construction of Ethnic Identity from Preclassic to Modern Times*, edited by Frauke Sachse, pp. 109–124. Acta Mesoamerica 19. A. Saurwein, Markt Schwaben.

Graham, Ian

1978 *Corpus of Maya Hieroglyphic Inscriptions*, vol. 2, pt. 2, *Naranjo, Chunhuitz, Xunantunich.* Peabody Museum of Archaeology and Ethnology, Harvard University, Cambridge, Mass.

Graham, Ian, and Eric von Euw

1975 *Corpus of Maya Hieroglyphic Inscriptions*, vol. 2, pt. 1, *Naranjo.* Peabody Museum of Archaeology and Ethnology, Harvard University, Cambridge, Mass.

Halperin, Christina T.

2008 Classic Maya Textile Production: Insights from Motul de San José, Peten, Guatemala. *Ancient Mesoamerica* 19(1):111–125.

2011 Late Classic Maya Textile Economies: An Object History Approach. In *Textile Economies: Power and Value from the Local to the Transnational*, edited by Walter E. Little and Patricia A. McAnany, pp. 125–145. Altamira Press, Lanham, Md.

Hammond, Norman, Arnold Aspinall, Stuart Feather, John Hazelden, Trevor Gazard, and Stuart Agrell

1977 Maya Jade: Source Location and Analysis. In *Exchange Systems in Prehistory*, edited by Timothy K. Earle and Jonathon E. Ericson, pp. 35–67. Academic Press, New York.

Harrison-Buck, Eleanor, and Patricia A. McAnany

2006 Terminal Classic Circular Shrines and Ceramic Material in the Sibun Valley, Belize: Evidence of Northern Yucatec Influence in the Eastern Maya Lowlands. In *Archaeological Investigations in the Eastern Maya Lowlands: Papers of the 2005 Belize Archaeology Symposium, Research Reports in Belizean Archaeology*, vol. 3, edited by John Morris, Sherilyne Jones, Jaime Awe, and Christophe Helmke, pp. 287–299. Institute of Archaeology, National Institute of Culture and History, Belmopan, Belize.

Harrison-Buck, Eleanor, Patricia A. McAnany, and Rebecca Storey

2007 Empowered and Disempowered during the Late to Terminal Classic Transition: Maya Burial and Termination Rituals in the Sibun Valley, Belize. In *New Perspectives on Human Sacrifice and Ritual Body Treatments in Ancient Maya Society*, edited by Vera Tiesler and Andrea Cucina, pp. 74–101. Springer, New York.

Hendon, Julia A.

2006 Textile Production as Craft in Mesoamerica. *Journal of Social Archaeology* 6(3):354–378.

Houston, Stephen D.

1997   A King Worth a Hill of Beans.
        Archaeology 50(3):40.

1998   Classic Maya Depictions of the Built
        Environment. In *Function and Meaning
        in Classic Maya Architecture*, edited
        by Stephen D. Houston, pp. 333–372.
        Dumbarton Oaks Research Library and
        Collection, Washington, D.C.

2000   Into the Minds of Ancients: Advances in
        Maya Glyph Studies. *Journal of World
        Prehistory* 14(2):121–201.

2006   Impersonation, Dance, and the Problem
        of Spectacle among the Classic Maya. In
        *Archaeology of Performance: Theaters of
        Power, Community, and Politics*, edited
        by Takeshi Inomata and Lawrence S.
        Coben, pp. 135–155. Altamira Press,
        Lanham, Md.

Houston, Stephen D., and Héctor L. Escobedo

1996   Descifrando la política maya: Perspec-
        tivas arqueológicas y epigráficas sobre
        el concepto de los estados segmen-
        tarios. In *X Simposio de Investigaciones
        Arqueológicas en Guatemala*, edited
        by Juan Pedro Laporte and Héctor
        L. Escobedo, pp. 463–481. Ministerio
        de Cultura y Deportes, Instituto de
        Antropología e Historia, and Asociación
        Tikal, Guatemala City.

Houston, Stephen D., and David Stuart

2001   Peopling the Classic Maya Court. In
        Royal Courts of the Ancient Maya, vol. 1,
        Theory, Comparison, and Synthesis,
        edited by Takeshi Inomata and Stephen
        D. Houston, pp. 54–83. Westview Press,
        Boulder, Colo.

Houston, Stephen D., David Stuart, and Karl A. Taube

1992   Image and Text on the "Jauncy Vase."
        In *The Maya Vase Book*, vol. 3, edited by
        Justin Kerr, pp. 499–512. Kerr Associates,
        New York.

2006   *The Memory of Bones: Body, Being, and
        Experience among the Classic Maya.*
        University of Texas Press, Austin.

Hutson, Scott R.

2000   Carnival and Contestation in the Aztec
        Marketplace. *Dialectical Anthropology*
        25:123–149.

Inomata, Takeshi

2001   The Power and Ideology of Artistic
        Creation. *Current Anthropology*
        42(3):321–349.

Inomata, Takeshi, and Stephen D. Houston

2001a   Opening the Royal Maya Court. In
        Royal Courts of the Ancient Maya, vol. 1,
        Theory, Comparison, and Synthesis,
        edited by Takeshi Inomata and Stephen
        D. Houston, pp. 3–23. Westview Press,
        Boulder, Colo.

Inomata, Takeshi, and Stephen D. Houston (editors)

2001b   *Royal Courts of the Ancient Maya*, vol. 1,
        Theory, Comparison, and Synthesis.
        Westview Press, Boulder, Colo.

2001c   *Royal Courts of the Ancient Maya*, vol. 2,
        Data and Case Studies. Westview Press,
        Boulder, Colo.

Jackson, Sarah, and David Stuart

2001   The Aj K'uhun Title: Deciphering a
        Classic Maya Term of Rank. *Ancient
        Mesoamerica* 12:217–228.

Karabell, Zachary

2010   Madness to the Method. *Time* 175(24):67.

Kepecs, Susan, and Sylviane Boucher

1996   The Pre-Hispanic Cultivation of
        Rejolladas and Stone-Lands: New
        Evidence from Northeast Yucatán. In
        *The Managed Mosaic: Ancient Maya
        Agriculture and Resource Use*, edited by
        Scott L. Fedick, pp. 69–91. University of
        Utah Press, Salt Lake City.

Knecht, R. J.

1994   *Renaissance Warrior and Patron: The
        Reign of Francis I.* Cambridge University
        Press, Cambridge.

Kovacevich, Brigitte

2007   Ritual, Crafting, and Agency at the
        Classic Maya Kingdom of Cancuen.
        In *Mesoamerican Ritual Economy:
        Archaeological and Ethnological
        Perspectives*, edited by E. Christian Wells
        and Karla L. Davis-Salazar, pp. 67–114.
        University Press of Colorado, Boulder.

Kowalski, Jeff Karl, and Cynthia Kristan-Graham
(editors)

2007   *Twin Tollans: Chichén Itzá, Tula,
        and the Epiclassic to Early Postclassic
        Mesoamerican World.* Dumbarton

Oaks Research Library and Collection,
Washington, D.C.

Lacadena, Alfonso

2008   El título *lakam*: Evidencia epigráfica
        sobra la organización tributaria y militar
        interna de los reinos mayas del clásico.
        Mayab 20:23–43.

Le Fort, Genevieve, and Robert Wald

1995   Large Numbers on Naranjo Stela 32.
        Mexicon 17:112–114.

Looper, Matthew G., and Thomas Tolles

2000   *Gifts of the Moon: Huipil Designs of
        the Ancient Maya*. Museum of Man,
        San Diego.

Lucero, Lisa J.

2007   Classic Maya Temples, Politics, and the
        Voice of the People. *Latin American
        Antiquity* 18(4):407–427.

Martin, Simon

2006   Cacao in Ancient Maya Religion: First
        Fruit from the Maize Tree and Other
        Tales from the Underworld. In *Chocolate
        in Mesoamerica: A Cultural History
        of Cacao*, edited by Cameron McNeil,
        pp. 155–183. University of Florida Press,
        Gainesville.

2007   Un informe provisional sobre los mura-
        les de la Estructura 1 de la Acrópolis de
        Chiik Nahb. Manuscript on file, Archivo
        del Proyecto Arqueológico Calakmul,
        Instituto Nacional de Antropología e
        Historia, Sureste, Mérida, Yucatan.

Martin, Simon, and Nikolai Grube

2000   *Chronicle of the Maya Kings and Queens:
        Deciphering the Dynasties of the Ancient
        Maya*. 1st ed. Thames and Hudson,
        London.

2008   *Chronicle of the Maya Kings and Queens:
        Deciphering the Dynasties of the Ancient
        Maya*. 2nd ed. Thames and Hudson,
        London.

Masson, Marilyn A., and David A. Freidel (editors)

2002   *Ancient Maya Political Economies*.
        Altamira Press, Walnut Creek, Calif.

Masson, Marilyn A., and Shirley B. Mock

2004   Ceramics and Settlement Patterns at
        Terminal Classic-Period Lagoon Sites
        in Northeastern Belize. In *The Terminal
        Classic in the Maya Lowlands: Collapse,
        Transition, and Transformation*, edited
        by Arthur A. Demarest, Prudence M.
        Rice, and Don S. Rice, pp. 367–401.
        University Press of Colorado, Boulder.

Masson, Marilyn A., and Carlos Peraza Lope

2007   Kukulkan/Quetzalcoatl, Death God,
        and Creation Mythology of Burial
        Shaft Temples at Mayapán. *Mexicon*
        29(3):77–85.

McAnany, Patricia A.

2007   Culture Heroes and Feathered Serpents:
        The Contribution of Gordon R. Willey
        to the Study of Ideology. In *Gordon
        R. Willey and American Archaeology:
        Contemporary Perspectives*, edited by
        Jeremy A. Sabloff and William L. Fash,
        pp. 209–231. University of Oklahoma
        Press, Norman.

2008   Shaping Social Difference: Political
        and Ritual Economy of Classic Maya
        Royal Courts. In *Dimensions of Ritual
        Economy*, edited by E. Christian Wells
        and Patricia A. McAnany, pp. 219–247.
        Research in Economic Anthropology 27.
        JAI Press, Bingley, U.K.

2010   *Ancestral Maya Economies in Archae-
        ological Perspective*. Cambridge
        University Press, New York.

2012   Terminal Classic Maya Heterodoxy
        and Shrine Vernacularism in the Sibun
        Valley, Belize. *Cambridge Archaeological
        Journal* 22(1):115–134.

McAnany, Patricia A., and Tomás Gallareta Negrón

2009   Bellicose Rulers and Climatological
        Peril? Retrofitting Twenty-First Century
        Woes on Eighth Century Maya Society.
        In *Questioning Collapse: Human
        Resilience, Ecological Vulnerability,
        and the Aftermath of Empire*, edited
        by Patricia A. McAnany and Norman
        Yoffee, pp. 142–175. Cambridge
        University Press, New York.

McAnany, Patricia A., and Shannon Plank

2001   Perspectives on Actors, Gender Roles,
        and Architecture at Classic Maya Courts
        and Households. In *Royal Courts of the
        Ancient Maya*, vol. 1, *Theory, Comparison,
        and Synthesis*, edited by Takeshi Inomata
        and Stephen D. Houston, pp. 84–129.
        Westview Press, Boulder, Colo.

McNeil, Cameron (editor)

2006   *Chocolate in Mesoamerica: A Cultural History of Cacao.* University of Florida Press, Gainesville.

Miller, Mary Ellen

2001   Life at Court: The View from Bonampak. In *Royal Courts of the Ancient Maya*, vol. 2, *Data and Case Studies*, edited by Takeshi Inomata and Stephen D. Houston, pp. 201–222. Westview Press, Boulder, Colo.

Miller, Mary Ellen, and Simon Martin

2004   *Courtly Art of the Ancient Maya.* Fine Arts Museum of San Francisco, San Francisco, and Thames and Hudson, New York.

Nicholson, H. B.

2000   The Iconography of the Feathered Serpent in Late Postclassic Central Mexico. In *Mesoamerica's Classic Heritage: From Teotihuacan to the Aztecs*, edited by Davíd Carrasco, Lindsay Jones, and Scott Sessions, pp. 145–164. University Press of Colorado, Boulder.

Perez Romero, Jose Alberto

1988   *Algunas consideraciones sobre cacao en el norte de la península de Yucatán.* Licenciatura thesis, Ciencias Antropológicas, Universidad Autónoma de Yucatán, Mérida.

Pillsbury, Joanne

1996   The Thorny Oyster and the Origins of Empire: Implications of Recently Uncovered *Spondylus* Imagery from Chan Chan, Peru. *Latin American Antiquity* 7(4):313–340.

Piña Chán, Román

1998   *Cacaxtla, fuentes históricas y pinturas.* Fondo de Cultura Económica, Mexico City.

Piperno, Dolores R., and Deborah M. Pearsall

1998   *The Origins of Agriculture in the Lowland Neotropics.* Academic Press, San Diego.

Reents-Budet, Dorie

2000   Feasting among the Classic Maya: Evidence from the Pictorial Ceramics. In *The Maya Vase Book*, vol. 6, edited by Justin Kerr, pp. 1022–1037. Kerr Associates, New York.

2001   Classic Maya Concepts of the Royal Court: An Analysis of Renderings on Pictorical Ceramics. In *Royal Courts of the Ancient Maya*, vol. 1, *Theory, Comparison, and Synthesis*, edited by Takeshi Inomata and Stephen D. Houston, pp. 195–231. Westview Press, Boulder, Colo.

Renfrew, Colin

1972   *The Emergence of Civilization: The Cyclades and the Aegean in the Third Millennium BC.* Methuen, London.

Restall, Matthew

1997   *The Maya World: Yucatec Culture and Society, 1550–1850.* Stanford University Press, Stanford.

Ringle, William M.

2004   On the Political Organization of Chichen Itza. *Ancient Mesoamerica* 15:167–218.

Ringle, William M., and George J. Bey III

2009   The Face of the Itzas. In *The Art of Urbanism: How Mesoamerican Kingdoms Represented Themselves in Architecture and Imagery*, edited by William L. Fash and Leonardo López Luján, pp. 329–383. Dumbarton Oaks Research Library and Collection, Washington, D.C.

Ringle, William M., Tomás Gallareta Negrón, and George J. Bey III

1998   The Return of Quetzalcoatl: Evidence for the Spread of a World Religion during the Epiclassic Period. *Ancient Mesoamerica* 9:183–232.

Saturno, William, Karl A. Taube, and David Stuart

2005   *The Murals of San Bartolo, El Petén, Guatemala*, pt. 1, *The North Wall.* Ancient America 7. Center for Ancient American Studies, Barnardsville, N.C.

Smith, Michael E.

2004   The Archaeology of Ancient State Economies. *Annual Review of Anthropology* 33:73–102.

Smith, Michael E., and Frances F. Berdan

2000   The Postclassic Mesoamerican World System. *Current Anthropology* 41(2):283–286.

Stanton, Travis W., and Aline Magnoni (editors)

2008   *Ruins of the Past: The Use and Perception of Abandoned Structures in the Maya Lowlands*. University Press of Colorado, Boulder.

Stuart, David

1998   "The Fire Enters His House": Architecture and Ritual in Classic Maya Texts. In *Function and Meaning in Classic Maya Architecture*, edited by Stephen D. Houston, pp. 373–425. Dumbarton Oaks Research Library and Collection, Washington, D.C.

2006a   Jade and Chocolate: Bundles of Wealth in Classic Maya Economics and Ritual. In *Sacred Bundles: Ritual Acts of Wrapping and Binding in Mesoamerica*, edited by Julia Guernsey and F. Kent Reilly, pp. 127–144. Boundary End Archaeology Research Center, Barnardsville, N.C.

2006b   The Language of Chocolate: References to Cacao on Classic Maya Drinking Vessels. In *Chocolate in Mesoamerica: A Cultural History of Cacao*, edited by Cameron McNeil, pp. 184–201. University Press of Florida, Gainesville.

Tate, Carolyn E.

1992   *Yaxchilan: The Design of a Maya Ceremonial City*. University of Texas Press, Austin.

Taube, Karl A.

1985   The Classic Maya Maize God: A Reappraisal. In *Fifth Palenque Round Table, 1983*, edited by Virginia M. Fields, pp. 171–181. Pre-Columbian Art Research Institute, San Francisco.

2000   The Breath of Life: The Symbolism of Wind in Mesoamerica and the American Southwest. In *The Road to Aztlan: Art from a Mythic Homeland*, edited by Virginia M. Fields and Victor Zamudio-Taylor, pp. 102–123. Los Angeles County Museum of Art, Los Angeles.

2005   The Symbolism of Jade in Classic Maya Religion. *Ancient Mesoamerica* 16:23–50.

Tedlock, Dennis

1985   *Popol Vuh: The Mayan Book of the Dawn of Life*. Simon and Schuster, New York.

Thompson, J. Eric S.

1964   Trade Relations between the Maya Highlands and the Lowlands. *Estudios de cultura maya* 4:13–48.

Tozzer, Alfred M.

1941 [ca. 1566]   *Landa's* Relación de las cosas de Yucatan: *A Translation*. Papers of the Peabody Museum of American Archaeology and Ethnology 18. The Peabody Museum, Cambridge, Mass.

Trigger, Bruce G.

2003   *Understanding Early Civilizations: A Comparative Study*. Cambridge University Press, New York.

Tuchman, Barbara W.

1978   *A Distant Mirror: The Calamitous Fourteenth Century*. Alfred A. Knopf, New York.

Tykot, Robert H.

2002   Contribution of Stable Isotope Analysis to Understanding Dietary Variation among the Maya. In *Archaeological Chemistry: Materials, Methods, and Meaning*, edited by Kathryn A. Jakes, pp. 214–230. American Chemical Society, Washington, D.C.

Vokes, Harold E., and Emily H. Vokes

1983   *Distribution of Shallow-Water Marine Mollusca, Yucatan Peninsula, Mexico*. Middle American Research Institute, Tulane University, New Orleans.

Weiner, Annette B.

1992   *Inalienable Possessions: The Paradox of Keeping-While-Giving*. University of California Press, Berkeley.

Widmer, Randolph J.

2009   Elite Household Multicrafting Specialization at 9N8, Patio H, Copan. *Archaeological Papers of the American Anthropological Association* 19(1):174–204.

Yoffee, Norman

2005   *Myths of the Archaic State: Evolution of the Earliest Cities, States, and Civilizations*. Cambridge University Press, Cambridge.

10

Craft Production and Distribution in the Maya Lowlands

A Jade Case Study

BRIGITTE KOVACEVICH

Aⁿ UNDERSTANDING OF THE ORGANIZA-tion of production and exchange of goods such as jade, shell, obsidian, chert, and textiles has proven to be quite challenging for Maya scholars. The answers to questions of who produced these items (i.e., elites or commoners, men or women), how they were transported and exchanged across the landscape, what routes were taken, and who consumed these objects still elude us to a great degree. Part of the problem may be due to the highly variable nature of Classic Maya polities, as well as changes in economic systems through time, but another contributing factor to these debates has been the traditional focus on elite contexts to the exclusion of commoner households (i.e., Robin 2003). This situation is beginning to be remedied, and new research is revealing an even more complicated picture than what was expected in many cases. The production and exchange of jade arti-facts highlight intertwined relationships between the status of the crafters, the location of the centers near valuable resources and trade routes, political

ties and alliances, and also the power of elites and nonelites over their political and economic des-tinies. Once argued to be the sole province of the Classic Maya elite, jade has been shown to have been crafted by commoners as well. Its exchange patterns are equally as confounding, possibly not restricted to spheres of elite exchange and maybe even traded in markets. Commoners not only cre-ated jade artifacts, but also they may have con-sumed them in some forms. The entangled nature of the production and exchange of jade reflects the intricacies of the Classic Maya economic system as a whole and can provide a window into these eco-nomic patterns. For this reason, I will focus here on how jade was produced and consumed during the Classic period, with an emphasis on evidence from the site of Cancuen, Guatemala (Figure 10.1).

Timothy Earle (1981) characterized the nature of the organization of production in preindustrial societies as including independent and attached forms of specialization. Independent craft spe-cialization refers to the creation of goods for an

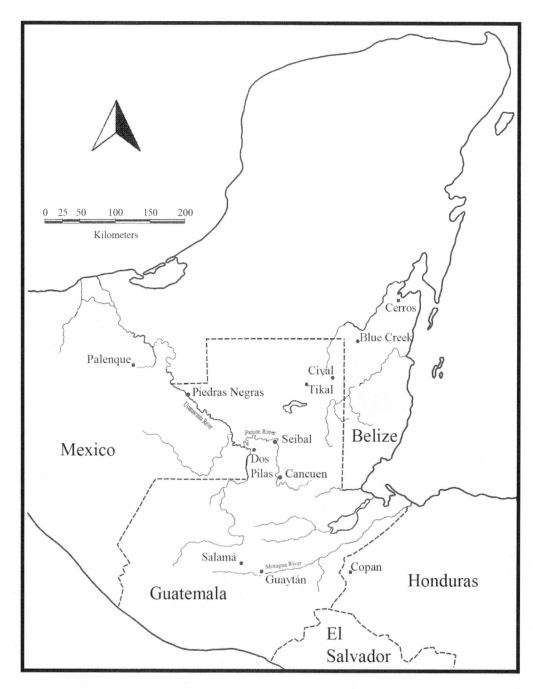

figure 10.1
Map of Guatemala showing the location of Cancuen. (Map created by Brigitte Kovacevich.)

unspecified demand crowd by persons working outside of elite control; attached specialization involves production for a specific elite demand crowd who control part or all of production and derive power and prestige from the control of production and/or products (Brumfiel and Earle 1987; Earle 1981).

According to these definitions, independent specialists generally make subsistence or utilitarian goods, usually distributed widely, for an unspecified demand crowd. This type of production usually arises in response to unevenly distributed resources and/or economic and demographic stress. Attached specialists typically (but not always) manufacture prestige goods, wealth items, or weapons for a specific demand crowd; these items are usually distributed in a restricted manner among elites. This type of production could have been stimulated by increasing political complexity and the emergence of elites (Brumfiel and Earle 1987; Costin 1991).

For many archaeologists, these categories were seen to form a polarized dichotomy, although this may not have been the original intent, and they were seen by the original proponents to form more along a continuum (see especially Costin 1991). These two categories have made it easy for many Maya scholars to dichotomize several issues in relation to craft production and exchange (see also Masson 2002:2–3). For example, as attached specialization is to independent, full-time specialization is to part-time, production and distribution of prestige and wealth items is to utilitarian items, and elite involvement is to nonelite involvement, facilitating a dual economy model. Recent studies in the Maya region have revealed the recondite nature of these relationships and suggested that simple dichotomized categories cannot explain the organization of Maya economic systems. As Patricia McAnany (2010:14), Christian Wells, and Karla Davis-Salazar (Wells 2007; Wells and Davis-Salazar 2007) have pointed out, the Maya economy is entangled in ritual process. Ritual may have been the original stimulus for craft production in many cases, and economic functions cannot be examined independently of ritual and ideological concerns. Following this path, the distinction between prestige and utilitarian items can also be problematic (Hirth 2009:4; Hruby 2003; Masson 2002:12), as many goods that circulated outside of elite or prestige spheres were ritually charged and could cross the boundary into items of wealth. Traditionally viewed luxury items, such as jade, may have been much more widely distributed among different social groups (e.g., Garber 1993; Guderjan 2007:81–88; Moholy-Nagy 1994:88, 1997:301; Palka 1995:20; Rochette 2009; Rochette and Pellecer Alecio 2008).

Scholars are also questioning the argument that economic power lies purely in the hands of the elite (Masson 2002; McAnany 2010; Wells 2007). As Rochette (2009) has demonstrated, commoners were involved in the creation of wealth items, such as jade in the Middle Motagua Valley in Guatemala, and as Potter and King (1995) have pointed out for chert production at Colha, Belize, nonelite producers were not always impoverished individuals attached to elites and dependent on them for their livelihoods. Research by Inomata (2001), Webster (1989, 1992), and Widmer (2009) have found that often elites were involved in the crafting of "prestige goods," but—at the same time—they may have been engaged in attached and independent forms of specialization (Inomata 2001). Nearly all of these contexts for specialized production took place within the household (e.g., Ball 1993; Freidel 1981; McAnany 1993, 1995), whether it was by elites or nonelites, and was often on a part-time basis, as evidence of multicrafting or intermittent crafting attest (Hirth 2009). Examples of "workshop"-type production as defined in the Old World (e.g., Peacock 1982; Van der Leeuw 1976) have not been discovered for the Maya (although, see Murata 2011). Nevertheless, many scholars have argued that this does not relegate the Maya to a lower level of political and economic complexity, and, in reality, the economic structure can be just as nuanced as Old World examples, yet not in the traditional sense (e.g., Costin 2000; Freidel 1981). The domestic and institutional sectors of the economy, as discussed by Hirth and Pillsbury (this volume), may have been linked and not disembedded from one another (e.g., Kovacevich 2007; Sheets 2000). In terms of distribution, the situation may have been equally as complicated, as market systems (Chase 1998; Fry 1979, 1980; West 2002), gifting and redistribution (Rice 1987; Sabloff and Rathje 1975; Tourtellot and Sabloff 1972), and tribute (McAnany et al. 2002) may have all existed simultaneously (Fry 1980; Masson 2002:8; Masson and Freidel, this volume; McAnany 2010; Sheets 2000). As Hirth and Pillsbury (this volume) point out, economic systems are accumulative and conservative, often retaining and articulating previous forms of production and distribution as changes occur.

As the data in this chapter will demonstrate, the production and exchange of jade objects in the Maya region during the Classic period (AD 600–900) support arguments for an economic system entangled in ritual and ideology with multiple interacting spheres. Although it was a wealth good, jade was also a raw material used to make ritual paraphernalia for the elite (Taube 2005); at the same time, jade was sometimes produced and used by nonelites (Kovacevich 2006, 2007, 2011; Rochette 2009). Its distribution may have followed two paths, not just along elite, vertical exchange networks (i.e., Marcus 1983), but also in less restricted spheres (i.e., Lesure 1999) and possibly even in the market, in some forms (Freidel 1993; Freidel et al. 2002). As unworked jade was apparently very difficult to restrict—and has not been recovered solely in elite contexts (Hirth 2009:4; Rochette 2009)—elites may have been able to regulate a part of this production and distribution possibly through sumptuary laws and ideological control (Kovacevich 2006). Certain finished jade artifacts were much more widely consumed than others. For example, jade beads at the site of Cancuen were much more widely distributed than were carved plaques or pendants. These distribution patterns also suggest that jade was created in attached and independent forms of craft production (see also Inomata 2001).

Jadeite and Its Properties

Jade is a general term for the minerals jadeite and nephrite. While it has been argued that both jadeite and nephrite occur in Mesoamerica, nephrite does not appear to have been exploited by ancient populations (Taube and Ishihara-Brito 2012). Jadeite is a pyroxene mineral composed of sodium, aluminum, and silicates ($NaAlSi_2O_6$). Depending on its chemical composition, jadeite in Mesoamerica can be green, blue, lavender, white, pink, or black in color. Green jade, highly prized by ancient Mesoamericans, derives its hue mainly from the presence of chromium and nickel (Kovacevich et al. 2005). To the ancient Maya, jade and the color green or green-blue symbolized maize, fertility,

centrality, axis mundi, nobility, and life's breath or essence (Coe 1988; Miller and Taube 1993; Schele and Freidel 1990; Taube 1996, 1998, 2000, 2005; Taube and Ishihara-Brito 2012). The production and possession of jade objects would certainly allude to the control of these forces and elevate the status of the possessor, but, as mentioned previously, jade was not necessarily restricted to elite contexts.

Jadeite is a very hard mineral, scoring 6.5 to 7.0 on Mohs scale of hardness, with talc as the softest at 1 and diamond being the hardest at 10. Other related minerals (i.e., albite, diopside, chloromelanite, etc.) are softer than jadeite (see also Kovacevich 2011). While jadeite was much more time-consuming and difficult to work (Lange and Bishop 1988), it yielded a better and longer-lasting polish and luster. Jadeite is also very rare: Guatemala has one of only six known sources of the mineral worldwide (Foshag and Leslie 1955), and the Motagua fault zone of Guatemala is, as of yet, the only source of jadeite outcrops in Mesoamerica (Kovacevich 2012). The scarcity and durability of jade certainly contribute to its value, in the past as well as today.

Hammond and colleagues (1977:61) have described the application of the term "jade" to nonjadeite greenstones as "social jade." They argue that patterns of jadeite inclusion in burials at Cuello demonstrate that the Maya could differentiate between jadeite and other greenstones: men were buried with jadeite artifacts, whereas women and children were laid to rest with social jade (Hammond 1999:58). As Hammond and colleagues (1977:61) note, other greenstones are often confused with jadeite by modern scholars, but these minerals have very different properties of workability and luster, making them inferior for use as adornments. The inclusion of these nonjadeite greenstones—as well as ceramic beads painted blue (i.e., at Piedras Negras; Kovacevich and Hruby 2005)—in royal tombs suggests that the color and the idea of jade were so highly prized that known fakes could be substituted and still convey elevated status and ritual importance. In fact, some scholars have suggested that highly valued artifacts often have similar counterparts or counterfeits that circulated more widely and contributed to the value of the original (Lesure 1999; Freidel et al. 2002). These gradations of value, as well as the existence of social jade, imply that jadeite and greenstones possibly circulated in multiple spheres of the economy. In addition, the evidence from Cuello and the following Postclassic Aztec example suggest that ancient Mesoamerican populations could distinguish between different qualities of jadeite and other greenstones, something that can prove to be more challenging for modern scholars. Jade in this work is used to refer to artifacts that are assumed to have jadeite as a major component, although some are certainly lesser-quality greenstones.

In Postclassic-period Aztec and Classic-period Maya society, there were different values attached to different greenstones, and they may be found in varying contexts, suggesting that jade and greenstones may have been exchanged in multiple economic spheres. Ethnohistoric sources often refer to greenstones as *chalchihuites* (more properly, *xalxihuitli*), meaning "herb-colored jewel" in Nahuatl (Foshag 1957:7). Sahagún (1950–1982:11:222–223) notes that the Aztecs used many terms to refer to the color and quality of greenstones. *Quetzalitztli* ("Quetzal obsidian") referred to bright, emerald-green stones that resembled Chinese "imperial" jade. *Quetzachalchihuitl* ("Quetzal greenstone") described high-quality, transparent stones without imperfections. *Chalchihuites* were green and of good quality, but opaque. Finally, *xihuitl* and *teoxihuitl* probably referred to common and fine turquoise. These identifications convey that certain jades were attributed to specific statuses during the Postclassic period, and such relegation also may have been the case for Classic-period Maya society based on distributions of jade at numerous sites, including Cuello. At many Classic-period Maya sites, jade is found in elite contexts, but it appears in certain forms in nonelite contexts as well. It seems that it was not necessarily the raw material that was restricted to the elite, but rather the form and quality of the finished product.

For example, at sites like Dos Pilas, jade was abundant in royal contexts, such as the tomb of Ruler 2 (Demarest et al. 1991) and the Lady of Cancuen (Wolley and Wright 1990), but jade was also recovered in lesser quantities and in less elaborate styles in middle-range and commoner households (Palka 1995, 1997). Guderjan (2007) also relates that at Blue Creek, Belize, jade is found in elite and nonelite contexts, especially in the case of an individual who appears to have been a nonelite community leader. His burial included several jade beads and bone earflares with jade inlays. At Copan, there is ample evidence of the use of jade in royal tombs (see Fash 1991 for examples), as well as elite lapidary work (Widmer 2009), including jade nodules that were in the process of being sawed (Willey et al. 1994). At the same time, Nancy Gonlin (2007:97) also found some evidence of jade in the ritual deposits of the households of the humblest Maya outside the Copan pocket, though the jade is not in an elaborate or incised form. As McAnany (this volume) notes, jade was part of the tactics of

0   1   2 cm

figure 10.2
Jade headdress ornaments recovered from tomb in Structure K7-3. (Drawing by Fernando Alvarez Andaverde.)

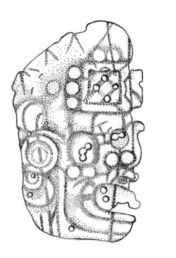
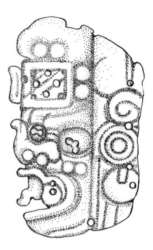

0 ⌐_____⌐ 5 cm

figure 10.3
Jade headdress ornament recovered
from cache beneath royal throne
room. (Drawing by Fernando Alvarez
Andaverde.)

cm

figure 10.4
Jade headdress ornament recovered from cache
beneath royal throne room. (Photograph by Brigitte
Kovacevich.)

elites to create a "weapon of exclusion," used to distinguish themselves from others, but it may have only been particular forms of jade that helped to authenticate this difference. While jade is often recovered in commoner contexts, it is not found in some specific forms which appear to have been exclusively restricted to the elite—for example, the tripartite "jester god" headdress, which represents a ripe maize plant (e.g., Fields 1991; Schele and Miller 1986:53). Such headdresses symbolized royal status and the power of the wearer to control fertility and abundance (see Figures 10.2–10.4). These examples suggest that jade objects circulated in institutional and domestic spheres simultaneously.

Jade Production

The two spheres of the economy, institutional and domestic, may have been economically linked by household production. As Masson and Freidel (this volume) note, the presence of craft production in the household can signal connectedness and interdependence of trade relationships. The part-time crafting of goods within Maya households may have occurred in attached and independent forms for vertical and horizontal trade in the institutional and domestic economies.

In many Classic Maya polities, specialized production of prestige goods, or items that are assumed to have circulated in the institutional economy (i.e., jade, textiles, marine shell, or pyrite), seems to have taken the form of small-scale elite production within the household, sometimes in the royal palace itself (i.e., Inomata 2001; McAnany, this volume). In other words, although these are artifacts that circulate in the institutional economy, they are still produced domestically, and not in institutional workshops or nondomestic settings. At Copan, there is evidence of specialization in shell carving from a royal court (Aoyama 1995), elite-controlled production of obsidian (Aoyama 1994), as well as scribal specialization (Fash 1991; Webster 1989). Convincing evidence of elite domestic multicrafting comes from excavations by Randolf Widmer (2009) of Structure N9-8, where de facto refuse from lapidary, textile, and feather work was left on elite residence floors. In addition, skeletal remains of a probable elite lapidary specialist (Widmer 2009:188) show exaggerated muscle attachments, further supporting the assertion that elites themselves were involved in crafting, even tackling the more strenuous tasks. It was just this kind of arduous level of production that lent value to the object being made (i.e., Appadurai 1986; Helms 1993; see Widmer 2009:182 for an archaeological example of "non-rational/economizing" elite crafting). It is possible, however, that elites were involved only in the finishing stages of a long operational chain of tasks (Costin 2007; Kovacevich 2006, 2007).

Evidence for nonelite participation in the creation of prestige goods in the Maya region has been largely absent until recently, but some scholars have suggested it (Ball 1993:264–265; Marcus 2004:262–263; Potter and King 1995:26). Notable recent findings include those of Rochette (2009) for jade production at Motagua Valley as well as at Cancuen (Kovacevich 2006, 2007). Due to the lack of this evidence, scholars previously had argued that the domestic/agrarian and prestige economies operated separately (Ball 1993:248, 264; McAnany 1993:70–71; Potter and King 1995:28; see

also Masson 2002:2), but the integration of these economies seems to be a possible organization of production for Mesoamerica (Kovacevich 2006, 2007; Sheets 2000; see also Wattenmaker 1994, 1998 for an Old World example). Elites and commoners appear to have been involved in the production and circulation of jade artifacts in different contexts. Jade as an item of wealth circulated not only in the institutional economy, but in the domestic economy as well.

Residential structures associated with large-scale production of jade at Cancuen, a Late Classic-period (AD 650–810) Maya center (Figure 10.1), generally appear to have invested a modest amount of labor in construction (Kovacevich 2003a). Low (i.e., a meter or less) earthen mounds supported perishable superstructures and exterior *laja* (or flagstone) patio floors. De facto refuse was often left on these floors during the abandonment of the site, sometimes including termination ritual deposits. There are also high-density sheet middens directly adjacent to the floors, containing lithic production refuse mixed with domestic refuse. These communal activity areas provide excellent data for studies of craft production at Cancuen, as the refuse derived from production is either directly on or adjacent to the crafting area, a feature not common at other lowland Maya sites (Moholy-Nagy 1990, 1997).

Nonelite households were initially identified by the amount of labor invested in construction and by the presence of certain architectural types (Kovacevich 2006:38–41). Typically, a sample of each patio group was excavated. Structure types, considered as a sample from a larger group, were then correlated with the presence or absence of specific portable items of material culture. As expected, the material culture of some households differed significantly from that of others. Excavated structures in Groups N9-1, N11-1, K7-1 had masonry architecture, stucco sculpture, tombs, hieroglyphic writing in associated monumental art, some evidence of jade working (usually its late stages), and finished jade artifacts. This last group included finely carved jade diadems and faces of the sort that, at many other sites, correlate with elite status and even kingship (see Eberl and Inomata 2001;

Friedel 1993:153–159; Friedel et al. 2002:45, 70; Schele and Friedel 1990:114–115, 121, 135, figs. 3.14, 3.19, 4.4).

Excavation of units in a nonelite structure group (M10-4 and M10-7) produced a total of 3,258 pieces of greenstone debitage (Figure 10.5) (Kovacevich 2003b, 2006, 2007; Kovacevich et al. 2002, 2003, 2004, 2005; Kovacevich and Pereira 2002). Thirty-two of these pieces, most of them with evidence of string-sawing, including a twenty-pound boulder, were left on the patio floor of Structure M10-4. Also recovered embedded in the patio floor of this same structure were large quantities of jade and quartzite microdebitage, which, as primary refuse, is an important indicator of lithic workshop production (Moholy-Nagy 1990). I believe that the pulverized quartzite was used in this case as an abrasive with the string-saw or drill as the actual cutting agent (Chenault 1986). Tools directly associated with jade working on the floors and middens include slate- and greenstone-polishing tools (West 1963), chert, greenstone, and quartzite hammerstones (Figure 10.6); chert and chalcedony drills (Figure 10.7); and string-saw anchors (Figure 10.8).

figure 10.6
Jade hammerstones and a pecking stone from middens in Structure M10-4. (Photograph by Brigitte Kovacevich.)

figure 10.5
Sample of jade debitage from the midden associated with Structure M10-4. (Photograph by Brigitte Kovacevich.)

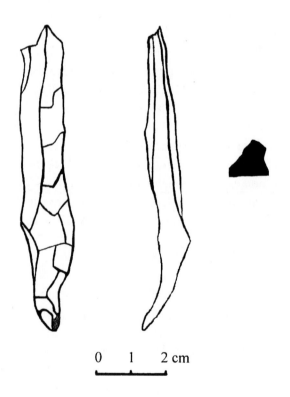

figure 10.7
Chert blade recovered from midden of Structure M10-4 associated with jade production. (Drawing by Brigitte Kovacevich.)

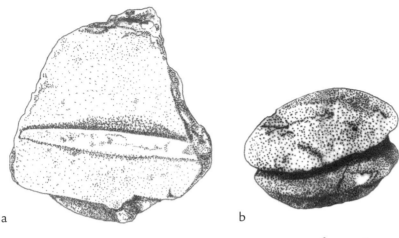

a   b

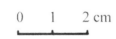

0   1   2 cm

figure 10.8
Artifacts found together on patio floor of
Structure M10-6: a) string-sawn piece of jade
(note convex septum break indicative of string-
sawing); and b) string-saw anchor used to protect
workers' hands. (Drawing by Laurie Greene.)

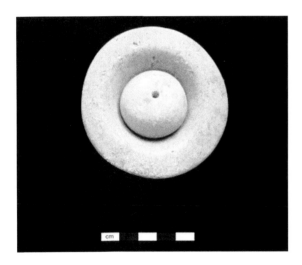

figure 10.9
Large jade earflare and bead recovered from the
cache beneath the royal throne room. (Photograph
by Brigitte Kovacevich.)

Also recovered were five spindle whorls, which I
previously interpreted to have been used possibly
as flywheels for pump drills for drilling jade (Digby
1972); however, they were most probably used in the
production of textiles because of their small size.
This evidence suggests multicrafting as described
by Hirth and colleagues (Hirth, ed. 2009).

Although excavations uncovered a high percentage of debitage that had been worked by percussion and string-sawing, there was little evidence
of the final stages of production (including incising), of jade artifacts, or of the finished products
themselves. Eight beads, including one large jade
bead that was in the process of being drilled (or was
possibly an earflare blank), were recovered from
middens or embedded within floors, a find that
suggests that at least some manufacture of beads or
early stages of artifact production did occur in this
area. But the only jade artifacts recovered from the
ten burials associated with the group were four possible jade inlaid teeth with Burial 25, although three
of the inlays were lost antemortem, and it cannot be
said for sure if the inlays were jade.

Other burials at Cancuen did contain finished
jade artifacts; however, these burials are associated
with elite architecture that required much more
labor investment for construction than the simple earthen mounds of the M10 group. For example, a cyst burial excavated by Erin Sears (2002) in
Structure K7-1 contained two large jade beads (one of
imperial green color), two light green jade earflares
with jade counterweights, and two intricately incised
headdress ornaments carved out of light green jade

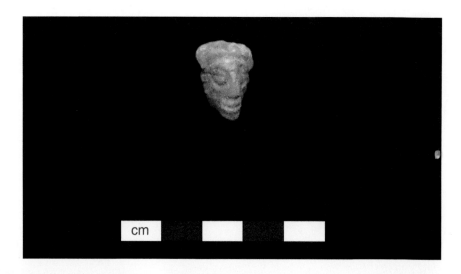

figure 10.10
Jade face pendant
from cache beneath
the royal throne
room. (Photograph by
Brigitte Kovacevich.)

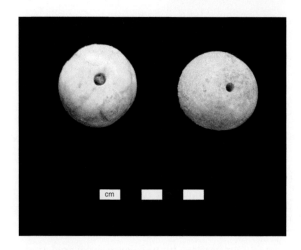

figure 10.11
Jade beads from cache beneath the royal throne
room. (Photograph by Brigitte Kovacevich.)

figure 10.12
String-sawn jade nodule from cache beneath the royal
throne room. (Photograph by Brigitte Kovacevich.)

figure 10.13
Limestone earflare
polisher recovered from
fill in the royal palace at
Cancuen. (Photograph by
Brigitte Kovacevich.)

with a vein of imperial green that were 1.89 milli-meters thick (see Figure 10.2). Michael Callaghan (2005) recovered beneath the royal throne room an elaborate cache with a royal headdress ornament (see Figures 10.3–10.4), a large jade earflare (Figure 10.9), a small jade face pendant (Figure 10.10), two large jade beads (Figure 10.11), and a string-sawn jade nodule (Figure 10.12). An earflare polisher was also found in the fill of Structure L7-9 within the royal palace (Figure 10.13), as well as in another vaulted elite structure (M9-1). While this evidence does not conclusively demonstrate elite engagement in this particular activity, documented elite craft participation at Aguateca and Copan supports elite involvement, and polishers such as these have been found in palatial contexts at other Maya sites, such as Kaminaljuyu (Kidder et al. 1946). Such findings suggest not only that elite residents of Cancuen were consuming finished jade products, but also that the final stages of jade production may have been car-ried out by elite artisans in elite residences.

For the institutional economy, the evidence points to segmented production of prestige goods in which nonelites or lesser elites completed the early stages. Commoner specialists may have been involved with only the initial phases of jade produc-tion, such as percussion, sawing, and drilling. The more intricate final steps, such as incising, may have been carried out by elites with the ritual and eso-teric knowledge necessary to incorporate these arti-facts into the political economy (Barber 1994; Childs 1998; Costin 1998, 2007; Inomata 2001; Reents-Budet 1998). This type of segmented production of jade artifacts has been inferred by Walters (1982) in the Motagua Valley workshop sites located directly adjacent to the Motagua jade source (although cf. Rochette 2009) and has been recognized at other sites in Mesoamerica and beyond (e.g., Berdan et al. 2009; Costin and Hagstrum 1995; Cross 1993; Urban and Schortman 1999). Elites owned and/or used these finished items, and someone was involved in their production; the evidence suggests domestic production by elites, possibly multiple family mem-bers within the household context (Kovacevich n.d.).

At Cancuen, early-stage jade producers had a few of the trappings of elite Classic Maya culture:

jade beads, dental modification, and exotic ceram-ics. At the same time, these indivduals lacked many more of the defining characteristics of elite mate-rial culture, including stone masonry structures, corbel-vaulted architecture, tombs, sculpture, hieroglyphic inscriptions, and high-quality carved jade plaques. The absence of these cultural corre-lates of elite status leads me to argue that the early-stage jade workers at Cancuen were commoners of elevated status (Kovacevich 2011). They negotiated and achieved their status and identity through the segmented production of jade.

In contrast, the earthen mounds of Structures M10-4, M10-6, M6-12, and K7-24 had simple buri-als and domestic refuse mixed with evidence of jade working, but only the early stages of it: no finished jade objects were found aside from small, scattered beads. There were other disparities in material culture, including higher amounts of Chablekal Fine Gray ceramics (Figure 10.14) asso-ciated with early-stage jade production, implying a somewhat elevated status and different identity for these producers (Callaghan et al. 2004; Kovacevich 2006:453–492; Kovacevich and Callaghan 2005). Such ceramics are a class of fine gray serving ves-sels. Extensive chemical analyses using instrumen-tal neutron activation analysis (INAA, see below) by Bishop and Rands (1982) suggest that this type of pottery was produced around the greater Palenque region of Mexico and appears in the archaeologi-cal record of Pasión/Usumacinta sites exclusively between AD 760 and 800 (Bishop and Rands 1982; Callaghan et al. 2004; Foias and Bishop 1997). The presence of this type of long-distance trade good in burials of individuals associated with houses containing evidence of the early stages of jade pro-duction suggests that it allowed these crafters an opportunity to negotiate their status within social networks at the site and in long-distance exchange relationships. It also strengthens the possibility of long-standing trade connections between Cancuen and the Palenque region.

To reiterate, jade, as a raw material, was not necessarily restricted to the elite of Maya society (Garber 1993; Guderjan 2007:81–88; Moholy-Nagy 1994:88, 1997:301; Palka 1995:20; Rochette 2009;

figure 10.14
Chablekal Fine Gray ceramics from Cancuen, showing portability. (Photograph by Michael Callaghan.)

Rochette and Pellecer Alecio 2008). But jade of high quality, and especially status symbols like head-dress ornaments and earflares, may have been restricted to the elite (Chase 1992:34–37; Haviland and Moholy-Nagy 1992:52–54). At Cancuen, com-moners did have access to jade, but it was sometimes of low quality, and it appeared in a limited number of forms. Although jade beads were present in nonelite structures, the jades were often of poor quality or of a related, likewise inferior green mineral (i.e., a mineral or rock softer than jadeite, with physical imperfections and/or a brownish or muddy green color). Many of these beads were found embedded in floors or in middens. We recovered very little jade from simple burials, and it was never found in the form of elaborately incised plaques or face pen-dants, symbols of kingship and nobility. Jade beads found in elite residences are significantly larger than those recovered from nonelite contexts (Kovacevich 2006:186–188, 2007), and the difference in quality is readily apparent. Raw or sawn jade was cached by

figure 10.15
Jade boulder showing marks of string-sawing recovered from termination cache in floor of Structure K7-24, a nonmasonry structure. (Photograph by Brigitte Kovacevich.)

people of lesser status—but only those who were jade crafters—in construction fill and termination rituals (Figure 10.15). This caching relates to the processes of identity formation and maintenance. At Cancuen, some commoners with achieved status identified themselves with the early stages of jade production and, by extension, with the divine act of creation (Kovacevich 2012). Caching also may have reflected a belief that all phases of jade working were sacred, as were the by-products of that activity (Hruby 2007:76; Sheets 1991:177; see Mills 2008 for a North American example). A cache beneath the royal throne room at Cancuen contained both sawn nodules and finished artifacts, as well as other exotic objects and ritual paraphernalia. Status and identity, therefore, can be seen in the distribution of production technologies, finished products, and ritual treatments of jade at the site of Cancuen.

Jade Sourcing and Exchange

Chemical compositional analyses can provide important information about the movement of commodities across the landscape. While the chemical compositional studies of jade are still in their infancy to some degree, they are essential to understanding changes in exchange patterns through time and across space. The following is a brief review of sourcing analysis for jade artifacts and some of the preliminary identifications of exchange patterns.

In 1978, the Brookhaven National Laboratory and the Boston Museum of Fine Arts launched the Maya Jade and Ceramic Research Project. This endeavor allowed Ronald Bishop and his colleagues to characterize source samples from Guatemala and Costa Rica, as well as artifacts from Guatemala, Belize, Honduras, and Costa Rica with the use of X-ray diffraction and INAA (Bishop et al. 1993; Bishop et al. 1984; Lange and Bishop 1988; Lange et al. 1981). The sampling in Guatemala focused primarily on the known source of jadeite in the Motagua Valley but was extended to include artifact samples from northwestern Costa Rica. A conclusive source for jadeite in Costa Rica was not found,

reinforcing the possibility that there were unidentified sources of jadeite in Guatemala and possibly Costa Rica (Lange and Bishop 1988; Lange et al. 1981). The primary findings of these studies demonstrated that there were almost certainly multiple jade sources utilized by Pre-Columbian peoples.

Others (e.g., Harlow 1993) point out that variation within the Motagua source can account for all of the variation in Classic Maya artifacts, and inadequate sampling is to blame for the lack of match between some Classic Maya jade artifacts and the one known source. Harlow argues that only the Motagua Valley has the geologic preconditions necessary for jadeite formation in Mesoamerica. He also argues that jadeite samples cannot be looked at as homogenous material, such as obsidian, when there are numerous distinct mineralogical compositions for each sample. Bishop and Lange (1993) address these arguments and point out that chemical compositional analysis used in conjunction with archaeological data strongly implies multiple sources. This debate has of yet not been completely resolved, and Taube and Ishihara-Brito (2012) suggest that the two arguments are not mutually exclusive.

Lange and Bishop (1988) assume that long-distance exchange functioned in the elite realm of ancient Mesoamerican society, and they apply Renfrew's (1975) model of prestige-chain-trade to better understand how jade moved from Guatemala to Costa Rica. This type of trade would occur over much longer distances and with much more gradual falloff curves than down-the-line or middleman trade. They note that while the paucity of jade in Costa Rica suggests that prestige-chain-trade did not exist, the analysis of other foreign materials may suggest otherwise. These conclusions demonstrate the difficulty in interpreting exchange patterns from the archaeological record, as many similar patterns may represent various modes of exchange. This study also highlights the importance of chemical sourcing as the directionality trade may be determined, the source can be identified through chemical compositional analysis, then production and consumption contexts can be determined archaeologically and matched with the compositional data. The prestige-chain-trade model suggests there was one sphere of vertical, elite exchange for jade objects moving from Guatemala to Costa Rica. This explanation is certainly feasible for long-distance exchange of elaborately carved jades found in elite contexts—probably gifts or tribute between elites at far distances—but it does not explain how some jades end up in nonelite settings.

Turning now to chemical sourcing analysis performed on jades from Cancuen (see also Kovacevich et al. 2005), these studies have added to previously mentioned research and show how chemical sourcing can shed light on the organization of jade production and exchange. Some of these analyses have posed more questions than answers, but they are beginning to promote an understanding of the movement of jade across the landscape. In 2001, twenty-seven pieces of greenstone debitage recovered from production contexts at Cancuen were subjected to Laser Ablation Inductively Coupled Plasma Mass Spectrometry (LA-ICP-MS). LA-ICP-MS is a nondestructive technique in chemical characterization analysis (see Speakman and Neff 2005).

This analysis was initiated in order to identify the mineralogical composition of the Cancuen greenstones, to identify a source for the procurement of the raw materials, and to look for compositional matches with finished products from other centers. These tests could aid in the interpretation of jade procurement patterns as well as distribution patterns. The primary research questions were: Did the residents of Cancuen procure jade from the known Motagua Valley source? Did any of the Cancuen jades match previously sampled artifacts from the highlands or the lowlands? (For a technical explanation of the methods used and a more complete discussion of the data in these tests, see Kovacevich et al. 2005.)

Data for the Cancuen samples were observed to form dark and light groups, as was previously found for the INAA analyses of the Motagua samples. The only previously sampled non-Cancuen artifacts linked with the Cancuen samples are three specimens from a single site in the Salama Valley, Alta Verapaz, that are included in the dark green group. At face value, this connection indicates that at least some of the jade from the Salama Valley was derived from the source favored by Classic-period Cancuen crafters. Besides the Cancuen-related composition, there are at least two other compositional profiles from Alta Verapaz (see also Sharer and Sedat 1987:appendix 3).

Overall, this research parallels the earlier INAA study quite closely in a number of respects. More generally, like the earlier Maya Jade and Ceramic Research Project, this analysis did not yield secure, specific source attributions for most of the artifacts. This last observation indicates that source sampling is as yet incomplete. Recent studies by Andrieu and colleagues (2011) have attributed the source of the Cancuen jades to the Salama Valley, making a further connection between the valley and the Cancuen jade industry. This sampling suggests that the jade of the Upper Motagua Valley is distinct from the Middle Motagua Valley samples collected by the Maya Jade and Ceramic Research Project. In any event, more research is needed in the identification of jade sources in Guatemala to reveal the full variation of chemical composition of the Motagua fault zone. What the research does suggest is the possibility of separate trade routes for different sources or at least different regions within the Motagua Valley.

Subsequent studies also found that the Cancuen jades compositionally match three tesserae of the funerary mask of K'inich Janahb' Pakal I of Palenque (Figure 10.16), the ruler of the powerful lowland center during the Classic period (Neff et al. 2010). As the southernmost Classic Maya site on the Pasión River, Cancuen occupied a strategic location for trade between the Guatemala Highlands and the lowland areas controlled by Classic Maya dynasties. Given the importance of craft production at Cancuen, especially jade working, it is perhaps not surprising that a powerful Maya king like Pakal would have been buried with a jade mosaic mask composed of pieces that may have passed through Cancuen and/or been gifted to the ruler. The chemical compositional results also reinforce the idea of a long-standing trade relationship between Cancuen and Palenque, a conclusion also

figure 10.16
Jade death mask of Pakal the Great of Palenque.
(Photograph by Emilio Labrador.)

supported by the presence of Chablekal Fine Gray ceramics (discussed above).

The compositions of most of the jade samples from Pakal's mask (apart from the three that match the Cancuen jades) match the previously identified Middle Motagua Valley source in Guatemala. Intriguingly, some, if not all, of the tesserae in the mask seem to be reused artifacts, such as beads (see the nostril of Figure 10.3) and pendants (some flat tesserae in the mask also have suspension holes). Such reincorporated pieces were possibly gifted, inherited, or even collected as tribute. Integrating jades from multiple kingdoms, sources, and ancestors could add to the power of the mask as a symbol of fertility, rebirth, and regeneration, which relates to Taube's (2005) argument for the symbolism of jade as life's breath or essence. For example, jade plaques, specifically one from Nakum, often express the comingling of the essence of the ancestor owner with the breath/essence of the inheritor, providing power for that individual (Finamore and Houston 2010:133, pl. 46). A jade mask with incorporated pieces could symbolize the same ideology—the comingling of life's vital essence with those that previously owned and/or wore the artifacts. While beads may have been employed as currency or served other utilitarian functions in some Mesoamerican contexts (e.g., Tozzer 1941 [ca. 1566]:19, 95–96, 130), other settings (such as those reincorporated into a mask) may have imbued the objects with even more value, instilling them with the vital essence of ancestors and/or powerful allies.

As of yet, these are the only trade connections that have been made using chemical characterization analysis, although future research will certainly find more. Clearly, more source and artifact sampling are needed. The artifact samples utilized in the Maya Jade and Ceramic Research Project were biased toward Belize. An important analytical method in establishing Cancuen as a trade center for jade and explaining how sites along the Pasión/Usumacinta were involved in that trade lies in chemical sourcing of jade artifacts. New samples from the Pasión/Usumacinta and central Peten sites could provide valuable data on these trade relationships, although testing of jades from Seibal by Andrieu and colleagues (2011) did not reveal a match in that case. Since LA-ICP-MS has performed at least as well as INAA in the chemical characterization of jade, we can continue to extrapolate information with the use of both datasets.

Discussion and Conclusions

As mentioned previously, Cancuen is located between the Maya Highlands and Lowlands, at a strategic point along the Pasión/Usumacinta River system (see Figure 10.1). Models for trade routes have been put forth, suggesting that rivers—including the Pasión/Usumacinta River system inland and the Motagua River for sea access—were primary trade arteries (see Figure 10.1). Unfortunately, the situation appears to be much more complex, as some major centers along these trade routes were not the recipients of large quantities of jade or obsidian flowing from the highlands. This condition casts doubt on the down-the-line trade models that imply each center along a trade route would have equal opportunity to the goods being exchanged; however, central-place models do seem to work in the case of obsidian at certain centers (i.e., Tikal [Moholy-Nagy 1997] and Copan [Aoyama 1994]). Yet other major centers, such as Calakmul, had a paucity of obsidian (Braswell 2010) but greater access to jade. Sites like Tikal in central Peten (reached by overland trade routes stemming from major rivers) and Palenque (along the Pasión/Usumacinta trade route) also had access to large quantities of jade. Specifically, Hattula Moholy-Nagy (1997) recorded 13,334 total jade artifacts at Tikal—of them, 7,611 were finished artifacts and 5,732 were jade debitage. Other centers along the Pasión/Usumacinta trade route, such as Piedras Negras, had very little jade, even in royal burials (Kovacevich and Hruby 2005). It appears that the Middle Usumacinta region was cut out of the major jade trade and that these items bypassed this part of the river. This exclusion may suggest that trade partnerships, and gifting in particular, occurred only between certain sites, calling into question the possibility of down-the-line trade as a probable mechanism in the distribution of jade. Jade distribution may not have followed simple economic and economizing models, and jade may have functioned largely as a product of political, social, and ideological ties.

Exchange of goods during the Classic period has been argued to have operated in two largely separate spheres: that of elite prestige goods and that of utilitarian goods (e.g., Potter and King 1995:26; Rice 1987:77; Tourtellot and Sabloff 1972). Many scholars contend that elite exchange took the form of gifting, often over long distances and vast interregional spheres, while utilitarian goods were traded locally and regionally, on the basis of kinship exchange systems. Still, other studies have questioned these two separate spheres of distribution, especially exchange of prestige and utilitarian ceramics (e.g., Fry 1979:510; Rands and Bishop 1980:43).

Trade of prestige goods such as jade ornaments, pyrite mirrors, and fine pottery most probably occurred as horizontal, long-distance exchange between elites of lowland polities (Marcus 1983). This type of trade probably took the form of emissary trade, as elite emissaries or the nobles themselves would have been sent with goods as gifts and/or tribute (McAnany 2010; Renfrew 1975; see also Tokovinine and Beliaev, this volume). These exchanges most likely did not take the form of economic exchanges as commodities or equivalencies (Appadurai 1986; Dalton 1965; Halperin 1993; Marx 1990 [1876]; Polanyi 1957; Weiner 1992:10). Exchanges of prestige goods probably took the form of gifting and served to create social ties, reinforcing the ideological power of the elite. Gifts of prestige goods would not always have immediate returns, but gift giving is calculated (Mauss 1990 [1925]), especially with regard to the symbolic and cultural value of the item (Bourdieu 1977:171–183). Many of these goods were probably inalienable possessions, made of exotic raw materials and transported over long distances. The may have passed through and/or may have been owned by many important individuals, inscribed with esoteric and ritual symbols, not able to be directly translated into an equivalent form (Kovacevich and Callaghan n.d.; McAnany 2010). Inalienable possessions can be either kept out of circulation completely or given to others in a form of exchange in which the rights of ownership are never actually transferred. The possession is still linked to the social and political identity of the original owner, not merely relating the temporary owner to the original one but creating an "emotional lien" upon the receiver. Inalienable possessions link their owners to the past and serve as vehicles to legitimate identities and authority in the present (Weiner 1992).

Other utilitarian objects used in everyday life may have been distributed in market or barter-type relationships. Evidence for marketplaces in the Maya world is sparse, but their presence has been suggested or inferred (Chase 1998; Coe 1967:73; Dahlin and Ardren 2002; Dahlin et al. 2010; Freidel 1981; Fry 1979; West 2002). Freidel (1981) has argued that market exchange corresponded to ritual and ceremonial events at major centers. Ethnohistoric and ethnographic sources suggest that market-places were an important feature of the ancient Mesoamerican economy (Berdan 1982, 1983; Carrasco 1983; Sahagún 1950–1982:bk. 11; Smith 1972, 1983), but their existence has been more convincingly demonstrated archaeologically outside the Maya realm (Feinman et al. 1984; Hirth 1998; Sheets 2000). This type of market exchange would coincide with Bohannan and Dalton's (1965:5) description of peripheral marketplaces where the "institution of the market-place is present, but the market principle does not determine the acquisition of subsistence or the allocation of land and other resources." Land and labor were not commodities, as Isaac points out (this volume).

Hirth (1998) has effectively argued for the identification of marketplaces through homogenous distributions of artifacts, with the presence of some workshops producing for the marketplace. Hirth's model provides promise for a new technique to identify marketplaces beyond the traditional structural and architectural features, which are not found in many Mesoamerican sites. Some structural evidence for marketplaces does exist in the Maya area: the East Plaza at Tikal contains a possible stone market structure, and many other market spaces may have been present at that large site (Jones 1996). Furthermore, there are possible depictions of market vendors at the Classic-period site of Calakmul (Carrasco Vargas et al. 2009; Masson and Freidel, this volume; Tokovinine and Beliaev, this volume).

Cancuen jade workers would have access to large quantities of raw jade debitage not suitable for ritual-good production and may have had the opportunity to produce beads for use as quasi-currency in the marketplace. The symbolic value of jade would have increased its currency value (Freidel et al. 2002). For example, gold coins in our own culture have an intrinsically high value because of the economic value of the substance, but this valuation comes from our ideology of gold as a precious substance, much like jade was to the ancient Maya. The lack of investment of esoteric knowledge in the production of beads may have

allowed them to exist outside of sumptuary laws, as opposed to incised plaques and pendants that were inscribed with cultural meaning possessed only by the elite. Freidel (1993) also notes that jade, because of its intrinsic qualities, was probably both treasure and currency, crosscutting our Western concepts of distinctions between the two mediums (see also Appadurai 1986). This duality may have allowed these producers a measure of economic freedom to trade for imported ceramics, other luxury goods, and/or utilitarian items that would have allowed artisans to negotiate their status in the social hierarchy. Intriguingly, at Cancuen, beads were recovered in nonelite households often from floor and midden contexts, not in burials as one might expect for a valued symbolic possession. The majority of these beads were associated with residences that participated in craft production and also had more access to imported Chablekal Fine Gray ceramics than did other households at the site (as discussed above). These beads were significantly smaller than those found in elite contexts such as burials and middens (see, for example, Figure 10.11 and Kovacevich 2007), and the beads were obviously of lesser quality (with a lesser hardness score than jadeite beads and an inferior, often brown or muddy, color). At the very least, there does seem to have been a difference in terms of the form and use of jade beads between elites and commoners at the site, and possibly these beads may have been used as equivalencies in a market situation.

Again, the economic systems of the Classic Maya, typified by Cancuen, seem to have been extremely complex (see also Freidel 1981), with many types of exchange and trade happening simultaneously. Gifting was an important part of elite power, based on possessions (often inalienable) representing cultural capital, which then established social bonds and social capital. Certainly market exchange existed, and jade forms may have been exchanged in this type of venue, but other forms of jade, especially carved plaques, almost certainly circulated in gifting and tribute spheres. The low volume of circulation of these objects supports this argument. Transfer of wealth through gifting was undoubtedly an important mechanism for the movement of finely crafted, high-quality jade objects in the Maya world. McAnany (2010, this volume) emphasizes the importance of tribute and tribute ransom as a means for acquiring wealth items, stimulating production, and state finance. Tribute is an underrecognized form of the movement of goods; it implies a forced and subordinate relationship that may not always require reciprocity, as does gifting. She also acknowledges the importance of gifting and inalienable possessions in the transfer of crafted items (McAnany 2010:304), and I have also done so myself (Kovacevich 2008, 2011; Kovacevich and Callaghan n.d.). Gifting is significant in that it can establish and at the same time defeat hierarchy in certain circumstances (see Mills 2004). It can create social asymmetry through reciprocal obligations but can also serve as an equalizing measure. I (Kovacevich n.d.) have also argued that we often ignore gifting as a significant mechanism for exchange in ancient civilizations due to our desire to identify market exchange as representative of the pinnacle of economic complexity. The movement of items, especially elaborate jades, throughout the Maya Highlands and Lowlands was not on a large scale in comparison with some other products. At the same time, recent investigations have shown that prestige items like jade can be found in commoner households and contexts (see Chase 1992; Haviland and Moholy-Nagy 1992; Kovacevich 2006, 2007; Moholy-Nagy 1997; Palka 1997; Rochette 2009), albeit in different forms than the elaborately carved plaques and large earflares worn almost exclusively by elites. Simpler jades may have circulated as equivalencies in market or barter-type exchanges (Freidel 1993;

Kovacevich 2007). Their relatively even distribution in many commoner residences may suggest market exchange (as per Hirth 1998), although more quantitative data are needed from many sites (although see Masson and Freidel, this volume). As discussed already, ethnohistoric sources frequently refer to jade beads as a form of currency in the Postclassic period. More elaborate artifacts that require esoteric knowledge and a higher degree of skill to produce may have circulated in different spheres of exchange, but the wider circulation of a less-valued form of the object can often add value to the more restricted forms (Freidel et al. 2002; Lesure 1999). Gifting and marketing cannot be ignored as simultaneous and significant economic and social forces that created reciprocal ties and moved objects throughout Mesoamerica.

The intent of this chapter was to highlight the entangled nature of Classic-period Maya economic systems. The production and distribution of jade reinforces arguments for this complexity. Jade was not restricted to the elite of Maya society, as once thought; it could be produced, distributed, and consumed by nonelite members of the society, possibly affording them some social mobility. Jade, as a valued item, brought economic and social power to elites and commoners. By extension, jade probably did not circulate only in horizontal, elite spheres of exchange, but in multiple spheres—including possibly that of the market. Gifting of jades, certainly an integral part of the movement of jades across the landscape, can account for the low volume of trade of jade at many Classic Maya sites. Jade production and distribution was inextricably linked to political and ideological structures within Maya society.

Andrieu, Chloé, Olaf Jaime Riveron, María Dolores
Tenorio, Thomas Calligaro, Juan Carlos Cruz
Ocampo, Melania Jiménez, and Mikhail
Ostrooumov

2011   Últimos datos sobre la producción
        de artefactos de jade en Cancuen. In
        *XXIV Simposio de Investigaciones
        Arqueológicas en Guatemala, 2010,*
        edited by Bárbara Arroyo, Lorena Paiz
        Aragón, and Adriana Linares Palma,
        pp. 1017–1026. Ministerio de Cultura
        y Deportes, Instituto de Antropología
        e Historia, and Asociación Tikal,
        Guatemala City.

Aoyama, Kazuo

1994   Microwear Analysis in the Southeast
        Maya Lowlands: Two Case Studies at
        Copan, Honduras. *Latin American
        Antiquity* 6(2):129–144.

1995   Socioeconomic Implications of Chipped
        Stone from the La Entrada Region,
        Western Honduras. *Journal of Field
        Archaeology* 21:133–145.

Appadurai, Arjun

1986   Introduction: Commodities and the
        Politics of Value. In *The Social Life
        of Things: Commodities in Cultural
        Perspective,* edited by Arjun Appadurai,
        pp. 3–63. Cambridge University Press,
        Cambridge.

Ball, Joseph

1993   Pottery, Potters, Palaces, and Politics:
        Some Socioeconomic and Political
        Implications of Late Classic Maya
        Ceramic Industries. In *Lowland Maya
        Civilization in the Eighth Century AD,*
        edited by Jeremy A. Sabloff and John
        Henderson, pp. 243–272. Dumbarton
        Oaks Research Library and Collection,
        Washington, D.C.

Barber, Elizabeth W.

1994   *Women's Work: The First 20,000 Years.*
        Norton, New York.

Berdan, Frances F.

1982   *The Aztecs of Central Mexico.* Holt,
        Rinehart, and Winston, New York.

1983   Markets in the Economy of Aztec
        Mexico. In *Markets and Marketing,*
        edited by Stuart Plattner, pp. 339–
        368. Monographs in Economic
        Anthropology 4. University Press of
        America, Lanham, Md.

Berdan, Frances F., Edward A. Stark, and Jeffrey D.
Sahagún

2009   Production and Use of Orchid Adhesives
        in Aztec Mexico: The Domestic Context.
        In *Housework and Domestic Production
        in Mesoamerica,* edited by Kenneth
        G. Hirth, pp. 148–156. Archaeological
        Papers of the American Anthropological
        Association 19. Wiley, Hoboken, N.J.

Bishop, Ronald L., and Frederick W. Lange

1993   Sources of Maya and Central
        American Jadeitites: Data Bases
        and Interpretations—A Summary.
        Compositional and Structural
        Characterization of Maya and Costa
        Rican Jadeitites. In *Precolumbian
        Jade: New Geological and Cultural
        Interpretations,* edited by Frederick W.
        Lange, pp. 125–130. University of Utah
        Press, Salt Lake City.

Bishop, Ronald L., and Robert Rands

1982   Maya Fine Paste Ceramics: A Compo-
        sitional Perspective. In *Excavations at
        Seibal: Analysis of Fine Paste Ceramics,*
        edited by Jeremy A. Sabloff. Memoirs of
        the Peabody Museum of Archaeology and
        Ethnology 15, no. 2. Peabody Museum
        of Archaeology and Ethnology, Harvard
        University, Cambridge, Mass.

Bishop, Ronald L., Edward V. Sayre, and Joan Mishara

1993   Compositional and Structural
        Characterization of Maya and Costa
        Rican Jadeitites. In *Precolumbian
        Jade: New Geological and Cultural
        Interpretations,* edited by Frederick W.
        Lange, pp. 30–60. University of Utah
        Press, Salt Lake City.

Bishop, Ronald L., Edward V. Sayre, and Lambertus
van Zelst

1984   Characterization of Mesoamerican
        Jade. In *Applications of Sciences in
        Examination of Works of Art,* edited
        by Lambertus van Zelst, pp. 151–156.
        Museum of Fine Arts, Boston.

Bohannan, Paul, and George Dalton

1965   Introduction to *Markets in Africa,* edited by Paul Bohannan and George Dalton, pp. 1–17. American Museum of Natural History, New York, and Doubleday and Anchor, Garden City, N.J.

Bourdieu, Pierre

1977   *Outline of a Theory of Practice.* Translated by R. Nice. Cambridge University Press, Cambridge.

Braswell, Geoffrey E.

2010   The Rise and Fall of Market Exchange: A Dynamic Approach to Ancient Maya Economy. In *Archaeological Approaches to Market Exchange in Ancient Societies,* edited by Christopher P. Garraty and Barbara L. Stark, pp. 127–139. University Press of Colorado, Boulder.

Brumfiel, Elizabeth M., and Timothy K. Earle

1987   Specialization, Exchange, and Complex Societies: An Introduction. In *Specialization, Exchange, and Complex Societies,* edited by Elizabeth M. Brumfiel and Timothy K. Earle, pp. 1–19. Cambridge University Press, Cambridge.

Callaghan, Michael

2005   Excavaciones en L7-1. In *Proyecto Cancuen: Informe Preliminar No. 6-Sexta Temporada,* edited by Arthur A. Demarest, Tomás Barrientos, Brigitte Kovacevich, Michael Callaghan, and Luis F. Luin, pp. 97–136. Instituto de Antropología e Historia, Guatemala City.

Callaghan, Michael, Cassandra Bill, Jeannette Castellanos, and Ronald L. Bishop

2004   Gris Fino Chablekal: Distribución y análisis socio-económico preliminar en Cancuen. In *XVII Simposio de Investigaciones Arqueológicas en Guatemala, 2003,* edited by Juan Pedro Laporte, Bárbara Arroyo, Héctor L. Escobedo, and Héctor E. Mejia, pp. 345–362. Museo Nacional de Arqueología y Etnología, Guatemala City.

Carrasco, Pedro

1983   Some Theoretical Considerations about the Role of the Market in Ancient Mexico. In *Economic Anthropology: Topics and Theories,* edited by Sutti Ortiz, pp. 62–82. University Press of America, Lanham, Md.

Carrasco Vargas, Ramón, Verónica A. Vázquez López, and Simon Martin

2009   Daily Life of the Ancient Maya Recorded on Murals at Calakmul, Mexico. *Proceedings of the National Academy of Sciences* 106(46):19245–19249.

Chase, Arlen F.

1992   Elites and the Changing Organization of Classic Maya Society. In *Mesoamerican Elites: An Archaeological Assessment,* edited by Diane Z. Chase and Arlen F. Chase, pp. 30–47. University of Oklahoma Press, Norman.

1998   Planeación cívica e integración de sitio en Caracol, Belize: Definiendo una economía administrada del periodo clásico maya. In *Las investigaciones de la cultura maya 6,* tomo 1, pp. 26–44. Universidad Autónoma de Campeche, Campeche.

Chenault, Mark L.

1986   Technical Analysis of Precolumbian Costa Rican Jadeite and Greenstone Artifacts. MA thesis, Department of Anthropology, University of Colorado, Boulder.

Childs, S. Terry

1998   Social Identity and Specialization among Toro Iron Workers in Western Uganda. In *Craft and Social Identity,* edited by Cathy Lynne Costin and Rita Wright, pp. 109–121. American Anthropological Association, Arlington, Va.

Coe, Michael D.

1988   Ideology of the Maya Tomb. In *Maya Iconography,* edited by Elizabeth P. Benson and Gillett G. Griffin, pp. 222–235. Princeton University Press, Princeton.

Coe, William R.

1967   *Tikal: A Handbook of the Ancient Maya Ruins.* University Museum of Pennsylvania, Philadelphia.

Costin, Cathy Lynne

1991   Craft Specialization: Issues Defining, Documenting, and Explaining the Organization of Production. In *Archaeological Method and Theory,* vol. 3, edited by Michael Schiffer, pp. 1–56. University of Arizona Press, Tucson.

1998   Introduction: Craft and Social Identity. In *Craft and Social Identity,* edited by Cathy Lynne Costin and Rita P. Wright, pp. 3–16. American Anthropological Association, Arlington, Va.

2000   The Use of Ethnoarchaeology for the Archaeological Study of Ceramic Production. *Journal of Archaeological Method and Theory* 7(4):377–403.

2007   Thinking about Production: Phenomenological Classification and Lexical Semantics. In *Rethinking Specialized Production in Archaeological Contexts*, edited by Zachary X. Hruby and Rowan K. Flad, pp. 143–162. Archaeological Papers of the American Anthropological Association 17. Wiley, Hoboken, N.J.

Costin, Cathy Lynne, and Melissa Hagstrum

1995   Standardization, Labor Investment, Skill, and the Organization of Ceramic Production in Late Prehispanic Highland Peru. *American Antiquity* 60(4):619–639.

Cross, John R.

1993   Craft Specialization in Nonstratified Societies. In *Research in Economic Anthropology,* vol. 14, edited by Barry Isaac, pp. 61–84. JAI Press, Greenwich, Conn.

Dahlin, Bruce H., and Traci Ardren

2002   Modes of Exchange and Regional Patterns: Chunchucmil, Yucatan. In *Ancient Maya Political Economies,* edited by Marilyn A. Masson and David Freidel, pp. 249–284. Altamira Press, Walnut Creek, Calif.

Dahlin, Bruce H., Daniel Bair, Tim Beach, Matthew Moriarty, and Richard Terry

2010   The Dirt on Food: Ancient Feasts and Markets among the Lowland Maya. In *Pre-Columbian Foodways: Interdisciplinary Approaches to Food, Culture, and Markets in Mesoamerica,* edited by John E. Staller and Michael Carrasco, pp. 191–232. Springer-Verlag, New York.

Dalton, George

1965   Primitive Money. *American Anthropologist* 67(1):44–65.

Demarest, Arthur, Takeshi Inomata, Héctor Escobedo, and Joel Palka (editors)

1991   *Proyecto Arqueológico Regional Petexbatún: Informe preliminar 3, tercera temporada 1991.* Instituto de Antropología e Historia, Guatemala City, and Department of Anthropology, Vanderbilt University, Nashville, Tenn.

Digby, Adrian

1972   *Maya Jades.* Rev. ed. Trustees of the British Muscum, London.

Earle, Timothy

1981   Comment on "Evolution of Specialized Pottery Production: A Trial Model" by Prudence M. Rice. *Current Anthropology* 22:230–231.

Eberl, Markus, and Takeshi Inomata

2001   Maya Royal Headband (sak hunal) from Aguateca. *Mexicon* 23(6):134–135.

Fash, William L.

1991   *Scribes, Warriors, and Kings: The City of Copan and the Ancient Maya.* Thames and Hudson, London.

Feinman, Gary M., Richard E. Blanton, and Stephen Kowaleski

1984   Market System Development in the Prehispanic Valley of Oaxaca, Mexico. In *Trade and Exchange in Early Mesoamerica,* edited by Kenneth G. Hirth, pp. 157–178. University of New Mexico Press, Albuquerque.

Fields, Virginia M.

1991   Iconographic Heritage of the Maya Jester God. In *Sixth Palenque Round Table, 1986,* edited by Virginia M. Fields, pp. 167–174. University of Oklahoma Press, Norman.

Finamore, Daniel, and Stephen D. Houston

2010   *Fiery Pool: The Maya and the Mythic Sea.* Yale University Press, New Haven.

Foias, Antonia, and Ronald Bishop

1997   Changing Ceramic Production and Exchange in the Petexbatun Region, Guatemala: Reconsidering the Classic Maya Collapse. *Ancient Mesoamerica* 8(2):275–292.

Foshag, William F.

1957   Mineralogical Studies on Guatemalan
        Jades. *Smithsonian Miscellaneous
        Collection* 135(2):1–57.

Foshag, William F., and Robert Leslie

1955   Jadeite from Manzanal, Guatemala.
        American Antiquity 21:81–83.

Freidel, David

1981   The Political Economics of Settlement
        Dispersion among the Lowland Maya.
        In *Lowland Maya Settlement Patterns,*
        edited by Wendy Ashmore, pp. 371–
        382. University of New Mexico Press,
        Albuquerque.

1993   The Jade Ahau: Toward a Theory of
        Commodity Value in Maya Civilization.
        In *Precolumbian Jade: New Geological
        and Cultural Interpretations*, edited
        by Frederick W. Lange, pp. 149–165.
        University of Utah Press, Salt Lake City.

Freidel, David, Kathryn Reese-Taylor, and David
        Mora-Marín

2002   The Origins of Maya Civilization: The
        Old Shell Game, Commodity, Treasure,
        and Kingship. In *Ancient Maya Political
        Economies,* edited by Marilyn A. Masson
        and David Freidel, pp. 41–86. Altamira
        Press, Walnut Creek, Calif.

Fry, Robert E.

1979   The Structure of Ceramic Exchange at
        Tikal, Guatemala: Models of Exchange
        for Serving Vessels. *American Antiquity*
        44(3):494–512.

1980   Models of Exchange for Major Shape
        Classes of Lowland Maya Pottery.
        In *Models and Methods in Regional
        Exchange*, edited by Robert E. Fry, pp.
        3–18. Society for American Archaeology,
        Washington, D.C.

Garber, James

1993   The Cultural Context of Jade Artifacts
        from the Maya Site of Cerros, Belize.
        In *Precolumbian Jade: New Geological
        and Cultural Interpretations,* edited
        by Frederick W. Lange, pp. 166–172.
        University of Utah Press, Salt Lake City.

Gonlin, Nancy

2007   Ritual and Ideology among Classic Maya
        Rural Commoners at Copan, Honduras.
        In *Commoner Ritual and Ideology in
        Ancient Mesoamerica*, edited by Nancy
        Gonlin and Jon C. Lohse, pp. 95–144.
        University of Press of Colorado, Boulder.

Guderjan, Thomas

2007   *The Nature of an Ancient Maya City:
        Resources, Interaction, and Power at Blue
        Creek, Belize*. University of Alabama
        Press, Tuscaloosa.

Halperin, Rhoda H.

1993   The Concept of Economic Equivalencies
        in Economic Anthropology. In *Research
        in Economic Anthropology 14,* edited
        by Barry Isaac, pp. 3–28. JAI Press,
        Greenwich, Conn.

Hammond, Norman

1999   The Genesis of Hierarchy: Mortuary and
        Offertory Ritual in the Pre-Classic at
        Cuello, Belize. In *Social Patterns in Pre-
        Classic Mesoamerica,* edited by David C.
        Grove and Rosemary A. Joyce, pp. 49–66.
        Dumbarton Oaks Research Library and
        Collection, Washington, D.C.

Hammond, Norman, Arnold Aspinall, Stuart Feather,
        John Hazelden, Trevor Gazard, and Stuart Agrell

1977   Maya Jade Source Location and
        Analysis. In *Exchange Systems in
        Prehistory,* edited by Timothy K. Earle
        and Jonathan E. Ericson, pp. 35–67.
        Academic Press, New York.

Harlow, George E.

1993   Middle American Jade: Geologic and
        Petrologic Perspectives on Variability
        and Source. In *Precolumbian Jade: New
        Geological and Cultural Interpretations*,
        edited by Frederick W. Lange, pp. 9–29.
        University of Utah Press, Salt Lake City.

Haviland, William, and Hattula Moholy-Nagy

1992   Distinguishing the High and
        Mighty from the Hoi-Polloi at Tikal,
        Guatemala. In *Mesoamerican Elites: An
        Archaeological Assessment,* edited by
        Diane Z. Chase and Arlen F. Chase, pp.
        50–60. University of Oklahoma Press,
        Norman.

Helms, Mary W.

1993   *Craft and the Kingly Ideal: Art, Trade, and
        Power.* University of Texas Press, Austin.

Hirth, Kenneth G.

1998   The Distributional Approach: A New Way to Identify Marketplace Exchange in the Archaeological Record. *Current Anthropology* 39(4):451–476.

2009   Housework and Domestic Craft Production: An Introduction. In *Housework and Domestic Production in Mesoamerica*, edited by Kenneth G. Hirth, pp. 1–12. Archaeological Papers of the American Anthropological Association 19. Wiley, Hoboken, N.J.

Hirth, Kenneth G. (editor)

2009   *Housework: Craft Production and Domestic Economy in Ancient Mesoamerica.* Archaeological Papers of the American Anthropological Association 19. Wiley, Hoboken, N.J.

Hruby, Zachary X.

2003   Re-evaluación de las categorías utilitarias y ceremoniales de artefactos mayas de piedra. En *XVI Simposio de Investigaciones Arqueológicas en Guatemala, 2002,* edited by Juan Pedro Laporte, Bárbara Arroyo, Héctor Escobedo, and Héctor Mejía, pp. 507–512. Museo Nacional de Arqueología y Etnología, Guatemala City.

2007   Ritualized Lithic Production at Piedras Negras, Guatemala. In *Rethinking Craft Specialization in Complex Societies: Archaeological Analyses of the Social Meaning of Production,* edited by Zachary X. Hruby and Rowan K. Flad, pp. 68–84. Archaeological Papers of the American Anthropological Association 17. Wiley, Hoboken, N.J.

Inomata, Takeshi

2001   The Power and Ideology of Artistic Creation: Elite Craft Specialists in Classic Maya Society. *Current Anthropology* 42(2):321–350.

Jones, Christopher

1996   *Excavations in the East Plaza of Tikal.* Tikal Report 16. University of Pennsylvania Museum of Archaeology and Anthropology, Philadelphia.

Kidder, Alfred V., Jesse Jennings, and Edwin M. Shook

1946   *Excavations at Kaminaljuyu, Guatemala.* Carnegie Institution of Washington Publication 561. Carnegie Institution of Washington, Washington, D.C.

Kovacevich, Brigitte

2003a   Programa de muestreo residencial en Cancuén: 1999–2003. In *Proyecto Cancuen: Informe Preliminar No. 5, Quinta Temporada,* Instituto de Antropología e Historia, Guatemala City.

2003b   A Large-Scale Jade Workshop at Cancuen: Implications for Economics and Production in the Classic Maya Civilization. Paper presented at the Annual Meeting of the Society for American Archaeology, Milwaukee, Wis.

2006   Reconstructing Classic Maya Economic Systems: Production and Exchange at Cancuen. PhD dissertation, Department of Anthropology, Vanderbilt University, Nashville, Tenn.

2007   Ritual, Crafting, and Agency at the Classic Maya Kingdom of Cancuen. In *Mesoamerican Ritual Economy: Archaeological and Ethnological Perspectives,* edited by E. Christian Wells and Karla Davis-Salazar, pp. 67–114. University Press of Colorado, Boulder.

2008   Jades as Inalienable Possessions among Elites and Nonelites. Paper presented at the Annual Meeting of the Society for American Archaeology, Vancouver.

2011   The Organization of Jade Production at Cancuen, Guatemala. In *The Technology of Maya Civilization: Political Economy and Beyond in Lithic Studies,* edited by Zachary X. Hruby, Oswaldo Chinchilla, and Geoffrey Braswell, pp. 149–161. Equinox Publishing, Sheffield.

2012   Jade en Guatemala: Una historia de investigación. Paper Presented at the XXV Simposio de Investigaciones Arqueológicas en Guatemala, Guatemala City.

n.d.   The Problem with "Workshops": Gender, Craft Specialization, and the State. In *Gendered Labor in Specialized Economies,* edited by Sofia Kelley

and Traci Ardren. University Press of
Colorado, Boulder, in press.

Kovacevich, Brigitte, Tomás Barrientos, Michael
Callaghan, and Karen Pereira

2002   La economía en el reino clásico de
Cancuen: Evidencia de produc-
ción, especialización e intercambio.
En *XV Simposio de Investigaciones
Arqueológicas en Guatemala, 2001,*
edited by Juan Pedro Laporte, Héctor
Escobedo, and Bárbara Arroyo, pp. 333–
349. Museo Nacional de Arqueología y
Etnología, Guatemala City.

Kovacevich, Brigitte, Ronald L. Bishop, Hector Neff,
and Karen Pereira

2003   Sistemas económicos y de producción
mayas: Nuevos datos y retos en Cancuén.
In *XVI Simposio de Investigaciones
Arqueológicas en Guatemala, 2002,*
edited by Juan Pedro Laporte, Bárbara
Arroyo, Héctor Escobedo, and Héctor
Mejia, pp. 143–158. Museo Nacional de
Arqueología y Etnología, Guatemala
City.

Kovacevich, Brigitte, and Michael Callaghan

2005   Architecture, Material Culture, and
Status at Classic Period Cancuen,
Guatemala. Paper presented at the
Southeast Conference on Mesoamerican
Archaeology and Ethnohistory,
University of South Florida, Tampa.

Kovacevich, Brigitte, and Michael Callaghan (editors)

n.d.   *The Inalienable in the Archaeology of
Mesoamerica.* Archaeological Papers
of the American Anthropological
Association, Arlington, Va., in press.

Kovacevich, Brigitte, Michael Callaghan, Patricia
Castillo, and Rodrigo Guzman

2012   Investigación de las dos primeras tempo-
radas en el sitio de Holtún, Guatemala.
Paper presented at the XXV Simposio
de Investigaciones Arqueológicas en
Guatemala, Guatemala City.

n.d.   Jades as Inalienable Possessions in
Mesoamerica. In *The Inalienable in the
Archaeology of Mesoamerica*, edited
by Brigitte Kovacevich and Michael
Callaghan. Archaeological Papers of the
American Anthropological Association,
Arlington, Va., in press.

Kovacevich, Brigitte, Duncan Cook, and Timothy
Beach

2004   Áreas de actividad doméstica en
Cancuén: Perspectivas basadas en datos
líticos y geoquímicos. In *XVII Simposio
de Investigaciones Arqueológicas en
Guatemala, 2003,* edited by Juan Pedro
Laporte, Bárbara Arroyo, Héctor L.
Escobedo, and Héctor Mejia, pp. 897–
912. Museo Nacional de Arqueología y
Etnología, Guatemala City.

Kovacevich, Brigitte, and Zachary X. Hruby

2005   Towards an Understanding of the Value
of Jade in Two Lowland Classic Maya
City Centers, Cancuen and Piedras
Negras. Paper presented at the Annual
Meeting of the Society for American
Archaeology, Salt Lake City.

Kovacevich, Brigitte, Hector Neff, and Ronald L.
Bishop

2005   Laser Ablation ICP-MS Chemical
Characterization of Jade from a Jade
Workshop in Cancuen, Guatemala. In
*Laser Ablation ICP-MS in Archaeological
Research*, edited by Robert J. Speakman
and Hector Neff, pp. 38–57. University of
New Mexico Press, Albuquerque.

Kovacevich, Brigitte, and Karen Pereira

2002   Operación CAN 24: Excavaciones en el
cuadrante M10. In *Proyecto Cancuen:
Informe preliminar no. 4, cuarta temporada*, edited by Arthur A. Demarest
and Tomás Barrientos, pp. 265–300.
Instituto de Antropología e Historia,
Guatemala City.

Lange, Frederick W., and Ronald L. Bishop

1988   Jade Exchange in Mesoamerica and
Central America. In *Costa Rican Art
and Archaeology*, edited by Frederick W.
Lange, pp. 65–88. University Press
of Colorado, Boulder.

Lange, Frederick W., Ronald L. Bishop, and
Lambertus van Zelst

1981   Perspectives on Costa Rican Jade:
Compositional Analyses and Cultural
Implications. In *Between Continents/
Between Seas: Precolumbian Art of Costa
Rica*, edited by Elizabeth P. Benson, pp.
167–175. H. N. Abrams, New York.

Lesure, Richard

1999   On the Genesis of Value in Early
        Hierarchical Societies. In *Material
        Symbols: Culture and Economy in
        Prehistory*, edited by John E. Robb, pp.
        23–55. Occasional Paper 26. Center for
        Archaeological Investigations, Southern
        Illinois University, Carbondale.

Marcus, Joyce

1983   Lowland Maya Archaeology at the
        Crossroads. *American Antiquity*
        48(3):454–488.

2004   Maya Commoners: The Stereotype and
        Reality. In *Ancient Maya Commoners*,
        edited by Jon C. Lohse and Fred Valdez
        Jr., pp. 255–284. University of Texas
        Press, Austin.

Marx, Karl

1990 [1876]   *Capital: A Critique of Political Economy.*
        Introduced by Ernest Mandel; translated
        by Ben Fowkes. Penguin, London and
        New York.

Masson, Marilyn A.

2002   Introduction to *Ancient Maya Political
        Economies,* edited by Marilyn A. Masson
        and David A. Freidel, pp. 1–30. Altamira
        Press, Walnut Creek, Calif.

Mauss, Marcel

1990 [1925]   *The Gift: Forms and Functions of
        Exchange in Archaic Societies.* Foreword
        by Mary Douglas; translated by W. D.
        Halls. Norton, New York.

McAnany, Patricia

1993   The Economics and Social Power
        of Wealth among Eighth-Century
        Maya Households. In *Lowland Maya
        Civilization in the Eighth Century AD,*
        edited by Jeremy A. Sabloff and John
        Henderson, pp. 65–89. Dumbarton
        Oaks Research Library and Collection,
        Washington, D.C.

1995   *Living with the Ancestors: Kinship and
        Kingship in Ancient Maya Society.*
        University of Texas Press, Austin.

2010   *Ancestral Maya Economies in Archae-
        ological Perspective.* Cambridge
        University Press, Cambridge.

McAnany, Patricia, Ben S. Thomas, Steven Morandi,
Polly A. Peterson, and Eleanor Harrison

2002   Praise the Ajaw and Pass the Kakaw:
        Xibun Maya and the Political Economy
        of Cacao. In *Ancient Maya Political
        Economies,* edited by Marilyn A. Masson
        and David A. Freidel, pp. 123–139.
        Altamira Press, Walnut Creek, Calif.

Miller, Mary Ellen, and Karl A. Taube

1993   *An Illustrated Dictionary of the Gods
        and Symbols of Ancient Mexico and the
        Maya.* Thames and Hudson, London.

Mills, Barbara J.

2004   The Establishment and Defeat of
        Hierarchy: Inalienable Possessions
        and the History of Collective Prestige
        Structures in the Pueblo Southwest.
        American Anthropologist 106(2):238–251.

2008   Remembering while Forgetting:
        Depositional Practices and Social
        Memory at Chaco. In *Memory Work:
        Archaeologies of Depositional Practice,*
        edited by Barbara J. Mills and William
        H. Walker, pp. 81–108. School of
        American Research, Santa Fe.

Moholy-Nagy, Hattula

1990   The Misidentification of Mesoamerican
        Lithic Workshops. *Latin American
        Antiquity* 1(3):268–279.

1994   Tikal Material Culture: Artifacts
        and Social Structure at a Classic
        Lowland Maya City. PhD disserta-
        tion, Department of Anthropology,
        University of Michigan, Ann Arbor.

1997   Middens, Construction Fill, and
        Offerings: Evidence for the Organization
        of Classic Period Craft Production
        at Tikal, Guatemala. *Journal of Field
        Archaeology* 24(3):293–313.

Murata, Satoru

2011   Maya Salters, Maya Potters: The
        Archaeology of Multicrafting on Non-
        Residential Mounds at Wits Cah Ak'al,
        Belize. PhD dissertation, Department of
        Archaeology, Boston University, Boston.

Neff, Hector, Brigitte Kovacevich, and Ronald L.
Bishop

2010   Caracterización de los compuestos de la
        jadeíta mesoamericana: Breve revisión
        a partir de los resultados obtenidos

durante el estudio de la máscara de K'inich Janaab' Pakal. In *Misterios de un rostro maya: La máscara funeraria de K'inich Janaab' Pakal de Palenque*, edited by Laura Filloy Nadal, pp. 131–138. Instituto Nacional de Antropología e Historia, Mexico City.

Palka, Joel

1995 Classic Maya Social Inequality and the Collapse at Dos Pilas, Peten, Guatemala. PhD dissertation, Department of Anthropology, Vanderbilt University, Nashville, Tenn.

1997 Reconstructing Classic Maya Socio-economic Differentiation and the Collapse at Dos Pilas, Peten, Guatemala. *Ancient Mesoamerica* 8(2):293–306.

Peacock, David P. S.

1982 *Pottery in the Roman World: An Ethnoarchaeological Approach.* Longman, London.

Polanyi, Karl

1957 Aristotle Discovers the Economy. In *Trade and Market in the Early Empires*, edited by Karl Polanyi, Conrad Arensberg, and Harry Pearson, pp. 64–96. Free Press, New York.

Potter, Daniel R., and Eleanor M. King

1995 A Heterarchical Approach to Lowland Maya Socioeconomies. In *Heterarchy and the Analysis of Complex Societies*, edited by Robert M. Ehrenreich, Carole L. Crumley, and Janet E. Levy, pp. 17–32. American Anthropological Association, Arlington, Va.

Rands, Robert, and Ronald L. Bishop

1980 Resource Procurement Zones and Patterns of Ceramic Exchange in the Palenque Region, Mexico. In *Models and Methods in Regional Exchange*, edited by Robert E. Fry, pp. 19–46. Society for American Archaeology Papers 1. Society for American Archaeology, Washington, D.C.

Reents-Budet Dorie

1998 Elite Maya Pottery and Artisans as Social Indicators. In *Craft and Social Identity*, edited by Cathy Lynne Costin and Rita P. Wright, pp. 71–89. American Anthropological Association, Arlington, Va.

Renfrew, Colin

1975 Trade as Interaction at a Distance: Questions of Integration and Communication. In *Ancient Civilization and Trade*, edited by Jeremy A. Sabloff and C. C. Lamberg-Karlovsky, pp. 3–60. University of New Mexico Press, Albuquerque.

Rice, Prudence

1987 Economic Change in the Lowland Maya Late Classic Period. In *Specialization, Exchange, and Complex Societies*, edited by Elizabeth M. Brumfiel and Timothy K. Earle, pp. 76–85. Cambridge University Press, Cambridge.

Robin, Cynthia

2003 New Directions in Classic Maya Household Archaeology. *Journal of Archaeological Research* 11(4):307–356.

Rochette, Erick

2009 Jade in Full: Prehispanic Domestic Production of Wealth Goods in the Middle Motagua Valley, Guatemala. In *Housework and Domestic Production in Mesoamerica*, edited by Kenneth G. Hirth, pp. 205–224. Archaeological Papers of the American Anthropological Association 19. Wiley, Hoboken, N.J.

Rochette, Erick, and Mónica Pellecer Alecio

2008 A quien está asociado?: La producción artesanal doméstica de bienes de estatus en la cuenca media del Río Motagua. In *XXI Simposio de Investigaciones Arqueológicas en Guatemala, 2007*, edited by Juan Pedro Laporte, Bárbara Arroyo, and Héctor Mejia, pp. 47–56. Museo Nacional de Arqueología y Etnologa, Guatemala City.

Sabloff, Jeremy A., and William L. Rathje

1975 The Rise of a Maya Merchant Class. *Scientific American* 233(4):73–82.

Sahagún, Bernardino de

1950–1982 *Florentine Codex: General History of the Things of New Spain.* Translated by Arthur J. O. Anderson and Charles E. Dibble. School of American Research, Santa Fe, and University of Utah, Salt Lake City.

Schele, Linda, and David A. Freidel

1990 *A Forest of Kings.* Morrow, New York.

Schele, Linda, and Mary Ellen Miller

1986 *The Blood of Kings: Dynasty and Ritual in Maya Art.* George Braziller, New York.

Sears, Erin L.

2002 Excavación e historia interpretativa de las Estructuras K7-1 y K7-3 de Cancuén. In *Proyecto Cancuen: Informe preliminar no. 4, cuarta temporada, 2002,* edited by Arthur A. Demarest, Tomás Barrientos, Brigitte Kovacevich, Michael Callaghan, and Luis F. Luin, pp. 115 144. Instituto de Antropología e Historia, Guatemala City.

Sharer, Robert J., and David W. Sedat

1987 *Archaeological Investigations in the Northern Maya Highlands, Guatemala: Interaction and Development of Maya Civilization.* University of Pennsylvania Museum of Archaeology and Anthropology, Philadelphia.

Sheets, Payson D.

1991 Flaked Lithics from the Cenote of Sacrifice, Chichen Itza, Yucatan. In *Maya Stone Tools: Selected Papers from the Second Maya Lithic Conference,* edited by Thomas R. Hester and Harry Shafer, pp. 163–188. Monographs in New World Archaeology 1. Prehistory Press, Madison, Wis.

2000 Provisioning the Ceren Household: The Vertical Economy, Village Economy, and Household Economy in the Southeastern Maya Periphery. *Ancient Mesoamerica* 11:217–230.

Smith, Carol A.

1972 Market Articulation and Economic Stratification in Western Guatemala. In *Food Research Institute Studies in Agricultural Economics, Trade, and Development* 2:203–233.

1983 Regional Analysis in World-System Perspective: A Critique of Tree Structural Theories of Uneven Development. In *Economic Anthropology: Topics and Theories,* edited by Sutti Ortiz, pp. 307–359. University Press of America, Lanham, Md.

Speakman, Robert J., and Hector Neff

2005 The Application of Laser-Ablation-ICP-MS to the Study of Archaeological Materials: An Introduction. In *Laser Ablation-ICP-MS in Archaeological Research,* edited by Robert J. Speakman and Hector Neff, pp. 1–16. University of New Mexico Press, Albuquerque.

Taube, Karl A.

1996 The Olmec Maize God: The Face of Corn in Formative Mesoamerica. *Res: Anthropology and Aesthetics* 29/30:39–81.

1998 The Jade Hearth: Centrality, Rulership, and the Classic Maya Temple. In *Function and Meaning in Classic Maya Architecture,* edited by Stephen D. Houston, pp. 427–478. Dumbarton Oaks Research Library and Collection, Washington, D.C.

2000 Lightning Celts and Corn Fetishes: The Formative and the Development of Maize Symbolism in Mesoamerica and the American Southwest. In *Olmec Art and Archaeology in Mesoamerica,* edited by John E. Clark and Mary E. Pye, pp. 297–337. National Gallery of Art, Washington, D.C.

2005 The Symbolism of Jade in Classic Maya Religion. *Ancient Mesoamerica* 16(1):23–50.

Taube, Karl A., and Reiko Ishihara-Brito

2012 From Stone to Jewel: Jade in Ancient Maya Religion and Rulership. In *Ancient Maya Art at Dumbarton Oaks,* edited by Joanne Pillsbury, Miriam Doutriaux, Reiko Ishihara-Brito, and Alexandre Tokovinine, pp. 135–153. Dumbarton Oaks Research Library and Collection, Washington, D.C.

Tourtellot, Gair, and Jeremy A. Sabloff

1972 Exchange Systems among the Maya. *American Antiquity* 37(1):126–135.

Tozzer, Alfred M.

1941 [ca. 1566] *Landa's* Relación de las cosas de Yucatan: *A Translation.* Papers of the Peabody Museum of American Archaeology and Ethnology 18. The Peabody Museum, Cambridge, Mass.

Urban, Patricia A., and Edward M. Schortman

1999 Thoughts on the Periphery: The Ideological Consequences of Core/Periphery Relations. In *World Systems Theory in Practice: Leadership,*

Production, and Exchange, edited by P. Nick Kardulias, pp. 125–152. Rowman and Littlefield, Lanham, Md.

Van der Leeuw, Sander E.

1976   *Studies of Technology of Ancient Pottery.* Organization for the Advancement of Pure Research, Amsterdam.

Walters, Gary Rex

1982   The Pre-Columbian Jade Processing Industry of the Middle Motagua Valley of East Central Guatemala. PhD dissertation, Department of Anthropology, University of Missouri, Columbia.

Wattenmaker, Patricia

1994   Household Economy and the Early State Society: Material Value, Productive Context, and Spheres of Exchange. In *The Economic Anthropology of the State,* edited by Elizabeth M. Brumfiel, pp. 93–118. Monographs in Economic Anthropology 11. University Press of America, Lanham, Md.

1998   Craft Production and Social Identity in Northwestern Mesopotamia. In *Craft and Social Identity,* edited by Cathy Lynne Costin and Rita P. Wright, pp. 47–55. American Anthropological Association, Arlington, Va.

Webster, David

1989   *The House of the Bacabs, Copan, Honduras.* Dumbarton Oaks Research Library and Collection, Washington, D.C.

1992   Maya Elites: The Perspective from Copán. In *Mesoamerican Elites: An Archaeological Assessment,* edited by Diane Z. Chase and Arlen F. Chase, pp. 135–156. University of Oklahoma Press, Norman.

Weiner, Annette B.

1992   *Inalienable Possessions: The Paradox of Keeping While Giving.* University of California Press, Berkeley and Los Angeles.

Wells, E. Christian

2007   Recent Trends in Theorizing Prehispanic Mesoamerican Economies. *Journal of Archaeological Research* 14(4):265–312.

Wells, E. Christian, and Karla Davis-Salazar (editors)

2007   *Mesoamerican Ritual Economies.* University Press of Colorado, Boulder.

West, Elizabeth H.

1963   Jade: Its Character and Occurrence. *Expedition* 592:2–11.

West, Georgia

2002   Ceramic Exchange in the Late Classic and Postclassic Maya Lowlands: A Diachronic Approach. In *Ancient Maya Political Economies,* edited by Marilyn A. Masson and David A. Freidel, pp. 140–196. Altamira Press, Walnut Creek, Calif.

Widmer, Randolf

2009   Elite Household Multicrafting Specialization at 9N-8 Copan, Honduras. In *Housework and Domestic Production in Mesoamerica*, edited by Kenneth G. Hirth, pp. 174–204. Archaeological Papers of the American Anthropological Association 19. Wiley, Hoboken, N.J.

Willey, Gordon R., Richard M. Leventhal, Arthur A. Demarest, and William L. Fash

1994   *Ceramics and Artifacts from Excavations in the Copán Residential Zone.* Papers of the Peabody Museum of Archaeology and Ethnology 80. Peabody Museum of Archaeology and Ethnology, Harvard University, Cambridge, Mass.

Wolley, Claudia, and Lori E. Wright

1990   Operación DP7: Investigaciones en el Grupo L4-4. In *Proyecto Arqueológico Regional Petexbatún: Informe preliminar 2, segunda temporada, 1990*, edited by Arthur A. Demarest and Stephen D. Houston, pp. 44–65. Instituto de Antropología e Historia, Guatemala City, and Department of Anthropology, Vanderbilt University, Nashville, Tenn.

11

Economic Mobility, Exchange, and Order in the Andes

Tom D. Dillehay

IN THIS ESSAY, I ADDRESS SOME OF THE FASH-
ionable themes related to ancient Andean economies and organizational structures, from early
forager mobility to late exchange systems of polities
and states. Competing mobility and political economic models in Andean studies have long privileged issues that addressed the connection between
the movement of resources and peoples across
different ecological zones, ritual and exchange
systems, and the impact of imperialism and colonialism on societies. Yet with a primary emphasis
on models such as transhumance (e.g., Lynch 1999),
verticality (e.g., Murra 1978), storage and redistribution, and, recently, diaspora and migration (e.g.,
Goldstein 2000, 2005; Owen 2005; Stanish 1992),
we have overlooked or given less attention to other
modes of exchange. Among them are informal barter fairs and markets (e.g., Contreras 2008; Larson
et al. 1995), mobile peddlers and long-distance
exchange networks (Bandy 2005; Goldstein 2000;
Vaughn 2006), feasting and exchange (e.g., Bray
2003; D'Altroy 1992; Jennings and Bowser 2009),

and the transfer of goods through the cyclical residency of families and individuals.

To consider the history of scholarly foci on
Andean economic strategies, we must examine the
foundations of mobility and exchange. An initial
theme I reflect upon is the long-term persistence
of widely ranging foragers and their continued
presence alongside and beyond areas inhabited by
farmers, fishers, and pastoralists: What role did
they play in establishing subsistence economic
principles throughout time and space? As part of
this persistence, the unevenness with which initial food production and sedentism spread provided opportunities for foragers and nonforagers
to make various exchange-based connections with
each other across multiple ecological zones. We
also need to consider the loss of mobility brought
about by sedentism and, subsequently, urbanism,
where different kinds of socioeconomic relations
occurred, and the related sociopolitical complica-
tions. In later, more developed societies, public ceremony, the exchange of prestige goods, storage and

figure 11.1
Map of the Central Andes. (Illustration by Tom D. Dillehay.)

redistribution, and other exchange modes have been seen as important components of Andean political economies (e.g., Contreras 2008; Larson et al. 1995; Murra 1978; Stanish 1992). Discussed below are several of these strategies, which represent all cultural periods in the Central Andes (Figure 11.1), with the most emphasis given to concepts of verticality and cyclical residency. Little to no attention is given to fairs, markets, and caravans as exchange systems because they are examined in other chapters (see Nielsen, this volume; Stanish and Coben, this volume). The broad, synthetic scope of this chapter requires generalization of most themes, although occasional specific case studies are presented.

Large-Scale Mobility and Exchange: Foraging Economies

Although the Late Pleistocene and Early Holocene environments of the Andes provided the resources and influenced the human response to procuring

them, people decided their own living conditions and organizations. The institutions and beliefs that people either controlled directly or indirectly, in turn, formed these conditions. The evidence from South America is clear: by ca. 9000 BC, technological and economic developments show long-distance mobility and cultural diversity as well as the establishment of increasingly distinct regional economic strategies (Bryan 1973; Dillehay 2000). We know that the first Andeans were generalized foragers, specialized maritime gatherers and hunters, specialized highland hunters, incipient horticulturalists, and other variations in a wide range of environmental contexts (Dillehay et al. 2004). These different economies necessitated many types of technological innovation, planning, uncertainty and risk management, resource sharing, mobility and territoriality, and social interaction across the entire continent.

More specific to the Central and South-Central Andes, contemporary scholars often favored the interpretative concept of early exchange called transhumance, which describes a scheduled seasonal migration to secure complementary resources at different elevation zones. Lynch (1999) initially postulated it as a strategy associated with the early development of pastoralism and agriculture in north and central Peru, northern Chile, and northwest Argentina. Not known is whether transhumance was the general rule or exception; as Lynch (1999:249) has noted, it appears to "have varied from place to place and time to time, depending on topography, climate, and distribution of resources and culturally conditioned preferences for certain resources." Yet the only hard evidence for transhumance comes from sites along the Pacific coast of south Peru and north Chile between the desert coast and the lower to intermediate highlands, and here it seems to be limited to few locations dated to the Terminal Pleistocene and Early Holocene periods (e.g., Santoro and Núñez 1987; cf. Sandweiss 2003). In these cases, the evidence usually consists of lithic raw materials from the highlands appearing in lower elevated sites and marine shells occurring in higher sites. The presence of these exotics may be explained by down-the-line exchange,

figure 11.2
Map showing selected major archaeological sites and general directions of the long-distance movement of resources and people during the Late Pleistocene and Early Holocene periods. (Illustration by Tom D. Dillehay.)

gradual demographic drift or migration over several generations, or transhumance.

Whether it be one or a combination of these initial modes of interregional exchange, long before the emergence of more complex economies, manufactured objects and other goods moved across the continent with migratory humans and across established social networks that mapped out shared arenas of communication, value, and consumption

(Figure 11.2). For instance, obsidian was transported or exchanged across long distances in the South-Central Andes (Méndez et al. 2008–2009), and food crops such as squash, manioc, and corn spread along rivers and trade routes across most of the Andean highlands and tropical lowlands (Pearsall 2008; Piperno 2006). As individuals and groups moved along routes between gatherings and social occasions in the Andes, the eastern tropical lowlands, or the southern grasslands of the continent, so they constructed local and regional social landscapes as they also formed economic landscapes of resource procurement and exchange. As objects were transferred between groups, they expressed relationships that must have referred to social networks increasingly stretched spatially and temporally by various mechanisms of direct or down-the-line exchange.

These relationships are important because the factors sustaining later, more complex ideological, technological, and subsistence developments during the later Preceramic and subsequent Initial Period (ca. 4000–2500 BC) were direct extensions of these earlier developments. Although the current evidence is too scanty to discern the specifics of all changes in all environments, two general transitions can be inferred. The first was a change in adaptive strategies and organizational abilities at the end of the Pleistocene period. This transition signifies the rapidly increasing ability of people to recognize the environmental potentials that existed in different settings and to develop the social organization required to exploit resources in both narrow and wider varieties of compressed environments, especially in the vertically stacked setting of the Andes. Second, early people learned many hunting and gathering techniques and on occasion employed them to domesticate select animals and plants and to begin a semisedentary or subterritorial lifestyle in some areas by at least ten thousand to eight thousand years ago, as especially indicated by the movement of a few exotic crops across parts of the Andes (Dillehay and Piperno n.d.; Piperno 2007). A related theme to consider is the long-term persistence of foraging and mobility alongside and beyond areas inhabited by farmers and pastoralists. There is growing evidence from several parts of the Andes, from Colombia to south-central Chile and Argentina, of foragers surviving alongside agriculturalists and pastoralists as late as AD 1000 (Dillehay 2011; Stackelback 2008). These mobile foragers probably accounted for some of the continued movement and exchange of exotic goods over long distances in selected areas.

Down-the-Line Exchange, Mobile Foragers and Farmers, and Food Production

It is important to briefly address early Andean agriculture and its related social and economic transformations within different environments. Farming began to develop during the Early Holocene period, and some of the major indigenous crops of South America were manioc, sweet potato, peanuts, squashes, *pehibaye* palm, potato, common and lima beans, quinoa, chili peppers, cotton, coca, and tobacco (Pearsall 2008; Piperno 2006).

During the mid-sixth millennium BC, several crops were translocated by migrating people or exchanged long distances from their area(s) of origin (Dillehay and Piperno n.d.; Pearsall 2008; Piperno 2006). For example, peanuts from southeastern Bolivia moved into the Zaña Valley of northern Peru by 9200 BC. Manioc from the eastern tropical lowlands occurs there by about 5000 BC; it is present in central Panama at about 5600 BC. Chili peppers were dispersed from western Amazonia by 3600 to 2600 BC. Corn from Mexico was dispersed into lower Central America by 5600 BC and moved into Colombia by 5000 BC. These and other plant foods reveal multidirectional, long-distance movement of crops (Figure 11.3). It is likely that technologies, ideas, and other goods were also moving along these same geographic vectors.

By the beginning of the second millennium BC, domestic forms of squash, manioc, maize, chili peppers, beans, and other plants were spread throughout most of the northern half of the Andes and along the Pacific coastal corridor (Piperno 2007). These crops were probably being diffused throughout a vast geographic network of social and economic interaction along down-the-line exchange routes that connected the tropical lowlands east of the Andes and the coasts of Ecuador, Peru, and north Chile (Dillehay and Piperno n.d.). This broad network of interaction was probably linked to camelid herding and mobility (e.g., llama, vicuña, and alpaca; cf. Rick 1980) in the Central and South-Central Andes sometime between the sixth and third millennia BC (Mengoni and Yacobaccio 2006; Stahl 2008). Herding must have transformed

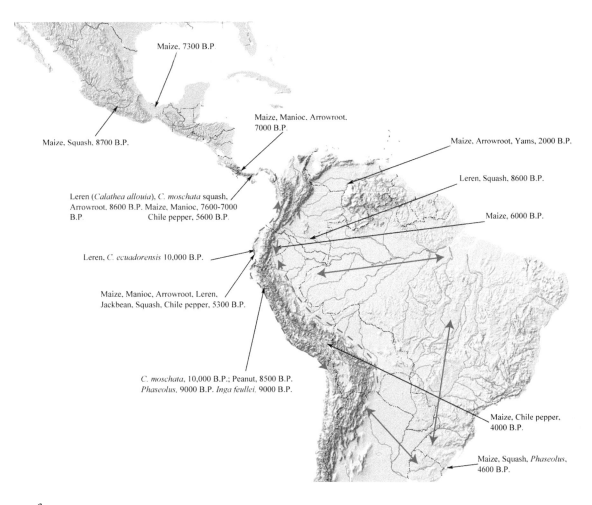

figure 11.3

Map showing the location and dates of early cultigens across the northern part of South America. The dashed line indicates the Andean region. The bipointed arrows demonstrate the multidirectional back and forth movement of crops and peoples between different regions. Note that dates are BP, before present, and not BC. (Map courtesy of Dolores Piperno.)

the scale and rhythm of intergroup interaction and the flow of objects, crops, and ideas between people (Bonavia 2008).

Throughout the second millennium BC, Andean societies continued to be influenced, in different ways, by developments in the eastern tropical lowlands of Colombia, Ecuador, Peru, and Bolivia (Burger 1992; Raymond 2008). This period ushered in the cultural and religious uniformity of many areas of the Central Andes. During the early first millennium BC, the cultural uniformity of the Central Andes subsided. As a result, human settlements began aggregating at nodal points along the coastal floodplains and highland valleys where

large-scale irrigation developed. It was at this time that farming began to play a more important role in Central Andean prehistory by providing more economic security at key nodes of interaction between adjacent coastal and highland valleys (e.g., Dillehay 2011; Kaulicke 2008; Moseley 1992).

Also important to the spread of agriculture lifeways were the demographic expansion and the assimilation of hunters and gatherers into farming and pastoral communities (Dillehay 2011; Núñez 2006). Fostering early social complexity in many regions of the Andes was the synergy created by combining camelid hunting/herding with cultivated crops, particularly from five thousand to four thousand years ago when the climate became less arid after the Middle Holocene period (cf. Sandweiss and Richardson 2008), and many coastal and highland environments supported economic intensification and human population growth.

Long-Distance Exchange and a Prestige-Goods Economy

I find the economies of the Late Preceramic, Initial, and Early Horizon periods of the Central Andes, collectively termed the Formative Period (ca. 3500–1000 BC), to be the most difficult to characterize. There is no formal exchange model in the literature to explain this period, although scholars presume that a combination of modes were operating at this time, including long-distance exchange of prestige goods, quasiverticality, storage and redistribution, and public ritual and exchange (cf. Burger 1992; Kaulicke 2008). But there is no reliable evidence to indicate that any of these modes served as primary mechanisms of exchange during these three periods.

To provide a few examples of these mechanisms, the Initial Period site of Pampa de las Llamas-Moxeke, in the Casma Valley on the Central Coast of Peru, contains possible storage units in the main temple (Pozorksi and Pozorski 1986), but their capacity suggests support of site-specific activity and not a larger population. Evidence for long-distance exchange is documented at several places, including La Galgada (Greider et al. 1988) on the central western slopes of the Peruvian Andes. There, elite burials were associated with grave offerings of elaborate jewelry, some made of exotic turquoise, and products from the tropical forest to the east. At Chavín de Huántar in the central highlands, the lower gallery of the site yielded a wide array of exotics, suggesting reciprocal relations and gift exchange between diverse centers of the late Initial Period and Early Horizon (Burger 1992; Kembel and Rick 2004). There is also fairly widespread evidence that long-distance exchange of exotics and trade networks increased during the later Early Horizon. Some sites of the Initial Period and especially of the Early Horizon, such as Chavín de Huántar, attest to the integration of

coastal, highland, and tropical forest traits through religious (Lathrap 1975; Roe 1978) and probably pilgrimage and marriage networks. For example, the Formative-period textiles recovered at Karwa, on the South Coast of Peru, illustrate clearly the extent of these exchange/communication networks. These textiles were possibly made on the North or Central Coast of Peru (Wallace 1991) and transported to the South Coast. They bear painted images that closely relate to those on stone carvings found in the northern highlands and which represent composites of coastal, sierra, and selva plants and animals. Burger (1992:60) summarized the economy of this period: "Economic interdependency between nearby communities in different habitats linked them at an intermediate level. Face-to-face contact with people of different centers within the same regional system was more restricted, but may have included occasional exchange of handicrafts, marriage ties, and attendance at large public events" (see also Burger, this volume).

Material and ideational transfers increased across the whole of the Andes and adjacent lowland tropics during the Formative Period, as revealed by the presence or greater quantities of small, but consistent, groups of marine shells and fish bones, minerals and ores, crops, among other items (see Burger 1992). Within the Central Andes, the procurement of such objects—and the images they often carried—coincided with a phase of unprecedented innovation in ceremonial and, to a lesser extent, funerary practices, which by the Early Intermediate Period had become a primary forum for competitive social transactions and ritual display.

Along these lines, current evidence suggests that some Initial Period and Early Horizon peoples throughout the Andes focused more on building a sense of social collectivity than on the strategic pursuit of individual power or prestige through the accumulation of wealth goods. These individuals privileged public ceremony and ritual feasting, the construction of both small- and large-scale monuments, and interaction networks. Such networks were probably fueled more by socio-ideational factors than by material wealth. At some point in the late Initial Period and in the Early

Horizon of the Central Andes, a critical moment was reached, however, when emphasis shifted to exotic wealth goods and perhaps individual, as opposed to group, leadership, as the more impressive elite burials and grave offerings at sites like La Galgada, Chongayape, Karwa, Kuntur Wasi, Shillicoto, Aspero, and Chavín de Huántar attest (Figure 11.4). Similar patterns are documented at Early Ceramic or Formative Period sites in northwest Argentina (Leoni and Acuto 2008), Alto Ramírez–phase sites in north Chile (Muñoz 1989), Chorrera sites in Ecuador (Zeidler 2008), and so forth (Guffroy 2008). These patterns intensify even more in the Early Intermediate Period of the Central Andes.

It seems that the concentration of exchange activity in the Andes during the Initial Period and Early Horizon cannot be understood without exploring wider regional and interregional patterns of interaction. As well as forming a changing material pattern of social life, exotic resources were necessary for participation in long-distance trade. Late Formative tombs of Peru contained an increasingly wide repertoire of items obtained through long-distance contacts and trade. Such objects seem best understood as forming the basis of a prestige-goods economy. The social mechanisms of a prestige-goods system, as defined by Rowlands and Frankenstein (1998:337), are "dominated by the political advantage gained through exercising control over access to resources that can only be obtained through external trade." The availability of such resources in many parts of the Andes increased significantly during this period, owing to the establishment of more road systems and camelid caravan routes crossing various parts of the Andes, especially the South-Central Andes, and the contemporaneous expansion of urban-rural trading systems in many regions. It can be hypothesized that maritime transport along the

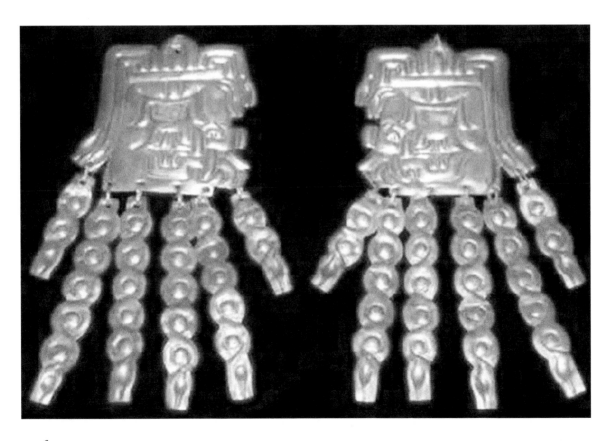

figure 11.4
Gold ear ornaments recovered from Kuntur Wasi, Cajamarca, Peru. Photograph by Yoshio Onuki.

Pacific Ocean was also probably essential in providing access to distant coastal trade routes.

The combination of circumstances surmised above created unique opportunities for groups of the Initial Period and Early Horizon to exercise control over wider networks of material, social, and ideological exchange. In the material and technological dimensions, this domination was also achieved by adding value to certain local resources through sophisticated manufacturing and decorating techniques (Lechtman 1984), by selecting a higher quality of material goods for manufacture and display, and by fostering and disseminating new forms of ritual practice and sumptuary codes. We might argue that a new cycle of development was set in motion during the Formative Period, whereby the acquisition of exotic trade goods stimulated local processes of technological innovation and social change, which, in turn, probably reinforced control over regional networks of circulation. By the end of the Formative Period, groups in many parts of the Andes were able to mobilize small but regular quantities of exotic materials and manufactured goods for deployment as funerary gifts and ritual paraphernalia. In the Central Andes and parts of the South-Central Andes, this pattern became clearer at both coastal and highland sites by the increased presence of elite tombs, many of which held more diverse and higher-quality grave offerings (cf. Burger 1992; Núñez 2006; Onuki 1995).

Craft Production and Specialization, Storage and Redistribution, and Feasting

In looking to the later cultures of the Central Andes—such as the Moche, Nazca, Vicús, Wari, Tiwanaku, Chimú, and Inca societies—some of the most accepted economic models relate to nonmarket strategies of accumulating and distributing goods, paying tribute and gathering surplus for storage and redistribution, and engaging in reciprocal exchange between elites (D'Altroy 1992; Earle and D'Altroy 1982; Lumbreras 1999; Moseley 1975; Murra 1980 [1955]; cf. Stanish 1992). The surplus derived from agricultural fields, fishing and

shellfish gathering, and/or the meat and wool from herds not only supported a redistribution economy and reciprocal exchange but also provided polities with an accumulation of goods that symbolized political power. Although storage facilities have been documented at several North Coast complexes of the Lambayeque and Chimú periods (ca. AD 1000–1450) and at sites in other areas of the Central Andes (Anders 1981), these facilities seem to be confined primarily to large urban sites, and they are not always present in these localities. For example, our surveys and excavations in two North Coast valleys have documented what we could term storage facilities at only twelve Lambayeque and Chimú sites (e.g., Dillehay et al. 2009), and even then the storage capacity was not enough to support large populations. What could have been supported, however, were elite-sponsored feasts held to strengthen elite and nonelite relations, give reverence to deities and ancestors, and so forth. A presumed important part of redistribution was also related to a reciprocal network, whereby polity rulers gave gifts to many hinterland lords, shrines, and other personnel.

Perhaps the economy of storage, redistribution, reciprocity, and feasting has been best considered archaeologically and ethnohistorically by the work of Craig Morris and Donald Thompson at the Inca site of Huánuco Pampa in the central highlands of Peru. There, "elaborate state-sponsored political and religious ceremonies [were used] as a way of establishing and maintaining the authority of the state over local groups" (Morris and Thompson 1985:20; see also Bray 2003; D'Altroy 1992; Jennings and Bowser 2009; Vaughn 2006). While the early Spanish writers emphasized military and bureaucratic aspects of control and administration, the emerging picture from the material record at Huánuco Pampa shows an "administrative center" that was committed to ceremonial acts and the economic activities that supported them. As Morris and Thompson (1985:24) noted, "the Inca political achievement was based on complicated administrative mechanisms, which operated and expanded within a structure defined and regulated through ritual." Numerous storage units were documented at Huánuco Pampa (Figure 11.5). The state housed

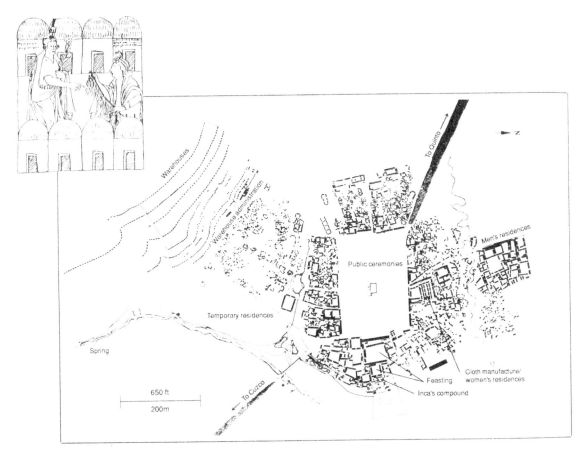

figure 11.5
Urban plan of Huánuco Pampa, north-central highlands of Peru (after Morris and Thompson 1985:fig. 3). Warehouses indicate the location of the storage units on a nearby hillside. The figure in the upper left corner represents a noble inspecting the *quipu* of a state accountant while standing in a cluster of storage units (after Moseley 1992:76).

sizable quantities of food, drink, and other goods in these facilities; some of the contents were shipped to distant areas to support state activities, and some were employed locally in regional festivals. Large quantities of broken *qero* vessels for *chicha* consumption abound, as do mortars and pestles. A large ceremonial area around the *ushnu* in the central plaza would have been where most feasting and political discourse took place. Morris and Thompson also discovered that Huánuco Pampa was not a typical urban center where a permanent population resided, but rather a seasonal center periodically used for religious ceremonial purposes: "At Huánuco Pampa traditional modes of sharing food and drink were probably used to cement loyalties and help motivate economic, political and military

collaboration" (Morris and Thompson 1985:91). The research at Huánuco Pampa represents one aspect of a major political economic model that in various forms has dominated (Bandy 2005; D'Altroy 1992; Owen 2005; Stanish 1992). The evidence suggests that state-sponsored feasting was a strategy that fits most state-level societies in the Central Andes, but the degree to which it can be applied to smaller nonstate polities is not known.

Andean Verticality

One reason for the lack of new explanatory models in the Andes has been the widespread popularity and initial uncritical acceptance of John Murra's model of verticality. Working from early colonial documents, Murra (2002:87–114) reconstructed the economic structure of five different regions of the Central Andes. Influenced by Karl Polanyi, Murra saw this type of structure was the major force shaping Andean political and economic structure. It was a way for ethnic polities to limit risk and maintain self-sufficiency through colonizing a variety of usually closely juxtaposed ecological zones (Figure 11.6). Publication of the vertical model and its various forms was an important moment for Andean studies, as Murra's work inspired two generations of anthropologists and historians who studied the distinctive ways in which Andean peoples, past and present, adapted to and worked with their physical and social environments (see Allen 1988; Brush 1978; Dillehay 1976, 1979; Goldstein, this volume, 2005; Isbell 1978; Mayer, this volume, 2002; Stanish 1992). While Murra's research was important in that it demonstrated the rich complexity of contemporary Andean societies, its focus on their uniqueness had the unintended consequence of conceptually separating the Andes not only from larger academic debates of social and economic theory, but also from contemporary political realities in Latin America (see Starn 1991).

Specifically, Murra's model of vertical archipelagos and colonies (*colonias*) addressed the economic, political, and demographic dimensions of community expansion and intercommunity or intergroup relations. The economic side of the model plays to the notion that by establishing colonies in distant ecological zones located at different elevations, expanding polities can control their access to varied resources and thus become more economically self-sufficient. Verticality thus constitutes an intra- and interpolity organization across a mosaic of natural and social terrain. The political side implies regulatory autonomy, because the home, or central base, of the polity administratively controls its *colonias* in distant zones. Yet these *colonias* are not always established in empty human landscapes. Therefore, they either enter into conflict and/or into coexisting agreements with competing groups also vying for occupation in or exploitation of the same resource zone (cf. Goldstein 2005; Owen 2006; Stanish 1992).

The political side points to more complex bureaucratic and centralized principles of intra- and intercommunity organization, which has strong implications for newly formed social structures (e.g., *ayllus*, a dual or moiety kinship format in the Andes) and the effectiveness of expanding administrative networks to regulate or control remote *colonias*. That is, by politically and logistically establishing and maintaining *colonias* in distant lands, home communities must have higher and more centralized levels of political organization and logistical complexity. This aspect of Murra's model has not received as much attention as the economic and demographic dimensions and warrants more research not only with respect to the spatial and social fragmentation of *colonia* kinship structures, but also with regard to the political implications of competing with other nonkin groups for access to different ecological zones. As a result, the presence of various groups in distant lands must have entailed multiple politico-economic strategies, ranging from coercive to voluntary intergroup relations.

Until recently, the practice by archaeologists has generally been an uncritical acceptance of the verticality model. Since the late 1970s, it has been the model employed by numerous scholars throughout many regions of the Andes to explain most late pre-Hispanic human movement and the presence of exotic goods. It was initially assumed by Andeanists that since vertical forms of organization persisted into the colonial period, they must have had a deep history within the Andes (Murra 1972; Pease 1992; see also Van Buren 1996:338), but this thinking has changed in recent years (e.g., Earle et al. 1987; Goldstein 2005; Núñez and Dillehay 1979; Stanish 2003; Topic and Topic 1985; Van Buren 1996). Not only is there now more caution in its application to earlier periods (see Burger, this volume), but some studies have questioned its utility for explaining late pre-Hispanic and early colonial patterns.

The degree of political centralization and control of the economy by colonizing groups has specifically come into question. For example, two of Murra's cases conform closely to the type of

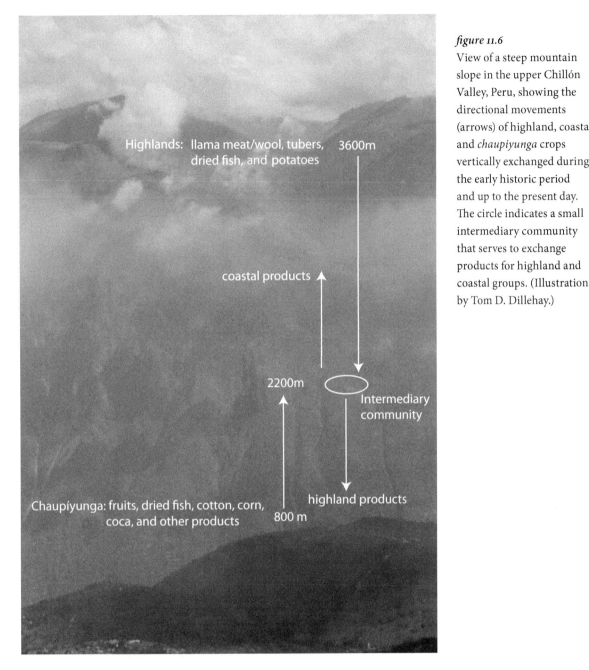

figure 11.6
View of a steep mountain slope in the upper Chillón Valley, Peru, showing the directional movements (arrows) of highland, coastal, and *chaupiyunga* crops vertically exchanged during the early historic period and up to the present day. The circle indicates a small intermediary community that serves to exchange products for highland and coastal groups. (Illustration by Tom D. Dillehay.)

Highlands: llama meat/wool, tubers, dried fish, and potatoes   3600m

coastal products

2200m   Intermediary community

Chaupíyunga: fruits, dried fish, cotton, corn, coca, and other products   800 m   highland products

economic organization described by Enrique Mayer's model of production zones (Mayer 2002). For Mayer, a production zone refers to a communally managed agricultural system where fields are distributed both upslope and downslope from a central community; control over resources is principally achieved through negotiation between the individual household and the community (Mayer 2002:245). In other cases, Assadourian (1994) has

found evidence for nonhierarchical "horizontal" exchange among various ethnic groups residing in the coastal plains of Peru. This finding challenges Murra's original paradigm.

One of Murra's specific case studies, the Chillón Valley in central Peru, warrants brief reconsideration here because it has been reassessed more than his other cases in terms of the applicability of verticality (Dillehay 1976, 1979, 1987). There is no doubt that at some point in time just prior to or at the time of the Inca invasion of the Chillón Valley, the coastal ruler (señorío), Collique, had access to resources in the Quivi polity of the *chaupiyunga* (a Quechua term meaning the place between the coast and highlands) in the middle valley, and that the latter paid tribute to the former. This seems to be a rather clear point in the colonial documents. But what is not clear is whether the Collique *señorío* actually "sent" his own people as colonists (*colonos*) to live in the Quivi area, either to protect his economic interests there, to protect the Quivi people from highland invaders, to provide extra labor to work the coca fields (*cocales*) and other crops, or any combination of these. It is also uncertain whether the Chillón case really represents verticality or some other politico-economic arrangement between the Quivi and the Collique—such as a simple resource exchange and protection agreement policy between these two neighboring groups. The ethnohistorically perceived relationship of domination and subordination between Collique and Quivi could represent just one of many different economic and political arrangements.

Other scenarios—most of which are directly mentioned in the document but not fully considered by ethnohistorians—include the Quivi people having sought military protection from the Collique *señorío* in return for access to the *cocales* and other *chaupiyunga* resources. This case does not necessarily imply that the Collique lord had *colonias* or his own lands in Quivi. Just prior to the arrival of the Inca, the Quivi people were threatened by several neighboring highland groups—including the Canta, who were in conflict with the Collique—and the Yauyos from the Huarochirí area to the southeast. Another scenario relates to down-valley water rights maintained between Quivi and Collique, with the former protecting the middle-valley uptakes (*boca tomas*) of canals irrigating the lower valley fields of the Collique, again perhaps in exchange for protection from marauding highland groups. Another option relates to the exchange of marriage partners between these groups. Other possible strategies include armed conflict, détente, out migration, and so forth. The point is that

nowhere in the document does it explicitly state that Collique sent what could be interpreted as *colonos* to live in Quivi. The text does imply, however, that the Collique lord had access to lands in Quivi and that the Quivi lord paid tribute to him. But such access was apparently achieved by a variety of different economic strategies.

During the AD 1400 to 1600 period represented by both the archaeological and ethnohistorical records, the archaeology indicates several different types of dominant–subordinate relationships between different coastal, *chaupiyunga*, and highland groups in the valley. Many archaeological sites in the *chaupiyunga* of the Chillón Valley—including Huancayo Alto, Santa Rosa de Quive (Quivi), Macas, and others—contain evidence of highland and coastal coresidency and occasional peaceful relations during this long period. Most interesting is that Santa Rosa de Quive is the only one characterized by a wide variety of coastal (probably Collique and perhaps other groups), *chaupiyunga*, and highland late ceramic styles; such an assortment suggests that the site was occupied, visited, and/or ruled by different coastal and highland groups during this time. (Unfortunately, most of the architecture at Quivi has been destroyed by modern-day activity, and little can be said about the functionality, chronology, and sequencing of coresidency arrangements between these groups.) Not known is whether the mixed artifact styles represent sequential episodes of: 1) coastal, *chaupiyunga*, or highland dominance of Quivi lands; or 2) coastal or highland *colonias* cosharing the Quivi lands through partnerships based on verticality and coresidency, marriage alliances, or other agreements that allowed for sharing of local resources (Figure 11.7). Any of these scenarios would produce the mixed architectural, ceramic, and other archaeological registers observed at Quivi. I suspect the same case can be argued for other examples of verticality in the Andes, whereby local and nonlocal peoples employed a wide range of situationally defined resource access and exchange strategies.

The Chillón case presents an interesting contrast between archaeological and ethnohistorical

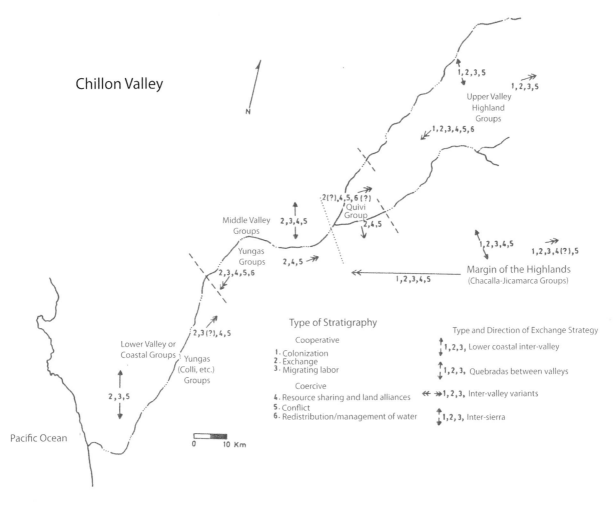

Chillon Valley

1,2,3,5

1,2,3,5

Upper Valley
Highland
Groups

1,2,3,4,5,6

2(?),4,5,6(?)
Quivi
Group

2,4,5

Middle Valley
Groups

2,3,4,5

1,2,3,4,5

1,2,3,4(?),5

Yungas
Groups
2,3,4,5,6

2,4,5

Margin of the Highlands
(Chacalla-Jicamarca Groups)

1,2,3,4,5

2,3(?),4,5

Type of Stratigraphy

Type and Direction of Exchange Strategy

Lower Valley or
Coastal Groups

Cooperative

Yungas
(Colli, etc.)
Groups

1. Colonization
2. Exchange
3. Migrating labor

1,2,3, Lower coastal inter-valley

Coercive

1,2,3, Quebradas between valleys

2,3,5

4. Resource sharing and land alliances
5. Conflict
6. Redistribution/management of water

1,2,3, Inter-valley variants

1,2,3, Inter-sierra

Pacific Ocean

0   10 Km

figure 11.7
Schematic map of archaeological sites in the Chillón Valley showing the hypothesized political and economic strategies employed by different lower-, middle-, and upper-valley groups as they accessed different ecological zones. (Illustration by Tom D. Dillehay.)

approaches to the study of verticality. While the written record has been interpreted as a rather clear-cut case for verticality, the archaeological record is ambivalent about the application of the model and suggests several different politico-economic strategies either operating sequentially or simultaneously between coastal, *chaupinyunga*, and highland groups during the period and place in question (Dillehay 1976, 1979, 1987). Which record is more correct in this case? Both are probably correct for different reasons. The ethno-historical record addresses a rather short period of time with regard to land tenure and intergroup relations between named leaders of Quivi and

Collique; it refers to the period just before the Inca conquest. After the Spanish conquest, several valley residents were interviewed by Spaniards to document who owned lands in the Quivi area and what the power relations were between *curacas* prior to the Inca's arrival. It is important to recognize that the documents speak to only that period when the named Collique *curaca* had access to Quivi lands, which probably was for only two to three decades, not to the longer period represented by the archaeological record. Thus, these different scenarios probably represent different historical moments when one strategy dominated the others.

In summary, there are questions related to the verticality model for which we have no answers but which warrant further attention. For instance, the split allegiance and tribute of *colonias* participating in archipelago expansion must have created tension in local political orders. Divided obligations must have involved a variety of kin-based structures, nonkin-based structures, ethnic groups, economic strategies, and/or social orientations and identities. How was order maintained for intergroup land use and tribute, for the control of population movements, for the regulation of water rights, and for rules of coresidency? If colonizing groups were to successfully cohere, they must have acquired a set of legitimizing principles in which all participants could achieve their objectives. What were they? What were the ground rules for legitimizing the authority of *curacas* overseeing the actions of groups? Were new ideological orders established for these types of intergroup relations?

Looking Beyond Verticality

The basic premise upon which most archaeologists applied the verticality model was the presence of foreign elements, such as architecture and ceramics, in distant lands (see Bandy 2005; Dillehay 1976; Goldstein 2005; Owen 2005). But this presence could imply other exchange strategies of intergroup contact and interaction, usually referred to as "zonal complementarity" (Masuda et al. 1985). Some of these are exchange and alliance-building (Berenguer 2004; Salomon 1986; Topic and Topic 1983, 1985); peaceful coresidency and resource sharing (Dillehay 1976, 1979); various modes of long-distance trade (Salomon 1986); production zones (Mayer 2002); diaspora/migration (Goldstein 2005; Owen 2005); raiding and warfare (Arkush 2008; Arkush and Stanish 2005); expansion/niche filling (Mayer 2002); and barter exchange and public feasting (Stanish and Coben, this volume). These strategies must have changed over the long and short term, most likely with different combinations of them employed simultaneously.

Specifically, work by Frank Salomon (1986) has shown that merchant networks were well developed in the Northern Andes (see also Topic, this volume). Centered in southern Ecuador, these trade networks stretched from western Mexico to the Central Coast of Peru and provided the circulation of such prestige goods as *Spondylus*, gold, and other preciosities. Another form of exchange is recorded at sites like Cerro Lorro on the North Coast of Peru, where axe-monies might have been used as an incipient type of currency during the late Lambayeque period (AD 1200–1500) (Jennings 2008). There is also maritime trade during all time periods; maritime ports along the littoral of western South America must have occupied considerable nodal positions between coastal populations and a growing network of interior areas, perhaps best exemplified by the Chincha lords in late pre-Inca and Inca times (Rostworowski 1970).

Recent studies of ethnic identity, hybridity, diaspora, and migration (Bandy 2005; Berenguer 2004; Goldstein 2005; Owen 2005) have also developed new perspectives for the relation of exchange and cultural interaction for both the pre- and postconquest periods. Goldstein (2000, 2005, this volume) has documented diaspora, migration, and long-distance exchange as constituting the pluralistic ethnic and cultural enclaves of late pre-Hispanic southern Peru. Investigations by Berenguer (2004), Browman (1981), Nielsen (this volume), and Núñez and Dillehay (1979), among others, demonstrate that herding and caravan trade functioned as a complex socioeconomic system that linked various ethnic groups in the South-Central Andes (Figure 11.8). Although camelid husbandry and caravans are usually seen to have been a critical part of the altiplano and puna economy, they also were key components of other highland zones, as well as some coast areas.

Given the considerable environmental and cultural variability within the South-Central Andes, there may well be correspondingly greater differences in the mode and nature of the exploitation and occupation of the Andean world, which included not only verticality but other economic modes, too. In this regard, the circuitous-axis

figure 11.8
A llama caravan transporting goods in the cordillera between Chile and Bolivia in 1978. (Photograph courtesy of Tom D. Dillehay.)

mobility model for arid northern Chile, southwest Bolivia, and northwest Argentina by Núñez and Dillehay (1979; cf. Berenguer 2004; Nielsen, this volume) may be helpful. This model posited symbiosis between foragers practicing transhumance, pastoralists, and agrarian communities located in dispersed oases or axis nodes in the highlands and in lower valleys. Circuitous caravans served the role of transport and exchange agents for these groups.

There is also the issue of markets and fairs in the Andes. Although the verticality paradigm stressed nonmarket exchange, Murra (2002:237–307) himself published evidence for pre-Hispanic "merchants" and long-distance "traders," and cited comparative studies suggesting that exchanges over hundreds of kilometers were organized as highly regulated, communal undertakings. There is also mounting evidence for postconquest Andeans participating in monetarized trade more broadly and creatively than the long-standing image of the

"self-sufficient Indian peasant." The link between participation in markets and ethnic identity has also received more attention. Thierry Saignes (1995) discussed Andean migrants during the seventeenth century and their strategies of rupture from or continued ties to their home communities as social change marked by a reduction in hierarchical vertical relations and growth of more horizontal and contractual trade and market relations (see also Larson 1995). As discussed by Stanish and Coben in this volume, there is also evidence to suggest the presence of pre-Hispanic markets and fairs.

Lastly, in considering the archaeological evidence for local fairs and markets, our research in the Jequetepeque Valley has located a few nonstorage structures of the Lambayeque and Chimú periods that were possibly used intermittently as staging areas for local informal exchange (Figure 11.9). These structures are typically about sixty by sixty meters in size and are found in areas where several roads

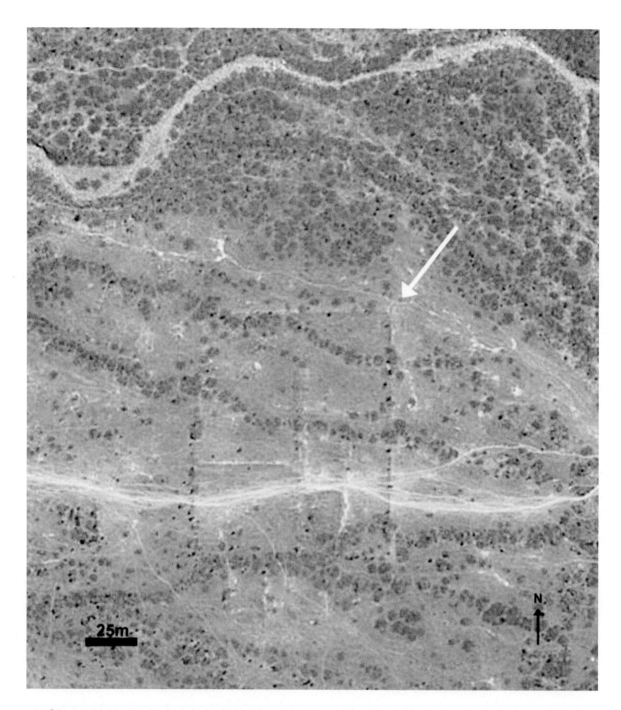

figure 11.9

Aerial view of an archaeological site in the upper-middle Zaña Valley showing low compound walls. A wide variety of Late Intermediate Period sherds and the presence of camelid dung suggest it may have functioned as a place of barter fairs or markets (© 2012 Google, modified by Tom D. Dillehay). Notice the well-worn trail passing through the site today, which is still used to connect exchange traffic between the highlands of Niepos to the east and the middle-valley people of Oyotun to the west.

and passageways converge; they are rarely associated with domestic or administrative settlements; and they reveal thin, intermittently used floors separated by eolian sand deposits, indicating occasional abandonment. They contain low internal benches and a wide variety of sherds, including Chimú, local Cajamarca, and other unidentified types; plant and animal food remains; and an abundance of animal, presumably camelid, dung. These remnants may be the signatures of places where informal and unsupervised product exchange occurred between local communities and caravans.

Mobility and Exchange of Cyclical Populations

In turning to a final theme, I focus on cyclical residency and its implications for exchange, economic diversification, risk management, and political order. It is well known that Andean people diversify their economic activities with livestock, plant gathering and harvesting, fishing, and occasionally rotating movement among multiple residences in different ecological zones (Altamirano 1988; Bourque 1997; Murra 1978). This is not a form of verticality whereby families or kin groups are sent by local rulers to colonize distant lands on a permanent basis. Nor is it migration whereby people choose to move permanently from one place to another or pilgrimages whereby sacred sites are periodically occupied by worshippers. Numerous ethnohistoric and ethnographic studies have indicated that residential shifts—whether from social, economic, or environmental causes—have been a common experience for Andean households in the past and present, and that these patterns are varied and not necessarily mandated by local rulers (e.g., Allen 1988; Isbell 1978; Mayer 2002; Skar 1994). The most visible, though certainly not the only, consequence of residential movement is the contribution made by local exchange to the overall economy and to wider networks of social harmony among kinsmen and trading partners. The cyclical paths, duration of residency, amount of moves, and numbers and categories of people moving all depend upon

the type of relationships that link residents, such as kinship structure, ethnic affiliation, mixed marriage alliances, preferential exchanges, and so forth. Ultimately, the routes and intensity of movement, both to and from places, is based on the kinship resourcefulness of those who are able to maximize economic diversification so as to ensure the maintenance of the household economy but also that of distant social contacts. Rather than a disintegrating element, cyclical movement between multiple localities is a solidifying action.

Did cyclical residency exist in the archaeological past, and, if so, can it be empirically identified in the archaeological record? I believe that the hard evidence for this form of mobility is manifested in the microstratigraphy of domestic sites—that is, the continuous and discontinuous sequences of occupational floors and floor fills. To explain, continuous floor/fill stratigraphy characterizes uninterrupted occupation (Figure 11.9). Discontinuous stratigraphy represents lapsing cycles of use and abandonment. Our research in the Zaña and Jequetepeque Valleys on the North Coast of Peru shows that these cycles are empirically evident in the microstratigraphy of domestic sites (Dillehay 2004a, 2004b; Dillehay and Kolata 2004a, 2004b, 2006). Unfortunately, this type of stratigraphy has not been given much emphasis in the Andes; instead, archaeologists have focused on macrostrata or architectural building phases expressed by the addition of walls and rooms, especially at large ceremonial centers. But by studying microstrata, we can examine the relationship between temporally and spatially discrete episodes of site use, abandonment, and reuse to identify continuities and discontinuities of residential permanency and mobility.

Alan Kolata and I (Dillehay 2006; Dillehay and Kolata 2006; Dillehay et al. 2009) have inferred residential mobility at several sites in the Jequetepeque Valley. We have argued that the repertoire of social and technological responses to environmental and social uncertainty during Moche to Chimú times (ca. AD 500–1450) was diverse, and it ranged from relocation or periodic abandonment of agricultural lands and domestic sites to technological interventions designed to mitigate or exploit major environmental impacts. For instance, one response was to extreme water resource fluctuation, which entailed the development of anticipatory agricultural infrastructure. This infrastructure included a network of redundant irrigation canals that supplied water to various sectors of the valley. Given the local hydrological regime, these canal systems could not have been supplied with sufficient river water to function simultaneously. At any given time, only part of the system could have drawn irrigation water. This use implies that settlements regulated the flow of irrigation water to different sectors of the valley through a coordinated means of water scheduling. The construction of redundant canal networks and the development of flexible, opportunistic agricultural systems served essentially as a diversification of landscape capital. If one part of the network was destroyed, fell into desuetude, or was abandoned for any reason— which was the case in the Jequetepeque Valley, as suggested by use and abandonment cycles revealed in canal stratigraphy and nearby domestic sites— then another part could be brought on line to compensate. Similar responses may be related to social events such as long- or short-term conflicts, avoidance of places more susceptible to environmental and social stresses, shifts in leadership, cyclical movement to different ecological zones to diversify economically, and so forth.

We also recorded anticipated resettlement or relocation to other areas within the valley (Dillehay and Kolata 2006), which we think led to an over-building of small to intermediate domestic settlements whereby people shifted residency according to demanding floods or political processes. This pattern is revealed in sand sheets and dune formations that choked irrigation canals, buried old cultivation surfaces, and covered residential floors and/or structures. We see this pattern clearly in the microstratigraphy of domestic sites in which residential and adjacent work areas of Moche, Lambayeque, and Chimú sites are completely or partially abandoned for short to lengthy periods of time and then reoccupied, as indicated by new floors built over sand and/or water deposits (Figure 11.10). These stratigraphic relationships reveal a pattern of

repeated shifts in the occupation of sectors of urban sites but mainly in rural sites. While we can reasonably assume that this type of mobility existed in the valley, it is difficult to judge the full extent of its importance for large urban sites, though we have recorded discontinuous occupational microstrata in domestic areas at such urban sites as Farfan Sur and Talambo. Given the presence of highly similar artifact styles and statistically indistinguishable radiocarbon dates recovered from tightly juxtaposed, discontinuous floor sequences in these domestic sites, we assume that most repeated occupations were by local people who also had access to other lands through kinship networks or simple rights of coresidency (Dillehay 1979).

Local land use patterns must have spatially shifted as a result of cyclical residency, even if movement was only a few kilometers away, to have accommodated new microstructural exchanges between traders, families, and individuals. This does not mean that all local populations, or portions of sites, were necessarily resettling simultaneously. But when small percentages of rotating people are added to multiple locations over the course of a year or decade, there could have been a significant reorganization of local settlement that involved social relationships not only within rural sites but within valley-wide economic networks in different habitats, whether those were agriculture, fishing, herding, or craft production. Although we have not yet figured out the details of these microshifts and their lasting impacts, it can be hypothesized that cyclical residency not only imposed a temporary new order in the formal community pattern, but also impacted the functional and social pattern of the settlements and probably the economic exchange patterns as well, particularly on the household and community levels.

In sum, if I am correct in interpreting the archaeological data from numerous sites on the North Coast of Peru—and at present I see no other plausible explanation—then they suggest the late pre-Hispanic societies in the Zaña and Jequetepeque Valleys practiced cyclical residency—probably within set politico-economic structures and kinship networks, and among

a

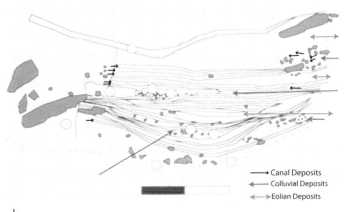

→ Canal Deposits
← Colluvial Deposits
←→ Eolian Deposits

b

c

figure 11.10

Microstratigraphy of domestic floor and fill sequences showing periods of occupation and abandonment: a) canal cut of the Late Intermediate Period in the Jequetepeque Valley showing thin layers of eolian, rainwater-induced alluvial, and silty canal deposits indicative of intermittent abandonment and use episodes; b) view of an adobe wall and floor placed on top of an eolian sand deposit indicative of cyclical occupation/ abandonment/occupation at an Early Intermediate Period site in the Jequetepeque Valley (after Dillehay and Kolata 2006); and c) intermittent layers of occupational floors and eolian sand deposits at a Late Moche settlement in the Zaña Valley. (Illustrations by Tom D. Dillehay.)

specific geographic places. This also suggests a countryside or rural stratum engaged in a "multiplicity of activities in a multiplicity of places" (Dillehay 2004b).

Presuming the existence of cyclical residency in late pre-Hispanic times, it probably was a more important component of economic and social integration in provinces where there was no dominant urban center. But even in urban areas, the economic links between small villages and large towns must have been multiple and partially established through the exchange of goods between individuals, households, and kin groups. Not only would cyclical movement have distributed goods in rural areas, but also the urban areas themselves would have become an integral part of the social and economic world of its hinterland and vice versa. An understanding of the potential complexity of this type of exchange is movement by a small sector of the local population, which would have involved a much larger area in these flows.

It can be hypothesized that acephalous and partially mobile demographic and economic structures existed in pre-Hispanic times (see Dillehay 2006), especially for Late-period urban and rural sites. Our idea of late Andean societies is usually associated with an image of absolute power as an expansionistic entity—one that is spatially fixed and focused in the administrative apparatus and the upper levels of the ruling elite, from which it spread outward across space and downward into the lives of the populace. Yet we are becoming more aware of those practices located outside of central power and places of tradition, change, or resistance. There must have been people who engaged in different activities, such as cyclical residency, barter markets, and other forms of ecological complementarity.

We do not know if cyclical movement was the intention of a political ideology that stressed hierarchical order of local societies within the regular layout of the settlement system, or whether it was a rural-based practice that had existed for centuries. We also do not know the extent to which dissolving localized socioeconomic relationships and moving them among other social and economic categories might have created new tensions or opportunities. To move, even on a temporary basis, may have involved considerations of communal ownership, resource rights, reciprocal labor obligations (*minga*), investment, and access—all of which were likely socially negotiated either between *curacas* or individual *ayllus* and families. But if cyclical movement was a habitual, albeit periodic, pattern, it is unlikely that it caused much social and economic disruption. Residential shifts probably operated within a widely spaced kinship system organized to support such movement. Thus, a system that may logically appear as disorder and disorganization to us may not have been any less systematic and systemic to them.

I am thus suggesting the existence of at least two complementary exchange strategies in the Zaña and Jequetepeque Valleys. One was the integrated system of local divine rulers, such as *curacas*, who were at the summit of a formal hierarchical order that radiated the power of decision making and the movement of wealth and staple goods (D'Altroy and Earle 1985). The other was an informal strategy expressed in the residential mobility of families and individuals involved in multiple, cyclical exchange networks of foods, utilitarian items, and perhaps raw materials. This latter system represents local and regional exchange networks through which raw materials, finished products, and people moved over both short and long distances. The motor of this system was informal encounters, public ritual events, barter markets, and traveling merchants, all perhaps fettered as they might have been from time to time by higher-order interventions.

To conclude this theme, Andean archaeologists seem to focus more on elite-ordered societies at the top rather than lower-level nonelites and any independent groups acting without a formal authority. No doubt *curacas* retained knowledge of lower-level exchange systems as well as some control over their own their people and their products; at the same time, however, informal social and economic relationships were probably constantly reordered in creative and multifaceted restructuring through the mobility of individuals and families. This mobility must have allowed the formation of new identities linked to coresidence in various places and the forging of new ties through a floating access to crops, goods, and people.

The existence of mobile or floating populations had to have been based on rational decisions made in response to the need to diversify, to avoid stress, and/or to maintain social contacts in distant areas. Kin groups and residential mobility had to have been complementary realities and one of the principal ways in which population sectors were linked. This, in turn, implies that past social and political orders may have been more complex, if not more varied, than we had imagined before. The likely existence of residential mobility in many areas was probably manifested in many forms, and was surely a key stabilizing element in the Andean past, especially during times of social and economic unrest, and even today where economic opportunities are few and ever-changing.

Epilogue

Generally speaking, Andean exchange can come about in many ways, such as through the movement of people via vertical colonies, migration, diaspora, and expansion/niche filling, and through trade networks, feasting, and so forth. Several new directions need to be taken in order to advance our understanding of these systems. First, we need to use the ecological conditions of production and the resource structures of population distributions to explore the shifting organization and relationships through time of different scales of foragers, horticulturalists, fisherfolk, agriculturalists, and pastoralists. The result is a picture of widespread and systematic relationships between what is often viewed as "separate" coastal, highland, and tropical peoples with separate maritime, agricultural, or pastoral economies. In this regard, models like ecological complementarity encourage us to look for development and control by a single economic mode when, in fact, elusive and less conspicuous forms of trade and exchange, economic synchronization, and interaction also must have existed to link these various peoples. The shifting connections among these peoples surely have been a long-term feature in the regional dialogue through which ethnic identities were eventually fashioned and transformed into the corporate styles of polities and state societies. Certain research questions can guide us in the ways these different societies operated in terms of their practical deployment of different material conditions; the way that practice reworked the structured social and economic principles of organization; the way practice and social agency mutually worked to meet historical contingencies; and the way they accessed different sets of material conditions and

the mechanism of interaction operating between them. Another research direction should involve more household archaeology, as it would help to counter the temple, palace, and elite architecture bias in the archaeology of the Central Andes. Future work also needs to define better regional chronologies and to excavate larger areas in sites to identify and study activity areas and the internal spatial structure that comprise local and regional exchange systems.

Common to our vision of the Andean past is that economies were ordered and prioritized, dominated by agriculture, pastoralism, and fishing systems of production. Yet it is most likely that there were mixtures of economies of differing values according to the environment, political economy, and other factors. The vision is one where no economy is pure, that all contain elements in which economies run over their edges and flow into one another, channeled to some extent by the political and economic strategies of the society.

REFERENCES CITED

Allen, Catherine J.
   1988   *The Hold Life Has: Coca and Cultural Identity in an Andean Community.* Smithsonian Institution Press, Washington, D.C.

Altamirano, Teófilo
   1988   *Cultura andina y pobreza urbana: Aymaras en Lima metropolitiana.* Fondo Editorial, Pontificia Universidad Católica del Perú, Lima.

Anders, Martha B.
   1981   Investigation of State Storage Facilities in Pampa Grande, Peru. *Journal of Field Archaeology* 8(4):391–404.

Arkush, Elizabeth
   2008   War, Chronology, and Causality in the Titicaca Basin. *Latin American Antiquity* 19:339–373.

Arkush, Elizabeth, and Charles Stanish
   2005   Interpreting Conflict in the Ancient Andes: Implications for the Archaeology of Warfare. *Current Anthropology* 46(1):3–28.

Assadourian, Carlos Sempat
   1994   *Transiciones hacia el sistema colonial andino.* Colegio de México, Fideicomiso Historia de las Américas, Instituto de Estudios Peruanos, Lima.

Bandy, Matthew S.
   2005   Trade and Social Power in the Southern Titicaca Basin Formative. *Archaeological Papers of the American Anthropological Association* 14:91–111.

Berenguer, José R.
   2004   *Caravanas, interacción y cambio en el desierto de Atacama.* Museo Chileno de Arte Precolombino, Santiago.

Bonavia, Duccio

2008   *The South American Camelids.* Cotsen Institute of Archaeology, University of California, Los Angeles.

Bourque, L. Nichole

1997   Making Space: Social Change, Identity, and the Creation of Boundaries in the Central Ecuadorian Andes. *Bulletin of Latin American Research* 16(2):153–167.

Bray, Tamara (editor)

2003   *The Archaeology and Politics of Food and Feasting in Early States and Empires.* Kluwer/Plenum Press, New York.

Browman, David L.

1981   New Light on Andean Tiwanaku. *American Scientist* 69:408–419.

Brush, Stephen B.

1978   *Subsistence Strategies and Vertical Ecology in an Andean Community, Uchucmarca, Peru.* University Microfilms International, Ann Arbor, Mich.

Bryan, Alan L.

1973   Paleoenvironments and Cultural Diversity in Late Pleistocene South America. *Quaternary Research* 3:237–256.

Burger, Richard L.

1992   *Chavín and the Origins of Andean Civilization.* Thames and Hudson, New York.

Contreras, Carlos (editor)

2008   *Economía prehispánica*, vol. 1. Instituto de Estudios Andinos, Lima.

D'Altroy, Terence N.

1992   *Provincial Power in the Inka Empire.* Smithsonian Institution Press, Washington, D.C.

D'Altroy, Terence N., and Timothy K. Earle

1985   Staple Finance, Wealth Finance, and Storage in the Inka Political Economy. *Current Anthropology* 26:187–205.

Dillehay, Tom D.

1976   *Competition and Cooperation in a Prehispanic Multi-Ethnic System in the Central Andes.* PhD dissertation, Department of Anthropology, University of Texas, Austin.

1979   Pre-Hispanic Resource Sharing in the Central Andes. *Science* 204(6):24–31.

1987   *Informe técnico de la temporada de 1985 en el Valle de Zaña, Perú.* Manuscript on file, Instituto Nacional de Cultura, Lima.

2000   *The Settlement of the Americas: A New Prehistory.* Basic Books, New York.

2006   Town and Country in Late Moche Times: A View from Two Northern Peru. In *Moche Art and Archaeology in Ancient Peru,* edited by Joanne Pillsbury, pp. 259–285. National Gallery of Art, Washington, D.C.

n.d.   Sedentism(s) in South America. DAI-KAA, Bonn, Germany, in press.

Dillehay, Tom D. (editor)

2011   *From Foraging to Farming in the Andes: New Perspectives on Food Production and Social Organization.* Cambridge University Press, Cambridge.

Dillehay, Tom D., Duccio Bonavia, and Peter Kaulicke

2004   The First Settlers. In *Andean Archaeology,* edited by Helaine Silverman, pp. 16–34. Blackwell, Malden, Mass.

Dillehay, Tom D., and Alan L. Kolata

2004a   Preindustrial Human and Environmental Interaction on the North Coast of Peru. *Journal of Holocene Studies* 18:345–364.

2004b   State Systems, Environmental Change, and Anticipatory Infrastructure. *Proceedings of the National Academy of Sciences* 25:178–183.

2006   *Informe técnico de la temporada de 1990 en el Valle de Jequetepeque, Perú.* Manuscript on file, Instituto Nacional de Cultura, Lima.

Dillehay, Tom D., Alan L. Kolata, and Edward R. Swenson

2009   *Paisajes culturales en el Valle de Jequetepeque: Los yacimientos arqueológicos.* Ediciones SIAN, Trujillo.

Dillehay, Tom D., and Dolores R. Piperno

n.d.   Agricultural Origins and Social Implications in South America. In *Cambridge Handbook of World Archaeology,* edited by Colin Renfrew and Paul Bahn. Cambridge University Press, Cambridge, in press.

Earle, Timothy K., and Terence N. D'Altroy

1982   Storage Facilities and State Finance in the Upper Mantaro Valley, Peru. In

Contexts for Prehistoric Exchange, edited by Jonathon E. Ericson and Timothy K. Earle, pp. 265–90. Academic Press, New York.

Earle, Timothy K., Terence N. D'Altroy, Christine A. Hastorf, Catherine J. Scott, Cathy Lynne Costin, Glenn S. Russell, and Elsie Sandefur

    1987   *Archaeological Field Research in the Upper Mantaro, Peru, 1982–1983: Investigations of Inka Expansion and Exchange*. Cotsen Institute of Archaeology, University of California, Los Angeles.

Goldstein, Paul S.

    2000   Communities without Borders: The Vertical Archipelago and Diaspora Communities in the Southern Andes. In *The Archaeology of Communities: A New World Perspective*, edited by Marcelo A. Canuto and Jason Yaeger, pp. 194–221. Routledge, London.

    2005   *Andean Diaspora: The Tiwanaku Colonies and the Origins of South American Empire*. University Press of Florida, Gainesville.

Grieder, Terence, Alberto B. Mendoza, Charles E. Smith Jr., and Robert Malina

    1988   *La Galgada, Peru: A Preceramic Culture in Transition*. University of Texas Press, Austin.

Guffroy, Jean

    2008   Cultural Boundaries and Crossings: Ecuador and Peru. In *Handbook of South American Archaeology*, edited by Helaine Silverman and William H. Isbell, pp. 889–902. Springer, New York.

Isbell, Billie Jean

    1978   *To Defend Ourselves: Ecology and Ritual in an Andean Village*. University of Texas Press, Austin.

Jennings, Justin

    2008   Catastrophe, Revitalization, and Religious Change on the Prehispanic North Coast of Peru. *Cambridge Archaeological Journal* 18(2):177–194.

Jennings, Justin, and Brenda J. Bowser (editors)

    2009   *Drink, Power, and Society in the Andes*. University Press of Florida, Gainesville.

Kaulicke, Peter

    2008   La economía en el periodo formativo. In *Economía prehispánica*, vol. 1, edited by Carlos Contreras, pp. 127–230. Instituto de Estudios Andinos, Lima.

Kembel R., Ann, and John W. Rick

    2004   Building Authority at Chavín de Huántar: Models of Social Organization and Development in the Initial Period and Early Horizon. In *Andean Archaeology*, edited by Helaine Silverman, pp. 51–76. Blackwell, London.

Larson, Brooke

    1995   Andean Communities, Political Cultures, and Markets: The Changing Contours of a Field? In *Ethnicity, Markets, and Migration in the Andes: At the Crossroads of History and Anthropology*, edited by Brooke Larson and Olivia Harris, with Enrique Tandeter, pp. 5–54. Duke University Press, Durham, N.C.

Larson, Brooke, and Olivia Harris, with Enrique Tandeter (editors)

    1995   *Ethnicity, Markets, and Migration in the Andes: At the Crossroads of History and Anthropology*. Duke University Press, Durham, N.C.

Lathrap, Donald W.

    1975   Influences of the Formative on the Emerging Civilizations of Mesoamerica and Peru. In *Ancient Ecuador—Culture, Clay, and Creativity, 3000–300 BC*, edited by Donald W. Lathrap, Donald Collier, and Helen Chandra, pp. 3–22. Field Museum of Natural History, Chicago.

Lechtman, Heather

    1984   Andean Value Systems and the Development of Prehistoric Metallurgy. *Technology and Culture* 25:1–36.

Leoni, Juan B., and Felix A. Acuto

    2008   Social Landscapes in Pre-Inca Northwestern Argentina. In *Handbook of South American Archaeology*, edited by Helaine Silverman and William H. Isbell, pp. 105–120. Springer, New York.

Lumbreras, Luis

    1999   Andean Urbanism and Statecraft. In *The Cambridge History of the Native Peoples of the Americas*, vol. 3, *South America*, pt. 1, pp. 518–576. Cambridge University Press, Cambridge.

Lynch, Thomas F.

1999   The Earliest American Lifeways. In *The Cambridge History of the Native Peoples of the Americas,* vol. 3, *South America,* pt. 1, pp. 188–263. Cambridge University Press, Cambridge.

Masuda, Shozo, Izumi Shimada, and Craig Morris (editors)

1985   *Andean Ecology and Civilization: An Interdisciplinary Perspective on Andean Ecological Complementarity.* University of Tokyo Press, Tokyo.

Mayer, Enrique

2002   *The Articulated Peasant: Household Economies in the Andes.* Westview Press, Boulder, Colo.

Méndez, César, Charles Stern, and Oscar Reyes

2008–2009   Transporte de obsidianas a lo largo de los Andes de Patagonia Central (Aisén, Chile). *Cazadores-Recolectores del Cono Sur* 3:51–68.

Mengoni Gonalons, Guillermo L., and Hugo D. Yacobaccio

2006   The Domestication of South American Camelids. In *Documenting Domestication: New Genetic and Archaeological Paradigms,* edited by Melinda A. Zeder, Douglas G. Bradley, Emily Emschwiller, and Bruce D. Smith, pp. 228–244. University of California Press, Berkeley.

Morris, Craig, and Donald E. Thompson

1985   *Huánuco Pampa: An Inca City and Its Hinterland.* Thames and Hudson, London.

Moseley, Michael E.

1975   Chan Chan: Andean Alternative of the Pre-Industrial City? *Science* 187:219–225.

1992   *The Incas and Their Ancestors.* Thames and Hudson, New York.

Muñoz, Ivon

1989   El período formativo en el Norte Grande. In *Culturas de Chile: Prehistoria, desde sus orígenes hasta los albores de la conquista,* edited by Jorge Hidalgo L., Virgilio Schiappacasse, Hans Niemeyer, Carlos Aldunate, and Iván

Solimano, pp. 107–128. Editorial Andrés Bello, Santiago.

Murra, John V.

1972   El control vertical de un máximo de pisos ecológicos en la economía de las sociedades andinas. In *Visita de la provincia de León de Huánuco en 1562,* vol. 2, by Iñigo Ortiz de Zuñiga, pp. 429–476. Universidad Nacional Hermilio Valdizán, Huánuco.

1978   *La organización económica del estado Inca.* Siglo Veintiuno, Mexico City.

1980 [1955]   *The Economic Organization of the Inka State.* JAI Press, Greenwich, Conn.

2002   *El mundo andino: Población, medio ambiente, y economía.* Fondo Editorial, Pontificia Universidad Católica del Perú, Lima.

Núñez, Lautaro

2006   Asentamientos formativos complejos en el centro-sur andino: Cuando la periferia se constituye en núcleo. *Boletín de Arqueología* PUCP 10:321–356.

Núñez, Lautaro, and Tom D. Dillehay

1979   *Movilidad giratoria, armonía social y desarrollo en los Andes meridionales: Patrones de tráfico e interacción económica.* Universidad Católica del Norte, Antofagasta.

Onuki, Yoshio (editor)

1995   *Kuntur Wasi y Cerro Blanco. Dos sitios del formativo en el norte del Perú.* Hokusen-sha, Tokyo.

Owen, Bruce D.

2005   Distant Colonies and Explosive Collapse: The Two Stages of Tiwanaku Diaspora in the Osmore Drainage. *Latin American Antiquity* 16:45–80.

Pearsall, Deborah M.

2008   Plant Domestication and the Shift to Agriculture in the Andes. In *Handbook of South American Archaeology,* edited by Helaine Silverman and William H. Isbell, pp. 105–120. Springer, New York.

Pease G. Y., Franklin, and Duccio Bonavia

1992   *Perú: Hombre e historia, entre el siglo XVI y el XVIII.* EDUBANCO, Lima.

Piperno, Dolores R.

2006   The Origins of Plant Cultivation and Domestication in the Neotropics: A Behavioral Ecological Perspective. In *Behavioral Ecology and the Transition to Agriculture*, edited by Douglas Kennett and Bruce Winterhalder, pp. 137–166. University of California Press, Berkeley.

2007   Prehistoric Human Occupation and Impacts on Neotropical Forest Landscapes during the Late Pleistocene and Early/Middle Holocene. In *Tropical Rainforest Responses to Climatic Change*, edited by Mark B. Bush and John R. Flenley, pp. 193–218. Springer, in association with Praxis Publishing, Berlin and New York.

Pozorski, Shelia G., and Tom G. Pozorski

1986   Recent Excavations at Pampa de las Llamas-Moxeke, a Complex Initial Period Site in Peru. *Journal of Field Archaeology* 13:381–401.

Raymond, J. Scott

2008   The Process of Sedentism in Northwestern South America. In *Handbook of South American Archaeology*, edited by Helaine Silverman and William H. Isbell, pp. 79–90. Springer, New York.

Rick, John W.

1980   *Prehistoric Hunters of the High Andes.* Academic Press, New York.

Roe, Peter G.

1978   Recent Discoveries in Chavín Art: Some Speculations on Methodology and Significance in the Analysis of a Figural Style. *El Dorado* 3:1–41.

Rostworowski de Diez Canseco, María

1970   Mercadores del valle de Chincha en la época prehispánica: Un documento y unos comentarios. *Revista española de antropología americana* 15:135–177.

Rowlands, Michael, and Susan Frankenstein

1998   The Internal Structure and Regional Context of Early Iron Age Society in South-Western Germany. In *Social Transformations in Archaeology: Global and Local Perspectives*, edited by Kristian Kristiansen and Michael J. Rowlands, pp. 334–368. Routledge, London.

Saignes, Thierry

1995   Indian Migration and Social Change in Seventeenth-Century Charcas. In *Ethnicity, Markets, and Migration in the Andes: At the Crossroads of History and Anthropology*, edited by Brooke Larson and Olivia Harris, with Enrique Tandeter, pp. 167–195. Duke University Press, Durham, N.C.

Salomon, Frank

1986   *Native Lords of Quito in the Age of the Incas: The Political Economy of North Andean Chiefdoms.* Cambridge University Press, New York.

Sandweiss, Daniel H.

2003   Terminal Pleistocene through Mid-Holocene Archaeological Sites as Paleoclimatic Archives for the Peruvian Coast. *Palaeogeography, Palaeoclimatology, Palaeoecology* 194:23–40.

Sandweiss, Daniel H., and James B. Richardson III

2008   Central Andean Environments. In *Handbook of South American Archaeology,* edited by Helaine Silverman and William H. Isbell, pp. 93–104. Springer, New York.

Santoro, Calogero, and Lautaro Núñez

1987   Hunters of the Dry Puna and the Salt Puna in Northern Chile. *Andean Past* 1:57–110.

Skar, Sarah Lund

1994   *Lives Together—Worlds Apart: Quechua Colonization in Jungle and City.* Scandinavian University Press, Oslo.

Stackelback, Kary L.

2008   Adaptational Flexibility and Processes of Emerging Complexity: Early to Mid-Holocene Foragers in the Lower Jequetepeque Valley, Northern Perú. PhD dissertation, Department of Anthropology, University of Kentucky, Lexington.

Stahl, Peter W.

2008   Animal Domestication in South America. In *Handbook of South American Archaeology*, edited by Helaine Silverman and William H. Isbell, pp. 121–130. Springer, New York.

Stanish, Charles

1992   *Ancient Andean Political Economy.* University of Texas Press, Austin.

2003   *Ancient Titicaca: The Evolution of Complex Society in Southern Peru and Northern Bolivia.* University of California Press, Berkeley.

Starn, Orin

1991   Missing the Revolution: Anthropologists and the War in Peru. *Current Anthropology* 6(1):63–91.

Topic, John, and Teresa Topic

1983   Coast-Highland Relations in Northern Peru: Some Observations on Routes, Networks, and Scales of Interaction. In *Civilization in the Ancient Americas: Essays in Honor of Gordon R. Willey,* edited by Richard Leventhal and Alan L. Kolata, pp. 237–260. University of New Mexico Press, Albuquerque.

1985   Coast Highland Relations in Northern Highland Peru: The Structure and Strategy of Interaction. In *Status, Structure, and Stratification: Current Archaeological Reconstructions; Proceedings of the Sixteenth Annual Conference,* edited by Mark Thompson, Maria Teresa Garcia, and François J. Kense, pp. 55–66. University of Calgary Archaeological Association, Calgary.

Van Buren, Mary

1996   Rethinking the Vertical Archipelago: Ethnicity, Exchange, and History in the South Central Andes. *American Anthropologist* 98:338–351.

Vaughn, Kevin J.

2006   Craft Production, Exchange, and Political Power in the Pre-Incaic Andes. *Journal of Archaeological Research* 14:313–344.

Wallace, Dwight T.

1991   A Technical and Iconographic Analysis of Carhua Painted Textiles. In *Paracas Art and Architecture: Object and Context in South Coastal Peru,* edited by Anne Paul, pp. 61–109. University of Iowa Press, Iowa City.

Zeidler, James A.

2008   The Ecuadorian Formative. In *Handbook of South American Archaeology,* edited by Helaine Silverman and Wiliam H. Isbell, pp. 459–488. Springer, New York.

12

In the Realm of the Incas

ENRIQUE MAYER

In the realm of the Incas ... the social product neither circulated as a commodity nor was distributed by means of exchange.

KARL MARX
Capital: A Critique of Political Economy
(Marx 1992 [1867–1894]:2:226)

ADAM SMITH POPULARIZED THE NOTION OF man's innate, pleasurable tendency to "barter and truck" as a universal condition. The institutionalization of this human trait into markets and their consequent evolutionary potential has always been implicit in any argument about the presence or absence of markets on a worldwide scale. The Inca were already known in the nineteenth century not to have had money and were, therefore, interesting more as an exception to a then-unilineal view of the process of development of civilizations.

The Inca, it seems, had neither coinage nor money, neither markets nor merchants. The early reports of marketplaces by the sixteenth-century chroniclers are confusing: just because the Spanish saw large groups of people convening at a certain place and time does not necessarily mean that those gatherings were marketplaces. Those urban markets the chroniclers did describe were clearly in contexts of postconquest society—such as urban Lima, Cusco, and Potosí—and not easily linked to preconquest situations. Furthermore, because the state taxed through labor rather than through goods, there was no state incentive to issue coinage. High-end luxury items such as *cumbi* textiles were not traded but were, instead, used in elaborate ritual and ceremonial exchanges. The chroniclers' descriptions of storage, textiles, roads, and bridges emphasized how the Inca state forbade trade in sumptuary goods, reserving for itself a monopoly over their production, transportation, and redistribution as part of the art of statecraft and control. Despite his Karl Polanyi–influenced antimarket predisposition, John Murra in his 1956 dissertation "Economic Organization of the Inca State" argued that markets did exist in the Inca Empire but that they were not that important (Murra 1956:ch. 5).

I will argue here that in subsequent years he tended to dismiss his own evidence for markets.

A decade later, there was a significant shift in Murra's thinking. His homecoming to U.S. academia in 1967, after many years of work in Peru, was strongly tinged by the concept of "verticality," a discovery he was busily propagandizing (Murra 1972). By "verticality," Murra meant that Andeans tended to use colonization of a maximum number of vertically stacked ecological niches for direct production, transportation, and redistribution. His evidence showed that the model operated at the sub-Inca ethnic group level (*kurakasgos* or *señoríos*), such as the Chupaychu, Lupaqa, or Cantas. The main products were salt, cotton, chili peppers, coca, cotton fiber, wood, and feathers—items not easily produced in their home territories. These items could have been obtained through trade, but they evidently were not.

Acceptance of the verticality model—the direct control of ecological niches—makes the exchange of goods through market mechanisms and marketplaces seem contradictory at an intellectual level. Murra, of course, would have liked to have had clear evidence that vertical arrangements for the direct production, together with redistributive mechanisms, operated at all levels of social complexity and geographical locations throughout the Andes and through time as well. Evidence for markets would have weakened his verticality argument. When confronted with clear evidence of the existence of barter, he would say that barter was a second option, an alternative when verticality failed.

Verticality propelled Murra to an unprecedented level of international fame and prestige. It latched on to then-fashionable cultural ecology arguments and further bolstered fascination with the possibility that exotic civilizations could thrive without markets. Murra's reiteration of Karl Polanyi's antimarket position was part of a populist echo in those years that Murra deftly exploited. In the 1930s, when Polanyi wrote, the Soviet Union was a great social experiment in building a society in which an ever-present organized political party supervised a strong coercive state with central planning—rather than the market—was to be

the driving force in the economy, with the intention of building a classless socialism. The Inca state fascinated scholars because it could be considered a non-Western precedent to socialist ideals. Margaret Mead, for example, was absorbed by Louis Baudin's *A Socialist Empire: The Incas of Peru* (Baudin 1961; Mead 1972).[1]

The idea of the market as a negative influence resurfaced in the 1980s—but in a different context. Andean peasants who opted to resist market forces (by using barter, for example) or found ways to circumvent it (through verticality or reciprocity) were of special interest to intellectuals because of the argument that markets were a necessary element in capitalism. A debate then ensued among scholars, some of whom contended that the lack of market integration made contemporary Andean households precapitalist, or noncapitalist (Harris 1982, 2000; Larson et al. 1995; Platt 1982). This perspective made Andeans courageous resisters. For other scholars, evidence of market penetration showed the pernicious inroads of capitalism and, therefore, a weakened Andean cultural identity (Montoya 1980; Sánchez 1982). Scholars from both points of view contributed to an edited volume with the appropriate title *Ecology and Exchange in the Andes*. In his introduction to the volume, the editor David Lehmann (1982) used sophisticated Marxism to argue how marketless and moneyless contemporary Andean peasants nonetheless could be part of the world capitalist system.

This debate also involved a chronological issue because the penetration of the market could clearly be dated to the setting up of the Spanish colonial economy in the sixteenth century (Wallerstein 1974), with varying degrees of success and/or resistance by the conquered people. The effects of market penetration over time as well as over space were important because the impact of colonial markets depended on whether the people studied were within the colonial core economic institutions—such as estates (*haciendas*), mines, workshops (*obrajes*), roads, cities, and ports—or whether they were differently affected because they were in the peripheral hinterlands in isolated indigenous territories in *encomiendas* and resettlements (*reducciones*); or, as we now know, constantly perambulating between the two poles (Assadourian 1982; Larson 1995; Stern 1995).

The issue of chronology and geography was important to Murra, too, and not simply for his verticality argument. His sentiments were against the European invasion—the arrival of Europeans in the sixteenth century. The more the people of the Andes resisted colonial, modern, and contemporary markets, the more they were, and are, asserting the "Andean" way of doing things.

In 1983, Brooke Larson, Olivia Harris, and Enrique Tandeter organized a conference in Sucre, Bolivia, to examine the issues of trade and markets in the Andes before and after the Spanish invasion. The publication, available in Spanish as *La participación inidígena en los mercados surandinos* (Harris et al. 1987) and in English as *Ethnicity, Markets, and Migration in the Andes: At the Crossroads of History and Anthropology* (Larson et al. 1995) is one of the most outstanding volumes on post-Spanish invasion market penetration in the Southern Andes, specifically Argentina, Bolivia, and Peru. At the same time, it is also a remarkable record of how Andean peoples of different classes and regions survived, reconfigured themselves, and redrew ethnic lines. The symposium was a notable collaborative encounter of anthropologists and historians, but archaeologists were not summoned, so the question of whether one can extend the Inca model of a marketless society backward in time was not broached there. But the transition from nonmarket Inca to colonial market economies itself can provide some idea of how the pendulum could potentially swing in both directions.

Murra was, of course, invited and had a star role in the Sucre conference. There, he restated his antitrade and antimarket position for the Inca. Leaning heavily on Bronislaw Malinowski, he reiterated that Inca trade was not commercial: "With Marcel Mauss, Karl Polanyi, Marshall Sahlins, and Paul Bohannan we have learned that all over the precapitalist world, exchanges did and do take place in a variety of noncommercial contexts. I suggest that in the Andean zones long-distance, maritime exchange of precious goods (rain-making *Spondylus,* unworn textiles that took literally years

to weave and were then buried with the dead, and fancy metals that imitated gold) took place in contexts which it is our task to unravel, not to dismiss with Western labels such as 'trade,' 'tribute,' or 'markets'" (Murra 1995:68).

Another international symposium was convened in Coral Gables, Florida, in 1983, to examine the verticality idea. The papers of that conference were published by the organizers, Izumi Shimada, Craig Morris, and Shozo Masuda (Masuda et al. 1985). In that volume, Murra's two short pieces attempted to respond to challenges about verticality made by colleagues (Murra 1985a, 1985b). One quote may summarize how Murra's persistent argument for the uniqueness of Andean solutions did not involve market mechanisms:

> In the Mesoamerican civilizations, the incomes of the kings and the state were based (although not exclusively) on tribute extorted from the conquered ethnic groups, parallel to this, a flourishing commerce existed, moving the resources from one ecological level to others; fairs and gigantic market places facilitated exchange and macro-economic integration; a guild of professional merchants, the *pochteca,* not only organized interzonal traffic but also served the political ends of the state apparatus. In contrast, there was no tribute in the Andean kingdoms; political authorities received their incomes in the form of human energy invested in the cultivation of *papakancha,* the expansion of irrigation works or the colonization of new environmental niches. . . . Although there was, no doubt, occasional trade of high mountain and low valley products, the traffic of Andean resources from one ecological tier to another was realized not through commerce but through mechanisms maximizing the reciprocal use of human energies (Murra 1985b:15).

Thus, by the 1980s, Murra had hardened his antimarket position, staking a lot on his verticality idea. Even if there is agreement with Murra's view, it still is possible to make the following arguments. First, if people were already used to markets—and even though the Inca may have attempted to suppress them—then markets quickly rose to prominence as soon as the antimarket pressures of the Inca state ceased. For contemporary examples, one can look at the rapid and sometimes violent and vicious ways in which markets and market ideology reasserted themselves in the former Soviet Union, Eastern Europe, and China to get an analogous idea of the chaotic transition in the former Inca Empire after 1532.

The second issue was the way ethnicity and gender issues crisscrossed in the market of Potosí in the sixteenth century and how these components illuminate pre-Inca conditions (Choque Canqui 1987; Murra 2002; Tandeter et al. 1987). For example, Murra (2002) noted that a male Andean lord (*kuraka*) of Lupaqa ethnicity owned scattered lands and llamas, and he regularly procured a great number of baskets of Andean *capsicum* (*uchu*), which he sent to his male Spanish agent in Potosí. The agent then resold it to indigenous women retailers of Caranga ethnic identity, described by the Spanish-Quechua term as *gateras* (from the Quechua term for market, *ccatu*), who then sold the spice in the marketplaces to the indigenous population. Male Spanish chroniclers had long noted the presence of women bartering in the *ccatu*, but Garcilaso de la Vega had dismissed their economic significance (Garcilaso de la Vega 1966 [1617]:2:31). Maybe the supposed absence of markets among the Incas is an issue of gender blindness.[2]

Among kernels of ideas that might be worth exploring in archives and through archaeological research is whether *kuraka* entrepreneurship followed up on commoner initiatives or whether the *kurakas* were pioneers in opening up production and trade possibilities in new ecological niches (Mayer 2002:66–67). The following questions should be further investigated: Were there alternate ways of obtaining the goods that *kurakas* also redistributed, such as coca or salt? What happens when *kurakas* fail to live up to expectations? Could commoner barter, vertical control, and redistribution have positive feedback relationships to each other, rather than the contradictory and negative ones initially postulated under Murra's

antimarket influences? Did *kurakas* have a double role as authority figures as well as merchants or traders (Ramírez 1982; Spalding 1973)? Conceivably, *kurakas* could have traded among each other for the goods they redistributed, or directly produced, in distant colonies.

Despite the elevation of Andean *campesinos* to heroic anticapitalist resistors in the work of Murra's followers, contemporary fieldwork shows that quite the opposite case is, in fact, far more common. Avid acceptance of money and market participation as a way to make a living or to realize a modest profit in money is now a fact of contemporary life (Harris 1995a; Mayer 2002, 2005; Mayer and Glave 1999). Andean ethnographic studies of peasant markets (Valcarcel 1946) lagged behind more spectacular reports of the colorful markets in Oaxaca (Beals 1975; Cook and Diskin 1976; Malinowski and de la Fuente 1982), Guatemala (Tax 1963), and elsewhere in Latin America (Wolf 1955), and theoretical orientations (Wolf 1966) in the sixties and seventies. Since then, contemporary studies in the Andes have closed the gap with excellent descriptions of success stories in market-oriented ventures. It may no longer only be about how to make a living in the extractive internal food market for the cities (Babb 1998; Seligmann 2004), but the expansion into the globalized commodity markets where indigenous peoples successfully sell their culture (Colloredo-Mansfield 1999; Meisch 2002; Zorn 2000) or use their gender and ethnicity for advantages in creating market niches for themselves as traders (Weismantel 2001) or entrepreneurs (Buechler and Buechler 1996).

I have recently become interested in cheating, informality, and illegality as integral aspects of economic behavior, and this might be a good place to speculate about how to project these aspects into the distant archaeological past. I am often struck by how archaeological studies assume docile and obedient peasant citizens in the Inca Empire and how colonial historians prefer to document Andean's anti-Spanish/capitalist resistance (Spalding 1970), while social anthropologists tend to underline individual agency and irreverence against officialdom (Mayer 1971, 1984, 2002:chs. 3–6).

I always admired Murra's efforts to document furtive stealing as resistance against the Inca state. He particularly wanted to check out the chroniclers' assertions of the existence of two bridges across the deep gorges in Peru, one for the state and the other for the plebeians (Murra 1962:3; Thompson and Murra 1966:638). He wanted archaeologists to find the checkpoints on the highways and *tambos* to figure out how smugglers might circumvent the posted guards (he would have been intrigued by the work of Axel Nielsen in this volume, for example). Murra also wanted to find out what the chroniclers meant when they used the phrase "payment of tolls" (Hyslop 1984:327). For those of us who prefer to drive along the *vía expresa* and pay tolls instead of using the slower and potholed *vía libre* in Latin America's privatized highways, this kind of double arrangement is not as uncommon or as weird as the chroniclers' assertions of double bridges once may have sounded. Maybe the modern writer Hernando de Soto (1989)—who praises the energetic push of today's street vendors into creating unsightly marketplaces on street corners and in squares, and have a way of expanding trade as "informals" who challenge and erode elitist prohibitions and rules—could benefit from Murra's subversive reading of Inca material and vice versa. Temple plazas and marketplaces are not necessarily either/ or places: Jesus of Nazareth, after all, with whip in hand, expelled money changers from the Temple in Jerusalem. We tend to follow this Durkheimian separation of sacred and profane into prehistory at the cost of misunderstanding non–Judeo-Christian religious, social, and economic systems.

For archaeologists and art historians, the question of identifying and interpreting the social uses of copies and forgeries in Inca, Aztec, and Maya cultures becomes an interesting question of potentially subversive behavior that undermines economic and social structures. In our modern luxury art market, forgeries have a role, but even in conjecture, I can't figure out what a forgery might mean in a redistributive context. Another question I am sure archaeologists have had more to say about is the role of mass production and replication of objects. Logically, redistributive and gift economies should

favor unique pieces that would symbolize the singularity of the relationship that is being expressed through the material gift. But what does it mean when the maker, the giver, and the receiver of a Moche portrait vessel know that it is mold-made and replicable? Why were these goods created, and how did they circulate? How many portraits and little red books of Chairman Mao does the Chinese collective production system require? In a market, we know that replicas, limited editions, and mass-produced goods have their meaning, roles, places, prices, and profit rates. We can do this even for reproductions and simulacra of the Virgin of Lourdes and Saint Anthony. Following Murra's call to heed Malinowski, what non-Western meanings can we attach in pre-Hispanic, premarket times to the circulation of mass-produced craft items, in pathways that we do not yet know in the Americas? Remembering Malinowski's roving eye while he was observing the ceremonial exchange of Kula arm shells and necklaces between magically embellished Polynesian males, he was also noticing, out of the corner of his eye, how women were crowding the boats and actively doing *gimwali* trading for more useful stuff.

In conclusion, I would like to refer to my chapter in the *Handbook of Economic Anthropology* (Mayer 2005). In it, I make the point that the word "market" in the singular is meaningless, and I stress that even in the most market-driven capitalist systems, there are many kinds of markets, each with its own commodities (futures, derivatives, junk bonds, indulgencies, stolen or looted antiquities, refined essence of coca leaf, stamps—not to mention slaves, body parts, hair, semen, eggs, DNA, and so on). Markets also differ among their participants, locations, specialized traders, means of exchange, rules, legalities and systems of arbitrations, punishment, and kinds of state support that make it the stuff of history, art history, and archaeology. The question of markets' existence is meaningless unless we immediately attach further questions to the original ones, such as: In which goods? Between which places? For whom and how transacted? For whose benefits and whose loss? How long did it last, and how did it fluctuate? How were items transported? How were they valued? How did the commodities cross geographic, symbolic, social, and cultural barriers? It is the predicates to the question of whether markets existed or not that make it interesting, not the research into a yes-or-no answer.

We need to be very aware that research on these issues is far more important than whether markets existed in the Americas or not. As an abstract term, the word "market" has its dangers because it alludes to some organizational principle that has become a totalizing concept. Since the fall of the Berlin Wall, there has been a resurgence of the free market as ideology because economics as a discipline (with its optimizing logic and the attached postulates that it produces greater efficiency) has become extremely influential as a pretend science and as a religion. Neoliberalism wants us to believe that there is only one single abstract market principle, which is spreading its tentacles onto one single global system as if this were as an unquestioned truth with the same level of absoluteness as that of the prophecies of a messianic Second Coming. And it says that those who do not get on board are going to be the losers.

The questions asked and the answers provided in this volume may help deflate such attempts to elevate the market into divine dimensions. If I have learned something as an economic anthropologist with sympathies toward history and archaeology, it is that markets are very unstable and that they originate, rise, grow, reach their zenith, and fall. And their demise, in the *longue durée*, is entirely predictable.

NOTES

1 Murra told me that Baudin was an anti-Communist who used the Inca case to illustrate how despotic the Incas were. This is somewhat in line with Karl Wittfogel's (1957) ideas on the same issue. Wittfogel was a refugee from Germany, who, in the Cold War, shared a political agenda with Baudin. Wittfogel had been a Communist before he was persecuted in Germany.

2 Even today, the race and gender issues related to market activities significantly cloud social relations. Olivia Harris (1995b:375) showed that in Andean Latin America, Indian participation is restricted to petty buying and selling in the local marketplace on market day. This is in stark contrast to male *mestizos* and *blancos,* who assume the wholesale, merchant, banking, and administrative functions. The rates of profitability go up as one moves from the numerically predominant Indian market women *cholas* to the privileged *comerciantes* who actually control the market. *Chola* is a term that has ethnic, lower-class, and risqué gender connotations to describe independent-minded women whose brashness, astuteness, and imputed nonfamily-oriented sexual mores are part of their allure (both as attraction or as repulsive fascination). The term also references descent from an Indian status. The importance of *cholas* as traders in Andean markets allows us, following Seligmann (2004) and Weismantel (2001), to note that the profession of low-level trader in the marketplace has a strong influence in the creation of a subethnic category based on Indians but differentiated by their occupation. Weismantel (2001) noted that the transgressive behavior of *cholas* could usefully be analyzed with notions derived from queer theory in gender studies.

Assadourian, Carlos Sempat

    1982   *El sistema de la economía colonial: Mercado interno, regiones y espacio económico.* Instituto de Estudios Peruanos, Lima.

Babb, Florence E.

    1998   *Between Field and Cooking Pot: The Political Economy of Marketwomen in Peru.* Rev. ed. University of Texas Press, Austin.

Baudin, Louis

    1961   *A Socialist Empire: The Incas of Peru.* Translated by Katherine Woods; edited by Arthur Goddard. Van Nostrand, Princeton.

Beals, Ralph L.

    1975   *The Peasant Marketing System of Oaxaca, Mexico.* University of California Press, Berkeley.

Buechler, Hans C., and Judith-Maria Buechler

    1996   *The World of Sofía Velazquez: The Autobiography of a Bolivian Market Vendor.* Columbia University Press, New York.

Choque Canqui, Roberto

    1987   Los caciques aymaras y el comercio en el Alto Peru. In *La participación indígena en los mercados surandinos: Siglos XVI a X*, edited by Olivia Harris, Brooke Larson, and Enrique Tandeter, pp. 357–377. Centro de Estudios de la Realidad Económica y Social (CERES), La Paz.

Colloredo-Mansfield, Rudolf Josef

    1999   *Native Leisure Class: Consumption and Cultural Creativity in the Andes.* University of Chicago Press, Chicago.

Cook, Scott, and Martin Diskin (editors)

    1976   *Markets in Oaxaca.* University of Texas Press, Austin.

Garcilaso de la Vega, El Inca

    1966 [1617]   *Royal Commentaries of the Incas, and General History of Peru.* 2 vols. Translated by Harold V. Livermore. University of Texas Press, Austin.

Harris, Olivia

    1982   Labour and Produce in an Ethnic Economy, Northern Potosí, Bolivia. In *Ecology and Exchange in the Andes*, edited by David Lehmann, pp. 70–96. Cambridge University Press, Cambridge.

    1995a   Sources and Meanings of Money: Beyond the Market Paradigm in an *Ayllu* of Northern Potosí. In *Ethnicity, Markets, and Migration in the Andes: At the Crossroads of History and Anthropology*, edited by Brooke Larson and Olivia Harris, with Enrique Tandeter, pp. 297–328. Duke University Press, Durham, N.C.

    1995b   Ethnic Identity and Market Relations: Indians and Mestizos in the Andes. In *Ethnicity, Markets, and Migration in the Andes: At the Crossroads of History and Anthropology*, edited by Brooke Larson and Olivia Harris, with Enrique Tandeter, pp. 351–390. Duke University Press, Durham, N.C.

    2000   *To Make the Earth Bear Fruit: Ethnographic Essays on Fertility, Work, and Gender in Highland Bolivia.* Institute of Latin American Studies, London.

Harris, Olivia, Brooke Larson, and Enrique Tandeter (editors)

    1987   *La participación indígena en los mercados surandinos: Siglos XVI a X.* Centro de Estudios de la Realidad Económica y Social (CERES), La Paz.

Hyslop, John

    1984   *The Inka Road System.* Academic Press, New York.

Larson, Brooke

    1995   Andean Communities, Political Cultures, and Markets: The Changing Contours of a Field. In *Ethnicity, Markets, and Migration in the Andes: At the Crossroads of History and Anthropology*, edited by Brooke Larson and Olivia Harris, with Enrique Tandeter, pp. 5–53. Duke University Press, Durham, N.C.

Larson, Brooke, and Olivia Harris, with Enrique Tandeter (editors)

    1995   *Ethnicity, Markets, and Migration in the Andes: At the Crossroads of History and Anthropology.* Duke University Press, Durham, N.C.

Lehmann, David (editor)

1982   *Ecology and Exchange in the Andes.* Cambridge University Press, Cambridge.

Malinowski, Bronislaw, and Julio de la Fuente

1982   *Malinowski in Mexico: The Economics of a Mexican Market System.* Edited by Susan Drucker-Brown. Routledge and Kegan Paul, London.

Marx, Karl

1992   *Capital: A Critique of Political Economy.*
[1867–1894]   3 vols. Penguin Books, London.

Masuda, Shozo, Izumi Shimada, and Craig Morris (editors)

1985   *Andean Ecology and Civilization: An Interdisciplinary Perspective on Andean Ecological Complementarity.* University of Tokyo Press, Tokyo.

Mayer, Enrique

1971   Un carnero por un saco de papas: Aspectos del trueque en la zona de Chaupiwaranga (Pasco). *Actas y memorias de XXXIX Congreso Internacional de Americanistas* 3:184–196. Lima.

1974   Intercambios económicos en tiempos incáicos. In *Los campesinos y el mercado*, edited by Enrique Mayer, pp. 15–43. Pontificia Universidad Católica del Perú, Lima.

1984   A Tribute to the Household: Domestic Economy and the Encomienda in Colonial Peru. In *Kinship Ideology and Practice in Latin America*, edited by Raymond T. Smith, pp. 85–117. University of North Carolina Press, Chapel Hill.

2002   *The Articulated Peasant: Household Economies in the Andes.* Westview Press, Boulder, Colo.

2005   Households and Their Markets. In *Handbook of Economic Anthropology*, edited by James G. Carrier, pp. 405–422. Berg, Oxford.

Mayer, Enrique, and M. Glave

1999   Alguito para ganar (A Little Something to Earn): Profits and Losses in Peasant Economies. *American Ethnologist* 26(2):344–369.

Mead, Margaret

1972   *Blackberry Winter: My Earlier Years.* Morrow, New York.

Meisch, Lynn A.

2002   *Andean Entrepreneurs: Otavalo Merchants and Musicians in the Global Arena.* University of Texas Press, Austin.

Montoya, Rodrigo.

1980   *Capitalismo y no capitalismo en el Perú: Un estudio histórico de su articulación en un eje regional.* Mosca Azul, Lima.

Murra, John V.

1956   The Economic Organization of the Inca State. PhD dissertation, Department of Anthropology, University of Chicago, Chicago.

1962   An Archaeological "Restudy" of an Andean Ethnohistorical Account. *American Antiquity* 28(1):1–4.

1972   El "control vertical" de un máximo de pisos ecológicos en la economía de las sociedades andinas. In *Visita de la provincia de León de Huánuco en 1562 (Iñigo Ortíz de Zúñiga, visitador)*, vol. 2, edited by John V. Murra, pp. 427–476. Universidad Nacional Hermilio Valdizán, Huánuco.

1985a   "El Archipiélago Vertical" Revisited. In *Andean Ecology and Civilization: An Interdisciplinary Perspective on Ecological Complementarity*, edited by Shozo Masuda, Izumi Shimada, and Craig Morris, pp. 3–13. University of Tokyo Press, Tokyo.

1985b   The Limits and Limitations of the "Vertical Archipielago" in the Andes. In *Andean Ecology and Civilization: An Interdisciplinary Perspective on Ecological Complementarity*, edited by Shozo Masuda, Izumi Shimada, and Craig Morris, pp. 15–20. University of Tokyo Press, Tokyo.

1995   Did Tribute and Markets Prevail in the Andes before the European Invasion? In *Ethnicity, Markets, and Migration in the Andes: At the Crossroads of History and Anthropology*, edited by Brooke Larson and Olivia Harris, with Enrique Tandeter, pp. 57–72. Duke University Press, Durham, N.C.

2002   La correspondencia entre "un capitán de la mita" y su apoderado en Potosí. In *El mundo andino: Población, medio ambiente y economía*, pp. 223–234. Pontificia Universidad Católica del Perú and Instituto de Estudios Peruanos, Lima.

Platt, Tristan

1982   The Role of an Andean *Ayllu* in the Reproduction of the Petty Commodity Regime in Northern Potosi (Bolivia). In *Ecology and Exchange in the Andes*, edited by David Lehmann, pp. 27–69. Cambridge University Press, Cambridge.

Ramírez, Susan E.

1982   Retainers of the Lords or Merchants: A Case of Mistaken Identity? *Senri Ethnological Studies* 10:123–136.

Sánchez, Rodrigo.

1982   The Andean Economic System and Capitalism. In *Ecology and Exchange in the Andes*, edited by David Lehmann, pp. 157–190. Cambridge University Press, Cambridge.

Seligmann, Linda J.

2004   *Peruvian Street Lives: Culture, Power, and Economy among Market Women in Cuzco*. University of Illinois Press, Urbana.

Soto, Hernando de

1989   *The Other Path: The Invisible Revolution in the Third World*. Harper and Row, New York.

Spalding, Karen

1970   Social Climbers: Changing Patterns of Mobility among the Indians in Peru. *Hispanic American Historical Review* 50:645–664.

1973   Kurakas and Commerce: A Chapter in the Evolution of Andean Society. *Hispanic American Historical Review* 53:581–599.

Stern, Stephen J.

1995   The Variety and Ambiguity of Native Intervention in European Colonial Markets. In *Ethnicity, Markets, and Migration in the Andes: At the Crossroads of History and Anthropology*, edited by Brooke Larson and Olivia Harris, with Enrique Tandeter, pp. 73–100. Duke University Press, Durham, N.C.

Tandeter, Enrique, Villma Milletich, María Matilde Oliver, and Beatriz Ruibal

1987   Indians in Late Colonial Markets: Sources and Numbers. In *Ethnicity, Markets, and Migration in the Andes: At the Crossroads of History and Anthropology*, edited by Brooke Larson and Olivia Harris, with Enrique Tandeter, pp. 196–223. Duke University Press, Durham, N.C.

Tax, Sol

1963   *Penny Capitalism: A Guatamalan Indian Economy*. University of Chicago Press, Chicago.

Thompson, Donald E., and John V. Murra

1966   The Inca Bridges in the Huánuco Region. *American Antiquity* 31(5):632–639.

Valcarcel, Luis E.

1946   Indian Markets and Fairs in Peru. In *Handbook of South American Indians*, vol. 2, edited by Julian Steward, pp. 477–482. Cooper Square, New York.

Wallerstein, Immanuel M.

1974   *The Modern World-System: Capitalist Agriculture and the Origins of the European World-Economy in the Sixtheenth Century*, vol. 1. Academic Press, New York.

Weismantel, Mary

2001   *Cholas and Pishtacos: Stories of Race and Sex in the Andes*. University of Chicago Press, Chicago.

Wittfogel, Karl A.

1957   *Oriental Despotism: A Comparative Study of Total Power*. Yale University Press, New Haven.

Wolf, Eric R.

1955   Types of Latin American Peasantry: A Preliminary Discussion. *American Anthropologist* 57:452–471.

1966   *Peasants*. Prentice Hall, Englewood Cliffs, N.J.

Zorn, Elayne

2000   When Incas Travel Abroad: Tourism to and from Peru. In *Transforming Cultures in the Americas*, edited by Debra A. Castillo and Mary Jo Dudley, pp. 21–30. Latin American Studies Program, Cornell University, Ithaca, N.Y.

13

In the Realm of the Incas

An Archaeological Reconsideration of Household Exchange, Long-Distance Trade, and Marketplaces in the Pre-Hispanic Central Andes

RICHARD L. BURGER

If I have learned something as an economic anthropologist with sympathies toward history and archaeology, it is that markets are very unstable and that they originate, rise, grow, reach their zenith, and fall. And their demise, in the *longue durée*, is entirely predictable.

ENRIQUE MAYER
"In the Realm of the Incas" (this volume)

IN THE PRECEDING CHAPTER, MY COLLEAGUE and friend Enrique Mayer offers a commentary on the intellectual history of the antimarket position in the pre-Hispanic Andes as advocated by John Murra and provides his own proposal for a more nuanced position on this issue. I believe that he is correct when he suggests that part of the attraction of Murra's position was the antimarket bias of many anthropologists and archaeologists, including myself, who were sympathetic to the critiques of American market expansion and global imperialism in the late 1960s and 1970s. Of course, today the pendulum has swung to the right, and we

must be careful not to let the widespread admiration of the market system unduly color our interpretations of the ancient Andes.

My purpose in this chapter is to briefly explore some of the archaeological implications of Mayer's analysis and discussion. At the core of his commentary is that the antimarket position found in Murra's late writings is both oversimplified and unrealistic. There probably was always some market activity, even during Inca times, though not necessarily in formal marketplaces. This is a position foreshadowed in the writings of Patterson (1988, 1991), Salomon (1977, 1986), and Rostworowski (1970, 1975), but unlike these authors, Mayer does not focus on the northern frontier of the empire or the special case of the Chincha Valley; instead, he is concerned with everyday life in Tawantinsuyu, the core of the Inca Empire. For Mayer and me, the real question is the nature, not the existence, of markets in the ancient Central Andes. There must have been major changes in the kinds of goods exchanged, the direction of these exchanges, the actors involved, and the intensity and scale of these transactions. Moreover, even if John Murra was correct that between the late fifteenth and early sixteenth century, market activity was of relatively little significance in the political economy of Tawantinsuyu (Murra 1995), localized exchange for subsistence goods almost certainly continued to occur between households or villages, coexisting—as it does in modern times—with other kinds of transactions and economic relationships.

Perhaps what is most important, for those investigating Andean prehistory, is realizing that the situation in the 1530s, as observed by the Spaniards, was not the inevitable culmination of socioeconomic evolution in the Andean world, but rather a historically specific moment in which a unique social formation, the Inca state, seized the production and distribution of prestige goods as part of a strategy of imperial power. In doing so, the state suppressed market activity by circumscribing the goods that could be exchanged. Eliminating the most valuable goods from the equation greatly constrained the potential for market activity. Nonetheless, archaeologists have demonstrated that the scale and bureaucratic organization of Tawantinsuyu had no equivalent among earlier pre-Hispanic states, and, thus, there is no reason to assume that we can use the role of the market in the Inca Empire as a guide to visualizing market activity among its predecessors—particularly those in the culturally diverse regions that the Inca conquered. Just as Josef Stalin sought to suppress market activity in Soviet Union during the 1920s and 1930s, and Pol Pot tried to extinguish it in Cambodia in the 1970s—only for market exchange to return with force to Russia and Cambodia in the twenty-first century—so there exists a complex and nonlinear history for markets and exchange in the Pre-Columbian Andes of Peru.

To illustrate this line of reasoning, I will briefly touch upon some of the archaeological evidence relevant to the history of exchange and markets in the Callejón de Huaylas and Callejón de Conchucos, in what is now the northern Peruvian Andes. But before I do, it is worth considering the issue of merchants in ancient Peru from an archaeological perspective.

Searching for Merchants and Their Tools

Market activity does not require a group of full-time specialists devoted to exchange and, in contrast to colonial historical records for Ecuador and Mesoamerica, there is scant evidence that such a group existed in Peru prior to the Spanish conquest. If such a collective had existed, its continuing survival would have depended on the profit made by exchange, and, thus, its members would have had a special interest in maximizing the range and volume of items exchanged. In many ancient societies, such as Sumerian Mesopotamia or New Kingdom Egypt, such entities constituted significant interest groups that influenced political and economic decisions (Trigger 2003). This does not appear to have occurred in the prehistoric Andes of Peru.

A single historic document, the famous *Aviso* published by María Rostworowski (1970), states that there were six thousand merchants in the valley of Chincha during Inca times; this lone historical source has led to much speculation about the existence in Chincha of pre-Hispanic merchants with links to traders of exotic pink-colored *Spondylus* on the North Coast and even in Ecuador. During the four decades since the publication of the *Aviso* in English and Spanish, there has been abundant archaeological research seeking confirmation of Rostworowski's claim, but no evidence of these merchants or their activities has yet been found. As Craig Morris and Julián Idilio Santillana have written: "None of the research of several projects sponsored jointly by the American Museum of Natural History, Instituto Andino de Arqueología . . . and the Institute of Andean Research have found significant quantities of *Spondylus* . . . there is the possibility that the information of the 'Aviso' document is somehow inaccurate or exaggerated" (Morris and Santillana 2007:136). Attempting to salvage something of the *Aviso*'s credibility, Morris and Santillana offer the unlikely alternative that it was written as a blueprint for the future rather than as a description of historical reality. Not surprisingly, today most scholars remain skeptical about the accuracy of the *Aviso* and its interpretation, and of the existence of full-time pre-Hispanic merchants in general.

It is interesting in this light that two common tools used by merchants elsewhere in the world seem to be lacking or underdeveloped in the Central Andes: money and a standardized system of weights and measures. These two elements are particularly noteworthy because of the unambiguous traces they leave in the archaeological record. As a medium of exchange, money is designed to make transactions more fluid and to permit the accumulation of wealth. But exchanges can be made without money, and there are ways to accumulate wealth without the existence of money. Nonetheless, money—particularly in the form of precious metal coinage—has distinct benefits. In the Old World, metal coinage was first issued around 700 BC in Lydia or Aegina, and its advantages in market transactions account for its rapid adoption throughout the Aegean, Anatolia, and Persia over the following two centuries. Independent but distinctive inventions of metal coinage occurred in India and China, and its introduction there likewise resulted in a comparably rapid spread over large areas (Grierson 1977; Price 1983).

In the Central Andes, the introduction of possible special-purpose money known as *naipes* appears several centuries before the Inca; these have been found in Piura in deposits from the Lambayeque culture in the form of thin hammered-copper sheets (see also Topic, this volume). They have not been found in refuse, but they do occur as tomb offerings, sometimes in decimally organized packets tied with string (Hosler et al. 1990:18–20). Some archaeologists have suggested the *naipes* could have played a part in long-distance exchange (Shimada 1985), and others have even seen a link between these *naipes* and the mention in the *Aviso* document of the use of copper for exchange by the supposed Chincha merchants (Hosler et al. 1990). If specialized merchants had existed in ancient Peru during the late pre-Hispanic era, I would have expected the potential of the *naipes* as a medium of exchange would have been obvious—and that their use to have spread rapidly across ancient Peru, as did coinage in the Old World. But thus far no *naipes* have been found anywhere south of Lambayeque, and their adoption within the ancient Peruvian area

seems very limited. In contrast, the idea of distinctive standardized copper objects related to the *naipes* and known as axe-money seems to have found a more receptive audience further north, spreading first to Ecuador and then into west Mexico, eventually reaching as far as Oaxaca (Hosler et al. 1990). It may be significant that the zones that adopted the relatives of the *naipes* are areas where the presence of merchants is confirmed by ethnohistoric documents. In Ecuador, merchants known as *mindalaes* were reminiscent of the *pochteca* who thrived in Mexico during Aztec times (Salomon 1977, 1986; see also Nichols, this volume; Topic, this volume). One wonders, or at least I wonder, whether the lack of a robust class of merchants in ancient Peru may have been responsible for preventing the spread of the *naipes* to the south as a medium of exchange.

Similarly, in ancient Peru there was no institutionalized organization of weights or measures—at least not one that was mentioned in the ethnohistoric record—nor have sets of standardized weights been recovered from the archaeological record. According to Rowe (1946:324–325), although the Incas employed a system of distance measurement that was at least as exact as that used in sixteenth-century Europe, they did not have a standard system of weights. Examples of the pan balance (*aysana*) are known from some late prehistoric sites in Peru, but I am unaware of any examples of them that predate the Late Intermediate Period or that come from outside the coastal valleys. The absence of an accurate system of weights and measures would seem consistent with a tradition of exchange that emphasized barter and lacked specialized merchants.

In summary, the weak historic and archaeological evidence of specialized merchants and the lack of money and a system of measurement by weight or volume suggests that while some form of market exchange probably existed throughout pre-Hispanic times in the Central Andes, these activities may have remained underdeveloped in comparison to some parts of the Old World or even Mesoamerica. This hypothesis, however, should be reevaluated as new archaeological research comes to light and not taken as an established fact.

Searching for Prehistoric Markets and Marketplaces: A Speculative Case Study

The role of marketplaces is particularly tricky from an archaeological perspective. As Mayer notes, if female domination of marketplaces, documented by contemporary ethnographers in Peru, prevailed in antiquity, then the Spanish chroniclers may have systematically ignored these activities because of gender bias. Even in areas such as Mesoamerica, where marketplaces are recognized as being important in prehistory, they are difficult to identify archaeologically since they may involve few permanent structures and leave few residues (Stark and Garraty 2010). On the other hand, the presence of market activity may be detectable from macropatterns revealed through artifact analysis, so we should not give up hope (Hirth 1998; Stark and Garraty 2010).

Where should we begin our search for the elusive marketplaces of the pre-Hispanic Andes? If ethnography and ethnohistory can serve as a guide, then pilgrimage and cult centers may be a good place to start. In contemporary Peru, in both highland and coastal locations, syncretistic belief systems draw thousands of believers to sacred points on the landscape or chapels and churches with miraculous saints and virgins at crucial points of the year. While visitors often travel great distances to worship and participate in religious ceremonies,

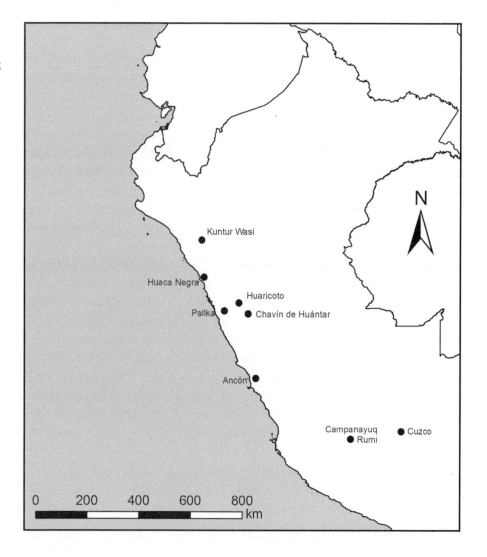

figure 13.1
Map of Peru indicating sites mentioned in the text. (Drawing by Richard Burger and Chris Milan.)

adjacent to the places of worship are usually large fairs or markets, which operate parallel to and largely independent of the cultic activities (e.g., see the description of the Cult of Wank'a and Qoyllur Rit'i in Sallnow 1987; the discussion of the celebration of the Virgen de Yauca in Silverman 1991; and Blanton, this volume).

Among the goods exchanged are secular items not produced or available in most rural communities as well as goods that relate specifically to the sacred place or the ceremonial practices carried out there. This pattern, of course, is not limited to the Andes. As British anthropologists Simon Coleman and John Elsner observed in their comparative study of Old World religious pilgrimages, "pilgrimage is as concerned with taking back some part of the charisma of a holy place as it is about actually going to the place. One of the most characteristic aspects of pilgrimage art in all the world religions is the proliferation of objects made available to pilgrims and brought home by them as reminders and even tangible channels of connection with

the sacred experience. In this way, the influence of the site can be retained in the domestic or mundane context into which a pilgrim has returned" (Coleman and Elsner 1995:100). Given this close association between markets and pilgrimage centers not only in the Andes but also in the Old World, it seems appropriate to consider the possibility that Chavín de Huántar could have served as an early hub of market activity (Figure 13.1).

At 3,150 meters above sea level (masl) in the northern highlands of Ancash, Peru, Chavín de Huántar is one of the best-known cult centers of pre-Hispanic Andes and has been the focus of archaeological investigations since Julio C. Tello's work in 1919 (Figure 13.2). Located at the junction of two natural routes of transportation across the glaciated Cordillera Blanca, Chavín would have occupied a crucial spot for those traveling from the coast or Callejón de Huaylas into the Callejón de Conchucos and adjacent Marañón drainage (Burger 1984, 1992). The site has been interpreted as an early pilgrimage complex (e.g., Burger 1988; Patterson

figure 13.2
Google Earth photograph of Chavín de Huántar with the locations of the Old Temple, New Temple, West Field, and Kotosh Religious Tradition shrine indicated. (© 2010 Google.)

1971; Sallnow 1987) that thrived from 1000 to 300 BC. Elsewhere, I have suggested that it was the dominant center of a network of branch oracles which were scattered from Nasca to Lambayeque on the coast and from Ayacucho to northern Cajamarca in the highlands (Burger 1988, 2008).

Much work has been carried out in Chavín de Huántar's temple sector. Archaeologists have documented an impressive complex of open plazas, inner chambers, and summit buildings all devoted to religious worship, as expressed in the depiction of supernatural beings and mythical processions in the stone sculpture that adorns the buildings. The interpretation of this monumental complex as fundamentally religious in character is reinforced by the ceremonial paraphernalia recovered from the excavations, such as mortars to grind hallucinogens, spoons to inhale psychotropic snuff, engraved shell trumpets, and the Lanzón, a remarkable cult object that remains in situ in the core of Chavín de Huántar's Old Temple.

Archaeological work within the Chavín site has documented abundant exotic materials brought to the religious center by people from the coast and highlands. One of the most famous sculptures, known in Peru as the Medusa Stone (Figure 13.3), shows the highland temple's main deity holding two shells, *Strombus* and *Spondylus*, both of which are native to the warm waters off the coast of Ecuador and northernmost Peru. This and other sculptures suggest that the identity of Chavín de Huántar's temple was closely linked with its access to distant goods of special power and value.

This iconographic claim has been more than confirmed by archaeological fieldwork (Figure 13.4). In the Ofrendas Gallery alone, Luis Lumbreras recovered more than three hundred ceramic vessels, most of which were brought from outside Chavín de Huántar (Lumbreras 1971, 2007; see also Burger 1984). The gallery contents included painted, single-necked ceramic bottles from Cajamarca; stirrup-spout bottles from the North Coast valleys of Chicama and Moche; heavily incised bowls from the Central Coast; a stone beaker from Jequetepeque; and a stone platter in the form a fish from Jaen. In 2001, in the nearby Caracolas

figure 13.3
The Medusa Stone, Chavín de Huántar. (Drawing by John Rowe, courtesy of Richard Burger.)

Gallery, John Rick unearthed twenty shell trumpets crafted from actual *Strombus* shell (Rick 2008:27–28); interestingly, many are incised with imagery typical of the highlands and the cloud forest (*ceja de selva*) zone near the Ecuador-Peruvian border. Elsewhere in the temple area, archaeologists have recovered obsidian from the Quispisisa source in Ayacucho and cinnabar, probably from the Santa Barbara mine of Huancavelica in the south-central highlands (Burger and Glascock 2000; Burger, Lau, Ponte, and Glascock 2006; Burger and Matos Mendieta 2002). These materials are probably not evidence of market activity. On the contrary, these objects should be interpreted as gifts or tribute brought to the temple by pilgrims from distant areas, perhaps from those places with branch oracles or shrines. The finds do, however, provide vivid evidence of the long-distance movement of peoples of different ethnic and linguistic backgrounds to the sacred center at Chavín de Huántar during the first millennium BC.

Possible evidence of market activity can be gleaned from excavations in the residential zone adjacent to the ceremonial sector (Figure 13.5). In my doctoral research in Chavín de Huántar, I documented that the residential zone spanned

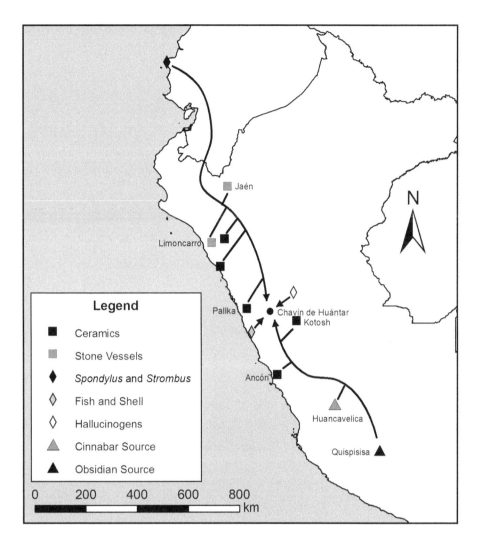

figure 13.4
Map showing the sources of exotic materials brought to the Chavín de Huántar temple. (Drawing by Richard Burger and Chris Milan.)

Legend

- ■ Ceramics
- ▨ Stone Vessels
- ◆ *Spondylus* and *Strombus*
- ◇ Fish and Shell
- ◇ Hallucinogens
- ▲ Cinnabar Source
- ▲ Obsidian Source

Jaén

Limoncarro

Pallka

Chavín de Huántar
Kotosh

Ancón

Huancavelica

Quispisisa

0   200   400   600   800
km

both sides of the Huachecsa and that it expanded from only a few hectares in the Urabarriu Phase (1000–700 BC) to more than thirty hectares along the western side of the Mosna River in the Janabarriu Phase (600–300 BC). Subsequent research by archaeologists from the Instituto Nacional de Cultura and the Stanford Project identified an additional residential zone of at least six hectares in La Banda along the eastern bank of the Mosna River across from the temple area; this occupation dates primarily to the Janabarriu Phase (Sayre 2010). I originally estimated that the peak population associated with the site at Chavín de Huántar may have reached between two and three thousand inhabitants (Burger 1984), and the recent research in La Banda only increases the plausibility of this

original estimate. I also argued that the residents to the north of the Huachecsa and further from the temple core seemed to be of lower status than those on the slopes adjacent to the temple area. I suggest here that the growth of a large resident population and the short-term presence of pilgrims and travelers at Chavín de Huántar during the Janabarriu Phase would have made it an attractive place for market exchange.

Hirth (1998) has observed that marketplace exchange makes a wide range of products available to all households, albeit tempered by differences in wealth, and that this pattern should be observable archaeologically. Judging from the evidence currently available, this pattern indeed appears in the Chavín residential areas. What is remarkable

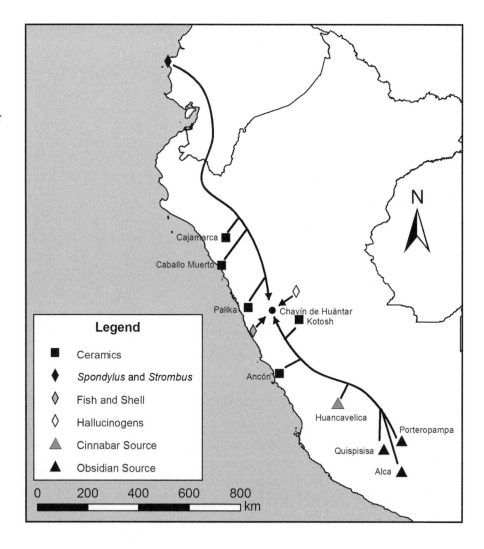

figure 13.5
Map showing the
sources of exotic
materials brought to
the Chavín de Huántar
settlement. (Drawing
by Richard Burger and
Chris Milan.)

Legend

- ■ Ceramics
- ◆ *Spondylus* and *Strombus*
- ◇ Fish and Shell
- ◊ Hallucinogens
- ▲ Cinnabar Source
- ▲ Obsidian Source

about the materials found in the residential areas is the quantity of exotic items associated with both the lower- and upper-status households. Access to exotic goods was not limited to one or two items; on the contrary, it applied to a variety of goods from many parts of the Peruvian highlands and coast. For example, considering the abundance of exotic styles, the ceramic vessels used in the residential areas included pottery from the Moche and Chicama Valleys on the North Coast, Huánuco in the central highlands, and Cajamarca in the northern highlands (Burger 1984). A petrographic and X-ray fluorescence study of ceramics from the Chavín residential area by Isabel Druc concluded that a substantial portion (36 percent) of the pottery came from nonlocal sources. Although most

fragments could not be identified, some were attributed to Pallka in the middle Casma Valley and Huaricoto in the central Callejón de Huaylas (Druc 1998:309–310). This situation at Chavín de Huántar was in sharp contrast to the other public coeval centers on the coast and in the highland studied by Druc, all of which utilized locally produced pottery almost exclusively (Druc 1998; Druc et al. 2001).

The pattern of exotic household ceramics at Chavín is paralleled by the lithic remains recovered. In domestic refuse from the Janabarriu Phase, the chipped lithics consist almost entirely of obsidian artifacts, which were common in all of the excavations regardless of household status (Burger 1984:248). This pattern of abundant obsidian debitage and tools from household contexts was likewise encountered by Matthew Sayre in his 2005 excavations in La Banda (Sayre 2010:161). A study of eighty-six of the obsidian artifacts collected by Burger revealed that about 95 percent came from the Quispisisa source located near Huanca Sancos in central Ayacucho, some six hundred kilometers to the south (Burger and Glascock 2000), while small amounts came from even more distant sources: the Alca source in the Cotahuasi Valley in the Department of Arequipa and the Potreropampa source in the Department of Apurimac (Burger 1998:248, cuadro 21; Burger et al. 1998; Burger, Fajardo, and Glascock 2006).

Access to nonlocal items by Chavín residents extended even to the food they ate. A significant number of fish bones were recovered in the Chavín de Huántar midden, and all proved to come from the Pacific shores, probably in dried and salted form; at least three species were consumed (Burger 1998:238, cuadro 18). There was also evidence of mollusk shells in both the lower- and upper-status areas, with at least thirteen different species represented; clams, mussels, and sea snails were all identified from the Burger excavations. Sayre likewise encountered numerous fragments of Pacific shells in the La Banda residential area, including most of the species found in the household areas on the other side of the Mosna (Sayre 2010:156). While a few of these mollusks may have been acquired for shell-ornament production, most seem to have been consumed as food. I have suggested elsewhere that marine fish and shellfish, as a source of iodine, were especially valuable in highland diets in order to avoid goiter (Burger 1985:276). Both Sayre and Burger also recovered rare pieces of unmodified coral, which likewise must have come from coastal waters and been transported to the site (Sayre 2010:160). Like obsidian and exotic pottery, Pacific shell appears to have been available to the Chavín de Huántar population regardless of social status.

Finally, rare finds in household refuse of exotic items—such a *Spondylus* bead (Sayre 2010), a tiny fragment of soldered gold jewelry (Burger 1998:436–443; Lechtman 1998), and a polished chlorite earspool covered with bright cinnabar pigment (Burger 1998:187–188)—suggest that some

distinctive costume items made of rare raw materials were also obtained by the local population.

The presence of these nonlocal materials by Chavín de Huántar residents can be explained if they had access to a marketplace or some other market activity. Particularly notable at Chavín de Huántar is the ample distribution of exotics among the households and the wide range of materials involved. The pattern just described for Chavín de Huántar differs sharply from the patterning that has been documented at Inca sites. For example, in the Huánuco Pampa region, exotics are totally absent from most households and when they occur, they are usually limited to a very few items distributed by the Inca elite to local ethnic leaders collaborating with them (e.g., Morris and Thompson 1985).

If the exotic items in the household refuse of the Chavín de Huántar residents were acquired by market mechanisms from pilgrims and/or traders, it is reasonable to wonder what was received in exchange. One possibility is that the goods were exchanged for food and lodging, neither of which would leave easily identifiable archaeological traces. But it is also possible that items were produced locally for exchange. Some of these could have been of purely local origin—such as potatoes from the upper slopes above the temple, the freeze-dried llama meat (*charki*) that the Chavín de Huántar villagers consumed in their own homes, or the freeze-dried tubers (*chuño*) produced in the high grasslands above Chavín de Huántar (Burger and Van der Merwe 1990; Miller and Burger 1995). While plausible, these possibilities are difficult to evaluate archaeologically at this time.

In contrast, there is ample evidence of local craft activities that may have produced objects for exchange as well as for local consumption. For example, artifacts of llama bone were common in the residential area of Chavín de Huántar throughout the first millennium BC (Burger 1998; Sayre 2010). As mentioned, pilgrims frequently obtain objects from sacred centers in order to take back part of the charisma of the holy place to their homes and to demonstrate to others that they have successfully completed a difficult pilgrimage. Carved spatulas and other bone ornaments carved with

Chavín religious iconography have been found throughout the Peruvian coast and highlands, and are often used to illustrate the spread of the Chavín cult (Figures 13.6–13.9). Could some of these carved bones have been produced in the Chavín de Huántar residential area for the purpose of market exchange?

Some additional support for this idea comes from Sayre's recent work in La Banda, where he found evidence of craft activity in a residential area. Four bones were highly modified with Chavín imagery, and two bore simple carvings etched into their surfaces. He further observed that "bone pieces similar to these appear across the site and may have been an artifact easily carried away by pilgrims and other visitors to the site" (Sayre 2010:154).

Other items possibly crafted for exchange from high grasslands (puna) products include thread and textiles spun and woven from camelid wool and products made from the skins of slaughtered llamas, such as leather sandals. The latter possibility receives some support from one set of excavations in the Chavín de Huántar residential area, where a unique concentration of unifaces and drills were encountered; these tools may have been used in the manufacture of leather goods, such as footwear (Burger 1998:39–40, 183).

The residents of the Chavín de Huántar settlement also created items from exotic raw materials that were hard to acquire. For example, I found evidence that one upper-status household in the area to the west of the temple was involved in making beads and pendants from *Spondylus* shell (Burger 1998:203, cuadros 14–15, fig. 432). More recently, Sayre has documented the production of carved and polished ornaments from what appears to be whalebone (Sayre 2010:157–158). The latter cases are particularly interesting, since they suggest that not only did the local population have access to a wide range of foods and household objects for personal use but that they also acquired exotic raw materials to work and presumably to exchange with others.

The evidence reviewed here provides a case for early market activity in the Peruvian Andes, perhaps one with no parallel in Inca times. It is tempting to speculate where such a marketplace

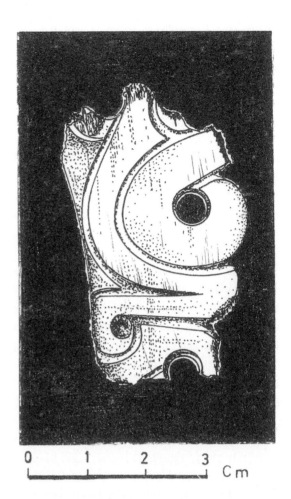

0   1   2   3   Cm

figure 13.6
Carved bone spatula from Huaricoto, Callejón de Huaylas. (Drawing courtesy of Richard Burger.)

would have been located at Chavín de Huántar. The large plazas and terraces of the temple would have been an option, but this seems unlikely given the sacred nature of the temple space and the activities carried out there. Moreover, excavations in the open plaza areas have not found evidence of market activity. Following ethnographic examples, it seems more likely that such activities would have been carried out behind the temple. One possibility would have been the area referred to locally as the West Field (Figure 13.2). The zone is poorly known; however, in Janabarriu times, it featured a series of broad terraces supported by masonry walls. Since the two trails across the Cordillera Blanca funnel into this zone, it would

a

b

figure 13.7
Carved bone spatula: (a) front and
(b) back view, Kuntur Wasi, upper
Jequetepeque Valley. (Photographs
courtesy of Kuntur Wasi Archaeological
Project.)

figure 13.9
Carved bone spatula,
Campanayuq Rumi,
Vilcashuaman, Ayacucho.
(Photograph by Yuichi
Matsumoto.)

figure 13.8
Carved bone spatula,
Ofrendas Gallery,
Chavín de Huántar
(Drawing by Jo Brady,
after Lumbreras 2007.)

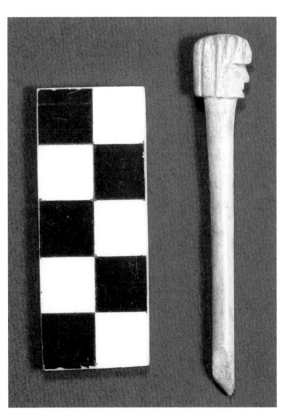

be a convenient place to establish a marketplace to serve the arriving pilgrims and other travelers. This is one of the few areas outside the temple where domestic architecture has not been encountered. Near the northwestern portion of this zone, Daniel Contreras (2010) found what appears to be a small ceremonial structure of the Kotosh Religious Tradition (KRT). I interpret it as a non-Chavín religious structure possibly built for visitors from the Callejón de Huaylas and other areas where these traditional highland ceremonial practices were still popular during the Early Horizon (Burger and Salazar 1985). This structure predates the open Janabarriu terraces, and little is known about the context of the small KRT building. It is possible that this structure was buried to create the open terraces, a space that would have been suitable as a marketplace, or alternatively, the marketplace could have already existed in this area and this KRT shrine could have been located adjacent to it. More research is needed in this zone to evaluate these admittedly speculative hypotheses.

Before ending this exploration of the idea of marketplace exchange in Chavín de Huántar during the first millennium BC, I would like to briefly mention one other line of relevant evidence. Beginning in the late Initial Period, roughly around the time of Chavín de Huántar's establishment, there is the first evidence for the use of llamas in long-distance transport. Harnessed llamas were left as offerings at the Templo de las Llamas at the Huaca Negra in the Virú Valley (Strong and Evans 1952); the animals are depicted on stirrup-spouted bottles recovered in North Coast cemeteries; and occasional llama bones have been found at North Coast sites such as Huaca Lucia (Shimada and Shimada 1985). More recently, analyses of faunal remains from Campanayuq Rumi, a Chavín ceremonial center near Vilcashuaman, Ayacucho, and excavated by Yuichi Matsumoto (2010), indicated that llamas were being herded by 1000 BC. This is germane because Campanayuq Rumi may have been pivotal in the acquisition and distribution of Quispisisa obsidian to Chavín de Huántar. This process would have been greatly facilitated by the existence of llama caravans traveling from the high grasslands of Ayacucho

during the first millennium BC (Browman 1974, 1975). The role of llama caravans organized by puna dwellers as a seasonal activity has been well documented ethnographically in southern Peru and northern Bolivia (e.g., Flores 1968; Tripcevich 2007), and pre-Hispanic versions of these camelid caravans may prove to be more relevant than the *mindalaes* of Ecuador and the *pochteca* of Mesoamerica for understanding exchange and market activity in the pre-Hispanic Andes.

As suggested at the outset of this chapter, the role of market exchange in the Central Andes is not a linear one. While there seems to be some evidence for market activity at Chavín de Huántar during the first millennium BC, there is equally convincing proof that this region of highland Ancash became increasingly isolated during the nine centuries after the collapse of the temple complex at Chavín de Huántar. Foreign items from the coast or other parts of the highlands are virtually absent at sites that belong to the Huarás and Recuay cultures during the terminal Early Horizon and the Early Intermediate Period. Obsidian completely disappears, as does coastal shell and fish bone (Burger, Lau, Ponte, and Glascock 2006; Lau 2005, 2010). No imported pottery from the coastal Salinar and Moche cultures has been encountered in the highland sites. The lack of access to exotics by any mechanism, market or otherwise, is exemplified by the local production of faux *Strombus* shell trumpets (*pututus*) made of ceramic.

It is not until the eighth century AD with the demise of Recuay and the subsequent expansion of Wari influence into the area that this insular pattern breaks down and foreign materials begin to appear again at both large and small sites (Burger, Lau, Ponte, and Glascock 2006; Lau 2005). This trend reaches its peak during the late Middle Horizon (AD 850–950), and Ruth Shady has suggested that the abundant ceramics and other exotics that appear at these sites may have more to do with increased market exchange than they do with a Wari conquest and/or state control (Shady 1988). But this apparent expansion of market activity was short lived. By AD 1000, the Callejón de Huaylas and the Callejón de Conchucos return to a state of relative isolation with little evidence of long-distance exchange or market activity during the poorly known Late Intermediate Period.

Final Remarks

To conclude, I would simply observe that the evidence from highland Ancash illustrates the danger of trying to essentialize the Central Andes as a nonmarket civilization based on the Inca case. The Central Andes saw the rise and fall of a multitude of civilizations, probably some with robust market activity and others with market activity reduced to a low level on a local scale. While powerful states and empires existed in the Central Andes long before the Incas, Tawantinsuyu may have been unusual or even unique in using state power to suppress market activity to the point where it was barely visible to Spanish invaders.

Acknowledgments

Special thanks to Kenneth Hirth and Joanne Pillsbury for encouraging my joint participation in the presentation with Enrique Mayer in the 2010 Dumbarton Oaks Pre-Columbian Studies symposium and for their willingness to allow us to divide the talk into two independent chapters for publishing purposes. I also appreciate comments on the manuscript by Ken Hirth, Jason Nesbitt, Joanne Pillsbury, Jeffrey Quilter, and Lucy Salazar, and the assistance on the maps from Christopher Milan. Finally, many of the ideas here came out of discussions with my friend Enrique Mayer.

REFERENCES CITED

Browman, David L.

1974   Pastoral Nomadism in the Andes. *Current Anthropology* 15(2):188–196.

1975   Trade Patterns in the Central Highlands of Peru in the First Millennium BC. *World Archaeology* 6(3):322–329.

Burger, Richard L.

1984   *The Prehistoric Occupation of Chavín de Huántar, Peru.* University of California Publications in Anthropology 14. University of California Press, Berkeley.

1985   Concluding Remarks: Early Peruvian Civilization and Its Relation to the Chavín Horizon. In *Early Ceremonial Architecture in the Andes*, edited by Christopher Donnan, pp. 269–289. Dumbarton Oaks Research Library and Collection, Washington, D.C.

1988   Unity and Heterogeneity within the Chavín Horizon. In *Peruvian Prehistory*, edited by R. W. Keatinge, pp. 99–144. Cambridge University Press, Cambridge.

1992   *Chavín and the Origins of Andean Civilization.* Thames and Hudson, London.

1998   *Excavaciones en Chavín de Huántar.* Fondo Editorial, Pontificia Universidad Católica del Perú, Lima.

2008   Chavín de Huántar and Its Sphere of Influence. In *Handbook of South American Archaeology*, edited by Helaine Silverman and William Isbell, pp. 681–703. Springer, New York.

Burger, Richard L., Frank Asaro, Paul Trawick, and Fred Stross

1998   The Alca Obsidian Source: The Origin of the Raw Material for Cuzco Type Obsidian Artifacts. *Andean Past* 5:185–202.

Burger, Richard L., Fidel Fajardo, and Michael D. Glascock

2006   Potreropampa and Lisahuacho Obsidian Sources: The Geological Origins of Andahuaylas A and Andahuaylas B Type Obsidians in the Province of Amaraes, Department of Apurimac. *Ñawpa Pacha* 28:109–127.

Burger, Richard L., and Michael D. Glascock

    2000   Locating the Quispisisa Obsidian Source in the Department of Ayacucho, Peru. *Latin American Antiquity* 11(3):258–268.

Burger, Richard L., George F. Lau, Victor Ponte, and Michael D. Glascock

    2006   The History of Prehispanic Obsidian Procurement in Highland Ancash. In *La complejidad social en la sierra de Ancash: Ensayos sobre paisaje, economía, y continuidades culturales*, edited by A. Herrera, C. Orsini, and K. Lane, pp. 103–120. Civiche Raccolte d'Arte Applicata del Castello Fozesco, Milan.

Burger, Richard L., and Ramiro Matos Mendieta

    2002   Atalla: A Center on the Periphery of the Chavín Horizon. *Latin American Antiquity* 13(2):153–177.

Burger, Richard L., and Lucy Salazar

    1985   The Early Ceremonial Center of Huaricoto: A Diachronic View. In *Early Ceremonial Architecture in the Andes*, edited by Christopher Donnan, pp. 111–138. Dumbarton Oaks Research Library and Collection, Washington, D.C.

Burger, Richard L., and Nicholaas van der Merwe

    1990   Maize and the Origin of Highland Chavín Civilization: An Isotopic Perspective. *American Anthropologist* 92(1):86–96.

Coleman, Simon, and John Elsner

    1995   *Pilgrimage: Past and Present*. British Museum Press, London.

Contreras, Daniel

    2010   A Mito-Style Structure at Chavín de Huántar: Dating and Implications. *Latin American Antiquity* 21(1):1–19.

Druc, Isabelle

    1998   *Ceramic Production and Distribution in the Chavín Sphere of Influence (North-Central Andes)*. BAR International Series 731. BAR, Oxford.

Druc, Isabelle, Richard L. Burger, Regina Zamojska, and Pierre Magny

    2001   Ancón and Garagay Ceramic Production at the Time of Chavín de Huántar. *Journal of Archaeological Science* 2(1):29–43.

Flores, Jorge

    1968   *Los pastores de Paratía: Una introducción a su estudio*. Instituto Indigenista Interamericano, Mexico City.

Grierson, Philip

    1977   *Origins of Money*. Athlone Press, London.

Hirth, Kenneth G.

    1998   The Distributional Approach: A New Way to Identify Marketplace Exchange in the Archaeological Record. *Current Anthropology* 39(4):451–476.

Hosler, Dorothy, Heather Lechtman, and Olaf Holm

    1990   *Axe-Monies and Their Relatives*. Dumbarton Oaks Research Library and Collection, Washington, D.C.

Lau, George F.

    2005   Core-Periphery Relations in the Recuay Hinterlands: Economic Interaction at Chinchawas, Peru. *Antiquity* 79:78–99.

    2010   House Forms and Recuay Culture: Residential Compounds at Yayno (Ancash, Peru), a Fortified Hilltop Town, AD 400–800. *Journal of Anthropological Archaeology* 29:327–351.

Lechtman, Heather

    1998   Examen técnico de un objecto de aleación de oro procedente de Chavín de Huántar. In *Excavaciones en Chavín de Huántar*, by Richard Burger, pp. 252–256. Fondo Editorial, Pontificia Universidad Católica del Perú, Lima.

Lumbreras, Luis G.

    1971   Towards a Re-evaluation of Chavín. In *Dumbarton Oaks Conference on Chavín*, edited by Elizabeth Benson, pp. 1–28. Dumbarton Oaks Research Library and Collection, Washington, D.C.

    2007   *Chavín: Excavaciones arqueológicas.* 2 vols. Universidad Alas Peruanas Press, Lima.

Matsumoto, Yuichi

    2010   The Prehistoric Ceremonial Center of Campanayuq Rumi: Interregional Interactions in the Peruvian South-central Highlands. PhD dissertation, Department of Anthropology, Yale University, New Haven.

Miller, George, and Richard L. Burger

1995   Our Father the Cayman, Our Dinner the Llama: Animal Utilization at Chavín de Huántar, Peru. *American Antiquity* 60(3):421–458.

Morris, Craig, and Julián Idilio Santillana

2007   The Inca Transformation of the Chincha Capital. In *Variations in the Expression of Inka Power*, edited by Richard L. Burger, Craig Morris, and Ramiro Matos Mendieta, pp. 135–163. Dumbarton Oaks Research Library and Collection, Washington, D.C.

Morris, Craig, and Donald Thompson

1985   *Huanuco Pampa: An Inca City and Its Hinterland*. Thames and Hudson, London.

Murra, John V.

1995   Did Tribute and Markets Prevail in the Andes before the European Invasion? In *Ethnicity, Markets, and Migration in the Andes: At the Crossroads of History and Anthropology*, edited by Brooke Larson and Olivia Harris, with Enrique Tandeter, pp. 57–72. Duke University Press, Durham, N.C.

Patterson, Thomas C.

1971   Chavín: An Interpretation of Its Spread and Influence. In *Dumbarton Oaks Conference on Chavín*, edited by Elizabeth Benson, pp. 229–248. Dumbarton Oaks Research Library and Collection, Washington, D.C.

1988   Merchant Capital and the Formation of the Inca State. *Dialectical Anthropology* 12:217–227.

1991   *The Inca Empire: The Formation and Disintegration of a Pre-Capitalist State*. Berg, New York.

Price, Martin

1983   Thoughts on the Beginning of Coinage. In *Studies in Numismatic Method Presented to Philip Grierson,* edited by C. N. L. Brooke, B. H. I. Stewart, J. G. Pollard, and T. R. Volk, pp. 1–10. Cambridge University Press, Cambridge.

Rick, John

2008   Context, Construction, and Ritual in the Development of Authority at Chavín de Huántar. In *Chavín: Art, Architecture,* *and Culture*, edited by William Conklin and Jeffrey Quilter, pp. 3–34. Cotsen Institute of Archaeology, University of California, Los Angeles.

Rostworowski de Diez Canseco, María

1970   Mercaderes del valle de Chincha en la época prehispánica: Un documento y unos comentarios. *Revista española de antropología americana* 5:135–177.

1975   Pescadores, artesanos y mercaderes costeños en el Perú prehispánico. *Revista del Museo Nacional* 41:311–351. Lima.

Rowe, John Howland

1946   Inca Culture at the Time of the Spanish Conquest. In *Handbook of South American Indians*, vol. 2, edited by Julian H. Steward, pp. 183–330. Cooper Square, New York.

Sallnow, Michael J.

1987   *Pilgrims of the Andes: Regional Cults in Cusco*. Smithsonian Institution Press, Washington, D.C.

Salomon, Frank

1977   Pochteca and Mindalá: A Comparison of Long-Distance Traders in Ecuador and Mesoamerica. *Journal of the Steward Anthropological Society* 9(2):231–246.

1986   *Native Lords of Quito in the Age of the Incas: The Political Economy of North Andean Chiefdoms*. Cambridge University Press, Cambridge.

Sayre, Matthew

2010   Life across the River: Agricultural, Ritual and Production Practices at Chavín de Huántar, Peru. PhD dissertation, Department of Anthropology, University of California, Berkeley.

Shady, Ruth

1988   La época Huari, como interracción de las sociedades regionales. *Revista andina* 6:67–99.

Shimada, Izumi

1985   Perception, Procurement, and Management of Resources: An Archaeological Perspective. In *Andean Ecology and Civilization*, edited by Shozo Masuda, Izumi Shimada, and Craig Morris, pp. 357–399. University of Tokyo Press, Tokyo.

Shimada, Melody, and Izumi Shimada

    1985   Prehistoric Llama Breeding and Herding on the North Coast of Peru. *American Antiquity* 50:3–26.

Silverman, Helaine

    1991   The Ethnography and Archaeology of Two Andean Pilgrimage Centers. In *Pilgrimage in Latin America*, edited by N. Ross Crumrine and Alan Morris, pp. 215–228. Greenwood Press, New York.

Stark, Barbara L., and Christopher P. Garraty

    2010   Detecting Marketplace Exchange in Archaeology: A Methodological Review. In *Archaeological Approaches to Market Exchange in Ancient Societies*, edited by Christopher P. Garraty and Barbara L. Stark, pp. 33–58. University of Colorado Press, Boulder.

Strong, William Duncan, and Clifford Evans

    1952   *Cultural Stratigraphy in the Viru Valley, Northern Peru: The Formative and Florescent Epochs*. Columbia University Studies in Archaeology and Ethnology 4. Columbia University Press, New York.

Trigger, Bruce

    2003   *Understanding Early Civilizations*. Cambridge University Press, Cambridge.

Tripcevich, Nicholas

    2007   Quarries, Caravans, and Routes to Complexity in the South-Central Andes. PhD dissertation, Department of Anthropology, University of California, Santa Barbara.

14

Exchange on the Equatorial Frontier

A Comparison of Ecuador and Northern Peru

JOHN R. TOPIC

A PROMINENT THEME OF THIS VOLUME IS the contrast between the more commercial economic systems characteristic of Mesoamerica and the more redistributive systems characteristic of the Central Andes. I explore that theme in microcosm by comparing the pre-Hispanic economic systems of Ecuador and northern Peru. These systems have been described by various scholars using slightly different but contrasting terms. Peru has been depicted as centralized and vertically oriented, with redistributive political economies striving for self-sufficiency. The literature on Ecuador stresses interdigitated economies linked by exchange relationships and markets where individual households have more responsibility for their own provisioning.

Richard Burger (2003:481) has commented on the distinctions between the regions and notes that there were already profound cultural, ideological, political, and economic differences by the end of the Formative Period. These differences were also recognized by Wendell Bennett (1948) in his definition

of the Peruvian co-tradition and are reflected in the boundaries that Gordon Willey (1971) defined for the Intermediate Area. They also underlay the creation of a separate Audiencia of Quito during the early colonial period and the establishment of Gran Colombia after the wars of independence.

The long-term distinctions between these areas imply the existence of a frontier (Hocquenghem et al. 1993) that deserves further study (Guffroy 2008; Montes Sánchez and Martínez Borrero 2010). Bennett (1948) drew the northern edge of the Peruvian co-tradition to include the Lambayeque complex of rivers in northern Peru and the adjacent highlands (Figure 14.1); this is some distance south of the present border. Anne-Marie Hocquenghem (1998) describes a frontier that moves gradually northward through time from a Formative Period location about where Bennett drew the line on his map to near the modern border between Ecuador and Peru by late pre-Incaic times.

The frontier was porous: people, raw materials, artifacts, and ideas moved across it via maritime

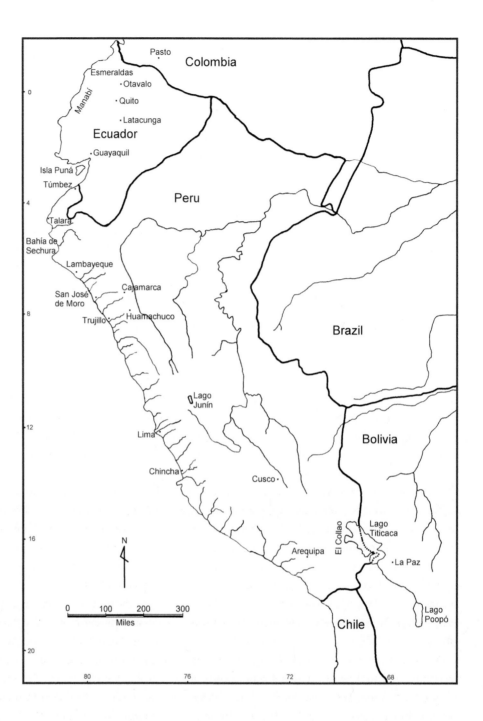

figure 14.1

A general map of
Peru and Ecuador
with some of the
locations mentioned
in this chapter
marked. (Drawing
by John Topic.)

or overland transport. But, as with many fron-
tiers, it was differentially porous. An interesting example is the trade in *Spondylus* shell from
Ecuador southward into the Andes but the complete lack of trade in obsidian. Burger et al. (1994)
have pointed to the fact that obsidian from mines
east of Quito was traded to the Ecuadorian coast,
near the modern border with Peru, while sites like
Pacopampa in the north Peruvian highlands were

supplied from mines in the central Peruvian highlands. Ecuadorian obsidian has not been found
in what is now Peruvian territory and vice versa.
Both *Spondylus* and obsidian are exotic processed
or semiprocessed materials with ritual and ceremonial importance (Blower 1996; Davidson 1981;
Paulsen 1974; Stothert 2003). The differential distribution can be partially explained by the fact that
Spondylus does not occur in the cold waters south

of Cabo Blanco (Carter 2008). On the other hand, areas of northern Peru could have been more efficiently supplied with obsidian from Ecuadorian sources than from the central Peruvian ones.

For decades, the literature has drawn a sharp distinction between a more commercial pattern of exchange in Ecuador—for example, Jacinto Jijón y Caamaño's (1988 [1941]) "league of coastal merchants"—and the administered exchange managed by the political elite in Peru (Murra 1980). By the 1970s, John Murra (1972; see also Mayer, this volume) had elaborated the idea of self-sufficient ethnic polities that directly exploited a range of resources by controlling productive zones distributed vertically across the Andes; the products from these diverse zones were then redistributed within the ethnic/political unit by its leader or lord. In contrast to Murra's model for Peru and Bolivia, Udo Oberem (1981 [1976]) presented a model for highland Ecuador that allowed for multiple modes of exchange. One of these modes involved semiautonomous elite exchange specialists, the *mindalaes*, whom Frank Salomon (1977–1978) described as being similar to the Aztec *pochteca* (see also Burger, this volume).

Murra (1971) called for an increased focus on trying to understand the means by which *Spondylus* shell was traded into the Central Andean area. At the same time, Rostworowski (1970, 1975, 1977a) had begun to contrast the economic organization of the Peruvian coast with the highland pattern described by Murra. She argued for much more occupational specialization on the coast and for the presence of exchange specialists, including long-distance traders based in the southern coastal valley of Chincha. She suggested that these traders might have been one link in the *Spondylus* trade. Jorge Marcos (1977–1978; Marcos and Norton 1981) then elaborated a stimulating model of maritime trade, centered on the movement of *Spondylus* through ports-of-trade in Ecuador, which joined cultures on the Pacific coast from Mesoamerica to Chincha. As Chantal Caillavet (2000a) has noted, however, these global theories often lacked substantive detail.

Instead of dealing in global models, I will focus on northern Peru and Ecuador to see where there are similarities and differences in exchange patterns. I

will focus on late pre-Incaic times (approximately AD 1000–1470), with a few comments on earlier developments. I am less interested in exchange between Peru and Ecuador than in comparing the economic patterns recognizable within each area. My main conclusion is that the differences across this frontier have been exaggerated. As Burger (this volume) comments, it is important not to essentialize the Inca. Hence, I will be trying to examine economic patterns in the period prior to the Inca expansion into northern Peru and Ecuador. I will draw on a combination of archaeological and historical data.[1]

The North Coast of Peru

Of the areas to be discussed, the best known during late pre-Incaic times is the North Coast of Peru, especially the section between the Lambayeque complex and the modern city of Trujillo (Figures 14.1–14.2). In this region, Mochica was spoken in the north and Quingnam in the south, with an area of overlap between the two languages (Netherly 2009). The distributions of these languages reflect different histories of development, which may affect the details of exchange relationships.

María Rostworowski's (1975, 1977a, 1977b) pioneering ethnohistorical work has provided a model of economic and political organization for the coast. The population was divided into *parcialidades* under the authority of a lord.[2] The *parcialidades* were characterized by occupational specialization, including farmers, fishermen, artisans, and maize-beer (*chicha*) brewers. The local documents repeatedly state that the *chicha* brewers did not grow maize, farmers did not fish, and fishermen did not farm (Netherly 1977, 1990). These specialized *parcialidades* were grouped into larger political units under ever more powerful lords whose success was judged by how well they managed the affairs of the polity, including the economy (Ramírez 1995b, 1996). A large polity might control resource zones extending from the ocean, several tens of kilometers inland, to the foothills of the Andes and would include many different *parcialidades* of specialists

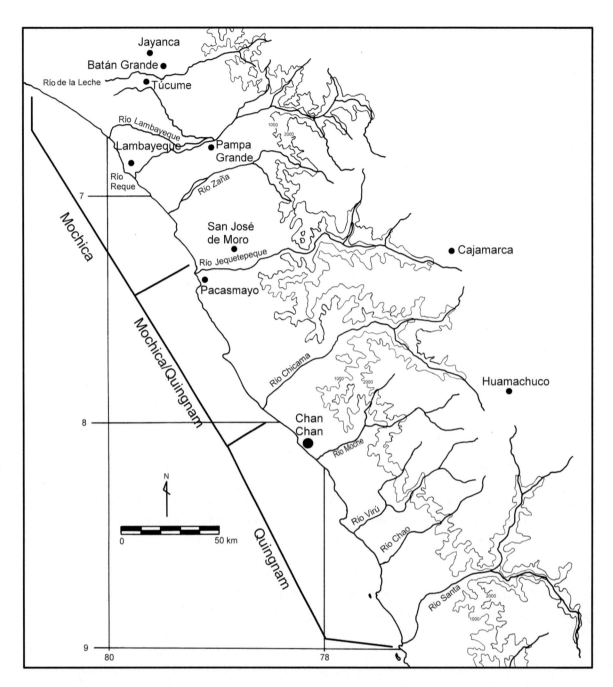

figure 14.2

The North Coast of Peru. The locations of sites mentioned in the chapter are given, as are the approximate distributions (after Netherly 2009) of some language groups. (Drawing by John and Theresa Topic.)

(Netherly 1977; Ramírez 1985; Ramírez Horton 1982; Shimada 1980, 1985).

The leaders of these polities could also diversify access to resources through what Tom Dillehay (1976, 1979, this volume) and Susan Ramírez (1985: 436) have termed resource sharing: one lord would delegate the use of resources under his control to another lord who would exploit those resources with the labor of his own subjects. In the colonial literature, these transactions are described in terms of one lord renting out lands to another for a portion of the harvest (Ramírez 1985, 1996).

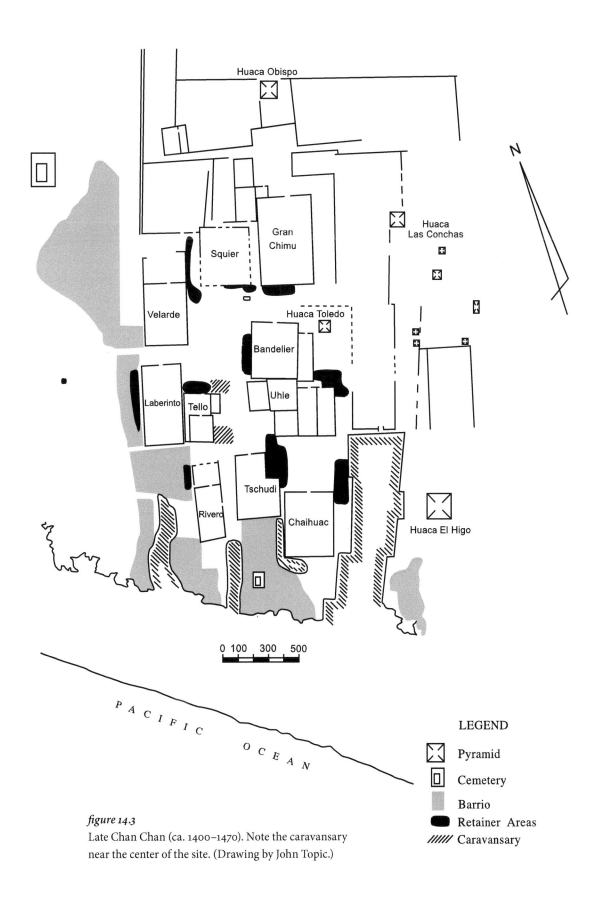

Huaca Obispo

Gran
Chimu

Squier

Huaca
Las Conchas

Velarde

Huaca Toledo

Bandelier

Uhle

Laberinto

Tello

Tschudi

Rivero

Chaihuac

Huaca El Higo

N

0 100 300 500

PACIFIC

OCEAN

LEGEND

Pyramid

Cemetery

Barrio

Retainer Areas

Caravansary

figure 14.3
Late Chan Chan (ca. 1400–1470). Note the caravansary
near the center of the site. (Drawing by John Topic.)

The lords managed the productive activities of their subjects; however, the extent to which the lords redistributed all the products of the specialized *parcialidades* is not entirely clear. Certainly, the lords sponsored *chicha* brewing and craft production in some cases (Topic 1990), but barter is also mentioned in colonial documents and most likely did take place between individuals and households. Merchants are also mentioned in colonial documents (Netherly 1977; Rostworowski 1977a, 1977b), but their presence may be due to the breakdown of the indigenous system under pressure from the colonial tribute regime and depopulation (Ramírez Horton 1982).

A well-documented case of the managed nature of North Coast economies is Chan Chan. This site, the capital of the Chimú kingdom, had at its height a population of about thirty thousand people (Topic and Moseley 1985) (Figure 14.3). In addition to residences of the kings and nobles, which incorporated large-scale storage facilities (Day 1982; Klymyshyn 1982), there were extensive areas containing the artisans' workshops and residences (Day 1982; Klymyshyn 1982; Topic 1982, 1990, 2009). These artisans, who may have numbered about six thousand households, were primarily engaged in metalworking and weaving; they received food and raw materials from the king's stores, and they had their products redistributed by the king's agents (Pozorski 1982; Topic 1990, 2009).

Raw materials, such as metal ingots and wool yarn, were brought into the site from the highlands by llama caravan. A caravansary was located near the center of the site; a small temple inside the caravansary contained sacrificed llamas, among other offerings. There were also corral-like areas, rooms with multiple sleeping benches, and a single large kitchen to serve the drovers. Exotic raw materials found in the caravansary included a macaw skeleton and *mishpingo* (*Nectandra* sp.) seeds—objects that suggest contact with the eastern slopes of the Andes—and a wool textile that was surely woven in the highlands (Topic 1977, 1990). While barter between households undoubtedly took place, the evidence is primarily for a redistributive economy

and administered exchange rather than for commercial exchange.

As the seat of the king's court, Chan Chan is an exception, as sites outside of the capital follow a different pattern. There is very little storage space at provincial sites and much less evidence for bureaucratic control (Topic 2003:268–270). The data suggest that lower-ranking lords would not have been able to sponsor the same concentration of artisans found at Chan Chan (Ramírez 1986:226–227; Topic 1990:170–171), and they might also have had difficulty accessing raw materials. Various sources for metals and other materials were available on the North Coast and in the highlands, however, and lords could obtain raw materials through resource sharing or other means. Arsenical copper ores were mined and smelted on the coast at Batán Grande (Shimada 1985; Shimada et al. 1983). The lord of Túcume had access to a silver mine in the highlands of Guambos (Netherly 1977:152), and fields there were worked by subjects of the lord of Jayanca (Ramírez 1985:426–428)—a case of resource sharing. Lords might also have administered trade with their counterparts in the highlands in order to access exotic materials (Netherly 1977).

A distinct ethnic group, located in the middle to upper valleys (*chaupiyungas*), may have served as intermediaries in this managed trade from an early date.[3] We located a site in the *chaupiyungas* zone of the Moche Valley, Cruz Blanca, dating to about 200 BC to AD 200, that had imported small decorated bowls from both the Callejón de Huaylas and Cajamarca (Topic and Topic 1983). These highland areas are not immediately adjacent to the Moche Valley, so the bowls were exchanged across some distance (Figure 14.4). We have argued that this exchange represents trade between independent groups rather than evidence for an archipelago-type example of highland colonies. The *chaupiyungas* zone would have been attractive to both coastal and highland people especially because of the ability to grow coca there. The *chaupiyungas* ethnic group was controlled by the Chimú during the Late Intermediate Period but was administered through the highlands under the Inca (Topic 1998).

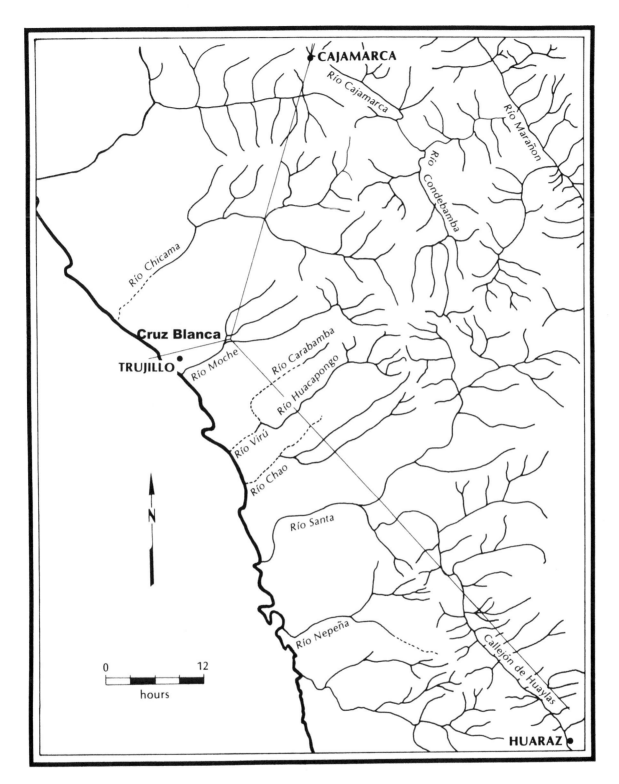

figure 14.4

Cruz Blanca as a floating node. The map has been transformed to reflect travel times rather than airline miles. The three lines, which join at 120-degree angles, are the shortest paths connecting the Moche Valley, the Callejón de Huaylas, and the Cajamarca area (after Topic and Topic 1983). (Drawing by John Topic.)

The Northern Peruvian Highlands

The northern highlands are best known from the Cajamarca and Huamachuco areas, adjacent to the coastal strip just discussed (Figure 14.5). These provinces seem to have spoken different languages, with Culli-speaking Huamachuco neighboring the Quingnam-speaking coastal area and the Den-speaking Cajamarca inland from the Mochica-speaking coastal area (Netherly 2009; Topic 1998; Torrero 1989).

The *chaupiyunga* population is well defined as a separate group in the Moche and Virú Valleys, west of Huamachuco. Ancient footpaths climb ridges from the *chaupiyungas* up into the cis-Andean highlands on the slopes west of the continental divide (Topic and Topic 1983). Chimú pottery is quite common on sites in these areas, the largest of which (e.g., Carpaico, Sulcha, Huasochugo, and Tantarica) tend to overlook the coast along the routes that descend down to the *chaupiyungas*. These large sites served as gateway

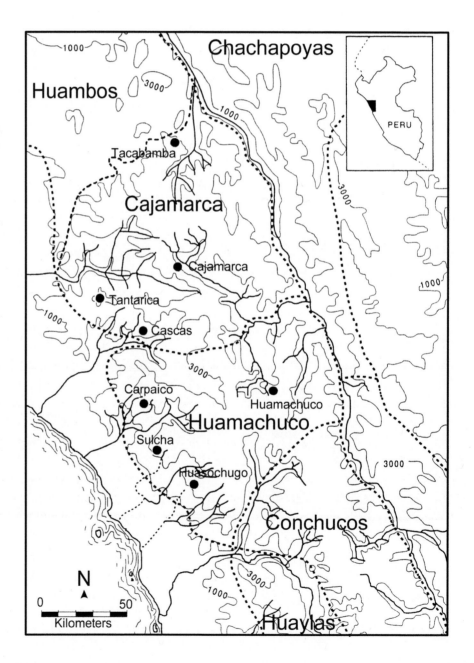

figure 14.5
The northern highlands of Peru, with the Incaic provinces as well as sites mentioned in the chapter. (Drawing by John Topic.)

communities into the highlands west of Cajamarca and Huamachuco (Coupland 1979; Hirth 1978; Jaeckel and Melly Cava 1987). In our experience in Huamachuco, Chimú ceramics are much less common across the continental divide, suggesting that the large sites on the western slopes mediated exchange with the coast in the Late Intermediate Period—and did so to their advantage.

There were several different mechanisms of exchange between the coast and the highlands. One involved reciprocal gift giving between the lords; for example, gifts or "rents" were given by coastal lords to their highland counterparts for water rights (Netherly 1977; Ramírez Horton 1982; Rostworowski 1992). Gift giving, however, probably did not secure the metal ingots and processed wool yarn used at Chan Chan. Since the control of labor was the fundamental basis of economic power in the pre-Hispanic Andes, it is important to understand how labor was mobilized to produce the materials and artifacts that were being exchanged within or between polities.

Labor and Exchange

The historical documents tell us that the lords had to request labor formally on each occasion and reciprocate with generosity, which meant offering, at least, large amounts of *chicha*. The labor was applied to a resource, generally agricultural land, but also mines. If fiber was provided, the labor to spin yarn and weave cloth could also be requested. Lords managed the work of their subjects in order to benefit the community; the importance of competent management is a recurring theme of political legitimacy (for an example from the North Coast, see Ramírez 1996:20–25).

In the example of artisanal production at Chan Chan, the king maintained a very large contingent of full-time specialists in his personal service (*yanakona*) by marshaling the labor of his agriculturalist and fisher subjects to produce the food to support them.[4] It is possible that some of the craft products were exported through administered exchange for raw materials from the highlands, while other products were probably given away to subordinate lords and subjects as an expression of generosity.

The parallel case would be for highland lords to mobilize the labor of their subjects to produce the raw materials in exchange for the finished products from the coast. The lords would then administer the exchange and control the redistribution of exchanged goods within their territories. This model fits well with the evidence of the caravansary in Chan Chan and the large cis-Andean gateway sites, especially in the western part of the Huamachuco province.

Another very different model was proposed by John Murra (1972) and documented in central and southern Peru. His vertical archipelago model proposes that polities or ethnic groups established colonies in different ecological zones in order to obtain direct access to the products of those zones. This direct access increased the self-sufficiency of the unit and decreased the economic interconnections between units. The vertical archipelago is usually associated with highland groups seeking lower-elevation lands in order to produce crops—such as *ají*, coca, and gourds—that cannot be grown at higher elevations. Highland colonies on the coast or in the *chaupiyungas* have not been documented archaeologically or ethnohistorically for this area of northern Peru.

An interesting variation on the theme of direct access, however, is represented by the cases of the aforementioned coastal lords who apparently had access to lands and mines in the highlands. Susan Ramírez (1985, 1996:16–20) has suggested that this is an example of resource sharing; in this case, labor is supplied by the coastal lords, who acknowledge the sovereignty of the highland lords by sharing part of the production. She draws on the distinction between *dominio directo* and *dominio útil* to explain that while one lord may "own" the resource, another may exploit it by applying the labor of his subjects to it (Ramírez 1985). She also notes that resource sharing might account for the pattern of discontinuous territoriality (*territorialidad discontinua*) that María Rostworowski (1992) had identified in the highlands of Cajamarca.

The evidence for discontinuous territoriality is found in the 1572–1578 *Visita* of Cajamarca (Remy 1992; Rostworowski 1992). To simplify the point greatly: subjects of one highland lord were enumerated as residents of towns in the core territories of other lords. It should be remembered that political units were defined more by the social relations of subject to lord than by the control of contiguous territory, so this could simply be a situation where a lord controlled a patchwork of territories (Rostworowski 1992); indeed, many of the subjects enumerated outside of their lords' core territories were located near the border areas between polities. Other subjects, however, resided in two settlements on the extreme northeastern and southwestern edges of the ethnic unit (Tacabamba and Cascas). As Pilar Remy (1992) notes, the concentration of the subjects of multiple lords into "frontier" settlements suggests strategic concerns, possibly involving interaction with the coast and the eastern slopes, respectively.

Two other distributions are interesting but difficult to explain with our current knowledge. In one case, patronyms in which the letter *F* occurs are found throughout the highland territory of Cajamarca (Rostworowski 1992). Rostworowski argues that the letter *F* only appears in coastal languages; hence, the presence of people with names including that letter indicates population movement into the highlands at an unspecified but pre-Incaic date. Although the names are scattered throughout Cajamarca, they are more common in the area along the northwestern margin.

The distribution of patronyms with the letter *F* is complemented by the dispersal of a pottery style called Coastal Cajamarca; Izumi Shimada (1980) dates its first appearance to about AD 700–750. The style was initially viewed as related to that of highland Cajamarca ceramics, but it is made in a different paste and is quite distinctive. Now, two substyles of Coastal Cajamarca are recognized: one style was made in the middle part (i.e., the *chaupiyungas* zone) of the Jequetepeque Valley (Luis Jaime Castillo Butters, personal communication 2010), while another was made in the Lambayeque area (Montenegro and Shimada 1998).

Coastal Cajamarca does not dominate at any site in the coastal zone but occurs mixed in tombs and in refuse, at times related to feasting, from at least the Jequetepeque Valley to the Lambayeque area (Julien 1993; Montenegro and Shimada 1998; Prieto Burmester et al. 2008; Shimada 1980).

All of these examples—the cases of coastal lords having access to highland resources, the patronyms with the letter *F*, the Coastal Cajamarca pottery, and the discontinuous territoriality of the highland *parcialidades*—are associated with the northern part of the region under discussion (that is, the Mochica-speaking area on the coast north of Pacasmayo, and Cajamarca and Guambos in the highlands). The impression I have is that there were somewhat different patterns of access to resources between this northern region and the southern one—the Quingnam-speaking coast near Trujillo and the adjacent highland Huamachuco area. In the southern region, centrally administered exchange may have taken place between groups that were more bounded territorially. In the northern region, lords may have had access to spatially dispersed resource zones, and those lords then exploited them by using the labor of their own subjects as well as by using centrally administered exchange between political units. In both areas, *chaupiyungas* populations may have acted as intermediaries between the coastal and highland groups.

Finally, Rostworowski (2009:345–347) urged archaeologists to look more closely at pilgrimage as a mechanism for the dispersal of ceramic styles and other exotic goods (see also Burger, this volume; Hartmann 1971). Theresa Topic and I have studied two pilgrimage sites in the Huamachuco area (Topic 2008; Topic and Topic 1992; Topic et al. 2002). Cerro Amaru, dating from the Early Intermediate Period and Middle Horizon, has abundant evidence for exotic materials, including imported ceramic styles, obsidian, and *Spondylus* shell, while the shrine of Catequil, a famous oracle dating from the Early Intermediate Period to the beginning of the colonial period, has very little in the way of exotic material. Hence, pilgrimage may at times be related to exchange, but exchange is not necessarily a concomitant of pilgrimage.

The Ecuadorian Highlands

As noted above, scholars working in the Ecuadorian Highlands have emphasized the lack of evidence for a Peruvian-style vertical archipelago model (Oberem 1981 [1976]:54; Salomon 1986). Instead, they have emphasized the multiplicity of different economic patterns at varying scales of interaction (Caillavet 2000c; Oberem 1981 [1976]; Salomon

1986). In general, political organization in the pre-Hispanic Ecuadorian Highlands was similar to that already discussed for Peru: political units were headed by lords who were owed service by their subjects in return for generosity in the form of feasts and the redistribution of some products.[5] The core territory of each unit was the area most heavily managed by the lord. In many cases, however, the lords also sponsored long-distance exchange specialists. The

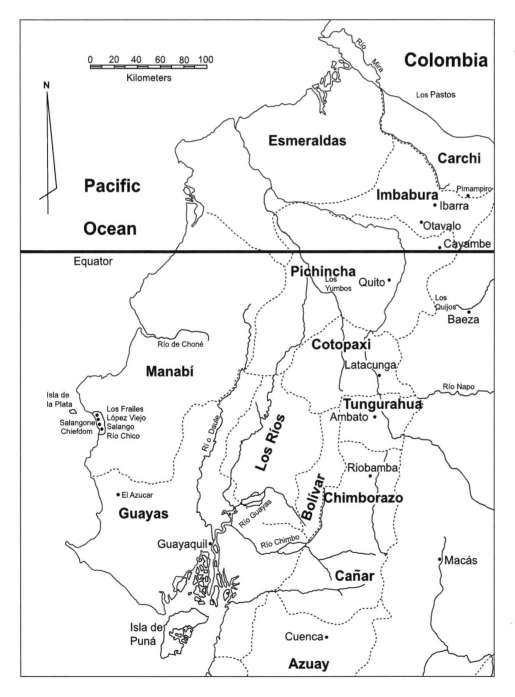

figure 14.6
Ecuador with the sites and areas mentioned in the chapter marked. (Drawing by John Topic.)

best-documented examples come from those areas where there was less Inca influence (i.e., northern Ecuador, from Latacunga into the Pasto territory of southern Colombia, and Quijos and Pimampiro to the east) (Figure 14.6). Specialized traders associated with marketplaces circulated elite goods such as coca, salt, cloth, medicinal plants, bead wealth, and gold between different political units and ethnic groups (Bray 1998, 2005; Hartmann 1971; Oberem 1974, 1981 [1976]; Salomon 1977–1978, 1986). Frank Salomon (1986) has made a strong argument that the marketplace in Quito, at least, was pre-Hispanic in date. Traders (*mindalaes*) administered this market and others in northern Ecuador and southern Colombia.

The *mindalaes*, in turn, were sponsored by lords who appropriated part of the goods traded in exchange for their sponsorship. In Ecuador, the *mindalaes* were only associated with the largest chiefdoms in each valley, whereas in southern Colombia almost all the communities had *mindalaes* (Salomon 1977–1978:236). The differences between the administered trade just discussed for northern Peru and the *mindalá* trade is, first, that the *mindalaes* engaged in trade on their own account as well as in the role of agents of the lord, and, second, that the *mindalaes* were associated with well-recognized marketplaces. In the case of the caravan drovers at Chan Chan, it seems clear that they were part of an exchange system administered by the lords, but it is unclear whether they could also trade on their own account or trade in established marketplaces (see Dillehay, this volume).

Microverticality was also practiced (Oberem 1981 [1976]), with individual households working fields within a day's walk of their community to produce such crops as maize, yucca, sweet potatoes, coca, cotton, *ají*, and fruits. A related activity was direct bartering between highland households and the neighboring Yumbos groups on the western slopes of the Andes (Lippi 1998; Salomon 1986), especially for salt, *ají*, and cotton.[6]

Less well understood, at least in terms of the extent to which we are dealing with a pre-Incaic pattern, is the use of *camayos* to farm fields or extract resources in nearby territories.[7] Salomon

(1986) feels that the use of *camayos* is probably an Inca introduction or that the pattern was intensified under the Inca. Noting that *camayos* were more common in areas that the Inca had already consolidated into the empire, Salomon (1986:111–114) relates the use of *camayos* to the development by the Inca of vertical archipelagos as defined by Murra (1972) for Peru and Bolivia. Oberem (1981 [1976]) notes that the phrase "from the time of the Inca," which is often found in documentary sources dealing with the *camayos*, could refer more generally to the pre-Hispanic past and not just the time of the Inca occupation. Certainly the term *camayos* occurs also in areas that were still in the process of consolidation (Borja 1992 [1591]), suggesting that the practice may predate the Inca occupation.

The *camayos* working lands in neighboring territories also had to farm for the host lord (Salomon 1986:112). This arrangement is similar to the accounts of Peruvian lords paying "rent" for access to fields outside their own territories. Although resident in a foreign territory, the *camayos* were counted as subjects of their lord of origin (i.e., the lord who sent them to work the fields) (Oberem 1981 [1976]:57). One of the more famous cases, but not the only example of this pattern, is the coca fields at Pimampiro in northern Ecuador. These were exploited in part by the Pastos who had permanent residents in Pimampiro to cultivate the fields and by other Pastos who came to help with the harvest. It is said that the local lords did not have to cultivate the coca with their own people because they had this other source of labor. Other outsiders—from Otavalo, Caranque, and even Latacunga—also exploited the coca at Pimampiro. Coca was traded for silver, gold, cloth, pigs, and sheep (Borja 1992 [1591]:481–482, 486; Oberem 1981 [1976]:56), and this trade could involve the *mindalaes*. Although Salomon (1986:191, 198–200, 211) believes that the *camayo* pattern was either an Inca introduction or was intensified by the Inca, he considers the practice of sharing part of the crop with the host lord to be indigenous and pre-Inca. This is a point that I wish to emphasize since it is similar to the pattern of resource sharing that was discussed for the Lambayeque and Cajamarca areas in northern Peru.

In some cases, *camayos* from multiple ethnic groups were exploiting resources within the same area (Oberem 1981 [1976]:55; Salomon 1986:112). In the Pimampiro region, Tamara Bray (2005) has documented archaeologically the presence of a multiethnic community at the site of Shanshipampa. While she notes that the site satisfies three of the five criteria for a port-of-trade (2005:137), she concludes that the model of a multiethnic community of *camayos*, as described by Borja (1992 [1591]), may offer a better interpretive model. In another case, salt was processed by a multiethnic enclave at Mira, close to Pimampiro (Caillavet 2000c). The salt source was "owned" by the Otavalos and exploited directly by them via microverticality; however, it was also exploited by *camayos* from all over the Quito province, and they paid two pesos plus part of the salt produced in "rent" during the colonial period. The salt was also traded by *mindalaes*, reminding us that several different mechanisms were used to extract and circulate the same resource in the Ecuadorian Highlands.

Chaquira, or bead wealth, was certainly traded by the *mindalaes*, but there is no indication that it was used by them as currency (Oberem 1981 [1976]:59, 62; Salomon 1986:94; Wassen 1955). There appear to have been several different types of bead wealth in circulation, and Chantal Caillavet (2000a) has helped to clarify some of the confusion surrounding the different types. First, the term *chaquira* may be of Panamanian origin (Caillavet 2000a:87). In Gonzalo Fernández de Oviedo y Valdés's *Historia general de las Indias* (ca. 1535–1557), which provides a description of the first encounter by the Spanish with a balsa raft manned by indigenous sailors off the coast of Manta, the term *chaquira* is used to describe the strings of shell beads that were one of the objects of trade carried by the raft (as cited in Holm 1988 [1981]; Jijón y Caamaño 1988 [1941]). Oviedo compares them to beads from the Canary Islands that the Portuguese used in the African trade. Indeed, glass beads were introduced to Ecuador early in the colonial period, and they were quickly adopted by indigenous people and are found in early colonial tombs in the Milagro-Quevedo area (Holm 1983:27). These glass versions were also referred to

as *chaquira*, and Caillavet cautions us to be careful not to confuse these with the *chaquira de la tierra* (Holm 1983:87–88), which consisted of various materials including gold, silver, stones, insects, and shell (Caillavet 2000a:87–88; Salomon 1986:90–92).

For the most part, it is not clear whether there was standardization within the classes of *chaquira*, something one might expect in a primitive money. For the Quijos area on the eastern slopes of the Andes, a variant, known as *carato*, may have been somewhat standardized. *Carato* were strings consisting of twenty-four beads of red and white "bone" (*hueso*) (Oberem 1981 [1976]:62). Caillavet notes that in the sixteenth century the term *hueso* could be used to describe any hard organic matter; the *carato* might actually have been made of *Spondylus* shell. During the colonial period, *carato* was valued at the equivalent of one day's work, one night with a woman, or one tomín (Oberem 1981 [1976]:62). The Quijos paid their tribute in *carato* in 1604 (Oberem in Salomon 1986:91).

In another case, Don Diego Collín left two strings of "chaquira de la tierra" (the material is not specified) in his will so that masses would be recited for his soul. He also left eight other strings to his direct heirs to be worn during fiestas, "as is the custom among lords" ("como es costumbre entre curacas") (Caillavet 2000b:447). The *chaquira* are included in the same section of the will as tapestry (*cumbi*) tunics, feather cloth, and drinking cups. The Collín example indicates both that *chaquira* had a commercial value during the colonial period (i.e., they could be converted to money to pay for the masses) and that they were accumulated by lords and worn as personal ornaments appropriate to the chiefly office (Salomon 1986:124). *Chaquira* were clearly valued, but the indigenous value may have been more associated with the insignia of chiefly status.

The Ecuadorian Coast

More than any other area in the Andean region, the Ecuadorian coast has been characterized as a center of commerce. A very brief report by the Spanish official Bartolomé Martín de Carranza (1992 [1569]:70) mentions a town called Siscala in Esmeraldas province. Carranza, who does not appear to have actually visited Siscala himself, described the town as a free-trade area, where the neighboring groups, even though at war with each other, would go in peace to trade salt, fish, clothing, and cotton.

Even more famous is Salangone (Calangome, Çalangone), the area from which the balsa raft captured by Bartolomé Ruiz in 1526 came. The most reliable account of this raft and its contents is the Samano-Xerez version, which has been published numerous times (Caillavet 2000a includes a transcription of part of the account). The raft was carrying merchandise—gold and silver jewelry, cloth and clothing, drinking cups and other items manufactured in Salangone—to exchange for seashells, most likely *Spondylus*. Caillavet (2000a:92) points out that there is no reason to believe, on the basis of the account itself, that the balsa was involved in anything more than local trade up and down the coast to obtain shells from fishing villages.

Jacinto Jijón y Caamaño reviewed these two accounts and noted that early descriptions of the people up and down the coast, from Esmeraldas to perhaps the Isla de Puná, portrayed a relatively homogenous culture (1988 [1941]:114–119). Based on this limited evidence, he characterized the population as a league of merchants, an interpretation that is still widely accepted (Marcos 1977–1978; Marcos and Norton 1981:149; Norton 1988 [1985]; cf. Damp and Norton 1987).

All the artifact types described on the raft have been found archaeologically in the area (Holm 1988 [1981]:179–181), but the *Spondylus* has attracted the most attention. There is abundant evidence for working the shell in late pre-Hispanic sites along the coast, but the industry was abruptly interrupted by the Spanish conquest (Norton 1988 [1985]:269). As Caillavet (2000a:91) points out, the information about Salangone is largely based on just the Samano-Xerez account, and that description is based on hearsay from the three indigenous sailors who were taken onto the Spanish craft rather than on direct observation by Bartolomé Ruiz or the other Spaniards.

Spondylus was made into beads, among other uses. Tombs on the Ecuadorian coast have large quantities of the beads (Holm 1988 [1981]:179), and strings of them are one of the forms of *chaquira* mentioned previously. The area of Salangone has been investigated, and four large urban sites have been identified: Salango, Puerto López, Machalilla, and Agua Blanca (Norton 1988 [1985]:268).

Studies of these sites and others (Carter 2008; Currie 1995; Holm 1988 [1981]; Marcos and Norton 1981; Masucci 1995; Mester 1985) have found abundant evidence for working shell—*Spondylus* in particular, but also others such as mother of pearl (*Pinctada mazatlanica* and *Pteria sterna*). A recent comparative study by Alexander Martín (2010) points out that shell working takes place in domestic contexts on the coast of Ecuador. The shell remains included species involved in the export trade and mollusks consumed as part of the subsistence diet. This observation supports Maria Masucci's (1995:78–80) interpretation of shell working as a part-time, nonspecialized, and informally organized industry. Martín (2010) characterizes shell working as low intensity, but large scale, since it involved a substantial proportion of the population.

Masucci studied the site of El Azúcar, located some twenty-five kilometers from the coast. She (1995:78) suggests that the shells were obtained from coastal villages through informal trade, which would mean a form of down-the-line trade, with processing taking place at a number of points along the line. Alternatively, material from different localities might have been accumulated at a port-of-trade, like Siscala, where it could be acquired by *mindalaes*. For Siscala, however, we have only the very brief documentary account by Carranza mentioned above. Marcos and Norton (1981) had argued that Isla de la Plata served as a port-of-trade for the export of shells and shell artifacts to Peru in part through the Chincha merchants discussed below. That interpretation has been critiqued by Damp and Norton (1987), who now consider Isla de la Plata to be a ritual site visited periodically rather than a permanently occupied port-of-trade.

Shell working has also been documented for North Coast sites in Peru, such as Cabeza de

Vaca, Rica Playa, Túcume, and Pampa Grande (Heyerdahl et al. 1996; Hocquenghem and Peña Ruiz 1994; Shimada 1980). Such locations might again suggest down-the-line trade into Peru, but the Chimú state might also have administered the exchange into its territory. *Spondylus*, especially, was very closely associated with Chimú kingship, and securing the supply line might have been one motive for imperial expansion northward (Netherly 2009; Pillsbury 1996). The trade in *Spondylus,* including both whole shells and worked pieces, from Ecuador to the North Coast of Peru expanded greatly during Sicán (Lambayeque) and Chimú times (AD 900–1470) (Carter 2008; Netherly 2009; Pillsbury 1996; Shimada 1985).

Maritime Trade

There has been considerable debate about the role of balsa rafts in moving *Spondylus* down the coast (see also Burger, this volume). Rostworowski (1970) proposed that merchants in Chincha, a valley south of Lima, used balsa rafts to trade to Ecuador. Her argument was based on a sixteenth-century document referred to as the *Aviso*, whose author is unknown. The *Aviso* purports to give a brief description of Chincha as it was at the time of the founding of Lima in 1534. It says that there were thirty thousand tribute-paying men of whom twelve thousand were agriculturalists, ten thousand were fishermen, each with a balsa, and six thousand were merchants (it is unclear who the other two thousand were). The merchants were quite wealthy and traveled from Chincha to Puerto Viejo in Ecuador. From Ecuador they brought gold beads and emeralds back to Peru.[8] They used copper money to buy and sell, and they also had scales to weigh gold and silver.

Ramírez (1995a:140, 156–157n16) pointed out that the *Aviso* (which may date to 1575 or 1585–1586) is the later of two documents that deal with the Chincha Valley. The earlier description of Chincha, the *Relación de Chincha* (Castro and Ortega Morejón 1974 [1558]), makes no mention of merchants, commerce, or seagoing trade. On the other

hand, Rostworowski (1977b:253) also cites the 1534 *encomienda*[9] grant of the indigenous population of Chincha to Hernando Pizarro along with "the traders and silversmiths that they have outside of their territory" (translation by the author). I would add that the *Aviso* specifies that the fishermen had balsas, but it does not mention balsas in conjunction with the merchants. Indeed, the way that the trade is described suggests an overland route ("they went from Chincha to Cuzco and through all of Collao, and others went to Quito and to Puerto Viejo" [Rostworowski 1970:171; translation by the author]). According to Bernabé Cobo (1990 [1653]:236), the people on the Peruvian coast did not use the balsa log rafts, but rather reed balsas of which he specifies two different sizes: one capable of holding one or two people and the other, larger one, capable of carrying a dozen people (Pillsbury 1996:329). Although models of log rafts are found in tombs on the South Coast of Peru and in northern Chile, the paddles are double-bladed (like kayak paddles), indicating that the pilot of the raft sat astride it (Bird 1943); these were not models of the large Ecuadorian sailing rafts.

It is also very difficult to sail south from Ecuador against the prevailing winds and currents (Borah 1954; Hocquenghem 1993). Artifacts found in the Galápagos Islands indicate that pre-Hispanic navigators reached those islands, but Holm (1988 [1981]) considers these remains to be the result of ephemeral occupations by people blown off course. Hocquenghem (1993; see also Edwards 1965) observes that balsa sailing technology changed and improved after contact, as new rigging allowed for better sailing against the currents. Even in 1820, sailing south to Paita and Sechura was common, but noteworthy, and sometimes the rafts reached as far as Pacasmayo, on the North Coast of Peru. The balsas that traveled to Paita, Sechura, and Pacasmayo were smaller than those navigating between Guayaquil and Tumbes, and were rigged differently (Baleato 1988 [1820]:102). Clinton Edwards (1965:113) felt that if certain wooden implements from Ica turned out not to be daggerboards, then the pre-Hispanic distribution of sailing rafts was probably only along the Manabí coast and southward to Sechura; D. Peter Kvietok (1987) has studied these wooden implements and considers them to be agricultural tools rather than daggerboards.

Axes, Axe-Monies, and *Naipes*

Related to both *chaquira* and to the possible role of sailing rafts for long-distance exchange are the so-called axe-monies. These thin axe-shaped objects were 6.5 to 8.9 centimeters high and were made of copper-arsenic alloy sheet metal (Hosler et al. 1990). Axe-monies are related to axes, which are much larger (some are nearly forty centimeters in height) cast objects found in large numbers in tombs in the southern Ecuadorian Highlands. These axes seem to have been symbolic as well as functional. Some of them may have served as functional axes at some point, but others did not show use wear. Regardless of their use as tools, they would certainly have been a source of metal wealth buried with elite individuals (Hosler et al. 1990:51). Lope de Atienza (1931 [1572–1575]; see also Hosler et al. 1990:52; Salomon 1986:92–93) also describes axes as bride wealth.

What are referred to as axe-monies, however, are quite distinct from axes. These small, thin objects are found stacked and in packets in tombs on the coast and in the Guayas Basin and down into Peru as far as Talara. There are a number of different types of axe-monies as well as variants, including "feathers" and *naipes* found in Ecuador and Peru. The *naipes* (so called because they resemble playing cards in shape) are confined essentially to the Lambayeque area in northern Peru, where they have been found in large numbers at the site of Batán Grande (Shimada 1980, 1985). The feathers (so called for their plume shape) are found both in the Lambayeque area and in Los Ríos province in Ecuador (Hosler et al. 1990:22). All of these objects were made of copper-arsenic bronze, and they are very thin (less than 0.12 centimeter). They were bundled into packets of five, ten, twenty, etc., and placed in graves, often in great quantities.

The naipes from the Lambayeque area date to the Middle Sicán period (AD 900–1050), possibly

slightly earlier than the Ecuadorian axe-monies discussed above. Because the axe-monies, *naipes*, and feathers all go out of use before the Conquest, we do not have any Spanish observations on their function. Hosler et al. (1990:67) point out that the *naipes*, since they are limited to a single valley, cannot be considered a medium of exchange between northern Peru and the Ecuadorian coast. I would add that if we just focus on Ecuador rather than the possible connection between Ecuador and Mesoamerica, then the distribution of axe-monies is essentially limited to the Manteño-Huancavilca and Milagro-Quevedo culture areas. Axe-monies are not found farther south than Talara, so they were not part of the possible Chincha trade, nor were they found in the highlands, so they were not part of the *mindalá* trade.

I agree with Hosler et al. (1990:67) that the *naipes* were grave wealth, much like the larger axes just mentioned for the southern highlands of Ecuador. As Lechtman (1981:96–97) has pointed out, copper-arsenic digging stick points and other large repositories of metal also occur on the North Coast in caches or hoards. While the *naipes* are reported only for the Lambayeque area, these other objects are reported as far south as the Moche Valley. The *naipes* probably did not function as a medium of exchange, and it is unlikely that the Ecuadorian axe-monies functioned in any way like a primitive currency. Arguments for their status as money are circumstantial, related to their role in possible trade to Mexico and the possible use of *chaquira* as currency. There is continuity between the contexts in which we find hoards of axe-monies, axes, and digging stick points, however. Many became grave goods, whether they were used at one point or not, and they were certainly a form of accumulating wealth.

There is also continuity between the bundling of axe-monies in sets of five, ten, twenty, and larger groups of round numbers, and the earlier Moche practice of burying offerings (*ofrendas, crisoles*) in tombs, usually in sets of five, ten, twenty, or other round numbers. *Ofrendas* are small, crudely made pots that were either unused or only slightly used and found in large numbers in burials (Costin 1999; Donnan 2009; Rengifo et al. 2008).[10] Christopher

Donnan, the first to note the pattern of offerings in round numbers, sees a similar pattern in objects of gold, silver, and copper, as well as decorative motifs and architectural elements in clusters of five and ten (Donnan 2009:177–178). He notes that this pattern occurs at a limited number of sites from the Jequetepeque Valley north to the Piura Valley (Donnan 2009:178).

Conclusions

As noted above, over the years scholars have compared and contrasted the economies of pre-Hispanic Peru and Ecuador. When comparisons are drawn between Ecuador and the Inca state, or between Ecuador and more southerly parts of Peru (see chapters by Goldstein, Nielsen, and Stanish and Coben in this volume), the differences in economic practice and organization are marked. But this chapter's comparison of Ecuador with northern Peru has not surprisingly found significant continuities and similarities between the two areas.

The pattern of resource sharing documented for the Lambayeque area, Cajamarca, and Guambos has many similarities to the pattern of *camayo* exploitation present in highland Ecuador. In both cases, the subjects of one lord are involved in productive activities away from their core territories and share the results of production with the host lords. Although the Spaniards characterized the exchange as rent, it is better to describe the relationship as one of resource sharing, in which the host allows the resource to be exploited by subjects of another lord. In this sense, Murra's (1980) often emphasized point—that lords only ask for the labor of their subjects and that subjects do not pay tax in kind—fits both cases.

The Moche practice of providing *ofrendas* in sets of five, ten, and twenty, and other larger groups of round numbers may well be the precedent for bundling Lambayeque *naipes* in similar sets. Rather than commercial transactions, both practices are best seen as related to death and burial. Ecuadorian axe-monies, in turn, are related to the Lambayeque *naipes*. Again, the context in which

these objects are found indicates that they were part of burial practice. If they circulated as a form of primitive money, it was within a relatively small area; however, I see no evidence that they circulated as currency.

Unlike axe-monies, *chaquira* made of shell continued to circulate in the colonial period and, at least in Quijos, seem to have been standardized in form and have had a recognized exchange value. In other cases, it is uncertain whether the *chaquira* mentioned in documents were made of gold, *Spondylus*, or imported glass beads, and more effort must be made to clarify the type of *chaquira* described. It is clear, however, that *chaquira* were associated with status and, in highland Ecuador at least, were part of chiefly accoutrements along with fine tapestry tunics and special drinking cups. Feathers, variants of axe-monies and *naipes*, may have had a similar role in chiefly regalia, perhaps as head ornaments, before they were buried in tombs.

The argument for ports-of-trade in coastal Ecuador rests on one sentence describing the town of Siscala. The evidence for a league of merchants is strongly tied to the description of one balsa raft from 1526. On the one hand, these observations are potential glimpses of indigenous institutions that had not yet been modified by the Spanish occupation, tribute extraction, and demographic collapse. On the other hand, in 1526, Spaniards had no context in which to understand these observations, and their reports were not followed in later years by more detailed descriptions of an indigenous merchant enterprise along the coast. Balsa rafts, critical for large-scale coastal trade, are well documented for the coast of Ecuador, including the Gulf of Guayaquil and the Isla de Puná, but their role in trade to the south into Peru beyond Sechura is not, in my opinion, well documented for the pre-Hispanic period.

Trade in *Spondylus* is very well documented in both Ecuador and Peru. It is likely that a number of different modes of production and exchange were involved in different places (Carter 2008). We have some images of the harvesting of the shells (Pillsbury 1996), but we do not know much about the motivations or organization of the divers. In

Ecuador, shell processing may have been organized as a household activity, while in Peruvian sites like Túcume and Pampa Grande, there is more direct evidence for elite sponsorship. *Mindalaes* certainly were involved in the transport and exchange process in Ecuador; transport into Peru may have been at least in part organized as administered exchange.

The site of Chan Chan provides a good example of what a centralized, redistributive economy looks like archaeologically: large storage capacity, craft production sponsored by the lord, provision of food and raw materials from the lord's resources to the artisans, and redistribution of their products. In this case, however, the city was essentially an extension of the king's household, and the artisans served him full-time (*yanakonas*) (Topic 2009). It is not clear that all goods from the specialists—be they farmers, fishermen, or brewers—were redistributed directly by the lords; some barter undoubtedly took place. There seems to have been no standard of exchange for products in the pre-Hispanic period: even in the 1560s, indigenous people petitioned the Spanish officials for a standard exchange rate to be set for maize and fish (Ramírez Horton 1982:129).

In contrast, highland Ecuador provides a good example of what a decentralized resource procurement situation looks like: individual households were responsible for more of their own domestic economy, but the lord facilitated the importation of exotic and luxury goods and redistributed some commodities. The lord could draw on the collective labor of his subjects as well as on that of a large household that included multiple wives and large numbers of personal retainers (*yanakona*) (Salomon 1986:127–131). Markets were more formalized and were served by specialist traders who were sponsored by the highest-ranking lords. Still, the evidence suggests a low level of commercialization, as defined by Michael Smith (2004:79), and there is only limited evidence for a standard medium of exchange (i.e., primitive money). Exchange in the marketplace was by barter (Hartmann 1971; see also Stanish and Coben, this volume).

This chapter has attempted to review in detail pre-Hispanic Ecuador and northern Peru,

essentially four relatively large and complex regions, yet much information has had to be presented in a very cursory manner or left out completely. The comparison of economic organization across these areas, however, even in a somewhat perfunctory fashion, stimulates some new interpretive perspectives and questions. As noted in the introduction, Hocquenghem (1998) has described the frontier between the areas as gradually moving northward through time. While that may be a Peruvianist perspective, another way of characterizing the process is simply one of increasing integration across the area. This is especially demonstrated by the increasing trade in *Spondylus* and the similarities between *naipes* and axe-monies. Indeed, the differences outlined above between the Lambayeque coast and Cajamarca highland areas, and the Moche Valley coast and Huamachuco highland areas, if borne out, could suggest a southward movement of a frontier, where Cajamarca and Lambayeque are benefiting from their intermediary status in the exchange process.

In the same way, but on a smaller scale, the *chaupiyungas* and west-slope groups in northern Peru and the Yumbos and Quijos in Ecuador seem to have benefited from their status as intermediaries in exchange processes. Those processes may have included resource sharing, direct barter, administered trade, and specialized trader exchange, depending on the time and the place. It might be fruitful to compare sites like Shanshipampa to the towns in Cajamarca with mixed populations, especially Cascas and Tacabamba. Are sites on the western slopes of Huamachuco, such as Carpaico, Cerro Sulcha, and Huasochugo—sites that seem to serve as gateway communities—different from Shanshipampa only, or mainly, because they are not multiethnic? Finally, why did *Spondylus* move so readily across the Ecuador-Peru frontier, particularly in later periods, while obsidian did not? As noted in the introduction, both were widely traded and had ritual significance. Is it a matter of ecology? *Spondylus* is not available south of Cabo Blanco so it had to be imported into Peru, whereas obsidian sources were relatively abundant across the Andean region. Or is it a matter of trade preference shifting over time? Does the trade in obsidian decline as the trade in *Spondylus* increases? Or do changes in exchange routes, such as a shift to more coastal trade, benefit the exchange of *Spondylus* more than obsidian?

Archaeology and ethnohistory have advanced our understanding of the dynamic economic systems that characterized the diverse polities and ethnic groups of the more northerly expanses of the Central Andes in late prehistory and in the first decades after the Spanish conquest. As I have endeavored to document in this chapter, there is an increased awareness of intriguing similarities in many aspects of production and exchange across these wide regions. Full explanation of these commonalities will require renewed focus on this important realm of social life, and I expect there will be stimulating new research on pre-Hispanic economics in both Ecuador and northern Peru in the next few years.

NOTES

1 I am well aware that the historical data are colonial in date, that culture is not static, and that it is difficult to project historical information into the prehistoric past. I have tried to be judicious in my use of the historical material. Many of the authors cited in this paper have wrestled with this same problem (e.g., Bray 2005; Julien 1993; Lippi 1998; Netherly 1977; Rostworowski 1970, 1992; Salomon 1986; Topic 1998; Topic et al. 2002).

2 *Parcialidad* is a Spanish term that, in the sense used here, indicates part of a larger sociopolitical unit. It is sometimes used in a manner equivalent to moiety, lineage, or census units of one hundred or one thousand families. A *parcialidad* connotes a community at least partially integrated by ties of kinship with a leader (though not necessarily a high-ranking leader); its members might not all reside in a single settlement (see Rostworowski 1981).

3 The term *chaupiyungas* (as also the terms *quechua* and *yungas*) can refer both to an ecological zone (see Dillehay, this volume) and to the people inhabiting that zone. I am using the term in both senses.

4 Although *yanakona* is a Quechua word (plural of *yana*), John Rowe (1948:47) pointed out that the word *yaná* existed in the Muchic (Mochica) language and referred to domestic servants; he suggested that "it is quite possible that the Incas borrowed the idea of a social class of public servants from a similar institution in the Kingdom of Chimor." I have recently argued that the status of the artisans at Chan Chan was, indeed, similar to that of the Inca *yanakona* (Topic 2009:239–240).

5 On the nature of political units in the Ecuadorian Highlands, see Salomon (1986:ch. 5); he (1986:117–122) also provides a preliminary demographic analysis for the populations subject to individual chiefs in the Quito area. He characterizes these polities as smaller, though not necessarily less complex or less centralized, than those just discussed for the northern Peruvian highlands. Bray (2008) groups these individual chiefdoms into larger "ethno-political" units that are more similar to Incaic provinces in northern Peru.

6 Salomon (1986:241) defines Yumbo as a "member of an ethnic and perhaps linguistic group inhabiting the western slopes of the Andes near Quito."

7 The term *camayo* (plural *camayos*) is Hispanicized from Quechua and generally used to designate a specialist (a *quipu camayoc* keeps the knotted string records; a *coca camayoc* cultivates coca; a *cumbi camayoc* weaves the finest grade of cloth). In historical documents from the Ecuadorian Highlands, however, the term refers to families who cultivated products or produced salt at some distance from the home territory of their lord. This usage varies from the Central Andean norm since they had to pay tribute to both their home lord and their host lord. Their production was in part distributed by their home lord and in part bartered by the families themselves.

8 Hocquenghem (1993:705–707) notes that the *Aviso* mentions emeralds and *chaquira* of gold, rather than *Spondylus*. In fact, very little *Spondylus* has been found in Chincha (Sandweiss 1992:142).

9 *Encomienda*, as it applies here, was a colonial institution. An *encomienda* was a grant to the *encomendero* (grantee) of the right to extract tribute from a specific group of indigenous people. The *encomendero* was usually a Spaniard, but there were also indigenous *encomenderos*. The *encomendero* was obliged to provide military service to the crown and to ensure the conversion of the indigenous population to Catholicism.

10 Costin (1999), noting that *ofrendas/crisoles* are not always found in round numbers, suggests that they may represent the offerings of individuals attending the burial ceremony.

REFERENCES CITED

Atienza, Lope de

1931   Compendio historial del estado de
[1572–1575]   los indios del Perú. In *La religión del imperio de los Incas, Apendices, I*, edited by Jacinto Jijón y Caamaño, pp. 1–235. Escuela Tipográfica Salesiana, Quito.

Baleato, Andrés

1988 [1820]   Monografía de Guayaquil. In *La balsa en la historia de la navegación ecuatoriana: Compilación de crónicas, estudios, gráficas y testimonios*, edited by Jenny Estrada, pp. 98–105. Instituto de Historia Marítima, Guayaquil.

Bennett, Wendell C.

1948   The Peruvian Co-tradition. In *A Reappraisal of Peruvian Archaeology*, edited by Wendell C. Bennett, pp. 1–7. Society for American Archaeology and Institute of Andean Research, Menash, Wis.

Bird, Junius B.

1943   *Excavations in Northern Chile*. American Museum of Natural History, New York.

Blower, David

1996   *The Quest for Mullu: Concepts, Trade, and the Archaeological Distribution of Spondylus in the Andes*. MA thesis, Trent University, Peterborough, Ontario.

Borah, Woodrow

1954   *Early Colonial Trade and Navigation between Mexico and Peru*. Ibero Americana 38. University of California Press, Berkeley and Los Angeles.

Borja, Antonio

1992 [1591]   Relación en suma de la doctrina y beneficio de Pimampiro y de las cosas notables que en ella hay. In *Relaciones histórico-geográficas de la Audiencia de Quito (siglo XVI–XIX)*, vol. 1, edited by Pilar Ponce Leiva, pp. 480–488. MARKA Instituto de Historia y Antropología Andina y Abya Ayala, Quito.

Bray, Tamara L.

1998   Monos, monstruos y mitos: Conexiones ideológicas entre la sierra septentrional y el oriente del Ecuador. In *Intercambio y comercio entre costa, Andes y selva: Arqueología y etnohistoria de Suramérica*, edited by Fernando Cardenas-Arroyo and Tamara L. Bray, pp. 135–154. Universidad de los Andes, Bogotá.

2005   Multi-Ethnic Settlement and Inter-regional Exchange in Pimampiro, Ecuador. *Journal of Field Archaeology* 30(2):119–141.

2008   Late Prehispanic Chiefdoms of Highland Ecuador. In *Handbook of South American Archaeology*, edited by Helaine Silverman and William H. Isbell, pp. 527–543. Springer, New York.

Burger, Richard L.

2003   Conclusions: Cultures of the Ecuadorian Formative in Their Andean Context. In *Archaeology of Formative Ecuador*, edited by J. Scott Raymond and Richard L. Burger, pp. 465–486. Dumbarton Oaks Research Library and Collection, Washington, D.C.

Burger, Richard L., Frank Asaro, Helen V. Michel, Fred H. Stross, and Ernesto Salazar

1994   An Initial Consideration of Obsidian Procurement and Exchange in Prehispanic Ecuador. *Latin American Antiquity* 5(3):228–255.

Caillavet, Chantal

2000a   Conchas marinas y rutas de intercambio prehispánico. In *Etnias del norte: Etnohistoria e historia de Ecuador*, edited by Chantal Caillavet, pp. 85–99. Ediciones Abya-Yala, Instituto Frances de Estudios Andinos, and Casa de Velázquez-EHEH, Quito.

2000b   Jerarquía autóctona y cultura material: El legado de un señor étnico del siglo XVI. In *Etnias del norte: Etnohistoria e historia de Ecuador*, edited by Chantal Caillavet, pp. 437–454. Ediciones Abya-Yala, Instituto Frances de Estudios Andinos, and Casa de Velázquez-EHEH, Quito.

2000c   La sal de Otavalo. Continuidades indígenas y rupturas coloniales. In *Etnias del norte: Etnohistoria e historia de Ecuador*, edited by Chantal Caillavet, pp. 59–84. Ediciones Abya-Yala, Instituto Frances de Estudios Andinos, and Casa de Velázquez-EHEH, Quito.

Carranza, Bartolomé Martín de

1992 [1569]   Relación de la provincia de Esmeraldas que fue a pacificar Andres Contero. In *Relaciones histórico-geográficas de la Audiencia de Quito (siglo XVI–XIX)*, vol. 1, edited by Pilar Ponce Leiva, pp. 66–71. MARKA Instituto de Historia y Antropología Andina y Abya-Ayala, Quito.

Carter, Benjamin Philip

2008   Technology, Society, and Change: Shell Artifact Production among the Manteño (AD 800–1532) of Coastal Ecuador. PhD dissertation, Department of Anthropology, Washington University, Saint Louis.

Castro, Cristóbal de, and Diego de Ortega Morejón

1974 [1558]   Relación y declaración del modo que este valle de Chincha y sus comarcanos se governavan antes que oviese Yngas y despues q(ue) los vuo hasta q(ue) los Cristianos entraron en esta tierra. *Historia y cultura* 8:91–104.

Cobo, Bernabé

1990 [1653]   *Inca Religion and Customs*. Translated by Roland Hamilton. University of Texas Press, Austin.

Costin, Cathy Lynne

1999   Formal and Technological Variability and the Social Relations of Production: *Crisoles* from San José de Moro, Peru. In *Material Meanings: Critical Approaches to the Interpretation of Material Culture*, edited by Elizabeth S. Chilton, pp. 85–102. University of Utah Press, Salt Lake City.

Coupland, Gary

1979   *A Survey of Prehistoric Fortified Sites in the North Highlands of Peru*. MA thesis, Trent University, Peterborough, Ontario.

Currie, Elizabeth J.

1995   Archaeology, Ethnohistory, and Exchange along the Coast of Ecuador. *Antiquity* 69:511–526.

Damp, Jonathan, and Presley Norton

1987   Pretexto, contexto y falacías en la Isla de la Plata. *Miscelánea antropológica ecuatoriana* 7:109–121.

Davidson, Judith R.

1981   El *Spondylus* en la cosmología Chimú. *Revista del Museo Nacional* 45:75–87. Lima.

Day, Kent C.

1982   Ciudadelas: Their Form and Function. In *Chan Chan: Andean Desert City*, edited by Michael E. Moseley and Kent C. Day, pp. 55–66. University of New Mexico Press, Albuquerque.

Dillehay, Tom D.

1976   *Competition and Cooperation in a Prehispanic Multi-Ethnic System in the Central Andes*. PhD dissertation, Department of Anthropology, University of Texas, Austin.

1979   Pre-Hispanic Resource Sharing in the Central Andes. *Science* 204:24–31.

Donnan, Christopher B.

2009   The Moche Use of Numbers and Number Sets. In *Andean Civilization: A Tribute to Michael E. Moseley*, edited by Joyce Marcus and Patrick Ryan Williams, pp. 165–180. Cotsen Institute of Archaeology, University of California, Los Angeles.

Edwards, Clinton

1965   *Aboriginal Watercraft on the Pacific Coast of South America.* University of California Press, Berkeley and Los Angeles.

Guffroy, Jean

2008   Cultural Boundaries and Crossings: Ecuador and Peru. In *Handbook of South American Archaeology,* edited by Helaine Silverman and William H. Isbell, pp. 889–902. Springer, New York.

Hartmann, Roswith

1971   Mercados y ferias prehispánicos en el área andina. *Boletín de la Academia Nacional de Historia* 54:214–235. Quito.

Heyerdahl, Thor, Daniel H. Sandweiss, Alfredo Narváez, and Luis Millones

1996   *Túcume.* Colección Arte y Tesoros del Perú. Banco de Crédito del Perú, Lima.

Hirth, Kenneth G.

1978   Interregional Trade and the Formation of Gateway Communities. *American Antiquity* 43(1):35–45.

Hocquenghem, Anne-Marie

1993   Rutas de entrada del mullu en el extremo norte del Perú. *Boletín de la Academia Nacional de Historia* 22(3):701–719. Quito.

1998   *Para vencer la muerte: Piura y Tumbes— raíces en el bosque seco y en la selva alta—horizontes en el Pacifico y en la Amazonía.* Instituto Frances de Estudios Andinos and Instituto de la Naturaleza y el Conocimiento Ambiental Humano, Lima.

Hocquenghem, Anne-Marie, Jaime Idrovo, Peter Kaulicke, and Domenique Gomís

1993   Bases del intercambio entre las socie- dades norperuanas y surecuatorianas: Una zona de transición entre 1500 AC y 600 DC. *Bulletin de l'Institut Français d'Etudes Andines* 22(2):1–24. Lima.

Hocquenghem, Anne-Marie, and Manuel Peña Ruiz

1994   La talla del material malacológico en Tumbes. *Bulletin de l'Institut Français d'Etudes Andines* 23(2):209–229. Lima.

Holm, Olaf

1983   *Cultura Milagro-Quevedo.* 2nd ed. Museo Antropológico y Pinacoteca del Banco Central, Guayaquil.

1988 [1981]   Las Islas Galápagos en la prehistoria ecuatoriana. In *La balsa en la historia de la navegación ecuatoriana: Compilación de crónicas, estudios, gráficas y testi- monios,* edited by Jenny Estrada, pp. 169–185. Instituto de Historia Marítima, Guayaquil.

Hosler, Dorothy, Heather Lechtman, and Olaf Holm

1990   *Axe-Monies and Their Relatives.* Dumbarton Oaks Research Library and Collection, Washington, D.C.

Jaeckel, Paul, and Alfredo Melly Cava

1987   [Untitled Summary of 1984 Fieldwork]. *Willay: Newsletter of the Andean Anthropological Research Group* 25:7–9. Cambridge, Mass.

Jijón y Caamaño, Jacinto

1988 [1941]   Ojeada general sobre la composición étnica de la costa ecuatoriana. In *La balsa en la historia de la navegación ecuatoriana: Compilación de crónicas, estudios, gráficos y testimonios*, edited by Jenny Estrada, pp. 111–128. Instituto de Historia Marítima, Guayaquil.

Julien, Daniel G.

1993   Late Pre-Inkaic Ethnic Groups in Highland Peru: An Archaeological- Ethnohistorical Model of the Political Geography of the Cajamarca Region. *Latin American Antiquity* 9(1):246–273.

Klymyshyn, Alexandra M. Ulana

1982   Elite Compounds in Chan Chan. In *Chan Chan: Andean Desert City,* edited by Michael E. Moseley and Kent C. Day, pp. 119–143. University of New Mexico Press, Albuquerque.

Kvietok, D. Peter

1987   Digging Sticks or Daggerboards? A Functional Analysis of Wooden Boards from the Ica Region. *Andean Past* 1:247–274.

Lechtman, Heather

1981   Copper-Arsenic Bronzes from the North Coast of Peru. In *Annals of the New York Academy of Sciences*, vol. 367, edited by Anne-Marie Cantwell, James B. Griffin, and Nan A. Rothschild, pp. 77–121. New York Academy of Sciences, New York.

Lippi, Ronald D.

1998   Encuentros precolombinos entre serranos y costeños en el País Yumbo (Pichincha Occidental, Ecuador). In *Intercambio y comercio entre costa, Andes y selva: Arqueología y etnohistoria de Suramérica*, edited by Felipe Cárdenas-Arroyo and Tamara L. Bray, pp. 115–134. Universidad de los Andes, Bogota.

Marcos, Jorge G.

1977–1978   Cruising to Acapulco and Back with the Thorny Oyster Set: A Model for a Lineal Exchange System. *Journal of the Steward Anthropological Society* 9(1–2):99–132.

Marcos, Jorge G., and Presley Norton

1981   Interpretación sobre la arqueología de la Isla de La Plata. *Miscelánea antropológica ecuatoriana* 1:136–154.

Martín, Alexander J.

2010   Comparing the Role of the Export Sector in Prehistoric Economies: The Importance of Shell Manufacture to the Livelihood of Coastal Ecuadorian Populations. In *Comparative Perspectives on the Archaeology of Coastal South America*, edited by Robyn E. Cutright, Enrique López-Hurtado, and Alexander J. Martin, pp. 77–100. Center for Comparative Archaeology, University of Pittsburgh, Pittsburgh.

Masucci, Maria A.

1995   Marine Shell Bead Production and the Role of Domestic Craft Activities in the Economy of the Guangala Phase, Southwestern Ecuador. *Latin American Antiquity* 6(1):70–84.

Mester, Ann M.

1985   Un taller manteño de la concha madre de perla del sitio Los Frailes, Manabí. *Miscelánea antropológica ecuatoriana* 5:101–111.

Montenegro, Jorge, and Izumi Shimada

1998   El "Estilo Cajamarca Costeño" y la interacción Sicán-Cajamarca en el norte del Perú. In *Intercambio y comercio entre costa, Andes y selva: Arqueología y etnohistoria de Suramérica*, edited by

Felipe Cárdenas-Arroyo and Tamara L. Bray, pp. 255–296. Universidad de los Andes, Bogota.

Montes Sánchez, Macarena, and Juan Martínez Borrero (editors)

2010   *I Encuentro de arqueólogos del norte del Perú y sur del Ecuador: Memorias; Relaciones interregionales y perspectivas de futuro.* Gobierno Provincial del Azuay Universidad de Cuenca, Cuenca.

Murra, John V.

1971   El trafico de mullu en la costa del Pacifico. Paper presented at the Primer Simposio de Correlaciones Antropológicas Andino-Mesoamericano, Salinas, Ecuador.

1972   El "Control Vertical" de un máximo de pisos ecológicos en la economía de las sociedades andinas. In *Visita de la provincia de Leon de Huánuco [1562]*, by Iñigo Ortiz de Zúñiga, visitador, vol. 2, pp. 429–476. Universidad Nacional Hermilio Valdizán, Huánuco.

1980   *The Economic Organization of the Inca State.* JAI Press, Greenwich, Conn.

Netherly, Patricia J.

1977   *Local Level Lords on the North Coast of Peru.* PhD dissertation, Department of Anthropology, Cornell University, Ithaca, N.Y.

1990   Out of Many, One: The Organization of Rule in the North Coast Polities. In *The Northern Dynasties: Kingship and Statecraft in Chimor*, edited by Michael E. Moseley and Alana Cordy-Collins, pp. 461–487. Dumbarton Oaks Research Library and Collection, Washington, D.C.

2009   Landscape as Metaphor: Resources, Language, and Myths of Dynastic Origin on the Pacific Coast from the Santa Valley (Peru) to Manabí (Ecuador). In *Landscapes of Origin in the Americas: Creation Narratives Linking Ancient Places and Communities*, edited by Jessica Joyce Christie, pp. 123–196. University of Alabama Press, Tuscaloosa.

Norton, Presley

    1988 [1985] El señorío de Salangone y la liga de mercaderes. In *La balsa en la historia de la navegación ecuatoriana: Compilación de crónicas, estudios, gráficas y testimonios*, edited by Jenny Estrada, pp. 255–274. Instituto de Historia Marítima, Guayaquil.

Oberem, Udo

    1974 Trade and Trade Goods in the Ecuadorian Montana. In *Native South Americans*, edited by Patricia J. Lyon, pp. 346–357. Little, Brown, and Company, Boston.

    1981 [1976] El acceso a recursos naturales de diferentes ecologías en la sierra ecuatoriana (siglo XVI). In *Contribución a la etnohistoria ecuatoriana*, edited by Segundo Moreno Yánez and Udo Oberem, pp. 45–71. Instituto Otavaleño de Antropología, Otavalo.

Paulsen, Alison C.

    1974 The Thorny Oyster and the Voice of God: *Spondylus* and *Strombus* in Andean Prehistory. *American Antiquity* 39(4):597–607.

Pillsbury, Joanne

    1996 The Thorny Oyster and the Origins of Empire: Implications of Recently Uncovered *Spondylus* Imagery from Chan Chan, Peru. *Latin American Antiquity* 7(4):313–340.

Pozorski, Shelia G.

    1982 Subsistence Systems in the Chimú State. In *Chan Chan: Andean Desert City*, edited by Michael E. Moseley and Kent C. Day, pp. 177–196. University of New Mexico Press, Albuquerque.

Prieto Burmester, O. Gabriel, Solsire Cusicanqui Marsano, and Francesco Fernandini Parodi

    2008 Estudio de la cerámica Cajamarca Tardía y de la cerámica de estilos Huari del Área 35, San José de Moro, valle de Jequetepeque. In *Programa Arqueológico San José de Moro, Temporada 2007*, edited by Luis Jaime Castillo Butters and Carlos E. Rengifo Chunga, pp. 163–219. Pontificia Universidad Católica del Perú, Lima.

Ramírez, Susan

    1985 Social Frontiers and the Territorial Base of Curacazgos. In *Andean Ecology and Civilization: An Interdisciplinary Perspective on Andean Ecological Complementarity*, edited by Shozo Masuda, Izumi Shimada, and Craig Morris, pp. 423–442. University of Tokyo Press, Tokyo.

    1986 Notes on Ancient Exchange: A Plea for Collaboration. In *Andean Archaeology: Papers in Memory of Clifford Evans*, edited by Ramiro Matos Mendieta, Solveig A. Turpin, and Herbert H. Eling Jr., pp. 225–238. Cotsen Institute of Archaeology, University of California, Los Angeles.

    1995a Exchange and Markets in the Sixteenth Century: A View from the North. In *Ethnicity, Markets, and Migration in the Andes: At the Crossroads of History and Anthropology*, edited by Brooke Larson and Olivia Harris, with Enrique Tandeter, pp. 135–164. Duke University Press, Durham, N.C.

    1995b An Oral History of the Valley of Chicama, circa 1524–1565. *Journal of the Steward Anthropological Society* 23(1–2):299–342.

    1996 *The World Upside Down: Cross-Cultural Contact and Conflict in Sixteenth-Century Peru*. Stanford University Press, Stanford.

Ramírez Horton, Susan

    1982 Retainers of the Lords or Merchants: A Case of Mistaken Identity? In *El hombre y su ambiente en los Andes centrales*, edited by Luis Millones and Hiroyasu Tomoeda, pp. 123–136. Senri Ethnological Studies 10. Museo Nacional de Etnología, Osaka.

Remy, Pilar

    1992 El documento. In *Las visitas a Cajamarca 1571–72/1578*, vol. 1, edited by María Rostworowski and Pilar Remy, pp. 37–109. Instituto de Estudios Peruanos, Lima.

Rengifo, Carlos E., Daniela Zevallos, and Luis Muro

    2008 Excavaciones en las Áreas 28, 33, 34, 40 y 43: La ocupación mochica en el sector norte de San José de Moro. In

Programa Arqueológico San José de Moro, Temporada 2007, edited by Luis Jaime Castillo Butters and Carlos E. Rengifo Chunga, pp. 118–161. Pontificia Universidad Católica del Perú, Lima.

Rostworowski de Diez Canseco, María

1970   Mercaderes del valle de Chincha en la época prehispánica: Un documento y unos comentarios. *Revista española de antropología americana* 5:135–178.

1975   Pescadores, artesanos, y mercaderes costeños en el Perú prehispánico. *Revista del Museo Nacional.* 41:311–349. Lima.

1977a   Coastal Fisherman, Merchants, and Artisans in Pre-Hispanic Peru. In *The Sea in the Pre-Columbian World*, edited by Elizabeth P. Benson, pp. 167–186. Dumbarton Oaks Research Library and Collection, Washington, D.C.

1977b   *Etnia y sociedad: Costa peruana prehispánica*. Historia Andina 4. Instituto de Estudios Peruanos, Lima.

1981   La voz parcialidad en su contexto en los siglos XVI y XVII. In *Etnohistoria y antropología andina: Segunda jornada del Museo de Historia*, pp. 35–45. Museo Nacional de Historia, Lima.

1992   Etnias forasteros en la visita toledana a Cajamarca. In *Las visitas a Cajamarca 1571–72/1578*, vol. 1, edited by María Rostworowski and Pilar Remy, pp. 9–36. Instituto de Estudios Peruanos, Lima.

2009   Apuntes de etnohistoria. In *La arqueología y la etnohistoria: Un encuentro andino*, edited by John R. Topic, pp. 341–354. Instituto de Estudios Andinos and Institute of Andean Research, Lima.

Rowe, John Howland

1948   The Kingdom of Chimor. *Acta americana* 6(1–2):26–59.

Salomon, Frank

1977–1978   Pochteca and Mindalá: A Comparison of Long Distance Traders in Ecuador and Mesoamerica. *Journal of the Steward Anthropological Society* 9(1–2):231–248.

1986   *Native Lords of Quito in the Age of the Incas: The Political Economy of North Andean Chiefdoms*. Cambridge University Press, Cambridge.

Sandweiss, Daniel H.

1992   *The Archaeology of Chincha Fishermen: Specialization and Status in Inka Peru*. Bulletin of the Carnegie Museum of Natural History 29. Carnegie Museum of Natural History, Pittsburgh.

Shimada, Izumi

1980   Horizontal Archipelago and Coast-Highland Interactions in North Peru: Archaeological Models. In *El hombre y su ambiente en los Andes Centrales*, edited by Luis Millones and Hiroyasu Tomoeda, pp. 137–210. Museo Nacional de Etnología, Osaka.

1985   Perception, Procurement, and Management of Resources: Archaeological Perspectives. In *Andean Ecology and Civilization: An Interdisciplinary Perspective on Andean Ecological Complementarity*, edited by Shozo Masuda, Izumi Shimada, and Craig Morris, pp. 357–399. University of Tokyo Press, Tokyo.

Shimada, Izumi, Stephen M. Epstein, and Alan F. Craig

1983   The Metallurgical Process in Ancient North Peru. *Archaeology* 36(5):38–45.

Smith, Michael E.

2004   The Archaeology of Ancient State Economies. *Annual Review of Anthropology* 33:73–102.

Stothert, Karen E.

2003   Expression of Ideology in the Formative Period of Ecuador. In *Archaeology of Formative Ecuador*, edited by J. Scott Raymond and Richard L. Burger, pp. 337–421. Dumbarton Oaks Research Library and Collection, Washington, D.C.

Topic, John R.

1977   *The Lower Class at Chan Chan: A Qualitative Approach*. PhD dissertation, Department of Anthropology, Harvard University, Cambridge, Mass.

1982   Lower Class Social and Economic Organization at Chan Chan. In *Chan Chan: Andean Desert City*, edited by Michael E. Moseley and Kent C. Day, pp. 145–176. University of New Mexico Press, Albuquerque.

1990   Craft Production in the Kingdom of Chimor. In *The Northern Dynasties: Kingship and Statecraft in Chimor*, edited by Michael E. Moseley and Alana Cordy-Collins, pp. 145–176. Dumbarton Oaks Research Library and Collection, Washington, D.C.

1998   Ethnogenesis in Huamachuco. *Andean Past* 5:109–127.

2003   From Stewards to Bureaucrats: Architecture and Information Flow at Chan Chan, Peru. *Latin American Antiquity* 14(3):243–274.

2008   El santuario de Catequil: Estructura y agencia; Hacia una comprensión de los oráculos andinos. In *Adivinación y oráculos en el mundo andino antiguo*, edited by Marco Curatola Petrocchi and Mariusz S. Ziołkowski, pp. 71–95. Fondo Editorial de la Pontificia Universidad Católica del Perú and Instituto Francés de Estudios Peruanos, Lima.

2009   Domestic Economy as Political Economy at Chan Chan, Peru. In *Domestic Life in Prehispanic Capitals: A Study of Specialization, Hierarchy, and Ethnicity*, edited by Linda Manzanilla and Claude Chapdelaine, pp. 221–242. Museum of Anthropology, University of Michigan, Ann Arbor.

Topic, John R., and Michael E. Moseley

1985   Chan Chan: A Case Study of Urban Change in Peru. *Ñawpa Pacha* 21:153–182.

Topic, John R., and Theresa Lange Topic

1983   Coast-Highland Relations in Northern Peru: Some Observations on Routes, Networks, and Scales of Interaction. In *Civilization in the Ancient Americas: Essays in Honor of Gordon R. Willey*, edited by Richard M. Leventhal and Alan L. Kolata, pp. 237–259. University of New Mexico Press, Albuquerque, and Peabody Museum of Archaeology and Ethnology, Harvard University, Cambridge, Mass.

1992   The Rise and Decline of Cerro Amaru: An Andean Shrine during the Early Intermediate Period and Middle Horizon. In *Ancient Images, Ancient Thought: The Archaeology of Ideology*, edited by A. Sean Goldsmith, Sandra Garvie, David Selin, and Jeannette Smith, pp. 167–180. University of Calgary Archaeology Association, Calgary.

Topic, John R., Theresa Lange Topic, and Alfredo Melly

2002   Catequil: The Archaeology, Ethnohistory, and Ethnography of a Major Provincial Huaca. In *Andean Archaeology I: Variations in Sociopolitical Organization*, edited by William H. Isbell and Helaine Silverman, pp. 303–336. Kluwer Academic/Plenum Press, New York.

Torrero, Alfredo

1989   Areas toponímicas e idiomas en la sierra norte peruana: Un trabajo de recuperación lingüística. *Revista andina* 7(1):217–257.

Wassen, S. Henry

1955   Algunos datos del comercio precolombino en Colombia. *Revista colombiana de antropología* 4:87–109. Bogota.

Willey, Gordon R.

1971   *An Introduction to American Archaeology,* vol. 2, *South America.* Prentice Hall, Englewood Cliffs, N.J.

15

Embedded Andean Economic Systems and the Expansive Tiwanaku State

A Case for a State without Market Exchange

PAUL S. GOLDSTEIN

The complexity of the human condition calls for a large dose of theoretical humility, but this, alas, is hard to find, especially in the dominant marginal utility theory paradigm. Value theorists need to perceive the limits to the generality of their particular theory. This requires them to accept that the economy, both market and nonmarket, has varied over time and place, and that ideas about the functioning of the economy reflect this geographical and historical variation. Whenever one group claims universality for their particular theory of value there can be no dialogue.

> C. A. GREGORY
> "Anthropology, Economics, and
> Political Economy" (Gregory 2000:1008)

The assumption of market essentialism forecloses considerations of alternative forms of exchange relations and structures. Given the historical and comparative diversity of market relations and institutions, there is at least a prima facie reason to consider alternative arrangements.

> JOHN LIE
> "Sociology of Markets" (1997:353)

Markets versus Embedded Exchange

ANDEAN CIVILIZATIONS ARE THE QUINTES- sential home of alternative economic arrangements. One key theme of this volume is the debate over a kind of Andean economic exceptionalism— the question of whether the Andean states and empires are unique, in the comparative economic anthropology of state societies, for the absence of significant price-fixing and entrepreneurial traditions. As the chapters in this volume attest, the early Spanish chroniclers described the astounding complexity of Mesoamerican craft and trading systems, and reported dozens of ethnosemantic categories about market exchange involving entrepreneurial traders. The evidence for Mesoamerican market trade includes a god of trade, long-standing commodity equivalencies, the recognition of transport costs and distance decay patterns, and attention to market reliability and fairness. All of these factors made Mesoamerican marketplaces somewhat familiar to modern scholars of economics. Clearly, commerce, entrepreneurship, and market exchange were every bit as important as engines of civilizational development in Mesoamerica as they were in the Old World (Adams 1978; Algaze 1993; Berdan 1982; Hassig 1985; Hirth 1978, 1984; Isaac 1993, 1996; Smith 2001; Stein 1999).

This is a tough act to follow for Andeanists. For while Spanish chroniclers in Mesoamerica wrote in awestruck detail about the strange, yet familiar, workings of the great markets and merchant classes of the Aztec Empire, a similar group of Spanish observers in the Andes failed to describe marketplaces to any comparable extent and reported little about pricing or entrepreneurial commerce (Murra 1980 [1955]; Stanish et al. 2010). Indeed, the absence of market institutions and standard equivalencies of exchange in the Andes frustrated the early Spanish bureaucrats, who eventually learned to document and exploit the complex web of mit'a (labor tax extraction), attached craft production, and strategic colonization that they inherited from the Inca Empire (Stanish 2000).

The problem that comparativists are addressing in this volume is not only one of finding (or not finding) evidence of market exchange, marketplaces, equivalencies, or professionalized entrepreneurs in the Andes. It is that the Andean states pose an existential threat to the dominant marginal utility theory paradigm for the rise of state societies. Central features of the classic economic formations of most Old World and Mesoamerican states include the florescence of entrepreneurial spirit, the commoditization of goods and labor, and the assumption of an economizing logic and profit motive (Blanton and Fargher 2010). A state society without all the habits of market rationality runs counter to our expectations of how state economies should work. Are the Andean states the exception to the rule? Was there not only an Inca

mode of production (Godelier 1977; Murra 1985), but an Andean mode of economic thought, one that emphasized reciprocity, with minimal market rationality, profit, and commoditization? Or have Andeanists simply not looked hard enough? If these questions recall twentieth-century debates between formalist and substantivist positions on economic theory, then perhaps it is because a range of economic modes may have existed in very different proportion in various ancient complex societies (Smith 2004:79). It helps to view the Andean economic formations through the prisms of both formal and culturalist theories.

In what follows, I will make a case that the economic integration of the Tiwanaku state (AD 500–1000) shows no evidence of significant markets, price-fixing rationality, or entrepreneurial exchange. I will argue that Tiwanaku's domestic and political economies were overwhelmingly what Karl Polanyi would have called "embedded" economies typified by reciprocity and redistribution within socially nested networks of agropastoral and craft production (Polanyi 1957; Smith 1976).

The Andean Debate

Supportive of culturally informed approaches to economic behavior, Polanyi imagined "embedded" economies as systems that met human needs through reciprocity and redistribution, without the individual economizing behavior assumed by the dominant marginal utility theory paradigm (Halperin 1994). Following Marx, Polanyi posited that in embedded economic relations, the functions of satisfying wants were not primarily motivated by considerations of supply and demand, but were instead "embedded" in social relations: "In such a community, the idea of profit is barred, higgling and haggling is decried, giving freely is acclaimed as a virtue; the supposed propensity to barter, truck, and exchange does not appear. The economic system is, in effect, a mere function of social organization" (Polanyi 1944:48). Polanyi argued that societies with primarily embedded economies were the norm for most of human history, with the transition to primarily market exchange being a relatively recent shift.[1] I stress the word "primarily" because, contrary to readings of all of his work as a fixed institutional typology, Polanyi elsewhere admitted that shades of reciprocity, redistribution, or market exchange are found in any society to some degree (Halperin 1994). Thus, some utilitarian negotiated exchange ("higgling and haggling") no doubt occurred within and between every hunting band. Conversely, even the most modern market systems are closely embedded in networks of human relations, with action predicated on goals of sociability, approval, status, and power, as well as economizing rationality (Granovetter 1985). The same logic allows for the existence of some complex societies where embedded exchange modes contingent on other kinds of social actions could outweigh the commercial market-based exchange (Blanton and Fargher 2010:221).

A second prerequisite for debating Andean economic exceptionalism, of course, involves defining an "ancient" or premodern market. Not surprisingly, proponents of marginal utility paradigms favor the projection of market behaviors into deep history by employing definitions of market exchange that include transactions where the forces of supply and demand are merely visible, though not necessarily paramount. With such an inclusive definition, it is possible to consider reciprocal gifts, bride wealth, and even the classic *moka* of highland New Guinea as forms of "market exchange" (Hirth 2010:229). While this position has a certain classical analytic clarity, the focus on the utilitarian aspect is at odds with specialists who see these institutions to be predominantly socially embedded (Akin and Robbins 1999).

I here will define "market exchange" as the realm of economic transactions that are primarily based on individual rational economizing behavior (i.e., in which negotiations over price, under forces of supply and demand, are the dominant transactional considerations). To be a market exchange, a transaction's motivation must be primarily one of pricing and predominantly disembedded from social context (i.e., "shorn of social relations, institutions, or technology and . . . devoid of elementary

sociological concerns such as power, norms, and networks" [Lie 1997:342]). I will argue that Tiwanaku's economy did not meet this standard any more than those of traditional highland New Guinea. The concept of an Andean states' exception to the market exchange assumption came to Andean studies not from Polanyi, but by way of that *amauta* of Andean economic anthropology, John Murra. His 1955 dissertation and related articles on Inca imperial production and exchange (Murra 1962, 1980 [1955]), followed by a distinct series of articles focusing on relations of reciprocity within smaller Andean polities (Murra 1968, 1972), are now accepted as paradigmatic statements of the dominance of nonmarket economic modes in native Andean states (Morris 1979). Since Murra, the political economy of Pre-Columbian Andean states is widely conceived of as something between the Inca's centrally directed command economy funded through *mit'a* labor taxes (La Lone 1982; LeVine 1992; Morris 1986) and a complex web of embedded social relationships defined by ethnicity and kinship (Stanish 1997). Under either scheme, Andean economic production and the allocational movement of goods and services took place in a network of households, extended agrarian communities known as *ayllus*, and far-flung productive enclaves that Murra described as an archipelago. In Murra's vision, market exchange and entrepreneurial action were subdued or even entirely absent from the Pre-Columbian Andes.

Some papers in this volume may question this interpretation, citing a small but oft-cited group of exceptions that test the rule, notably the "*mollo chasqui camayoc*" (*Spondylus* messenger-worker) who traded *Spondylus* shell along the North Coast of Peru (Rostworowski 1988:210) and the *mindalae* trading class known in contact-period Ecuador (Salomon 1986; see also Burger, this volume; Dillehay, this volume; Topic, this volume). While these groups may have specialized as intermediaries, it is unclear whether either was supported or motivated by profit, or simply by attachment to elite patrons or the Inca state. Other scholars point to a few colonial descriptions of regional fairs as potential barter markets for interchange with foreign groups (Murra 1980 [1955]:146; Stanish et al. 2010); however, as these authors note, fairs were also embedded within complex social, ritual, and political networks, and their association with even limited "market exchange" or entrepreneurial motives is unclear.

Still other authors suggest that Murra's ideology, formed in the streets of Romania, Spain, and Chicago, left him prone to a polemic primitivism (Figure 15.1). The question, though, is not whether John Murra had an interesting past and some biases (Mayer, this volume), but whether his analyses of the Inca command economy and Andean reciprocity were largely correct. Trained as an anthropologist, Murra was informed by a wide reading of structural functionalism and a worldwide comparative stance, not naive ideology or a coffeehouse reading of Polanyi. Murra's revolutionary interpretations incorporate previously underappreciated

figure 15.1
John Murra in Spain, May 1938. (Photograph courtesy of the Abraham Lincoln Brigade Archives, Fifteenth International Brigade Photographic Unit Collection, Tamiment Library, New York University.)

economic data from *visitas* (royal censuses) and notarial records, as well as traditional chronicle sources. Ironically, this innovative perspective on Inca political economy arose in part from the denial of a U.S. passport to Murra until 1958, which kept him away from ethnographic research and forced him into the library (Salomon 2007). On balance, it is not Murra's politics but his pragmatic and data-driven approach that explains why many of his interpretations remain valid after five decades.

Archipelagos, *Ayllus*, and Diasporas

Several years after proposing the Inca as a non-market state society, Murra (1964, 1968, 1972, 1985) suggested another Andean economic mode in a form of economic colonization and reciprocal exchange practiced in the South-Central Andes at the time of the Spanish invasion. Murra described such systems as "archipelagos" because ethnic polities seemed to establish extended communities with "islands" of settlement in multiple productive zones, all linked by ethnic and kin networks.[2] The most cited, but least compelling, aspect of Murra's archipelago phenomenon is the functional truism of "vertical" ecological complementarity across the altitude-defined environment of the Andes (Van Buren 1996:340).

More interesting, however, are the archipelago model's structural implications about the importance of complex and enduring social identities in the ancient Andes. Elsewhere, I have compared Murra's model of multiethnic colonization to recent considerations of some migrant streams as "diasporas." Diasporas, like archipelago colonies, are expatriate communities that maintain a strong connection to their original homeland and see the ancestral home as a place of eventual return, and whose consciousness and solidarity are importantly defined by this continuing relationship with their parent communities in the homeland (Clifford 1994:304). In the Andes, early Spanish bureaucrats were intrigued because certain enclave settlements invariably insisted on being counted with their distant community of origin, even after generations of residence in the colonized location (Murra 1972:431). Equally surprising to the Spaniards, although colonists maintained permanent residence in new locations, their settlements shared each colonized resource zone interspersed with enclaves of other ethnic polities. In 1571, the *visitador* Juan Polo de Ondegardo noted with bewilderment the lack of territorial exclusivity among enclaves in one lowland valley, writing, "In accounting for and distributing the things they bring, it is curious and difficult to believe, but no one is wronged" (Julien 1985). A similar "multi-ethnic rubbing of shoulders" was described in a 1595 litigation that affirmed simultaneous settlements of "indios lupacas, yungas, huarinas y achacaches" in the valley of Larecaja, Bolivia (Saignes 1986), and among colonies of Lupaqa, Colla, Pacaxe, and coastal Camanchaca affiliation in the western oasis valleys of Moquegua, Sama, Caplina, and Azapa in Peru and Chile (Hidalgo Lehuedé 1996; Hidalgo Lehuedé and Focacci Aste 1986; Murra 1972; Pease G. Y. 1980, 1984; Rostworowski 1986; Van Buren 1996).

It is important to stress that multiethnic coexistence does not mean that colonized regions were melting pots. In fact, it means just the opposite. As expatriate colonies carefully maintained their identities and economic ties with their parent communities, they had relatively limited contact with neighboring colonies of different ethnic origins. In lowland resource zones, this segregation makes functional sense because neighboring colonies within a resource zone tended to produce similar products, leaving little incentive for exchange between them.

Ongoing ethnographic research also suggests that multiethnic coexistence between lowland colonies could be facilitated by the separation of each colonial enclave into a distinct irrigation group (Fortier and Goldstein 2006). Interviews were conducted in two recently settled agrarian colonies at Trapiche, a location at 1,300 meters above sea level (masl) in the Moquegua Valley in southern Peru (Figure 15.2). These two irrigation groups comprise separate communities of first-generation immigrants from the highland hamlets of Muylaque (3,300 masl)

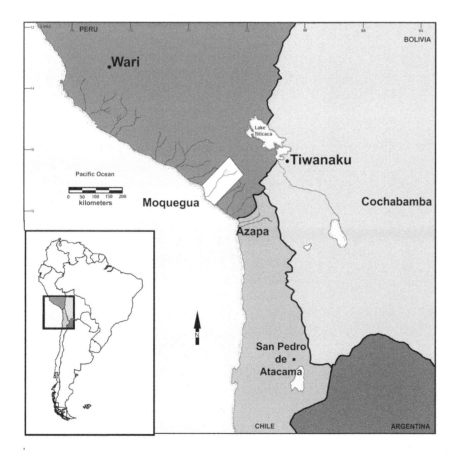

figure 15.2
Map of the South-Central Andes, showing principle locations in text. (Drawing by Paul S. Goldstein.)

a

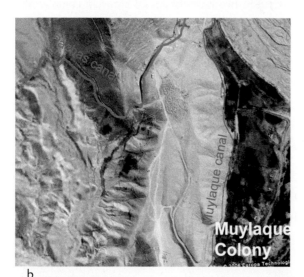

b

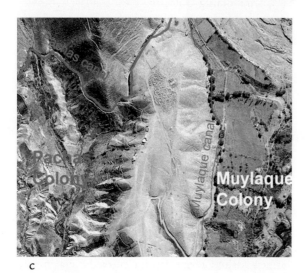

c

figure 15.3
Images of Trapiche *denuncia*: a) 1997 photograph, showing
Muylaque canal under construction; b) 2006 photograph,
showing Muylaque agrarian colony (© 2006 Google);
and c) 2011 photograph, showing Muylaque and Pachas
agrarian colonies (© 2011 Google).

and Pachas (3,600 masl). Together with the inter-
view data, aerial images from the years 1997, 2006,
and 2011 demonstrate the two enclaves' separate histories and mutual independence. The Muylaque colony's canal, indicated in the 1997 air photo (Figure
15.3a), was created by a group of pioneer women and
men from the Aymara-speaking parent community
of Muylaque. The Muylaque group gradually brought
more family members to complete the canal and to
successfully irrigate and cultivate the area first visible in the 2006 photo (Figure 15.3b). Later, a different
coalition of men and women from the Quechua-
speaking town of Pachas constructed a separate,
higher, and much longer canal, first indicated in the
2006 photo, which brought an entirely separate area
to fruition in the 2011 photo (Figure 15.3c). Our interviews found that these neighboring communities
have little contact with each other, each primarily
maintaining relationships with their homeland communities. Significantly, the Muylaque and Pachas
groups choose different crops to plant; use different planting and land forming technologies; recount
different self-descriptions of origins, kin ties, settlement histories, and identity; and, most relevant here,
employ distinct named categories of reciprocal and
nonmarket labor relations, such as *ayni* (mutual aid)
(Figure 15.4) (Fortier and Goldstein 2006).

A final theoretical note is that the workings of
socially embedded economies are intricately linked
to social and structural reproduction. In the case of
archipelago colonies past and present, this would
imply that colonial enclaves maintain strong identities by reproducing the social structure and practice
of their parent communities. Thus, historic Lupaqa
colonies replicated the division of the two homeland moieties, Aransaya and Urinsaya, and each
colony reported specific allegiance to and traded
with their respective moiety (Murra 1968:126). More

figure 15.4

Ayni (mutual labor aid) canal construction by the Pachas Association, Trapiche *denuncia*, Moquegua, 2005. (Photograph by Paul S. Goldstein.)

fine-grained ethnic, occupational, or status categories were also each represented within archipelago colonies, many of them glossed under the recursive structure known as the *ayllu*.

The Andean *ayllu*, as understood from ethnography and ethnohistory in Quechua and Aymara-speaking regions of the South-Central Andes, is a corporate body of ascriptive identity held together by shared conceptions of behavior, history, and common ancestry. Structurally, an *ayllu* is a "group or unit of social, political, economic, and ritual cohesion and action" (Astvaldsson 2000; Urton 1993). *Ayllu* membership may be determined by literal or fictive descent, adoption, geographical origins, political negotiation, marriage, alliance, or other criteria (Abercrombie 1998:341; Albarracin-Jordan 1996a; Isbell 1997:99; Salomon 1991). *Ayllus* typically exhibit recursive structure and binary oppositions, splitting by moiety (Platt 1986) and forming "recursive"

(Urton 1993), "nested" (Albarracin-Jordan 1996b), or "Chinese box" hierarchical arrangement of component parts (Astvaldsson 2000:148; Bouysse-Cassagne 1986:207). Functional definitions emphasize the *ayllu* as a landholding collective (Brush 1977:41; Rowe 1946:255); the proprietor and ritual superintendent of water rights (Sherbondy 1982); an economically autonomous kin collective (Moseley 1992:49); and the key suprahousehold unit of a "communal mode of production" for exchange and productive labor organization above the level of the nuclear family (Patterson and Gailey 1987).

The archipelago model proposes several principles testable in the archaeological record: 1) permanent residence in complementary resource zones; 2) multiple colonies who explicitly maintained identity with distinct homeland parent communities; 3) reproduction of the social structure of the homeland; and 4) multiethnicity, or the sharing of resource zones by colonies of various ethnic, political, or social affiliations. Archaeological differences in cultural practice and material culture among contemporary settlements would lend support for multiethnicity. If, as Murra posits, the principal mode of exchange in the South-Central Andes was embedded in the archipelago's extended communities, we would expect to find relative homogeneity of exchanged goods within community groups and heterogeneity between groups. Finally, demonstrating multiethnic coexistence in the archaeological record further requires settlement-pattern evidence showing contemporary colonial enclaves of distinct affiliations coexisting in proximity. John Murra himself sketched out a hypothesis that could only be tested through research on both archaeological identity and regional settlement patterns: "I wouldn't be surprised if we find in one single valley settlements of diverse antecedents without any temporal stratification between them. These would simply be peripheral colonies established in the lowlands by cores that were contemporary, but diverse in material culture" (Murra 1972:441). In what follows, I examine the Tiwanaku state colonies of southern Peru and propose that a diasporic archipelago model best explains Tiwanaku's productive organization and its nonmarket system of integration.

Tiwanaku Expansion—Pluralism in Diaspora

The civilization we call Tiwanaku created the largest and most cosmopolitan city the Andes had yet seen with a far-flung network of towns and ceremonial centers in outlying regions, near and far. Some find that Tiwanaku bears comparison to hierarchical archaic states elsewhere in the world and envision "Tiwanaku" as a unitary political actor with a centralized government, territorial governance, and class-stratified society (Goldstein 1993a; Janusek and Kolata 2004; Kolata 1993, 2003)—or at least a centralized tributary political economy, perhaps like that of the Inca (Stanish 2002). Others, however, see Tiwanaku as a segmentary confederation in which component groups recognized a cultural unity and

some form of maximal polity but reckoned social affiliations and conducted daily business at the level of *ayllus* or some similar form of autonomous local corporate organizations (Albarracin-Jordan 1996a, 1996b; Berenguer 1998; Bermann 1994, 1997; Janusek 1999, 2002, 2004; McAndrews et al. 1997).

In the following discussion of Tiwanaku colonization and economic integration of the maize-producing region of Moquegua, I suggest that Tiwanaku could act as a unitary state for ceremonial and political purposes, but its day-to-day systems of economic production and distribution functioned through reciprocity and redistribution integrated on a community level. Reciprocity depends on identity and trust, and Tiwanaku reciprocity was articulated through units smaller than the state. I argue that socially embedded exchange was articulated through enduring and largely autonomous recursive corporate groupings within the greater Tiwanaku civilization, rather than a unitary political economy, hierarchical tributary, or administrative infrastructure. Tiwanaku civilization's component corporate groups were the principal organizational agents of Tiwanaku economic production, and these segments replicated themselves in the settlement patterns and domestic habitus of colonized regions.

Since the turn of the twentieth century, the extent of Tiwanaku material culture in the south-central Andean region has suggested a wide area of cultural influence. Recent empirical and methodological advances have succeeded in contextualizing the scale and integration of this Tiwanaku expansion, and the emergence of a problem-oriented mortuary and household archaeology makes it possible to associate peripheral Tiwanaku practices with social structure, group identity, and power relations. Diacritics for shared social identity may be evident archaeologically in spatially discernible variations and microvariations in costume, utensils, household, ceremonial, mortuary, or other practices and materials. Variability appears to correspond to nested levels of scale, such as polity, ethnicity, moiety, or major and minor *ayllus*.

Ongoing mortuary archaeology in the Tiwanaku colonies focuses on identifying such microaffiliations within the Tiwanaku culture through detailed studies of Tiwanaku mortuary behavior, tomb construction, burial positioning, and clothing (Baitzel and Goldstein 2011; Buikstra 1995; Korpisaari 2006; Plunger 2009). Subtle but significant differences in Tiwanaku mortuary treatment include differences in burial wrapping procedures; the use of litters, timing, placement, and associations of surface mourners' offerings; and the appearance of feathered headdresses on Tiwanaku mummy bundles in some cemeteries (Figure 15.5).

Studies of the variations in intentional cranial deformation provide particularly strong evidence for the intergenerational maintenance of distinct identities. Cranial deformation is a stylistic behavior that is imposed on children by their parents and leaves a permanent and unchangeable record on the body. For this reason, it can be a particularly telltale marker of social identity on several levels of scale. Widely held norms about desirable head shape might mark shared group identity for entire ethnic groups (Blom 1999, 2005; Buikstra 1995; Buikstra et al. 1990; Hoshower et al. 1995; Sutter 2000; Torres-Rouff 2002). For much of the Tiwanaku culture, the preferred head shape involved variants of fronto-occipital deformation (Figure 15.6). At the same time, individual communities achieved more subtle variants of general norms with specific choices about particular deforming devices, such as facial deformers designed to flatten the cheekbones (Figure 15.7).

As social identity is at least partially affiliated with kinship and marriage patterns, skeletal biological distance studies also offer insight into genetic relationships among Tiwanaku populations across time and space (Blom 1999; Blom et al. 1998; Lozada Cerna 1998; Rothhammer et al. 1989; Rothhammer and Santoro 2001; Sutter 2000); paleodietary and isotopic origin studies confirm migratory patterns and point to unique regional origins, agricultural practices, or cuisines among different groups (Knudson 2008; Knudson et al. 2004; Sandness 1992; Tomczak 2003).

Recent advances in household archaeology studies are particularly important for understanding the link between Tiwanaku's nonmarket institutions and its larger social and cultural systems. Household archaeology has given us a window into

figure 15.5
Tiwanaku mummy with feathered headdress and cane feather holders, Río Muerto M70 R1. (Photograph by Paul S. Goldstein.)

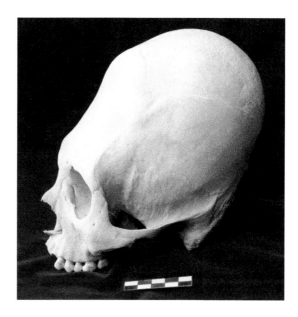

figure 15.6
Fronto-occipital cranial deformation, Río Muerto M70 cemetery, Tiwanaku Omo–style, Moquegua. (Photograph by Paul S. Goldstein.)

figure 15.7
Facial deformer mask, Río Muerto
M43B, R52, Tiwanaku style,
Moquegua. (Photograph by
Paul S. Goldstein.)

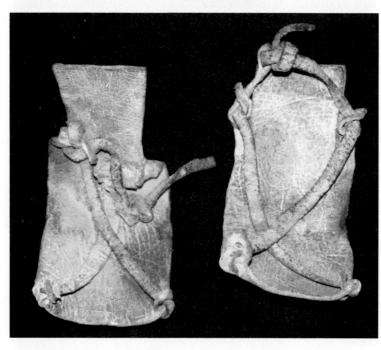

figure 15.8
Tiwanaku X-strap leather sandal, Río Muerto M43 Tiwanaku site, Moquegua.
(Photograph by Paul S. Goldstein.)

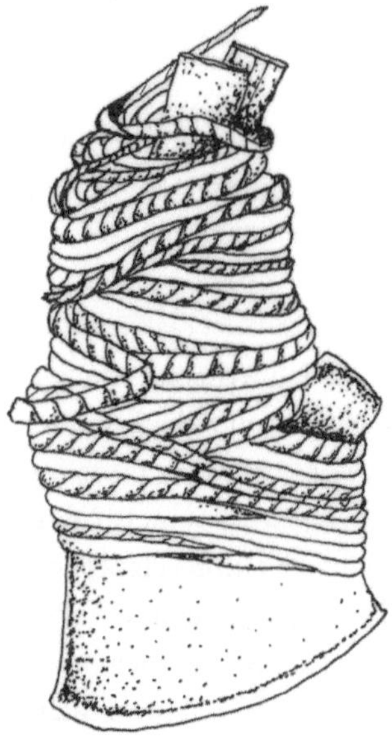

figure 15.9
Camelid mandible polisher,
Río Muerto M43 site. (Illustration
by Paul S. Goldstein.)

daily life, household agrarian and craft production, storage, and consumption in the Tiwanaku culture, both in the altiplano heartland and abroad (Bermann 1994, 1997; Goldstein 1993b, 2005; Janusek 1999, 2002, 2004). Implements for farming and crop processing, tool making, food preparation, and textile production appear in most households, suggesting local household production of most quotidian goods for the individual household and the extended community. Common patterns evident in household goods—such as one-piece leather sandals and camelid mandible polishers—indicate the reproduction of universally shared Tiwanaku artifact types and technological styles that must have reinforced common identity (Figures 15.8–15.9). At the same time, microvariability in house plan and construction,

figure 15.10
Embroidered coca
bag, M43=4516,
Tomb R52, M43 "A."
(Photograph by
Paul S. Goldstein.)

tools, clothing, vessels, and household dedicatory practices suggest stylistic affiliation with one or another subgroup. Bodily marking and adornment similarly announced affiliation with and the reproduction of a cultural identity, with diacritical information encoded in an astounding array of technical, decorative, and formal variability in the textile arts (Murra 1962; Oakland 1992) as well as group-specific techniques of body modification, such as cranial and facial deformation (Figure 15.10).

Finally, systematic settlement pattern studies allow us to consider the intersection of identity and exchange with the Tiwanaku settlement system (Albarracin-Jordan 1996a; Janusek and Kolata 2004; McAndrews et al. 1997; Stanish 2003). Many of these studies have considered the case for settlement hierarchy as a proxy for the degree of central state integration in the Tiwanaku homeland. What I will focus on here for the Moquegua colonies might also include settlement heterarchy: how settlement pattern analysis, building on the increasingly sophisticated understanding of Tiwanaku social and cultural variability from household and mortuary archaeology, can also map distinct contemporary settlements with different social identities across a colonized region.

Tiwanaku Diaspora Settlement Patterns— Two Archipelagos, One Valley

In some peripheral regions, Tiwanaku expansion was typified by agrarian colonization.[3] Lowland valley regions provided complementary temperate crop resources such as maize, coca, peppers, and beans, all of which are unavailable in Tiwanaku's altiplano core region. In exchange, this core region provided highland products and a large agrarian labor force in the form of expatriate colonists. Our best case study of Tiwanaku colonization is in the Moquegua (also known as Middle Osmore) Valley of southern Peru, approximately three hundred kilometers west of the Tiwanaku site. Since 1993, the Moquegua Archaeological Survey (MAS) has systematically surveyed the area (150 square kilometers) of the Middle Moquegua Valley, which is between 900 and 2,000 masl. A total of 531 Pre-Columbian site components of all periods were recorded, classified as habitation sites (207 components, covering 220 hectares), cemeteries (168 components, covering 47 hectares), agricultural fields and canals (20 components), ceremonial structures (11 components), and *apachetas* (small ritual or offering sites, 6 components).

Tiwanaku and later Tiwanaku-derived settlements collectively occupied more than 141 hectares of residential sites in the Middle Moquegua Valley (Figures 15.11–15.12). The Tiwanaku settlers preferred large settlements on plateaus above the river floodplain and evidently avoided the existing valley-bottom settlements of the Huaracane, effectively partitioning the valley territory in a form of multiethnic coexistence. I will focus here on the eighty-three hectares of Tiwanaku occupation, which comprised two contemporary Tiwanaku migrant communities from the altiplano, known as the Omo- and Chen Chen–style occupations.

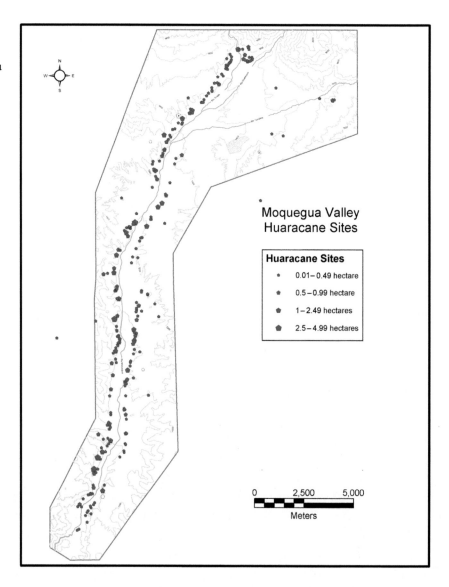

figure 15.11
Indigenous pre-Tiwanaku settlement distribution in the Moquegua Valley. (Illustration by Paul S. Goldstein.)

Moquegua Tiwanaku sites were open and unfortified, suggesting that the Tiwanaku colonists averted direct conflict with the region's indigenous inhabitants. Paleodemography and strontium isotope analysis support archaeological interpretations that the Moquegua Tiwanaku sites were inhabited by first-generation altiplano immigrants and their descendents, rather than acculturated local populations (Baitzel 2008; Knudson 2008). These Tiwanaku colonists, already experienced with collective land reclamation from Tiwanaku's altiplano raised fields (Kolata 1996; Kolata and Ortloff 1996), chose terrain near springs and canal-irrigable lands deeper in the desert. A major El Niño event circa AD 700 may also have played a role in this choice. Middle

valley effects of this event may have been complex, potentially wiping out the fields of indigenous farmers dependent on valley-bottom lands while, at the same time, attracting Tiwanaku settlement by recharging springs in lowland Moquegua in a year likely characterized by highland drought (Goldstein and Magilligan 2011; Magilligan and Goldstein 2001; Magilligan et al. 2008; Manners et al. 2007).

Contrary to expectations for agrarian landscapes in many state societies, the MAS systematic survey found no evidence of a Tiwanaku settlement hierarchy in the Moquegua colonies. Specifically, there were virtually no small Tiwanaku hamlets or individual farmstead sites. The Tiwanaku settlement in Moquegua was instead concentrated

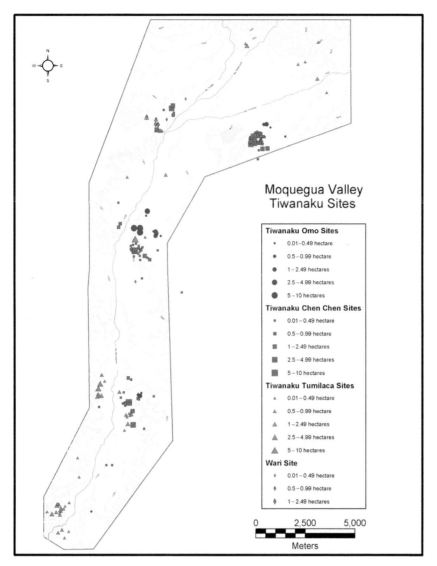

figure 15.12
Tiwanaku settlement
distribution in the Moquegua
Valley. (Illustration by Paul S.
Goldstein.)

Moquegua Valley
Tiwanaku Sites

Tiwanaku Omo Sites
- 0.01–0.49 hectare
- 0.5–0.99 hectare
- 1–2.49 hectares
- 2.5–4.99 hectares
- 5–10 hectares

Tiwanaku Chen Chen Sites
- 0.01–0.49 hectare
- 0.5–0.99 hectare
- 1–2.49 hectares
- 2.5–4.99 hectares
- 5–10 hectares

Tiwanaku Tumilaca Sites
- 0.01–0.49 hectare
- 0.5–0.99 hectare
- 1–2.49 hectares
- 2.5–4.99 hectares
- 5–10 hectares

Wari Site
- 0.01–0.49 hectare
- 0.5–0.99 hectare
- 1–2.49 hectares

0   2,500   5,000
Meters

in large residential sectors in four large townsite enclaves in locations that were not inhabited previously—the Omo-, Chen Chen–, Río Muerto–, and Cerro Echenique–site groups. These four Tiwanaku areas are all located some distance from the valley floodplain and are connected by desert caravan trails and a series of llama geoglyphs still visible on hillsides near Chen Chen (Figure 15.13).

Mapping Moquegua's Tiwanaku-contemporary colonization is instructive on the socially embedded nature of Tiwanaku economy because the Tiwanaku presence may be subdivided into two distinct contemporary sets of residential components, designated as the Omo and Chen Chen styles. Omo- and Chen Chen–style occupations are found in distinct

residential sectors within each site group. This dispersal indicates simultaneous colonial settlement by different segments of the Tiwanaku population who resided separately and maintained their distinct affiliations and lifeways.

Omo-style Tiwanaku ceramics predominated at fifteen site components covering a total of 28.7 hectares. This presence suggests an Omo-style colonial population of perhaps three thousand people, almost all of whom clustered in large residential sectors at the site groups of Omo, Chen Chen/Los Cerrillos, and Río Muerto. The Omo-style sectors of these townsites are the farthest away from the irrigable valley floodplain and closest to the caravan routes, a placement that could suggest the

figure 15.13
Llama and *qero* geoglyphs, Omo site group. (Photograph by Paul S. Goldstein.)

Omo-style Tiwanaku colonists may have arrived as pastoralists or caravan drovers. Omo-style residential remains consisted of multiroom structures constructed of mats or skins suspended from poles and arrayed in community sectors around plazas for public assembly (Goldstein 1993b, 2000, 2005). The Omo-style colonists brought with them traditions and lifeways that marked their identity with Tiwanaku culture and a wide range of everyday tools and implements that linked their everyday habitual behaviors to those of their homeland. While utilitarian ceramics and some utensils may have been locally made, their formal and functional identity with altiplano Tiwanaku prototypes confirms that they were made by Tiwanaku-trained craftspeople for Tiwanaku consumers adhering to a Tiwanaku way of doing things, and there can be little question that these Tiwanaku colonists were of altiplano

origin. Within this general identity with Tiwanaku origins, specific variants of household practice and material culture were also specific to the Omo style.

Either simultaneously or shortly after the initial Omo-style Tiwanaku colonization, a second set of Tiwanaku towns appeared in Moquegua, and they are associated with a distinct subset of Tiwanaku material culture known as the Chen Chen style (Figure 15.14). Chen Chen–style settlements are found adjacent to the Omo-style sites at the site groups in the Middle Moquegua Valley, covering a total of 54.6 hectares of domestic area, with an additional 10.4 hectares occupied by forty-eight distinct cemeteries (Figure 15.12); this arrangement suggests a mortuary population between ten thousand and twenty thousand burials (Goldstein 2005; Goldstein and Owen 2001). Biometric and isotopic analysis has confirmed the altiplano origins of these

figure 15.14
Chen Chen–style Red Ware *qero*. (Photograph by
Paul S. Goldstein.)

settlers (Blom 1999; Blom et al. 1998; Knudson et al.
2004), and the paleodemography of the Chen Chen
settlement suggests a pattern of adult return migration consistent with long-standing ties to altiplano
parent communities (Baitzel 2008). Typical Chen
Chen Tiwanaku domestic remains included densely
occupied household habitation areas with extensive evidence of agricultural processing and storage
attached to household complexes. Multiple cemeteries were located around the residential sites' peripheries, and some Chen Chen–style settlements were
often also surrounded by informal "suburban" areas
that may have served as temporary housing for tran-
sient laborers. Excavation indicates that Chen Chen
houses were of *quincha* (cane) construction and consisted of autonomous patio groups with functionally
specific activity areas, contiguous roofed rooms,
and open patios. Domestic compounds included
large numbers of subsurface mud-plastered stone
cists and above ground plastered rectangular stone
storage features. The domestic compounds of the
Chen Chen–style sites differ from the Omo-style

occupations in household organization, size, and
productive activities, and the Chen Chen–style
occupation also includes the only example of a
Tiwanaku sunken court temple in the region at the
Omo M10 site (Goldstein 1993a).

Chen Chen–style sites show ample evidence of
intensive cultivation of maize, cotton, coca, peppers, and other temperate crops for export to parent
communities. A massive presence of chipped stone
hoes, large rocker *batanes,* or grinding stones, and
numerous underground storage cists in household
complexes further attest to intensive farming. The
number and size of the *batanes* indicates a focus on
maize processing for both local use and for export
to the altiplano. Ongoing isotopic and paleoethno-
botanical research indicate a prevalence of maize
consumption among the colonists (Muñoz et al.
2009; Sandness 1992), and Moquegua maize kernels have been identified at the site of Tiwanaku
(Hastorf et al. 2006), confirming that production
indeed exceeded demands of the colony and that
surplus was shipped to trade partners in Tiwanaku
and other altiplano communities. Maize was a vital
political resource, essential for the success of the
state and the leaders of its component *ayllus,* in
that it fueled Tiwanaku's ritual cycle in the form
of *chicha,* or maize beer. In Andean societies, the
acceptance of political leadership mandated the
sponsorship of competing festival drinking bouts
critical to economic, social, and political relations.
Because maize cannot grow in the Tiwanaku
homeland due to frost, access to maize from lowland regions would have been a powerful motiva-
tor for each parent community to establish its own
affiliated colonies in lowland regions.

Embedded Economies in the Tiwanaku Colonies

Consideration of Tiwanaku settlement patterns
in Moquegua does not find a well-integrated single hierarchy of site size that would indicate either
market efficiency or a unitary command economy.
Instead, the distinction we see between two separate, crosscutting groups of Tiwanaku colonists

suggests simultaneous migrant streams with distinct origins and allegiances within the Tiwanaku core region. The structured sharing of space in Moquegua between Omo-style and Chen Chen–style colonists may reflect the transplantation of distinct diasporas from two or more autonomous segments of Tiwanaku society. These groups operated as separate social, political, and economic networks, with distinct material cultures and practices, yet their adjacent settlements coexisted within large townsites in the colonies and at the Tiwanaku-type site itself (Bouysse-Cassagne 1986; Kolata 1993:101, 2003).

The prevalence of polished black serving wares and other ceramic types in the Omo-style assemblage suggests affiliations with parent communities on the southwestern shore of Lake Titicaca[4] and sister sites such as Piñami, in the distant Cochabamba Valley of Bolivia (Anderson 2009). This interregional distribution of blackware suggests one corporately linked archipelago extending from the Omo-style colonies of Moquegua to a mirror colony of the same ethnic group on the eastern slopes of the Andes. The contemporary Chen Chen–style sites in Moquegua did not equally participate in the Omo-style network; they instead seem to belong

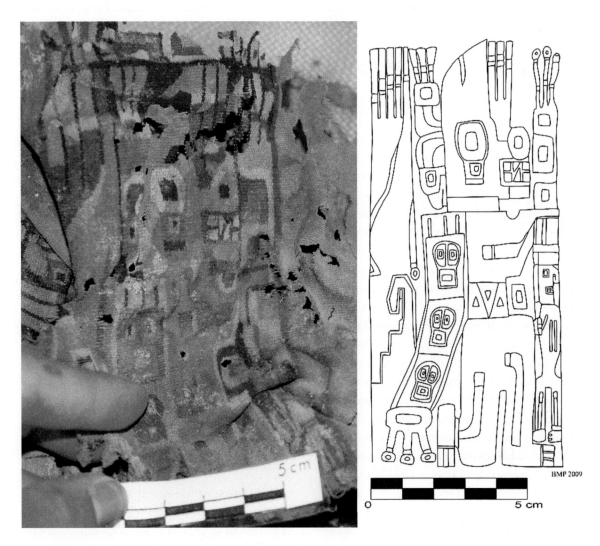

figure 15.15
Tapestry tunic, detail, Río Muerto M43=4507, M43A Tomb R52 (after Plunger 2009). (Photograph by Paul S. Goldstein; reconstruction drawing by Elizabeth Plunger.)

to a distinct subtradition of the greater Tiwanaku style represented in the Tiwanaku site itself and distinct sites in the altiplano and Cochabamba.

It appears that the vast majority of goods and services in the Tiwanaku colonies circulated through something very much like Murra's "archipelagos." Exchanges were embedded in networks of noncontiguous settlements that could crosscut and coexist with one another in different resource zones across the Tiwanaku sphere. These corporate networks mobilized staple and industrial agricultural products (maize, potatoes, coca, legumes, peppers, cotton, wool, meat, and hides), a variety of corvée and communal labor pools, and most craft products (textiles, ceramics, wood, basketry, reed mats, and bone and leather goods). The frequencies of specific substyles of Tiwanaku products, such as black polished serving ware, do not seem to show a typical distance decay pattern that might be expected under market exchange conditions. Instead, high frequencies of blackware ceramics clump in the Copacabana peninsula and in the "islands" of "Omo-style" colonization in Cochabamba and Moquegua. While these items moved between ecological zones, their movement was always embedded in social context—that is, within networks of socially linked parent and sister communities, rather than as alienated commodities in market interactions.

Were there some true commodities in Tiwanaku that pose commercial exceptions to this embedded economic system? The Omo and Chen Chen settlement archipelagos in Moquegua were in contact with one another and traded some goods and services between them, particularly if the two groups truly represent pastoralists, drovers, and agrarian ethnic specialists—a hypothesis that bears further research. Certainly highly specialized craftspeople, and concentration of some rare raw materials, are indicated by some of the Tiwanaku culture's finer serving ceramics, stone and shell beadwork, and most elaborate and labor-intensive textiles. But Tiwanaku-made highly crafted preciosities such as tapestry tunics (Figure 15.15) betray less uniformity and standardization than their Inca counterparts, and are actually quite rare, suggesting that they may have been produced by highly skilled weaver

households and circulated as highly valued and emblematic prestations, rather than through markets or the highly specialized attached workshops and regulated sumptuary redistribution, envisioned for the Inca state's *cumbi* cloth (Murra 1962).

A more compelling possibility for truly commercial market exchange might be sought in external trade between the Tiwanaku colonies and non-Tiwanaku partners. While internal exchange within the expanded Tiwanaku cultural sphere accounted for the vast majority of economic activity for its peoples, the Southern Andes also had a long-standing tradition of long-distance caravan trade between distant regions (Dillehay, this volume; Nielsen, this volume). For Tiwanaku, such intercultural exchange could have included interactions with local groups (Green and Goldstein 2010; Owen 2005; Owen and Goldstein 2001), the Wari colony on Cerro Baúl (Moseley et al. 2005; Williams and Nash 2002), and more distant, non-Tiwanaku "others." Exchange with strangers can be confrontational and fraught with peril (Blanton, this volume), yet extramural trade would have been the only way to obtain certain exotic products or raw materials that were unavailable within the Tiwanaku social sphere. Such goods include *Spondylus* shell from Ecuador, macaw feathers, animal pelts, medicines, and dyes and hallucinogens from the Amazonian region (Figure 15.16), all of which must have been obtained from non-Tiwanaku peoples or via intermediaries, conditions suggestive of disembedded negotiated equivalencies and entrepreneurial action. Further research on obsidian, a sourceable raw material heavily used in the Wari culture but rare in Tiwanaku lithic industries, may be a promising avenue of investigation here. Obsidian is extremely rare in Moquegua Tiwanaku contexts, but what has been found has been traced to Wari-controlled sources, indicating that at least some goods were obtained outside of polity, ethnic, or *ayllu* boundaries (Burger et al. 2000; Goldstein 2005). But when compared to the robust usage of imported obsidian at the nearby Cerro Baúl site (Williams et al. 2001), the minuscule quantity of obsidian found at the Moquegua Tiwanaku sites suggests that there was probably not open market

figure 15.16
Hallucinogenic snuff kit, Río Muerto M43 cemetery A, R30; the snuff kit includes a wooden tablet, net bag, bone tube and spatula, and an animal paw fur container. (Photograph by Paul S. Goldstein.)

exchange across the cultural divide between Wari and Tiwanaku. Indeed, other exchange mode possibilities such as theft, pillage, or even projectile exchange might explain the quantities present. Moreover, in the vast majority of Tiwanaku households and tombs, extracultural exotic commodities from outside the Tiwanaku sphere seldom appear and may have been replaced with internally available import substitutes. Thus, virtually all jewelry and offerings use regionally available *Choromytilus* and oliva shell instead of exotic *Spondylus*; altiplano flamingo feathers replace Amazonian macaw; and white chert, rather than obsidian, is the raw material of choice for the vast majority of small stone tools.

Conclusion

We began by wondering whether new case studies might give cause to question the Murra thesis of Andean economic exceptionalism—that nonmarket economic logics were far more dominant in indigenous Andean states than in the Old World and Mesoamerican civilizations. Could this

"conventional wisdom" have been overstated, or could it even be an artifact of Murra's own substantivist leanings? My consideration of Tiwanaku's agrarian colonies finds support for both Murra's early general statement on the socially embedded nature of Andean economics and his later prediction of "archipelagos" as reciprocal trade networks in colonized resource zones. Tiwanaku has still produced no evidence of marketplaces, commodification, alienation, or systems of equivalencies that suggest trucking or bartering in a price-fixing market.

Nor does it seem that the Tiwanaku colonies responded to a centralized "command economy" like that of the Inca in Murra's initial formulation. At least part of the Inca economic system was a highly centralized top-down redistribution of land and labor, with highly standardized craft production for hegemonic impression-management and emblematic state gifts subject to sumptuary laws, such as uniform tapestry tunics and headgear that embodied both congealed labor value and a centrally regulated social status (Murra 1962). The Inca, of course, also funded massive infrastructural investment in roads, storage, and communication

(D'Altroy 1992, 2001; Hyslop 1990; LeVine 1992; Morris 1986). In contrast, Tiwanaku had few standardized emblematic sumptuary goods to attest to fully attached specialist communities, and luxury goods seem more diverse in manufacture and origin. Neither do Tiwanaku colonized regions nor intervening zones reveal much of the centralized logistical infrastructure in the form of warehouses, roads, *tambos*, and other centrally administered installations that are so emblematic of Inca rule (Goldstein 2005; Stanish et al. 2010).

Instead, the Tiwanaku colonies better fit Murra's later description of a Southern Andean tradition of "reciprocity writ large" (Murra 1982). The scale of settlement represented by the Omo- and Chen Chen–style towns indicates that thousands of Tiwanaku settlers colonized the Moquegua region for agropastoral production. Yet the colonists' principal economic partners appear to have been their own parent communities in the altiplano. Most productive and exchange relationships for labor, produce, and other goods were articulated neither through markets nor through a single centralized command, but through a web of relationships that were continually reproduced and reinforced through social action. All the while, the Tiwanaku colonies retained their segmentation into at least two distinct groups and probably a series of nested subgroups, each with its own parent community counterpart in the homeland and other resource zones. In some lowland valleys like Azapa and Cochabamba with dense indigenous agrarian populations and well-developed political systems, resource allocation was carefully negotiated with local populations across a complex political landscape. In Moquegua, the sheer scale of the Tiwanaku presence indicates that each Tiwanaku corporate subunit sent its own diaspora of colonists to establish productive reciprocal partners to meet its own increasing demands for maize, coca, and cotton for the parent communities in the highlands. These embedded exchange relationships probably included both balanced reciprocity for staple goods between partners of similar status, and asymmetrical reciprocal relationships within Tiwanaku's corporate groups between commoners and their elite patrons for items of political importance, like maize and coca.

In the end, what do the data on provincial Tiwanaku economy tell us about the Murra thesis, the possibility of Andean merchants, and the problem of Andean economic exceptionalism? First, the vast majority of economic transactions in Tiwanaku's extended communities were deeply embedded in social relationships. Whether trade for labor, services, staples, or even preciosities, most exchanges took place between familiar parties who carefully reckoned their social relationships and obligations, rather than "rational" strangers who competed according to utilitarian considerations of supply and demand. Certainly, some "higgling and haggling" no doubt occurred, notably perhaps with strangers offering exotic items from beyond the social boundaries of Tiwanaku settlement. Perhaps some exotic imports—such as Ecuadorian *Spondylus* shell, Amazonian macaw feathers and medicinals, or foreign obsidian (for which Tiwanaku had poor internal sources)—can be thought of as commodified in this way and changed hands via professional merchants in the disembedded, even hostile, conceptual space of market exchange. But the rarity of these items in domestic contexts tells us that they never enjoyed the widespread market distribution of such goods in Mesoamerican societies. True market commerce, even in the distribution of exotic imports, is not evident in Tiwanaku. Instead, the preponderance of evidence from the Tiwanaku colonies supports an outside reliance on socially embedded reciprocity and productive colonization for exchanging virtually all categories of goods and services. If Tiwanaku merchants are to be found, then future research must look to the acquisition of rare commodities that come from well outside the margins of Tiwanaku's powerfully integrated social world.

NOTES

1 Some archaeological critics discount Polanyi
entirely for suggesting that the "great transformation" to market relations occurred only with the
advent of capitalism. Rejecting the substantivist contribution due to this overstatement would
be akin to rejecting the archaeological adaptation
of World Systems Theory to premodern societies
because Wallerstein made a similar overstatement.

2 Lupaqa colonies included up to several hundred
households (Murra 1972:443). Lupaqa colonists
maintained their privileges and obligations as
members of specific homeland communities.

3 In other regions, far smaller Tiwanaku enclaves
settled amid indigenous majority traditions, as in
the Azapa Valley (Dauelsberg 1985; Goldstein 1996;
Muñoz Ovalle 1996; Muñoz Ovalle and Santos 1998;
Rivera Diaz 1999; Rivera 2002), the neighboring

Chaca, Camarones, and Lluta Valleys of northern
Chile (Santoro 1980), and the Locumba, Sama, and
Caplina Valleys of southern Peru (Disselhoff 1968;
Flores Espinoza 1969; Lynch 1983; Trimborn 1973;
Uhle 1919; Vela Velarde 1992). A similar pattern
may hold for the valleys of the Cochabamba region
(Anderson 2009; Goldstein 1996, 2005; Higueras
1996), but it is as yet difficult to detect migration
streams or Tiwanaku's internal sociopolitical
structure in these regions.

4 Black polished ceramics were excavated by Adolph
Bandelier in the cemeteries of Ciriapata and Titin-
uayni on the Island of the Sun and the lakeside
sites of Mocachi and Copacabana, while the prevalence of the continuous volute motif also suggests
connections to Lukurmata and the Katari Valley
(Bermann 1994; Goldstein 2005; Janusek 2003).

REFERENCES CITED

Abercrombie, Thomas
1998 *Pathways of Memory and Power:
Ethnography and History among an
Andean People.* University of Wisconsin
Press, Milwaukee.

Adams, Robert M.
1978 Strategies of Maximization, Stability,
and Resilience in Mesopotamian
Society, Settlement, and Agriculture.
*Proceedings of the American Philosophi-
cal Society* 122(5):329–335.

Akin, David, and Joel Robbins (editors)
1999 *Money and Modernity: State and Local
Currencies in Melanesia.* University of
Pittsburgh Press, Pittsburgh.

Albarracin-Jordan, Juan
1996a Tiwanaku Settlement Systems: The
Integration of Nested Hierarchies in the
Lower Tiwanaku Valley. *Latin American
Antiquity* 3(3):183–210.
1996b *Tiwanaku: Arqueología regional y
dinámica segmentaria.* Editores Plural,
La Paz.

Algaze, Guillermo
1993 *The Uruk World System: The Dynamics
of Early Mesopotamian Civilization.*
University of Chicago Press, Chicago.

Anderson, Karen
2009 Tiwanaku Influence on Local Drinking
Patterns in Cochabamba, Bolivia. In
Drink, Power, and Society in the Andes,
edited by Justin Jennings and Brenda
J. Bowser, pp. 167–199. University of
Florida Press, Gainesville.

Astvaldsson, Astvaldur
2000 The Dynamics of Aymara Duality:
Change and Continuity in Sociopolitical
Structures in the Bolivian Andes. *Journal
of Latin American Studies* 32(1):145–174.

Baitzel, Sarah I.
2008 No Country for Old People: A
Paleodemographic Study of Tiwanaku
Return Migration in Moquegua,
Peru. MA thesis, Department of
Anthropology, University of California,
San Diego.

Baitzel, Sarah I., and Paul S. Goldstein

2011   Manifesting Ethnic Identity in an Ancient Society: Evidence from a Tiwanaku Cemetery in Moquegua, Peru. In *Ethnicity from Various Angles and through Varied Lenses*, edited by Christine Hunefeldt and León Zamosc, pp. 30–44 . Sussex Academic Press, Sussex.

Berdan, Frances F.

1982   *The Aztecs of Central Mexico: An Imperial Society*. Holt, Rinehart, and Winston, New York.

Berenguer, José R.

1998   La iconografía del poder en Tiwanaku y su rol en la integración de zonas de frontera. *Boletín del Museo Chileno de Arte Precolombino* 7:19–37.

Bermann, Marc P.

1994   *Lukurmata: Household Archaeology in Prehispanic Bolivia*. Princeton University Press, Princeton.

1997   Domestic Life and Vertical Integration in the Tiwanaku Heartland. *Latin American Antiquity* 8(2):93–112.

Blanton, Richard E., and Lane F. Fargher

2010   Evaluating Causal Factors in Market Development in Premodern States: A Comparative Study with Critical Comments on the History of Ideas about Markets. In *Archaeological Approaches to Market Exchange in Ancient Societies*, edited by Christopher P. Garraty and Barbara L. Stark, pp. 207–226. University Press of Colorado, Boulder.

Blom, Deborah E.

1999   Tiwanaku Regional Interaction and Social Identity: A Bioarchaeological Approach. PhD dissertation, Department of Anthropology, University of Chicago, Chicago.

2005   Embodying Borders: Human Body Modification and Diversity in Tiwanaku Society. *Journal of Anthropological Archaeology* 24(1):1–24.

Blom, Deborah E., Benedikt Hallgrímsson, Linda Keng, María C. Lozada C., and Jane. E. Buikstra

1998   Tiwanaku "Colonization": Bioarchaeological Implications for Migration in the Moquegua Valley, Peru. *World Archaeology* 30(2):238–261.

Bouysse-Cassagne, Thérèse

1986   Urco and Uma: Aymara Concepts of Space. In *Anthropological History of Andean Polities*, edited by John V. Murra, Nathan Wachtel, and Jacques Revel, pp. 201–227. Cambridge University Press, Cambridge.

Brush, Stephen B.

1977   *Mountain, Field, and Family: The Economy and Human Ecology of an Andean Valley*. University of Pennsylvania Press, Philadelphia.

Buikstra, Jane E.

1995   Tombs for the Living . . . or . . . For the Dead: The Osmore Ancestors. In *Tombs for the Living: Andean Mortuary Practices*, edited by Tom D. Dillehay, pp. 229–280. Dumbarton Oaks Research Library and Collection, Washington, D.C.

Buikstra, Jane E., Susan R. Frankenberg, and Lyle W. Konigsberg

1990   Skeletal Biological Distance Studies in American Physical Anthropology: Recent Trends. *American Journal of Physical Anthropology* 82:1–7.

Burger, Richard L., Karen L. Mohr Chávez, and Sergio J. Chávez

2000   Through the Glass Darkly: Prehispanic Obsidian Procurement and Exchange in Southern Peru and Northern Bolivia. *Journal of World Prehistory* 14(3):267–362.

Clifford, James

1994   Diasporas. *Cultural Anthropology* 9(3):302–338.

D'Altroy, Terence N.

1992   *Provincial Power in the Inka Empire*. Smithsonian Institution Press, Washington, D.C.

2001   Politics, Resources, and Blood in the Inka Empire. In *Empires: Perspectives from Archaeology and History*, edited by Susan E. Alcock, Terence N. D'Altroy, Kathleen D. Morrison, and Carla M. Sinopoli, pp. 201–226. Cambridge University Press, Cambridge.

Dauelsberg, Percy

1985   Desarrollo regional en los valles costeros del norte de Chile. *La problemática*

Tiwanaku-Huari en el contexto panan-dino del desarrollo cultural, edited by M. A. Rivera, pp. 277–287. Universidad de Tarapacá, Arica, Chile.

Disselhoff, Hans D.

1968   Huari und Tiahuanaco: Grabungen und Funde in Sud-Peru. *Zeitschrift fur Ethnologie* 93:207–216.

Flores Espinoza, Isabel

1969   Informe preliminar sobre las investiga-ciones arqueológicas de Tacna. Paper presented at the Mesa Redonda de Ciencias Prehistóricas y Antropológicas, Lima.

Fortier, Jane, and Paul S. Goldstein

2006   Agrarian Diasporas Past and Present: Highland Colonization in the South Central Andes. Paper presented at the 105th Annual Meeting of the American Anthropological Association, San Jose, Calif.

Godelier, Maurice

1977   *Perspectives in Marxist Anthropology.* Translated by Robert Brain. Cambridge University Press, Cambridge.

Goldstein, Paul S.

1993a   Tiwanaku Temples and State Expansion: A Tiwanaku Sunken Court Temple in Moquegua, Peru. *Latin American Antiquity* 4(3):22–47.

1993b   House, Community, and State in the Earliest Tiwanaku Colony: Domestic Patterns and State Integration at Omo M12, Moquegua. In *Domestic Architecture, Ethnicity, and Comple-mentarity in the South-Central Andes*, edited by Mark Aldenderfer, pp. 25–41. University of Iowa Press, Iowa City.

1996   Tiwanaku Settlement Patterns of the Azapa Valley, Chile—New Data, and the Legacy of Percy Dauelsberg. *Diálogo andino* 14–15:57–73.

2000   Communities without Borders: The Vertical Archipelago, and Diaspora Communities in the Southern Andes. In *The Archaeology of Communities: A New World Perspective*, edited by Jason Yaeger and Marcelo Canuto, pp. 182–209. Routledge Press, London.

2005   *Andean Diaspora: The Tiwanaku Colonies and the Origins of South American Empire.* University Press of Florida, Gainesville.

Goldstein, Paul S., and Francis J. Magilligan

2011   Hazard, Risk, and Agrarian Adaptations in a Hyperarid Watershed: El Niño Floods, Streambank Erosion, and the Cultural Bounds of Vulnerability in the Andean Middle Horizon. *Catena* 85:155–167.

Goldstein, Paul S., and Bruce D. Owen

2001   Tiwanaku en Moquegua: Las colonias altiplánicas. *Boletín de arqueología* PUCP 5:139–168.

Granovetter, Mark S.

1985   Economic Action and Social Structure: The Problem of Embeddedness. *American Journal of Sociology* 91(3):481–510.

Green, Ulrike Matthies, and Paul S. Goldstein

2010   The Nature of Wari Presence in the Mid-Moquegua Valley: Investigating Contact at Cerro Trapiche. In *Beyond Wari Walls: Exploring the Nature of Middle Horizon Peru Away from Wari Centers*, edited by Justin Jennings, pp. 19–36. University of New Mexico Press, Albuquerque.

Gregory, C. A.

2000   Anthropology, Economics, and Political Economy: A Critique of Pearson. *History of Political Economy* 32(4):999–1009.

Halperin, Rhoda H.

1994   *Cultural Economies Past and Present.* University of Texas Press, Austin.

Hassig, Ross

1985   *Trade, Tribute, and Transportation: The Sixteenth-Century Political Economy of the Valley of Mexico.* University of Oklahoma Press, Norman.

Hastorf, Christine A., William T. Whitehead, Maria C. Bruno, and Melanie F. Wright

2006   Movements of Maize into Middle Horizon Tiwanaku, Bolivia. In *Histories of Maize: Multidisciplinary Approaches to the Prehistory, Linguistics, Biogeography, Domestication, and Evolution of Maize*, edited by John E. Staller, Robert H. Tykot, and Bruce F. Benz, pp. 429–447. Elsevier Academic Press, Burlington, Mass.

Hidalgo Lehuedé, Jorge

1996 Relaciones protohistóricas interétnicas entre las poblaciones locales y altiplánicas en Arica. In *La integración surandina: Cinco siglos después*, compiled by Xavier Albó, María Inés Arratia, Jorge Hidalgo, Lautaro Nuñez, Agustín Llagostera, María Isabel Remy, and Bruno Revesz, pp. 161–174. Centro de Estudios Regionales Andinos "Bartolomé de Las Casas," Cuzco, and Universidad Católica del Norte, Antofagasta.

Hidalgo Lehuedé, Jorge, and Guillermo Focacci Aste

1986 Multietnicidad en Arica S. XVI: Evidencias etnohistóricas y arqueológicas. *Chungará* 16–17:137–147.

Higueras, Alvaro

1996 Prehispanic Settlement and Land Use in Cochabamba, Bolivia. PhD disseration, Department of Anthropology, University of Pittsburgh, Pittsburgh.

2001 El periodo intermedio (horizonte medio) en los valles de Cochabamba: Una perspectiva del análisis de asentamientos humanos y uso de tierras. *Boletín de arqueología* PUCP 5:623–646.

Hirth, Kenneth G.

1978 Interregional Trade and the Formation of Prehistoric Gateway Communities. *American Antiquity* 43(1):35–45.

1984 *Trade and Exchange in Early Mesoamerica*. University of New Mexico Press, Albuquerque.

2010 Finding the Mark in the Marketplace: The Organization, Development, and Archaeological Identification of Market Systems. In *Archaeological Approaches to Market Exchange in Ancient Societies*, edited by Christopher P. Garraty and Barbara L. Stark, pp. 227–248. University Press of Colorado, Boulder.

Hoshower, Lisa M., Jane E. Buikstra, Paul S. Goldstein, and Ann D. Webster

1995 Artificial Cranial Deformation at the Omo M10 Site: A Tiwanaku Complex from the Moquegua Valley, Peru. *Latin American Antiquity* 6(2):145–164.

Hyslop, John

1990 *Inka Settlement Planning*. University of Texas Press, Austin.

Isaac, Barry L.

1993 Retrospective on the Formalist-Substantivist Debate. *Research in Economic Anthropology* 14:213–233.

1996 Approaches to Classic Maya Economies. *Research in Economic Anthropology* 17:297–334.

Isbell, William H.

1997 *Mummies and Mortuary Monuments: A Postprocessual Prehistory of Central Andean Social Organization.* University of Texas Press, Austin.

Janusek, John W.

1999 Craft and Local Power: Embedded Specialization in Tiwanaku Cities. *Latin American Antiquity* 10(2):107–131.

2002 Out of Many, One: Style and Social Boundaries in Tiwanaku. *Latin American Antiquity* 13(1):35–61.

2003 Vessels, Time, and Society: Toward a Ceramic Chronology in the Tiwanaku Heartland. In *Tiwanaku and Its Hinterland: Archaeology and Paleoecology of an Andean Civilization*, edited by Alan L. Kolata, pp. 30–91. Smithsonian Institution Press, Washington, D.C.

2004 *Identity and Power in the Ancient Andes: Tiwanaku Cities through Time.* Routledge, New York.

Janusek, John W., and Alan L. Kolata

2004 Top-down or Bottom-up: Rural Settlement and Raised Field Agriculture in the Lake Titicaca Basin, Bolivia. *Journal of Anthropological Archaeology* 23(4):404–430.

Julien, Catherine

1985 Guano and Resource Control in the Southern Sixteenth-Century Arequipa. In *Andean Ecology and Civilization: An Interdisciplinary Perspective on Andean Ecological Complementarity*, edited by Shozo Masuda, Izumi Shimada, and Craig Morris, pp. 185–232. University of Tokyo Press, Tokyo.

Knudson, Kelly J.

2008 Tiwanaku Influence in the South Central Andes: Strontium Isotope Analysis and Middle Horizon Migration. *Latin American Antiquity* 19(1):3–23.

Knudson, Kelly J., T. Douglas Price, Jane E. Buikstra, and Deborah E. Blom

2004   The Use of Strontium Isotope Analysis to Investigate Tiwanaku Migration and Mortuary Ritual in Boliva and Peru. *Archaeometry* 46(1):5–18.

Kolata, Alan L.

1993   *The Tiwanaku: Portrait of an Andean Civilization.* Blackwell, Cambridge, Mass.

2003   The Social Production of Tiwanaku: Political Economy and Authority in a Native Andean State. In *Tiwanaku and Its Hinterland: Archaeology and Paleoecology of an Andean Civilization,* vol. 2, *Urban and Rural Archaeology,* edited by Alan L. Kolata, pp. 449–472. Smithsonian Institution Press, Washington, D.C.

Kolata, Alan L. (editor)

1996   *Tiwanaku and Its Hinterland: Archaeology and Paleoecology of an Andean Civilization,* vol. 1, *Agroecology.* Smithsonian Institution Press, Washington, D.C.

Kolata, Alan L., and Charles Ortloff

1996   Agroecological Perspectives on the Decline of the Tiwanaku State. In *Tiwanaku and Its Hinterland: Archaeology and Paleoecology of an Andean Civilization,* edited by Alan L. Kolata, pp. 181–202. Smithsonian Institution Press, Washington, D.C.

Korpisaari, Antti

2006   *Death in the Bolivian High Plateau.* BAR, Oxford.

La Lone, Darrell E.

1982   The Inca as a Nonmarket Economy: Supply on Command versus Supply and Demand. In *Contexts for Prehistoric Exchange,* edited by Jonathon E. Ericson and Timothy K. Earle, pp. 291–316. Academic Press, New York.

LeVine, Terry Y. (editor)

1992   *Inka Storage Systems.* University of Oklahoma Press, Norman.

Lie, John

1997   Sociology of Markets. *Annual Review of Sociology* 23:341–360.

Lozada Cerna, Maria Cecilia

1998   The Señorio of Chiribaya: A Bio-Archaeological Study in the Osmore Drainage of Southern Peru. PhD dissertation, Department of Anthropology, University of Chicago, Chicago.

Lynch, Thomas F.

1983   Camelid Pastoralism and the Emergence of Tiwanaku Civilization in the South Central Andes. *World Archaeology* 15:1–14.

Magilligan, Francis J., and Paul S. Goldstein

2001   El Niño Floods and Culture Change: A Late Holocene Flood History for the Rio Moquegua, Southern Peru. *Geology* 29(5):431–434.

Magilligan, Francis J., Paul S. Goldstein, and R. J. Manners

2008   Climate Change, Floods, and Alluvial Adjustments in a Hyper-Arid Watershed in the Atacama Desert: Links to the El-Niño-Southern Oscillation. Paper presented at the Binghamton Geomorphology Symposium, "Fluvial Deposits and Environmental History," Austin.

Manners, Rebecca B., Francis J. Magilligan, and Paul S. Goldstein

2007   Floodplain Development, El Niño, and Cultural Consequences in a Hyperarid Andean Environment. *Annals of the Association of American Geographers* 97(2):229–248.

McAndrews, Tim, Juan Albarracin-Jordan, and Marc P. Bermann

1997   Regional Settlement Patterns of the Tiwanaku Valley of Bolivia. *Journal of Field Archaeology* 24:67–83.

Morris, Craig

1979   Review of *La organización económica del estado Inca,* by John V. Murra. *American Antiquity* 81:922–923.

1986   Storage, Supply, and Redistribution in the Economy of the Inka State. In *Anthropological History of Andean Polities,* edited by John Murra, Nathan Wachtel, and Jacques Revel, pp. 59–68. Cambridge University Press, Cambridge.

Moseley, Michael E.

1992   *The Incas and Their Ancestors: The Archaeology of Peru.* Thames and Hudson, New York.

Moseley, Michael E., Donna J. Nash, Patrick Ryan
    Williams, Susan D. de France, A. Miranda, and
    M. Ruales
    2005   Burning Down the Brewery: Estab-
            lishing and Evacuating an Ancient
            Imperial Colony at Cerro Baúl, Peru.
            *Proceedings of the National Academy of
            Sciences of the United States of America*
            102(48):17264–17271.

Muñoz, L., D. J., Paul S. Goldstein, A. Boswell, and
    A. Somerville
    2009   Growing Tiwanaku: Social Identity and
            Plant Use in Domestic and Funerary
            Contexts. Paper presented at the 74th
            Annual Meeting of the Society for
            American Archaeology, Atlanta.

Muñoz Ovalle, Iván
    1996   Integración y complementariedad en las
            sociedades prehispánicas en el extremo
            norte de Chile: Hipótesis de trabajo. In
            *La integración surandina: Cinco siglos
            después*, edited by Xavier Albó, María
            Inés Arratia, Jorge Hidalgo, Lautaro
            Nuñez, Agustín Llagostera, María Isabel
            Remy, and Bruno Revesz, pp. 117–134.
            Centro de Estudios Regionales Andinos
            "Bartolomé de Las Casas," Cuzco,
            and Universidad Católica del Norte,
            Antofagasta.

Muñoz Ovalle, Iván, and Mariela Santos
    1998   Desde el período Tiwanaku al indígena
            colonial: Uso del espacio e interacción
            social en la Quebrada de Miñita, norte
            de Chile. *Diálogo andino* 17:71–114.

Murra, John V.
    1962   Cloth and Its Functions in the Inka
            State. *American Anthropologist*
            64:710–728.
    1964   Una apreciación etnológica de la
            visita. In *Visita hecha a la provincia
            de Chucuito*, edited by John V. Murra,
            pp. 419–442. Casa de la Cultura del
            Perú, Lima.
    1968   An Aymara Kingdom in 1567.
            Ethnohistory 15:115–151.
    1972   El "control vertical" de un máximo
            de pisos ecológicos en la economía de
            las sociedades andinas. In *Visita de
            la Provincia de León de Huánuco en
            1562 por Iñigo Ortiz de Zuñiga*, vol. 2,
            edited by John V. Murra, pp. 427–476.

            Universidad Nacional Hermilio
            Valdizan, Huánuco.
    1980 [1955] *The Economic Organization of the Inka
            State*. JAI Press, Greenwich, Conn.
    1982   The Mit'a Obligations of Ethnic Groups
            to the Inka State. In *The Inca and Aztec
            States, 1400–1800*, edited by George
            Collier, R. Rosaldo, and J. Wirth, pp. 237–
            264. Academic Press, New York.
    1985   "El Archipiélago Vertical" Revisited:
            Limits and Limitations of the "Vertical
            Archipelago" in the Andes. In *Andean
            Ecology and Civilization: An Interdisci-
            plinary Perspective on Andean Ecological
            Complementary*, edited by Shozo Masuda,
            Izumi Shimada, and Craig Morris, pp. 3–
            20. University of Tokyo Press, Tokyo.

Oakland, Amy
    1992   Textiles and Ethnicity: Tiwanaku in San
            Pedro de Atacama, North Chile. *Latin
            American Antiquity* 3(4):316–340.

Owen, Bruce D.
    2005   Distant Colonies and Explosive
            Collapse: The Two Stages of the
            Tiwanaku Diaspora in the Osmore
            Drainage. *Latin American Antiquity*
            16(1):45–80.

Owen, Bruce D., and Paul S. Goldstein
    2001   Tiwanaku en Moquegua: Interacciones
            regionales y colapso. *Boletín de arque-
            ología PUCP* 5:169–188.

Patterson, Tom, and C. W. Gailey
    1987   Power Relations and State Formation.
            In *Power Relations and State Formation*,
            edited by Tom Patterson and C. Gailey,
            pp. 1–27. American Anthropological
            Association, Washington, D.C.

Pease G. Y., Franklin
    1980   Las relaciones entre las tierras altas y la
            costa del sur del Perú: Fuentes documen-
            tales. *Bulletin of the National Museum of
            Ethnology* 5(1):301–310. Osaka.
    1984   Indices notariales de Moquegua,
            siglo XVI: Una introducción. In
            *Contribuciones a los estudios de los Andes
            centrales*, edited by S. Masuda, pp. 151–
            383. University of Tokyo Press, Tokyo.

Platt, Tristan
    1986   Mirrors and Maize: The Concept of
            Yanantin among the Macha of Bolivia.

In *Anthropological History of Andean Polities*, edited by John V. Murra, Nathan Wachtel, and Jacques Reve, pp. 228–259. Cambridge University Press, Cambridge.

Plunger, E. M.

2009   Woven Connections: Group Identity, Style, and the Textiles of the "A" and "B" Cemeteries at the Site of Rio Muerto (M43), Moquegua Valley, Southern Peru. MA thesis, Department of Anthropology, University of California, San Diego.

Polanyi, Karl

1944   *The Great Transformation.* Beacon Press, Boston.

1957   The Economy as Instituted Process. In *Trade and Market in Early Empires*, edited by Karl Polanyi, C. Arensburg, and H. Pearson, pp. 243–270. Free Press, Glencoe, Ill.

Rivera, Mario A.

1999   Prehistory of the Southern Cone. In *The Cambridge History of the Native Peoples of the Americas,* vol. 3, *South America*, edited by Frank Salomon and Stuart Schwartz, pp. 734–768. Cambridge University Press, Cambridge.

2002   *Historias del desierto: Arqueología del norte de Chile.* Editorial del Norte, La Serena.

Rostworowski de Diez Canseco, María

1986   La región del Colesuyu. *Chungará* 16–17:127–135.

1988   *Historia del Tahuantinsuyu.* Instituto de Estudios Peruanos, Lima.

Rothhammer, Francisco, José Cocilovo, Elena Llop, and Silvia Quevedo

1989   Orígenes y microevolución de la población chilena. In *Culturas de Chile, prehistoria desde sus orígenes hasta los albores de la conquista*, edited by J. Hidalgo L., V. Schiappacasse F., H. Niemeyer F., C. Aldunate, and I. Solimano R., pp. 403–413. Editorial Andrés Bello, Santiago.

Rothhammer, Francisco, and Calogero Santoro

2001   El desarrollo cultural en el Valle de Azapa, extremo norte de Chile y su vinculacion con los desplazamientos poblacionales altiplanicos. *Latin American Antiquity* 12(1):59–66.

Rowe, John H.

1946   Inca Culture at the Time of the Spanish Conquest. In *Handbook of South American Indians*, vol. 2, edited by Julian H. Steward, pp. 183–330. Cooper Square, New York.

Saignes, Thierry

1986   The Ethnic Groups in the Valley of Larecaja: From Descent to Residence. In *Anthropological History of Andean Polities*, edited by John V. Murra, Nathan Wachtel, and Jacques Revel, pp. 311–341. Cambridge University Press, Cambridge.

Salomon, Frank

1986   Vertical Politics on the Inka Frontier. In *Anthropological History of Andean Polities*, edited by John V. Murra, Nathan Wachtel, and Jacques Revel, pp. 89–117. Cambridge University Press, Cambridge.

1991   Introductory Essay: The Huarochirí Manuscript. In *The Huarochirí Manuscript*, edited by Frank Salomon and George L. Urioste, pp. 1–38. University of Texas Press, Austin.

2007   John Victor Murra (1916–2006). *American Anthropologist* 109:792–796.

Sandness, K.

1992   Temporal and Spatial Dietary Variability in the Osmore Drainage, Southern Peru: The Isotope Evidence. MA thesis, Department of Anthropology, University of Nebraska, Lincoln.

Santoro, Calogero

1980   Estratigrafía y secuencia cultural funeraria: Fase Azapa, Alto Ramírez y Tiwanaku. *Chungará* 6:24–45.

Sherbondy, Jeanette

1982   The Canal Systems of Hanan Cuzco. PhD dissertation, Department of Anthropology, University of Illinois, Urbana-Champaign.

Smith, Carol A.

1976   Regional Economic Systems: Linking Geographical Models and Economic Problems. In *Regional Analysis*, edited by Carol A. Smith, pp. 3–63. Academic Press, New York.

Smith, Michael E.

2001 The Aztec Empire and the Meso-american World System. In *Empires: Perspectives from Archaeology and History*, edited by Susan E. Alcock, Terence N. D'Altroy, Kathleen D. Morrison, and Carla M. Sinopoli, pp. 128–154. Cambridge University Press, Cambridge.

2004 The Archaeology of Ancient Economies. *Annual Review of Anthropology* 33:73–102.

Stanish, Charles

1997 Nonmarket Imperialism in the Prehispanic Americas: The Inka Occupation of the Titicaca Basin. *Latin American Antiquity* 8(3):195–216.

2000 Negotiating Rank in an Imperial State: Lake Titicaca Basin Elite under Inca and Spanish Control. In *Hierarchies in Action, Qui Bono?*, edited by Michael W. Diehl, pp. 317–339. Center for Archaeo-logical Investigations, Southern Illinois University, Carbondale.

2002 Tiwanaku Political Economy. In *Andean Archaeology*, vol. 1, *Variations in Sociopolitical Organization*, edited by William H. Isbell and Helaine Silverman, pp. 169–198. Kluwer Academic/Plenum, New York.

2003 *Ancient Titicaca: The Evolution of Complex Society in Southern Peru and Northern Bolivia.* University of California Press, Berkeley.

Stanish, Charles, Edmundo de la Vega, Michael E. Moseley, Patrick R. Williams, Cecilia J. Chávez, Benjamin Vining, and Karl LaFavre

2010 Tiwanaku Trade Patterns in Southern Peru. *Journal of Anthropological Archaeology* 29(4):524–532.

Stein, Gil J.

1999 *Rethinking World Systems: Diasporas, Colonies, and Interaction in Uruk Mesopotamia.* University of Arizona Press, Tucson.

Sutter, Richard C.

2000 Prehistoric Genetic and Culture Change: A Bioarchaeological Search for Pre-Inka Altiplano Colonies in the Coastal Valleys of Moquegua Valley, Perú, and Azapa, Chile. *Latin American Antiquity* 11(1):43–70.

Tomczak, Paula D.

2003 Prehistoric Diet and Socioeconomic Relationships within the Osmore Valley of Southern Peru. *Journal of Anthropological Archaeology* 22:262–278.

Torres-Rouff, Christina

2002 Cranial Vault Modification and Ethnicity in Middle Horizon San Pedro de Atacama, Chile. *Current Anthropology* 43:163–171.

Trimborn, Hermann

1973 Investigaciones arqueológicas en el departamento de Tacna. In *Atti del XL Congreso Internazionale Degle Americanisti*, vol. 1, pp. 333–335. Genoa.

Uhle, Max

1919 La arqueología de Arica y Tacna. *Boletín de la Sociedad Ecuatoriana de Estudios Históricos Americanos* 3:1–48.

Urton, Gary

1993 Moieties and Ceremonialism in the Andes: The Ritual Battles of the Carnival Season in Southern Peru. In *El mundo ceremonial andino*, edited by Luis Millones and Yoshio Onuki, pp. 117–142. Senri Ethnological Studies 37. National Museum of Ethnology, Osaka.

Van Buren, Mary

1996 Rethinking the Vertical Archipelago. *American Anthropologist* 98(2):338–351.

Vela Velarde, Carlos

1992 Tiwanaku en el Valle de Caplina (Tacna). *Pumapunku*, new series, 1(3):31–45.

Williams, Patrick Ryan, J. Isla C., and Donna J. Nash

2001 Cerro Baúl: Un enclave wari en interac-ción con Tiwanaku. *Boletín de arque-ología PUCP* 5:169–188.

Williams, Patrick Ryan, and Donna J. Nash

2002 Imperial Interaction in the Andes: Huari and Tiwanaku at Cerro Baúl. In *Andean Archaeology*, vol. 1, *Variations in Sociopolitical Organization*, edited by William H. Isbell and Helaine Silverman, pp. 243–265. Kluwer Academic/Plenum, New York.

16

Circulating Objects and the Constitution
of South Andean Society (500 BC–AD 1550)

AXEL E. NIELSEN

BROADLY CONCEIVED AS THE MUTUALLY appropriative movement of things between agents (Polanyi 1953:234), exchange is the most basic expression of the social nature of human action. As such, trade offers a privileged vantage point for studying the reproduction of society and culture. Building on this simple premise, I explore in this paper the relationship between interregional circulation practices and social change in the Southern Andes between 500 BC and AD 1550. In so doing, I discuss widely shared ideas about the role of long-distance trade, merchants, and market principles in the history of this area.

As the southernmost division of the Andean world, the Southern Andes include northwestern Argentina, northern Chile, and southwestern Bolivia (Figure 16.1). This area shares with the more famous Central Andes some characteristics, such as the pronounced, altitude-dependent environmental diversity and the ensuing need for human populations to access resources from different ecozones. But it also has differences, three of which

need to be stressed here. First, it is more arid, colder, and shows a significantly lower primary productivity; patches suitable for human settlement are small and separated by vast deserts, salt pans, and high mountains. These conditions resulted in lower demographic densities with relatively small population aggregates occupying fertile valleys or oases, separated by wide stretches of scarcely inhabited land. Second, at the core of the south Andean highlands is a vast high plateau (> 3,500 meters above sea level [masl]) called altiplano (in Bolivia) or puna (in Argentina), which offers the best conditions for llama herding. Consequently, the Southern Andes had a large stock of pack animals in the New World and developed a strong emphasis on pastoralism. Third, if we consider state-level institutions, urbanism, monumental architecture, and large-scale productive infrastructure as hallmarks of social complexity, then Southern Andean societies were never complex; states only reached this area as a result of the Inca conquest in the fifteenth century. These conditions offer a good opportunity for

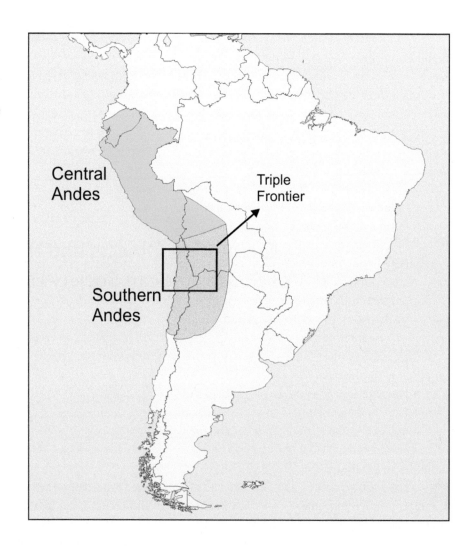

figure 16.1
Map of the Southern
Andes, showing the
location of the Triple
Frontier. (Map by
Axel E. Nielsen.)

assessing the existence and relative importance of market practices and institutions in societies without cities or states.

The first archaeologists working in the Southern Andes were well aware of the high frequency of nonlocal items and, therefore, they acknowledged the significance of long-distance trade in the area (Boman 1991 [1908]; Latcham 1909). For this reason, Murra's (1975) thesis regarding the limited importance of interethnic trade in Andean economies at the time of the Incas seemed at odds with the archaeological evidence then. The reaction to this apparent contradiction came in the form of alternative models that sought to grasp the particularities of South Andean society, mainly by stressing the role of llama herders and their part in exchange. Browman's (1980) "altiplano mode"—applied

mainly to Tiwanaku and its associated interaction sphere—emphasized specialization and commerce through llama caravans. In the Titicaca Basin and farther south, according to Browman, economic mechanisms of integration prevailed over the political and ethnic bonds highlighted by verticality in Murra's model. More influential, however, was Núñez and Dillehay's (1979) "circuit mobility," which embraced the influential substantivist stand of Murra, dissociating the notion of caravan trade from market principles and commerce. In their model, which included a sequence of historical scenarios from the Archaic Period through the Spanish conquest, herders and their caravans played a central part since the Formative Period, but they were seen as operating through reciprocal and redistributive arrangements.

In its original formulation, however, circuit mobility was quite vague on the social context of trade (Dillehay and Núñez 1988:615). Given the limited data available at the time, the authors avoided such questions as: Who ran these caravans? How did they relate to nonpastoral groups or their authorities? What were the political consequences of caravan trade? In practice, some of the questions were addressed in various ways by those who applied their ideas to specific cases (Berenguer 2004; Céspedes and Lecoq 1998; Nielsen 2001a; Núñez 1994; Pérez 2000:252), resorting mostly to the political models of trade associated with cultural evolutionism and Marxism, which were influential in the anglophone literature on the origins of social complexity of the 1980s and 1990s (e.g., Brumfiel and Earle 1987; Friedman and Rowlands 1978).

As a result, the most common framework used today in the Southern Andes to interpret the significance of archaeological evidence of trade is a flexible, usually implicit, combination of ideas that can be summarized in the form of three general, nonexclusive models that I label "no-market," "caravan mobility," and "elite control."

No-Market Model

It is generally believed that markets were absent in Andean economies (Llagostera 1996; Núñez and Dillehay 1979; but see also Browman 1980). Given the multiple connotations of this term, let me define briefly what I mean by this and other related concepts addressed in this chapter. Market exchange refers to transactions in goods or services. It is ruled mainly by the forces of supply and demand (Pryor 1977:104), with barter being its simplest expression. Items transferred in this way are commodities, meaning that exchangeability is the main source of their value and that their circulation does not create lasting obligations among the trade parties (Appadurai 1986; Gregory 1994). Market exchange is frequently, but not necessarily, associated with other practices, settings, and institutions to form market systems. Important among them are marketplaces—locations that regularly concentrate

market exchange—and merchants, or "distribution specialists" (Hirth and Pillsbury, this volume). At the most general level, the market can also be conceived as a structuring principle (Giddens 1984): when market systems are well developed, they may permeate noneconomic fields of action, providing symbols, logics, and dispositions that are drawn upon in multiple social practices. It is in this sense that Polanyi (1953) referred to the market as a principle of social integration that characterized modern capitalism.

Most archaeologists working in the Southern Andes believe that goods circulated mostly through the obligations of reciprocity and redistribution among kin-based or ethnic groups. The Andean economy, therefore, was strongly embedded in kinship, political, and religious institutions. Originally, this view rejected the existence of: 1) barter or any other form of market exchange; 2) merchants; and 3) marketplaces. Over the years, positions regarding these points have become more flexible without abandoning the general no-market thrust of Murra's work (see Mayer, this volume).

Caravan Mobility Model

Since the beginning of the Formative Period, llama caravans were the main agents responsible for moving goods across regions (Browman 1980; Núñez and Dillehay 1979). The wide acceptance of this idea brought some implicit amendments to the no-market thesis. Most of the circulation of goods involved interethnic exchange or barter, although in certain periods some caravan traffic may have operated within corporate, self-sufficient economies (i.e., transporting goods within vertical ethnic territories under reciprocal or redistributive arrangements). Moreover, some caravan drovers (i.e., herders) may have acted as traders.

Elite Control Model

Elites or political institutions controlled—at least partially—the circulation of goods. This control was one of the main sources of their power and, in early times, it played a crucial role in the development of social complexity (chiefdoms). There are three nonexclusive variants of this model. In the first one, Murra's (1975) "vertical economies," chiefs controlled within ethnic territories (dispersed or not) the circulation of resources (mostly consumables) and gained prestige through their redistribution (Van Buren 1996). In the second, the elites of South Andean peer polities maintained a restricted circulation of prestige goods through personal alliances and gift exchanges, and/or attached caravans. These exotica could be used to bestow prestige through display or to legitimize high status and privileges through religious involvement (Berenguer 2004; Nielsen 2001a; Núñez 2006). In the third variant, states like Tiwanaku or Tawantinsuyu maintained hegemony over distant territories by controlling the distribution of goods with corporate iconography, style, and/or craftsmanship that reproduced official ideology and political domination. This control was achieved by placing colonies in the periphery, maintaining client elites who provided valuables in exchange for state support, and/or sponsoring caravans and other official trade expeditions (Berenguer 1998; Browman 1980; Kolata 1993). Sometimes these ideas are combined into more complex arguments. For example, prestige-good exchange among high-ranking individuals and redistribution of staples within vertical economies reinforced each other to consolidate the power of chiefly elites, who gained further support through their connections with Tiwanaku (Llagostera 1996:22).

In this chapter, I critically assess these three models by taking into account research conducted during the past two decades. In particular, I incorporate into the discussion new data on the archaeology of the "internodes"—that is, areas between the most densely occupied regions that acted as the consumer nodes of the trade network (Nielsen 2006a). I develop my argument in four sections. In the first section, the internodal approach is defined, as is the area and methodology of this study. The second section analyzes trends in caravan trade over space and time, and the third section outlines an alternative form of interregional circulation referred to here as embedded trade. The last section discusses the implications of these data through the interpretive framework of the internodal approach.

An Internodal Approach to South Andean Trade

Archaeological studies of interregional trade have relied mostly on nonlocal items found in domestic or mortuary contexts of sedentary settlements, as exemplified by Myriam Tarragó's (1989) study of foreign materials in the tombs of San Pedro de Atacama. Working with this evidence alone is problematic because it offers little information about the actual practices responsible for the circulation of goods. Some archaeologists have tried to palliate this limitation by looking at variations in the function of nonlocal items, the contexts in which they are found (Stanish 1992), and, more recently, the origins of the people who may have been involved in trafficking these objects (Knudson 2008).

Another way of dealing with this problem is to look at the internodal areas between sedentary settlements or densely populated regions, places where archaeological traces of the practices and agents responsible for the circulation of goods should exist in the form of roads or trails, resting places (shelters and campsites), shrines, and signals of various sorts. Following the pioneering studies of Núñez (1976, 1985) on the relationship between rock art and caravan routes, an internodal approach that combines ethnoarchaeological research with detailed studies of circulation-related sites, features, and refuse has taken shape among archaeologists working in the Southern Andes over the last decade (Berenguer 2004; Berenguer and Pimentel 2010; Nielsen 2006a). Internodal studies of circulation are based on the premise that we can build arguments relating the small and scattered remains left in the internodes with relevant issues concerning the social organization of trade.

This approach is particularly useful for an agency-centered perspective on interregional interaction because it shifts attention from abstract, systemic forces—market principles, economic policies, adaptation—to the very practices of circulation and the opportunities they offer for people pursuing multiple projects. The Southern Andes is an area well suited to the application of this approach. The region's highly circumscribed resource distribution leaves large and sparsely populated internodes—mountain ranges, frigid high plateaus, hyperarid deserts—where the subtle archaeological traces of traffic can be identified and interpreted with little interference from other activity traces.

The internodal research reported in the next section focused on the Triple Frontier of Bolivia, Chile, and Argentina (Figure 16.1). This is an arbitrary spatial frame that includes parts of two subareas commonly recognized by archaeologists: the Southern Altiplano and the Circumpuna. One of the reasons for choosing this area was the existence of the largest funerary collection of the Southern Andes, coming from San Pedro and other oases of the Atacama Basin, which permits tracing changes in the presence of nonlocal items in mortuary contexts from circa 500 BC to the Spanish conquest.

The geography of the Triple Frontier can be examined in two ways. One of them is ecological, or vertical, since altitude is the main factor conditioning the distribution of life forms and economic production. Based on different classifications proposed by several scholars, the following "ecozones" can be distinguished: 1) the Pacific coast, rich in marine resources; 2) low-altitude valleys apt for macrothermic crops (coca, squash, and some varieties of maize); 3) mid-altitude valleys and oases appropriate for mesothermic crops (maize); 4) high-altitude valleys suitable for frost-resistant tubers and grains (quinoa and potatoes); 5) puna, the ideal zone for herding; and 6) unproductive mountain heights.

The Triple Frontier can also be divided "horizontally"—that is, by considering regions that encompass multiple ecozones. Since ecological strata are closely juxtaposed, regions differ in their combinations of ecozones and, therefore, in the possibilities they offer for the development of diversified productive systems and for population aggregation. From this point of view, they can be classified into five types that support: (Ia)

agriculture of meso- and microthermic crops and herding; (Ib) herding and agriculture of microthermic crops; (Ic) agriculture of macrothermic crops; (IIa) herding only; and (IIb) maritime exploitation only. These regions are separated by areas unsuitable for permanent occupation, or internodes (III). The combination of ecological and regional divisions of the Triple Frontier is summarized in Table 16.1 and illustrated in Figure 16.2. It should be kept in mind that llama herding at this latitude is mostly practiced above 3,000 masl, so pastoralists running ancient caravans may have belonged—and probably did belong—to region types Ia and Ib, but especially IIa because, in keeping with specialized herders around the world (Khazanov 1984), these groups had to maintain regular exchange relationships with farmers and other groups.

At the beginning of this internodal research, I was mainly interested in identifying informal caravan routes in order to date the beginning of this practice and study changes in the trade network over time. The survey focused on the High Lakes region of the Western Cordillera, a high-altitude desert (> 4,200 masl) that is too hostile for permanent human occupation. I expected this area, interposed between the Atacama Desert and the altiplano, to bear traces of important interregional trade routes. Moreover, the high circumscription of resources that are critical for traveling caravans—water, pastures, and firewood—in this environment, should have generated high spatial redundancy in the activities associated with traffic, thus increasing the archaeological visibility of their material remains.

My previous ethnoarchaeological work on caravans (Nielsen 2001b) had indicated that overnight campsites (Figures 16.2–16.6) are the points along the routes that exhibit the highest rates of deposition, either through the loss or breakage of transported objects while loading or unloading the animals or through the normal discard associated with cooking, eating, repairing equipment, and manufacturing objects for trade (e.g., ropes). Still, depositions generated by any camping event are so scant that only repeatedly occupied places may concentrate enough refuse to become recognizable

figure 16.2

The Triple Frontier of the Southern Andes, its main nodal regions, and the internodal corridors surveyed. Atacama Oases (AO), Loa River (LR), Northern Lípez (NL), Intersalar (IS), Lake Poopó (LP), Southern Potosí Valleys (SPV), Río Grande de San Juan (RGSJ), Southeastern Lípez (SL), Northwestern Puna (NP), Guayatayoc (GC), and Quebrada de Humahuaca (QH). (Illustration by Axel E. Nielsen.)

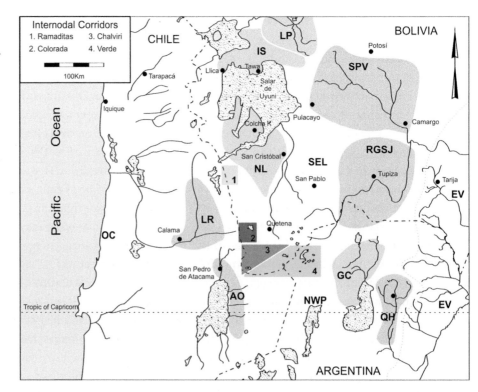

table 16.1

The main regions of the Triple Frontier and their related ecozones (see Figure 16.2)

ECOZONES (LOW–HIGH)	OCEAN COAST	ATACAMA DESERT	LOA RIVER; ATACAMA OASES	HIGH LAKES	SOUTHEASTERN LÍPEZ; NORTWESTERN PUNA	INTERSALAR; NORTHERN LÍPEZ; GUAYATAYOC	SOUTHERN POTOSÍ VALLEYS; RÍO GRANDE DE SAN JUAN; HUMAHUACA	EASTERN VALLEYS
MOUNTAIN HEIGHTS			×	×	×	×	×	
PUNA			×	×	×	×	×	
HIGH VALLEYS			×				×	×
MID-VALLEYS			×				×	×
LOW VALLEYS		×						×
COAST		×						
REGION TYPES	IIb	III	Ia	III	IIa	Ib	Ia	Ic

Notes: Herding develops mostly in the altitude range between the double lines. Darkly shaded regions (I) support agriculture and, therefore, relatively dense populations; lightly shaded regions (II) do not allow agriculture and support disperse populations only; and unshaded regions (III) do not support permanent human settlement.

archaeological sites. In order to record in a systematic way as many of these redundantly occupied places as possible, over such a vast area, the survey focused on four internodal corridors: Ramaditas (corridor 1); Colorada (corridor 2); Chalviri (corridor 3); and Verde (corridor 4) (Figure 16.2). These places, associated with marshes (*cienegos*) that concentrate pastures and water, attract travelers in search of good places to spend the night, and they have topographic constraints (mountain passes, valleys) that channel circulation along discrete stretches of land. I chose these corridors with the goal of intercepting traffic routes connecting the main nodes of the Triple Frontier, as indicated schematically in Table 16.2.

Following this method, dozens of campsites and other features left by ancient caravans were located, including shrines (particularly on mountain passes), cairns, rock art, trails, and artifacts lost along the way. Campsites range from one or two windbreaks with a few associated artifacts (Figure 16.7) to dozens of windbreaks, expedient shelters, U-shaped structures (Figures 16.8–16.9), corrals, offering pits, hastily buried human remains, and such refuse as pottery, lithic artifacts and debris, copper minerals, beads, fire-cracked rocks, and animal bones. On resource-rich segments along particularly important routes, these sites are closely spaced, attesting

to centuries or millennia of continuous use (Figure 16.10). Every campsite located was mapped and its surface collected. A few of them were excavated in order to obtain carbon samples for dating initial occupations. In most cases, however, the lack of spatial congruence among successive occupation events and the prevalence of deflation processes prevented the formation of stratified deposits and the establishment of secure associations through excavation.

Site chronology, then, was estimated using diagnostic ceramics from surface collections and excavations; in this way, 117 campsites were assigned to one or more of the following periods: Early (500 BC–AD 500); Middle (AD 500–1250); Late (AD 1250–1450); and Inca (AD 1450–1550). One of the advantages of working with internodes is that one can safely assume that all the pottery found was manufactured elsewhere. Moreover, at this scale, regional pottery traditions are different enough to allow a considerable number of fragments to be assigned roughly to particular nodes or groups of nodes.[1] Certainly, these identifications offer only a general approximation to the period of use of each site and the provenience of the materials discarded, taking into account the limited knowledge we have about South Andean ceramics. For this reason, a rather conservative approach was chosen in the analysis, using campsite components as the units of quantification when comparing

figure 16.3
Caravan campsite of Yuraj Cruz immediately after unloading the animals. Note the two basic components of these sites: the cooking area (charcoal-stained spot to the right) and the loading/unloading area at the center. (Photograph by Axel E. Nielsen, 1995.)

figure 16.4
Caravan campsites at the annual fair of Santa Catalina, Argentina. Note the llamas belonging to each caravan roped together by their necks to prevent stampedes during the night. (Photograph by Axel E. Nielsen, 1996.)

figure 16.5
The campsite of Supirapata (on the route between Lípez and Tarija) at dawn, before loading the caravan. Note the salt loads, saddlebags, and ropes piled to form a windbreak for overnight protection. (Photograph by Axel E. Nielsen, 1995.)

figure 16.6
Sun-drying meat for consumption along the journey on a windbreak at the caravan campsite of Sique Jara. Note the midden forming next to the hearth by the repeated cleaning of the cooking area. (Photograph by Axel E. Nielsen, 1997.)

table 16.2

Internodal corridors and nodal regions they probably connect (see Figure 16.2)

NON-ADJACENT NODES TO THE WEST	ADJACENT NODES TO THE WEST	INTERNODAL CORRIDOR (WESTERN CORDILLERA)	ADJACENT NODES TO THE EAST		NONADJACENT NODES TO THE EAST AND NORTH	
Pacific Coast (OC)	Loa River (LR)	1. Ramaditas	Northern Lípez (NL)		Intersalar (IS); Lake Poopo (LP); Cochabamba (CB); Titicaca Basin (TW)	EV
		2. Colorada				
	Atacama Oases (AO)	3. Chalviri	Southeastern Lípez (SEL)	Southern Potosí Valleys (SPV)		
		4. Verde		Río Grande de San Juan (RGSJ)	Eastern Valleys (EV)	
			Northwestern Puna (NWP)	Guayatayoc (GC)	Humahuaca (QH)	EV

figure 16.7
Ancient windbreaks at the Middle-to Late-period campsite of Vega de Pampa Jara 2 (Chalviri Corridor). (Photograph by Axel E. Nielsen.)

figure 16.8
U-shaped structure at the campsite of Silala 3, located between the Colorada and Ramaditas Corridors, used since the Early period. Ethnographically, these structures are used for corralling the animals in order to facilitate loading and unloading. Once the caravan is driven inside, the open side of the structure is easily closed with a rope. (Photograph by Axel E. Nielsen.)

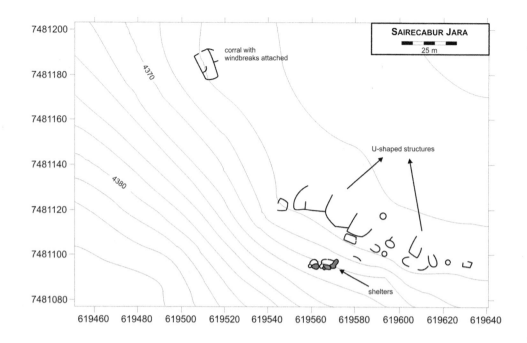

figure 16.9

Map of Sairecabur Jara, an intensively used Late-period campsite in the Chalviri Corridor. Note the combination of features characteristic of caravan campsites: windbreaks, corrals, U-shaped structures, and expediently built shelters. (Map by Axel E. Nielsen.)

figure 16.10

Caravan campsites, paths, and shrines located along the Huayllajara stream (Colorada Corridor), a route segment that connects the oases of Atacama (San Pedro) and the Loa River (Caspana) with the southern altiplano. (Illustration by Axel E. Nielsen.)

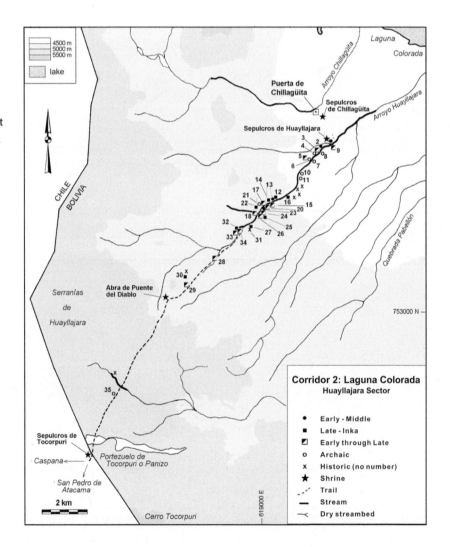

table 16.3

Caravan campsites and campsite components analyzed by corridor

INTERNODAL CORRIDOR	PERIOD				TOTAL COMPONENTS	TOTAL CAMPSITES
	EARLY	MIDDLE	LATE	INCA		
1. RAMADITAS	7	2	26	4	39	26
2. COLORADA	26	16	39	7	88	47
3. CHALVIRI	3	12	14	3	32	16
4. VERDE	11	4	21	6	42	28
TOTAL COMPONENTS	47	34	100	20	201	117

table 16.4

Frequency of components with regionally diagnostic ceramics by corridor

PERIOD	EARLY	MIDDLE						LATE – INCA							
Nodes (ceramic groups)	any region (Sequitor, Morros)	AO – LR (S Pedro Black Polished)	RGSJ (Calahoyo)	QH (Isla)	SPV (Yura, Cinti)	IS – LP (Puqui)	Tiwanaku	OA – LR (Red, Dupont, Aiquina)	RGSJ (Yavi)	GC (Queta, Aguas Calientes)	NL (Mallku)	SPV (Yura, Huuquilla)	IS – LP (Taltape, Chilpe)	Inca	TOTAL
1. RAMADITAS	7	2	-	-	-	-	-	15	2	-	24	2	2	4	58
2. COLORADA	26	10	-	-	10	1	3	36	1	-	22	-	4	7	120
3. CHALVIRI	3	1	-	3	9	5	-	11	5	-	7	2	6	3	55
4. VERDE	11	3	1	-	1	-	1	16	18	2	3	-	1	6	63
TOTAL	47	16	1	3	20	6	4	78	26	2	56	4	13	20	296

table 16.5

Percentage of components with regionally diagnostic ceramics by corridor and period

PERIOD	MIDDLE						LATE – INCA						
Nodes (ceramic groups)	AO – LR (S Pedro Black Polished)	RGSJ (Calahoyo)	QH (Isla)	SPV (Yura, Cinti)	IS – LP (Puqui)	TW (Tiwanaku)	OA – LR (Red, Dupont, Aiquina)	RGSJ (Yavi)	GC (Queta, Aguas Calientes)	NL (Mallku)	SPV (Yura, Huuquilla)	IS – LP (Taltape, Chilpe)	Inca
1. RAMADITAS	100	-	-	-	-	-	31	4	-	49	4	4	8
2. COLORADA	42	-	-	42	4	12	52	1	-	31	-	6	10
3. CHALVIRI	6	-	16	50	28	-	31	15	-	21	6	18	9
4. VERDE	50	17	-	17	-	16	34	39	4	6	-	2	13

Note: 100% = total components belonging to one period in one corridor.

corridors in terms of both the frequency of sites by period (Table 16.3) and their relative association with particular nodes (Tables 16.4–16.5).

Temporal and Spatial Trends in Caravan Trade

Evidence of interregional circulation of goods dates back to the Archaic period (8000–1500 BC) and seems to increase during the Late Archaic and Early Formative periods (1500–500 BC), when the domestication of llamas enhanced the capacity of early pastoralists-hunters-horticulturalists to transport bulky loads over great distances. The following analysis, however, starts around 500 BC. This was the time when a sedentary lifestyle associated with a stronger emphasis on agriculture began to consolidate in several nodal regions of the area, probably giving new breath and significance to long-distance exchange.

Early Period (500 BC–AD 500)

Consolidation of a new productive base resulted in the gradual appearance of small, but permanently occupied, villages in all the regions with potential for farming, although most people probably continued living in dispersed homesteads. Agriculture, herding, hunting, and gathering were combined into diversified economic strategies that required considerable mobility across ecological strata and resulted in forms of compressed verticality that varied depending on the possibilities offered by each region. Early occupations recorded in Southeastern Lípez and Northwestern Puna suggest that specialized herders, who likely hunted and gathered as well, were already present in the high altiplano regions during this period.

These early communities had access to many items from distant regions: marine shell and fish from the Pacific coast; copper and turquoise beads from the Atacama Oases and the Loa River; obsidian from the High Lakes; wood and cane (for bows and arrows), terrestrial shell (*Sthrophocheilus oblongus*, used as containers for pigments), psychotropic plants (*Anadenanthera* and *Nicotiana*, indirectly

attested by pipes and inhaling paraphernalia), and feathers from the subtropical forests of the Eastern Valleys; and ceramics from multiple regions. Metal objects made of copper, gold, or silver also began to circulate during this period. We may assume that some perishable items were being transported as well; this would be the case of maize and fruits (*Prosopys* sp., *Geoffrea* sp.) from the temperate valleys on both Andean flanks, coca leaves from the low valleys to the east, or salt from the highlands.[2]

Consistent with these observations, Table 16.3 shows that routes through all corridors were active during this time. These results and a radiocarbon date of 2750±60 BP (Beta 187356) obtained for a caravan campsite near Laguna Colorada (site 18, Figure 16.10) are consistent with the widely shared notion that, since the domestication of llamas, caravans were fully involved in interregional traffic (Núñez and Dillehay 1979). Moreover, the presence of several sites with Late Archaic components along the Huayllajara stream indicates that some of these routes were already in use, probably by earlier hunter-gatherers following their seasonal vertical circuits.

Who were operating these caravans? This question can be answered by considering the position and direction of the routes, as well as the presence of regionally diagnostic ceramics at campsites—under the assumption that some of them were part of the travel gear of the ancient drovers and were accidentally broken during the journey. Given the limited knowledge available on early ceramics, it can only be said that both sides of the Western Cordillera are represented in campsites. People from all highland nodes were involved in this traffic but perhaps to different degrees in each corridor. Thus, Loa River and Northern Lípez herders were probably more engaged in Ramaditas (corridor 1) caravans, while those from the Atacama Oases and Río Grande de San Juan were active mainly in Verde (corridor 4). Following this line of argument, corridors 2 and 3 were probably traveled not only by herders from the six agropastoral nodes surrounding them but also by specialized pastoralists from the vast Southeastern Lípez high plateau. This possibility adds complexity to the caravan traffic system because these two kinds of herders probably acted under different structural constraints; while the former were likely linked to local farmers through various reciprocal or redistributive relationships (with the ensuing obligations), the latter may have been free of these social entanglements but pressed to trade as a necessary aspect of their economy (like *llameros* today). If this case is true, then both barter and part-time traders would have been present in these early economies.

Based on a detailed analysis of foreign items found in funerary contexts around San Pedro de Atacama, Llagostera (1996) differentiates two spheres of exchange. One of them was restricted and composed of religious symbols such as pipes, inhaling tablets,[3] and psychotropic plants. These items tend to be associated with men, as were maces and, later, axes—both of which were considered symbols of power— and copper artifacts. The nonrestricted sphere is mainly represented by foreign ceramics, which are common both in burials and in domestic sites, such as Tulor. We could add to this second, more inclusive sphere wood, shell, some consumables (e.g., fish), and greenstone (malachite, azurite, and other copper minerals), which is ubiquitous in caravan campsites, both as a raw material and as beads. Importantly, Llagostera notes that objects in both spheres of exchange come from a variety of sources and do not tend to form consistent associations by place of origin. In other words, people were connected to several distant places and combined foreign items quite freely in both mortuary and domestic contexts, at least in San Pedro. If these tendencies applied to other nodes, they would result in an open network—that is, one in which all nodes are similarly connected without significant discontinuities.[4]

Middle Period (AD 500–1250)

The Middle period in the Triple Frontier is characterized by an increase in the frequency of nonlocal valuables, mainly in funerary contexts. Most famous among these goods are Tiwanaku-style items, such as beakers (*keros*), snuffing paraphernalia (Figure 16.11), and textiles. Such items are frequent in San Pedro de Atacama, almost absent in the Loa River,

and apparently exceptional in Guayatayoc and Humahuaca. It is not known whether they are present in other regions because little research has been done on Middle-period sites.

It should be stressed that Tiwanaku-style objects in San Pedro are intrusive in contexts dominated by local items and represent only a minority in nonlocal artifact classes. Tiwanaku's state iconography, for example, is found only in 10–30 percent of the snuffing tablets of any cemetery, while ceramics continue to be brought from multiple places, including the Mizque and Tarija Valleys, the Río Grande de San Juan, Quebrada de Humahuaca, and various places in northwestern Argentina. Tiwanaku material culture, then, was incorporated in similar ways to other foreign valuables of restricted circulation, following an open pattern already established during the Early period (Llagostera 1996:28–29).

The close association between inhaling paraphernalia and axes (interpreted as symbols of religious and civil power, respectively), as well as the tendency of both items to be found in tombs with more offerings and metal wealth, suggest to Llagostera (1996) that a more hierarchical chiefdom developed in San Pedro at this time. The high frequency of greenstone, copper, gold, and metalworking tools suggest that an increase in inequality was also linked to the rise of metallurgical specialization (Llagostera 1996:30). This view is elaborated by Núñez (2006), who argues that San Pedro elites and their attached metallurgic specialists achieved a privileged position in South Andean society through the production of significant metal surpluses for trade. According to Myriam Tarragó (2006), a similar increase in social inequality would be taking place at this time in Quebrada de Humahuaca. She grounds this interpretation on the presence of wealthy funerary contexts (including gold artifacts), a few Tiwanaku items, and indications of trade connections with San Pedro.

The interpretations of Llagostera, Núñez, and Tarragó are difficult to assess because of the limited research that has been conducted on Middle-period settlement patterns and domestic contexts in the Triple Frontier. But if it is assumed

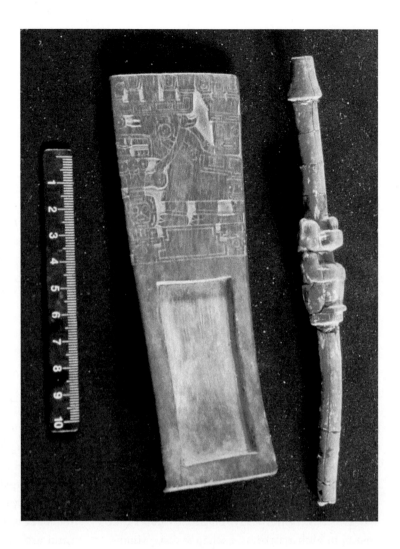

figure 16.11
Middle-period snuffing tube and
tablet found at San Pedro de Atacama.
(Photograph by Axel E. Nielsen.)

that these interpretations are correct, then what was Tiwanaku's role in San Pedro de Atacama? Following Kolata (1993:275–280), did Tiwanaku place colonists in San Pedro to promote official trade in luxury items, political influence, and religious proselytism? This model has to be rejected because strontium isotope analysis has demonstrated that even the individuals interred with the most sophisticated Tiwanaku textiles (Oakland 1992) were of local origin (Knudson 2008).

A second hypothesis, based on a core-periphery argument, posits that Tiwanaku controlled caravan trade with San Pedro through the cooperation of local client elites imbued in state ideology (Berenguer 1998; Kolata 1993). Caravan campsite data cast doubts on this interpretation, however. As Figure 16.12 shows, the northern routes are only associated with traffic between the Loa River

and Northern Lípez.[5] Materials from more distant places reached San Pedro de Atacama through the Colorada and Chalviri Corridors, which contain a large amount of pottery from the Southern Potosí Valleys (Yura, Cinti). It was probably through this node that some Puqui material from the Intersalar and Lake Poopó regions were also brought. Similar items are also found on the Verde route. The Tiwanaku material, then, was probably coming through some or all of these intermediate regions. I should emphasize that not only are Tiwanaku ceramics found along the routes, but so are other forms of wealth associated with Middle-period trade. In the Colorada Corridor, for example, a silver ring was found while excavating a campsite from this period, and gold trimmings were discovered from a mountain-pass shrine. Whatever the connections with Tiwanaku, the internodal data

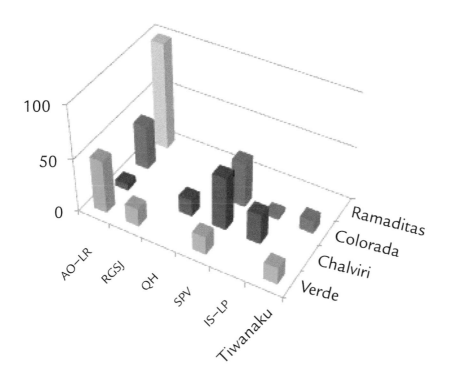

figure 16.12
Percentage of Middle-
period regionally
diagnostic ceramics
by corridor. Atacama
Oases (AO), Loa River
(LR), Río Grande de San
Juan (RGSJ), Guayatayoc
(GC), Northern Lípez
(NL), Southern Potosí
Valleys (SPV), Intersalar
(IS), and Lake Poopó
(LP). (Graph by Axel E.
Nielsen.)

show that during the Middle period caravan trade between San Pedro de Atacama and the Southern Potosí Valleys intensified, perhaps with specialized herders of Southeastern Lípez as middlemen.

Research by Céspedes and Lecoq (1998) in the Southern Potosí Valleys revealed several Middle-period settlements (dwellings, workshops, cemeteries, and storage areas) associated with Yura and other local ceramic types. They also found nonlocal pottery, mainly from the Cochabamba area, but only a few local Tiwanaku-style sherds. Céspedes and Lecoq think that these Yura groups were active members of the Tiwanaku interaction sphere but were connected mainly with the Cochabamba node by caravans and, again, by the presence of colonists devoted to the control of the southern trade network.

In the Lake Poopó region, Michel López (2008) has also documented Tiwanaku ceramics alongside Puqui, Yura, and other local styles in villages associated with intensive terrace agriculture and herding. For Michel López, these communities represent local developments built on the basis of Formative-period interaction networks, linked by ritual practices of the Tiwanaku tradition, but

without the direct participation of the state or of the Cochabamba or Titicaca Basin populations. Local groups interacted with multiple regions via llama caravans, as reflected by the wide distribution of Lake Poopó ceramic styles and basalt from the nearby Queremita outcrop.

The most important evidence for understanding the role of the Southern Potosí Valleys in Middle-period interaction comes from Pulacayo, on the southeastern corner of the Salar de Uyuni. A few years ago, the Museo de Arte Indígena (ASUR) in Sucre, Bolivia, acquired an archaeological collection from this area that included five bodies—some of them with traces of violence—and a remarkable assemblage of nonlocal items of both Tiwanaku and San Pedro de Atacama styles. These goods included tunics, hats, plumed headdresses, baskets, bows and arrows, snuffing paraphernalia, and other objects (Figures 16.13–16.14). Initially, these unusual offerings led to the speculation that the remains belonged to Tiwanaku caravan traders who had been killed while traversing this lonely region, but strontium isotope analysis of three of the bodies revealed that they were local people (Knudson et al. 2005).

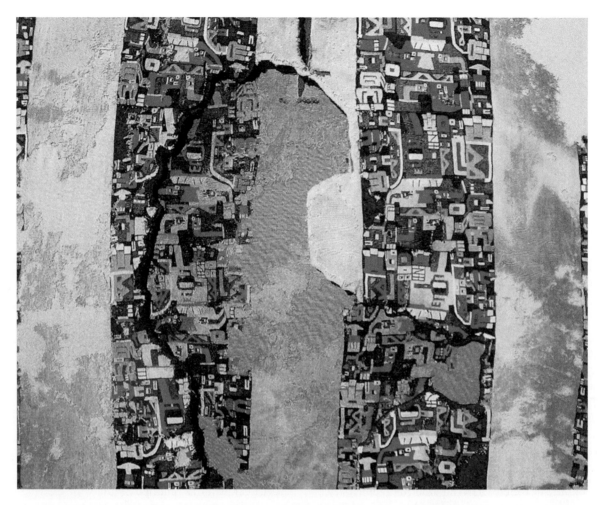

figure 16.13
Tiwanaku-style textile from Pulacayo.
(Photograph courtesy of Museo de Arte
Indígena, ASUR, Sucre, Bolivia.)

figure 16.14
Tiwanaku-style hat from Pulacayo.
(Photograph courtesy of Museo de Arte
Indígena, ASUR, Sucre, Bolivia.)

Recent survey and excavations in the area (Cruz 2009) provide some context to these findings. Cruz found twelve habitation sites and seventeen funerary caves with Middle-period components that have been radiocarbon dated to AD 500–900. The local pottery at these sites is of Yura and Puqui styles, but foreign Tiwanaku, Taltape (Intersalar), and Cabuza (Central Altiplano-Arica) materials are also present. Several sites showed evidence of metallurgy, and the excavations exposed sophisticated furnaces and other workshop contexts that represent all the steps of the copper production chain, including mining, mineral processing, smelting, and artifact finishing. Cruz concludes that sizable groups devoted to metallurgy and affiliated with the Southern Potosí Valleys lived permanently in Pulacayo. In his view (Cruz 2009:97), these people were in contact with the Titicaca Basin and San Pedro but also with the Intersalar, Lake Poopó, and Central Altiplano regions.

Taken together, these data ratify what is geographically apparent. The San Pedro–Tiwanaku relationship was probably not direct, as implied by the clientage model or in the maps of Tiwanaku's expansive period that typically show a straight line connecting the city with the San Pedro "periphery." Caravans loaded with prestige goods did not travel back and forth across the eight hundred kilometers that separate the two communities, a caravan journey of three to four months minimum, in a social vacuum. Instead, the circulation of Tiwanaku items must have been mediated by several communities living in between—like those in the Intersalar, Lake Poopó, and Southern Potosí Valleys—and probably also by specialized *llameros* residing in nonagricultural regions like Southeastern Lípez. If this is true, the whole notion of a political or economic expansion of the Tiwanaku state into the Southern Andes is hard to sustain. Instead, we see the world of many small communities[6] of the Southern Andes expand through intensified, but decentralized, multidirectional, and locally driven trade. After all, even in San Pedro, Tiwanaku paraphernalia is just one among several groups of items from multiple distant places. There are, for example, a number of Aguada-style objects, such as textiles, baskets, and

ceramics from the Valliserrana region of northwestern Argentina, which lies six hundred kilometers away but in the opposite direction, to the south.

Late Period (AD 1250–1450)

This period brought about many changes for South Andean peoples. One of them was rapid population aggregation, leading to the formation of densely occupied residential conglomerates that, in the Triple Frontier, hosted maximum community sizes of between six hundred and three thousand inhabitants, depending on the region. This process was closely related to the outbreak of endemic warfare, indicated by the defensive location and design of settlements (*pukaras*), the appearance of new weapons and armory (helmets, cuirasses), osteological trauma, and rock-art iconography representing warriors, weapons, and fighting themes. Some of the largest settlements have well-defined public spaces that could have accommodated marketplaces, but research conducted thus far in plazas of several regions does not support this interpretation (Nielsen 2006b). Differences in site size and the presence or complexity of public areas point to the emergence of hierarchical settlement structures and the formation of multicommunity polities.

This process also involved the constitution of new regional identities, as suggested by the emergence of emblematic ceramics, architecture, and textiles. Regional pottery styles are frequently associated with large containers and serving bowls, which were probably used in the communal consumption of food and maize beer (*chicha*) during public ceremonies. Some of the ethnonyms recorded by the Spanish in the sixteenth century (e.g., Atacamas, Chichas, Lipes, Casabindos, Humahuacas, Qaraqaras, and Quillacas) may have designated social collectives that were born during this era through the segmentary integration of corporate groups, who conceived of themselves as descendants from common ancestors. These ancestors were physically present in public spaces in the form of monuments (e.g., visible tombs, *chullpa* towers, and monoliths), interacting directly with community members who gathered periodically for political feasts (Nielsen 2006b). Two centuries later, at the time of the European invasion, these corporate groups were known as *ayllus*, who federated into nested hierarchies to form the ethnic confederations described in early historical documents (Platt 1987). In the case of the Triple Frontier, every region seems to have included more than one of these polities, indicating that these cultural collectives were not centralized or unified, but rather composed of several related but relatively autonomous political units, perhaps allied or federated in exceptional circumstances, or for specific purposes, like war.

In addition to maintaining their identity and influence within larger political superstructures, sixteenth-century *ayllus* held key resources in common (land, water, and pastures) that were shared by their members through vertical strategies of reciprocity and redistribution, as described by Murra (1975). Several lines of evidence suggest that corporate vertical economies of this kind, comprising pastoral transhumance and agriculture in different ecozones, had already developed in several regions of the Triple Frontier by the fourteenth century. Such formation is indicated, for example, by the presence of functionally complementary settlements (defensive residential conglomerates; pastoral homesteads; and extensive agricultural fields indicated by terraces, irrigation networks, and other features) distributed at different altitudes within the same regions and associated with the same material culture styles (ceramics, architecture, metals, and rock art).

I should stress, however, that none of these processes (i.e., aggregation, defensive actions, and political and economic integration) are found in regions without farming. Specialized pastoralists, or *llameros* in the highlands (type IIa regions, Table 16.1) and fishers in the Pacific coast (type IIb regions), continued a dispersed lifestyle with apparent autonomy from the corporate structures emergent in type I regions. Far from being isolated, however, these groups were fully integrated into interregional trade networks, as indicated by the great variety of pottery styles and lithic raw materials that characterize the homesteads of specialized herders–caravan drovers in Southeastern

López (Nielsen 2009), or the presence of metal artifacts from the highlands in coastal sites like Taltal (Núñez 2006). These groups of fishers and maritime collectors were actively engaged in traffic between the coast and the oases of the Loa River since the Early period, as demonstrated by recent internodal research conducted by Pimentel and colleagues (2011) in the desert strip that separates these two regions. The transactions associated with this traffic pattern provide another example of barter (maritime goods in exchange for agropastoral products).

In spite of war, trade items continued to abound, but there are changes in their distribution. Notably, with the dissolution of the Middle-period network, San Pedro apparently entered an era of relative isolation; tombs from this period have limited mortuary offerings, with a low frequency of metals and artifacts bearing complex iconography (Núñez and Dillehay 1979). By contrast, interregional trade thrived in other regions, like Northern López, Loa River, Guayatayoc, and Humahuaca. In the latter three regions, for example, objects for snuffing *sebil* (*Anadenanthera* sp.) are consistently present in funerary contexts, while domestic storage complexes in Northern López show evidence of widely consumed foreign goods, such as obsidian from the High Lakes, maize and *chañar* fruits from the temperate valleys and oases, and coca, wood, cane, and feathers from the eastern lowlands.

Figure 16.15 confirms the intensity of interregional traffic during this period and reveals some interesting patterns. Regionally diagnostic ceramics indicate that the Triple Frontier network broke down into at least two discrete traffic spheres (Figure 16.16). Setting aside the Atacama material present in every route, the two northern corridors are strongly associated with Northern López ceramics (Mallku) and some Intersalar–Lake Poopó material (Taltape, Chilpe, Carangas) probably coming through that region, while Río Grande de San Juan pottery (Yavi) dominates the southern routes through the Verde Corridor. The absence of Northern López material in the Río Grande de San Juan settlements, and vice versa, confirms this separation. Similar discrete circuits seem to exist beyond the Triple Frontier—for

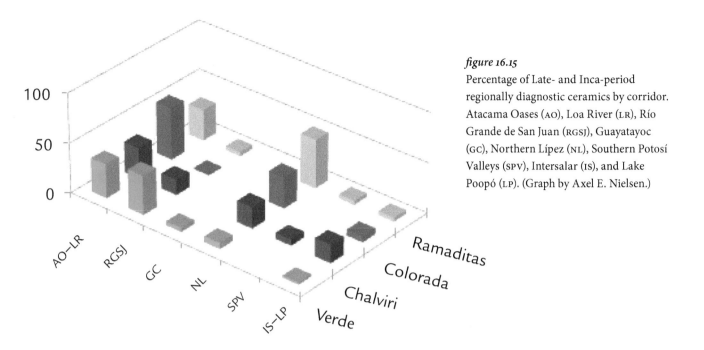

figure 16.15
Percentage of Late- and Inca-period regionally diagnostic ceramics by corridor. Atacama Oases (AO), Loa River (LR), Río Grande de San Juan (RGSJ), Guayatayoc (GC), Northern Lípez (NL), Southern Potosí Valleys (SPV), Intersalar (IS), and Lake Poopó (LP). (Graph by Axel E. Nielsen.)

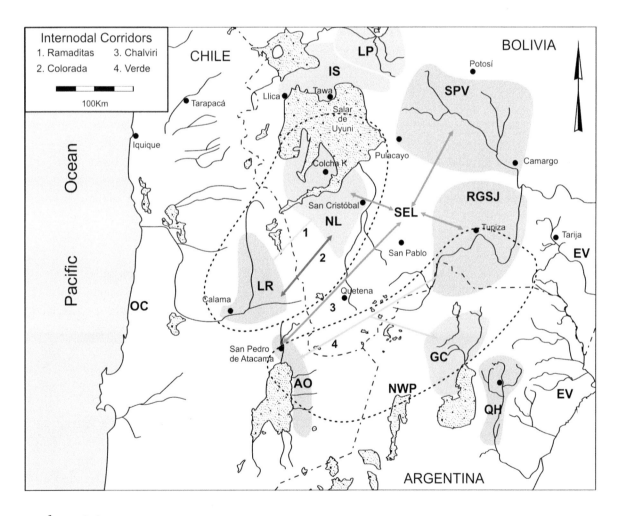

figure 16.16
Late-period circulation areas in the Triple Frontier. (Illustration by Axel E. Nielsen.)

example, the Tarapacá–Intersalar–Central Altiplano to the north and the Valle Calchaquí-Valliserrana region of northwestern Argentina to the south. These traffic areas involve not only ceramics but also lithic raw materials (Yacobaccio et al. 2004)—probably among many other items—suggesting that they correspond to actual discontinuities in the trade network.

It is still unclear, however, what these areas represent. Do they reflect alliances between emerging polities or closely interacting nodes with alternating periods of peaceful exchange and bellicosity? Some of the circulation through corridors 1 and 2 may have been intra-ethnic traffic, or verticality (e.g., Llagostera 2010)—connecting demographic nuclei in Northern Lípez with colonies settled during this period in the upper portion of the Loa River region in the Turi and Toconce areas, where they could cultivate maize and other crops under irrigation

(Aldunate 1993; Castro et al. 1984; Llagostera 2010). It should be emphasized, though, that the conflicts that may have ensued from such expansion by altiplano groups did not prevent interethnic exchange with groups from the Atacama Desert, as indicated by the high frequency of their pottery in the Western Cordillera campsites, and conversely, the abundance of Mallku ceramics from Northern Lípez in caravan campsites of the Middle Loa River (Núñez et al. 2003). Moreover, it is worth noting that some war-related artifacts (bows and arrows, quivers, and cuirasses; see Figure 16.17) are often made of nonlocal materials, as if they embodied an intimate relationship between trade and war. Perhaps we should consider the possibility that, like other ethnographically documented peoples (e.g., Wiessner 2009), ancient South Andeans viewed positive and negative reciprocity as alternating aspects of the same close relationships.

figure 16.17
Late-period cuirass made of alligator hide with applications of monkey fur, found in a cemetery near Chiu Chiu, Loa River. (Photograph by Ferenc Schwetz, courtesy of the Museum of World Culture, Göteborg.)

The problem becomes still more complex when one considers the existence of unaffiliated *llameros*, who were seemingly unaffected by war and free of the corporate constraints that burdened other herders. Could they be neutral traders bridging otherwise separate trade circuits or mediating between enemies? Would they take advantage of this neutrality to foster their own interests? Significantly, corridor 3 (Chalviri) that leads directly into the pastoral region of Southeastern Lípez continued channeling traffic in materials from multiple nodes, including not only Northern Lípez and Río Grande de San Juan, but also the more distant nodes of the Southern Potosí Valleys, Intersalar, and Lake Poopó (Figure 16.16). This mediating role is further indicated by the fact that Southeastern Lípez is the only region where both Northern Lípez and Río Grande de San Juan ceramics are found in the same sites, as if their inhabitants were connecting the two main circuits of the Triple Frontier. It would be interesting to assess whether a similar trend is present in other specialized pastoral regions beyond the Triple Frontier.

Inca Period (AD 1450–1550)

During the fifteenth century, the Southern Andes were incorporated into the Inca Empire (Tawantinsuyu), putting an end to the armed confrontations of the previous period. In order to take advantage of local skills and economic potential, labor taxes (*mit'a*) on state-owned facilities were imposed on the conquered groups. Documentary sources reveal that the state relied extensively on the corporate political structures formed during the Late period to build this productive infrastructure and to mobilize *mit'a* labor. The abundant Inca remains in the highland agricultural nodes of the Triple Frontier attest to their importance in the political economy of Tawantinsuyu. Humahuaca, Río Grande de San Juan, and Northern Lípez, for example, probably produced agricultural surpluses of different crops (maize, tubers, and quinoa), while Loa River and Río Grande de San Juan were important mining districts.

Again, the high-altiplano pastoralists of Northwestern Puna and Southeastern Lípez stand apart from their neighbors in their relationship with Tawantinsuyu. No Inca settlements have been reported in these two regions, although Inca-style artifacts are occasionally found in what were probably humble pastoral homesteads. Perhaps these groups remained relatively free in the interstices among areas intensively controlled by the state, as they apparently did during most of the Spanish colonial period. It is also possible that these groups were the ones who had to look after state-owned herds, but there is presently little material evidence to support this hypothesis.

As in earlier times, Inca-period nodal sites of the Triple Frontier also bear foreign items, including those with restricted circulation—such as metal artifacts, imperial ceramics, and fine textiles—as well as more common items, such as provincial Inca and other pottery styles, lithics, greenstone, coca leaves, and maize. The traffic areas of the Late period were formalized through the construction of two separate roads, one of them connecting the Loa River with Northern Lípez through corridor 1, the other going from San Pedro de Atacama into the High Lakes through corridor 4 (Figure 16.18), probably to reach the Río Grande de San Juan and Guayatayoc nodes (Nielsen et al. 2006). Interestingly, obsidian from the Laguna Blanca/Zapaleri source (located in corridor 4), which before did not spread to the north, is now present in roadside posts along the northern Inca road (*qhapaqñan*) in corridor 1. This presence suggests that the Incas consolidated some preexisting circulation patterns, including those involving pottery, but also introduced new ones, as indicated by the wider distribution of Laguna Blanca/Zapaleri obsidian.

It is worth emphasizing that Inca ceramics were found in all four corridors. This fact could either mean that the state used both newly constructed formal roads and preexisting informal paths or that the Inca effort to control trade was not totally successful. If one takes the *qhapaqñan* as an expression of an official circulation policy or ideal, sophisticated Inca objects found in caravan campsites away from the road system suggest that a lot of unofficial traffic was taking place at the time. If one applies this conclusion to the Inca attitude toward

figure 16.18
Full-standing
architecture at Inca
de Catalcito, a lodge
on the Inca road
that runs through
the Verde Corridor.
(Photograph by
Axel E. Nielsen.)

trade, conveyed in the Spanish sources, one may suspect that a lot more independent exchange and barter was taking place than Murra's no-market thesis would have us believe.

Circulation without Caravans: Embedded Trade

My survey of the Western Cordillera internode revealed not only caravan-related sites and features but also traces of temporary occupations by task groups from the adjacent nodal regions at lower elevations (Figure 16.19). After all, the High Lakes are too hostile for permanent habitation, but they offer important resources, such as prey for hunting (vicuñas and large rodents), flamingo eggs and feathers, obsidian, and basalt. These sites—which are present in all four internodal corridors and date to all periods—include temporary habitation settlements, lithic quarries and workshops, egg-processing loci, and hunting stands. Some of them (Huayllajara 1, Ramaditas 4) include Late Archaic components as well, revealing the earlier roots of such occupations and their remarkable persistence in spite of multiple changes in the economies in which they were immersed.

Three aspects of temporary occupations need to be emphasized. First, some activities—notably *vicuña* hunting by corralling—required large groups of people, a fact that is consistent with the presence of numerous structures in some hunting sites like Moroco or Ojo del Novillito (Figure 16.20). These collective hunts were described as late as the beginning of the twentieth century by Bowman (1924:268–270), who observed that in the late summer, some villages around the Salar de Atacama were left vacant because most adults were hunting in the high puna.

Second, similar temporary settlements were occupied by groups coming from both sides of the High Lakes, an inference based on ceramics and architecture. Thus, sites on the west share features with those in the nodes of the Atacama Desert (e.g., Early-period Ramaditas 4, Huayllajara 1, and Aguas Calientes, Late-period Puerta de Chillagüita and Moroco), while those on the east include artifacts and architectural styles from the altiplano or puna (e.g., Early-period Ojo del Novillito, Dulcenombre, and Zapaleri 1, Late-period Chillagua Grande). Others may have been used—perhaps alternatively—by people coming from both directions (e.g., Guayaques 3). This indicates that the High Lakes— and perhaps other internodal areas as well—were

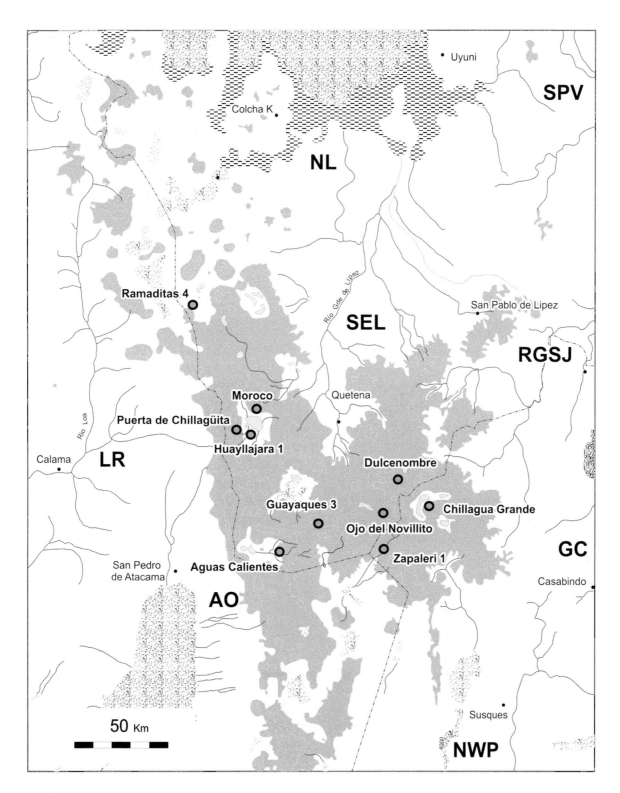

figure 16.19

Temporary settlements investigated in the High Lakes region. (Map by Axel E. Nielsen.)

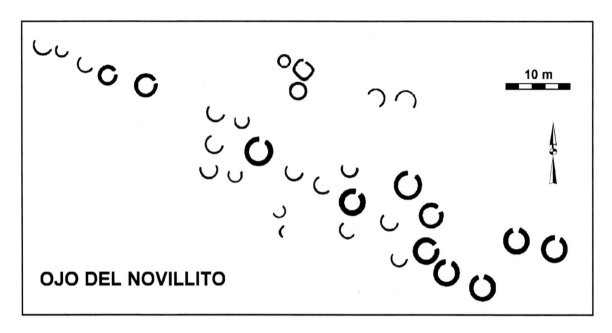

figure 16.20
Site map of the Early-period site of Ojo del Novillito at an elevation of 4,700 masl in corridor 4, associated with San Francisco ceramics from the eastern side of the Andes. (Illustration by Axel E. Nielsen.)

exploited seasonally by task groups coming from different regions and possibly belonging to different social collectives.

The third and most important point is that the same trade items recorded in these temporary sites were also found along caravan routes and in the agropastoral nodal regions. The list includes many of the same ceramic types, greenstone, beads, obsidian, basalt, flamingo bones, eggs, feathers, marine shell, maize, and *chañar* fruits. Such similarities suggest that many of the same items transported over long distances by caravans were simultaneously exchanged directly by task groups from different regions who met periodically in the internodes. Objects exchanged in this context—as barter or gifts—could be later passed on to community members or outsiders in analogous contexts (for example, in a distant internode visited during a different season). Assuming that these transactions would be secondary to the main procurement goals that organized these occupations as part of the verticality schedule (hunting, gathering), I have called this form of circulation "embedded traffic" in contrast to the "specialized traffic" practiced by caravans

and other individuals traveling without animals (Nielsen 2006a). The association of embedded traffic with annual cycles driven by hunting and gathering schedules and the previously mentioned presence of earlier artifacts in some of the sites suggests that this was an important, perhaps the main, form of interregional circulation during the Archaic period.

Discussion

What are the implications of the internodal data for the three models on South Andean trade outlined in the first section? In my view, the data indicate that some of the earlier propositions are correct, while others deserve some amendments, and still others are in need of a strong revision.

I believe that the no-market model requires significant revision. The abundant evidence of caravan trade between socially different regional collectives demonstrates that a large amount of the transactions associated with long-distance traffic in all the periods analyzed took the form of interethnic trade or barter—that is, direct, immediate commodity exchange. Circulation of goods through reciprocity and, toward the later part of the sequence, redistribution certainly coexisted alongside interethnic exchange, but it probably was only significant at the local or regional level, among kin, or within Late-period ethnic federations.

Likewise, we must conclude that many of those involved directly in the interregional circulation of goods were traders: people who—at least partially—made a living through their involvement in exchange. This case must have been particularly true of specialized pastoralists but probably applied to some extent to many herders and caravan drovers of the area.

As to the existence of marketplaces, Núñez and Dillehay (1979) proposed that mobile fairs existed since the Middle period, and some scholars argue on theoretical grounds that they should have existed (Stanish and Coben, this volume), but to the best of my knowledge, nobody has presented archaeological data to sustain this hypothesis. Therefore, we can provisionally conclude that many transactions must have taken place in domestic settings, or as observed ethnographically, at caravan campsites on the outskirts of villages.

There is more evidence to support the caravan mobility model, one of the hallmarks of the Southern Andes. Nonetheless, it was never the only form of interregional traffic. It may have been responsible for transporting the bulk of trade items over long distances, but it always coexisted with embedded traffic—perhaps with multiple forms of it. Indeed, to approach the real complexity of the circulation system, we should also keep in mind that both forms probably included other variants that have not been pursued here. Specialized traffic, for example, probably involved exchange trips without pack animals as well, especially by people from the lower nodes where herding was not feasible, such as the Eastern Valleys or the Pacific coast (e.g., Pimentel et al. 2011). Likewise, direct, interethnic exchange must have also been embedded in other social contexts besides summer hunting in the high mountain internodes, such as direct visits to the nodes associated with matrimonial exchange and the renewal of friendship and political alliances.[7]

Summarizing the points made thus far we can say that, since the Early period, interregional trade was not a single activity but the result of multiple heterogeneous and redundant practices. The trade was heterogeneous in terms of activities (caravan journeys, seasonal trips into the internodes), transactions (barter, gift exchange), and participants (their interests and constraints). Herders from the agropastoral nodes (perhaps acting partially on behalf of a group of related households), specialized *llameros*, and members of various households engaged in regular activities of the (more or less collective) verticality schedule. It was redundant because different practices simultaneously moved many of the same goods between the same nodes—and probably some of the same consumers within them. Even if the economy was embedded in political and religious fields—as the no-market model suggests—a complex circulation system like this would be extremely difficult to control for any agent, group, or institutional power.

This brings us to the elite control model, which I believe should be strongly qualified. Local authorities may have mediated the redistribution of many goods—particularly staples—within ethnic territories organized according to verticality principles during the Late period, as the Inca did over the entire Andes during the last century before the European invasion. Nevertheless, the difficulties of controlling interregional circulation (i.e., of preventing the majority from obtaining circulating items) would have been enormous, particularly as the length of the circuits expanded to enchain several nodes and internodes. For this reason, I think that center-periphery interpretations of the Tiwanaku phenomenon in the Southern Andes, whether framed as conquest, colonization, or peripheral clientage, should be abandoned in favor of models that stress local agencies and the values that drove them. Furthermore, I have argued that even the Inca, who clearly made every effort to regulate interregional circulation in the provinces and mobilized massive resources to this effect, had only limited success.

This does not necessarily imply that trade items were used or consumed freely without any restriction. As mentioned before, the frequency and distribution of foreign goods in mortuary and domestic contexts show that throughout the sequence there are at least two distinct circulation spheres. The restricted sphere included psychotropic substances and tools for their consumption, certain weapons that may have served as political emblems (maces, axes), fine textiles or elaborate headdresses, and a variety of metal ornaments, particularly those made of gold and silver. The nonrestricted sphere included ceramics; greenstone and other lithics; wood and cane for bows, arrows, and other tools; feathers; less sophisticated textiles (ropes, bags, and clothes); marine and terrestrial shell; coca leaves; fish; maize; *chañar*; and probably a number of perishable goods (e.g., quinoa, tubers, peppers, and salt).

Certainly, it is possible that a few restricted items moved long distances under the close control of a small number of people. This could happen through the direct exchange of gifts between authorities or related elites; transactions during special visits to other nodes; peacemaking, weddings, and other special events; or even the mediation of particularly loyal caravaners. In my view, however, this possibility does not account for the existence of restricted spheres of exchange in the Southern Andes. Firstly, some of the same objects were circulating regularly along caravan routes, as illustrated by Tiwanaku ceramics and metals found along the Colorada Corridor, or Inca artifacts leaking into unofficial routes. Secondly, even if some of these objects were gifts between authorities, their use frequently committed conjoining items that were probably obtained by other means. Llagostera (1996:24), for example, notes that snuffing trays and tubes from a single tomb context at San Pedro often show different styles, implying that they came from different places. It is possible that the psychotropic plants consumed with them originated in another place and arrived via a different route and means of circulation. Finally, it would be extremely difficult to prevent access to some of these goods before exchange, in their places of origin, where they still seem to circulate in a restricted way. For example,

would it be feasible to constrain access to metals in areas such as the Atacama Desert, Northern Lípez, the Southern Potosí Valleys, or Río Grande de San Juan, where mines were abundant and metallurgy was a widespread activity? What about psychotropic plants in the Eastern Valleys or in the adjacent Humahuaca, areas where they abound?

I believe that discrete spheres associated with different value standards and restrictions on exchange did exist and were closely related to the development of social hierarchies. Their explanation, however, should be sought for in local value systems, such as in norms concerning the legitimate use and consumption of various goods and in the processes that brought them about. The insistence on elite control taken from the "archaeology of social complexity" ultimately reveals a narrow (formalist) conception of value as scarcity, and of power as accumulation and closure. It is the exclusion created by elite control over production and trade that turns the possession of scarce valuables into effective power indices ("prestige goods") and forces lower-ranking elites and commoners to enter into debt relationships in order to get them. Abandoning the elite control model invites us to consider other means through which objects can be assigned value and invites us to think about different ways of building power or gaining support for political projects.

Acknowledgments

The field research reported in this paper was partially funded by the National Geographic Society (Grant #7552-03) and kindly supported by the Viceministerio de Cultura de Bolivia and by Reserva Nacional de Fauna Andina "Eduardo Avaroa," who issued the corresponding permits to Proyecto Arqueológico Altiplano Sur. I would also like to express my gratitude to Joanne Pillsbury, Ken Hirth, and the Dumbarton Oaks staff for their warm hospitality.

NOTES

1 Some nodes and periods are underrepresented given the absence of diagnostic ceramics or the difficulties in applying the same chronological divisions to every region. For example, Sequitor ceramics from Atacama were all included in the Early period, although they continued in use until the end of the first millennium AD. There are no diagnostic ceramics for the pastoral regions of Southeastern Lípez or Northwestern Puna throughout the sequence, perhaps because specialized herders did not make pottery. Presently, the pastoralists of Southeastern Lípez trade in all the vessels they use from the Río Grande de San Juan during their annual long-distance caravan journeys to the Eastern Valleys (Nielsen 2001b).

2 Salt, a precious trade item in many parts of the world, is very common in the Southern Andean highlands; it was probably a significant element of exchange only toward the eastern flanks of the Southern Andes, where it was still traded by caravans in the 1990s.

3 Inhaling paraphernalia (e.g., tablets, tubes, and spatulae) appear at the beginning of the first millennium AD. Initially, they are associated with pipes and, toward the end of the Early period, they completely replace smoking as a medium to consume psychotropic substances.

4 The Late Formative site of Turi-2 (Upper Loa River), for example, has yielded pottery from multiple distant nodes, from Lake Titicaca (Kalassasaya) to the Valliserrana region of northwest Argentina (Ciénaga and Condorhuasi [Castro et al. 1994]).

5 Northern Lípez and Guayatayoc are not represented in the graph (although both must have been involved in this trade) because Middle-period pottery diagnostics for these areas are still not well established.

6 Given the exceptional character of the San Pedro de Atacama funerary sample, it is difficult to establish if the high frequency of trade items known from there reflects some centralization of the South Andean network by this node, or if similar proportions of foreign items exist in other regions, waiting to be discovered.

7 The importance of matrimonial exchange for securing access to distant productive zones in the Southern Andes has been forcefully argued by Martínez (1990) on the basis of ethnohistoric data.

REFERENCES CITED

Aldunate, Carlos
1993 Arqueología en el Pukara de Turi. In *Actas del XII Congreso Nacional de Arqueología Chilena*, edited by Hans Niemeyer Fernández, pp. 61–77. Sociedad Chilena de Arqueología, Santiago, Dirección de Bibliotecas, Archivos y Museos, and Museo Regional de la Araucanía, Temuco.

Appadurai, Arjun
1986 Introduction: Commodities and the Politics of Value. In *The Social Life of Things: Commodities in Cultural Perspective*, edited by Arjun Appadurai, pp. 3–63. Cambridge University Press, Cambridge.

Berenguer, José
1998 La iconografía del poder en Tiwanaku y su rol en la integración de zonas de frontera. *Boletín del Museo Chileno de Arte Precolombino* 7:19–37.
2004 *Caravanas, interacción y cambio en el desierto de Atacama*. Ediciones Sirawi, Santiago.

Berenguer, José, and Gonzalo Pimentel
2010 Arqueología de los "espacios vacíos": Una aproximación internodal a las relaciones intersocietales. In *Actas del XVII Congreso Nacional de Arqueología Chilena*, pp. 1305–1308. Universidad Austral de Chile, Valdivia.

Boman, Eric

1991 [1908] *Antigüedades de la región andina de la República Argentina y del desierto de Atacama.* Universidad Nacional de Jujuy, San Salvador de Jujuy.

Bowman, Isaiah

1924 *Desert Trails of Atacama.* American Geographical Society, New York.

Browman, David L.

1980 Tiwanaku Expansion and Altiplano Economic Patterns. *Estudios arqueológicos* 5:107–120.

Brumfiel, Elizabeth M., and Timothy K. Earle

1987 Specialization, Exchange, and Complex Societies: An Introduction. In *Specialization, Exchange, and Complex Societies,* edited by Elizabeth M. Brumfiel and Timothy K. Earle, pp. 1–9. Cambridge University Press, Cambridge.

Castro, Victoria, Carlos Aldunate, and José Berenguer

1984 Orígenes altiplánicos de la fase Toconce. *Estudios atacameños* 7:209–235.

Castro, Victoria, Carlos Aldunate, José Berenguer, Luis Cornejo, Carole Sinclaire, and Varinia Varela

1994 Relaciones entre el noroeste argentino y el norte de Chile: El sitio TU-02 Vegas de Turi. In *De costa a selva,* edited by María Ester Albeck, pp. 215–236. Instituto Interdisciplinario Tilcara, Tilcara.

Céspedes, Ricardo, and Patrice Lecoq

1998 El horizonte medio en los Andes meridionales de Bolivia (Potosí). In *Los desarrollos locales y sus territorios: Arqueología del NOA y sur de Bolivia,* compiled by María Beatriz Cremonte, pp. 103–129. Universidad Nacional de Jujuy, San Salvador de Jujuy.

Cruz, Pablo

2009 Tumbas, metalurgia y complejidad social en un páramo del altiplano surandino. *Revista andina* 49:71–103.

Dillehay, Tom D., and Lautaro Núñez

1988 Camelids, Caravans, and Complex Societies in the South-Central Andes. In *Recent Studies in Pre-Columbian Archaeology,* edited by Nicholas J. Saunders and Olivier de Montmollin, pp. 603–633. BAR, Oxford.

Friedman, Jonathan, and Michael Rowlands

1978 Notes towards an Epigenetic Model of the Evolution of "Civilization." In *The Evolution of Social Systems,* edited by Jonathan Friedman and Michael Rowlands, pp. 201–276. Duckworth, London.

Giddens, Anthony

1984 *The Constitution of Society: Outline of the Theory of Structuration.* Polity Press, Oxford.

Gregory, C. A.

1994 Exchange and Reciprocity. In *Companion Encyclopedia of Anthropology,* edited by Tim Ingold, pp. 911–939. Routledge, London.

Khazanov, Anatoly M.

1984 *Nomads and the Outside World.* Cambridge University Press, Cambridge.

Knudson, Kelly J.

2008 Tiwanaku Influence in the South Central Andes: Strontium Isotope Analysis and Middle Horizon Migration. *Latin American Antiquity* 19:3–23.

Knudson, Kelly J., Tiffiny A. Tung, Kenneth C. Nystrom, T. Douglas Price, and Paul D. Fullagar

2005 The Origin of the Juch'uypampa Cave Mummies: Strontium Isotope Analysis of Archaeological Human Remains from Bolivia. *Journal of Archaeological Science* 32:903–913.

Kolata, Alan L.

1993 *The Tiwanaku: Portrait of an Ancient Civilization.* Blackwell, New York.

Latcham, Ricardo E.

1909 *El comercio precolombino en Chile y otros países de América.* Imprenta Cervantes, Santiago.

Llagostera, Agustín

1996 San Pedro de Atacama: Nodo de complementariedad reticular. In *La integración sur andina cinco siglos después,* edited by Xavier Albó, María Inés Arratia, Jorge Hidalgo, Lautaro Núñez, Agustín Llagostera, María Isabel Remy, and Bruno Revesz, pp. 17–42. Centro de Estudios Regionales Andinos "Bartolomé de Las Casas," Cuzco.

2010   Retomando los límites y limitaciones del "archipiélago vertical." *Chungará* 42(1):283–295.

Martínez, José L.

1990   Interetnicidad y complementariedad en el Altiplano meridional: El caso atacameño. *Andes: Antropología e historia* 1:11–30. Salta.

Michel López, Marcos

2008   Patrones de asentamiento precolombino del altiplano boliviano: Lugares centrales de la región de Quillacas, Departamento de Oruro, Bolivia. PhD dissertation, Uppsala University, Uppsala.

Murra, John V.

1975   *Formaciones económicas y políticas en el mundo andino.* Instituto de Estudios Peruanos, Lima.

Nielsen, Axel E.

2001a   Evolución social en Quebrada de Humahuaca (AD 700–1536). In *Historia Argentina prehispánica,* edited by Eduardo E. Berberián and Axel E. Nielsen, pp. 171–264. Editorial Brujas, Córdoba.

2001b   Ethnoarchaeological Perspectives on Caravan Trade in the South-Central Andes. In *Ethnoarchaeology of Andean South America: Contributions to Archaeological Method and Theory,* edited by Lawrence A. Kuznar, pp. 163–201. International Monographs in Prehistory, Ann Arbor, Mich.

2006a   Estudios internodales e interacción interregional en los Andes circum-puneños: Teoría, método y ejemplos de aplicación. In *Esferas de interacción prehistóricas y fronteras nacionales modernas: Los Andes sur centrales,* edited by Heather Lechtman, pp. 29–62. Instituto de Estudios Peruanos—Institute of Andean Research, Lima.

2006b   Plazas para los antepasados: Descentralización y poder corporativo en las formaciones políticas preincaicas de los Andes circumpuneños. *Estudios atacameños* 31:63–89.

2009   Pastoralism and the Non-Pastoral World in the Late Precolumbian History of the Southern Andes (AD 1000–1535). *Nomadic Peoples* 13(2):17–35.

Nielsen, Axel E., José Berenguer R., and Cecilia Sanhueza T.

2006   El *Qhapaqñan* entre Atacama y Lípez. *Intersecciones* 7:217–234.

Núñez, Lautaro

1976   Geoglifos y tráfico de caravanas en el desierto chileno. *Homenaje al Dr. R. P. Gustavo Le Paige S. J.,* pp. 147–201. Universidad del Norte, Antofagasta.

1985   Petroglifos y tráfico en el desierto chileno. *Estudios en arte rupestre,* edited by Carlos Aldunate del Solar, José Berenguer R., and Victoria Castro R., pp. 243–263. Museo Chileno de Arte Precolombino, Santiago.

1994   Cruzando la cordillera por el norte: Señoríos, caravanas y alianzas. In *La cordillera de los Andes: Ruta de encuentros,* by Francisco Mena Larraín, translated by María Teresa Contreras and Adriana Pineda, pp. 9–21. Museo Chileno de Arte Precolombino, Santiago.

2006   La orientación minero-metalúrgica de la producción atacameña y sus relaciones fronterizas. In *Esferas de interacción prehistóricas y fronteras nacionales modernas: Los Andes sur centrales,* edited by Heather Lechtman, pp. 205–251. Instituto de Estudios Peruanos—Institute of Andean Research, Lima.

Núñez, Lautaro, Carolina Agüero, Bárbara Cases, and Patricio Souza

2003   El campamento minero Chuquicamata 2 y la explotación cuprífera prehispánica en el desierto de Atacama. *Estudios atacameños* 25:7–34.

Núñez, Lautaro, and Tom D. Dillehay

1979   *Movilidad giratoria, armonía social y desarrollo en los andes meridionales: Patrones de tráfico e interacción económica.* Universidad Católica del Norte, Antofagasta.

Oakland, Amy

1992   Textiles and Ethnicity: Tiwanaku in San Pedro de Atacama. *Latin American Antiquity* 3:316–340.

Pérez, José A.

2000   El jaguar en llamas (la religión en el antiguo noroeste argentino). In *Nueva historia Argentina*, vol. 1, edited by Myriam Noemí Tarragó, pp. 229–256. Sudamericana, Buenos Aires.

Pimentel, Gonzalo, Charles Rees, Patricio de Souza, and Lorena Arancibia

2011   Viajeros costeros y caravaneros. Dos estrategias de movilidad en el período formativo en el desierto de Atacama, Chile. In *En ruta: Arqueología, historia y etnografía del tráfico sur andino*, edited by Lautaro Núñez and Axel Nielsen, pp. 43–81. Editorial Encuentro, Córdoba.

Platt, Tristan

1987   Entre *ch´axwa* y *muxsa*: Para una historia del pensamiento político aymara. In *Tres reflexiones sobre el pensamiento andino*, by Thérèse Bouysse Cassagne et al., pp. 61–132. Hisbol, La Paz.

Polanyi, Karl

1953   *Semantics of General Economic History.* Columbia University Press, New York.

Pryor, Frederic L.

1977   *The Origins of the Economy: A Comparative Study of Distribution in Primitive and Peasant Economies.* Academic Press, New York.

Stanish, Charles

1992   *Ancient Andean Political Economy.* University of Texas Press, Austin.

Tarragó, Myriam N.

1989   Contribución al conocimiento arqueológico de las poblaciones de los oasis de Atacama en relación con otros pueblos puneños. PhD dissertation, Universidad Nacional de Rosario, Rosario.

2006   Espacios surandinos y la circulación de bienes en época de Tiwanaku. In *Esferas de interacción prehistóricas y fronteras nacionales modernas: Los Andes sur centrales*, edited by Heather Lechtman, pp. 331–369. Instituto de Estudios Peruanos—Institute of Andean Research, Lima.

Van Buren, Mary

1996   Rethinking the Vertical Archipelago. *American Anthropologist* 98:338–351.

Wiessner, Polly

2009   Warfare and Political Complexity in an Egalitarian Society: An Ethnohistorical Example. In *Warfare in Cultural Context: Practice, Agency, and the Archaeology of Violence*, edited by Axel E. Nielsen and William H. Walker, pp. 165–189. University of Arizona Press, Tucson.

Yacobaccio, Hugo D., Patricia Escola, F. X. Pereyra, Marisa Lazzari, and Michael Glascock

2004   Quest for Ancient Routes: Obsidian Research Sourcing in Northwestern Argentina. *Journal of Archaeological Science* 31:193–204.

17

Barter Markets in the Pre-Hispanic Andes

CHARLES STANISH AND LAWRENCE S. COBEN

THE TRADITIONAL VIEW THAT MARKET systems did not exist in the prehistoric Andes is based on a large corpus of historical data. Unlike Central Mexico, where market systems were described in substantial detail in early colonial documents, markets and marketplaces were barely mentioned in Andean texts of the same era. We have no accounts of large marketplaces, few descriptions of independent traders except on the margins of the empire, no discussion of media of exchange or any description of a legal structure to regulate such trade. Instead of markets and complex tribute rolls, Andean sources tell of labor taxation (*mit'a*). Known as corvée in the Western feudal world, this arrangement is unpaid labor conscripted on a regular basis by a political authority. Yet in spite of this, evidence for small marketplaces exists in the pre-Hispanic Central Andes. Local fairs flourished, and there was a brisk trade in many goods, both basic commodities and products of highly specialized labor. Long-distance interregional exchange of many kinds of items was also robust and historically deep.

In this paper, we try to resolve some of these apparent contradictions. We apply a suite of theoretical tools to help us understand how one of the great empires in world history—the Inca—functioned without price-making market mechanisms while simultaneously existing in an economic landscape structured by regional fairs, intense specialized production, and vigorous interregional trade.

Background to the Debate

In certain ways, the debate begins with the historical observations of the earliest Europeans who chronicled the Andes. In Central Mexico, the chroniclers lavishly described markets and traders, and even talked about some kinds of money. As Kenneth Hirth (1998:451) noted, "the marketplace was the center of economic life in ancient Mesoamerica. It was here that countless products were bought and sold and all the riches of the New World were displayed." A mere dozen years later,

419

Spanish conquerors from the same class and background as those of Mexico also described the economy, political structure, religion, and other aspects of indigenous life in Andean South America. One of the first mentions of contact with the Andean world was a raft, off the coast of Ecuador, filled with commodities. Spanish writers interpreted its sailors to be traders like the *pochteca* they had come to know in Mexico (Pizarro 1978 [1571]:line 4280). Yet, in the months and years following the initial conquest, markets and marketplaces were barely mentioned in the Andean historical literature. We have few or no descriptions of large markets or independent traders, and virtually no discussion of currencies, market equivalencies, and the like. Regional fairs are occasionally noted, but compared to texts concerning Central Mexico, these are incidental and almost invisible.

The Inca economy was enormous and profoundly complex. We do get descriptions of the massive production of items by the Inca state as well as the movement of goods across the landscape. Craft specialization and exchange were a cornerstone of both the local and imperial economies. But the way this economic activity took place was very different from that of the Aztec landscape. The Inca, like their counterparts in Central Mexico, were able to extract an impressive amount of resources from their provinces; however, in place of the institution of markets and complex tribute rolls of Central Mexico is the theme of labor taxation in the Andes, or *mit'a*. *Mit'a* is an indigenous term meaning "turn" in the sense of fulfilling an obligation—that is, in each community every taxpayer had to take their turn in meeting the labor tax imposed by the authorities. In the same way that the institution of the market dominates the observations of the Europeans in Central Mexico, the institution of the *mit'a* dominates the literature on the Andean peoples.

Spanish writers independently described the elaborate labor arrangements for producing everything from buildings to beer, for supplying the army with troops to filling the ubiquitous storehouses that lined the great road system. Catherine Julien (1988:264), echoing a generation of Andean

scholars, is emphatic about this point: "The Inca system of exactions was unlike the Spanish system in that all that was assessed from local people was their labor.... Products might be elaborated with this labor donation, but the resources that were converted into product were held by the state."

It was in this intellectual context that the now tired substantivist-formalist debate in economic anthropology played out with the Andean data. As late as the early 1980s, substantivists like George Dalton were still arguing that markets could not exist without money: "What is wrong ... is to postulate ... that important market sectors existed before money existed" (Dalton 1982:183).[1] Most Andean historians and ethnohistorians concerned with economic history and anthropology were in the substantivist camp and drew the obvious conclusion: since there were no pre-Hispanic currencies in the Andes, there were no markets.

Perhaps the single greatest figure in this literature was the Andean ethnohistorian John Murra (Murra 1962, 1980 [1956], 1985a, 1985b, 1995; see also Mayer, this volume). Murra's theoretical work focused on the alleged uniqueness of the Andean landscape. His model of "verticality" or "zonal complementarity" was based on the fact that the ecozones for agricultural production and pastoralism depended upon altitude. This dependency resulted in a highly compact and stratified set of resource zones up and down the vast Andean chain. According to Murra, this ecological fact promoted nonmarket systems over other types of exchange. Instead of independent traders, Andean peoples used kinship ties to establish colonial settlements in multiple ecological zones. Exchange was robust, but it was an exchange through redistribution and reciprocity, not market mechanisms.

Murra and his colleagues used this supposed unique nature of the Andean environment to create what was in so many words an "Andean mode of production." Theorists who never worked in the Andes began to compare the region with various forms of the "Asiatic" mode of production (e.g., Godelier 1977). Murra took it a step further, at least by implication: underlying his theoretical work was the idea that verticality was a newly discovered way to structure noncapitalist society. For Murra, this was the basis of a new mode of production in Marxist economic anthropology. By the late 1970s and early 1980s, the notion that the Andes were different than other areas of the world was entrenched in much of the literature.

The verticality concept has been increasingly criticized (Stanish 1989; Van Buren 1996; see also Burger, this volume; Mayer, this volume). It is important to remember that the other great economic and social historian of this period, María Rostworowski, subtly but firmly criticized Murra's theoretical attempts to create a new mode of production from the Andean data (1977, 1981). Rostworowski has consistently maintained that craft specialization and market-like exchange characterized at least the coastal societies of central Peru in prehistory. Her rich ethnohistoric data demonstrate a brisk trade up and down the coast, and her work—most notably her book *Etnía y sociedad: Costa peruana prehispánica* (1977)—has always existed as a theoretical counter to Murra and the verticality theories of his colleagues.

The empirical base of zonal complementarity or verticality, the concept of "lo Andino" (that is, Andean society as a timeless and unchanging social reality), has now been challenged as a classic case of theoretical "essentializing" (see Paerregaard 2000). Comparative studies likewise suggest that the Andes are not all that different than many areas of the world in terms of ecological zonation. Regions such as the Basin of Mexico also display degrees of ecological stratification based on altitude. Timothy Earle (1977), another early critic of Murra's theory, noted that similar environmental diversity existed in Hawaii without the use of extensive exchange. Even in the Andes, altitude is not as stark as imagined. For instance, most of the major Andean crops can be grown in the areas from fifteen hundred to 2,800 meters above sea level (masl). From an economic perspective, there are far fewer ecozones, with perhaps the coast and coastal plain, the highlands, and the forest being the principal resource areas. This is not much different from many parts of the world where there are mountains or patchy

resource distribution. Finally, a close look at the archaeological record indicates that expected patterns of colonization are rare and can be explained without recourse to a unique Andean mode of production. In fact, these patterns can be understood with general comparative social science concepts drawn from a full range of case studies from around the world in space and time (Stanish 1992; Van Buren 1996).

There has likewise been a significant shift in attitude among social scientists in the last two decades or so regarding markets in the non-Western world. This rethinking has been particularly true for anthropological archaeologists. The idea that market systems are "rational" in the economic sense leads some to forcefully argue that non-Western peoples were, in fact, "rational" as well. From this logic, non-Western people also structured their economic life with market principles. The problem begins with the word *rational*. Semantically, particularly in European languages, *rational* has positive moral and cognitive connotations, while *irrational* has the opposite implication. When used in the colloquial sense, *rational* behavior is simply that which most effectively allows one to achieve a particular goal. Calling somebody irrational implies that they lack some basic human cognitive capacity. Using the colloquial sense for an entire culture is even worse and represents the epitome of uninformed ethnocentrism. The argument follows that non-Western people also had markets for rational action, though these were mediated and structured in culturally specific ways. In fact, modern behavioral economics came about for precisely this reason—people behaved or could be led to behave in intelligent but "irrational" ways.

Ironically, it was not long ago that anthropologists bristled at the notion that non-Western peoples had market systems. The observation by Scott Cook (1966) that the substantivist approach embodied an "anti-market mentality" remained valid for verticality theory into the 1980s. The idea that non-Western people had markets was seen as ethnocentric and theoretically untenable, an attempt to interpret non-Westerners through the lens of Western economics. In the words of Richard

Blanton and Lane Fargher (2010:208), this led many to "an unfortunate and mistaken anthropological consensus that rational action and market exchange could not have been important aspects of premodern complex societies." We now recognize this latter position to be inaccurate, as ethnography and history teaches us the highly sophisticated and varied means by which peoples around the world structure their economic lives.

The Core of the Issue:
What Exactly Is a Market?

Defining the term *market* is perhaps the most intractable problem facing comparative research on Andean economies. The literature in economic anthropology and economic history contains a plethora of definitions, ranging from the most general and encompassing to the most restrictive (see below). All of these classifications can be useful concepts, depending on the analytical goals one seeks to achieve. General definitions center on the idea that a market is simply a place where goods and services can be exchanged. A typical broad definition in this sense is "an organized public gathering of buyers and sellers of commodities meeting at an appointed place at regular intervals" (Hodder 1965:57). Quoting this very definition in their review of marketplace trade in Latin America, R. J. Bromley and Richard Symanski elaborate:

> These markets are held in open market squares or plazas, in streets and open spaces, at roads junctions, and in public, municipal market buildings. Locally, markets are referred to by such names as *ferias*, *plazas*, or *mercados* in Spanish-speaking Latin America . . . *feiras* in Brazil, *tianguis* in Indian areas of Central Mexico, *catus* in some Quechu-speaking Andean areas, and *marches* in French-speaking countries. Generally found in medium to large nucleated settlements, markets are also encountered in very small hamlets, particularly those located at nodal points in communication networks. A settlement may have one or more different market locations. . . . Places with

one or more markets are generally referred to as market centers (Bromley and Symanski 1974:3).

Kenneth Hirth is one of the leading theoreticians of markets in Mesoamerica and of trade in ancient states. Echoing a consensus in the literature, he classifies markets to include those venues where exchange occurs with either barter or currencies. He notes that "[t]hese exchanges [in markets] may occur as single balanced and reciprocal events or in clusters as they do in a marketplace" (Hirth 1998:451–452). In this perspective, a market is both a place and system where goods and services are exchanged via a number of mechanisms (see Hirth 1996).

Such a definition of a market is quite useful. It focuses our research on the variety of means by which goods and services were exchanged in the premodern world. It also allows us to effectively compare how different societies created exchange mechanisms and overcame resource patchiness, developed specialist groups, moved goods over short and long distances, and achieved economic efficiencies in alternate ways. Most importantly, again citing Hirth, is that the existence of markets "has a tremendous effect on the demand for resources, the quantity of items exchanged, and the efficiency with which they move" (Hirth 1998:452). The creation of market institutions, by this definition, puts them at the center of the development of complex chiefdoms and states. Markets redirect and concentrate human economic efforts. They facilitate the emergence of efficient systems of exchange and are the basis for the development of state around the world.

This broad definition effectively covers the exchange of goods in most settled village societies known in the ethnographic and historical record. It would even cover mobile groups who periodically met to exchange goods, information, and so forth in a predetermined place. As argued above, this definition is useful because it allows for cross-cultural comparisons among many different social and historical contexts. And by this definition, there certainly were markets in the Andes, going back at least to the second millennium BC and continuing up to the Inca and early colonial periods. Accepting this point of view, our debate is effectively over: there were markets in the prehistoric Andes. Andean markets were based on barter exchange without the use of currencies, price swings, and an independent class of traders.

Distinguishing Markets: Places versus Rules

We are still faced, however, with the rather glaring discrepancies between the historical data of market exchange in the Andes versus that of Central Mexico. Although it is generally agreed that while both areas had robust exchange of goods in periodic places, the economic organization of the empires and states that ruled each area differed considerably. This empirical reality most likely explains the disparities in reports from the early Spanish writers.

As Darrell E. La Lone (1982:300) noted thirty years ago, we must distinguish between marketplace, market economy, and market. There exists, in fact, in the study of exchange in the premodern world, another tradition that creates distinctions between various kinds of markets. Economists and economic historians have largely developed this tradition. This is a view of the market "as an institutional set of rules" and not necessarily as a place where exchange takes place. We argue that this perspective allows us to understand the important question regarding the differences between the Andes and Mesoamerica.

Donald Kurtz raised this issue, with special reference to Mesoamerica, a generation ago:

The markets with which anthropologists have traditionally been concerned are the sites and places in which goods and services are traded and exchanged. This is a considerably different concept of the market from that with which economists are concerned. The market of the economist is a specific institution with rules of its own which function to regulate the supply of goods and services in relationship to demand and considerations of price so that presumed infinite human wants may be satisfied with the finite resources at hand (Kurtz 1974:686).

This perspective makes the distinction between the "market as an institution" and the "market as a concentrated place for exchange between buyers and sellers." This more restrictive definition centers on the means by which value is established and the nature of transaction costs (in the sense defined by North 1984). Such a view makes the distinction between market *places* and the market *as a specific set of rules and/or strategies for exchange.*

The classic market occurs when transacting actors engage in decentralized, arm's-length bargaining, the parties are generally informally organized and remain autonomous, each actor presses his/her own interests vigorously, and contracting is relatively comprehensive. Actors then specify preferences and prices through contracts that, when completed, are self-liquidating and require no further interaction among the transacting parties. Moreover, the identities of the parties do not influence the terms of the exchange . . . no durable relation is observed among economic actors, and the only purpose of the market adjustments is to make on-the-spot, coherent instantaneous transactions, without any concern about future strategies (Hollingsworth and Boyer 1997:7).

This "rule" or "strategy-based" definition of a market, plus the broader ones provided above, give us the theoretical tools to understand the historical data from the sixteenth-century accounts of markets in Central Mexico and the Central Andes. By focusing on the nature of economic interactions, we can see that there were some substantial differences in the ways exchange took place in various marketplaces in both areas. Likewise, this focus helps us understand the state economies that developed in the late pre-Hispanic imperial systems in both regions.

Price-Making versus Barter Markets

Richard Wilk (1996:469) makes an important point that "markets come in a variety of shapes and sizes, that there is no single market principle, and that markets can be integrated into a remarkable variety of economic systems." The strategy-based definition of markets provided above describes what economists call "price-fixing markets" or "price-making markets" (North 1977), as opposed to other kinds of exchange systems. A price-making market is one in which prices are determined by negotiation between autonomous buyers and sellers without much regard to social class or status. Supply and demand is the principal force behind the negotiation and the ultimate exchange value reached, expressed almost always in a "price" by some kind of independent unit of exchange, or currency. Money or some kind of medium of exchange, in fact, is virtually a prerequisite for the efficient operation of price-making markets. While in theory a price-making market can exist with various media of exchange or even no money at all, a customarily recognized currency is usually associated with these systems. The first metal coinage was produced in either Thrace or India in the sixth century BC, coming rather late in the world of price-making markets that had developed at least fifteen hundred years earlier. Other kinds of currencies include beads, cacao, ingots, feathers, standardized metal rings, bullae (accounting devices of clay balls), and the like that go back millennia or more and are found around the world in a variety of cultural contexts, both in the Old World and in the Americas (Silver 2010).

The social context of exchange tends to be different in price-making markets than in other kinds of market systems. Hirth (1998:455) notes that "buyers and sellers interacted within the marketplace independent of their social rank." He goes on to characterize this system as one in which there were no "enduring relationships" between buyers and sellers. Households, the basic unit of production, operated free from interference by social or political authorities. All of this comes together to produce a "centralized but nonhierarchical provisioning network that operates independently of other sociopolitical relationships in the society" (Hirth 1998:455).

Another type of marketplace exchange that we see in the ethnographic and historical data is based on barter, a form of exchange found in every society. A barter exchange is one in which goods and services are traded directly without the use of currencies. These exchanges use customarily agreed-upon equivalencies that also fluctuate, but they fluctuate far less than that seen in price-making markets. A basket of corn for a bushel of wheat, or a stone axe for a worked marine shell, epitomizes this kind of exchange. There are an infinite number of variations of these exchange equivalencies that employ other goods, all without the use of money. As with all economic transactions, supply and demand affect the relative equivalencies (Smith 1980:876), but they do so within a larger social context. That social context involves kin groups, political and religious authorities, and the like.

The key point is that in both kinds of market exchanges—price-making markets and barter—people act rationally, in the colloquial sense, to maximize utilities. In economics, a utility is simply a measure of satisfaction that an agent receives from the consumption of a good or service. People seek to get wealthy, achieve social status, and vie with one another for advantage in each of these systems. As anthropologists, we understand that different cultures value goods and services in different ways. It is almost self-evident for the anthropologist to note that the utility of goods and services in every society will be culturally determined. Less obvious perhaps is the observation that what differs between these various kinds of exchange systems are the rules of competition and the corresponding strategies used to maximize utilities, culturally determined as they are. And, of course, the two systems are not mutually exclusive: barter and price-making markets frequently coexist, even in today's modern globalized world (Prendergast and Stole 2000).

The Different Strategies of Competition in Price-Making Markets and Barter Exchange

As mentioned, the idea that people in non-Western societies did not engage in any kind of profit motive was naive and a bit patronizing. Quite to the contrary, most comparative behavioral and social scientists who look at this problem would maintain that actors in all kinds of exchange systems seek to maximize utilities. We agree with the great Raymond Firth, in his critique of Malinowski, that the desire to maximize individual advantage is a universal human trait (and see Schneider 2002:66 for a different interpretation of this "neo-formalist" assumption). But, as anthropologists, we realize that the advantages that are maximized (utilities) are not universal: different cultures value different things, and this fundamental anthropological fact must always be part of any analysis of any economy. Furthermore, since the contexts in which the exchange takes place are distinct in barter versus price-making market exchanges, the corresponding maximizing strategies are likewise appropriate to the particular system in which wealth is distributed.

In price-making markets, competition between individual traders is played out via price negotiation. Individual sellers maximize advantage by selling more commodities at appropriate prices that fluctuate on a supply-and-demand basis. Buyers, in contrast, seek to bring the price down as much as possible. In economic terms, the price reaches equilibrium between supply and demand. Merchants enrich themselves by finding the right price to maximize profit, selling to a buyer with little regard to other factors. The principles of price-making markets are such a staple of Western economies that they require little explanation in this paper.

In a barter market, however, prices are more stable. Fluctuations in equivalencies are much slower through time, though ultimately supply and demand affect the values as well. In most of the ethnographies that we have, most households and certainly entire villages are largely self-sufficient in producing basic life-sustaining commodities. In economic terms, we would say that supply is relatively elastic for most of the basic goods (though not all), including those that are naturally available. Major added value from economic activity comes not only from collecting or making something rare but also from the transport of those goods from producer to buyer. In fact, compared to modern Western economies, transaction costs from transport are extremely high in premodern contexts. Therefore, the supply of commodities tends to be less important than the transaction costs of making the exchange (an example would be obsidian—there is virtually an endless and cost-free supply at volcanic sources, but getting the raw material from the source to the consumers is a huge cost, particularly if there is regional conflict). Of course, high transaction costs lead to scarcities that affect supply even in these situations. But compared to price-making market exchange in premodern contexts for rare objects, the barter economy stands out in that the exchange values of goods tend to be more stable.

Another way to put it is that this elasticity in supply and high transport costs leads to relatively stable prices in barter markets vis-à-vis price-making markets—that is, prices are "customarily" accepted and notions of fairness and reputation rigidly maintained. Important exceptions occur, and when there is a scarce item of value, barter markets tend to take on the attributes of price-making markets for that particular commodity. Malinowski himself noted that negotiation takes place in the barter for common goods, a trade called *gimwali,* "where one article is traded against another, with direct assessment of equivalence and even with haggling" (Malinowski 1921:13). But he quickly qualifies this by observing that "in all cases trade follows customary rules, which determine what and how much shall be exchanged for any given article" (Malinowski 1921:13). The obvious conclusion from this and many other observations by ethnographers like Malinowski is that barterers are not haggling over the actual customary values that are generally inflexible; rather, they are haggling over the quality and nature of the traded objects themselves in an attempt to get a better deal by "reclassifying" the object into a different quality class.

As a general rule, actors in barter markets customarily understand the exchange value of goods and services: "All the trade is carried on in exactly the same way—given the article, and the communities between which it is traded, anyone would know its equivalent, rigidly prescribed by custom" (Malinowski 1921:14). Instead of rapidly shifting prices determined by individual negotiations, prices in barter markets result from a broader social consensus involving buyers, sellers, producers, and political authorities.

Scarcity of an otherwise obtainable item occurs when a political entity restricts access to a naturally occurring good, or when the commodities are created by highly specialized labor that cannot meet demand. In these instances, supply is obviously less elastic. But in both of these instances, supply is often controlled by entities above the household. The ideal of the price-making market in which exchange partners trade with little regard to social caste or class is lost where supply is directly monitored by political authorities. To go back to our obsidian example, when a political entity controls the volcanic source, they can restrict its access to various subgroups in a society. Households that do not have access to this source cannot barter or sell in the marketplace; they instead have to work within a larger social context for procurement (production) and exchange to take place.

In barter markets, exchange partners are maintained by elaborate social rules, another difference from price-making markets. Economic exchange is highly ritualized, much more so than in price-making markets. The Kula ring of the Trobriand Islanders is one of countless examples of the ritualized nature of trade in a barter system. Individual traders have partners for life with whom they must trade. As Rolf Ziegler (1990:143), reflecting J. P. Singh Uberoi's earlier work (1971), notes, "the Kula exchange does not take place in an anonymous market but within stable, usually lifelong, partnerships being transferred to the heirs by mortuary rites symbolizing the stability of the relationship." Kula traders can have many or few partners, depending on their social status. The partner's status shifts through time based on the quality and quantity of the Kula items each man acquires (bracelets and necklaces). There is a debate in the literature as to whether the Kula trade is connected to the parallel trade in domestic items (Hann 2006:210; Strathern and Stewart 2005). We view the two as inseparable and see the status of the Kula partners as directly linked to their success in the domestic trade, at

least during the turn of the last century, when Malinowski completed his famous ethnographic studies.[2] Status goes up or down, depending on whether one provides quality goods during trading expeditions. From the perspective that sees the Kula as the ritualized framework for domestic exchange, the quality of the Kula items reflects the value that each trader adds to the domestic exchange. The Kula ring also shows us that some traders get rich while others get poor, and this condition is likewise tied to their status. Since supply is elastic, the customary prices of commodities remain relatively stable—rather, it is the quantity of partners that determines the relative success of each Kula trader.

The most important theoretical point here is this: *The key strategy of a trader getting rich in a barter system is not to sell more at a constantly negotiated price, as in price-making markets, but rather to increase his/her social network and therefore increase the number of trade partners.* Given that the exchange values in barter market systems tend to remain relatively stable compared to price-making markets, where fluctuations are required for profits to be earned, *people in barter markets get rich by acquiring more partners in their factions and not by undercutting the competition.*

All of the faction-building strategies that anthropologists have studied come into play in these contexts. Hosts feast their partners, seek strategic alliances with other families or factions, engage in strategic intermarriage, build up their household numbers with fictive and real kin, try to accumulate deferred debts to be converted in major events (such as potlatches), and keep their competitors at bay with force or forceful persuasion. In the Kula ring, we see this process at work:

The exchange of gifts creates or reinforces relationships of alliance between individuals and the groups of which they are representative. . . . In the *kula* ring, the partnership establishes an alliance with political overtones . . . It opens the channels of substantial trade and social intercourse. But a man's position in the ring is not predetermined and static. A participant starts from a position of relative capital advantage or disadvantage . . . from this position, if he is ambitious, he may maneuver to increase the number and scale of alliances, and hence his command over the flow of wealth and the degree to which his good will is sought, and hence his status and prestige (Belshaw 1955:19).[3]

In other words, as the social network increases, so does the number of trade "partners." The maximization of advantage is achieved by increasing the number of trading partners through noneconomic incentives, not by just earning a profit over price differentials. This is the fundamental difference between barter and price-making markets.

The Andean Fair as Barter Markets

> Throughout the entire kingdom of Peru . . . there were large *tiangues* that are markets where the locals conducted their business (Cieza de León 1967 [1553]:capítulo cx).[4]

The historical data are quite clear that there were few price-making markets, but substantial barter markets, in the Andes. In a telling example from the historical data, the Aymara-Spanish dictionary by Ludovico Bertonio of 1612 demonstrates that there was an emic distinction between European and indigenous ways of trading. One entry is "mercader a nuestro modo: mircatori ves Tintani" and immediately below this entry is "mercader a modo de indios, Hanrucu, Alasiri." The word for the former is obviously an Aymarization of the Spanish *mercado* (Aymara today still occasionally pronounce the E's like I's). In other words, two generations after the conquest, there was no indigenous word for "marketing" the "European way," and, to express the concept, they had to borrow from the Spanish. These two modest dictionary entries in a sense comprise one of the earliest anthropological descriptions on record for Andean economies: two cultures, coexisting in the same landscape, structured their economic lives in such different ways that they literally required a separate vocabulary to describe and understand them. Hirth's chapter in this volume reinforces this

distinction between Mesoamerica and the Andes. He provides numerous references to merchants who "profit," in a manner immediately recognizable to the Spaniards who recorded these practices.

That vocabulary distinguishes between the Spanish (and Central Mexican) concepts of price-making markets and the Andean concept of barter. These barter markets were referred to as *ferias*, *mercados*, or *tiangues* in the ethnographic and historical literature (e.g., Cieza de León 1967 [1553]:32, 96, 110; Cobo 1890–1893 [1653]:libro 1, capítulo 8), and as La Lone (1982:299–300) noted, they should not be confused with price-making markets in the European or Mesoamerican sense.

For those of us who have worked for many years in the highland Andes, the periodic (weekly, monthly, or annual) trade fair is a common phenomenon. Fairs are still found throughout the highlands on a regular basis, and merchants from distant places ply their wares there. In the Titicaca region, for instance, livestock fairs are a huge enterprise. People from throughout the region will congregate in a specified village or town to trade cattle, sheep, goats, camelids, and other animals. Smaller, but similar, fairs are held on a weekly basis in virtually all towns.

That barter markets should be found throughout the Andes is not surprising. The nature of Andean society obviates the need for the development of price-making markets by ameliorating the theoretical weaknesses of a barter market. The two primary weaknesses (Jevons 1879 [1871])—want of coincidence and want of a measure of value—are, for the most part, resolved by the structure of Andean society and markets, and help to explain the ethnohistoric descriptions of Andean fairs.

Consider the most commonly ascribed weakness of barter markets—the want of coincidence, or the double coincidence of wants. This term refers to the possibility that those who possess the goods for which you want to trade will not want your goods, or that the people who want what you have to sell will not have something you want with which to barter. Yet this theoretical formulation ignores the social relationships among Andean market participants. Most of them live near the markets they attend. They know most, if not all, of the other participants in that marketplace, and they are aware of complex kinship relationships that bind individuals. Furthermore, people understand what, how much, and the quality of the products available.

Knowledge and social practice would, therefore, make a want of coincidence unlikely, if not impossible, except for a first-time or infrequent visitor to the market. This visitor would lack this knowledge. In the event of an abnormal shortage, while some price adjustment would occur as in a price market, barterers with such goods would likely favor their closer relationships/better customers.

Similarly, in cyclically repeated markets with participants who share a community, such as those that likely characterized the pre-Hispanic Andes, establishment of measures of value and exchange is a socialized and habituated process that does not require complicated price lists, as suggested by the theoretical literature on barter. The classic work of William S. Jevons notes that in a barter market,

> the price-current list would be a most complicated document, for each commodity would have to be quoted in terms of every other commodity, or else complicated rule-of-three sums would become necessary. Between one hundred articles there must exist no less than 4950 possible ratios of exchange, and all these ratios must be carefully adjusted so as to be consistent with each other, else the acute trader will be able to profit by buying from some and selling to others (Jevons 1879 [1871]:7).

Yet modern barter markets in the Andes exist without such complicated lists and apparently without "acute" arbitrageurs gaming the system, and we propose that pre-Hispanic markets likely did the same. At a series of modern food barter markets in the Lares Valley of Peru, known as *chalayplasa*, "products are measured in units or handfuls, according to traditional social agreements" (Argumedo and Pimbert 2010:345). Like a Kula ring, "these principles have been institutionalized into exchange and participation rules through ritualized customs that express generosity and solidarity"

(Argumedo and Pimbert 2010:345). No currency is exchanged, no exchange-price lists exist, and yet the markets function well. Argumedo and Pimbert argue that barter markets improve food security and nutrition, as well as agricultural diversity, while maintaining local control over the food supply.

A reputed advantage of currency is the ability to store and transport value. In other words, you can sell a good in market A and carry money, rather than commodities, to market B to make purchases. Currency also permits the storing of value until such time as the holder desires to expend it, which would be impossible, at least in the case of nondurable goods. Yet the ability to store and transport value is not required in the subsistence food markets that likely dominated pre-Hispanic Andean life. Value could still be stored and transported in durable goods, such as obsidian and textiles, and perhaps even storable foodstuffs such as *chuño* and *charki*. Transporting value would also depend on these goods being available in sufficient quantity to make long-distance trade worthwhile, transportable at some reasonable cost, and desired. This makes these goods tradable in other markets. Long-distance trade, then, is a highly specialized profession, as traders must constantly be moving goods at the right time to the appropriate market and have the requisite knowledge and resources to do so. Due to this constant movement, it is not surprising that there would be little documentary evidence or description of any such traders. Given the required resources, is it surprising that effective long-distance trade would best be managed by a state-like entity, such as the program of redistribution found in the Inca Empire? Without or in addition to government sponsorship, long-distance trade could operate through a series of interregional fairs that met for short periods of time in different locations, with their well-known schedule providing a template for long-distance traders.

Examples of Andean Fairs

A 1573 official survey (*relación geográfica*) from Quito (Jiménez de la Espada 1965 [1897]:220, no. 115) provided a virtual textbook description of a barter market and emphasized the difference with Spanish monetarized systems of exchange: "The Indians hold their markets in their villages, moving them day to day.... Among themselves there are no weights and measures but they conduct business by bartering one thing for another. [In contrast], the Spaniards use the Avila system of weights and measures."[5]

In places like Pucara, the annual fair in July is a spectacular event. Even today, the fame of this market extends to the neighboring countries of Argentina, Chile, and Bolivia. People from the coast and the southern altiplano vie with Cusqueños, people from Carabaya, Ilave, and many other places to sell their goods. Modern Kalawaya continue their ancient trade in medicine. The justly famous potters of Pucara bring out their best. Any and all sorts of goods abound in these markets.

While spectacular to the modern eye, the markets are apparently a pale reflection of their earlier glory. Summarizing the observations of several nineteenth-century European and Peruvian travelers—such as Antonio Raimondi, Clements Markham, Jorge Basadre, and Paul Macoy—G. M. Wrigley poetically writes that the town of "Pucara, 'one hundred mud huts set down in the silence of the Pampa' of Puno, was also during one fortnight of the year transformed into 'a commercial and industrial Babel'" (Wrigley 1919:78).

While Pucara was an important market, it was neither the largest nor most famous. The honor of being the greatest periodic fair in the northern Titicaca Basin was apparently found at the now charming but nondescript town of Vilque. In the nineteenth century, Vilque was transformed into a vast marketplace for two weeks a year:

The fair of Vilque, today abandoned but once the most famous of all Peru, is a good example. Vilque is a sad little town on the desolate puna, six leagues west of Puno, the port of Titicaca. During the greater part of the year the chance traveler found the place practically destitute of resources, but at Whitsuntide! Outside the town there were thousands of mules from Tucuman;... in the plaza were booths full of every description of Manchester and Birmingham goods; in more

retired places were gold dust and coffee from Caravaya, silver from the mines, bark and chocolate from Bolivia, Germans with glassware and woolen knitted work, French modistes, Italians, Quechua and Aymara Indians.... Alpaca wool and cinchona were other important articles of sale. The number of people assembled has been stated at 15,000 (Wrigley 1919:78).

Documented fairs were held throughout the Andes during the colonial and early Republican period. At the great fair of Huari, near the mining town of Potosí in Bolivia, Wrigley writes that people were drawn from an area larger than the country of France to this annual fair, bringing every conceivable good to sell: "During the great part of the year Huari leads a desolate and monotonous existence, but for the fort-night succeeding Holy Week the transformation is complete. Huari is a busy mart; a gathering of 10,000 people is not unusual" (Wrigley 1919:69). The Huari fair was noteworthy for the wide variety of goods and for the numerous places from which merchants traveled to sell their wares in this mining region:

The visitors to the fair are drawn from a wide area and bring with them a great diversity of products. From the Argentine pampas by way of Salta and La Quiaca come mules, donkeys, bullocks, leather goods. More beasts that have been fattening during the preceding summer in the alfalfa meadows of the high valleys of Los Andes come over the Puna de Atacama. And today those not salable in the nitrate fields are likewise taken to Huari. Grain comes from Tupiza and Sucre and other upper valley regions; wine from Cinti; fruit and coca from the warmer valleys, such as Mizque; sugar, rice, brandy from Santa Cruz. From the altiplano itself come woolen fabrics, wrought silver, chuño (the frozen potato), and vicuña and chinchilla skins from the desolate region of Lipez, southern Bolivia. Trade in the last-named article, diminished today, has long constituted one of the leading features of the Huari fair. The larger towns—La Paz, Oruro, Potosi—send European goods. Southward, where the influence of the fair extends for the greatest distance, its attraction is felt at least 500 miles 'as the condor flies' (Wrigley 1919:69–70).

Major fairs in the South-Central Andes were held at other towns—Yunguyu (August), Sauces (August), Mocomoco (September), and La Quiaca (October) (Wrigley 1919:70). Some towns that were practically abandoned and desolate for most of the year came alive for about two weeks with a huge congregation of people who traveled from far and wide. Other towns like Yunguyu (which still has a huge weekly regional market) were large towns with considerable residential areas. While these observations were made in the early twentieth century, they reflect patterns of earlier times and are supported by historical and archaeological data.

The existence of the institution of the Andean fair as a barter market is, in our view, the key to resolving the questions of markets in the pre-Hispanic

Andes. Markets abounded where people would barter a plethora of goods. As in price-making markets, people acted rationally and sought to maximize advantages in a system where commodity prices were relatively stable, with an elastic supply meeting demand rather quickly for most items.

Perhaps the biggest added value in Andean exchange was through the transport of goods from one region to another. We have good data from the early colonial period from the inspection (*visita*) of the crown administrator Garci Diez de San Miguel 1964 [1567]. This, of course, was a generation into the colonial period, and price-making markets strategies were already spreading as the native Andeans quickly adapted to the introduction of currency. As seen in Table 17.1, transportation costs were quite high in at least the South-Central Andes. The movement of maize a mere two hundred kilometers increased the value from seven tomines to five to six pesos, a massive jump in value added for

table 17.1
Prices of selected commodities in the visita of Diez de San Miguel (in pesos and tomines)

IN THE TITICACA BASIN		
One fanega of flour	5–8 p.	
One fanega of maize	5–6 p.	
One fanega of chuño	4–7 p.	
One camelid		5–6 p.
One pig		3.5–4 p.
One fanega of potatoes	2 p.	
One bird (*perdiz*)	0.5 t.	
IN THE SAMA VALLEY		
One cotton *manta*	4 p.	
One jug of wine		4 p.
One fanega of wheat	1.5–1.75 p.	
One fanega of maize	7 t.	
Small basket of cotton	3 t.	

p. = peso, t. = tomín (8 tomines/peso)
Note: A fanega is a dry measure of weight of approximately fifty-five liters.

transport. In the region, maize was, and is, a highly valued crop used for food but more importantly for the brewing of *chicha* beer. The valley of Sama is a maize-growing region, while the Titicaca Basin had very little indigenous maize production. We can presume that this supply-and-demand equilibrium existed in the pre-Hispanic period as well and that the barter equivalencies reflected this reality.

We contend that barter fairs were the means by which most commodities were traded in the Andes prior to and even during the Inca Empire. There was undoubtedly a state imperial economy that produced and moved large quantities of goods outside of any barter or other kind of market. But at the daily, domestic level, people most likely produced and traded goods, at least locally, if not regionally, outside of the state economy. But the empire did not create a state economy based on the barter market system. It is most likely that the *mit'a* system can be seen as a logical outgrowth of this historical context. It required an elaborate bureaucracy with the entire population of taxpayers throughout the empire theoretically ranked into a decimal organization. It is likely that the barter markets continued to exist during the Inca period while the state overlaid the corvée system.

In short, the indigenous peoples of the Andes indeed engaged in vigorous trade, met in marketplaces, and exchanged goods via barter. Equivalencies, established by custom, were indirectly affected by supply and demand. Currencies did not exist, nor were they needed. Independent traders most likely existed. They competed with each other for "greater market share" not by reducing prices but by increasing their political and kin networks. The Andean example provides us with yet one more fascinating case study in economic history, one that demonstrates the enormous adaptability and ingenuity of peoples around the world to acquire, produce, and exchange goods.

NOTES

1 The full quote: "There is no question that when many different goods become priced in money, market exchanges become enormously facilitated to the advantage of buyers and sellers. What is wrong with the example is to postulate as ever having actually existed in the real world economies of time and place a situation of widespread barter; that market exchanges ever were frequent, quantitatively important, or transacted an appreciable range of natural resources, labor, goods, or services before money came into use; that important market sectors existed before money existed" (Dalton 1982:183).

2 Annette Weiner (1988) describes the Kula after the introduction of speedboats and market economies. The traditional Kula exchange adapted to these changed conditions.

3 From North (1977:712), citing a reanalysis of Malinowski's data by Belshaw (1955) in Uberoi (1971).

4 "En todo este reino del Peru ... hubo grandes tiangues, que son mercados, donde los naturales contrataban sus cosas."

5 The full passage: "Entre los indios hacen sus mercados en sus pueblos, de manera que hoy se hace en un pueblo y mañana en otro más cercano, y ansí andan por su rueda. Entrellos no tienen peso ni medida, sino su contratación es trocar una cosa por otra, y esto es a ojo. Los españoles se rigen por el peso y marco de Avila y la hanega es algo mayor que en estos reinos."

Argumedo, Alejandro, and Michel Pimbert

2010   Bypassing Globalization: Barter Markets as a New Indigenous Economy in Peru. *Development* 53(3):343–349.

Belshaw, Cyril S.

1955   In Search of Wealth: A Study of the Emergence of Commercial Operations in the Melanesian Society of Southeastern Papua. Memoirs of the American Anthropological Association, 80. American Anthropological Association, Washington, D.C.

Blanton, Richard E., and Lane F. Fargher

2010   Evaluating Causal Factors in Market Development in Premodern States: A Comparative Study, with Critical Comments on the History of Ideas about Markets. In *Archaeological Approaches to Market Exchange in Ancient Societies*, edited by Christopher P. Garraty and Barbara L. Stark, pp. 207–226. University Press of Colorado, Boulder.

Bromley, R. J., and Richard Symanski

1974   Marketplace Trade in Latin America. *Latin American Research Review* 9(3):3–38.

Cieza de León, Pedro

1967 [1533]   *El señorío de los incas: Segunda parte de la crónica del Perú.* Edited by Carlos Aranibar. Instituto de Estudios Peruanos, Lima.

Cobo, Bernabé

1890–1893 [1653]   *Historia del nuevo mundo, por el P. Bernabé Cobo.* Edited by Marcos Jiménez de la Espada. E. Rasco, Seville.

Cook, Scott

1966   The Obsolete Anti-Market Mentality: Critique of the Substantive Approach to Economic Anthropology. *American Anthropologist* 68(2):323–345.

Dalton, George

1982   Barter. *Journal of Economic Issues* 16(1):181–190.

Diez de San Miguel, Garci

1964 [1567]   *Visita hecha a la Provincia de Chucuito por Garci Diez de San Miguel en año 1567.* Casa de la Cultura del Perú, Lima.

Earle, Timothy K.

1977   A Reappraisal of Redistribution: Complex Hawaiian Chiefdoms. In *Exchange Systems in Prehistory*, edited by Timothy K. Earle and Jonathon E. Ericson, pp. 213–239. Academic Press, New York.

Godelier, Maurice

1977   *Perspectives in Marxist Anthropology.* Cambridge University Press, Cambridge.

Hann, Chris

2006   The Gift and Reciprocity: Perspectives form Economic Anthropology. In *Handbook of the Economics of Giving, Altruism, and Reciprocity*, vol. 1, edited by Serge-Christophe Kolm and Jean Mercier Ythier, pp. 208–223. Elsevier, Amsterdam.

Hirth, Kenneth G.

1996   Political Economy and Archaeology: Perspectives on Exchange and Production. *Journal of Archaeology Research* 4(3):203–239.

1998   The Distributional Approach: A New Way to Identify Marketplace Exchange in the Archaeological Record. *Current Anthropology* 39(4):451–478.

Hodder, B. W.

1965   The Distribution of Markets in Yorubaland. *Scottish Geographical Magazine* 81:48–58.

Hollingsworth, J. Rogers, and Robert Boyer

1997   Coordination of Economic Actors and Social Systems of Production. In *Contemporary Capitalism*, edited by J. R. Hollingsworth and R. Boyer, pp. 1–48. Cambridge University Press, Cambridge.

Jevons, William Stanley

1879 [1871]   *The Theory of Political Economy.* Macmillan, London.

Jiménez de la Espada, Marcos

1965 [1897]   *Relaciones geográficas de indias del Perú*, vol. 3. Biblioteca de Autores Españoles 84. Atlas, Madrid.

Julien, Catherine

1988   How Inca Decimal Administration Worked. *Ethnohistory* 35:257-279.

Kurtz, Donald V.

    1974   Peripheral and Transitional Markets: The Aztec Case. *American Ethnologist* 1(4):685–705.

La Lone, Darrell E.

    1982   The Inca as a Nonmarket Economy: Supply on Command versus Supply and Demand. In *Contexts for Prehistoric Exchange*, edited by Jonathan E. Ericson and Timothy K. Earle, pp. 291–316. Academic Press, New York.

Malinowski, Bronislaw

    1921   The Primitive Economics of the Trobriand Islanders. *The Economic Journal* 21:1–16.

Murra, John V.

    1962   An Archeological "Restudy" of an Andean Ethnohistorical Account, *American Antiquity* 28(1):1–4.

    1980 [1956]   *The Economic Organization of the Inca State*. Research in Economic Anthropology. JAI Press, Greenwich, Conn.

    1985a   "El Archipiélago Vertical" Revisited. In *Andean Ecology and Civilization: An Interdisciplinary Perspective on Andean Ecological Complementary*, edited by Shozo Masuda, Izumi Shimada, and Craig Morris, pp. 3–13. University Press of Tokyo, Tokyo.

    1985b   The Limits and Limitations of the "Vertical Archipelago" in the Andes. In *Andean Ecology and Civilization: An Interdisciplinary Perspective on Andean Ecological Complementary*, edited by Shozo Masuda, Izumi Shimada, and Craig Morris, pp. 15–20. University Press of Tokyo, Tokyo.

    1995   Did Tribute and Markets Prevail in the Andes before the European Invasion? In *Ethnicity, Markets, and Migration in the Andes: At the Crossroads of History and Anthropology*, edited by Brooke Larson and Olivia Harris, with Enrique Tandeter, pp. 57–72. Duke University Press, Durham, N.C.

North, Douglass C.

    1977   Markets and Other Allocation Systems in History: The Challenge of Karl Polanyi. *Journal of European Economic History* 6:703–716.

    1984   Transaction Costs, Institutions, and Economic History. *Journal of Institutional and Theoretical Economics* 140:7–17.

Paerregaard, Karsten

    2000   Procesos migratorios y estrategias complementarias en la sierra peruana. *European Review of Latin American and Caribbean Studies* 69:69–80.

Pizarro, Pedro

    1978 [1571]   *Relación del descubrimiento y conquista del Perú*. Fondo Editorial, Pontificia Universidad Católica del Perú, Lima.

Prendergast, Canice, and Lars Stole

    2000   Barter Relationships. In *The Vanishing Rouble: Barter Networks and Non-Monetary Transactions in Post-Soviet Societies*, edited by Paul Seabright, pp. 35–70. Cambridge University Press, Cambridge.

Rostworowski de Diez Canseco, María

    1977   *Etnía y sociedad: Costa peruana prehispánica*. Instituto de Estudios Peruanos, Lima.

    1981   *Recursos naturales renovables y pesca, siglos XVI y XVII: Curacas y sucesiones, costa norte*. Instituto de Estudios Peruanos, Lima.

Schneider, Jane

    2002   World Markets: Anthropological Perspectives. In *Exotic No More: Anthropology on the Front Lines*, edited by Jeremy MacClancy, pp. 64–85. University of Chicago Press, Chicago.

Silver, Morris

    2010   Ancient Economies. Electronic document, http://sondmor.tripod.com/index-7.html, accessed June 8, 2010.

Smith, Michael E.

    1980   The Role of the Marketing System in Aztec Society and Economy: Reply to Evans. *American Antiquity* 45(4):876–883.

Stanish, Charles

    1989   An Archaeological Evaluation of an Ethnohistorical Model in Moquegua. In *Ecology, Settlement, and History in the*

Osmore Drainage, edited by Don Rice, Charles Stanish, and P. Scarr, pp. 303–320. BAR, Oxford.

1992   *Ancient Andean Political Economy.* University of Texas Press, Austin.

Strathern, Andrew, and Pamela J. Stewart

2005   Ceremonial Exchange. In *A Handbook of Economic Anthropology*, edited by James Carrier, pp. 230–245. Edward Elgar, Cheltenham, U.K.

Uberoi, J. P. Singh

1971   *Politics of the Kula Ring: An Analysis of the Findings of Bronislaw Malinowski.* The University Press, Manchester.

Van Buren, Mary

1996   Rethinking the Vertical Archipelago: Ethnicity, Exchange, and History in the South Central Andes. *American Anthropologist* 98(2):338–351.

Weiner, Annette

1988   *The Trobrianders of Papua New Guinea.* Thomson, Belmont, Calif.

Wilk, Richard

1996   *Economies and Cultures: Foundations of Economic Anthropology.* Westview Press, Boulder, Colo.

Wrigley, G. M.

1919   Fairs of the Central Andes. *Geographical Review* 7(2):65–80.

Ziegler, Rolf

1990   The Kula: Social Order, Barter, and Ceremonial Exchange. In *Social Institutions: Their Emergence, Maintenance, and Effects*, edited by Michael Hechter, Karl-Dieper Opp, and Reinhard Wippler, pp. 141–157. Aldine de Gruyter, Hawthorne, N.Y.

18

Discussion

BARRY L. ISAAC

A S AN ECONOMIC ANTHROPOLOGIST, I SHALL focus upon two key dimensions of the general economic framework within which trade and exchange took place in Pre-Columbian civilizations. The first is the extent to which their economies were commercialized, that is, the scope and intensity of the market as both a place of exchange and a cultural institution (see Blanton, this volume; Kurtz 1974:686; Stanish and Coben, this volume). The second key dimension is the political context in which the economic activities occurred (see Smith 2004:77–82). While mindful of this volume's inherently comparative perspective, I lean heavily upon the Aztec case. It was the most extensively commercialized economy and has by far the richest ethnohistorical documentation, and it is the case I know best.

The Commercial Sector

Mesoamerican economies were remarkable for their extent of commercial exchange and partial monetization, especially during the Postclassic period in both the Central Highlands and the Maya region (Smith 1990; Smith and Berdan 2003). Both areas had long-distance merchants who were important politically and economically, as well as ritually, in both Classic and Postclassic times. The incidence, or even existence, of marketplaces is still controversial for the Classic period in both areas, however, and even for the Maya Postclassic period (see McAnany 2010:253–268), although periodic market fairs were prominent in the Maya region at Spanish contact (Berdan et al. 2003:101). In contrast, Late Postclassic Central Mexico featured enormous marketplaces that astonished the first Spanish observers. Colonial writers (especially Bernardino de Sahagún) focused on the Aztec professional merchants (*pochteca*), but the Spanish conquerors were agape, instead, at the many thousands of producer-vendors, most of whom were only part-time marketers, as well as the numerous regional merchants in the Aztec Empire (Berdan 1986; Nichols, this volume).

Stanish and Coben (this volume) argue that, like the Spanish conquerors, we are so bedazzled by the great daily marketplaces of Central Mexico that we tend to view Pre-Columbian Andean economies mainly in terms of their lack of them. Thus, we largely overlook other forms or venues of exchange that were integral to Andean economies (also see Burger, this volume; Nielsen, this volume). Speaking more generally, our enthusiasm for marketplace exchange often leads us to ignore or underestimate the nonmarket context of most of the preindustrial economy, especially reciprocity and the routine domestic activities, in both production and exchange. In the Maya area, for instance, noncommercial exchange was important at all social levels, and appreciable amounts of elite as well as common goods were distributed through reciprocal gifting (see Kovacevich, this volume). The same is true of the Aztec Empire, where the exchange of refined craft products among elites was a "means of validating status and sociopolitical relationships," initiating or affirming military alliances, or "soliciting favors from one's superiors" (Brumfiel 1987:111–112; also see Berdan et al. 2003:105–106; Brumfiel 1998). In the Andes of Inca times, huge amounts of cloth "flowed in many directions" (Costin 1998:123) by nonmarket means, not only between subordinates and superiors but also ubiquitously among commoners to celebrate birth, puberty, marriage, and death (Costin 1998:123). "No [Inca] political, military, social, or religious event was complete without textiles volunteered or bestowed, burned, exchanged, or sacrificed" (Murra 1989:293; see also Murra 1980:65ff). Nor was any such event complete without distributions of maize beer and other foods in Tiwanaku as well as in Inca times (Bray 2009; Goldstein 2003, this volume).

Stanish and Coben (this volume) highlight the Andean area's periodic market fairs, which transacted both mundane and refined products. These authors contrast Central Andean and Central Mexican structured exchange at the moment of the Spanish conquest by noting that the Andean market fairs were based on barter exchange and that they lacked money as well as an independent class of traders. Barter equivalencies would have been

set and adjusted by the supply-and-demand forces that operate in any large market, but they would have fluctuated less and/or more slowly than monetary prices in similar settings. While the apparent lack of currencies in the Andean area in both pre-Inca and Inca periods (see Burger, this volume; Goldstein, this volume; Stanish and Coben, this volume; Topic, this volume) is striking in view of their widespread occurrence in Mesoamerica (see Berdan et al. 2003:102; Blanton, this volume; Hirth, this volume), I caution against overdrawing the contrast. In fact, direct barter was also the most usual mode of exchange in Central Mexican marketplaces (see Berdan 1982:43–44; Kurtz 1974:695–696). At the same time, it is possible that the mere existence of exchange currencies in Mesoamerica—even though they applied to only a restricted range of transactions—had some measure of feedback upon the setting of barter exchange equivalents there (see Berdan 1982:44).

In general, we must take care not to exaggerate the extent of commercialization or monetization in Postclassic Mesoamerica, even in the Central Mexican Highlands. In the aggregate, Aztec economy—the most commercialized in the Pre-Columbian New World—was mainly noncommercial and nonmonetary. The great majority of the Aztec Empire's inhabitants were rural peasants whose main production aim was household provisioning; even most rural artisans were only part-time specialists who made much (probably most) of their living from agriculture (see Brumfiel 1998:147), as did most rural marketers (Berdan 1986:288–289). Furthermore, neither land nor labor was generally for sale (see below). Thus, instead of saying that "the marketplace was the center of economic life in ancient Mesoamerica" (Hirth 1998:451), I suggest we speak more modestly of marketplaces as simply the principal urban exchange venues in the Mexican Central Highlands during the Late Postclassic period.

Factor Markets in Aztec Economy

A key feature of Aztec economy—again, the most highly commercialized in the Pre-Columbian New World—is the scant development of factor markets, whether rural or urban. In the first place, there is not even a hint of a capital market—that is, borrowing at interest for purposes of investment in productive assets.

Secondly, there was only a rudimentary market in land. The overwhelming majority of all productive land belonged to city-states, and it was administered by local governments in conjunction with the *calpolli* (ward, barrio) council, which allocated usufruct shares or, in an alternative interpretation, adjudicated tenure rights among its constituent households (Harvey 1984). On the other hand, some land in newly conquered areas was awarded as private property to distinguished nobles and war-hero commoners, and these lands apparently could indeed be sold or wagered freely (Harvey 1984:86–89). Outright sale of *calpolli* lands is doubtful, however. While Sahagún (1950–1982:3:9) does provide a single instance in which a man who was impoverished by ceremonial obligations "sold his land" when he had nothing else to sell, the nature of the transaction is unclear. The passage reads: "or sold his land, which he had enclosed or somewhere placed in another's hands; somewhere he arranged a loan. And so he did in connection with whatever land; he did it with *calpulli* land. . . ." Lockhart (1992:154) interprets this passage as a case of reallocation, in which the current allottee accepted a payment for giving up his usufruct rights, allowing the governing bodies to reallocate usufruct to the fee-payer. I suggest it was an instance of pawning without redemption, which would explain the otherwise puzzling reference to arranging a loan. At any rate, occasional events of this nature do not constitute a customary land market (see Carrasco 1983:71).

Third, the labor market was rudimentary. Only a small fraction of the total Aztec population—most notably porters, prostitutes, barbers, and "private" (independent) master craftsmen who did commissioned work (Brumfiel 1987:102, 1998; Hassig 1985:28–40; Sahagún 1950–1982:9:91, 10:94)—made a living by selling their labor as such. In fact, almost all labor that was not performed by individuals for their own households' provisioning was recruited through corvée (labor taxation),

seignorial rights on noblemen's landholdings, and kinship and neighborhood reciprocity.

Slavery was another labor device, but it was of very minor economic importance. Aztec slaves, who were never numerous, were mainly engaged in domestic duties in urban noble households or, in the case of women, were slave-concubines. Their noble masters also gave them as gifts or as tax payments, wagered them in gambling games, and offered them for sacrifice (Shadow and Rodríguez 1995:318–320). Furthermore, some of the "slaves" noted by the Spaniards were actually pawns whose families could redeem them later; when agriculture revived after the 1454 Famine of One Rabbit, for instance, "the plenty was such that foodstuffs were more than sufficient and parents were able to ransom their sons and daughters" whom they had sold to the Totonacs in exchange for maize during the famine (Durán 1994 [1579–1581]:240–241).

"Peripheral Market" Redux

For the foregoing reasons, I believe a modified form of George Dalton's "peripheral market" concept is still useful, even in the Aztec case. Outside of the major Aztec cities, it appears that "most sellers [did] not acquire the bulk of their livelihood . . . [nor did] buyers [acquire] the bulk of their daily . . . goods and services, via the marketplace sales and purchases" (Dalton 1967a:75). In both rural and urban areas, the near absence of factor markets meant that marketplace transactions could not have functioned "as an integrative mechanism to allocate resources [factors] of production" (Dalton 1967b:266) to the extent that they would in an economy with robust factor markets. In an economy lacking them, marketplace prices "are determined by familiar supply and demand forces, [but] there is absent that crucial feedback effect which links change in market[place] price to production decisions" (Dalton 1967a:75). We need to qualify this last statement somewhat. Instead of saying that market feedback upon the allocation of land and labor was "absent," we should say that marketplace prices were not the major allocative mechanism. After all, many things were produced specifically for marketplace sale, especially in the urban setting, and land or raw materials and labor were allocated to their production. What we can indeed say is that "land utilization [was] organized differently from labor utilization" and that "*each* of the factor ingredients ... enter[ed] production lines through *different* institutional channels" (Dalton 1967a:66; emphasis his). Land (productive property) was mobilized through one channel, labor through another, and raw materials through yet another.

Regulation of Aztec Marketplaces

Until recently, most scholars held that trade and exchange were strongly controlled by the governments of preindustrial states, including those of the Pre-Columbian New World. This stance is now in retreat (Garraty and Stark 2010; Smith 2004), although no one would deny that states typically regulate their economies to some extent. The range of regulation is large, however: the Inca Empire seems to have actively discouraged formal marketplaces and some kinds of entrepreneurship within its core area (cf. Burger, this volume; Stanish and Coben, this volume), whereas the Aztec state actively promoted these activities. Nevertheless, even the Aztecs kept tight rein on the behavior of professional traders (see below), leaving open the question of governmental control over other aspects of commerce. Here, I shall discuss three such matters, all of which are controversial because they are subject to quite different interpretations: 1) price-setting in urban marketplaces, 2) governmental provisioning of marketplaces, and 3) administration of long-distance trade.

First, were prices in Aztec urban marketplaces regulated or fixed by governmental agencies or set independently by supply-and-demand forces? Our best ethnohistorical source, Bernardino de Sahagún (1950–1982), contributes uncertainty on this point. He states that "they [principal *pochteca*] regulated well everything: all in the market place which was sold; what price it would be" (Sahagún 1950–1982:9:24). Again: "Each of the [marketplace] directors took care ... that no one might deceive another, and how [articles] might be priced and sold" (Sahagún 1950–1982:8:67). Did the principal *pochteca* enforce their notion of "fair prices"

(Berdan 1978:193)? Or set "price ceilings" (Kurtz 1974:697)? Or simply ensure accurate counts and measures (Hutson 2000:129)? On the other hand, we are told indirectly that the price of maize fluctuated seasonally. In the eighth month (July 3–22), when household stores were depleted but the next harvest was some seventy to one hundred days away, there was "much hunger" because "at this time dried grains of maize were costly" (Sahagún 1950–1982:2:98). Clearly, supply and demand were at work in setting the price of this staple food. All in all, I concur with Kurtz (1974:697) that given "the enormous variety of goods which were for sale"— and the huge numbers of buyers and sellers—"it does not seem likely that market officials set a price on each commodity" independently of supply-and-demand forces.

Second, if the Aztec government did not directly set market prices, did it nevertheless influence them by channeling tax goods through the marketplaces? Because of the extensive overlapping of items sold in urban marketplaces and those demanded in tax (Berdan 1993:83), some researchers have suggested that the Aztec state channeled certain tax goods, especially elite raw materials, through the marketplaces. Good evidence of this practice is lacking, however (Berdan 1993:79–82; Blanton 1996:48). Rather, the flow between marketplaces and tax demands was mainly in the opposite direction—that is, taxpayers obtained some of their required items in the marketplaces (see below). There was some observable counterflow, however, because the recipients of tax revenues given to them as "gifts and commissions" often exchanged some or all of their awards— which probably consisted mainly of cloth—in the marketplaces (see Berdan 1982:39–40; Brumfiel 1980:466, 1987:109).

Third, advocates of the "administered trade" and "ports-of-trade" models (see Polanyi et al. 1957) have argued that tax revenues were used to supply long-distance trade. These authors have pointed to Sahagún's (1950–1982:9:7–8, 17–19) account of Aztec king Ahuitzotl's giving the *pochteca* sixteen hundred large cotton capes and sending them off to trade in Xicalango on the Gulf of Mexico. To my knowledge, this is the only recorded instance of state financing of long-distance trade. Sahagún repeatedly ties the story specifically to the reign of King Ahuitzotl and his efforts to expand the empire southward along the Gulf coast. The policies of Moctezuma, the succeeding Tenochca king, are stated only as florid platitudes about the *pochteca's* exalted status. He "continued the customs, followed the way, honored well the calling of the merchants" and "honored the principal merchants" at state functions (Sahagún 1950–1982:9:23). The "continued the customs" phrase is part of the recursive sequence "continued . . . followed . . . honored"—a common literary flourish in classic Nahuatl discourse. It is a chain of repetitive honorifics, not a trade policy. Thus, I am unwilling to generalize the singular story about Ahuitzotl's use of the treasury for long-distance trading (see Isaac 1986:331–333). Indeed, the administered trade idea may be one whose time has come and gone (see Berdan 1978; Smith 1990). Although we still hear occasional echoes of it in Maya and Andean studies, it is being vigorously challenged there, even in its weaker "elite control of trade" form (see Graham 2002:413–415; Kovacevich, this volume; Masson and Freidel, this volume; Nielsen, this volume; West 2002).

The Ambivalent Position of Merchant Specialists

Interregional trade was a feature of both Mesoamerica and the Andes, in both Classic and Postclassic times, as several chapters in this volume make clear. Mesoamerica had professional merchants who specialized in long-distance trade during both periods and in both highland Central Mexico and the Maya area. The intensity of interregional trade is still controversial for the Inca Empire's Peruvian heartland, but there is good evidence of professional merchants and other traders in the Ecuadorian Highlands (see Salomon 1986:102–115; Stanish 2010; Topic, this volume). In the Southern Andes, interregional trade is evident in the Late Formative period (500 BC–AD 500)

and continues through Inca domination (Nielsen, this volume).

Two chapters address the apparent ambivalence, even hostility, of the Maya elite toward their specialized merchants, who were dealers in the very preciosities and sumptuary goods that were the iconic material accoutrements of elite power, the corporate emblems that legitimated it (see Helms 1988, 1993). These merchants required a certain extent of freedom to travel and to negotiate trade, but they could not be allowed to accumulate these power symbols for themselves, lest they threaten the ruling stratum's power.

We do not know the specific details of elite control over specialized merchants in the Classic Maya period, although Tokovinine and Beliaev (this volume) and McAnany (this volume) posit religious controls—on either the merchant status itself or on specific behaviors, or both. We have no knowledge of control mechanisms with reference to the specialized merchants in the Inca Empire's northern highlands (Topic, this volume).

For the Aztecs, we have considerable information. Aztec *pochteca*, professional merchants, occupied a legally defined stratum with specific rights and duties, such as internal self-governance (e.g., their own judicial courts), marketplace control, and certain sumptuary and religious privileges (Blanton, this volume; Hicks 1999; Hutson 2000). In this regard, they resembled nobility but were not members of it. The distinguished *pochteca* elders attended certain state functions, at which the king "set them right by his side, even like the noblemen, the rulers" (Sahagún 1950–1982:9:23). In short, *pochteca* were "like" nobles, but still distinctive. Although the last two independent Aztec kings (Ahuitzotl and Moctezuma) are said to have regarded the *pochteca* elders "like . . . sons" (Sahagún 1950–1982:9:19, 23), these rulers certainly intended them to be obedient, nonthreatening sons, and the *pochteca* were at pains to appear humble and poor in both dress and demeanor (Sahagún 1950–1982:9:31–32). When they returned from a successful trading expedition, the *pochteca* entered the city (Tenochtitlan-Tlatelolco) at night and hid the profits of their venture in the houses of the *pochteca* elders. And if they succeeded in accumulating a great fortune, they converted it into food and clothing (capes and breechcloths for men, skirts for women) for a spectacular giveaway to the nobility, the distinguished soldiers, the *pochteca* community, the poor, and the gods (Sahagún 1950–1982:9:34–38, 41, 47). After a wealthy *pochteca* had thusly impoverished himself, he was admonished by the elders to remain humble and to get back to work quickly (Sahagún 1950–1982:9:43).

The *pochteca* had good reason to follow these practices and admonitions. Although the king loved them "like his sons" when they were humble, he "was saddened" and inclined to condemn them to death "by means of false testimony" if they appeared "no longer . . . of good heart" (Sahagún 1950–1982:9:32). This statement of dire punishment applied specifically to the "disguised merchants" who often traveled into foreign territories as trader-spies. Perhaps the king feared their opportunities to plot against him by colluding with foreign enemies. Nevertheless, the repeated admonitions of humility and feigned poverty aimed at the entire *pochteca* stratum surely signal that a lack of these qualities would have endangered any of them.

Ruler-merchant tensions of this sort occurred widely in preindustrial states with elite-oriented traders (see Lenski 1966:248–256; Oka and Kusimba 2008). We have good documentation for medieval Europe, where such merchants lived in fear of the nobility, who alone could grant the privileges and exemptions necessary to the conduct of business but who capriciously "violated their own laws, rescinded privileges, forged documents, clipped coins, and imposed arbitrary taxes" (Bergel 1962:314). Accordingly, the medieval European elite-oriented trader "was no proud merchant prince but a humble petitioner" (Bergel 1962:314). Nevertheless, the relationship was basically symbiotic because nobles needed these traders and, in fact, were their best customers.

Furthermore, the European nobility was most clearly dominant over the elite traders when the state was strong, and advantage swung to the merchants when the state was weak (Bergel 1962:314), a relationship widely posited for preindustrial states

(Smith 2004:93). A similar situation has been postulated for the Maya area following the demise of the strong states of the Classic period, although the argument remains controversial (Masson and Freidel, this volume; McAnany, this volume). In Mexico's Central Highlands, in contrast, the Postclassic period saw the simultaneous—and, apparently, causally linked—flowering and integration of trade and empire (see Nichols, this volume). It is worth noting that a similarly fruitful political-mercantile synergy also occurred in the Islamic Empire circa AD 622–850 (Ibrahim 1990).

Political Economy, Part I: State Expenditures (Aztec and Inca)

The Aztec and Inca states, especially the latter, had very substantial governmental (noncommercial) sectors to their economies. We know less about this aspect of Maya states, but they apparently were similar. This sector included both taxation and governmental expenditures. I eschew the term "redistribution" with reference to this public component, as it has no precise meaning. If defined broadly, to include all disbursements of tax revenues, redistribution is synonymous with the governmental sector of the economy. If defined narrowly, to include only that portion of the revenue that subsequently flows outward from the centers—always much less than what flows into them (Blanton and Fargher 2010; Carneiro 1981:58–65)—it is synonymous with transfer payments and operational expenditures.

Aztec Transfer Payments

At least in the core cities, the Aztec state's array of civil, military, and religious officials was impressive. "This nation had a special functionary for every activity, even minor ones. . . . There were even officials in charge of sweeping," wrote Diego Durán (1994 [1579–1581]:309). Relatively few of them were supported directly by the state, though. Temple personnel were self-supporting through private donations (Berdan 2007:255–256), and the lower-level civil workers would have performed their duties as part of regular labor tax. Some of the upper-level officials would have supported themselves from lands or tribute areas awarded them by the state, although most middle- and upper-level civil and military officials, mainly nobles, probably lived at least partly from public revenues, which some of them collected or supervised (see Durán 1994 [1579–1581]:309; Hicks 1999).

On the other hand, the Aztec core state expended heavily on "gifts and commissions" (Berdan 1982:39–40) to "attendant nobles, valiant warriors, skilled artisans, disabled veterans, widows, and orphaned children" (Brumfiel 1980:466, 1987:109; also see Berdan 1987:161; Berdan et al. 2003:105–106). The proportion of Tenochtitlan's large population (often estimated at 150,000–200,000) that was directly supported by such redistribution is variously estimated at one-fourth, one-third, and one-half (see Brumfiel 1987:109). Even the lowest of these estimates is probably an exaggeration.

More impressively, the Aztec core state annually sponsored an eight-day public feast—for "the poor of Mexico [Tenochtitlan] and those who tilled the fields," for "the common folk," and for the military estate as well as youths who had been to war (Sahagún 1950–1982:2:14–15, 96–107)—in the eighth month (July 3–22), the annual hungry season. While supplies lasted, each person could go through the line up to three times, receiving each time a generous handful of tamales and one or two gourd-fuls of *chiampinolli* (maize-chia gruel) mixed with honey (Sahagún 1950–1982:2:96–97). Distributions of food and/or clothing also were made to the poor on certain state occasions, such as coronations, war victory celebrations, or major human sacrifices (Durán 1994 [1579–1581]:306, 341, 400, 408, 415); the coronation giveaways had a direct parallel in the Inca state (Murra 1989:291–292). The Aztec state provided famine relief, as well, most famously during the 1454 Famine of One Rabbit, when the rulers of the three core capitals (Tenochtitlan, Texcoco, and Tlacopan) gave food to the resident commoners for about a year (Hassig 1981); they did likewise during the famine of 1506 (Alva Ixtlilxóchitl 1977 [ca. 1625]:2:ch. LXXI:179; Torquemada 1975 [1615]:1:ch. LXXII:279–280).

Aztec Public Works

The Aztec state commanded the construction of temples, palaces, and other public buildings (see Berdan 2007), as well as large-scale hydraulic works (see Doolittle 1990:121ff.; Espinosa Pineda 1996:345–382). The materials and labor for these projects were requisitioned as special tax levies (see Durán 1994 [1579–1581]:328, 365, 373), and the laborers were fed from provisions also levied specifically for the project or, more usually, they were local recruits who ate at home (see, e.g., Alvarado Tezozomoc 1980 [ca. 1598]:ch. CII:662; Durán 1994 [1579–1581]:477). In other words, Aztec corvée workers were not routinely fed from state storehouses, as was the case in the Inca Empire (D'Altroy and Earle 1992; Morris and Thompson 1985:94–112).

On the other hand, the reconstruction of all the public areas of Aztec Tenochtitlan following its nearly complete destruction by flood in 1499 was "paid for by [King] Ahuitzotl. . . . He distributed mantles, breechcloths, cacao, chiles, beans, all taken from his treasury" (Durán 1994 [1579–1581]:373). He probably "paid" only the skilled workers and/or supervisors, as King Moctezuma did when he rewarded the stonemasons who had carved his statue, giving them "many loads of maize, beans, and chiles, also mantels and clothing for their wives and children . . . [and] cacao . . . and each sculptor received a slave to serve him" (Durán 1994 [1579–1581]:481; see Alvarado Tezozomoc 1980 [ca. 1598]:ch. CII:666–667).

Inca Governmental Disbursements

The governmental economic sector was especially prominent in the Inca Empire, which supported a large bureaucracy to extract and channel the tax labor (corvée) that tilled state and sacred fields, herded and sheared government camelids, and spun and wove vast amounts of wool and cotton from raw fibers supplied by the state (see Murra 1980, 1982). Tax labor also built and stocked the impressive chains of storehouses (LeVine 1992) from which these same or other tax laborers were fed while working on government projects. The fruits of tax labor likewise supported extensive rituals and feasting designed to increase Inca legitimacy (Costin 1998; LeVine 1992; Morris and Thompson 1985:83–91). Inca distribution of military supplies, not only food but also cloth, from state storehouses to the common soldiers, was especially impressive (Costin 1998; Murra 1980:65ff.). A notable feature of Inca state expenditures was their tight focus on providing raw materials and foodstuffs for such state projects or functions as public construction, military maintenance and reward, and ceremonial support. Very little if any government revenues were expended simply to promote the general welfare. All in all, the public economic sector looms very large in the Inca Empire, simply because its government had to carry out many of the supply and distribution functions that were handled by markets in the Aztec case.

Political Economy, Part II: Tax Policy (Aztec versus Inca)

The Aztecs taxed mostly in material items, although we must not overlook the considerable extent of labor taxation (corvée) for everything from farming nobles' lands to military service, porterage, road maintenance, public construction, temple service, and even spinning of fibers (Berdan 2007:256; Hicks 1984; Parsons 1975). The Incas, in contrast, taxed almost entirely in labor. The relatively minor exceptions were: 1) "things gathered, creatures hunted, and items otherwise 'raw' . . . [which] were owed in kind" (Murra 1982:238–239; see also Murra 1980:89–119); and 2) a relatively small quantity of refined craft products that were sent directly to Cuzco, whether explicitly as tax or as tax "phrased as gifts" (D'Altroy and Earle 1992:39ff.). Even when a product (such as cloth) was submitted in fulfillment of this obligation, however, its tax value was conceptualized as the labor that went into its production, because the materials for it typically were supplied by the state or produced on state facilities (Costin 1998; Murra 1980:69ff.). This was probably true of the pre-Inca Andean states as well (see Goldstein, this volume; Topic, this volume).

The purposes of taxation in both empires were highly similar—to support and exalt the nobility and to fund the state's political, military, and ceremonial activities—but their divergent policies had vastly different collateral effects. First, the Aztec tax policy promoted marketplace development whereas the Inca policy did not. Aztec policy forced many primary producers of both foodstuffs and specialized goods to sell some of their production in the marketplaces to obtain the required tax stuffs (see Gutiérrez, this volume). Most dramatically, the state accomplished this effect by taxing some communities in items that were not available locally or that could not be produced there, and which the commoners had to obtain in the marketplaces. Even in the more usual case, though, where taxes were payable in local materials or goods (Berdan 1996:124–132), many commoners probably had to exchange some of their own products (food, crafts, and raw materials) for at least some of their tax contribution.

Secondly, the Inca policy of taxing in labor rather than in goods or raw materials impelled the state to intervene much more directly in the lives of subject populations because of the state's need to reorganize labor in newly conquered provinces (Stanish 2010; Wernke 2006). The Aztecs, in contrast, largely let conquered rulers and their subjects work out their own means of acquiring tax goods, often via markets—although, as mentioned earlier, the Aztecs also taxed in labor to some extent.

Thirdly, in promoting market exchange, the Aztec state simultaneously promoted urbanism. A network of marketplaces provides a low-cost, nonbureaucratic way of achieving "economic integration of the city with the sustaining area" (Stanish 2010:201). The Inca state, on the other hand, did not promote (indeed, it seems to have discouraged) marketplace development, leaving its urban areas (mainly towns rather than cities) largely dependent upon governmental provisioning through a costly bureaucracy. The same corvée system used to produce and transport foodstuffs through work projects had to be "marshaled to transport the grains and tubers that fed the state workers, bureaucracy, church, and military" (Stanish 2010:203). Thus,

Inca urban zones were surprisingly small compared with those of Mesoamerican states. In addition to tax policy, Inca resettlement policy also may have inhibited urban growth (see Hyslop 1990).

Finally, these two very different taxation policies had very different implications for another important aspect of the economy, namely, storage. As Michael Smyth (1996) has pointed out, large-scale taxation in labor requires large-scale public storage facilities. This is so for two reasons: 1) laborers require provisioning; and 2) the fruits of large amounts of labor applied to specific production tasks usually are not disbursed simultaneously or exhaustively. In contrast, taxation in material items—even on a large scale—does not necessarily require large-scale centralized storage, as each taxation unit (households or whole communities) can produce the tax items gradually, hold them a short time at the point of production, and then send them to the center on a periodic schedule.

This latter option was the Aztec pattern. For instance, the royal granaries that were famously "opened" during the 1454 Famine of One Rabbit were in the tributary city-states, not in the core capitals; furthermore, the state ordered that the famine relief arrive as fully prepared food (tamales and *atole* or *pinole*) ready for immediate distribution, obviating the need for storage or cooking facilities in the capitals (see Berdan 1996:125; Durán 1994 [1579–1581]:238–239; Hassig 1981). These procedures, in addition to the state's inability to prevent either hunger or starvation in the two major reported famines (1454 and 1506), its policy of providing famine relief mainly or only to nobles until the situation became dire (Hassig 1981:177; Sahagún 1950–1982:8:41), and the horrible famine that occurred in Tenochtitlan after only seventy-five days of siege in 1521 (Sahagún 1950–1982:12:104), all argue persuasively against Sahagún's assertion that the royal granary in Tenochtitlan held "a store of twenty years for the city" (Sahagún 1950–1982:12:44). Apparently, the only extensive urban storage facilities were the six state armories in Tenochtitlan and the one in Texcoco. Even most war supplies were not stockpiled in advance, however. Rather, "each *calpolli* [ward] and subject town provided food . . . as well

as equipment," and in Tenochtitlan, some food was prepared for the occasion by marketplace vendors; however, much of the army's provisions were, in fact, supplied by towns along the route (Hassig 1988:46, 60–62).

To date, large-scale centralized storage facilities have not been identified at Classic-period Teotihuacan either, which suggests that it also taxed mainly in material items rather than in labor (after Smyth 1996). We also lack evidence for such large-scale facilities in the Maya area for either Classic or Postclassic periods, indicating similar taxation systems there. In contrast, substantial storage facilities have great antiquity in the Andean region, beginning more than three thousand years ago and reaching their apogee during the Inca period (see Goldstein, this volume; LeVine 1992; Pozorski and Pozorski 1991; Topic, this volume), a duration that implies that taxation mainly in labor has a long antiquity there. Because these two forms of taxation can have different implications for the development of market systems, as we have seen, it seems likely that commercial exchange was a more important component of Mesoamerican than of Andean state economies even in Classic times.

Concluding Thoughts

The most striking contrast afforded by this volume is the great importance of commerce in Postclassic Mesoamerica and its much lesser importance in the Andes at that time. Even in the former area, though, the private economic sector included a huge noncommercial component, most evident among the masses of peasants who supplied their own labor and produced mainly for their own households, almost entirely without purchased inputs. Furthermore, in both areas, noncommercial economic reciprocity was important among elites and likely ubiquitous among ordinary folk, as it is today.

The governmental economic sectors in all of our cases also were almost entirely noncommercial in their operations, making few if any market purchases—quite unlike their counterparts in postindustrial states. This sector was substantial for the Aztecs and truly huge in the Inca Empire. As we have seen, this difference in scope reflects, mainly, their very different forms of taxation. Unfortunately, the Maya area is relatively poor in ethnohistorical materials, but the information we do have (see, e.g., Foias 2002; Kovacevich, this volume; Masson and Freidel, this volume; McAnany, this volume; Tokovinine and Beliaev, this volume), as well as the apparent absence of large-scale storage facilities, suggests that Maya political economies more closely resembled those of Central Mexico than those of the Andes.

In the aggregate, then, commercial transactions of all forms constituted a minority economic component in all cases covered in this volume. This is not to say that commercial exchange was unimportant, of course, only that we must keep it in perspective. Mesoamerican civilizations would look enormously different without their commercial sectors, even in the Maya region, which largely (perhaps entirely) lacked the huge daily or weekly marketplaces that were so notable in the Central Mexican Highlands. In the Inca Empire, merchants were important in both the northern and southern portions, and there were large periodic market fairs and substantial reciprocal trade networks elsewhere in the empire.

Finally, while each of the economies covered in this volume had predominant tendencies, none was of a "pure" type. Nor did any exist apart from other aspects of culture; each was intertwined with (embedded in) politics and religion. Mercifully, we have left behind the essentialist dichotomies and tendentious debates of the recent past with regard to ethnohistoric and prehistoric economies (see Dale 2010a, 2010b; Garraty and Stark 2010; Hann and Hart 2009; Isaac 1993, 2005; McAnany 2010; Smith 2004; Wells and Davis-Salazar 2007; Wells and McAnany 2008). We are no longer debating whether the New World's Pre-Columbian economies were organized by "redistribution" or by markets, whether they were embedded or disembedded, or whether they were integrated by verticality or by exchange. We can now accept as axiomatic that all state economies are embedded in (tangled up with) social, political, and religious systems; that all display both governmental (public) and private economic sectors; and that the private sector includes both commercial and noncommercial components.

At the same time, as the studies in this volume demonstrate, we have preserved the good ideas that we indeed had in the late twentieth century. We are still employing such concepts as reciprocity; we are still sensitive to both cross-cultural and cross-temporal variation; we are still attempting to construct anthropologically sound concepts and models for pre- and protohistoric economies; and we are still resisting the urge to make capitalists or socialists out of the ancient Americans.

REFERENCES CITED

Alva Ixtlilxóchitl, Fernando de

1977 [ca. 1625]   *Obras históricas*, vol. 2, edited by Edmundo O'Gorman. 3rd ed. Universidad Nacional Autónoma de México, Mexico City.

Alvarado Tezozomoc, Hernando

1980 [ca. 1598]   *Crónica mexicana*. 3rd ed. Biblioteca Porrúa 61. Editorial Porrúa, Mexico City.

Berdan, Frances F.

1978   Ports of Trade in Mesoamerica: A Reappraisal. In *Mesoamerican Communication Routes and Cultural Contacts*, edited by Thomas A. Lee Jr. and Carlos Navarrete, pp. 187–198. New World Archaeological Foundation, Brigham Young University, Provo, Utah.

1982   *The Aztecs of Central Mexico: An Imperial Society*. Holt, Reinhart, and Winston, New York.

1986   Enterprise and Empire in Aztec and Early Colonial Mexico. In *Economic Aspects of Prehispanic Highland Mexico*, edited by Barry L. Isaac, pp. 281–302. JAI Press, Greenwich, Conn.

1987   The Economics of Aztec Luxury Trade and Tribute. In *The Aztec Templo Mayor*, edited by Elizabeth Hill Boone, pp. 161–183. Dumbarton Oaks Research Library and Collection, Washington, D.C.

1993   Trade and Tribute in the Aztec Empire. In *Current Topics in Aztec Studies: Essays in Honor of Dr. H. B. Nicholson*, edited by Alana Cordy-Collins and Douglas Sharon, pp. 71–84. San Diego Museum Papers 30. San Diego Museum of Man, San Diego.

1996   The Tributary Provinces. In *Aztec Imperial Strategies*, edited by Frances F. Berdan, Richard E. Blanton, Elizabeth Hill Boone, Mary G. Hodge, Michael E. Smith, and Emily Umberger, pp. 115–135. Dumbarton Oaks Research Library and Collection, Washington, D.C.

2007   Material Dimensions of Aztec Religion and Ritual. In *Mesoamerican Ritual Economy: Archaeological and Ethnological Perspectives*, edited by E. Christian Wells and Karla L. Davis-Salazar, pp. 245–266. University Press of Colorado, Boulder.

Berdan, Frances F., Marilyn A. Masson, Janine Gasco, and Michael E. Smith

2003   An International Economy. In *The Postclassic Mesoamerican World*, edited by Michael E. Smith and Frances F. Berdan, pp. 96–108. University of Utah Press, Salt Lake City.

Bergel, Egon E.

1962   *Social Stratification*. McGraw-Hill, New York.

Blanton, Richard E.

1996   The Basin of Mexico Market System and the Growth of Empire. In *Aztec Imperial Strategies*, edited by Frances F. Berdan, Richard E. Blanton, Elizabeth Hill Boone, Mary G. Hodge, Michael E. Smith, and Emily Umberger, pp. 47–84. Dumbarton Oaks Research Library and Collection, Washington, D.C.

Blanton, Richard E., and Lane F. Fargher

2010   Evaluating Causal Factors in Market Development in Premodern States: A Comparative Study, with Critical Comments on the History of Ideas about Markets. In *Archaeological Approaches to Market Exchange in Ancient Societies*, edited by Christopher P. Garraty and Barbara L. Stark, pp. 207–226. University Press of Colorado, Boulder.

Bray, Tamara

2009   The Role of Chicha in Inca State Expansion: A Distributional Study of Inca Aríbalos. In *Drink, Power, and Society in the Andes*, edited by Justin Jennings and Brenda J. Bowser, pp. 108–132. University Press of Florida, Gainesville.

Brumfiel, Elizabeth M.

1980   Specialization, Market Exchange, and the Aztec State: A View from Huexotla. *Current Anthropology* 21(4):459–478.

1987   Elite and Utilitarian Crafts in the Aztec State. In *Specialization, Exchange, and Complex Societies*, edited by Elizabeth M. Brumfiel and Timothy K. Earle, pp. 102–118. Cambridge University Press, Cambridge.

1998   The Multiple Identities of Aztec Craft Specialists. In *Craft and Social Identity*, edited by Cathy Lynne Costin and Rita P. Wright, pp. 145–152. American Anthropological Association, Arlington, Va.

Carneiro, Robert L.

1981   The Chiefdom: Precursor of the State. In *The Transition to Statehood in the New World*, edited by Grant D. Jones and Robert R. Kautz, pp. 37–79. Cambridge University Press, Cambridge.

Carrasco, Pedro

1983   Some Theoretical Considerations about the Role of the Market in Ancient Mexico. In *Economic Anthropology: Topics and Theories*, edited by Sutti Ortiz, pp. 67–82. University Press of America, Lanham, Md.

Costin, Cathy Lynne

1998   Housewives, Chosen Women, Skilled Men: Cloth Production and Social Identity in the Late Prehispanic Andes. In *Craft and Social Identity*, edited by Cathy Lynne Costin and Rita P. Wright, pp. 123–141. American Anthropological Association, Arlington, Va.

Dale, Gareth

2010a   *Karl Polanyi: The Limits of the Market*. Polity, Cambridge.

2010b   Review of *Market and Society: The Great Transformation Today*, edited by Chris Hann and Keith Hart. *Dialectical Anthropology* 34:29–41.

Dalton, George

1967a   Traditional Production in Primitive African Economies. In *Tribal and Peasant Economies: Readings in Economic Anthropology*, edited by George Dalton, pp. 61–80. American Museum of Natural History, New York.

1967b   Primitive Money. In *Tribal and Peasant Economies: Readings in Economic Anthropolgy*, edited by George Dalton, pp. 254–281. American Museum of Natural History, New York.

D'Altroy, Terence N., and Timothy K. Earle

1992   Staple Finance, Wealth Finance, and Storage in the Inka Political Economy. In *Inka Storage Systems*, edited by Terry Y. LeVine, pp. 31–61. University of Oklahoma Press, Norman.

Doolittle, William E.

1990   *Canal Irrigation in Prehistoric Mexico: The Sequence of Technological Change*. University of Texas Press, Austin.

Durán, Fray Diego

1994   *The History of the Indies of New Spain*.
[1579–1581]   Translated by Doris Heyden. University of Oklahoma Press, Norman.

Espinosa Pineda, Gabriel

1996   *El embrujo del lago: El sistema lacustre de la Cuenca de México en la cosmovisión mexica*. Instituto de Investigaciones Antropológicas, Instituto de Investigaciones Históricas, Universidad Nacional Autónoma de México, Mexico City.

Foias, Antonia E.

2002   At the Crossroads: The Economic Basis of Political Power in the Petexbatun Region. In *Ancient Maya Political Economies*, edited by Marilyn A. Masson and David A. Freidel, pp. 223–248. Altamira Press, Walnut Creek, Calif.

Garraty, Christopher P., and Barbara L. Stark (editors)

2010   *Archaeological Approaches to Market Exchange in Ancient Societies*. University Press of Colorado, Boulder.

Goldstein, Paul S.

2003   From Stew-Eaters to Maize-Drinkers: The Chicha Economy and Tiwanaku Expansion. In *The Archaeology and Politics of Food and Feasting in the Early States and Empires*, edited by Tamara L. Bray, pp. 143–172. Kluwer Academic/Plenum, New York.

Graham, Elizabeth

2002   Perspectives on Economy and Theory. In *Ancient Maya Political Economies*, edited by Marilyn A. Masson and David A. Freidel, pp. 398–418. Altamira Press, Walnut Creek, Calif.

Hann, Chris, and Keith Hart (editors)

2009   *Market and Society: The Great Transformation Today*. Cambridge University Press, Cambridge.

Harvey, H. R.

1984   Aspects of Land Tenure in Ancient Mexico. In *Explorations in Ethnohistory: Indians of Central Mexico in the Sixteenth Century*, edited by H. R. Harvey and Hanns J. Prem, pp. 83–102. University of New Mexico Press, Albuquerque.

Hassig, Ross

1981   The Famine of One Rabbit: Ecological Causes and Social Consequences of a Pre-Columbian Calamity. *Journal of Anthropological Research* 37:172–182.

1985   *Trade, Tribute, and Transportation: The Sixteenth-Century Political Economy of the Valley of Mexico*. University of Oklahoma Press, Norman.

1988   *Aztec Warfare: Imperial Expansion and Political Control*. University of Oklahoma Press, Norman.

Helms, Mary W.

    1988   *Ulysses' Sail: An Ethnographic Odyssey of Power, Knowledge, and Geographical Distance.* Princeton University Press, Princeton.

    1993   *Craft and the Kingly Ideal: Art, Trade, and Power.* University of Texas Press, Austin.

Hicks, Frederic

    1984   Rotational Labor and Urban Development in Prehispanic Tetzcoco. In *Explorations in Ethnohistory: Indians of Central Mexico in the Sixteenth Century,* edited by H. R. Harvey and Hanns J. Prem, pp. 147–174. University of New Mexico Press, Albuquerque.

    1999   The Middle Class in Ancient Central Mexico. *Journal of Anthropological Research* 55:409–427.

Hirth, Kenneth G.

    1998   The Distributional Approach: A New Way to Identify Marketplace Exchange in the Archaeological Record. *Current Anthropology* 39(4):451–476.

Hutson, Scott R.

    2000   Carnival and Contestation in the Aztec Marketplace. *Dialectical Anthropology* 25:123–149.

Hyslop, John

    1990   *Inka Settlement Planning.* University of Texas Press, Austin.

Ibrahim, Mahmood

    1990   *Merchant Capital and Islam.* University of Texas Press, Austin.

Isaac, Barry L.

    1986   Notes on Obsidian, the Pochteca, and the Position of Tlatelolco in the Aztec Empire. In *Economic Aspects of Prehispanic Highland Mexico,* edited by Barry L. Isaac, pp. 319–343. JAI Press, Greenwich, Conn.

    1993   Retrospective on the Formalist-Substantivist Debate. *Research in Economic Anthropology* 14:213–233.

    2005   Karl Polanyi. In *A Handbook of Economic Anthropology,* edited by James G. Carrier, pp. 14–25. Edward Elgar, Cheltenham, U.K.

Kurtz, Donald V.

    1974   Peripheral and Transitional Markets: The Aztec Case. *American Ethnologist* 1:685–704.

Lenski, Gerhard E.

    1966   *Power and Privilege: A Theory of Social Stratification.* McGraw-Hill, New York.

LeVine, Terry Y. (editor)

    1992   *Inka Storage Systems.* University of Oklahoma Press, Norman.

Lockhart, James

    1992   *The Nahuas after the Conquest: A Social and Cultural History of the Indians of Central Mexico, Sixteenth through Eighteenth Centuries.* Stanford University Press, Stanford.

McAnany, Patricia A.

    2010   *Ancestral Maya Economies in Archaeological Perspective.* Cambridge University Press, Cambridge.

Morris, Craig, and Donald E. Thompson

    1985   *Huánuco Pampa: An Inca City and Its Hinterland.* Thames and Hudson, London.

Murra, John V.

    1980   *The Economic Organization of the Inka State.* JAI Press, Greenwich, Conn.

    1982   The Mit'a Obligations of Ethnic Groups to the Inka State. In *The Inca and Aztec States 1400–1800,* edited by George A. Collier, Renato I. Rosaldo, and John D. Wirth, pp. 237–262. Academic Press, New York.

    1989   Cloth and Its Function in the Inka State. In *Cloth and Human Experience,* edited by Annette B. Weiner and Jane Schneider, pp. 275–302. Smithsonian Institution Press, Washington, D.C.

Oka, Rahul, and Chapurukha M. Kusimba

    2008   The Archaeology of Trading Systems, Part 1: Towards a New Trade Synthesis. *Journal of Archaeological Research* 16:340–395.

Parsons, Mary H.

    1975   The Distribution of Late Postclassic Spindle Whorls in the Valley of Mexico. *American Antiquity* 40:207–215.

Polanyi, Karl, Conrad M. Arensberg, and Harry W.
  Pearson (editors)

  1957   *Trade and Market in the Early Empires:
          Economies in History and Theory.* Free
          Press, Glencoe, Ill.

Pozorski, Shelia, and Thomas Pozorski

  1991   Storage, Access Control, and Bureau-
          cratic Proliferation: Understanding the
          Initial Period (1800–900 BC) Economy
          at Pampa de las Llamas-Moxeke, Casma
          Valley, Peru. *Research in Economic
          Anthropology* 13:341–371.

Sahagún, Bernardino de

  1950–1982   *Florentine Codex: General History of
              the Things of New Spain.* Translated by
              Arthur J. O. Anderson and Charles E.
              Dibble. School of American Research,
              Santa Fe, and University of Utah, Salt
              Lake City.

Salomon, Frank

  1986   *Native Lords of Quito in the Age of
          the Incas: The Political Economy of
          North-Andean Chiefdoms.* Cambridge
          University Press, Cambridge.

Shadow, Robert D., and María J. Rodríguez V.

  1995   Historical Panorama of Anthropological
          Perspectives on Aztec Slavery. In *Arque-
          ología del norte y del occidente de México:
          Homenaje al Doctor J. Charles Kelley,*
          edited by Barbro Dahlgren and María
          de los Dolores Soto de Arechavaleta,
          pp. 299–323. Universidad Nacional
          Autónoma de México, Mexico City.

Smith, Michael E.

  1990   Long-Distance Trade under the Aztec
          Empire. *Ancient Mesoamerica* 1:153–169.

  2004   The Archaeology of Ancient State Econo-
          mies. *Annual Review of Anthropology*
          33:73–102.

Smith, Michael E., and Frances F. Berdan

  2003   Postclassic Mesoamerica. In *The Post-
          classic Mesoamerican World,* edited by
          Michael E. Smith and Frances F. Berdan,
          pp. 3–13. University of Utah Press, Salt
          Lake City.

Smyth, Michael P.

  1996   Storage and the Political Economy: A
          View from Mesoamerica. *Research in
          Economic Anthropology* 17:335–355.

Stanish, Charles

  2010   Labor Taxes, Market Systems, and
          Urbanization in the Prehispanic
          Andes: A Comparative Perspective. In
          *Archaeological Approaches to Market
          Exchange in Ancient Societies,* edited by
          Christopher P. Garraty and Barbara L.
          Stark, pp. 185–205. University Press of
          Colorado, Boulder.

Torquemada, Juan de

  1975 [1615]   *Monarquía indiana,* vol. 1. 3rd ed.
               Universidad Nacional Autónoma
               de México, Mexico City.

Wells, E. Christian, and Karla L. Davis-Salazar

  2007   *Mesoamerican Ritual Economy:
          Archaeological and Ethnological
          Perspectives.* University Press of
          Colorado, Boulder.

Wells, E. Christian, and Patricia A. McAnany

  2008   *Dimensions of Ritual Economy.* Emerald,
          JAI Press, Bingley, U.K.

Wernke, Steven A.

  2006   The Politics of Community and Inka
          Statecraft in the Colca Valley, Peru.
          Latin American Antiquity 17:177–208.

West, Georgia

  2002   Ceramic Exchange in the Late Classic and
          Postclassic Maya Lowlands: A Diachronic
          Approach. In *Ancient Maya Political
          Economies,* edited by Marilyn A. Masson
          and David A. Freidel, pp. 140–196.
          Altamira Press, Walnut Creek, Calif.

CONTRIBUTORS

Dmitri Beliaev is an archaeologist and epigrapher whose research interests include Mesoamerican writing systems, the formation of complex societies and early states, and political anthropology. As a recipient of the Russian Presidential Stipend in 1996–1997, Dmitri did part of his undergraduate studies at the Universidad Autónoma de Yucatán, Mexico. He received his doctoral degree in history at the Russian State University for Humanities in 2001 (his doctoral research centered on the formation and evolution of ancient Maya polities). Beliaev participated in several field projects, including the Central Mixteca Alta Settlement Patterns Project in 1999 in Oaxaca, Mexico. He is currently assistant professor at the Knorozov Center for Mesoamerican Studies at the Russian State University for Humanities and research associate of the Centro Knórosov de Estudios de la Lengua y Epigrafía Maya del Parque Xcaret, Mexico.

Richard E. Blanton is professor of anthropology at Purdue University. His research and publications represent a productive combination of archaeology and cross-cultural comparative method. His archaeological career began in the Basin of Mexico on Bill Sanders's Teotihuacan Valley survey with Jeff Parsons, and also at Tikal, where he worked on a settlement pattern survey; he then continued with more regional archaeological research in the Texcoco and Ixtapalapa regions of the basin as well as a similar survey of the Valley of Oaxaca, Mexico. Additional regional archaeological work followed in Rough Cilicia, in the south coastal region of Turkey, but he has recently returned to his Central Mexican archaeological roots in a new and ongoing project, with Lane Fargher, in Tlaxcala, Mexico. Beginning with his paper on the origins of markets, presented at the inaugural meeting of the Society for Economic Anthropology in 1983, Blanton has consistently encouraged his anthropological archaeology colleagues to embrace market study in their research efforts. His own interest in, and research on, markets, has continued, as attested by an analysis of Postclassic market evolution in the Basin of Mexico published in *Aztec Imperial Strategies* (with Frances F. Berdan, 1996), and, most recently, in a chapter in *Archaeological Approaches to Market Exchange in Ancient Societies* (edited by Christopher P. Garraty and Barbara L. Stark, 2010).

Richard L. Burger is an anthropological archaeologist with more than three decades of field experience in highland and coastal Peru. In addition to directing excavations at Chavín de Huántar, Pojoc, Huaricoto, Cardal, Mina Perdida, and Manchay Bajo, he has also devoted himself to studying the changing patterns of prehistoric Andean obsidian exchange in Peru and Ecuador, and searching for the geological sources of the volcanic glass utilized in the past. Burger joined the faculty of Yale University in 1981 and is currently the Charles J. MacCurdy Professor of Anthropology there. He served as the director of the Peabody Museum of Natural History for eight years and has been the chairman of the anthropology and archaeological studies departments. Burger has written and edited numerous books and many articles on early Andean civilization, including *Excavaciones en Chavín de Huantar* (1998); *Emergencia de la civilización en los Andes: Ensayos de interpretación* (1993); *Chavin and the Origins of Andean Civilization* (1992); *Archaeology of Formative Ecuador* (with J. Scott Raymond, 2003); *The Life and Writings of Julio C. Tello* (2009); and *Arqueología del período formativo de la Cuenca Baja de Lurín* (with Krzysztof Makowski, 2009).

David M. Carballo is assistant professor in the department of archaeology at Boston University. His research focuses on the archaeology of Formative and Classic-period Central Mexico through excavation projects at Teotihuacan and in the state of Tlaxcala. He is the author of *Obsidian and the Teotihuacan State: Weaponry and Ritual Production at the Moon Pyramid* (2011) and the editor of *Cooperation and Collective Action: Archaeological Perspectives* (2012). Other publications cover household archaeology, ritual and religion, obsidian exchange, transportation corridors, and archaeological theory on pre-Hispanic households, the origins of deities, obsidian exchange, and highland transportation corridors, among other topics. He was formerly a visiting scholar in the Center for U.S.-Mexican Studies, University of California at San Diego, and is currently active in the archaeology of Teotihuacan and the state of Tlaxcala.

Lawrence S. Coben is the founder and executive director of Sustainable Preservation Initiative (SPI). SPI, an organization dedicated to the preservation of the world's cultural heritage, provides sustainable economic opportunities to poor communities where endangered archaeological sites are located. Coben is also an affiliated archaeologist at the University of Pennsylvania, and his most recent work focuses on Inca imperial expansion and the role of spectacles, rituals, and theatricality in ancient societies. He directed Proyecto Incallajta, a multidisciplinary project at the Inca site of that name in Bolivia. He coedited *Archaeology of Performance: Theaters of Power, Community, and Politics* (with Takeshi Inomata, 2006), a volume that examines the importance and use of theatrical

performance at public events, rituals, and spectacles in ancient societies to create and govern states and empires. He has also written numerous articles on the Inca, sustainable preservation, performance, and complex societies.

Tom D. Dillehay is the Rebecca Webb Wilson University Professor and Distinguished Professor in the Department of Anthropology at Vanderbilt University and Profesor Extraordinaire at the Universidad Austral de Chile. He has carried out numerous archaeological and anthropological projects in South America and the United States. His main interests are migration, the long-term transformative processes leading to political and economic change, and the interdisciplinary and historical methodologies designed to study those processes. He has been a visiting professor at several universities around the world, including the Universidad de Chile; Universidad Nacional Mayor de San Marcos, Lima; Universidade de Sao Paulo; Universidad Nacional Autónoma de México; Cambridge University; University of Tokyo; and the University of Chicago. Professor Dillehay has published fifteen books and more than two hundred refereed journal articles. He currently codirects with the University of Chicago an interdisciplinary project focused on long-term human and environmental interaction on the North Coast of Peru. He has begun an excavation project at Huaca Prieta, Peru. He directs another project sponsored by the Guggenheim Foundation and the National Science Foundation on the political identity of the Araucanians in Chile and Argentina. Professor Dillehay, a recipient of numerous international and national awards for his research, books, and teaching, is a member of the American Academy of Arts and Sciences.

David A. Freidel is professor of anthropology at Washington University in Saint Louis. His interest in Maya markets, commerce, and political economy started with his settlement pattern study of the pilgrimage center of Cozumel Island under the direction of Jeremy Sabloff and William Rathje. He continued to explore these issues in his first project at the Preclassic trading port of Cerros in Belize. His second project was at Yaxuna in Yucatan, another trading city linking eastern and western sectors of the northern lowlands. This work focused on regional commercial and military interaction in the Late Classic period. Yaxuna also revealed Early Classic evidence of interaction with forces allied with Teotihuacan as well as Middle Preclassic interaction with Olmec horizon people. He currently directs research at the site of El Perú, ancient Waka', in northwestern Peten. He is coauthor of *A Forest of Kings: The Untold Story of the Ancient Maya* (with Linda Schele, 1990) and *Maya Cosmos* (with Linda Schele and Joy Parker, 1993); he is coeditor of *Ancient Maya Political Economies* (with Marilyn Masson, 2002).

Paul S. Goldstein is associate professor of anthropology at University of California, San Diego. He received his doctorate from the University of Chicago and has held postdoctoral fellowships at the American Museum of Natural History and Dumbarton Oaks, and he was associate professor of anthropology at Dartmouth College. His area of interest lies in the origins of Pre-Columbian civilizations of the Andes, with a particular focus on the role of colonization, diasporic migration, and trade in the growth of ancient states and empires. Much of his ongoing research centers on fieldwork on the Tiwanaku culture of Bolivia, Peru, and Chile, where he has directed numerous excavation and survey projects. He is the director of the Moquegua Archaeological Survey (MAS), a long-term study of ancient settlement patterns in southern Peru, and the author of *Andean Diaspora: The Tiwanaku Colonies and the Origin of South American Empire* (2005). Recently, he has worked on relating the history of "El Niño" flood events to the Pre-Columbian archaeological record of the expansion, integration, and collapse of early empires, and on the poorly understood interaction of Wari and Tiwanaku state systems along their frontier.

Gerardo Gutiérrez is assistant professor of anthropology at the University of Colorado, Boulder. He received a PhD in anthropological archaeology in 2002 from the Pennsylvania State University, an MA in urban studies from El Colegio de México, and a Licenciatura (BA) in archaeology from the Escuela Nacional de Antropología e Historia, Mexico. He has done archaeological and ethnohistorical investigations in many areas of Mexico, including the southern Huaxtec region; the Zapotec, Mixe, and Chinantec regions of northern Oaxaca; the Mixtec-Tlapanec-Nahua-Amuzgo region of eastern Guerrero; and the Soconusco coast. He has written articles on a variety of topics, including Huaxtec religion and settlement patterns as well as the archaeology and ethnohistory of Guerrero, in particular the Postclassic Tlapa-Tlachinollan kingdom. He is the senior author of *Códice Humboldt Fragmento 1 (Ms. amer. 1) y Códice Azoyú 2 reverso: Nómina de tributos de Tlapa y su provincia al Imperio Mexicano* (bilingual edition, 2009) and *Toponimia náhuatl en los códices Azoyú 1 y 2: Un estudio crítico* (2008).

Kenneth G. Hirth is professor of anthropology in the department of anthropology at Pennsylvania State University. He is an archaeologist and economic anthropologist interested in the comparative analysis of domestic and political economy in the Pre-Columbian world. He has authored, edited, and coedited fourteen books on different aspects of Mesoamerican economy and political economy. These volumes include: *Housework: Craft Production and Domestic Economy in Ancient Mesoamerica* (2009); *Obsidian Craft Production in Ancient Central Mexico* (2006); *Mesoamerican Lithic Technology: Experimentation and Interpretation* (2003); *Ancient Urbanism at Xochicalco* (2000); and *Trade and Exchange in Early Mesoamerica* (1984). He is a recipient of the Excellence in Lithic Studies Award from the Society of American Archaeology (1998) and the Chairman's Award for Career Achievement in Archaeology by the National Geographic Society (2000). His current research is on the role and organization of merchants in Mesoamerica.

Barry L. Isaac is emeritus professor of anthropology at the University of Cincinnati. An economic anthropologist, he was the editor of *Research in Economic Anthropology* from 1982 to 2000. That venue published both research annuals covering economic anthropology in general and occasional thematic volumes devoted to prehistoric economies. This latter group includes *Economic Aspects of Prehispanic Highland Mexico* (1986); *Prehistoric Economies of the Pacific Northwest Coast* (1988); *Prehistoric Maya Economies of Belize* (coedited with Patricia McAnany, 1989); *Early Paleoindian Economies of Eastern North America* (coedited with Kenneth Tankersley, 1990); *Long-Term Subsistence Change in Prehistoric North America* (coedited with Dale Croes and Rebecca Hawkins, 1992); and *Economic Aspects of Water Management in the Prehispanic New World* (coedited with Vernon Scarborough, 1993). His geographical area of specialization is highland Mexico, on which he has coauthored two books with Hugo G. Nutini: *Los Pueblos de Habla Náhuatl de la Región de Puebla y Tlaxcala* (1974) and *Social Stratification in Central Mexico, 1500–2000* (2009). His current research focus is Aztec ethnohistory, especially warfare, human sacrifice, and alleged cannibalism.

Brigitte Kovacevich is assistant professor of anthropology at Southern Methodist University. She received her BA from the University of Arizona and PhD from Vanderbilt University. Her interests include the complex interplay between technology, power, economic systems, social action, and culture change in the past and present. She primarily carries out her research in Guatemala, but she has also worked in Mexico, Arizona, Tennessee, Kentucky, and the U.S. Virgin Islands. Her areas of specialization comprise Mesoamerican archaeology, lithic analysis, household archaeology, gender, identity, and political economy. Recent publications include "Ritual, Crafting, and Agency at the Classic Maya Kingdom of Cancuen," a chapter in *Mesoamerican Ritual Economy* (2007) as well as "Laser Ablation ICP-MS Chemical Characterization of Jade from a Jade Workshop in Cancuen, Guatemala" in *Laser Ablation ICP-MS in Archaeological Research* (2005). She has also coauthored papers and an article (in the *Journal of Archaeological Science*) on the geochemical analyses of soils from activity areas at Cancuen, as well as papers and articles on the chemical analyses of jade and obsidian. She organized a symposium on gifting and inalienable possessions in the past for the 2008 Society for American Archaeology, the papers from which will be published in the Archaeological Papers of the American Anthropological Association. A book chapter in *The Technology of Maya Civilization: Political Economy and Beyond in Lithic Studies* was published in 2011.

Marilyn A. Masson is associate professor in anthropology at the University at Albany–SUNY. Her research focuses on ancient economies of the Maya area, with recent emphases on household archaeology and the urban organization of Mayapan, the largest Maya political capital of the Postclassic period. She is the author and editor of three books: *In the Realm of Nachan Kan* (2000); *Ancient Civilizations of Mesoamerica* (with Michael E. Smith, 2000); and *Ancient Maya Political Economies* (with David A. Freidel, 2002). She has served as principal investigator on two major archaeological research projects, including the Belize Postclassic Project (1996–2002) and the Economic Foundations of Mayapan Project (2001 to present, supported by the National Science Foundation and the National Geographic Society). Currently, her research at Mayapan examines occupational heterogeneity, affluence, and modes of governance within the city's neighborhoods.

Enrique Mayer is an anthropologist with more than forty years of specialization in Andean agricultural systems and Latin American peasantries. He is professor of social anthropology at Yale University. He did graduate work at Cornell University under the supervision of John V. Murra. His work on peasants and their agricultural systems demonstrates that regions characterized by diversity (such as mountainous environments, small islands, and "marginal" lands) and unsuitable for agribusiness are exploited by peasants in strikingly similar ways. Peasant forms of production predominate and persist in these environments worldwide. His book *The Articulated Peasant* makes a point of describing how household economies function in theory and in actual Andean practice. His book *Ugly Stories of the Peruvian Agrarian Reform* (2009) focuses on how people remember the reform that took place forty years ago and assesses the impact it has had in the rural areas of Peru.

Patricia A. McAnany is Kenan Eminent Professor of Anthropology at the University of North Carolina–Chapel Hill and external faculty at the Santa Fe Institute. A Maya archaeologist, she is principal investigator of the Xibun Archaeological Research Project, coprincipal investigator of Proyecto Arqueológico Colaborativo del Oriente de Yucatán, and executive director of the nonprofit InHerit: Indigenous Heritage Passed to Present. She is particularly interested in the intersection of ritual and economy and in cultural heritage rights for descendant Maya peoples. She is the author or coeditor of several books, including *Textile Economies: Power and Value from the Local to the Transnational* (2011, coedited with Walter E. Little), *Ancestral Maya Economies in Archaeological Perspective* (2010), *Questioning Collapse: Human Resilience, Ecological Vulnerability, and the Aftermath of Empire* (2009, coedited with Norman Yoffee), and *Dimensions of Ritual Economy* (2008, coedited with E. Christian Wells). Her journal articles include "Terminal Classic Maya Heterodoxy and Shrine Vernacularism in the Sibun Valley, Belize," *Cambridge Archaeological Journal* 22 (2012); "Casualties of Heritage Distancing: Children, Ch'ortí Indigeneity, and the Copán Archaeoscape" (coauthored with Shoshaunna Parks), *Current Anthropology* 53 (2012); "Thinking about Stratigraphic Sequence in Social Terms" (coauthored with Ian Hodder), *Archaeological Dialogues* 16 (2009); "Rational Exuberance: Mesoamerican Economies and Landscapes in the Research of Robert S. Santley" (coauthored with Christopher A. Pool), *Journal of Anthropological Research* 64 (2008); and "America's First Connoisseurs of Chocolate" (coauthored with Satoru Murata), *Food and Foodways* 15 (2007). She has been the recipient of several research awards from the National Science Foundation and of fellowships from the Institute for the Arts and Humanities (University of North Carolina–Chapel Hill), National Endowment for the Humanities, Radcliffe Center for Advanced Study at Harvard University, and Dumbarton Oaks. Currently, she works with organizations in southern Mexico, Belize, Guatemala, and western Honduras to provide local communities with opportunities to dialogue about the value and conservation of cultural heritage.

Deborah L. Nichols is the William J. Bryant 1925 Professor of Anthropology at Dartmouth College and the chair of the department of anthropology. She has coedited four books, including *Social Violence in the Prehispanic Southwest* (2008), *Archaeology Is Anthropology* (2003), and *Archaeology of City-States* (1997). She has authored and coauthored numerous articles for professional journals, including "The Rise of Civilization and Urbanism" in *Encyclopedia of Archaeology* (2008); "Artisans, Markets, and Merchants" in *The Aztecs* (2008); and book chapters "Chiconautla, Mexico: A Crossroads of Aztec Trade and Politics" (2009) and "Aztec Studies" (2011). She has participated in and directed numerous archaeological projects in Mexico. She is currently codirector with George Cowgill of the research project "Spanning the Classic to Postclassic Transition at a Teotihuacan Regional Center," which is sponsored by the National Science Foundation.

Axel E. Nielsen is professor of archaeology at the University of Córdoba and tenured investigator of Consejo Nacional de Investigaciones Científicas y Técnicas (Argentina). He has been working in the Southern Andes since the mid-1980s. He conducted ethnoarchaeological and ethnographic research among llama pastoralists and caravan traders in the southern Bolivian altiplano and has been applying the results of this work to the archaeological study of caravan routes that date from the last three millennia. His general interests include the ways in which interregional interaction (e.g., trade and warfare) shape processes of social change. Some of his recent publications are *Warfare in Cultural Context: Practice, Agency, and the Archaeology of Violence* (coedited with William Walker, 2009); "The Materiality of Ancestors: Chullpas and Social Memory in the

Late Prehispanic History of the South Andes" (in *Memory Work: Archaeologies of Material Practices*, edited by Barbara Mills and William Walker, 2008); "Plazas para los antepasados: Descentralización y poder corporativo en las formaciones políticas preincaicas de los Andes circumpuneños" (*Estudios Atacameños* 31, 2006); and "Estudios internodales e interacción interregional en los Andes circumpuneños: Teoría, método y ejemplos de aplicación" (in *Esferas de interacción prehistóricas y fronteras nacionales modernas: Los Andes sur centrales*, 2006). His current project focuses on the study of late pre-Hispanic public spaces, with a special interest on how practices developed in these settings contributed to the constitution of corporate political subjects.

Joanne Pillsbury is the former director of Pre-Columbian Studies at Dumbarton Oaks and the associate director of the Getty Research Institute. She holds a PhD and an MA in art history and archaeology from Columbia University and a BA in anthropology from the University of California, Berkeley. She has been the recipient of grants and fellowships from the Fulbright Commission, the Metropolitan Museum of Art, Dumbarton Oaks, and the Samuel H. Kress Foundation, and she has conducted archaeological field research in Peru, West Africa, and California. She is the editor of *Past Presented: Archaeological Illustration and the Ancient Americas* (2012); the three-volume *Guide to Documentary Sources for Andean Studies, 1530–1900* (2008); and *Moche Art and Archaeology in Ancient Peru* (2001). She is coeditor of *Palaces of the Ancient New World* (with Susan Toby Evans, 2004) and *Ancient Maya Art at Dumbarton Oaks* (with Miriam Doutriaux, Reiko Ishihara-Brito, and Alexandre Tokovinine, 2012). Her recent articles have addressed topics in eighteenth-century archaeology, the history of collecting, *Spondylus* in ritual and representation, and architectural sculpture of the late pre-Hispanic period in the Andes.

Charles Stanish, a professor of anthropology, holds the Lloyd Cotsen Chair in Archaeology at the University of California at Los Angeles (UCLA). He is a specialist in Pre-Columbian Lake Titicaca Basin cultures, with a theoretical interest in political and economic organization. He is currently the director of the Cotsen Institute of Archaeology at UCLA. He has authored, edited, or coedited nine books, including *Ancient Titicaca* (2003), *Ritual and Pilgrimage in the Ancient Andes* (with Brian Bauer, 2001) and *Ancient Andean Political Economy* (1992). He is a fellow of the American Academy of Arts and Sciences and a senior fellow at Dumbarton Oaks. His current research focuses on the development of complex societies in the northern Titicaca Basin.

Alexandre Tokovinine is a Maya epigrapher and archaeologist. He has participated in several projects in Guatemala, including the Holmul Archaeological Project and Proyecto Arqueológico de Investigación y Rescate Naranjo, and he recently received a PhD in anthropology from Harvard University. His doctoral research centered on Classic Maya place names and was supported by a junior fellowship at Dumbarton Oaks. His recent research projects include 3-D documentation of Classic Maya sculpture and contributions to *Ancient Maya Art at Dumbarton Oaks* (with Joanne Pillsbury, Miriam Doutriaux, and Reiko Ishihara-Brito, 2012). He is currently a research associate of the Corpus of Maya Hieroglyphic Inscriptions, Peabody Museum, as well as a lecturer at the department of anthropology, Harvard University.

John R. Topic received his PhD from Harvard in 1977 and is professor emeritus at Trent University, where he has served as chair and director of the graduate program. His research has focused on the Inca and pre-Incaic cultures of Peru and Ecuador, exploring themes such as urbanism, craft production, warfare, bureaucracy, ethnic identity, and religious cults. He has served as an associate editor of *Latin American Antiquity* and is currently treasurer of the Institute of Andean Research. In 2002, he was named a Huésped Ilustre by the city of Huamachuco, Peru, and in 2003, he won Trent's Distinguished Research Award. He was named to the Orden de José Faustino Sánchez Carrión in 2007 by the Municipalidad Provincial de Sánchez Carrión (Huamachuco) and was visiting professor in the Programa de Estudios Andinos at the Pontificia Universidad Católica del Peru in 2008.

INDEX

Carrasco, Pedro, 131
Carrasco, Ramón, 210
Casas, Bartolomé de las, 171, 241
Cascas, 352
Caso Barrera, Laura, 239
Catequil, 344
Ceibal, 238
censers: Mayapan incense burners depicting God M, 191; Otumba, 62, 63; theater-style censers, Teotihuacan, 128, 129, 129–130
Central Andes, Pre-Columbian economy of, 1, 2–4, 3, 11–14, 16–17. See also archaeological perspectives on economy of Central Andes; barter markets in Andes; caravan trade in Southern Andes; comparison of exchange practices in Ecuador and northern Peru; models of Andean economy; Tiwanaku; vertical model for Andean economy
ceramics: caravan trade in Southern Andes and, 395, 400, 401–405, 403, 406–408, 407, 409, 414, 415n1; chaupiyunga bowls, 340, 344; Chavín de Huántar, objects brought to, 324–326, 325, 326; distance traded in Mesoamerica, 96, 96–97, 97; Otumba, ceramic production at, 62, 62–63, 66–73, 67–72; source studies for Otumba region, 66–73, 67–72; Teotihuacan, 96, 97, 121, 128–131, 129, 130. See also specific types and classifications
Ceren, 218
Cerro Amaru, 344
Cerro Baúl, 377
Cerro Echenique-site groups, 373
Cerro Lorro, 296
Cerro Portezuelo, 51, 70, 71, 72, 73
Cerro Sulcha, 352
Céspedes, Ricardo, 403
Chablekal Fine Gray ceramics, 265, 266, 269, 271
Chadwick, John, 232
Chahk, 188, 193, 194
chalayplasa, 428
chalchihuites, 259
Chalco, 66, 67, 69, 70, 72, 74
Chama-style vessels with procession of travelers, 179, 179–180
Chan Chan, 339, 340, 343, 346, 352, 353n4
Chan Noohol, 218
Chapab Modeled ware, 214
chaquira (bead wealth), 347, 348, 350, 351
Charlton, Cynthia Otis, 63
Charlton, Thomas H., 50, 58, 59, 64, 65, 71, 73, 123
chaupiyungas, 340, 341, 342, 344, 352, 353n3
Chavín de Huántar, 13, 288, 289, 323–326, 323–330
cheating and stealing as economic behavior, 312–313
Chen Chen–style occupations, 371, 373, 374–375, 375, 376–377
Chen Chen–style red ware, 375
Chi, Gaspar Antonio, 220
chiampinolli (maize-chia gruel), 441
Chiapa de Corzo, 232

chicha (maize beer) and chicha brewing, 291, 337, 340, 343, 375, 405, 431
Chichen Itza: circular shrine structures at, 242, 243–244; Court of One-Thousand Columns, 210, 211; disc from, 192; Great Cenote, 191; heterodoxy at, 243; marketplace, 32; Temple of the Owls decorations, 187; Temple of the Warriors murals, 183, 184, 194
Chichimec peoples, 36
Chiconautla, 61, 66, 70, 72, 73
Chiepetlan, 151, 152
Chile, 284, 286, 288, 296–297, 297, 349, 365, 389, 393–400, 429. See also Triple Frontier of Bolivia, Chile, and Argentina, caravan trade on
chili peppers, trade in, 95
Chillón Valley, 293–295, 293, 295
Chimalhuacan, 73
Chimú pottery, 299, 342–343
Chimú state, 290, 297, 300, 340, 349
Chincha Valley, 12, 16, 319–321, 337, 348, 349, 350, 353n8
Chincha lords, 296
Chinese market systems, 23, 30
Chochola-style vessels, 184, 187
Ch'ok Wayis, 175–177, 177
cholas, 314n2
Chongayape, 289
Christensen, Mark, 106–107
Chunchucmil, 210–211, 218, 221
Cieza de León, Pedro, 427
cinnabar, 324, 325, 326, 327
circuit mobility theory, 390–391
circuitous-axis mobility model for northern Chile, 297
circular shrine structures, 242, 243–245, 244
civil servants in Aztec state, 440–441
Clark, John, 122
classical Greece: Athenian Agora, boundary marker of, 28, 29; marketplaces of, 28, 29, 29–30, 39n11; palace economies of Aegean Bronze Age, 231, 232
climatic-vegetation zones: ecological diversity of Central Mexico and, 98, 98–99, 99, 104; Maya trade in staple goods and, 218–220, 219; vertical model of Central Andean economy and, 292, 293, 421
Coastal Cajamarca ware, 344
coastal trade, Peruvian-Ecuadorean, 349–350, 351–352, 420
coatequitl (public works labor), 131, 143, 157, 441
Coatsworth, John, 118
Coben, Lawrence S., 7, 12, 14, 16, 297, 419–434, 436, 450
Cobo, Bernabé, 349
Cochabamba, 376–377, 379, 380n3, 397, 403
cochineal production at Otumba, 64–65
codices: Azoyú 1, 162; Azoyú 2-Reverse, 144; Dresden, 186, 187, 188, 191, 192, 193, 194; Florentine, 53, 106; Humboldt Fragment 1, 144; Madrid, 191, 192, 193, 193; Mendoza, 96, 142, 143, 144, 151, 151, 153, 156, 157, 165n9, 209; Otlazpan, 165n9; Tepeucila, 158
Coixtlahuaca, 39n9
Coleman, Simon, 323
Collique, 294–295

colonialism and verticality, 310–311

colonias, 292, 294, 296

comal (ceramic griddle), 51, 73, 75, 90

commercialization of Pre-Columbian economy, extent of, 103–104, 221, 435–439, 443–444. *See also* Pre-Columbian economy

comparison of exchange practices in Ecuador and northern Peru, 13, 335–354; centralized, redistributive economy in Peru, 352; *chaquira* (bead wealth), 347, 348, 350, 351; coast of Ecuador, 347–349; decentralized resource procurement economy in Ecuador, 352; ethnic groups as trade intermediaries, 340, *341,* 342, 344, 346, 352–353; frontier area between Peru and Ecuador, 335–337, 352; highlands of Ecuador, *345,* 345–347; highlands of northern Peru, *342,* 342–343; historiographic distinction between, 335, 337; labor and exchange models for Peru, 343–344; map of Peru and Ecuador, *336;* maritime trade, 349–350, 351–352; North Coast of Peru, 337–340, *338, 339, 341;* obsidian trade between Peru and Ecuador, lack of, 336–337, 352–353; *ofrendas* (axe-monies, axes, and *naipes),* 350–351, 352; resource sharing, 338–340, 343–344, 346, 351, 352; *Spondylus* shell, coastal trade in, 348, 349, 351–353

competition strategies in price-making and barter markets, 424–427

Conides, Cynthia, 130

Contreras, Daniel, 330

Cook, Scott, 421

cooperation theory of markets, 24–25

Copan, 218, 230, 259, 261, 265, 270

copies and forgeries, 313

Córdova Frunz, José Luís, 125–126

Cortés, don Juan, 241

Cortés, Hernán, 143

corvée labor (labor taxation), 5; in Aztec state *(coatequitl),* 131, 143, 157, 437, 441, 442; in Inca state *(mit'a),* 362, 363, 377, 409, 419, 420, 431, 441–442; in Maya state *(patan),* 175, 188, 209, 236, 238

Cosotlan 23, figurine and censer production at, 130

cost-path analysis, Teotihuacan, *119,* 120–121, 132

Costin, Cathy Lynne, 354n10

cotton: distance traded in Mesoamerica, *95,* 95–96; Otumba, fiber production at, *63,* 63–64; in royal presentation scenes, 239–240; Teotihuacan cotton industry, 121, 126–128, *127*

Cowgill, George, 129

Cozumel, 32

cranial deformation, intentional, *369, 369–370,* 371

Cruz Blanca, 340, *341*

Cruz, Pablo, 405

Cuauhtitlan, 55, 66, 74

Cuello, 258–259

Cuexcomate, 218

cuirass of alligator hide, Chiu Chiu, *408*

Culbert, T. Patrick, 213

Culhuacan, 66

cult. *See* religion and ritual

cultural evolutionism, 23, 37, 391

cumbi cloth, 309, 347, 377

curacas, 12, 13, 295–296, 302. *See also kuraka* entrepreneurship

currency: axe-monies, 296, 321, 350–351, 352; Central Andean lack of, 309, 321; *chaquira* (bead wealth), 347, 348, 350, 351; jade, currency value of, 271; *mantas de tributo* or *quachtli* (tributary cloth) as standard of exchange, 142, *156,* 156–163, *157, 159,* 165n9; Maya use of currency units, 220; *naipes,* 321, 350, 351, 352; price-making versus barter markets, 424, 428; substantivist-formalist debate and, 420

cyclical residency, 299–302, *301*

D

Dahlin, Bruce, 210, 230–231

Dalton, George, 271, 420, 437–438

D'Altroy, Terence, 92, 105n1, 202

Damp, Jonathan, 348

Davis-Salazar, Karla, 257

demons bedeviling travelers, 190–191, *191*

Diakhanké marketplaces, Mali, 31–32

diasporas in Central Andes, 296, *297,* 364–365

Díaz del Castillo, Bernal, 92, 143

Díaz Oyarzábal, Clara, 126

Diccionario de San Francisco, 170

Diccionario grande del siglo XVI, 170

dichotomized explanations of craft production, problems with, 255–257

Diez de San Miguel, Garci, 430–431, *430*

Dillehay, Tom D., 12–13, 16, 283–308, *296, 297,* 299–300, *338,* 390–391, 413, 450

discontinuous territoriality, 343–344

distance of trade in staple goods, 86, *92,* 92–99, *94–99,* 104

divine myths indicating conflicts between merchants and royal courts, 234–235

divine patrons of merchants, 171, 184–194, *185, 186, 188–193*

domestic sector of economy, 4, 7

Domínguez, Silvia, 122

dominio directo and *dominio útil,* 343

Donnan, Christopher, 350–351

Dos Pilas, 172, 238, 259

double coincidence of wants/want of coincidence, 427–428

Dresden Codex, *186,* 187, 188, *191, 192, 193,* 194

Druc, Isabel, 326

Durán, Diego, 35, 39n10, 93, 148, 150, 440

E

Earle, Timothy, 202, 255, 421

ebeet (messengers or emissaries), 10, 16, 175–179, *177,* 186, 194, 238, 239

ecological zones. *See* climatic-vegetation zones

Ecology and Exchange in the Andes (Lehmann, ed., 1982), 310

economy, Pre-Columbian. *See* Pre-Columbian economy

Ecuador. *See* comparison of exchange practices in Ecuador and northern Peru; *mindalaes*

Edwards, Clinton, 349

Ek' Chuwah, 191

El Azúcar, 348

El Durazno, 100

elasticity, 121, 131, 425

elite control model, 391–392, 413–414, 438–439

Elsner, John, 323

embedding of economy within sociocultural institutions, 6, 14; caravan trade and, 410–412, *411, 412,* 413; marketplaces and, 23–25, 37; at Otumba, 52; at Teotihuacan, 113; at Tiwanaku, 362–363, 366, 375–379. *See also* redistributive economies

environmental zones. *See* climatic-vegetation zones

ethnicity: diasporas in Central Andes, 296, *297,* 364–365; identity, hybridity, diaspora, and migration in Central Andes, 296, *297;* irrigation groups and multiethnic coexistence, 365–366, *366, 367;* mythic history, and marketplaces in Central Mexico, 36–37; northern Peru and Ecuador, ethnic groups as trade intermediaries in, 340, *341,* 342, 344, 346, 352–353

Ethnicity, Markets, and Migration in the Andes (Larson et al., 1995), 311

Etnía y sociedad: Costa peruana prehispánica (Rostworowski, 1977), 421

European comparative studies. *See* classical Greece; medieval Europe

exchange, defined, 6–7. *See also* Pre-Columbian economy

F

facial deformers, 369, *370,* 371

factor markets in Aztec economy, 436–437

fairs. *See* marketplaces

Famine of One Rabbit (1454), 437, 441, 443

Fargher, Lane, 422

farming, at Otumba, *64,* 64–65, 73

feasting: Aztec public feasts in hungry season, 441; Central Andes feasting-based economies, 290–291, *291;* gift exchanges, *ikaatz* transactions as, 175; at royal Maya courts, 232, *233*

feathered headdresses on Tiwanaku mummy bundles, *369*

"feathers," bronze, 350

feathers, quetzal, in royal presentation scenes, 240–241

Feldman, Lawrence H., 32, 170, 241

festivals, tributary, 144–148, 150, *153,* 164n6

fibers and textiles: from Chavín de Huántar, 328; Karwa, Formative-period textiles discovered at, 288; *mantas de tributo* or *quachtli* (tributary cloth) as standard of exchange, 142, *156,* 156–163, *157, 159,* 165n9; in Mayapan, 207; Otumba, fiber production at, *63,* 63–64; public distribution of clothing, 441; Pulacayo, Tiwanaku-style textile and hat from, 403, *404;* royal Maya courts, textile production at, 233–234, 240, 242; spindle whorls, 8, 59, *63,* 63–64, 70, 71, 233, 240, 263; tapestry tunic, Río Muerto, *376, 377;* as tribute item,

153–156; women as textile workers, 127, 233–234, 240, 242. *See also specific fibers and textiles*

figurine makers at Otumba, *62, 63,* 71

Firth, Raymond, 425

fish and seafood consumed at Chavín de Huántar, *325, 326,* 327

fishing industry, 218

Flannery, Kent, 103

Florentine Codex, 53, 106

forgeries and copies, 313

formalist-substantivist debate, 420–422

Frankenstein, Susan, 289

Freidel, David, 10, 16, 201–228, *207,* 220, 230, 238, 241, 260, 270, 271, 450–451

fruit: caravan trade in Southern Andes and, 400; distance traded, 93, 105n3–4; Teotihuacan sources, 126

Fry, Robert E., 213

funerary goods and practices. *See* mortuary behavior

G

Galápagos Islands, 349

Gallareta, Tomás, 201

game theory, 25, 38n1

García Cook, Ángel, 128

García-Des Lauriers, Claudia, 131

Garcilaso de la Vega, El Inca, 312

Garraty, Christopher P., 66, 74–75, 207

Gazzola, Julie, 122

geoglyphs of llamas, Moquegua Valley, 373, *374*

geographic information systems (GIS), 120

gift exchanges: alliance formation and, 6; barter markets and, 426; caravan trade in Southern Andes and, 392, 412, 413, 414; civil servants, transfer payments to, 441; *ebeet* (messengers or emissaries), 10, 16, 175–179, *177,* 186, 238, 239; forgeries and copies, meaning of, 313; *ikaatz* transactions, 174–175, 240; importance in Pre-Columbian economy, 436; jade production and use at Cancuen, 11, 267–272; luxury manufacture and, 208; between northern Peruvian coast and highlands, 343; in northern Peruvian highlands, 343; restricted markets and, 25, 32–33

gimwali, 313, 425

Glascock, Michael, 74, 122

God D, as merchant patron, 172, 174, 186, 188–190

God L, as merchant patron, 11, 174, 184–194, *185, 186, 188, 189,* 234, 235, 238, 242, *243*

God M, as merchant patron, 191–194, *192, 193*

gods. *See* divine myths indicating conflicts between merchants and royal courts; divine patrons of merchants; *specific gods*

gold dust, as tributary item, 153

Goldstein, Paul S., 13–14, 296, 361–387, 451

Gonlin, Nancy, 259

Gormsen, Erdmann, 93

government control. *See* political authority and influence

Graham, Elizabeth, 238

Granovetter, Mark, 25

graves. *See* mortuary behavior
Great Temple, Tenochtitlan, 150
Greece, classical. *See* classical Greece
greenstones. *See* jade production and use at Cancuen
Gregory, C. A., 361
Grube, Nikolai, 177–178, 234
Guambos, 340, 344, 351
Guayaquil, 349
Guayatayoc, *394, 397,* 401, *403,* 406, *407,* 409, 415n5
Guderjan, Thomas, 259
Guerrero, 93, 95, 144
Gutiérrez, Gerardo, 9, 15, 141–167, 231, 451

H

hallucinogens and psychotropics, 324, 377, *378,* 400, 401,
     402, 414, 415n3
Hammond, Norman, 258
Handbook of Economic Anthropology (Mayer, 2005), 313
Harlow, George E., 267
Harris, Olivia, 311, 314n2
Hassig, Ross, 56
Hero Twins, 174, 184, 187, 188, 189, 190, 235
Hidalgo, 125, 126
High Lakes region, 393, *394,* 400, 406, 409, 410, *411*
Hirth, Kenneth G., 1–22, 8–9, 15, 85–112, 106, 126, 128, 141,
     230, 257, 263, 271, 325, 419–420, 422, 424, 451
*Historia de la provincia de San Vicente de Chiapa y
     Guatemala,* 208
Historia eclesiastica indiana (Mendieta), 100, 105n9
Historia general de las Indias (Oviedo y Valdés, ca.
     1535–1557), 347
historiography of Pre-Columbian economy, 309–314, 319,
     362, 364, 420–422
Hocquenghem, Anne-Marie, 335, 349, 352
Holm, Olaf, 349
Homo economicus, 24, 25, 37
Hosler, Dorothy, 350
Houston, Stephen D., 232, 237, 238
Huaca Lucia, 330
Huaca Negra, Templo de las Llamas at, 330
Huamachuco, 342, 343, 344, 352
Huancavelica, 324
Huánuco Pampa, 290–291, *291,* 327
Huari, annual fair at, 429–430
Huasochugo, 342, 352
Huayllajara stream area, 395, *398,* 400
Huitzamola, 151, *152*
Humahuaca, *394, 397,* 401, 406, 409, 414
Codex Humboldt Fragment 1, 144
Hunal, 181
Hutson, Scott R., 35, 231

I

Ichcateopan, 151, *152*
ikatz/ikaatz or *ikitz* transactions, 172–175, *176,* 236, 239
illegality as economic behavior, 312–313
INAA (instrumental neutron activation analysis), 59, 66,
     73, 265, 267, 268, 269

Inca. *See* Central Andes, Pre-Columbian economy of
Inca de Catalcito, 409, *410*
incense burners. *See* censers
independent versus attached specialization, 255–257, 258
Información de 1554, 142, 143, 144, *151,* 151–153, *156, 157,* 158,
     164, 164n6
informal economy, 312–313
inhaling paraphernalia, *378,* 401, *402, 403,* 406, *414,* 415n3
institutional sector of economy, 4–5, 7
instrumental neutron activation analysis (INAA), 59, 66,
     73, 265, 267, 268, 269
internodal approach to caravan trade in Southern
     Andes, 392–400, *394–399,* 406
interregional exchange in highland Mesoamerica, 8–9,
     85–104; climatic-vegetation zones and ecological
     diversity, 98, *98–99, 99,* 104; commercial nature of
     world, 103–104; distance of trade in staple goods, 86,
     92, 92–99, 94–99, 104; merchants, concepts of, 86, *87,
     87–91, 89–91,* 103–104; Nahautl economic vocabulary,
     88, 106, *106–107,* 164n1; profitability model for
     itinerant obsidian blade production, 86, 99–103, *102,*
     104; transportation issues, 2, 85, *86, 87,* 92
Intersalar region, *394, 397, 402, 403, 405,* 406, *407, 408,*
     409
irrigation groups and multiethnic coexistence, 365–366,
     366, 367
Isaac, Barry L., 14–15, 16, 220, 271, 435–448, 451–452
Ishihara-Brito, Reiko, 267
Isla de la Plata, 348
Isla de Puná, 348, 351
itinerant obsidian blade production in Mesoamerica,
     profitability model for, 86, 99–103, *102,* 104
Itzamk'anak, 171
Itzamnaaj B'ahlam, 235
Itzimte altar fragment and Stela 7, *182,* 183–184

J

Jackson, Sarah, 241
jade in royal presentation scenes, 240
jade production and use at Cancuen, 11, 255–272;
     attached versus independent specialization in,
     255–257, 258; both elite and commoner use of jade
     items, 257, 259–260; dichotomized explanations of
     craft production, problems with, 255–257; distribution
     of production technologies, finished products, and
     ritual treatments, 260–267, *262–264, 266;* in elite
     and nonelite burials, *259,* 263–265, *266;* in elite and
     nonelite domestic households, 260–263, *262, 263;*
     gift exchanges, 11, 267–272; headdress ornaments,
     259–260, 260; map of Guatemala showing Cancuen,
     256; physical properties of jadeite and other green-
     stones, 258–259; ritual and ideology, economic system
     intertwined with, 257–258, 267; royal courts and,
     240; from royal throne room cache, *263, 264, 265,*
     267; segmented production system, 265; sourcing of
     jade, 267–269, *269;* trade patterns for jade, 269–272;
     as tribute item, 272; values attached to greenstones in
     Maya culture, 258–260

Jaguar God of the Underworld (JGU), 184, 191–193, *193*
Jasaw Chan K'awiil I of Tikal, tomb of, 236–238, *237,* 241
Jayanca, 340
Jequetepeque Valley, 13, 297–302, *298, 301,* 324, 344, 351
Jevons, William S., 428
Jijón y Caamaño, Jacinto, 337, 348
Jonuta, panel fragment from, 175, *176*
Julien, Catherine, 420
Juun Ajaw (Hero Twin), 189, *190*

K
K'ahk' Tiliw Chan Chahk, 174
Kaminaljuyu, 265
K'an Joy Chitam II of Palenque, 238
Karwa, 288, 289
K'awiil, 187, *188*
K'awiil Chan K'inich, 172
Kepecs, Susan, 35
K'inich Ajaw (sun god), 234–235
K'inich Janahb' Pakal I of Palenque: funerary mask, 268–269, *269*; sarcophagus, 240
Kolata, Alan, 299–300
Kolb, Charles, 128–129
Kotosh Religious Tradition, *323,* 331
Kovacevich, Brigitte, 11, 16, 207, 230, 255–282, 452
Kristan-Graham, Cynthia, 37
Kula ring, Trobriand Islanders, 426, 428, 431n2
Kuntur Wasi, *289*
kuraka entrepreneurship, 312. *See also curacas*
Kurtz, Donald, 423, 438
Kusimba, Chapurukha M., 56, 73
Kvietok, D. Peter, 350

L
La Banda, 325, 327, 328
La Galgada, 288, 289
LA-ICP-MS (Laser Ablation Inductively Coupled Plasma Mass Spectrometry), 268, 269
La Quiaca, 430
La Sufricaya murals, *180,* 180–181, *181,* 184, 194
labor market: commodities with labor-added value, 121; Peru, labor and exchange models for, 343–344; rudimentary nature in Aztec economy, 437; tributary system of Aztec Empire, labor payment in, 143
labor taxation. *See* corvée labor
Lacadena, Alfonso, 231, 235–236
Lady K'ab'aal Xook of Yaxchilan, 233, 235
Laguna Blanca, 409
Laguna Colorada, 400
Laguna de On, 218
lakam (district governor), 175, 179, 231, 236
Lake Poopó, *397,* 402–403, *403,* 405, 406, *407,* 409
Lake Titicaca/Titicaca Basin, 376, 390, *397,* 403, 405, 415n4, 427, 429–431
Lambayeque, 290, 296–297, 300, 321, 324, 335, 337, 344, 346, 349, 350, 351, 352
Landa, Diego de, 10, 32, 33, 169, 171, 193–194, 209, 218, 220
Lange, Frederick W., 267

Lanzón, Chavín de Huántar, 324
Larson, Brooke, 311
Laser Ablation Inductively Coupled Plasma Mass Spectrometry (LA-ICP-MS), 268, 269
Latacunga, 346
Lechtman, Heather, 350
Lecoq, Patrice, 403
Lehmann, David, 310
Lie, John, 361
lime industry at Teotihuacan, 121, *125,* 125–126, 132
liminal spaces, marketplaces as, 28–29, *29*
linguistic evidence of exchange: in lowland Maya languages, 171–172, *173*; Nahautl cconomic vocabulary, 88, 106, *106–107,* 164n1
Lira López, Yamile, 128
Llagostera, Agustín, 401, 414
llamas and other pack animals: archaeological evidence for late Initial Period use of llamas, 330; feed for, 105n2; geoglyphs of llamas, Moquegua Valley, 373, *374*; Huaca Negra, Templo de las Llamas at, 330. *See also* caravan trade in Southern Andes
llameros, 401, 405, 406, 409, 413
Loa River area, *397, 398,* 400–401, *402, 403,* 406, *407, 408, 408,* 409
Looper, Matthew G., 233
Los Cerrillos-site groups, 373
Los Teteles de Ocotítla, 128
Lumbreras, Luis, 324
Lumholtz, Carl, 93, 97
Lynch, Thomas F., 284

M
Machalilla, 348
Macoy, Paul, 429
Madrid Codex, 191–193, *192, 193*
maguey and cotton fiber production at Otumba, *63,* 63–64
maize: caravan trade in Southern Andes and, 400; *chiampinolli* (maize-chia gruel), 441; *chicha* (maize beer) and *chicha* brewing, 337, 340, 343, 375, 405; distance traded, 93; itinerant obsidian blade production in Mesoamerica and, 103; Maya trade in, 220; price fluctuations, 438; in Tiwanaku, 368, 375, 377, 379; wholesale price of, 105n9
maize god, 178, 187, *188,* 194, 220, 234
Malinaltepec, 151, *152*
Malinowski, Bronislaw, 311, 313, 425, 426
Maltrata region, 128
mantas de tributo or *quachtli* (tributary cloth) as standard of exchange, 142, *156,* 156–163, *157, 159,* 165n9
Manzanilla, Linda, 118, 120, 126–127, 128, 131, 132
Maquixco Bajo, 131
Marcos, Jorge G., 337, 348
marital exchange, 25, 34, 239, 288, 294, 299, 367, 369, 413, 415n7, 426, 436
maritime trade along Peruvian-Ecuadorean coast, 349–350, 351–352, 420

mindalaes, 4, 13, 321, 330, 337, 346–348, 352, 363

mining at Otumba, *65,* 65–66

Mira, 347

mit'a (Inca system of labor taxation or corvée labor), 362, 363, 409, 419, 420, 431, 441–442

Mixteca Alta, marketplaces in, *33,* 33–34

Mixtequilla region, 127

"Moan Bird," 187, 193

Mocomoco, 430

Moctezuma II, 161, 162, 439, 441

models of Andean economy, 12–13, 283–303; archipelago model, 363, 364–368, *366, 367,* 377; cyclical residency, 299–302, *301;* early agricultural and pastoral economy (middle sixth to middle third millennium BC), 286–288, *287;* foraging economies (late Pleistocene and early Holocene periods), 284–286, *285;* Formative Period (ca. 3500–1000 BC), long-distance and prestige-goods trade in, 288–290, *289;* map of Central Andes, *284;* markets and fairs, 297–299, *298;* nonmarket economic strategies of later Central Andean cultures, 290–291, *291;* northern Peru, labor and exchange models for, 343–344; post-vertical explanations for foreign elements, 296–299, *297;* transhumance, 284–285, 297. *See also* caravan trade in Southern Andes; vertical model for Andean economy

Moholy-Nagy, Hattula, 214

Molina, Alonso de, 106, 165n9

mollo chasqui camayoc (*Spondylus* messenger-worker), 363

momoztli symbol, 209

money. *See* currency

Motagua Valley jadeite, 240, 257, 258, 261, 265, 267, 268

Moon Goddess, 188, 194

Moquegua Valley colonies of Tiwanaku, 368, 371–378, *372–376, 378, 379*

Morelos, 39, 93, 100, 103, 125, 126, 143, 144

Morris, Craig, 290–291, 311, 320

mortuary behavior: bundled grave goods (*ofrendas*), 350–351; Cancuen burials, elite and nonelite, jade in, *259,* 263–265, *266;* caravan trade in Southern Andes and, 401, 403–405, *404;* funerary mask of K'inich Janahb' Pakal I of Palenque, 268–269, *269;* Palenque, jadeite in tombs of, 240; in Tiwanaku, 368–369, *369. See also specific tombs*

Motul de San José, 174–175

Múnera Bermúdez, Carlos, 129

Murakami, Tatsuya, 126

Murra, John: archaeological perspectives on economy of Central Andes and, 319, 320; on *ayllus,* 406; barter markets in Andes and, 420–421; caravan trade and, 390, 392; comparison of northern Peru and Ecuador and, 337, 343, 351; photograph of, *364;* on *pochteca,* 311; Tiwanaku's embedded economy and, 363, 364, 368, 377, 378–379; vertical model for Andean economy and, 11, 13, 16, 291–293, 297, 309–311, 314n1, 343, 364, 392, 420–421

mythic history, ethnicity, and marketplaces in Central Mexico, 36–37

N

Nahautl economic vocabulary, 88, 106, *106–107,* 164n1

naipes, 321, 350, 351, 352

Nakum, 269

Naranjo: Stela 12 at, 174, *236,* 238; Stela 22 at, 188; Stela 30 at, *193;* Stela 32 at, 174, 177–178, 236, *237;* Stela 43 at, 187; vessels from, 171, *172,* 184, 187, 188–189, *189*

Neff, Hector, 122, 129

neo-Romanticism, 23, 28

nephrite, 258. *See also* jade production and use at Cancuen

Nezahuacoyotl, 58

Nichols, Deborah L., 8, 15, 16, 23, 49–83, 88, 453

Nielsen, Axel E., 12, 13–14, 16, 296, 313, 389–418, 453–454

no-market model of caravan trade in Southern Andes, 391, 412–413

Nohmul, 245

Nonoalca, 32

North, Douglass C., 25

Northern Lípez, *394, 397,* 400, 402, *403,* 406, *407, 408,* 409, 414

northern Peru. *See* comparison of exchange practices in Ecuador and northern Peru

Northwestern Puna, *394, 397,* 400, 409, 415n1

Norton, Presley, 348

Núñez, Lautaro, 296, 297, 390–391, 392, 401, 413

O

Oaxaca, marketplaces in, 33–34, 46

Oberem, Udo, 337, 346

obsidian: in barter markets versus price-making markets, 425, 426; Calakmul's lack of, 218, 221, 270; caravan trade in, 330, 409; Chavín de Huántar, objects brought to, 324, *325,* 326, 326–327; Ecuador and northern Peru, lack of trade between, 336–337, 352–353; Maya nonlocal consumption of, *215–217,* 215–218, 221; Otumba mining and crafting of, *58,* 59–61, *60,* 65, 65–66, 74, 76; problem of reconstructing market systems from, 220; production output for blades, 101–103, *102;* profitability model for itinerant obsidian blade production in Mesoamerica, 86, 99–103, *102,* 104; source studies for Otumba region, 66–73, *67;* in Tiwanaku, 377–378, *379*

occupational specialization. *See* specialization

Ocoapan, 151, *152*

ofrendas, 350–351

Ojo del Novillito, 410, *412*

Oka, Rahul, 56, 73

Olmeca-Xicallanca, 32

Omo-style occupations, *369,* 371, 373–374, 376, 377

Omo-style Tiwanaku ceramics, 373

Orange Ware, 66

Orizaba, 128

Ostrom, Elinor, 131

Codex of Otlazpan, 165n9

Otumba, 8, 49–77; after Spanish conquest, 76; basalt, *61,* 61–62; ceramic production, 62, 62–63; city-state and archaeological site, 56–59, *57, 58;* cochineal production, 64–65; commercial intensification through large communities, 16; in context of Aztec state, 49–51, 50, 51; cotton and maguey fiber production, 63, 63–64; craft industries in, 58, 59–66, 60–65; farming, 64, 64–65, 73; in Late Postclassic period, 69–73, 71, 72; marketplaces of Aztec confederations, 51–52; merchants and market activity in, 73–76, 75; in Middle Postclassic period, 66–69, 69, 70; mining, 65, 65–66; obsidian, 58, 59–61, 60, 65, 65–66, 74, 76; pochteca of, 7, 8, 61, 70, 73–74, 75, 76; political influence on market development of, 73, 76; source studies of ceramics and obsidian, 66–73, 67–72; Teotihuacan obsidian industry and, 122; types of merchants in Aztec marketplaces and, 52–56, 53

Otumba Polished Tan bowls, 63, 72
Oviedo y Valdés, Gonzalo Fernández de, 347
oztomeca, 7, 87

P

Pacasmayo, 344, 349
Pachuca obsidian, 59, 60, 65, 69, 74, 76, 101, 120, 122, 122–123, 132
pack animals. *See* llamas and other pack animals
Paita, 349
Pakal Na, 245
palace economy. *See* royal courts in Maya economy
Palenque: Bundle Panel, 238–239; Cancuen, trade with, 265, 266, 268–269, 269; funerary mask of K'inich Janahb' Pakal I, 268–269, 269; jade, access to, 270; jadeite in tombs of, 240; Temple 12 tomb, 240; Temple of the Inscriptions, 174; Temple of the Sun, 185, 186, 188
Pallka, 326
Pampa de las Llamas-Moxeke, 288
Pampa Grande, 349, 352
Panquetzaliztli, 56, 148
Papamalil, 177
parcialidades, 337–340, 344, 353n2
Paredon obsidian, 60, 123
Pastos, 346
Pastrana, Alejandro, 122
patan, 175, 188, 236, 238
patronyms with letter *F* in northern Peru, 344
Patterson, Thomas C., 319
peripheral market, concept of, 437–438
Petexbatun, 177
petlacalcatl (steward in charge of tribute storage facility), 143, 161
Piedras Negras: Burial 5 at, 240; jade artifacts from, 258; jade, lack of, 270; Panel 2 at, 178; Panel 3 at, 175, 232; Throne 1 at, 174
Pik Chan Ahk, 187
pilgrimage. *See* religion and ritual
Pillsbury, Joanne, 1–22, 23, 141, 230, 257, 454
Pimampiro, 346, 347
Pimbert, Michel, 428
Pimentel, Gonzalo, 406
Piñami, 376

pinole, 93, 443
Pizarro, Hernando, 349
Plain Orange Ware, 66, 72, 75
Pluckhahn, Thomas J., 34
pochteca, 52–56; ambivalent position of, 439–440; cities inhabited by, 54–55, 55; coastal Andean traders compared, 420; cooperation theory of marketplaces and, 35–36, 37; defined, 53–54; different types of, 56, 66; government control of long-distance trade and, 438–439; Hispanic focus on, 435; indigenous and Spanish concepts of merchants and, 87, 87–91; llama caravans, relevance compared to, 330; management of marketplace by, 438; *mindalaes* and, 321, 337; Murra on, 311; in Otumba, 7, 8, 61, 70, 73–74, 75, 76; producer-vendors compared, 104; profitability of travel for, 100; significance of, 50–51; social status and wealth, 55–56, 439–440; of Tenochtitlan, 35, 133; tribute collection and, 141, 158
Pohl, John M. D., 34
Polanyi, Karl, 2, 11, 23, 26, 30, 37, 292, 309, 310, 311, 362–363, 364, 380n1, 391
political authority and influence, 14–15, 52, 440–443; control of production versus control of distribution, 206, 206–207; marketplaces, regulation and management of, 30–32, 31, 438–439; merchants, ambivalence of elites regarding, 234–235, 439–440; *mit'a* or corvée labor for Inca government projects, 362, 363, 409, 419, 420, 431, 441–442; nonmarket economic strategies of later Central Andean cultures, 290; Otumba, market development of, 73, 76; public works of Aztec state, 441; Staple and Wealth finance, 202; stimulation of trade and markets by expansion of Aztec Empire, 141–142; tax policies, 442–443 (*See also* tributary system of Aztec Empire; tributary system of Maya culture); Teotihuacan, organization of economy in, 131, 132; Tiwanaku, as unitary political state, 368; transfer payments in Aztec state, 440–441. *See also* royal courts in Maya economy
Polo de Ondegardo, Juan, 365
pottery. *See* ceramics
Pre-Columbian economy, 1–17, 435–444; antimarket bias regarding, 11–13, 23, 30, 37, 38n11, 309–314, 319; in Central Andes, 1, 2–4, 3, 11–14, 16–17 (*See also* archaeological perspectives on economy of Central Andes; barter markets in Andes; caravan trade in Southern Andes; comparison of exchange practices in Ecuador and northern Peru; models of Andean economy; Tiwanaku; vertical model for Andean economy); commercialization, extent of, 103–104, 221, 435–439, 443–444; comparative study of economic systems and, 4; comparing Aztec and Maya economies, 203; conservative and accumulative nature of, 5–6; definitions pertinent to, 6–7, 363, 391, 422–423, 424; dual domestic and institutional sectors, 4–5, 7; embedded (*See* embedding of economy within sociocultural institutions); hemispheric perspective, importance of, 2–4; historiography of, 309–314, 319, 362, 364, 420–422; importance of studying, 1–4;

maps of key sites and areas, 2, 3; marketplaces, 8, 17–38 (*See also* marketplaces); in Maya region, 1, 2, 4, 9–11, 16 (*See also* jade production and use at Cancuen; Maya market exchange; representations of merchants and trade in Maya texts and images; royal courts in Maya economy); in Mexican Highlands, 1, 2, 7–9, 15–16 (*See also* interregional exchange in highland Mesoamerica; Otumba; Teotihuacan; tributary system of Aztec Empire); Nahautl economic vocabulary, 88, 106, *106–107,* 164n1; new understanding of, 16–17; political context of, 14–15, 52, 440–443 (*See also* political authority and influence); principles of, 5–7; urbanism and market exchange, 15, 16, 442–443; variety of exchanged goods, importance of considering, 220

prestige-chain-trade model, 267–268

price-making versus barter markets, 423–427

processualism, 23

production zones model of Andean economy, 293

profitability model for itinerant obsidian blade production in Mesoamerica, 86, 99–103, *102,* 104

psychotropics and hallucinogens, 324, *377, 378,* 400, 401, *402,* 414, 415n3

public works labor *(coatequitl),* 131, 143, 157, 441

Pucara, 429

Puebla, 93, 95, 96, 105, 115, 125, 126, 128, 129, 132, 186

Puerto López, 348

Puerto Viejo, 349

Pulacayo, 403–405, *404*

Puqui ceramics, 402, 403, 405

Putun, 32

Q

quachtli or *mantas de tributo* (tributary cloth) as standard of exchange, 142, *156,* 156–163, *157, 159,* 165n9

Quebrada de Humahuaca, 401

quetzachalchihuitl, 259

quetzal feathers, in royal presentation scenes, 240–241

Quetzalcoatl, 36

quetzalitztli, 259

Quijos, 346, 347, 351, 352

Quintana Roo, 219

Quispisisa obsidian source, 324, 327, 330

Quito, 346, 347

Quivi people and lands, 294, 295

R

Raimondi, Antonio, 429

rainfall. *See* climatic-vegetation zones

Ramírez, Susan, 338, 343, 349

ransoming captives, 236–239

Rathje, William, 214

rationality of market systems, 421–422, 424

real property market, 437

Red Ware, 52, 59, 63, 66, 70, 72

redistributive economies, 11–14, 444; antimarket mentality and, 309–310, 312; Aztec tributary system and, 141; barter markets in Andes and, 420, 428;

caravan trade and, 390, 391, 392, 401, 406, 413; in comparison of Ecuador and northern Peru, 335, 337, 340, 343, 345, 352; forgeries and copies, meaning of, 313; jade production and use at Cancuen, 257; Maya market exchange and, 201, 202, 203, 207, 208; models of Central Andean economies involving, 283, 284, 290–291; representations of merchants and trade in Maya art and, 170; at Teotihuacan, 118; Tiwanaku and, 362–363, 368, 377, 378; traditional accounts of Pre-Columbian economy and, 1, 3, 6, 9, 11–14, 16, 17; transfer payments by Aztec state, 440–441

regional-scale commerce: Maya marketplace and market exchange, 203–204, *205,* 218; significance in Pre-Columbian economy, 439. *See also* interregional exchange in highland Mesoamerica

Relación de Chincha, 349

Relaciones geográficas, 16, 90, 92–93, 96

religion and ritual: barter markets, ritualized nature of exchange in, 426; caravan trade in Southern Andes and, 401; economic system intertwined with, 257–258; exchange and dispersal of goods, pilgrimage and cult sites as mechanisms for, 13, 34, 243, 288, 299, 344; jade production and use at Cancuen, 257–258, 267; marketplaces piggybacking on religious authorities and sites, 30–31, *31,* 34, 35, 207, 322–324, 327–330, *328, 329, 396;* nonmarket economic strategies of later Central Andean cultures, 290–291, *291;* Teotihuacan, organization of economy in, 131, 132; termination rituals, 242, 261, 267; transfer payments by Aztec state, 440–441

Remy, Pilar, 344

Renfrew, Colin, 25, 231, 267

representations of merchants and trade in Maya texts and images, 10, 169–194; cacao-related titles in inscriptions, *182,* 183–184, 194; canoes, people associated with, *178,* 178–179; Classic texts and imagery, 171–184, *172, 173, 176–183;* demons bedeviling travelers, 190–191, *191;* divine patrons of merchants, 171, 184–194, *185, 186, 188–193; ebeet* (messengers or emissaries), depictions of, 10, 16, 175–179, *177,* 186; Late Postclassic–early colonial ethnohistorical sources, 169–171; linguistic evidence of exchange, 171–172, *173;* market scenes in Calakmul North Acropolis mural, 10, 16, *181,* 181–183; merchants and travelers, *183,* 184; Naranjo workshop drinking cup dedicatory text, 171, *172;* subroyal households with tradable commodities, *179;* toad merchant narrative, 189–190, *190;* traveling and trade, identity of, 170; traveling scenes, *179,* 179–181, *180, 181;* tribute, *ikaatz* or *ikitz,* and payment transactions, 172–175, *176;* types of merchants, distinguishing, 169–170

resource sharing, 284, 296, 338–340, 343–344, 346, 351, 352

Restall, Matthew, 242

restricted markets, 25, 26–27, 32–34

Rica Playa, 349

Ricardo, David, 38n5

Rick, John, 324

SRTM (Shuttle Radar Topographic Mission), *119*, 120, 123, 126, 128, 129

stairways, hierarchic and dramaturgical nature of, 236–237

Stanish, Charles, 7, 12, 14, 16, 297, 419–434, 436, 454

staple goods: distance of trade in, 86, *92*, 92–99, *94–99*, 104; in Maya market exchange, 218–220, *219*; Staple and Wealth finance theory, 142, 202, 246. *See also specific staples*

Stark, Barbara L., 36

state control. *See* political authority and influence

stealing and cheating as economic behavior, 312–313

storage: in Central Andes, 290–291, *291*; tax policies and, 443

Strombus shell, 324, *325, 326*, 330

strontium isotope analysis, 372, 402, 403

Stuart, David, 174, 236–241

substantivist-formalist debate, 420–422

Sulche Black ware, 214

Sullivan, Kristin, 129–130

sun god, 187, 188, 194, 234–235

Sunraiser Jaguar of Pomona, 239

Supirapata, 393, *396*

Symanski, Richard, 422

T

Tacabamba, 352

Tacuba, 142, 164

Tah Itza, 239

Taltal, 406

Taltape ceramics, 405

Tandeter, Enrique, 311

tapestry tunic, Río Muerto, *376*, 377

Tarascan merchants and marketplaces, *89*, 97

Tarragó, Myriam, 392, 401

Taube, Karl A., 184, 191, 193, 234, 267, 269

Tawantinsuyu, 319–320, 331, 392, 409

tax policies, 442–443. *See also* corvée labor; tributary system of Aztec Empire; tributary system of Maya culture

Tayel Chan K'inich, 174

Techotlalatzin of Texcoco, 58

Tehuantepec, 95, 96, 98

Tello, Julio C., 323

temporary settlements: caravan trade in Southern Andes and, 410–412, *411, 412*; cyclical residency at, 299–302, *301*; transhumance, 284–285, 297

Tenochca people, 142–143, 439

Tenochtitlan: Amantla Barrio, 8; commercial intensification through large communities, 15; cotton provided to, 96, 105n5; daily markets, 51; *pochteca* of, 35, 133; pottery produced in, 51, 74; public works of Aztec state in, 441; special merchant barrios in, 54–55; storage facilities, 443; Tepenaca, break from, 49; transfer payments, 441

Teopancazco, 126, 127, 128, 132

Teotihuacan, 9, 113–133; apartment houses as public housing project, 132; art, trade-related items and themes in, *117*, 117–118, *118*; ceramics, 96, 97, 121, 128–131, *129, 130*; chronology of, *114*; as city-state and archaeological site, 113, *114*; Ciudadela, 122, 131; cotton, 121, 126–128, *127*; economic foundations of, 115, 115–117, *116*; export pottery, 121, 128–131, *129, 130*; Feathered Serpent Pyramid, 122; figurine workshops at, 63; fruit, sources of, 126; Great Compound, 132; heterogeneity of economy, 130–131; La Ventilla Barrio, 124; lime at, 121, *125*, 125–126, 132; maps, *115, 116*; Merchants' Barrio, 127, 132, 133; migration to and cosmopolitanism of, 132–133; Moon Pyramid, 122, 123, *124*, 131; Oaxaca Barrio, 125; obsidian at, 121–124, *122–123, 124*; organization of mercantile and production activities in, 130–133; Otumba and, 58, 59, 73; Oztoyahualco compound, 125, 132; political-religious authorities, role of, 131, 132; scale of market exchange at, 118; spindle whorls at, 240; storage facilities, 443; Temple of Agriculture mural, *118*; Temple of the Feathered Shells, *125*; Tetitla mural, *117*; Tlajinga Barrio, 129–130, 131; transportation issues, 118–121, *119, 120–121*, 132; Zacuala mural, *117*, 118; Zapotec Barrio, 132

teoxihuitl, 259

Tepeaca, 93, 105n4

Tepenaca, 49, *51*

Tepeucila, 158

Tepolzingo obsidian, 60

tequitlato (local tribute officer), 143, 157, 158

termination rituals, 242, 261, 267

Terraciano, Kevin, 34

Terry, Richard, 210

Tetenanco, 151, *152*

Texcoco: Otumba and, 49, *51*, 54–55, 58, 63, 66, 69, 71–74, 76; storage facilities, 441, 443; tributary system and, 142, 158, 164

Texcoco Fabric Marked pottery, 73, 76

textiles. *See* fibers and textiles

Tezcatlipoca, 36

theater-style incense burners, Teotihuacan, 128, *129*, 129–130

Thin Orange ware, *96*, 96–97, *97*, 128–129, *129*

Thompson, Donald, 290–291

Tikal: Calakmul, conflict with, 218, 221, 238; court officials seldom represented or mentioned at, 172; craft activities, identifying, 213; East Market Plaza, *210*, 211, 271; jade, access to, 270; Jasaw Chan K'awiil I, tomb of, 236–238, *237*, 241; nonlocal valuables, consumption of, 214, *215, 216*, 218, 221; occupational specialization at, 218; population levels, 230; regional markets and exchange, importance of, 203, 204, *205*; staple goods trade and, 219; stucco vase with *ebeet* from, 177

Titicaca Basin/Lake Titicaca, 376, 390, *397*, 403, 405, 415n4, 427, 429–431, *430*

Tiwanaku, 13–14, 361–380; "altiplano mode" in, 390; Andean exceptionalism, problem of, 361–364; archipelago model, ethnic diasporas, and *ayllus*, 363, 364–368, *366, 367*, 377; caravan trade and, 392, 401–405, *404*, 413, 414; as embedded economy with reciprocity and redistribution, 362–364, 366, 368, 375–379; map of area, *365*; material culture, social status, and identity in, 368–371, *369–371*; Moquegua Valley colonies, 368, 371–378, *372–376, 378, 379*; patterns and mechanisms of exchange, 377–378, *379*; as unitary political state, 368

tlaciuitiani, tlaciuiti (solicitors and purchasing agents), 91

tlacochcalco (state armories), 131

tlacocoalnamac (itinerant peddlers), 91

Tlacopan, 49, 441

tlameme (human porters), goods moved via, 85, *86*, 92–93, 104–105n1

tlanamacac (producer-vendors), 52–53, 88, 89–90, *90*

tlanecuilo (regional merchants or retailers), 52–53, 56, 72, 74, 76, 88, 89, 90–91, *91*

Tlapa. *See* tributary system of Aztec Empire; *Tribute Record of Tlapa*

tlapatlac (exchange merchants or money changers), 91

tlapatlani (small-scale peddlers), 141

Tlatelolco: marketplace at, 35, 51; merchants operating in, 88, 89–91; salt sold at, 95; Spanish descriptions of, 15, 49, 86; special merchant barrios in, 54–55

Tlaxcala, 76, 93, 115, 123, 128–129, 132, 242

toad merchant narrative, 189–190, *190*

Tobler, Waldo, 120, 123

Tochtepec, 35

tojool (payment), 175

Tokovinine, Alexandre, 10, 16, 169–200, 202, 230, 235, 238, 439, 454

Tolles, Thomas, 233

Toltec civilization, 36, 126, 184

tombs. *See* mortuary behavior

Tonina, 238–239; Monument 89 at, *182*, 183–184

Topic, John R., 13, 16, 335, 454

Topic, Theresa, 344

Topiltzin Quetzalcoatl, 36

Topoxte, 175

Torre, Tomás de la, 171

Totomixtlahuacan, 151, *152*

Totonac people, 93, 437

trade, defined, 6. *See also* Pre-Columbian economy

traders. *See* merchants

transfer payments by Aztec state, 440–441

transhumance, 284–285, 297

transportation issues: in Maya territory, 218–219, *219*; in Mesoamerica, 2, 85, *86*, 87, 92, 118–121, *119, 120–121*, 132; as transaction costs in premodern economies, 425. *See also* caravan trade in Southern Andes; llamas and other pack animals

travel and travelers: demons bedeviling travelers, 190–191, *191*; Maya images of, *179*, 179–181, *180, 183*, 184; trade and travel, linguistic identity of, 170

tributary system of Aztec Empire, 9, 141–164; basic operation of, 143, 156–157, 164; *calpixqui* (tribute collectors), 9, 141, 142, 143, 148, 150, 157, 158, 163–164; capitulation ceremony and first assessment at Tlapa, 148–150, *149, 150*; Codex Mendoza, 142, 143, 144,

151, 156, *157*, 165n9; definition of Aztec Empire and people, 142–143; documentary sources of, 142, 143; end of, 163; exchange values for tributary items, 142; festivals, tributary, 144–148, 150, *153*, 164n6; flexibility and negotiability of, 142, 156, 163–164; gold dust, 153; increase in tribute amounts from Tlapa over time, 158–163, *159, 160, 162*; *Información de 1554*, 142, 143, *151*, 151–153, *156, 157*, 164, 164n6; *manta* standard of exchange, 142, *156*, 156–163, *157, 159*, 165n9; materials and quantities of tribute items from Tlapa, *151–155*, 151–156; *Matrícula de Tributos*, 142, 143, 144, *151, 152*, 153, 156, *157*, 164n2; payment in goods or labor, 143; *petlacalcatl* (steward in charge of tribute storage facility), 143, 161; problems with reconstruction of, 143–144; stimulation of trade and markets by, 141–142, 231; as tax policy, 442–443; *tequitlato* (local tribute officer), 143, *157*, 158; textiles, 153–156; *tlacatecatl* (provincial governor) of Tlapa, 150, 164

tributary system of Maya culture: collapse of, 231; jade as tribute item, 272; provisioning of royal courts via, 235–239, *236, 237*, 241–242; representations of tribute or payment transactions in texts and images, 172–175, *176*; royal status of tribute collector, *237*, 241

Tribute Record of Tlapa, 144–148; capitulation ceremony and first assessment, *149, 150*; *Codex of Otlazpan* contradicted by, 165n9; as documentary source for tributary system of Aztec Empire, 142, 163; increase in tribute amounts after, 158; key pictorial items, 144–148, *146*; *manta* standard of exchange, 156, *157*; materials and quantities of tribute items from Tlapa, *151, 153, 154, 155*; quantities of tributary goods and their equivalents, *147*, 148; spreadsheet system, 144, *145*

Trigger, Bruce, 235

Triple Alliance, 49, 54, 58, 142, 144, 151, 153, 157, 162

Triple Frontier of Bolivia, Chile, and Argentina, caravan trade on, 393–400, *394–399*. *See also* caravan trade in Southern Andes

Tuchman, Barbara W., 239, 241

Túcume, 340, 349, 352

Tula, 36–37, 126

Tulancingo obsidian, 60, 123

Tumbes, 349

Turner, Edith L. B., 37

Turner, Victor, 28, 29, 37, 38n7

Tuxtla region, 127

Tzotzil people, 170–171

U

Uberoi, J. P. Singh, 426

Ucanal, 177–178

Uitzilopcho, 55

urbanism and market exchange, 15, 16, 442–443

utilities, market exchanges as means of maximizing, 424, 425

V

Valdivia shipwreck (1511), 203

Van Zantwijk, Rudolph, 52–53

Vega, Garcilaso de la, 312

vegetation zones. *See* climatic-vegetation zones

vertical model for Andean economy, 12–13, 291–296, 309–312; caravan trade and, 392; challenges to, 292–296, *295*, 311–312; climatic-vegetation zones, 292, *293*, 421; conferences on, 311; defined, 292, *293*, 310; factors influencing acceptance of, 292, 309–311; labor and exchange in northern Peru and, 343; microverticality in Ecuador and, 346; Murra and, 11, 13, 16, 291–293, 297, 309–311, 314n1, 343, 364, 392, 420–421

Vilque, 429

Visita of Cajamarca (1572–1578), 344

W

Walters, Gary Rex, 265

want of coincidence/double coincidence of wants, 427–428

war and trade: caravan trade in Southern Andes and, *408*; provisioning of royal Maya courts via martial competition and tribute extraction, 235–239, *236*, *237*, 241–242

Wari culture, 377–378

Wauchope, Robert, 201

Weber, Max, 28, 37

weights and measures, 321

Weiner, Annette, 233, 431n2

Wells, E. Christian, 257

whalebone, 328

Widmer, Randolph, 131, 132, 261

Wilk, Richard, 423–424

Willey, Gordon, 335

women: marketplace, female participation in, 13, 28, 33, 35, 90, 312, 314n2; as textile workers, 127, 233–234, 240, 242; as *tlanamacac* (producer-vendors), 52, 90

Wrigley, G. M., 429–430

X

X-ray diffraction, 267

X-ray fluorescence, 326

Xalapa, 128

Xaltocan, 58, 66, *70, 72*

xihuitl, 259

Xochicalco, 100, 103

Xocotla, 151, *152*

Xuenkal, 240

Y

Yacatecuhtli, 191

yanakonas, 343, 352, 353n4

Yauyos people, 294

Yich'aak Bahlam of Ceibal, 238

Yihk'in Chan K'awiil, 172

Yoallan, 151, *152*

Yuhkno'm Yich'aak K'ahk', 175

Yumbos, 346, 352, 353n6

Yunguyu, 430

Yura ceramics, 402, 403, 405

Yuraj Cruz, 393, *395*

Z

Zacapoaxtla, 93, 105n4

Zaña Valley, 286, *298*, 299–302, *301*

Zapaleri, 409

Ziegler, Rolf, 426

zonal complementarity, 296, 421

Zumpango, 125, 126

DUMBARTON OAKS PRE-COLUMBIAN
SYMPOSIA AND COLLOQUIA

PUBLISHED BY DUMBARTON OAKS RESEARCH LIBRARY
AND COLLECTION, WASHINGTON, D.C.

The *Dumbarton Oaks Pre-Columbian Symposia and Colloquia* series volumes are based on papers presented at scholarly meetings sponsored by the Pre-Columbian Studies program at Dumbarton Oaks. Inaugurated in 1967, these meetings provide a forum for the presentation of advanced research and the exchange of ideas on the art and archaeology of the ancient Americas.

Further information on Dumbarton Oaks Pre-Columbian series and publications can be found at www.doaks.org/publications.

Dumbarton Oaks Conference on the Olmec, edited by Elizabeth P. Benson, 1968

Dumbarton Oaks Conference on Chavín, edited by Elizabeth P. Benson, 1971

The Cult of the Feline, edited by Elizabeth P. Benson, 1972

Mesoamerican Writing Systems, edited by Elizabeth P. Benson, 1973

Death and the Afterlife in Pre-Columbian America, edited by Elizabeth P. Benson, 1975

The Sea in the Pre-Columbian World, edited by Elizabeth P. Benson, 1977

The Junius B. Bird Pre-Columbian Textile Conference, edited by Ann Pollard Rowe, Elizabeth P. Benson, and Anne-Louise Schaffer, 1979

Pre-Columbian Metallurgy of South America, edited by Elizabeth P. Benson, 1979

Mesoamerican Sites and World-Views, edited by Elizabeth P. Benson, 1981

The Art and Iconography of Late Post-Classic Central Mexico, edited by Elizabeth Hill Boone, 1982

Falsifications and Misreconstructions of Pre-Columbian Art, edited by Elizabeth Hill Boone, 1982

Highland-Lowland Interaction in Mesoamerica: Interdisciplinary Approaches, edited by Arthur G. Miller, 1983

Ritual Human Sacrifice in Mesoamerica, edited by Elizabeth Hill Boone, 1984

Painted Architecture and Polychrome Monumental Sculpture in Mesoamerica, edited by Elizabeth Hill Boone, 1985

Early Ceremonial Architecture in the Andes, edited by Christopher B. Donnan, 1985

The Aztec Templo Mayor, edited by Elizabeth Hill Boone, 1986

The Southeast Classic Maya Zone, edited by Elizabeth Hill Boone and Gordon R. Willey, 1988

The Northern Dynasties: Kingship and Statecraft in Chimor, edited by Michael E. Moseley and Alana Cordy-Collins, 1990

Wealth and Hierarchy in the Intermediate Area, edited by Frederick W. Lange, 1992

Art, Ideology, and the City of Teotihuacan, edited by Janet Catherine Berlo, 1992

Latin American Horizons, edited by Don Stephen Rice, 1993

Lowland Maya Civilization in the Eighth Century AD, edited by Jeremy A. Sabloff and John S. Henderson, 1993

Collecting the Pre-Columbian Past, edited by Elizabeth Hill Boone, 1993

Tombs for the Living: Andean Mortuary Practices, edited by Tom D. Dillehay, 1995

Native Traditions in the Postconquest World, edited by Elizabeth Hill Boone and Tom Cummins, 1998

Function and Meaning in Classic Maya Architecture, edited by Stephen D. Houston, 1998

Social Patterns in Pre-Classic Mesoamerica, edited by David C. Grove and Rosemary A. Joyce, 1999

Gender in Pre-Hispanic America, edited by Cecelia F. Klein, 2001

Archaeology of Formative Ecuador, edited by J. Scott Raymond and Richard L. Burger, 2003

Gold and Power in Ancient Costa Rica, Panama, and Colombia, edited by Jeffrey Quilter and John W. Hoopes, 2003

Palaces of the Ancient New World, edited by Susan Toby Evans and Joanne Pillsbury, 2004

A Pre-Columbian World, edited by Jeffrey Quilter and Mary Ellen Miller, 2006

Twin Tollans: Chichén Itzá, Tula, and the Epiclassic to Early Postclassic Mesoamerican World, edited by Jeff Karl Kowalski and Cynthia Kristan-Graham, 2007

Variations in the Expression of Inka Power, edited by Richard L. Burger, Craig Morris, and Ramiro Matos Mendieta, 2007

El Niño, Catastrophism, and Culture Change in Ancient America, edited by Daniel H. Sandweiss and Jeffrey Quilter, 2008

Classic Period Cultural Currents in Southern and Central Veracruz, edited by Philip J. Arnold III and Christopher A. Pool, 2008

The Art of Urbanism: How Mesoamerican Kingdoms Represented Themselves in Architecture and Imagery, edited by William L. Fash and Leonardo López Luján, 2009

New Perspectives on Moche Political Organization, edited by Jeffrey Quilter and Luis Jaime Castillo B., 2010

Astronomers, Scribes, and Priests: Intellectual Interchange between the Northern Maya Lowlands and Highland Mexico in the Late Postclassic Period, edited by Gabrielle Vail and Christine Hernández, 2010

The Place of Stone Monuments: Context, Use, and Meaning in Mesoamerica's Preclassic Transition, edited by Julia Guernsey, John E. Clark, and Barbara Arroyo, 2010

Their Way of Writing: Scripts, Signs, and Pictographies in Pre-Columbian America, edited by Elizabeth Hill Boone and Gary Urton, 2011

Past Presented: Archaeological Illustration and the Ancient Americas, edited by Joanne Pillsbury, 2012

Merchants, Markets, and Exchange in the Pre-Columbian World, edited by Kenneth G. Hirth and Joanne Pillsbury, 2013